Looking for a particular kind of employer? Each **JOB BANK** Book features a comprehensive cross-index, which lists entries both by industry and, in multi-state job markets, by state. This means a person seeking a job in, say, finance, can identify major employers quickly and accurately.

Hundreds of discussions with job-hunters show they prefer information organized geographically, because most people look for jobs in specific areas. The **JOB BANK SERIES** offers sixteen regional titles, from Minneapolis to Houston, and from Washington, D.C., to San Francisco. The future employee moving to a particular area can review the local employment data and get a feel not only for the type of industry most common to that region, but also for major employers.

A condensed, but thorough, review of the entire job search process is presented in the chapter, 'The Basics of Job Winning', a feature that has received many compliments from career counselors. In addition, each **JOB BANK** directory is completed by a section on resumes and cover letters **The New York Times** has acclaimed as "excellent".

The **JOB BANK SERIES** gives job-hunters the most comprehensive, most timely, and most accurate career information, organized and indexed to facilitate the job search. An entire career reference library, **JOB BANK** books are the consummate employment guides.

The Metro
New York
JobBank
1992

Managing Editor
Carter Smith

Associate Editor
Peter Weiss

Editorial Assistants
Michelle Bevilacqua
Sharon C. Cook
Elizabeth Gale
Lynne Griffin

BOB ADAMS, INC.
PUBLISHERS
Holbrook, Massachusetts

Top career publications from Bob Adams, Inc.:

THE JobBank SERIES:

The Atlanta JobBank ($12.95)
The Boston JobBank ($12.95)
The Chicago JobBank ($12.95)
The Dallas-Ft. Worth JobBank ($12.95)
The Denver JobBank ($12.95)
The Detroit JobBank ($12.95)
The Florida JobBank ($12.95)
The Houston JobBank ($12.95)
The Los Angeles JobBank ($12.95)
The Minneapolis-St. Paul JobBank ($12.95)
The New York JobBank ($12.95)
The Ohio JobBank ($12.95)
The Philadelphia JobBank ($12.95)
The Phoenix JobBank ($12.95)
The San Francisco JobBank ($12.95)
The Seattle JobBank ($12.95)
The St. Louis JobBank ($12.95)
The Washington DC JobBank ($12.95)

The JobBank Guide to Employment Services (covers 50 states: $129.95)
The National JobBank ($199.95)

CAREERS

Campus-Free College Degrees ($9.95)
Careers and the College Grad ($12.95)
Careers and the Engineer ($12.95)
Careers and the MBA ($14.95)

The Complete Guide to Washington Internships ($12.95)
Cover Letters that Knock 'em Dead ($7.95)
The Elements of Job Hunting ($4.95)
Harvard Guide to Careers in Mass Media ($7.95)
How to Get a Job in Education ($6.95)
International Careers ($12.95)
Job Search Handbook ($6.95)
Knock 'em Dead with Great Answers to Tough Interview Questions ($6.95)
The Minority Career Book ($9.95)
Over 40 and Looking for Work ($7.95)
Resume Handbook ($5.95)
Resumes that Knock 'em Dead ($7.95)
Which Niche? (Answers to the Most Common Questions About Careers and Job Hunting) ($4.95)

To obtain a copy of any of these books, please check your local bookstore. If unavailable, please call 1-800-USA-JOBS toll free. (In Massachusetts call 617-767-8100).

HOW TO USE THIS BOOK

A copy of *The Metropolitan New York JobBank* is one of the most effective tools you can find for your professional job hunt. Use this guide for the most up-to-date information on most major businesses in the Big Apple. It will supply you with specific addresses, phone numbers, and personnel contact information.

Separate yourself from the flock of candidates who answer the help-wanted advertisements "looking for a job." The method this book offers, direct employer contact, boasts twice the success rate of any other. Exploit it.

Read and use *The Metropolitan New York JobBank* to reveal new opportunities. Here's how:

Read the introductory economic overview section in order to gain insight on what the overall trends are for Metropolitan New York's economy.

Map out your job-seeking strategy by reading the "Basics of Job Winning" section. It's a condensed review of the most effective job search methods.

Write a winning resume and learn how to sell yourself most effectively on paper, by using the "Resumes and Cover Letters" section.

Focus your career goals by reading the "Jobs in Each Industry" section. This chapter features descriptions of many of the most common professional occupations, as well as background requirements, and forecasts for future growth.

Formulate a target list of potential employers in your field. Consult the company listings in the "Primary Metro New York Employers" section. Use that information to supplement your own research, so that you'll be knowledgeable about the firm - before the interview.

Increase your knowledge of your field, as well as your connections within it, by using our listings of some of the region's major professional and trade associations.

Whether you are just out of college starting your first job search, looking for a new position in your current field, or entering an entirely new sector of the job market, *The Metropolitan New York JobBank* will give you an idea of the incredible diversity of employment possibilities in one of the the country's most dynamic employment centers. Your ultimate success will largely depend upon how rigorously you use the information provided herein. This one-of-a-kind employment guide can lead you to a company, and a job, that would otherwise have remained undiscovered. With a willingness to apply yourself, a positive attitude, and the research within these covers, you can attain your career objective.

TABLE OF CONTENTS

INTRODUCTION/11

A complete and informative economic overview designed to help you understand all of the forces shaping the Metropolitan New York job market.

PART ONE: THE JOB SEARCH

The Basics of Job Winning/17

A condensed review of the basic elements of a successful job search campaign. Includes advice on developing an effective strategy, time planning, preparing for interviews, interview techniques, etc.

Resumes and Cover Letters/33

Advice on creating a strong resume. Includes sample resumes and cover letters.

PART TWO: OCCUPATION PROFILES

Jobs In Each Industry/51

Descriptions of many of the most common professional positions, with forecasts of their growth potential for the 1990's.

PART THREE: WHERE THE JOBS ARE

Primary Metro New York Employers/109

Metro New York organized according to industry. Includes the address, phone number, description of the company's basic product lines and services, and for most firms, the name of the contact person for professional positions.

Professional Employment Services/381

Includes the address, phone number, description of each company's services, contact name, and a list of positions commonly filled.

Professional & Trade Associations/447

Includes both local and national addresses and phone numbers for professional and trade associations in each field.

INTRODUCTION

Introduction

For many people, landing a good job in New York City is tantamount to making it in the "Big Time." As one of the world's leading centers of finance, trade, industry, advertising, publishing, fashion, and the arts, New York is fast paced, exciting, and challenging. And throughout most of the 1980's, its economy was booming.

Times have certainly changed. Among New York's problems are a growing level of poverty and a dangerously unskilled workforce that has led to a shortage of prepared workers and a growing dependence on highly specialized service industries.

The turning point in New York's fortunes is symbolized by the October, 1987 stock market crash. In the months immediately following "Black Monday," Wall Street was forced to lay off 9,000 workers, a major setback for the industry that had become New York's hottest and most rapidly expanding. Unfortunately, according to area economists and executives, the city's problems have only grown more serious since then.

Among New York's biggest problems is a growing level of poverty and a dangerously unskilled workforce.

New York's problems are far deeper than those affecting Wall Street. Symptomatic of this is the serious long term decline of the city's manufacturing sector.

TOUGH TIMES FOR BIG APPLE MANUFACTURERS

When most people think of closing factories, warehouses, and other manufacturing operations, they often think of the industrial Midwest. What many don't know, however, is that no American city -- not Detroit, nor Cleveland, nor Chicago has lost manufacturing jobs as rapidly as New York.

According to a report released by the Office of the Mayor during the administration of longtime Mayor Edward Koch, the total number of manufacturing jobs in New York declined 30% between 1977 and 1987. Since that time, the trend has not only continued, but the rate of decline has gotten steadily worse. In 1988, another 5,100 manufacturing jobs were lost followed by another 10,600 in 1989, and then still another *22,000* jobs in 1990. Even the headquarters of large manufacturing companies -- traditionally drawn to New

York because of the city's role as the nation's leading financial center, have been abandoning the city.

> ## No other American city -- other than Washington, D.C. has a lower percentage of its workforce in manufacturing.

In fact, according to the U.S. Department of Labor, employment in metro New York administrative offices of industrial companies has dropped a whopping 45% during the past 10 years. Today, no other American city -- other than Washington, D.C. has a lower percentage of its workforce in manufacturing. Putting the shape of New York's manufacturing sector in more tangible terms, it is interesting to note that even as far back as 1987, the largest commodity being shipped out of New York Harbor -- as measured in raw tonnage -- was wastepaper bound for recycling in the Far East. Exactly how much of that recycled paper is then sold back to the United States at a considerable markup is a matter of speculation.

THE NEW SERVICE ECONOMY AND "THE JOBS MISMATCH"

While wastepaper is the largest commodity shipped out of New York in terms of weight, the export from the city that generates the greatest income is now legal services. In fact, according to *The New York Times*, the city has been redefining the term "service economy." Instead of being led by restaurant and hotel workers, or retail clerks as is the case in most service economies, New York has become increasingly dependant on "advanced services" like management consulting, computer software design and legal services -- in short the kind of employers that hire only the highest level of professionals while leaving little opportunity for everyone else.

According to area analysts, this reliance on advanced services is leading to a "jobs mismatch" wherein the city's poorest residents -- or those with insufficient skills to find anything better than the lowest level of jobs -- have little chance of advancement in the expanding services market. Symptomatic of this problem was the recent case of New York Telephone, in which the company had to test 60,000 applicants in order to come up with 3,000 qualified new operators.

> ## New York Telephone recently had to test 60,000 applicants in order to find 3,000 New Yorkers qualified to become operators.

To address a problem of this magnitude, a long-term, concerted effort on the part of the government and business leaders alike seems more necessary than ever. Some initial steps have been taken to address the problem. American Express, one of New York's largest employers, is one of many companies that have begun to assist the public schools.

Unfortunately, New York is currently faced with an enormous budgetary crisis. In response, Mayor David Dinkins has proposed slashing the city's already overburdened civil services. Many executives worry that this will make it increasingly difficult to attract professional workers from outside of the Tri-State area, since New York already has a cost of living well above that of most other American cities.

THE OUTLOOK FOR THE FUTURE

In total, over 44,000 people lost their jobs in New York City during 1990, the largest employment decline for the city in 14 years. As mentioned, manufacturers have been especially hard hit, losing 22,000 workers. The trade sector had an even higher number of lost jobs, with 24,000 jobs disappearing.

In the Finance, Insurance, and Real Estate sector, the bad news that began with the Crash of '87 will continue as financial companies maintain their policies of retrenchment. In fact job cutbacks on Wall Street have amounted to 30,000 since late 1989 alone. Construction employment fell in 1990 for the second year in a row, down another 8,000 jobs from 1989.

> ### New York still offers the college graduate with skills and experience a dynamic range of professional opportunities.

Despite the many foreboding signs, New York still offers the college graduate with skills and experience a dynamic range of professional opportunities. Even as all other private industries registered job declines, over 16,000 new employees were added to the services sector in 1990, down only slightly from the 23,000 added in 1989, but up from the 14,000 added in 1988.

No one would suggest that the boom times of the 1980's will return soon, if ever. By the same token, New York will always be a city for passionate, driven, creative, and hard-working people who thrive on the excitement and challenges that only the Big Apple can provide. Most New Yorkers have long taken Frank Sinatra's words to heart when he sang "if you can make it there, you'll make it anywhere!" And as the city that never sleeps heads towards the 21st Century, those words ring truer than ever before.

Metropolitan New York's Largest Companies

Company	Revenue (in Billions)	Type of Business
1. IBM, *Armonk, NY*	54.2	Computers
2. AT&T (NY), *New York, NY*	51.2	Telecommunications
3. Mobil, *New York, NY*	50.5	Petroleum
4. General Electric, *Fairfield, CT*	49.4	Electronics, appliances
5. Texaco, *White Plains, NY*	35.3	Petroleum
6. AT&T (NJ), *Basking Ridge, NJ*	33.5	Telecommunications
7. Citicorp, *New York, NY*	27.9	Banking
8. Phillip Morris, *New York, NY*	27.6	Cigarettes, Food
9. Aetna Life, *Farmington, CT*	24.2	Insurance
10. ITT Corporation, *New York, NY*	19.5	Diversified
11. Travelers Corp., *Hartford, CT*	18.9	Insurance
12. United Technologies, *Hartford, CT*	18.0	Aerospace
13. Xerox Corporation, *Stamford, CT*	16.4	Office Machinery
14. American Express Co., *New York, NY*	14.7	Financial Services
15. NYNEX, *New York, NY*	12.0	Telecommunications
16. American Brands, *Old Greenwich, CT*	11.9	Tobacco
17. Pepsico, Inc., *Purchase, NY*	11.4	Food and Beverages
18. American Intl. Group, *New York, NY*	11.2	Insurance
19. Merrill Lynch & Co., *New York, NY*	10.8	Financial Services
20. Chase Manhattan, *New York, NY*	10.7	Banking

PART ONE:
THE JOB SEARCH

The Basics of Job Winning

THE BASICS OF JOB WINNING: A CONDENSED REVIEW

The best way to obtain a better professional job is to contact the employer directly. Broad-based statistical studies by the Department of Labor show that job seekers have found employment more successfully by contacting employers directly, than by using any other method.

However, given the current diversity, and increased specialization of both industry and job tasks it is possible that in some situations other job seeking methods may prove at least equally successful. Three of the other most commonly used methods are: relying on personal contacts, using employment services, and following up help wanted advertisements. Many professionals have been successful in finding better jobs using one of these methods. However, the Direct Contact method has an overall success rate twice that of any other method and it has been successfully used by many more professionals. So unless you have specific reasons to believe that another method would work best for you, the Direct Contact method should form the foundation of your job search effort.

The Objective

With any business task, you must develop a strategy for meeting a goal. This is especially true when it comes to obtaining a better job. First you need to clearly define your objectives.

Setting your job objectives is better known as career planning (or life planning for those who wish to emphasize the importance of combining the two). Career planning has become a field of study in and of itself. Since most of our readers are probably well-entrenched in their career path, we will touch on career planning just briefly.

If you are thinking of choosing or switching careers, we particularly emphasize two things. First, choose a career where you will enjoy most of the day-to-day tasks. Sure, this sounds obvious, but most of us have at one point or another been attracted by a glamour industry or a prestigious sounding job without thinking of the most important consideration: Would we enjoy performing the everyday tasks the position entailed?

The second key consideration is that you are not merely choosing a career, but also a lifestyle. Career counselors indicate that one of the most common problems people encounter in job seeking is a lack of consideration for how well-suited they are for a particular position or career. For example, some people, attracted to management consulting by good salaries, early responsibility and high level corporate exposure, do not adapt well to the long hours, heavy travel demands, and the constant pressure to produce. So be sure to determine both for your career as a whole and for each position that you apply for, if you will easily adapt to both the day-to-day duties that the position entails and the working environment.

The Strategy

Assuming that you have now established your career objectives, the next step of the job search is to develop a strategy. If you don't take the time to develop a strategy and lay out a plan you will probably find yourself going in circles after several weeks making a random search for opportunities that always seem just beyond your reach.

Your strategy can be thought as having three simple elements:

1. Choosing a method of contacting employers.

2. Allocating your scarce resources (in most job searches the key scarce resource will be time, but financial considerations will become important in some searches too.)

3. Evaluating how the selected contact method is working and then considering adopting other methods.

We suggest you give serious consideration to using the Direct Contact method exclusively. However, we realize it is human nature to avoid putting all your eggs in one basket. So, if you prefer to use other methods as well, try to expend at least half your effort on the Direct Contact method, spending the rest on all of the other methods combined. Millions of other job seekers have already proven that Direct Contact has been twice as effective in obtaining employment, so why not benefit from their effort?

With your strategy in mind, the next step is to develop the details of the plan, or scheduling. Of course, job searches are not something that most people do regularly so it is difficult to estimate how long each step will take. Nonetheless, it is important to have a plan so that your effort can be allocated the way you have chosen, so that you can see yourself progressing, and to facilitate reconsideration of your chosen strategy.

It is important to have a realistic time frame in mind. If you will be job searching full-time, your search will probably take at least two months and very likely, substantially longer. If you can only devote part-time effort, it will probably take four months.

You probably know a few people who seem to spend their whole lives searching for a better job in their part time. Don't be one of them. Once you begin your job search on a part-time basis, give it your whole-hearted effort. If you don't really feel like devoting a lot of energy to job seeking right now, then wait. Focus on enjoying your present position, performing your best on the job, and storing up energy for when you are really ready to begin your job search.

Those of you currently unemployed should remember that job hunting is tough work physically and emotionally. It is also intellectually demanding -- requiring your best. So don't tire yourself out by working on your job campaign around the clock. It would be counter-productive. At the same time, be sure to discipline yourself. The most logical approach to time management is to keep your regular working hours.

For those of you who are still employed, job searching will be particularly tiring because it must be done in addition to your regular duties. So don't work yourself to the point where you show up to interviews appearing exhausted and slip behind at your current job. But don't be tempted to quit! The long hours are worth it - it is much easier to sell your skills from a position of strength (as someone currently employed).

If you are searching full-time and have decided to choose a mixture of contact methods, we recommend that you divide up each week allowing some time for each method. For instance, you might devote Mondays to following up newspaper ads because most of them appear in Sunday papers. Then you might devote Tuesdays, and Wednesday mornings to working and developing the personal contacts you have, in addition to trying a few employment services. Then you could devote the rest of the week to the Direct Contact method. This is just one plan that may succeed for you.

By trying several methods at once, job-searching will be more interesting for you, and you will be able to evaluate how promising each of the methods seems, altering your time allocation accordingly. Be very careful in your evaluation, however, and don't judge the success of a particular method just by the sheer number of interviews you obtain. Positions advertised in the newspaper, for instance, are likely to generate many more interviews per opening than positions that are filled without being advertised.

If you are searching part-time and decide to try several different contact methods, we recommend that you try them sequentially. You simply won't have enough time to put a meaningful amount of effort into more than one method at once. So decide how long your job search might take. (Only a guess, of course.) And then allocate so many weeks or months for each contact method you choose to use. (We suggest that you try Direct Contact first.)

If you are expected to be in your office during the business day, then you have an additional time problem to deal with. How can you work interviews into the business day? And if you work in an open office, how can you even call to set up interviews? As much as possible you should keep up the effort and the appearances on your present job. So maximize your use of the lunch hour, early in the morning and late in the afternoon for calling. If you really keep trying you will be surprised how often you will be able to reach the executive you are trying to contact during your out-of-office hours. The lunch hour for different executives will vary between 12 and 3. Also you can catch people as early as 8 AM and as late as 6 PM on frequent occasions. Jot out a plan each night on how you will be using each minute of your precious lunch break.

Your inability to interview at any time other than lunch just might work to your advantage. If you can, try to set up as many interviews as possible for your lunch hour. This will go a long way to creating a relaxed rapport. (Who isn't happy when eating?) But be sure the interviews don't stray too far from the agenda on hand.

Lunchtime interviews will be much easier for the person with substantial career experience to obtain. People with less experience will often find that they have no alternative other than taking time off for interviewing. If you have to take time off, you have to take time off. But try to do this as little as possible. Usually you should take the whole day off so that it is not blatantly obvious that you are job searching. Try to schedule in at least two, or at the most three, interviews for the same day. (It is very difficult to maintain an optimum level of energy at more than three interviews in one day.) Explain to the interviewer why you might have to juggle your interview schedule -- he/she should honor the respect you are showing your current employer by minimizing your days off and will probably appreciate the fact that another prospective employer is showing an interest in you.

Once again we need to emphasize if you are searching for a job, especially part-time, get out there and do the necessary tasks to the best of your ability and get it over with. Don't let your job search drag on endlessly.

Remember that all schedules are meant to be broken. The purpose of a schedule in your job search is not to rush you to your goal, its purpose is to map out the road ahead of you and evaluate the progress of your chosen strategy to date.

The Direct Contact Method

Once you have scheduled a time, you are ready to begin using the job search method that you have chosen. In the text we will restrict discussion to use of the Direct Contact method. Sideboards will comment briefly on developing your personal contacts and using newspaper advertisements.

The first step in preparing for Direct Contact is to develop a check list for categorizing the types of firms for which you would prefer working. You might categorize firms by their product line, their size, their customer-type (such as industrial or consumer), their growth prospects, or, of course by their geographical locations. Your list of important considerations might be very short. If it is, good! The shorter it is, the easier it will be to find appropriate firms.

Then try to decide at which firms you are most likely to be able to obtain employment. You might wish to consider to what degree your particular skills might be in demand, the degree of competition for employment, and the employment outlook at the firm.

Now you are ready to assemble your list of prospective employers. Build up your list to at least 100 prospects. Then separate your prospect list into three groups. The first tier of maybe 25 firms will be your primary target market, the second group of another 25 firms will be your secondary market, and remaining names you will keep in reserve.

DEVELOPING YOUR CONTACTS

Some career counselors feel that the best route to a better job is through somebody you already know or through somebody to whom you can be introduced. The counselors recommend you build your contact base beyond your current acquaintances by asking each one to introduce you, or refer you, to additional people in your field of interest.

The theory goes like this: You might start with 15 personal contacts, each of whom introduces you to 3 additional people, for a total 45 additional contacts. Then each of these people introduces you to three additional people which adds 135 additional contacts. Theoretically, you will soon know every person in the industry.

Of course, developing your personal contacts does not usually work quite as smoothly as the theory suggests because some people will not be able to introduce you to several relevant contacts. The further you stray from your initial contact base, the weaker your references may be. So, if you do try developing your own contacts, try to begin with as large an initial group of people you personally know as possible. Dig into your personal phone book and your holiday greeting card list and locate old classmates from school. Be particularly sure to approach people who perform your personal business such as your lawyer, accountant, banker, doctor, stockbroker, and insurance agent. These people develop a very broad contact base due to the nature of their professions.

This book will help you greatly in developing your prospect list. Refer to the primary employers section of this book. You will notice that employer listings are arranged according to industry, beginning with Accounting, followed by Advertising, and so on through to Utilities. If you know of a firm, but you're unsure of what industry it would be classified under, then refer to the alphabetically ordered employer index at the rear of the book to find the page number that the firm's listing appears on.

At this stage, once you have gotten your prospect list together and have an idea of the firms for which you might wish to work, it is best to get to work on your resume. Refer to formats of the sample resumes included in the Resumes and Cover Letters section that follows this chapter.

Once your resume is at the printer, begin research for the first batch of 25 prospective employers. You will want to determine whether you would be happy working at the firms you are researching and also get a better idea of what their employment needs might be. You also need to obtain enough information to sound highly informed about the company during phone conversations and in mail correspondence. But don't go all out on your research yet! At some of these firms you probably will not be able to arrange interviews, so save your big research effort until you start to arrange interviews. Nevertheless, you should plan to spend about 3 or 4 hours, on average, researching each firm. Do your research in batches to save time and energy. Go into one resource at a time and find out what you can about each of the 25 firms in the batch. Start with the easiest resources to use (such as this book.) Keep organized. Maintain a folder on each firm.

If you discover something that really disturbs you about the firm (i.e. perhaps they are about to close their only local office) or if you discover that your chances of getting a job there are practically nil (i.e. perhaps they just instituted a hiring freeze) then cross them off your prospect list.

If possible, supplement your research efforts with contacts to individuals who know the firm well. Ideally you should make an informal contact with someone at the particular firm, but often a contact at a direct competitor, or a major supplier or customer will be able to supply you with just as much information. At the very least try to obtain whatever printed information that the company has available, not just annual reports, but product brochures and anything else. The company might very well have printed information about career opportunities.

Getting The Interview

Now it is time to arrange an interview, time to make the Direct Contact. If you have read many books on job searching you have probably noticed that virtually all tell you to avoid the personnel office like the plague. It is said that the personnel office never hires people, they just screen out candidates. In some cases you may be able to identify and contact the appropriate manager with the authority to hire you. However, this will take a lot of time and effort in each case. Often you'll be bounced back to personnel. So we suggest that you begin your Direct Contact campaign through personnel offices. If it seems that in the firms on your prospect list that little hiring is done through personnel, you might consider an alternative course of action.

The three obvious means of initiating Direct Contact are:

-Showing up unannounced
-Phone calls
-Mail

Cross out the first one right away. You should never show up to seek a professional position without an appointment. Even if you are somehow lucky enough to obtain an interview, you will appear so unprofessional that you will not even be seriously considered.

Mail contact seems to be a good choice if you have not been in the job market for a while. You can take your time to prepare a careful letter, say exactly what you want, tuck your resume in, and then the addressee can read the material at leisure. But employers receive many resumes every day. Don't be surprised if you do not get a response to your inquiry. So don't spend weeks waiting for responses that never come. If you do send a cover letter, follow it up (or precede it) with a phone call. This will increase your impact, and underscore both your interest in the firm and the fact that you are familiar with it (because of the initial research you did.)

Another alternative is to make a "Cover Call." Your Cover Call should be just like your cover letter: concise. Your first sentence should interest the employer in you. Then try to subtly mention your familiarity with the firm. Don't be overbearing; keep your introduction to three sentences or less. Be pleasant, self confident and relaxed. This will greatly increase the chances of the person at the other end of the line developing the conversation. But don't press. When you are asked to follow up "with something in the mail" don't try to prolong the conversation once it has ended. Don't ask what they want to receive in the mail. Always send your resume and a highly personalized follow-up letter, reminding the addressee of the phone conversation. Always include a cover letter even if you are requested to send a resume. (It is assumed that you will send a cover letter too.)

Unless you are in telephone sales, making smooth and relaxed cover calls will probably not come easily. Practice them on your own and then with your friends or relatives (friends are likely to be more objective and hence, better participants.)

If you obtain an interview over the telephone, be sure to send a thank you note reiterating the points you made during the conversation. You will appear more professional and increase your impact. However, don't mail your resume once an interview has been arranged unless it is specifically requested. Take it with you to the interview instead.

DON'T BOTHER WITH MASS MAILING OR BARRAGES OF PHONE CALLS

Direct Contact does not mean burying every firm within a hundred miles with mail and phone calls. Mass mailings rarely work in the job hunt. This also applies to those letters that are personalized -- but dehumanized -- on an automatic typewriter. Don't waste your time or money on such a project; you will fool no one but yourself.

The worst part of sending out mass mailings or making unplanned phone calls is that you are likely to be remembered as someone with little genuine interest in the firm, as someone who lacks sincerity, and as somebody that nobody wants to hire.

HELP WANTED ADVERTISEMENTS

Only a small fraction of professional job openings are advertised. Yet a majority of job seekers -- and a lot of people not in the job market -- spend a lot of time studying the help wanted ads. As a result, the competition for advertised openings is often much more severe.

A moderate-sized Manhattan employer told us about an experience advertising in the help wanted section of a major Sunday newspaper:

It was a disaster. We had over 500 responses from this relatively small ad in just one week. We have only two phone lines in this office and one was totally knocked out. We'll never advertise for professional help again.

If you insist on following up on help wanted ads, then research a firm before you reply to an ad so that you can ascertain if you would be a suitable candidate and that you would enjoy working at a particular firm. Also such preliminary research might help to separate you from all of the other professionals responding to that ad, many of whom will only have a passing interest in the opportunity. That said, your chances of obtaining a job through the want-ads are still much smaller than they are if you use the Direct Contact method.

Preparing For The Interview

Once the interview has been arranged, begin your in-depth research. You have got to arrive at the interview knowing the company upside down and inside out. You need to know their products, their types of customers, their subsidiaries, their parent, their principal locations, their rank in the industry, their sales and profit trends, their type of ownership, their size, their current plans and much more. By this time you have probably narrowed your job search to one industry, but if you haven't then you need to be familiar with the trends in this firm's industry, the firm's principal competitors and their relative performance, and the direction that the industry leaders are headed. Dig into every resource you can! Read the company literature, the trade press, the business press, and if the company is public, call your stockbroker and ask for still additional information. If possible, speak to someone at the firm before the interview, or if not, speak to someone at a competing firm. Clearly the more time you spend, the better. Even if you feel extremely pressed for time, you should set aside at least 12 hours for pre-interview research.

If you have been out of the job market for some time, don't be surprised if you find yourself tense during your first few interviews. It will probably happen every time you re-enter the market, not just when you seek your first job after getting out of school.

Tension is natural during an interview, but if you can be relaxed you will have an advantage over the competition. Knowing you have done a thorough research job should help you relax for an interview. Also make a list of questions that you think might be asked in an interview. Think out your answers carefully. Then practice reviewing them with a friend. Tape record your responses to the questions he/she raises in the role as interviewer. If you feel particularly unsure of your interviewing skills, arrange your first interviews at firms in which you are not very interested. (But remember it is common courtesy to seem excited about the possiblity of working for any firm at which you interview.) Then practice again on your own after these first few interviews. Go over each of the questions that you were asked.

How important is the proper dress for a job interview? Buying a complete wardrobe of Brooks Brothers pinstripes, donning new wing tip shoes and having your hair trimmed every morning is not enough to guarantee your obtaining a career position as an investment banker. But on the other hand, if you can't find a clean, conservative suit and a narrow tie, or won't take the time to polish your shoes and trim and wash your hair -- then you are just wasting your time by interviewing at all.

Very rarely will the final selection of candidates for a job opening be determined by dress. So don't spend a fortune on a new wardrobe. But be sure that your clothes are adequate. Men applying for any professional position should wear a suit; women should either wear a dress or a suit (not a pant suit.) Your clothes should be at least as formal or slightly more formal and more conservative than the position would suggest.

Top personal grooming is more important than finding the perfect clothes for a job interview. Careful grooming indicates both a sense of thoroughness and self-confidence.

Be sure that your clothes fit well and that they are immaculate. Hair must be neat and clean. Shoes should be newly polished. Women need to avoid excessive jewelry and excessive makeup. Men should be freshly shaven, even if the interview is late in the day.

Be complete. Everyone needs a watch and a pen and pad of paper (for taking notes.) Finally a briefcase or folder (containing extra copies of your resume) will help complete the look of professionalism.

Sometimes the interviewer will be running behind schedule. Don't be upset, be sympathetic. He/she might be under pressure to interview a lot of candidates and to quickly fill a demanding position. So be sure to come to your interview with good reading material to keep yourself occupied. This will help increase your patience and ease your tenseness.

The Interview

The very beginning of the interview is the most important part because it determines the rapport for the rest of it. Those first few moments are especially crucial. Do you smile when you meet? Do you establish enough eye contact, but not too much? Do you walk into the office with a self-assured and confident stride? Do you shake hands firmly? Do you make small talk easily without being garrulous? It is human nature to judge people by that first impression, so make sure it is a good one. But most of all, try to be yourself.

Often the interviewer will begin, after the small talk, by proceeding to tell you about the company, the division, the department, or perhaps, the position. Because of your detailed research, the information about the company will be repetitive for you and the interviewer would probably like nothing better than to avoid this regurgitation of the company biography. So if you can do so tactfully, indicate to the interviewer that you are very familiar with the firm. If he/she seems intent on providing you with background information, despite your hints, then acquiesce. But be sure to remain attentive. If you can manage to generate a brief discussion of the company or the industry at this point, without being forceful, great. It will help to further build rapport, underscore your interests and increase your impact.

Soon (if it didn't begin that way) the interviewer will begin the questions. This period of the interview falls into one of two categories (or somewhere in between): either a structured interview, where the interviewer has a prescribed set of questions to ask; or an unstructured interview, where the interviewer will ask only leading questions to get you to talk about yourself, your experiences and your goals. Try to sense as quickly as possible which direction the interviewer wishes to proceed and follow along in the direction he/she seems to be leading. This will make the interviewer feel more relaxed and in control of the situation.

SOME FAVORITE INTERVIEW QUESTIONS

Tell me about yourself...

Why did you leave your last job?

What excites you in your current job?

What are your career goals?

Where would you like to be in 5 years?

What are your greatest strengths?

What are your greatest weaknesses?

Why do you wish to work for this firm?

Where else are you seeking employment?

Why should we hire you?

Many of the questions will be similar to the ones that you were expecting and you will have prepared answers. Remember to keep attuned to the interviewer and make the length of your answers appropriate to the situation. If you are really unsure as to how detailed a response the interviewer is seeking, then ask. Query if he/she would prefer more details of a particular aspect.

As the interview progresses, the interviewer will probably mention what he/she considers to be the most important responsibilities of the position. If applicable, draw parallels between your experience and the demands of the position as seen by the interviewer. Describe your past experience in the same manner that you did on your resume: emphasizing results and achievements and not merely describing activities. If you listen carefully (listening is a very important part of the interviewing process) the interviewer might very well mention or imply the skills in terms of what he/she is seeking. But don't exaggerate. Be on the level.

Try not to cover too much ground during the first interview. This interview is often the toughest, with many candidates being screened out. If you are interviewing for a very competitive position, you will have to make an impression that will last. Focus on a few of your greatest strengths that are relevant to the position. Develop these points carefully, state them again in other words, and then try to summarize them briefly at the end of the interview.

Often the interviewer will pause towards the end and ask if you have any questions. Particularly in a structured interview, this might be the one chance to really show your knowledge of and interest in the firm. Have prepared a list of specific questions that are of real interest to you. Let your questions subtly show your research and your knowledge of the firm's activities. It is wise to have an extensive list of questions, as several of them may have already been answered during the interview.

Do not allow your opportunity to ask questions to become an interrogation. Avoid bringing your list of questions to the interview. And ask questions that you are fairly certain the interviewer can answer (remember how you feel when you cannot answer a question during an interview.)

Even if you are unable to determine the salary range beforehand, do not ask about it during the first interview. You can always ask about it later. Above all, don't ask about fringe benefits until you have been offered a position. (Then be sure to get all the details.) You should be able to determine the company's policy on fringe benefits relatively easily before the interview.

Try not to be negative about anything during the interview. (Particularly any past employer or any previous job.) Be cheerful. Everyone likes to work with someone who seems to be happy.

Don't let a tough question throw you off base. If you don't know the answer to a question, say so simply -- do not apologize. Just smile. Nobody can answer every question -- particularly some of the questions that are asked in job interviews.

Before your first interview, you may have been able to determine how many interviews the employer usually has for positions at your level. (Of

YOU'RE FIRED!!

You are not the first and will not be the last to go through this traumatic experience. Thousands of professionals are fired every week. Remember, being fired is not a reflection on you as a person. It is usually a reflection of your company's staffing needs and its perception of your recent job performance. Share the fact with your relatives and friends. Being fired is not something of which to be ashamed.

Don't start your job search with a flurry of unplanned activity. Start by choosing a strategy and working out a plan. Now is not the time for major changes in your life. If possible, remain in the same career and in the same geographical location, at least until you have been working again for a while. On the other hand, if the only industry for which you are trained is leaving, or is severely depressed in your area, then you should give prompt consideration to moving or switching careers.

Register for unemployment compensation immediately. A thorough job search could take months. After all, your employers have been contributing to unemployment insurance specifically for you ever since your first job. Don't be surprised to find other professionals collecting unemployment compensation as well. Unemployment compensation is for everybody who is between jobs.

Be prepared for the question, "Why were you fired?", during job interviews. Avoid mentioning you were fired while arranging interviews. Try especially hard not to speak negatively of your past employer and not to sound particularly worried about your status of being temporarily unemployed. But don't spend much time reflecting on why you were fired or how you might have avoided it. Look ahead. Think positively. And be sure to follow a careful plan during your job search.

course it may differ quite a bit within one firm.) Usually you can count on at least three or four interviews, although some firms, such as some of the professional partnerships, are well-known to give a minimum of six interviews for all professional postions.

Depending on what information you are able to obtain you might want to vary your strategy quite a bit from interview to interview. For instance if the first interview is a screening interview then try to have a few of your strengths really stand out. On the other hand, if later interviews are primarily with people who are in a position to veto your hiring, but not to push it forward (and few people are weeded out at these stages), then you should primarily focus on building rapport as opposed to reiterating and developing your key strengths.

If it looks as though your skills and background do not match the position your interviewer was hoping to fill, ask him or her if there is another division or subsidiary that perhaps could profit from your talents.

After The Interview

Write a follow-up letter immediately after the interview, while it is still fresh in the interviewer's mind. Then, if you have not heard from the interviewer within seven days, call him/her to stress your continued interest in the firm and the position and to request a second interview.

A parting word of advice. Again and again during your job search you will be rejected. You will be rejected when you apply for interviews. You will be rejected after interviews. For every job you finally receive you will probably have received a multitude of rejections. Don't let these rejections slow you down. Keep reminding yourself that the sooner you go out and get started on your job search and get those rejections flowing in, the closer you will be to obtaining the better job.

Resumes and Cover Letters

RESUMES AND COVER LETTERS

THIS SECTION CONTAINS:

1. Resume Preparation

2. Resume Format

3. Resume Content

4. Should You Hire A Resume Writer?

5. Cover Letters

6. Sample Resumes

7. General Model For A Cover Letter

8. Sample Cover Letters

9. General Model For A Follow-up Letter

RESUMES/OVERVIEW

When filling a position, a recruiter will often have 100 plus applicants, but time to interview only the 5 or 10 most promising ones. So he or she will have to reject most applicants after a brief skimming of their resume.

Unless you have phoned and talked to the recruiter -- which you should do whenever you can -- you will be chosen or rejected for an interview entirely on the basis of your resume and cover letter. So your resume must be outstanding. (But remember -- a resume is no substitute for a job search campaign. YOU must seek a job. Your resume is only one tool.)

RESUME PREPARATION

One page, usually.

Unless you have an unusually strong background with many years of experience and a large diversity of outstanding achievements, prepare a one page resume. Recruiters dislike long resumes.

8 1/2 x 11 Size

Recruiters often get resumes in batches of hundreds. If your resume is on small sized paper it is likely to get lost in the pile. If oversized, it is likely to get crumpled at the edges, and won't fit in their files.

Typesetting

Modern photocomposition typesetting gives you the clearest, sharpest image, a wide variety of type styles and effects such as italics, bold facing, and book-like justified margins. Typesetting is the best resume preparation process, but is also the most expensive.

Word Processing

The most flexible way to get your resume typed is on a good quality word processor. With word processing, you can make changes almost instantly because your resume will be stored on a magnetic disk and the computer will do all the re-typing automatically. A word processing service will usually offer you a variety of type styles in both regular and proportional spacing. You can have bold facing for emphasis, justified margins, and clear, sharp copies.

Typing

Household typewriters and office typewriters with nylon or other cloth ribbons are NOT good for typing the resume you will have printed. If you can't get word processing or typesetting, hire a professional with a high quality office typewriter with a plastic ribbon (usually called a "carbon ribbon.")

Printing

Find the best quality offset printing process available. DO NOT make your copies on an office photocopier. Only the personnel office may see the resume you mail. Everyone else may see only a copy of it. Copies of copies quickly become unreadable. Some professionally maintained, extra-high-quality photocopiers are of adequate quality, if you are in a rush. But top quality offset printing is best.

Proofread your resume

Whether you typed it yourself or had it written, typed, or typeset, mistakes on resumes can be embarrassing, particularly when something obvious such as your name is misspelled. No matter how much you paid someone else to type or write or typeset your resume, YOU lose if there is a mistake. So proofread it as carefully as possible. Get a friend to help you. Read your draft aloud as your friend checks the proof copy. Then have your friend read aloud while you check. Next, read it letter by letter to check spelling and punctuation.

If you are having it typed or typeset by a resume service or a printer, and you can't bring a friend or take the time during the day to proof it, pay for it and take it home. Proof it there and bring it back later to get it corrected and printed.

RESUME FORMAT

(See samples)

Basic data

Your name, phone number, and a complete address should be at the top of your resume. (If you are a university student, you should also show your home address and phone number.)

Separate your education and work experience

In general, list your experience first. If you have recently graduated, list your education first, unless your experience is more important than your education. (For example, if you have just graduated from a teaching school, have some business experience and are applying for a job in business you would list your business experience first.) If you have two or more years of college, you don't need to list high schools.

Reverse chronological order

To a recruiter your last job and your latest schooling are the most important. So put the last first and list the rest going back in time.

Show dates and locations

Put the dates of your employment and education on the left of the page. Put the names of the companies you worked for and the schools you attended a few spaces to the right of the dates. Put the city and state or city and country where you studied or worked to the right of the page.

Avoid sentences and large blocks of type

Your resume will be scanned, not read. Short, concise phrases are much more effective than long-winded sentences. Keep everything easy to find. Avoid paragraphs longer than six lines. Never go ten or more lines in a paragraph. If you have more than six lines of information about one job or school, put it in two or more paragraphs.

RESUME CONTENT

Be factual

In many companies, inaccurate information on a resume or other application material will get you fired as soon as the inaccuracy is discovered. Protect yourself.

Be positive

You are selling your skills and accomplishments in your resume. If you achieved something, say so. Put it in the best possible light. Don't hold back or be modest, no one else will. But don't exaggerate to the point of misrepresentation.

Be brief

Write down the important (and pertinent) things you have done, but do it in as few words as possible. The shorter your resume is, the more carefully it will be examined.

Work experience

Emphasize continued experience in a particular type of function or continued interest in a particular industry. De-emphasize irrelevant positions. Delete positions that you held for less than four months. (Unless you are a very recent college grad or still in school.)

Stress your results

Elaborate on how you contributed to your past employers. Did you increase sales, reduce costs, improve a product, implement a new program? Were you promoted?

Mention relevant skills and responsibilities

Be specific. Slant your past accomplishments toward the type of position that you hope to obtain. Example: Do you hope to supervise people? Then state how many people, performing what function, you have supervised.

Education

Keep it brief if you have more than two years of career experience. Elaborate more if you have less experience. Mention degrees received and any honors or special awards. Note individual courses or research projects that might be relevant for employers. For instance, if you are a liberal arts major, be sure to mention courses in such areas as: accounting, statistics, computer programming, or mathematics.

Job objective?

Leave it out. Even if you are certain of exactly the type of job that you desire, the inclusion of a job objective might eliminate you from consideration for other positions that a recruiter feels are a better match for your qualifications.

Personal data

Keep it very brief. Two lines maximum. A one-word mention of commonly practiced activities such as golf, skiing, sailing, chess, bridge, tennis, etc. can prove to be good way to open up a conversation during an interview. Do not include your age, weight, height, etc.

SHOULD YOU HIRE A RESUME WRITER?

If you write reasonably well, there are some advantages to writing your resume yourself. To write it well, you will have to review your experience and figure out how to explain your accomplishments in clear, brief phrases. This will help you when you explain your work to interviewers.

If your write your resume, everything in it will be in your own words -- it will sound like you. It will say what you want it to say. And you will be much more familiar with the contents. If you are a good writer, know yourself well and have a good idea of what parts of your background employers are looking for, you may be able to write your own resume better than anyone else can. If you write your resume yourself, you should have someone who can be objective (preferably not a close relative) review it with you.

When should you have your resume professionally written?

If you have difficulty writing in Resume Style (which is quite unlike normal written language), if you are unsure of which parts of your background you should emphasize, or if you think your resume would make your case better if it did not follow the standard form outlined here or in a book on resumes, then you should have it professionally written.

There are two reasons even some professional resume writers we know have had their resumes written with the help of fellow professionals. First, when they need the help of someone who can be objective about their background, and second, when they want an experienced sounding board to help focus their thoughts.

If you decide to hire a resume writer

The best way to choose a writer is by reputation -- the recommendation of a friend, a personnel director, your school placement officer or someone else knowledgeable in the field.

You should ask, "If I'm not satisfied with what you write, will you go over it with me and change it?"

You should ask, "How long has the person who will write my resume been writing resumes?"

There is no sure relation between price and quality, except that you are unlikely to get a good writer for less than $50 for an uncomplicated resume and you shouldn't have to pay more than $300 unless your experience is very extensive or complicated. There will be additional charges for printing.

Few resume services will give you a firm price over the phone, simply because some people's resumes are too complicated and take too long to do at any predetermined price. Some services will quote you a price that applies to almost all of their customers. Be sure to do some comparative shopping. Obtain a firm price before you engage their services and find out how expensive minor changes will be.

COVER LETTERS

Always mail a cover letter with your resume. In a cover letter you can show an interest in the company that you can't show in a resume. You can point out one or two skills or accomplishments the company can put to good use.

Make it personal

The more personal you can get, the better. If someone known to the person you are writing has recommended that you contact the company, get permission to include his/her name in the letter. If you have the name of a person to send the letter to, make sure you have the name spelled correctly and address it directly to that person. Be sure to put the person's name and title on both the letter and envelope. This will ensure that your letter will get through to the proper person, even if a new person now occupies this position. But even if you are addressing it to the "Personnel Director" or the "Hiring Partner," send a letter.

Type cover letters in full. Don't try the cheap and easy ways like photocopying the body of your letter and typing in the inside address and salutation. You will give the impression that you are mailing to a multitude of companies and have no particular interest in any one. Have your letters fully typed and signed with a pen.

Phone

Precede or follow your mailing with a phone call.

Bring extra copies of your resume to the interview

If the person interviewing you doesn't have your resume, be prepared. Carry copies of your own. Even if you have already forwarded your resume, be sure to take extra copies to the interview, as someone other than the interviewer(s) might now have the first copy you sent.

Functional Resume
(Prepared on a Word Processor and Letter-Quality Printer.)

Michelle Hughes
430 Miller's Crossing
Essex Junction, VT 05452
802/555-9354

Solid background in plate making, separations, color matching,
background definition, printing, mechanicals, color corrections, and supervision of personnel. A highly motivated
manager and effective communicator. Proven ability to:

* **Create Commercial Graphics**   * **Meet Graphic Deadlines**
* **Produce Embossing Drawings**   * **Control Quality**
* **Color Separate**   * **Resolve Printing Problems**
* **Analyze Consumer Acceptance**   * **Expedite Printing Operations**

Qualifications

Printing: Black and white and color. Can judge acceptability
of color reproduction by comparing it with original. Can make
four or five color corrections on all media. Have long
developed ability to restyle already reproduced four-color
artwork. Can create perfect tone for black and white match
fill-ins for resume cover letters.

Customer Relations: Work with customers to assure specifications are met and customers are satisfied. Can guide work
through entire production process and strike a balance between
technical printing capabilities and need for customer approval.

Management: Schedule work to meet deadlines. Direct staff in
production procedures. Maintain quality control from inception
of project through final approval for printing.

Specialties: Make silk screen overlays for a multitude of
processes. Velo bind, GBC bind, perfect bind. Have knowledge
to prepare posters, flyers, and personalized stationery.

Personnel Supervision: Foster an atmosphere that encourages
highly talented artists to balance high level creativity with
a maximum of production. Meet or beat production deadlines. Am
continually instructing new employees, apprentices and students in both artistry and technical operations.

Experience

Professor of Graphic Arts, University of Vermont, Burlington,
VT (1977-present).
Assistant Production Manager, Artsign Digraphics, Burlington,
VT (1981-present) Part time.

Education

Massachusetts Conservatory of Art, PhD 1977
University of Massachusetts, B.A. 1974

Chronological Resume
(Prepared on a Word Processor and Laser Printer.)

DAMIEN W. PINCKNEY

U.S. Address:
15606 Center Street
Bottineau, ND 58777
701/555-9320

Jamaican Address:
Oskarrataan Building, Room 1234
Hedonism II
Negril, Jamaica
809/555-6634

Experience

1984-present   **HEDONISM II,** Negril, Jamaica
Resident Engineer for this publicly owned resort with main offices in
Kingston. Responsibilities include:

Maintaining electrical generating and distribution equipment.

Supervising an eight-member staff in maintenance of refrigeration equipment, power and light generators, water purification plant, and general
construction machinery.

1982-1984   **NEGRIL BEACH HOTEL,** Negril Beach, Jamaica
Resident Engineer for a privately held resort, assigned total responsibility
for facility generating equipment.

Directed maintenance, operation and repair of diesel generating equipment.

1980-1982   Directed overhaul of turbo generating equipment in two Mid-Western localities
and assisted in overhaul of a turbo generating unit in Mexico.

1975-1980   **CAPITAL CITY ELECTRIC,** Washington, DC
Service Engineer for the power generation service division of this regional
power company, supervised the overhaul, maintenance and repair of large
generators and associated auxiliary equipment.

Education

1972-1975   **FRANKLIN INSTITUTE,** Baltimore, MD
Awarded a degree of Associate of Engineering. Concentration in Mechanical Power Engineering Technology.

Personal   Willing to travel and relocate.
Interested in sailing, scuba diving, deep sea fishing.

References available upon request.

Chronological Resume
(Prepared on an Office-Quality Typewriter.)

Lorraine Avakian
70 Monback Avenue
Oshkosh, WI 54901
Phone: 414/555-4629

Business Experience

1984-1991 **NATIONAL PACKAGING PRODUCTS**, Princeton, WI

1989-1991 **District Sales Manager.** Improved 28-member sales group from a company rank in the bottom thirty percent to the top twenty percent. Complete responsibility for personnel, including recruiting, hiring and training. Developed a comprehensive sales improvement program and advised its implementation in eight additional sales districts.

1986-1988 **Marketing Associate.** Responsible for research, analysis, and presentation of marketing issues related to long-term corporate strategy. Developed marketing perspective for capital investment opportunities and acquisition candidates, which was instrumental in finalizing decisions to make two major acquisitions and to construct a $35 million canning plant.

1984-1986 **Salesperson, Paper Division.** Responsible for a four-county territory in central Wisconsin. Increased sales from $700,000 to over $1,050,000 annually in a 15 month period. Developed six new accounts with incremental sales potential of $800,000. Only internal candidate selected for new marketing program.

AMERICAN PAPER PRODUCTS, INC., Oshkosh, WI
1983-1984 **Sales Trainee.** Completed the intensive six month training program and was promoted to salesperson status. Received the President's Award for superior performance in the sales training program.

HENDUKKAR SPORTING GOODS, INC., Oshkosh, WI
1983 **Assistant Store Manager.** Supervised six employees on the evening shift. Handled accounts receivable.

Education
1977-1982 **BELOIT COLLEGE**, Beloit, WI
Received Bachelor of Science Degree in Business Administration in June 1982. Varsity Volleyball. Financed 50% of educational costs through part-time and co-op program employment.

Personal Background
Able to relocate; Excellent health; Active in community activities.

Chronological Resume
(Prepared on a Word Processor and Laser Printer.)

Melvin Winter
43 Aspen Wall Lane
Wheaton, IL 60512
312/555-6923 (home)
312/555-3000 (work)

RELATED EXPERIENCE
1982-Present GREAT LAKES PUBLISHING COMPANY, Chicago, IL
Operations Supervisor (1986-present)
in the Engineering Division of this major trade publishing house, responsible for maintaining on line computerized customer files, title files, accounts receivable, inventory and sales files.

Organize department activities, establish priorities and train personnel. Provide corporate accounting with monthly reports of sales, earned income from journals, samples, inventory levels/value and sales and tax data. Divisional sales average $3 million annually.

Senior Customer Service Representative (1984-1986)
in the Construction Division. Answered customer service inquiries regarding orders and accounts receivable, issued return and shortage credits and expedited special sales orders for direct mail and sales to trade schools.

Customer Service Representative (1982-1983)
in the International Division. Same duties as for construction division except that sales were to retail stores and universities in Europe.

1980-1982 B. DALTON, BOOKSELLER, Salt Lake City, UT
Assistant Manager of this retail branch of a major domestic book seller, maintained all paperback inventories at necessary levels, deposited receipts daily and created window displays.

EDUCATION
1976-1980 UNIVERSITY OF MAINE, Orono, ME
Awarded a degree of Bachelor of Arts in French Literature.

LANGUAGES
Fluent in French. Able to write in French, German and Spanish.

PERSONAL
Willing to travel and relocate, particularly in Europe.

References available upon request.

General Model for a Cover Letter

Your Address
Date

Contact Person Name
Title
Company
Address

Dear Mr./Ms._____:

Immediately explain why your background makes you the best candidate for the position that you are applying for. Keep the first paragraph short and hard-hitting.

Detail what you could contribute to this company. Show how your qualifications will benefit this firm. Remember to keep this letter short; few recruiters will read a cover letter longer than half a page.

Describe your interest in the corporation. Subtly emphasize your knowledge about this firm (the result of your research effort) and your familiarity with the industry. It is common courtesy to act extremely eager to work for any company that you interview.

In the closing paragraph you should specifically request an interview. Include your phone number and the hours when you can be reached. Alternatively, you might prefer to mention that you will follow up with a phone call (to arrange an interview at a mutually convenient time within the next several days).

Sincerely,

(signature)

Your full name (typed)

Cover Letter

49 Chinwick Circle
Houston, TX 77031
October 5, 1993

Ms. Ruth Herman-George
V.P./Director of Personnel
Holly Rock Fire Insurance Group
444 Rolling Cloud Lane, Suite 24
Houston, TX 77035

Dear Ms. Herman-George:

I am a career-oriented individual who can successfully provide technical direction and training to pension analysts in connection with FKLE system.

My major and most recent background is directly involved in the administration of pension and profit sharing plans with TRMZ. Furthermore, my extensive experience both as a Group Pension Pre-Scale Underwriter and as a Pension Underwriter involves data processing knowledge and overall pension administration.

A prime function of mine is decision making with reference to group pension business. You specifically seek an idividual who can recommend changes and/or new procedures of plan administration and maintenance plus assistance in development of pension administration kits for use by the field force at Holly Rock. I feel that I possess the ability to fulfill your need dramatically.

I would welcome the practical opportunity to work directly with general agents and plan trustees in qualifying, revising and requalifying pension and profit sharing plans required by TRMZ. You will note in my resume my background in working with others in both an advisory and shirt-sleeve capacity.

I look forward to hearing from you.

Sincerely,

Henry Washington

Cover Letter

411 Looksee Avenue
Apt. 449
Medford, MA 02139
March 15, 1993

Mr. Benjamin Deiver
Sales Manager
Yankee Ski Products
456 Pillbox Lane
Denver, CO 80201

Dear Mr. Deiver:

I seek a position as a sales representative with Yankee Ski Products and I offer, in return, thorough industry experience and more than eleven years of solid practical background in sales.

As a sample of sales achievement, I increased my personal monthly gross sales volume to a point where it tripled the combined sales of three other full-time representatives for one ski manufacturer. Also, I have won numerous international and domestic sales awards.

As an experienced sales representative, I have succeeded in improving area or regional sales by employing a combination of aggressiveness, enthusiasm, and persistence, and I have been able to bring out these traits in those whom I have hired and trained in my capacity as National Sales Instructor for two companies.

I feel that your new line of competition skis offers an unbeatable price/performance combination for the serious racer. I am firmly convinced that I can improve your market penetration in the lucrative Upstate New York area at least to a top five position.

I am an avid skier. As such, I am familiar with not only the technical terms involved, but with the types of equipment available and the extent to which it is marketed.

I look forward to hearing from you.

Sincerely,

Christina Harges

Cover Letter

1286 136th Avenue
Newark, NJ 07101
December 10, 1992

Mr. Edward Buchanan
Personnel Manager
Caufield & Compson Engineering Services, Inc.
Central Park Square Building
New York, NY 10019

Dear Mr. Buchanan:

My diversity as well as my depth of engineering experience in the wastewater treatment field could prove to be a particularly strong asset for Caufield & Compson given the firm's current and continued commitment to being a pioneering innovator in the engineering and construction of wastewater treatment facilities.

I offer an extensive background in investigating, reporting and designing multimillion dollar wastewater treatment facilities, pumping facilities and sewer lines in New Jersey and in Puerto Rico. In addition, I have experience in coordinating engineering services during construction of sewers and pumping facilities in Hawaii.

One of my basic strengths is my ability to act as liaison for diverse engineering and non-engineering individuals and groups to keep a project on schedule and in line with funding constraints.

I have come to a point in my career where I desire to expand into areas where I might apply over 8 years of solid engineering experience. These areas include hazardous waste treatment, industrial wastewater and water treatment, and water supply.

I will be glad to furnish any additional information you desire. You may reach me during the day at 201/555-1100. I look forward to hearing from you.

Sincerely,

Raymond A. Gatz

Enc. Resume

General Model for a Follow-Up Letter

```
                                          Your Address
                                          Date

Contact Person Name
Title
Company
Address

Dear Mr./Ms._____:

Remind the interviewer of the position for which you were in-
terviewed, as well as the date. Thank him/her for the inter-
view.

Confirm your interest in the opening and the organization. Use
specifics to emphasize both that you have researched the firm
in detail and considered how you would fit into the company
and the position.

Like in your cover letter, emphasize one or two of you
strongest qualifications and slant them toward the various
points that the interviewer considered the most important for
the position. Keep the letter brief, a half-page is plenty.

If appropriate, close with a suggestion for further action,
such as a desire to have additional interviews. Mention your
phone number and the hours that you can best be reached. Alter-
natively, you may prefer to mention that you will follow up
with a phone call in several days.


                                          Sincerely yours,

                                          (signature)

                                          Your full name (typed)
```

PART TWO:
OCCUPATION PROFILES

Jobs In Each Industry

JOBS IN EACH INDUSTRY

The following chapter includes descriptions of many of the most common occupations, with an emphasis on those that have especially strong growth outlooks for the 1990's. For each position, you will find a brief description of what the position entails, the background or qualification you would need for entering and advancing in that occupation, the salary expectations for various levels within the occupational category, and a forecast of the job's growth potential for the 1990's.

The occupations listed are as follows:

Accountant/Auditor
Actuary
Administrator
Advertising Worker
Architect
Attorney
Bank Officer/Manager
Biochemist
Blue-Collar Worker Supervisor
Buyer/Merchandise Manager
Chemist
Claims Representative
Commercial Artist
Data Processing Specialist
Dietician/Nutritionist
Draftsperson
Economist
Engineer
Financial Analyst
Food Technologist
Forester
Geographer
Geologist/Geophysicist
Hotel Manager/Assistant Manager
Industrial Designer
Insurance Agent/Broker
Manager
Manaufacturer's Sales Worker
Personnel and Labor Relations Specialist
Physicist
Public Relations Worker

Purchasing Agent
Quality Control Supervisor
Reporter/Editor
Securities and Financial Services
Sales Representative
Statistician
Systems Analyst
Technical Writer/Editor
Underwriter

ACCOUNTANT/AUDITOR

DESCRIPTION:

Accountants prepare and analyze financial reports that furnish important financial information. Four major fields are public, management, and government accounting, and internal auditing. Public accountants have their own businesses or work for accounting firms. Management accountants, also called industrial or private accountants, handle the financial records of their company. Government accountants examine the records of government agencies and audit private businesses and individuals whose dealings are subject to government regulation. Accountants often concentrate on one phase of accounting. For example, many public accountants may specialize in auditing, tax, or estate planning. Others specialize in management consulting and give advice on a variety of matters. Management accountants provide the financial information executives need to make sound business decisions. They may work in areas such as taxation, budgeting, costs, or investments. Internal auditing, a specialization within management accounting, is rapidly growing in importance. Internal auditors examine and ensure efficient and economical operation. Government accountants are often Internal Revenue Service agents or are involved in financial management and budget administration.

About 60 percent of all accountants do management accounting. An additional 25 percent are engaged in public accounting through independent firms. Other accountants work for government, and some teach in colleges and universities. Accountants and auditors are found in all business, industrial, and governmental organizations.

BACKGROUND AND QUALIFICATIONS:

Although many graduates of business schools are successful, most public accounting and business firms require applicants for accountant and internal auditor positions to have at least a BA in Accounting or a closely related field. Many employers prefer those with a Master's degree in Accounting. Most large employers prefer applicants who are familiar with computers and their applications in accounting and internal auditing.

Previous experience in accounting can help an applicant get a job. Many colleges offer students an opportunity to gain experience through summer or part-time internship programs conducted by public accounting firms. Such training is invaluable in gaining permanent employment in the field.

Professional recognition through certification or licensing also is extremely valuable. Anyone working as a certified public accountant (CPA) must hold a certificate issued by a state board of accountancy. All states use the four-part Uniform CPA Exam, prepared by the American Institute of Certified Public Accountants, to establish certification. The CPA exam is very rigorous, and candidates are not required to pass all four parts at once. Most states require applicants to have some public accounting experience for a CPA certificate, and those with BA's often need two years of experience. New trends require the candidate to have a BA plus 30 additional semester hours.

The Institute of Internal Auditors confers the Certified Internal Auditor (CIA) certificate upon graduates from accredited colleges and universities who have completed three years internal auditing and who have passed a four-part exam. The National Association of Accountants (NAA) confers the Certificate in Management Accounting (CMA) upon candidates who pass a series of uniform exams and meet specific educational and professional standards. A growing number of states require both CPA's and licensed public accountants to complete a certain number of hours of continuing education before licenses can be renewed. Increasingly, accountants are studying computer programming so they can adapt accounting procedures to data processing.

Junior public accountants usually start by assisting with auditing work for several clients. They may advance to intermediate positions with greater responsibility in one or two years, and to senior positions within another few years. Those who deal successfully with top industry executives often become supervisors, managers, or partners, or transfer to executive positions in private firms. Beginning management accountants often start as ledger accountants, junior internal auditors, or as trainees for technical accounting positions. They may advance to chief plant accountant, chief cost accountant, budget director, or manager of internal auditing. Some become controllers, treasurers, financial vice-presidents, or corporation presidents.

OUTLOOK:

Employment of accountants and auditors is expected to grow much faster than the average for all occupations through the year 2000 due to the key role these workers play in the management of all types of businesses. Although increased demand will generate many new jobs, most openings win result from the need to replace workers who leave the occupation or retire. While accountants and auditors tend to leave the profession at a lower rate than members of most other occupations, replacement needs will be substantial because the occupation is large. Accountants rarely lose their jobs when other workers are laid off during hard economic times. Financial information must be developed and tax reports prepared regardless of the state of the economy.

ACTUARY

DESCRIPTION:

Actuaries design insurance and pension plans that can be maintained on a sound financial basis. They assemble and analyze statistics to calculate probabilities of death, sickness, injury, disability, unemployment, retirement, and property loss from accident, theft, fire, and other hazards. Actuaries use this information to determine the expected insured loss. The actuary calculates premium rates and determines policy contract provision for each type of insurance offered. Most actuaries specialize in either life and health insurance, or property and liability (casualty) insurance; a growing number specialize in pension plans. About two-thirds of all actuaries work for private insurance companies, the majority in life insurance. Consulting firms and rating bureaus employ about one-fifth of all actuaries. Other actuaries work for private organizations administering independent pension and welfare plans.

BACKGROUND AND EXPERIENCE:

A good educational background for a beginning job in a large life or casualty insurance company is a Bachelor's degree in Mathematics or Statistics; a degree in Actuarial Science is preferred. Courses in accounting, computer science, economics, and insurance also are useful. Of equal importance, however, is the need to pass one or more of the exams offered by professional actuarial societies. Three societies sponsor programs leading to full professional status in the specialty. The Society of Actuaries gives nine actuarial exams for the life and health insurance, and pension fields; The Casualty Actuarial Society gives 10 exams for the property and liability fields; and the American Society of Pension Actuaries gives nine exams covering the pension field. Actuaries are encouraged to complete the entire series of exams as soon as possible; completion generally takes from five to ten years. Actuaries who complete five exams in either the life insurance segment of the pension series, or seven exams in the casualty series are awarded "associate" membership in their society. Those who have passed an entire series receive full membership and the title "Fellow".

Beginning actuaries often rotate among different jobs to learn various actuarial operations and to become familiar with different phases of insurance work. At first, their work may be routine, such as preparing tabulations for actuarial tables or reports. As they gain experience, they may supervise clerks, prepare correspondence and reports, and do research. Advancement to more responsible positions such as assistant, associate, or chief actuary depends largely on job performance and the number of actuarial exams passed. Many actuaries, because of their broad knowledge of insurance and related fields, are selected for administrative positions in other company activities, particularly in underwriting, accounting, or data processing. Many advance to top executive positions.

OUTLOOK:

Employment of actuaries is expected to grow much faster than the average for all occupations through the year 2000. Most job openings, however, are expected to arise each year to replace actuaries who transfer to other occupations, or retire. Job opportunities should be favorable for college graduates who have passed at least two actuarial exams while still in school and have a strong mathematical and statistical background.

ADMINISTRATOR

DESCRIPTION:

Administrators perform a wide variety of office paperwork tasks. These tasks might range from preparing a summary of sales activity to filing and retrieving information. A lower-level administrator might serve primarily as a typist, office machine operator, or secretary, being closely supervised by an office superior. An upper-level administrator might supervise the work of many office workers and be responsible for a broad range of office duties that support an organization's activities.

BACKGROUND AND QUALIFICATIONS:

Because of the broad range of duties and responsibilities of administrators at different levels or within different organizations, the actual job and its requisite background and experience may vary greatly from one firm to the next, and from one position to the next. However, all but the highest managerial levels of administrative work require strong office skills, such as fast and accurate typing and the ability to prepare business correspondence. In larger organizations with more complex office tasks, a college background is becoming an increasingly valuable asset. Also, experience or familiarity with computers, word processors, or data processing equipment greatly improves an applicant's employability and chances for promotion.

OUTLOOK:

Despite the nearly universal use of computer and word processing automation in the office, administrative positions are still expected to offer above average growth. Also, with many new entrants to the job market trying to obtain junior managerial jobs and similar posts, administrative positions are likely to be less competitive than many other types of jobs. Administrators are found in all industries, but especially in banking, insurance, utilities, and other companies with a high volume of paperwork.

ADVERTISING WORKER

DESCRIPTION:

There are several different occupations commonly associated with the field of advertising. Advertising managers direct the advertising program of the business for which they work. They determine the size of the advertising budget, the type of ad and the medium to use, and what advertising agency, if any, to employ. Managers who decide to employ an agency work closely with the advertising agencies to develop advertising programs for client firms and individuals. Copywriters develop the text and headlines to be used in the ads. Media directors negotiate contracts for advertising for advertising space or air time. Production managers and their assistants arrange to have the ad printed for publication, filmed for television, or recorded for radio.

BACKGROUND AND QUALIFICATIONS:

Most employers prefer college graduates. Some employers seek persons with degrees in advertising with heavy emphasis on marketing, business, and journalism; others prefer graduates with a liberal arts background; some employers place little emphasis on the type of degree. Opportunities for advancement in this field generally are excellent for creative, talented, and hard-working people. For example, copywriters and account executives may advance to more responsible work in their specialties, or to managerial jobs if they demonstrate ability in dealing with clients. Some especially capable employees may become partners in an existing agency, or they may establish their own agency.

OUTLOOK:

Employment of advertising managers is expected to increase faster than the average for all occupations through the year 2000 as increasingly intense domestic and foreign competition in products and services offered to consumers requires greater marketing and promotional efforts. In addition to rapid growth, many job openings will occur each year to replace managers who move into the top positions or retire. However, the ample supply of experienced professional and technical personnel and recent college graduates seeking these management positions may result in substantial job competition.

ARCHITECT

DESCRIPTION:

Architects provide a wide variety of professional services to individuals, organizations, corporations, or government agencies planning a building project. Architects are involved in all phases of development of a building or project, from the initial discussion of general ideas through completion of construction. Their duties require a variety of skills, including design, engineering, managerial, and supervisory.

The architect and client first discuss the purposes, requirements, and cost of a project. The architect then prepares schematic drawings that show the scale and the mechanical and structural relationships of the building. If the schematic drawings are accepted, the architect develops a final design showing the floor plans and the structural details of the project.

Architects also specify the building materials and, in some cases, the interior furnishings. In all cases, the architect must ensure that the structure's design and specifications conform to local and state building codes, zoning laws, fire regulations, and other ordinances. After all drawings are completed, the architect assists the client in selecting a contractor and negotiating the construction contract. As construction proceeds, the architect visits the building site from time to time to ensure that the contractor is following the design using the specified materials.

Besides designing structures, architects may also help in selecting building sites, preparing cost and land-use studies, and long-range planning for site development. When working on large projects or for large architectural firms, architects often specialize in one phase of work, such as designing or administering construction contracts. This often requires working with engineers, urban planners, landscape architects, and others.

Most architects work for architectural firms or for builders, real estate firms, or other businesses that have large construction programs. Some work for governmental agencies. Although found in many areas, a large proportion of architects are employed in seven cities: Boston, Chicago, Los Angeles, New York, Philadelphia, San Francisco, and Washington, DC.

BACKGROUND AND QUALIFICATIONS:

Every state requires individuals to be licensed before they may call themselves architects, or contract for providing architectural services. To qualify for the licensing exam, a person must have either a Bachelor of Architecture degree followed by three years of acceptable practical experience in an architect's office, or a Master of Architecture degree followed by two years of experience. As a substitute for formal training, most states accept additional experience (usually 12 years) and successful completion of a qualifying test for admission to the licensing examination. Many architectural school graduates work in the field although they are not licensed. However, a registered architect is required to take legal responsibility for all work. New graduates usually begin as drafters for architectural firms, where they prepare architectural drawings and make models of structures under the direction of a registered architect. After several years of experience, they may advance to Chief or Senior Drafter responsible for all major details of a set of working drawings, and for supervising other drafters. Others may work as designers, construction contract administrators, or specification writers who prepare documents that specify the building materials, their method of installation, the quality of finishes, required tests, and many other related details.

OUTLOOK:

Employment of architects is expected to rise faster than the average for all occupations through the year 2000, although growth in employment will be slower than in recent years; however, demand for architects is highly dependent upon the level of construction, particularly of non-residential structures such as office buildings and shopping centers. Although rapid growth in this area is expected, construction is sensitive to cyclical changes in the economy. During recessions or slow periods for construction, architects will face competition for job openings or clients, and layoffs may occur.

ATTORNEY

DESCRIPTION:

Certain activities are common to nearly every attorney's work. Probably the most fundamental is interpretation of the law. Every attorney, whether representing the defendant in a murder trial, or the plaintiff in a lawsuit, combines an understanding of the relevant laws with knowledge of the facts in the case, to determine how the first affects the second. Based on this determination, the attorney decides what action would best serve the interests of the client.

A significant number specialize in one branch of law, such as corporate, criminal, labor, patent, real estate, tax, admiralty, probate, or international law. Communications lawyers, for example, may represent radio and television stations in their dealings with the Federal Communications Commission in such matters as preparing and filing license renewal applications, employment reports, and other documents required by the FCC on a regular basis. Lawyers representing public utilities before state and federal regulatory agencies handle matters involving utility rates. They develop strategy, arguments, and testimony, prepare cases for presentation, and argue the case. These attorneys also inform clients about changes in regulations and give advice about the legality of certain actions.

A single client may employ a lawyer full time. Known as House Counsel, this lawyer usually advises a company about legal questions that arise from business activities. Such questions might involve patents, governments regulations, a business contract with another company, or a collective bargaining agreement with a union. Some attorneys use their legal background in administrative or managerial positions in various departments of large corporations. A transfer from a corporation's legal department to another department is often viewed as a way to gain administrative experience and rise in the ranks of management. People may also use their legal background as journalists, management consultants, financial analysts, insurance claim adjusters, real estate appraisers, lobbyists, tax collectors, probation officers, and credit investigators.

BACKGROUND AND QUALIFICATIONS:

To practice law in the courts of any state, a person must be admitted to its bar. Applicants for admission to the bar must pass a written examination; however, a few states drop this requirement for graduates from its own law schools. Lawyers who have been admitted to the bar in one state may be admitted in another without taking an examination if they meet the state's standard of good moral character and have a specified period of legal experience. Federal courts and agencies set their own qualifications for those practicing before them. To qualify for the bar examination in most states, an applicant must complete at least three years of college, and graduate from a law school approved by the American Bar Association

OUTLOOK:

Rapid growth in the nation's requirements for lawyers is expected to bring job openings into rough balance with the relatively stable number of law school graduates each year and result in an easing of competition for jobs through the year 2000. During the 1970's, the annual number of law school graduates more than doubled, even outpacing the rapid growth of jobs. Although graduates with superior academic records from well-regarded law schools continued to enjoy excellent opportunities, most graduates encountered increasingly keen competition for jobs. Growth in the yearly number of law school graduates has tapered off during the 1980's, but, nevertheless, the number remains at a level high enough to tax the economy's capacity to absorb them. The number of law school graduates is expected to continue to remain near its present level through the year 2000, allowing employment growth to bring the job market for lawyers back into balance.

Employment of lawyers has grown very rapidly since the early 1970's, and is expected to continue to grow much faster than the average for all occupations through the year 2000. Increased population and growing business activity help sustain the strong demand for attorneys. This demand also will be spurred by growth of legal action in such areas as employee benefits, consumer protection, the environment, and safety, and an anticipated increase in the use of legal services by middle-income groups through legal clinics and prepaid legal service programs.

Turnover of jobs in this occupation is low because its members are well paid and enjoy considerable social status, and a substantial educational investment is required for entry. Nevertheless, most job openings will stem from the need to replace lawyers who transfer to other occupations or retire.

BANK OFFICER/MANAGER

DESCRIPTION:

Because banks offer a broad range of services, a wide choice of careers is available. Loan officers may handle installment, commercial, real estate, or agricultural loans. To evaluate loan applications properly, officers need to be familiar with economics, production, distribution, merchandising, and commercial law, as well as have a knowledge of business operations and financial analysis. Bank officers in trust management must have knowledge of financial planning and investment research for estate and trust administration. Operations officers plan, coordinate, and control the work flow, update systems, and strive for administrative efficiency. Careers in bank operations include electronic data processing manager and other positions involving internal and customer services. A correspondent bank officer is responsible for relations with other banks; a branch manager, for all functions of a branch office; and an international officer, for advising customers with financial dealings abroad. A working knowledge of a foreign country's financial system, trade relations, and economic conditions is beneficial to those interested in international banking. Other career fields for bank officers are auditing, economics, personnel administration, public relations, and operations research.

BACKGROUND AND QUALIFICATIONS:

Bank officers and management positions generally are filled by management trainees, and occasionally by promoting outstanding bank clerks and tellers. A Business Administration degree with concentrations in finance or a liberal arts curriculum, including accounting, economics, commercial law, political science, or statistics, serves as excellent preparation for officer trainee positions. In large banks that have special training programs, promotions may occur more quickly. For a senior officer position, however, an employee usually needs many years of experience. Although experience, ability, and leadership are emphasized for promotion, advancement may be accelerated by special study. The American Bankers Association (ABA) offers courses, publications, and other training aids to officers in every phase of banking. The American Institute of Banking, an arm of the ABA, has long filled the same educational need among bank support personnel.

OUTLOOK:

Employment of financial managers is expected to increase about as fast as the average for all occupations through the year 2000. Expanding automation - such as use of computers for electronic funds transmission and for data and information processing - may make financial managers more productive. However, the growing need for skilled financial management in the face of increasing domestic and foreign competition, changing laws regarding taxes and other financial matters, and greater emphasis on accurate reporting of financial data should spur demand for financial managers. New jobs will also be created by the increasing variety and complexity of services - including financial planning - offered by financial institutions. However, most job openings will result from the need to replace those who transfer to other fields or retire.

BIOCHEMIST

DESCRIPTION:

Biochemists study the chemical composition and behavior of living things. They often study the effects of food, hormones, or drugs on various organisms. The methods and techniques of biochemists are applied in areas such as medicine and agriculture. More than three out of four biochemists work in basic and applied research activities. Some biochemists combine research with teaching in colleges and universities. A few work in industrial production and testing activities. About one-half of all biochemists work for colleges or universities, and about one-fourth for private industry, primarily in companies manufacturing drugs, insecticides, and cosmetics. Some biochemists work for non-profit research institutes and foundations; others for federal, state, and local government agencies. A few self-employed biochemists are consultants to industry and government.

BACKGROUND AND QUALIFICATIONS:

The minimum educational requirement for many beginning jobs as a biochemist, especially in research and teaching, is an advanced degree. A PhD is a virtual necessity for persons who hope to contribute significantly to biochemical research and advance to many management or administrative jobs. A BS in Biochemistry, Biology, or Chemistry may qualify some persons for entry jobs as research assistants or technicians. Graduates with advanced degrees may begin their careers as teachers or researchers in colleges or universities. In private industry, most begin in research jobs, and with experience may advance to positions in which they plan and supervise research.

OUTLOOK:

Employment of biochemists is expected to increase about as fast as the average for all occupations through the year 2000. Most growth will be in private industry, primarily in genetic and biotechnical research and in production - using newly developed biological methods. Efforts to preserve the environment should also result in growth.

Biochemists are less likely to lose their jobs during recessions than those in many other occupations since most are employed on long-term research projects or in agriculture, activities which are not much affected by economic fluctuations.

BLUE-COLLAR WORKER SUPERVISOR

DESCRIPTION:

Supervisors direct the activities of other employees and frequently ensure that millions of dollars worth of equipment and materials are used properly and efficiently. While blue-collar worker supervisors are most commonly known as foremen or forewomen, they also have many other titles. In the textile industry, they are referred to as second hands; on ships, they are known as boatswains, and in the construction industry, they are often called overseers, strawbosses, or gang leaders. Supervisors make work schedules and keep production and employee records. They must use judgement in planning and must allow for unforeseen problems such as absent workers, or machine breakdowns. Teaching employees safe work habits and enforcing safety rules and regulations are among other supervisory responsibilities. Supervisors also may demonstrate timesaving or laborsaving techniques to workers, and train new employees. Worker supervisors tell their subordinates about company plans and policies; recommend good workers for wage increases, awards, or promotions; and deal with poor workers by issuing warnings or recommending that they be fired. In companies where employees belong to labor unions, supervisors meet with union representatives to discuss work problems and grievances. They must know the provisions of labor management contracts and run their operations according to these agreements.

BACKGROUND AND QUALIFICATIONS:

When choosing supervisors, employers generally look for experience, skill and leadership qualities. Most supervisors rise through the ranks; however, a growing number of employers are hiring trainees with a college background. This practice is most prevalent in industries with highly technical production processes, such as the chemical, oil, and electronics industries. Employers generally prefer backgrounds in business administration, industrial relations, mathematics, engineering, or science. The trainees undergo on-the-job training until they are able to accept supervisory responsibilities. Outstanding supervisors may move up to higher management positions. In manufacturing, for example, they may advance to jobs such as department head or plant manager. Some supervisors, particularly in the construction industry, use the experience and skills they gain to go into business for themselves.

OUTLOOK:

Employment of blue-collar worker supervisors is expected to increase more slowly than the average for all occupation through the year 2000. Although rising incomes will stimulate demand for goods such as air-conditioners, home entertainment equipment, personal computers, and automobiles, employment in manufacturing industries will decline, due in part to increasing foreign competition. The production-related occupations in manufacturing, including blue-collar worker supervisors, will be the ones most adversely affected. Offsetting the decline in the number of supervisors in manufacturing, however, will be an increase in jobs in non-manufacturing industries, especially in the trade and service sectors. In addition to the jobs resulting in increased demand for supervisors, many openings will arise from the need to replace workers who leave the occupation. Supervisors have a relatively strong attachment to the occupation, but because the occupation is so large, turnover results in a large number of openings. Because blue-collar worker supervisors are so important to the successful operation of a firm, they are often protected from layoffs during a recession. Supervisors in the construction industry, however, may experience periodic layoffs when construction activity declines.

BUYER/MERCHANDISE MANAGER

DESCRIPTION:

All merchandise sold in a retail store appears in that store on the decision of a buyer. Although all buyers seek to satisfy their stores' customers and sell at a profit, the type and variety of goods they purchase depends on the store where they work. A buyer for a small clothing store, for example, may purchase its complete stock of merchandise. Buyers who work for larger retail businesses often handle a few related lines of goods, such as men's wear, ladies' sportswear, or children's toys, among many others. Some, known as foreign buyers, purchase merchandise outside the United States. Buyers must be familiar with the manufacturers and distributors who handle the merchandise they need. They also must keep informed about changes in existing products and the development of new ones. Merchandise Managers plan and coordinate buying and selling activities for large and medium-sized stores. They divide the budget among buyers, decide how much merchandise to stock, and assign each buyer to purchase certain goods. Merchandise Managers may review buying decisions to ensure that needed categories of goods are in stock, and help buyers to set general pricing guidelines.

Some buyers represent large stores or chains in cities where many manufacturers are located. The duties of these "market representatives" vary by employer; some purchase goods, while others supply information and arrange for store buyers to meet with manufacturer's representatives when they are in the area. New technology has altered the buyers' role in retail chain stores. Cash registers connected to a computer, known as point-of-sale terminals, allow retail chains to maintain centralized, up-to-the-minute inventory records. With these records, a single garden furniture buyer, for example, can purchase lawn chairs and picnic tables for the entire chain.

BACKGROUND AND QUALIFICATIONS:

Because familiarity with the merchandise and with the retailing business itself is such a central element in the buyer's job, prior retailing experience sometimes provides sufficient preparation. More and more, however, employers prefer applicants who have a college degree. Most employers accept college grads in any field of study and train them on the job. In many stores, beginners who are candidates for buying jobs start out in executive training programs. These programs last from six to eight months, and combine classroom instruction in merchandising and purchasing with short rotations in various store jobs. This training introduces the new worker to store operations and policies, and provides the fundamentals of merchandising and management. The trainee's first job is likely to be that of assistant buyer. The duties include supervising sales workers, checking invoices on material received, and keeping account of stock on hand. Assistant buyers gradually assume purchasing responsibilities, depending upon their individual abilities and the size of the department where they work. Training as an assistant buyer usually lasts at least one year. After years of working as a buyer, those who show exceptional ability may advance to merchandise manager. A few find promotion to top executive jobs such as general merchandise manager for a retail store or chain.

OUTLOOK:

Employment of buyers is expected to grow more slowly than the average for all occupations though the year 2000 as more wholesale and retail trade establishments automate and centralize their purchasing departments. Productivity gains resulting from the increased use of computers to control inventory, maintain records, and reorder merchandise will be the principal factor restraining employment growth. Most job openings, therefore, will result from replacement needs, which occur as experienced buyers transfer to other occupations in sales or management, change careers, or stop working altogether. The number of qualified jobseekers will continue to exceed the number of openings because merchandising attracts many college graduates. Prospects are likely to be best for qualified applicants who enjoy the competitive, fast-paced nature of merchandising.

CHEMIST

DESCRIPTION:

Chemists search for and put into practical use new knowledge about substances. Their research has resulted in the development of a tremendous variety of synthetic materials, such as nylon and polyester fabrics. Nearly one-half of all chemists work in research and development. In basic research, chemists investigate the properties and composition of matter and the laws that govern the combination of elements. Basic research often has practical uses. In research and development, new products are created or improved. Nearly one-eighth of all chemists work in production and inspection. In production, chemists prepare instructions (batch sheets) for plant workers that specify the kind and amount of ingredients to use and the exact mixing time for each stage in the process. At each step, samples are tested for quality control to meet industry and government standards. Other chemists work as marketing or sales representative because of their technical knowledge of the products sold. A number of chemists teach in colleges and universities. Some chemists are consultants to private industry and government agencies. Chemists often specialize in one of several subfields of chemistry: analytical chemists determine the structure, composition, and nature of substances, and develop new techniques; organic chemists at one time studied only the chemistry of living things, but their area has been broadened to include all carbon compounds; inorganic chemists study noncarbon compounds; and physical chemists study energy transformations to find new and better energy sources.

BACKGROUND AND QUALIFICATIONS:

A BS with a major in Chemistry or a related discipline is sufficient for many entry-level jobs as a chemist. However, graduate training is required for many research jobs, and most college teaching jobs require a PhD. Beginning chemists with a Master's Degree can usually go into applied research. The PhD is generally required for basic research for teaching in colleges and universities, and for advancement to many administrative positions.

OUTLOOK:

Employment of chemists is expected to grow more slowly than the average for all occupations through the year 2000.

CLAIM REPRESENTATIVE

DESCRIPTION:

The people who investigate insurance claims, negotiate settlements with policy holders, and authorize payments are known as claim representative - a group that includes claim adjusters and claim examiners. When a casualty insurance company receives a claim, the claim adjuster determines whether the policy covers it and the amount of the loss. Adjusters use reports, physical evidence, and testimony of witnesses in investigating a claim. When their company is liable, they negotiate with the claimant and settle the case. Some adjusters work with all lines of insurance. Others specialize in claims from fire, marine loss, automobile damage, workers' compensation loss, or product liability. A growing number of casualty companies employ special adjusters to settle small claims. These workers, generally called inside adjusters or telephone adjusters, contact claimants by telephone or mail and have the policy holder send repair costs, medical bills, and other statements to the company. In life insurance companies, the counterpart of the claim adjuster is the claim examiner, who investigates questionable claims or those exceeding a specified amount. They may check claim applications for completeness and accuracy, interview medical specialists, consult policy files to verify information on a claim, or calculate benefit payments. Generally, examiners are authorized to investigate and approve payment on all claims up to a certain limit; larger claims are referred to a senior examiner.

BACKGROUND AND QUALIFICATIONS:

No specific field of college study is recommended. Although courses in insurance, economics, or other business subjects are helpful, a major in most college fields is adequate preparation. Most large insurance companies provide beginning claim adjusters and examiners with on-the-job training and home study courses. Claim representatives are encouraged to take courses designed to enhance their professional skills. For example, the Insurance Institute of America offers a six semester study program leading to an Associate's Degree in Claims Adjusting, upon successful completion of six exams. A professional Certificate in Insurance Adjusting also is available from the College of Insurance in New York City. The Life Office Management Association (LOMA), in cooperation with the International Claim Association, offers a claims education, program for life and health examiners. The program is part of the LOMA Institute Insurance Education Program leading to the professional designation FLMI (Fellow Life Management Institute) upon successful completion of eight written exams. Beginning adjusters and examiners work on small claims under the supervision of an experienced employee. As they learn more about claim investigation and settlement, they are assigned claims that are either higher in loss value or more complex. Trainees are promoted as they demonstrate competence in handling assignments and as they progress in their course work. Employees who show unusual competence in claims work or outstanding administrative skills may be promoted to department supervisor in a field office, or to a managerial position in the home office. Qualified adjusters and examiners sometimes transfer to other departments, such as underwriting or sales.

OUTLOOK:

Employment of claim representatives is expected to grow faster than the average for all occupations as the increasing volume of insurance sales results in more insurance claims. Shifts in the age distribution of the population will result in a large increase in the number of people who assume career and family responsibilities. People in this group have the greatest need for life and health insurance, and protection for homes, automobiles, and other possessions. A growing demand for insurance coverage for working women is also expected. New or expanding businesses will need protection for new plants and equipment and for insurance covering their employees' health and safety. Opportunities should be particularly good for claim representatives who specialize in complex business insurance such as marine cargo, workers' compensation, and product and pollution liability insurance.

COMMERCIAL ARTIST

DESCRIPTION:

A team of commercial artists with varying skills and specializations often creates the artwork in newspapers and magazines, and on billboards, brochures, and catalogs. This team is supervised by an art director, whose main function is to develop a theme or idea for an ad or advertising campaign. After the art director has determined the main elements of an ad or design, he or she will turn the project over to two specialists for further refinement. The sketch artist, also called a renderer, does a rough drawing of any pictures required. The layout artist, who is concerned with graphics rather than art work, constructs or arranges the illustrations or photographs, plans the typography, and picks colors for the ad. Other commercial artists, usually with less experience, are needed to turn out the finished products. Letterers put together headlines and other words on the ad. Mechanical artists paste up an engraver's guide of the ad. Paste-up artists and other less experienced employees do more routine work, such as cutting mats, assembling booklets, or running errands. Advertising artists create the concepts and artwork for a wide variety of items. These include direct mail advertising, catalogs, counter displays, slides, and filmstrips. They also design or lay out newspapers, magazines, and advertising circulars. Some commercial artists specialize in producing fashion illustrations, greeting cards, or book illustrations, or in making technical drawings for industry.

BACKGROUND AND QUALFICATIONS:

Persons can prepare for a career in commercial art by attending either a 2- or 4-year trade school, community college, college, or university offering a program in commercial art.

OUTLOOK:

The graphic arts fields have a glamorous and exciting image. Because formal entry qualifications are few, many people with a love for drawing and creative ability qualify for entry. As a result, competition for both salaried jobs and freelance work is keen. Freelance work may be hard to come by, especially at first, and many free-lancers earn very little until they acquire experience and establish a good reputation.

DATA PROCESSING SPECIALIST

DESCRIPTION:

The main function of a data processing specialist is to type data from documents such as checks, bills, and invoices quickly and accurately, and enter this information into a computer system. This is done with a variety of typewriter-like equipment. Many specialists use a machine that converts the information they type to magnetic impulses on tapes or disks. The information is then read into the computer from the tape or disk. Some specialists operate on-line terminals of the main computer system that transmit and receive data. Although brands and models of computer terminals and data entry equipment differ somewhat, their operation and keyboards are similar.

Some specialists working from terminals use data from the computer to produce business, scientific, and technical reports. In some offices, specialists also operate computer peripheral equipment such as printers and tape readers, and act as tape librarians.

BACKGROUND AND QUALIFICATIONS:

Employers usually require a high school education and the ability to key data in at a certain speed. Applicants are often tested for speed and accuracy. Some employers prefer applicants with experience or training in the operation of data entry equipment, and console operators are often required to have a college education. In some firms, other clerical workers such as tabulating and bookkeeping machine operators may be transferred to jobs as data processing specialists. Training in the use of data entry and similar keyboard equipment is available in high schools or private business schools.

OUTLOOK:

The employment rate of data processing specialists is expected to decline through the year 2000. Despite this decline, many openings, including part-time ones, will occur each year, due to the need to replace workers who transfer to other occupations or leave the labor force. Related occupations include secretaries, typists, receptionists, and typesetters and compositors.

DIETITIAN/NUTRITIONIST

DESCRIPTION:

Dietitians, sometimes called nutritionists, are professionals trained in applying the principles of nutrition to food selection and meal preparation. They counsel individuals and groups; set up and supervise food service systems for institutions such as hospitals, prisons, and schools; and promote sound eating habits through education and administration. Dietitians also work on education and research. Clinical dietitians, sometimes called therapeutic dietitians, provide nutritional services for patients in hospitals, nursing homes, clinics, or doctors' offices. They assess patients' nutritional needs, develop and implement nutrition programs, and evaluate and report the results. Clinical dietitians confer with doctors and nurses about each patient in order to coordinate nutritional intake with other treatments-medications in particular.

Community dietitians counsel individuals and groups on sound nutrition practices to prevent disease and to promote good health. Employed in such places as home health agencies, health maintenance organizations, and human service agencies that provide group and home-delivered meals, their job is to establish nutritional care plans, and communicate the principles of good nutrition in a way individuals and their families can understand. Research dietitians are usually employed in academic medical centers or educational institutions, although some work in common programs. Using established research methods and analytical techniques, they conduct studies in areas that range from basic science to practical applications. Research dietitians may examine changes in the way the body uses food over the course of a lifetime, for example, or study the interaction of drugs and diet. They may investigate the nutritional needs of persons with particular diseases, behavior modification, as it relates to diet and nutrition, or applied topics such as food service systems and equipment.

BACKGROUND/QUALIFICATIONS:

The basic educational requirement for this field is a bachelor's degree with a major in foods and nutrition or institution management. To qualify for professional credentials as a registered dietitian, the American Dietetic Association (ADA) recommends one of the following educational paths: Completion of a grow-year coordinated undergraduate program which includes 900 to 1,000 hours of clinical experience; completion of a bachelor's degree from an approved program plus an accredited dietetic internship; completion of a bachelor's or master's degree from an approved program and six month's approved work experience.

DRAFTSPERSON

DESCRIPTION:

Drafters prepare detailed drawings based on rough sketches, specifications, and calculations made by scientists, engineers, architects, and designers. Final drawings contain a detailed view of the object from all sides as well as specifications for materials to be used, procedures to be followed, and other information needed to carry out the job. There are two methods by which these drawings are prepared. In the traditional method, drafters sit at drawing boards and use compasses, dividers, protractors, triangles, and other drafting devices to prepare the drawing manually. In the new method, drafters use computer-aided drafting (CAD) systems. They sit at computer work stations and may make the drawing on a videoscreen. In some cases, the design may never be placed on paper. It may be stored electronically and, in some factories, may be used to guide automatic machinery. These systems free drafters from much routine drafting work and permit many variations of a design to be prepared easily. CAD systems allow a design to be viewed from various angles and perspectives not usually available with more traditional drafting methods so that design work can be better, faster, and more thorough. In addition to drafting equipment and CAD systems, drafters use technical handbooks, tables, and calculators in preparing drawings and related specifications.

BACKGROUND/REQUIREMENTS:

It is preferred that applicants have two years of post-high school training in technical institutes, junior and community colleges, or extension divisions of universities. Some persons receive training in the Armed Forces. Training for a career in drafting should include courses in mathematics, physical science, mechanical drawing, and drafting. Courses in shop practices and shop skills are also helpful, since most higher level drafting jobs require knowledge of manufacturing or construction methods. Many technical schools offer courses in structural design, architectural drawing, and engineering or industrial technology. Beginners usually start as junior drafters doing routine work under close supervision. After gaining experience, they do more difficult work with less supervision and may advance to senior drafter or supervisor with appropriate college education, they may become engineers, designers, or architects.

OUTLOOK:

Little change in employment of drafters is expected to occur through the year 2000. Related occupations include architects, engineering technicians, engineers, landscape architects, photogrammetrists, and surveyors.

ECONOMIST

DESCRIPTION:

Economists study the way a society uses scarce resources such as land, labor, raw materials, and machinery to produce goods and services. They analyze the costs and benefits of distributing and using resources in a particular way. Their research might focus on such topics as energy costs, inflation, business cycles, unemployment, tax policy, farm prices, and many other areas. Being able to present economic and statistical concepts in a meaningful way is particularly important for economists whose research is policy directed. Economists who work for business firms may be asked to provide management with information on which decisions such as the marketing or pricing of company products are made; to look at the advisability of adding new lines of merchandise, opening new branches, or diversifying the company's operations; to analyze the effects of changes in the tax laws; or to prepare economic or business forecasts. Business economists working for firms that carry on operations abroad may be asked to prepare forecasts of foreign economic conditions. About three of every economists work in private industry, including manufacturing firms, banks, insurance companies, securities and investment companies, economic research firms and management consulting firms. Some run their own consulting businesses. A number of economists combine a full-time job in government, business or an academic institution with part-time or consulting work in another setting.

BACKGROUND AND QUALIFICATIONS:

A Bachelors degree in Economics is sufficient for many beginning research, administrative, management trainee, and business sales jobs. However, graduate training is increasingly necessary for advancement to more responsible positions as economists. In government research organizations and consulting firms, economists who have Master's degrees can usually qualify for more responsible research and administrative positions. A PhD may be necessary for top positions in some organizations. Experienced business economists may advance to managerial or executive positions in banks, industrial concerns, trade associations, and other orginzations where they formulate practical business and administrative policy.

OUTLOOK:

Employment of economists is expected to grow faster than the average for all occupations through the year 2000. Most job openings, however, will result from the need to replace experienced economists who transfer to other occupations, retire, or leave the labor force for other reasons.

ENGINEER

DESCRIPTION:

Engineers apply the theories and principles of science and mathematics to tactical technical problems. Often, their work is the link between a scientific discovery and its useful application. Engineers design machinery, products, systems, and processes for efficient and economical performance. Engineering is a highly specialized field and the work an engineer does depends greatly upon the industry in which he/she is employed. The following descriptions outline the basic specialties and their respective employment outlooks.

Aerospace Engineer:

Aerospace engineers design, develop, test, and help produce commercial and military aircraft, missiles, spacecraft, and related systems. They play an important role in advancing the state of technology in commercial aviation, defense and space exploration. Aerospace engineers often specialize in an area of work like structural design, navigational guidance and control, instrumentation and communication, or production methods. They also may specialize in one type of aerospace product, such as passenger planes, helicopters, satellites, or rockets.

Outlook:

Employment of aerospace engineers is expected to grow more slowly than average for all occupations through the year 2000. During the 1980's, their employment grew very rapidly. However, because of recent Defense Department expenditure cuts for military aircraft, missiles and other aerospace systems, major growth is not expected.

Chemical Engineer:

Chemical engineers are involved in many phases of the production of chemicals and chemical products. They design equipment and chemical plants as well as determine methods of manufacturing these products. Often, they design and develop chemical processes such as those used to remove chemical contaminants from waste materials. Because the duties of the chemical engineer cut across many fields, these professionals must have knowledge of chemistry, physics, and mechanical and electrical engineering. This branch of engineering is so diversified and complex that chemical engineers frequently specialize in a particular operation such as oxidation or polymerization. Others specialize in a particular area such as pollution control or the production of a specific product like plastics or rubber.

Outlook:

Employment of chemical engineers is expected to grow about as fast as the average for all occupations through the year 2000.

Civil Engineer:

Civil engineers, who work in the oldest branch of the engineering profession, design and supervise the construction of roads, harbors, airports, tunnels, bridges, water supply and sewage systems, and buildings. Major specialties within civil engineering are structural, hydraulic, environmental/ sanitary, transportation, urban planning, and soil mechanics. Many civil engineers are in supervisory or administrative positions ranging from supervisor of a construction site, to city engineer, to top level executive Others teach in colleges and universities, or work as consultants.

Outlook:

Employment of civil engineers is expected to increase faster than the average for all occupations through the year 2000.

Electrical Engineer:

Electrical engineers design, develop, test and supervise the manufacture of electrical and electronic equipment. Electrical equipment includes power-generating and transmission equipment used by electrical utilities, electric motors, machinery controls, and lighting and wiring in buildings, automobiles, and aircraft. Electronic equipment includes radar, computers, communications equipment, and consumer goods such as television sets and stereos. Electrical engineers also design and operate facilities for generating and distributing electrical power.

Electrical engineers generally specialize in a major area, such as integrated circuits, computers, electrical equipment manufacturing, communications, or power distributing equipment, or in a subdivision of these areas, such as microwave communication or aviation electronic systems. Electrical engineers design new products, specify their uses, and write performance requirements and maintenance schedules.

Outlook:

The outlook for electrical engineers is estimated to be good through the year 2000.

Industrial Engineer:

Industrial engineers determine the most effective ways for an organization to use the basic factors of production--people, machines and materials. They are more concerned with people and methods of business organization than are engineers in other specialties, who generally are concerned more with particular products or processes, such as metals, power or mechanics. To solve organizational, production, and related problems most efficiently, industrial engineers design data processing systems and apply mathematical concepts. They also develop management control systems to aid in financial planning and cost analysis, design production planning and control systems to coordinate activities and control product quality, and design or improve systems for the physical distribution of goods and services. Industrial engineers also conduct plant location surveys, where they look for the best combination of sources of raw materials, transportation, and taxes, and develop wage and salary administration positions and job evaluation programs. Many industrial engineers move into managerial positions because the work is closely related.

Outlook:

Employment opportunities for industrial engineers are expected to be good; their employment is expected to grow faster than the average for all occupations through the year 2000. Most job openings, however, will result from the need to replace industrial engineers who transfer to other occupations or leave the labor force.

Metallurgical Engineer:

Metallurgical engineers develop new types of metals with characteristics that are tailored for specific requirements, such as heat resistance, lightweight strength, or high malleability. They also develop methods to process and convert metals into useful products. Most of these engineers generally work in one of three major branches of metallurgy: extractive or chemical, physical, or mechanical. Extractive metallurgists are concerned with extracting metals from ores, and refining and alloying them to obtain useful materials. Physical metallurgists deal with the nature, structure, and physical properties of metals and their alloys, and with the methods of converting refined metals into final products. Mechanical metallurgists develop methods to work and shape materials, such as casting, forging, rolling, and drawing.

Outlook:

Employment of metallurgical, ceramic, and materials engineers is expected to grow more rapidly than the average for all occupations through the year 2000.

Mining Engineer:

Mining engineers find, extract, and prepare minerals for manufacturing industries to use. They design open pit and underground mines, supervise the construction of mine shafts and tunnels in underground operations, and devise methods for transporting minerals to processing plants. Mining engineers are responsible for the economical and efficient operation of mines and mine safety, including ventilation, water supply, power, communications, and equipment maintenance. Some mining engineers work with geologists and metallurgical engineers to locate and appraise new ore deposits. Others develop new mining equipment or direct mineral processing operations, which involve separating minerals from the dirt, rock, and other materials they are mixed with. Mining engineers frequently specialize in the mining of one specific mineral such as coal or copper. With increased emphasis on protecting the environment, many mining engineers have been working to solve problems related to mined land reclamation, and water and air pollution.

Outlook:

The employment outlook for mining engineers is expected to remain constant through the year 2000, due to expected low growth in demand for coal, metals, and other minerals.

Petroleum Engineer:

Petroleum engineers are mainly involved in exploring and drilling for oil and gas. They work to achieve the maximum profitable recovery of oil and gas from a petroleum reservoir by determining and developing the best and most efficient methods. Since only a small proportion of the oil and gas in a reservoir will flow out under natural forces, petroleum engineers develop and use various artificial recovery methods, such as flooding the oil field with water to force the oil to the surface. Even when using the best recovery methods, about half the oil is still left in the ground. Petroleum engineers' research and development efforts to increase the proportion of oil recovered in each reservoir can make a significant contribution to increasing available energy resources.

Outlook:

Employment of petroleum engineers is expected to grow more slowly than the average for all occupations through the year 2000. With the drop in oil prices, domestic petroleum companies have curtailed exploration, resulting in poor employment opportunities.

BACKGROUND AND QUALIFICATIONS:

A bachelor's degree in engineering from an accredited engineering program is generally acceptable for beginning engineering jobs. College graduates trained in one of the natural sciences or mathematics also may qualify for some beginning jobs. Most engineering degrees may be obtained in branches such as electrical, mechanical, or civil engineering. College graduates with a degree in science or mathematics and experienced engineering technicians may also qualify for some engineering jobs, especially in engineering specialties in high demand. Graduate training is essential for engineering faculty positions but is not required for the majority of entry level engineering jobs. All 50 states require licensing for engineers whose work may affect life, health or property, or who offer their services to the public.

Beginning engineering graduates usually work under the supervision of experienced engineers, and in larger companies, may receive seminar or classroom training. As engineers advance in knowledge, they may become technical specialists, supervisors, or managers or administrators within the field of engineering. Some engineers obtain advanced degrees in business administration to improve their growth opportunities, while others obtain law degrees and become patent attorneys.

FINANCIAL ANALYST

DESCRIPTION:

A financial analyst prepares the financial reports required by the firm to conduct its operations and satisfy tax and regulatory requirements. Financial analysts also oversee the flow of cash and financial instruments and develop information to assess the present and future financial status of the firm.

BACKGROUND AND QUALIFICATIONS:

A bachelor's degree in accounting or finance is suitable academic preparation for a financial manager. An MBA degree in addition to a bachelor's degree in any field is acceptable to many employers.

OUTLOOK:

Employment of financial managers is expected to increase about as fast as the average for occupations through the year 2000.

FOOD TECHNOLOGIST

DESCRIPTION:

A food technologist studies the chemical, physical and biological nature of food to learn how to safely process, preserve, package, distribute, and store it. Some develop new products, while others insure quality standards. They are, like animal scientists, dairy scientists, horticulturists, soil scientists, animal and plant breeders, entomologists, and agriculturalists, classified generally as agricultural scientists by the U.S. Department of Labor.

BACKGROUND AND QUALIFICATIONS:

Educational requirements for the agricultural scientist depend a great deal upon the area and type of work performed. A PhD degree in agricultural science is usually required for college teaching, independent research, and for advancement to many administrative and management jobs. A bachelor's degree is sufficient for some sales, production management, inspection, and other nonresearch jobs, but, in some cases, promotions may be limited. Degrees in some related sciences such as biology, chemistry, or physics or in related engineering specialties also may be acceptable for some agricultural science jobs.

OUTLOOK:

Employment of agricultural scientists is expected to grow about as fast as the average for an occupations through the year 2000.

FORESTER

DESCRIPTION:

Foresters plan and supervise the growing, protection and harvesting of trees. They plot forest areas, approximate the amount of standing timber and future growth, and manage timber sales. Some foresters also protect the trees from fire, harmful insects, and disease. Some foresters also protect wildlife and manage watersheds; develop and supervise campgrounds, parks, and grazing lands; and do research. Foresters in extension work provide information to forest owners and to the general public.

BACKGROUND AND QUALIFICATIONS:

A bachelor's degree in forestry is the minimum educational requirement for professional careers in forestry. In 1986, 55 colleges and universities offered bachelor's or higher degrees in forestry, 47 of these were accredited by the Society of American Foresters.

OUTLOOK:

Employment of foresters and conservation scientists is expected to grow more slowly than the average for all occupations through the year 2000.

GEOGRAPHER

DESCRIPTION:

Geographers study the interrelationship of humans and the environment. Economic geographers deal with the geographic distribution of an area's economic activities. Political geographers are concerned with the relationship of geography to political phenomena. Physical geographers study physical processes in the earth and its atmosphere. Urban geographers study cities and metropolitan areas, while regional geographers specialize in the physical, climatic, economic, political and cultural characteristics of a particular region or area. Medical geographers study the effect of the environment on health.

BACKGROUND AND QUALIFICATIONS:

The minimum educational requirement for entry-level positions is a BA or BS degree in Geography. However, a Masters degree is increasingly required for many entry level positions. Applicants for entry level jobs would find it helpful to have training in a specialty such as cartography, photogrammerty, remote sensing data interpretation, statistical analysis including computer science, or environmental analysis. To advance to a senior research position in private industry and perhaps gain a spot in management, a geographer would probably be required to have an advanced degree.

OUTLOOK:

Average growth is predicted throughout the 1990's.

GEOLOGISTS AND GEOPHYSISICTS

DESCRIPTION:

Geologists study the structure, composition and history of the earth's crust. By examining surface rocks and drilling to recover rock cores, they determine the types and distribution of rocks beneath the earth's surface. They also identify rocks and minerals, conduct geological surveys, draw maps, take measurements, and record data. Geological research helps to determine the structure and history of the earth, and may result in significant advances, such as in the ability to predict earthquakes. An important application of geologists' work is locating oil and other natural and mineral resources. Geologists usually specialize in one or a combination of general areas: earth materials, earth processes, and earth history.

Geophysicists study the composition and physical aspects of the earth and its electric, magnetic and gravitational fields. Geophysicists usually specialize in one of three general phases of the science -- solid earth, fluid earth, and upper atmosphere. Some may also study other planets.

BACKGROUND AND QUALIFICATIONS:

A Bachelor's degree in geology or geophysics is adequate for entry to some lower level geology jobs, but better jobs with good advancement potential usually require at least a master's degree in geology or geophysics. Persons with strong backgrounds in physics, mathematics, or computer science also may qualify for some geophysics jobs. A PhD is essential for most research positions.

OUTLOOK:

Employment of geologists and geophysicists is expected to grow more slowly than the average for all occupations through the year 2000, mainly due to the reduction in energy exploration by oil companies.

HOTEL MANAGER/ASSISTANT MANAGER

DESCRIPTION:

Hotel managers are responsible for operating their establishments profitably and satisfying guests. They determine room rates and credit policy, direct the operation of the food science operation, and manage the housekeeping, accounting, security, and maintenance departments of the hotel. Handling problems and coping with the unexpected are important parts of the job. A small hotel or motel requires only a limited staff, and the manager may have to fill various front office duties, such as taking reservations or assigning rooms. When management is combined with ownership, these activities may expand to include all aspects of the business. General managers of large hotels usually have several assistants or department heads who manage various part of the operation. Because hotel restaurant and cocktail lounges are important to the success of the entire establishment, they are almost always operated by managers with experience in the restaurant field. Other areas that are usually handled separately include advertising, rental of banquet and meeting facilities, marketing and sales, personnel and accounting. Large hotel and motel chains often centralize some activities, such as purchasing and advertising, so that individual hotels in the chain may not need managers for these departments. Managers who work for chains may be assigned to organize a newly-built or purchased hotel, or to reorganize an existing hotel or motel that is not operating successfully.

BACKGROUND AND QUALIFICATIONS:

Experience is the most important consideration in selecting hotel managers. However, employers are increasingly emphasizing college education. A BA in Hotel/Restaurant Administration provides particularly strong preparation for a career in hotel management. Most hotels promote employees who have proven their ability, usually front office clerks, to assistant manager, and eventually to general manager. Hotel and motel chains may offer better employment opportunities because employees can transfer to another hotel or motel in the chain, or to the central office if an opening occurs

OUTLOOK:

Employment of salaried hotel managers is expected to grow much faster than the average for all occupations through the year 2000 as more large hotels and motels are built.

INDUSTRIAL DESIGNER

DESCRIPTION:

Industrial designers combine artistic talent with a knowledge of marketing, materials, and methods of production to improve the appearance and functional design of products so that they compete favorably with similar goods on the market. Although most industrial designers are engaged in product design, others are involved in different facets of design. To create favorable public images for companies and for government service, some designers develop trademarks or symbols that appear on the firm's products, advertising, brochures, and stationery. Some design containers and packages that both protect and promote their contents. Others prepare small display exhibits or the entire layout for industrial fairs. Some design the interior layout of special purpose commercial buildings such as restaurants and supermarkets.

Corporate designers usually work only on products made by their employer. This may involve filling the day-to-day design needs of the company, or long-range planning of new products. Independent consultants who serve more than one industrial firm often plan and design a great variety of products. Most designers work for large manufacturing companies designing either consumer or industrial products, or for design consulting firms. Others do freelance work, or are on the staffs of architectural and interior design firms.

BACKGROUND AND QUALIFICATIONS:

The normal requirement for entering this field of work involves completing a course of study in industrial design at an art school, university, or technical college. Most large manufacturing firms hire only industrial designers who have a Bachelor's degree in the field. Beginning industrial designers frequently do simple assignments. As they gain experience, they may work on their own, and many become supervisors with major responsibility for the design of a product or group of products. Those who have an established reputation and the necessary funds may start their own consulting firms.

OUTLOOK:

Employment in design occupations is expected to grow faster than the average for all occupations through the year 2000. Continued emphasis on product quality and safety, on design of new products for businesses and offices, and on high-technology products in medicine and transportation should expand the demand for industrial designers.

INSURANCE AGENT/BROKER

DESCRIPTION:

Agents and brokers usually sell one or more of the three basic types of insurance: life, casualty, and health. Underwriters offer various policies that, besides providing health benefits, may also provide retirement income, funds for education, or other benefits. Casualty insurance agents sell policies that protect individual policyholders from financial losses resulting from automobile accidents, fire, or theft. They also sell industrial or commercial lines, such as workers' compensation, products liability, or medical malpractice insurance. Health insurance policies offer protection against the high costs of hospital and medical care, or loss of income due to illness or injury. Many agents also offer securities, such as mutual fund shares or variable annuities.

An insurance agent may be either an insurance company employee or an independent who is authorized to represent one or more insurance companies. Brokers are not under exclusive contract with any single company, instead, they place policies directly with the company that best meets a company's needs.

Insurance agents spend most of their time discussing insurance needs with prospective and existing clients. Some time must be spent in office work to prepare reports, maintain records, plan insurance programs that are tailored to prospects' needs, and draw up lists of prospective customers. Specialists in group policies may help an employer's accountant set up a system of payroll deductions for employees covered by the policy.

BACKGROUND AND QUALIFICATIONS:

All insurance agents and most insurance brokers must obtain a license in the state where they plan to sell insurance. In most states, licenses are issued only to applicants who pass written examinations covering insurance fundamentals and the state insurance laws. Agents who plan to sell mutual fund shares and other securities also must be licensed by the state. New agents usually receive training at the agencies where they will work, and frequently at the insurance company's home office. Beginners sometimes attend company-sponsored classes to prepare for the examination. Others study on their own and accompany experienced sales workers when they call on prospective clients.

OUTLOOK:

Employment of insurance agents and brokers is expected to grow about as fast as the average for all occupations through the year 2000. Turnover is high because many beginners are able to establish a sufficiently large clientele in this highly competitive business. Most individuals and businesses consider insurance a necessity, regardless of economic conditions. Therefore, agents are not likely to face unemployment because of a recession.

MANAGER

DESCRIPTION:

Managers supervise employees and are accountable for the overall success of the operation which they direct. The scope and nature of a manager's responsibilities depend greatly upon the position and the size of his or her organization.

A department manager at a retail store, for example, may actually spend most of his or her time waiting on customers, and his or her managerial duties may be limited to scheduling employees' work shifts to properly staff the department, or to training new employees in such simple tasks as operating the check-out terminal, processing credit card purchases, and displaying merchandise.

A branch manager, even in a small store or service operation, might have considerably broader duties and responsibilities. He or she might, in addition to supervising and training employees, be responsible for hiring and firing decisions. He or she might have a limited ability to purchase items, and might have some control over a local advertising budget. He or she might also deal with local suppliers of goods and services. Some organizations, however, prefer to delegate rather limited responsibility to branch managers, and instead rely upon a strong network of regional managers who travel from branch to branch, making key operating decisions.

Factories or service firms with extensive processing requirements employ operations and production managers. While these managers typically supervise many people, their primary responsibility is the overall success of the operation, which may be dependent upon equipment, raw material, purchased goods, or outside vendors. The operations manager at a bank, for example, remains heavily dependent upon data processing equipment, and usually will have an extensive background in this area. The production manager at a petroleum refinery, for another example, remains heavily dependent upon a large variety of specialized equipment, and will usually have a background in engineering or chemistry.

The general manager is responsible for the overall day-to-day operations of the firm or operating unit. He or she must be acquainted with each part of the operation. In a small store, the general manager may spend most of his or her time performing nonmanagerial tasks such as making purchases, or even waiting on customers. In a large corporation, on the other hand, the general manager (who is often the executive vice president) will spend much of his or her time meeting with key executives in each department to ensure that company operations are being conducted successfully.

BACKGROUND AND QUALIFICATIONS:

The educational background of managers and top executives varies as widely as the nature of their diverse responsibilities. Most general managers and top executives have a bachelor's degree in liberal arts or business administration. Graduate and professional degrees are common. Many managers in administrative, marketing, financial, and manufacturing activities have a master's degree in business administration. Larger firms usually have some form of management training program, usually open to recent college graduates. While such programs are usually competitive, they generally offer an excellent opportunity to quickly familiarize oneself with many different aspects of a firm's business. Also, such programs are often open to a broad range of candidates, including both candidates with a BS in business administration, and liberal arts graduates as well.

OUTLOOK:

Employment of general managers and top executives is expected to grow about as fast as the average for all occupations through the year 2000.

MANUFACTURERS' SALES WORKERS

DESCRIPTION:

Most manufacturers employ sales workers to market their products to other businesses, mainly to other producers, wholesalers, and retailers. Manufacturers also sell directly to institutions such as schools, hospitals, and libraries. The sales workers who represent a manufacturer to prospective buyers are usually called manufacturers' representatives, although the job title may vary by product line.

Manufacturers' sales workers visit prospective buyers to inform them about the products they sell, analyze the buyer's needs, suggest how their products can meet these needs, and take orders. Sales workers visit firms in their territory, using an approach adapted to their line of merchandise. Sometimes sales workers promote their company's products at trade shows and conferences.

Manufacturers' sales workers spend most of their time visiting prospective customers. They also prepare reports on sales prospects or customers' credit ratings, plan their work schedules, draw up lists of prospects, contact the firm to schedule appointments, handle correspondence, and study literature about their products.

BACKGROUND AND QUALIFICATIONS:

Although a college degree is increasingly desirable for a job as a manufacturer's sales worker, many employers hire individuals without a degree who have previous sales experience. Most entrants to this occupation, even those with college degrees, transfer from other occupations, but some are recent graduates. Entrants are older, on the average, than entrants to other occupations. Sales representatives who have good sales records and leadership ability may advance to sales supervisor, branch manager, or district manager. Those with managerial ability eventually may advance to sales manager or other executive positions; many top executives in industry started as sales representatives. Some people eventually go into business for themselves as independent representatives, while others find opportunities in advertising and marketing research.

OUTLOOK:

Little or no change in employment is expected in the occupation through the year 2000. Increased reliance on electronic ordering systems and a trend toward increased utilization of wholesale distribution channels will limit future employment growth.

PERSONNEL AND LABOR RELATIONS SPECIALIST

DESCRIPTION:

Personnel and labor relations specialists provide the necessary link between management and employees which helps management make effective use of employees' skills, and helps employees find satisfaction in their jobs and working conditions. Personnel specialists interview, select, and recommend applicants to fill job openings. They handle wage and salary administration, training and career development, and employee benefits. Labor relations specialists usually deal in union-management relations, and people who specialize in this field work primarily in unionized businesses and government agencies. They help management officials prepare for collective bargaining sessions, participate in contract negotiations with the union, and handle day-to-day matters of labor relations agreements.

In a small company, personnel work consists mostly of interviewing and hiring, and one person usually handles all phases. By contrast, a large organization needs an entire staff, which might include recruiters, interviewers, counselors, job analysts, wage and salary analysts, education and training specialists, as well as technical and clerical workers. Personnel work often begins with the personnel recruiter or employment interviewer who travels around the country, often to college campuses, in the search for promising job applicants. These specialists talk to applicants, and then select and recommend those who appear qualified to fill vacancies. They often administer tests to applicants and interpret the results. Job analysts and salary and wage administrators examine detailed information on jobs, including job qualifications and worker characteristics, in order to prepare manuals and other materials for these courses, and look into new methods of training. They also counsel employees participating in training opportunities, which may include on-the-job, apprentice, supervisory, or management training.

Employee benefits supervisors and other personnel specialists handle the employer's benefits programs, which often include health insurance, life insurance, disability insurance, and pension plans. These specialists also coordinate a wide range of employee services, including cafeterias and snack bars, health rooms, recreational facilities, newsletters and communications, and counseling for worker-related personal problems. Counseling employees who are reaching retirement age is a particularly important part of the job. Labor relations specialists give advice on labor management relations. Nearly three out of four work in private industry, for manufacturers, banks, insurance companies, airlines, department stores, and virtually every other business concern.

BACKGROUND AND QUALIFICATIONS:

The educational backgrounds of personnel training, and labor relations specialists and managers vary considerably due to the diversity of duties and level of responsibility. While some employers look for graduates with degrees in Personnel Administration or Industrial and Labor Relations, others prefer graduates with a general business background. Still others feel that a well-rounded liberal arts education is the best preparation. A college degree in Personnel Administration, Political Science, or Public Administration can be an asset in looking for personnel work with a government agency. Graduate study in industrial or labor relations is often required for work in labor relations. Although a law degree is often required for entry-level jobs, most of the people who are responsible for contract negotiations are lawyers, and a combination of industrial relations courses and a law degree is becoming highly desirable. New personnel specialists usually enter formal or on-the-job training programs to learn how to classify jobs, interview applicants, or administer employee benefits. Next, new workers are assigned to specific areas in the employee relations department to gain experience. Later, they may advance within their own company, transfer to another employer, or move from personnel to labor relations work. Workers in the middle ranks of a large organization often transfer to a top job in a smaller company. Employees with exceptional ability may be promoted to executive positions, such as director of personnel or director of labor relations.

OUTLOOK:

The number of jobs in this field is projected to increase through the year 2000, although most job openings will be due to replacement needs. The job market is likely to remain competitive in view of the abundant supply of college graduates and experienced workers with suitable qualifications.

PHYSICIST

DESCRIPTION:

Through systematic observation and experimentation, physicists describe the structure of the universe and the interaction of matter and energy in fundamental terms. Physicists develop theories that describe the fundamental forces and laws of nature. The majority of physicists work in research and development. Some do basic research to increase scientific knowledge. Some engineering-oriented physicists do applied research and help develop new products. Many physicists teach and do research in colleges and universities. A small number work in inspection, quality control and other production-related jobs in industry, while others do consulting work.

Most physicists specialize in one or more branches of the science. A growing number of physicists are specializing in fields that combine physics and a related science. Furthermore, the practical applications of a physicist's work have become increasingly merged with engineering. Private industry employs more than one half of all physicists, primarily in companies manufacturing chemicals, electrical equipment, and aircraft and missiles. Many others work in hospitals, commercial laboratories, and independent research organizations.

BACKGROUND AND QUALIFICATIONS:

Graduate training in physics or a closely related field is almost essential for most entry-level jobs in physics, and for advancement into all types of work. A PhD is normally required for faculty status at colleges and universities, and for industrial or government jobs administering research and development programs. Those with a Master's Degree qualify for many research jobs in private industry and in the Federal Government. In colleges and universities, some teach and assist in research while studying for their PhD degrees. Those with a BA may qualify for some applied research and development positions in private industry and in government, and some holding Bachelor's degrees are employed as research assistants in colleges and universities while studying for advanced degrees. Many also work in engineering and other scientific fields. Physicists often begin their careers performing routine laboratory tasks. After gaining some experience, they are assigned more complex tasks and may advance to work as project leaders or research directors. Some work in top management jobs. Physicists who develop new products sometimes form their own companies or join new firms to exploit their own ideas.

OUTLOOK:

Physicists with a PhD should experience good employment opportunities by the late 1990s. The employment of physicists is expected to improve as retirements increase. Related industries: chemistry, geology, and geophysics.

PUBLIC RELATIONS WORKER

DESCRIPTION:

Public relations workers aid businesses, government, universities, and other organizations build and maintain a positive public image. They apply their talents and skills in a variety of different areas, including press, community, or consumer relations, political campaigning, interest-group representation, fund-raising, or employee recruitment. Public relations is more than telling the employer's story, however. Understanding the attitudes and concerns of customers, employees, and various other public groups, and effectively communicating this information to management to help formulate policy is an important part of the job.

Public relations staffs in very large firms may number 200 or more, but in most firms the staff is much smaller. The director of public relations, who is often a vice-president of the company, may develop overall plans and policies with a top management executive. In addition, large public relations departments employ writers, research workers, and other specialists who prepare material for the different media, stockholders, and other groups the company wishes to reach.

Manufacturing firms, public utilities, transportation companies, insurance companies, and trade and professional associations employ many public relations workers. A sizeable number work for government agencies, schools, colleges, museums, and other educational, religious, human service and other organizations. The rapidly expanding health field also offers opportunities for public relations work. A number of workers are employed by public relations consulting firms which furnish services to clients for a fee. Others work for advertising agencies.

BACKGROUND AND QUALIFICATIONS:

A college education combined with public relations experience is excellent preparation for public relations work. Although most beginners in the field have a college degree in communications, public relations, or journalism, some employers prefer a background in a field related to the firm's business. Other firms want college graduates who have worked for the news media. In fact, many editors, reporters, and workers in closely related fields enter public relations work. Some companies, particularly those with large public relations staffs, have formal training programs for new workers. In other firms, new employers work under the guidance of experienced staff members.

Promotion to supervisory jobs may come as workers demonstrate their ability to handle more demanding and creative assignments. Some experienced public relations workers start their own consulting firms. The Public Relations Society accredits public relations officers who have at least five years of experience in the field and have passed a comprehensive six-hour examination.

OUTLOOK:

Employment of public relations workers is expected to increase much faster than the average for all occupations through the year 2000.

PURCHASING AGENT

DESCRIPTION:

Purchasing agents, also called industrial buyers, obtain goods and services of the quality required at the lowest possible cost, and see that adequate supplies are always available. Agents who work for manufacturing maintenance and repair supplies; those working for government agencies may purchase such items as office supplies, furniture, business machines, or vehicles, to name some.

Purchasing agents usually specialize in one or more specific groups of commodities. Agents are assigned to sections, headed by assistant purchasing managers, who are responsible for a group of related commodities. In smaller organizations, purchasing agents generally are assigned certain categories of goods. About half of all purchasing agents work for manufacturing firms.

BACKGROUND AND QUALIFICATIONS:

Most large organizations now require a college degree, and many prefer applicants who have an MBA degree. Familiarity with the computer and its uses is desirable in understanding the systems aspect of the purchasing profession. Following the initial training period, junior purchasing agents usually are given the responsibility of purchasing standard and catalog items. As they gain experience and develop expertise in their assigned areas, they may be promoted to purchasing agent and then senior purchasing agent. Continuing education is essential for purchasing agents who want to advance their careers. Purchasing agents are encouraged to participate in frequent seminars offered by Professional societies, and to take courses in the field at local colleges and universities.

The recognized mark of experience and professional competence is the designation certified purchasing manager (CPM). This designation is conferred by the National Association of Purchasing Management, Inc. upon candidates who have passed four examinations and who meet educational and professional experience requirements

OUTLOOK:

Employment of purchasing agents and managers is expected to increase more slowly than the average for all occupations during the 1990's. Computerization of purchasing coupled with an increased reliance on a smaller number of suppliers should boost the productivity of purchasing personnel.

QUALITY CONTROL SUPERVISOR

DESCRIPTION:

A quality control supervisor may either be involved in the spot checking of items being manufactured or processed or in assuring that the proper processes are being followed. A quality control system involves selection and training of personnel, product design, the establishment of specifications, procedures and tests, the design and maintenance of facilities and equipment, the selection of materials, and recordkeeping. In an effective quality control system, all these aspects are evaluated on a regular basis, and modified and improved when appropriate.

BACKGROUND AND QUALIFICATIONS:

While some quality control positions involved with the supervision of the production of simpler items might require little background besides on-the-job training, many require a specialized degree in engineering, chemistry, or biology. While all manufacturing firms require some degree of quality control, this is especially important in the chemistry, food and drug industries. Some drug manufacturers for example, may assign one out of six production workers to quality assurance functions alone

OUTLOOK:

Varies greatly, depending upon the industry.

REPORTER/EDITOR

DESCRIPTION:

Newspaper reporters gather information on current events and use it to write stories for daily or weekly newspapers. Large dailies frequently assign teams of reporters to investigate social, economic, or political conditions, and reporters are often assigned to beats, such as police stations, courthouses, or governmental agencies, to gather news originating inthese places. General assignment reporters write local news stories on a wide range of topics, from public meetings to human interest stories.

Reporters with a specialized background or interest in a particular area write, interpret, and analyze the news in fields such as medicine, politics, foreign affairs, sports, fashion, art, theater, consumer affairs, travel, finance, social events, science, education, business, labor, religion, and other areas. Critics review literary, artistic, and musical works and performances while editorial writers present viewpoints on topics of interest. Reporters on small newspapers cover all aspects of local news, and may also take photographs, write headlines, lay out pages, and write editorials. On some small weeklies, they may also solicit advertisements, sell subscriptions, and perform general office work. Reporters must be highly motivated, and are expected to work long hours.

BACKGROUND AND QUALIFICATIONS:

Most newspapers will only consider applicants with a degree in journalism, which includes training in the liberal arts in addition to professional training in journalism. Others prefer applicants who have a bachelor's degree in one of the liberal arts and a master's degree in journalism. Experience as a part-time "stringer" is very helpful in finding full time employment as a reporter. Most beginning reporters start on weekly or small daily newspapers, with a small number of outstanding journalism graduates finding work with large daily newspapers, although this is a rare exception. Large dailies generally look for at least three years of reporting experience, acquired on smaller newspapers.

Beginning reporters are assigned duties such as reporting on civic and community meetings, summarizing speeches, writing obituaries, interviewing important community leaders or visitors, and covering police, government, or courthouse proceedings. As they gain experience, they may report on more important events, cover an assigned beat, or specialize in a particular field. Newspaper reporters may advance to large daily newspapers or state and national newswire services. However, competition for such positions is fierce, and news executives are flooded with applications from highly qualified reporters every year. Some experienced reporters become columnists, correspondents, editorial writers, editors, or top executives; these people represent the top of the field, and competition for these positions is extremely keen. Other reporters transfer to related fields, such as public relations, writing for magazines, or preparing copy for radio or television news programs.

OUTLOOK:

Employment of reporters and correspondents is expected to grow through the year 2000, primarily due to the anticipated increase in the number of small-town and suburban daily and weekly newspapers.

SECURITIES AND FINANCIAL SERVICES SALES REPRESENTATIVES

DESCRIPTION:

Securities Sales Representatives:

Most investors, whether they are individuals with a few hundred dollars or large institutions with millions to invest, use securities sales representatives when buying or selling stocks, bonds, shares in mutual funds, or other financial products. Securities sales representatives also provide many related services for their customers. Depending on a customer's knowledge of the market, the representative may explain the meaning of stock market terms and trading practices, offer financial counseling, devise an individual financial portfolio including securities, corporate and municipal bonds, life insurance, annuities, and other investments, and offer advice on the purchase or sale of particular securities.

Financial Services Sales Representative:

Financial services sales representatives call on various businesses to solicit applications for loans and new deposit accounts for banks or savings and loan associations. They also locate and contact prospective customers to present their bank's financial services and to ascertain the customer's banking needs. At most small and medium-sized banks, branch managers and commercial loan officers are responsible for marketing the bank's financial services. As banks offer more and increasingly complex financial services, for example, securities brokerage and financial planning - the job of financial services sales representatives - will assume greater importance.

BACKGROUND AND QUALIFICATIONS:

A college education is becoming increasingly important, as securities sales representatives must be well informed about economic conditions and trends. Although employers seldom require specialized academic training, courses in business administration, economics, and finance are helpful. Securities sales representatives must meet state licensing requirements, which generally include passing an examination and, in some cases, furnishing a personal bond. In addition, sales representatives must register as representatives of their firm according to the regulations of the securities exchanges where they do business or the National Association of Securities Dealers, Inc. (NASD). Before beginners can qualify as registered representatives, they must pass the General Securities Registered Representative Examination. Banks and other credit institutions prefer to hire college graduates for financial services sales jobs. A business administration degree with a specialization in finance or a liberal arts degree including courses in accounting, economics, and marketing serves as excellent preparation for this job. Financial services sales representatives learn through on-the-job training under the supervision of bank officers. Outstanding performance can lead to promotion to managerial positions.

OUTLOOK:

The demand for securities sales representatives fluctuates as the economy expands and contracts. Employment of securities sales representatives is expected to expand as economic growth, rising personal incomes, and greater inherited wealth increase the funds available for investment. Employment of financial services sales representatives is also expected to increase through the year 2000, as banks and credit institutions expand the financial services they offer, and issue more loans for personal and commercial use.

STATISTICIAN

DESCRIPTION:

Statisticians devise, carry out, and interpret the numerical results of surveys and experiments. In doing so, they apply their knowledge of statistical methods to a particular subject area, such as economics, human behavior, the natural sciences, or engineering. They may use statistical techniques to predict population growth or economic conditions, develop quality control tests for manufactured products, or help business managers and government officials make decisions and evaluate the results of new programs. Over half of all statisticians are in private industry, primarily in manufacturing, finance, and insurance firms.

BACKGROUND AND QUALIFICATIONS:

A bachelor's degree in statistics or mathematics is the minimum educational requirement for many beginning jobs in statistics. For other entry-level jobs in the field, however, a BA with a major in an applied field of study such as economics or a natural science, and a minor in statistics is preferable. A graduate degree in mathematics or statistics is essential for college and university teaching. Most mathematics statisticians have at least a BA in mathematics and an advanced degree in statistics. Beginning statisticians who have a BA often spend their time performing routine work under the supervision of an experienced statistician. Through experience, they may advance to positions of greater technical and supervisory responsibility. However, opportunities for promotion are best for those with advanced degrees.

OUTLOOK:

Employment opportunities for persons who combine training in statistics with knowledge of computer science or a field of application - such as biology, economics or engineering - are generally expected to be favorable through the year 2000.

SYSTEMS ANALYST

DESCRIPTION:

Systems analysts plan efficient methods of processing data and handling the results. Analysts use various techniques, such as cost accounting, sampling, and mathematical model building to analyze a problem and devise a new system. The problems that systems analysts solve range from monitoring nuclear fission in a powerplant to forecasting sales for an appliance manufacturing firm. Because the work is so varied and complex, Analysts usually specialize in either business or scientific and engineering applications. Most systems analysts work in manufacturing firms, banks, insurance companies, and data processing service organizations. In addition, large numbers work for wholesale and retail businesses and government agencies.

BACKGROUND AND QUALIFICATIONS:

College graduates are almost always sought for the position of systems analyst. For some of the more complex positions, persons with graduate degrees are preferred. Employers usually seek analysts with a background in accounting, business management, or economics for work in a business environment, while a background in the physical sciences, mathematics, or engineering is preferred for work in scientifically oriented organizations. A growing number of employers seek applicants who have a degree in Computer Science, Information Systems, or Data Processing. Regardless of the college major, employers seek those who are familiar with programming languages.

In order to advance, systems analysts must continue their technical education. Technological advances come so rapidly in the computer field that continuous study is necessary to keep computer skills up to date. Training usually takes the form of one and two-week courses offered by employers and software vendors. Additional training may come from professional development seminars offered by professional computing societies. An indication of experience and professional competence is the Certificate in Data Processing (CDP). This designation is conferred by the Institute for Certification of Computer Professionals, and is Granted to candidates who have five years experience and have passed a five-part examination.

OUTLOOK:

The demand for systems analysts is expected to rise through the year 2000, as advances in technology lead to new applications for computers. Factory and office automation, advances in telecommunications technology, and scientific research are just a few areas where use of computers will expand.

TECHNICAL WRITER/EDITOR

DESCRIPTION:

Technical writers and technical editors research, write, and edit technical materials, and also may produce publications and audiovisual materials. To ensure that their work is accurate, Technical Writers must be expert in the subject area in which they are writing. Editors are also responsible for the accuracy of material on which they work. Some organizations use job titles other than technical writer/editor, such as staff writer, publications engineer, communications specialist, publications engineer, communications specialist, industrial writer, industrial materials developer, and others.Technical writers set out either to instruct or inform, and in many instances they do both. They prepare manuals, catalogs, parts lists, and instructional materials needed by sales representatives who sell machinery or scientific equipment and by the technicians who install, maintain, and service it. Technical writers are often part of a team, working closely with scientists, engineers, accountants, and others. Technical editors take the material Technical writers produce and further polish it for final publication and use. Many writers and editors work for large firms in the electronics, aviation, aerospace, ordinance, chemical, pharmaceutical, and computer manufacturing industries. Firms in the energy, communications, and computer software fields also employ many technical writers, and research laboratories employ significant numbers.

BACKGROUND AND QUALIFICATIONS:

Employers seek people whose educational background, work experience, and personal pursuits indicate they possess both writing skills and appropriate scientific knowledge. Knowledge of graphics and other aspects of publication production may be helpful in landing a job in the field. An understanding of current trends in communication technology is an asset, and familiarity with computer operations and terminology is increasingly important. Many employers prefer candidates with a degree in science or engineering, plus a minor in English, journalism, or technical communications. Other employers emphasize writing ability and look for candidates whose major field of study was journalism, English, or the liberal arts. Depending on their line of business, these employees almost always require course work or practical experience in a specific subject as well, computer science, for example.

People with a solid background in science or engineering are at an advantage in competing for such jobs. Those with BA's or MA's in Technical Writing are often preferred over candidates with little or no technical background. Beginning technical writers often assist experienced writers by

With large writing staffs may eventually move to the job of technical editor, or shift to an administrative position in the publication or technical information departments. The top job is usually that of publications manager (and other titles), who normally supervises an of the people directly involved in producing the company's technical documents. The manager supervises not only the technical writers and editors, but also staff members responsible for illustrations, photography, reproduction, and distribution.

OUTLOOK:

Through the year 2000, the outlook for writing and editing jobs is expected to continue to be keenly competitive. With the increasing complexity of industrial and scientific equipment, more users will depend on the technical writer's ability to prepare precise but simple explanations and instructions.

UNDERWRITER

DESCRIPTION:

Underwriters appraise and select the risks their company will insure. Underwriters decide whether their insurance company will accept risks after analyzing information in insurance applications, reports from loss control consultants, medical reports, and actuarial studies. Most Underwriters specialize in one of the three major categories of insurance: life, casualty, and health. They further specialize in group or individual policies.

BACKGROUND AND QUALIFICATIONS:

For beginning underwriters, most large insurance companies seek college graduates with degrees in liberal arts or business administration. Underwriter trainees begin by evaluating routine applicants under the close supervision of an experienced risk appraiser. Continuing education is a necessity if the underwriter expects to advance to senior level positions. Insurance companies generally place great emphasis on completion of one or more of the many recognized independent study programs. Many companies pay tuition and the cost of books for those who successfully complete underwriting courses; some offer salary increases as an additional incentive. Independent study programs are available through the American Institute of Property and Liability Underwriters, the Health Insurance Association of America, and the Life Office Management Association.

As underwriters gain experience, they can qualify as a "Fellow" of the Academy of Life Underwriters by passing a series of examinations and completing a research paper on a topic in the field. Exams are given by the Institute of Home Office Underwriters and the Home Office Life Underwriters Association. The designation of "Fellow" is recognized as a mark of achievement in the underwriting field. Experienced underwriters who complete a course of study may advance to chief underwriter or underwriting manager. Some underwriting managers are promoted to senior managerial positions after several years.

OUTLOOK:

Employment of underwriters is expected to rise faster than the average for all occupations through the year 2000 as insurance sales continue to expand. Most job openings, however, are expected to result from the need to replace underwriters who transfer to other occupations or stop working altogether.

PART THREE:
WHERE THE JOBS ARE

Primary Metro New York Employers

For more information on professional opportunities in accounting or auditing, contact the following professional and trade organizations, as listed beginning on page 449:

AMERICAN INSTITUTE OF CERTIFIED PUBLIC ACCOUNTANTS
NATIONAL SOCIETY OF PUBLIC ACCOUNTANTS

New York

ARTHUR ANDERSEN & COMPANY
1345 Avenue of the Americas
12th Floor
New York NY 10105
212/708-4000
Contact Mr. Michael Denkensohn, Partner in charge of Recruiting. One of the largest certified public accounting and consulting firms in the world; operating offices in more than 40 countries. Operates in the following divisions: Audit, Tax, and Information Consulting. New York City location seeks experienced professionals with backgrounds in computer science, accounting, taxation, systems analysis, engineering, finance and marketing. Common positions include: Accountant; Computer Programmer; Civil Engineer; Electrical Engineer; Industrial Engineer; Mechanical Engineer; Financial Analyst; Marketing Specialist; Systems Analyst. Principal educational backgrounds sought: Accounting; Business Administration; Computer Science; Economics; Engineering; Finance; Liberal Arts; Mathematics. Company benefits include: medical insurance; dental insurance; pension plan; life insurance; disability coverage; profit sharing. Corporate headquarters location: Chicago, IL. Operations at this facility include: service to clients in the areas of accounting and auditing, financial consulting, tax consulting, information consulting, and strategic series consulting.

COOPERS & LYBRAND
1251 Avenue of the Americas
New York NY 10020
212/536-2323
Contact Joseph S. Rorro, Regional Director of Recruiting. Five area locations, including New York, NY; Parsippany, NJ; Princeton, NJ; Stamford, CT; and Huntington, NY. One of the largest certified public accounting firms, providing a broad range of services in the areas of accounting and auditing, taxation, management consulting, actuarial, benefits, and compensation consulting. Operates 100 offices in the United States; more than 510 offices in 95 foreign locations. Corporate headquarters location. International. Common positions include: Accountant; Actuary; Data Processing Specialist; Tax Specialist; Management Consultant.

DELOITTE & TOUCHE
1633 Broadway
New York NY 10019
Contact Director of Personnel. Multiple area locations. One of the largest ('Big Six') certified public accounting organizations in the world. Provides accounting, auditing, management consultation, tax, and actuarial services to clients through a wide network of offices throughout the world. Common positions include: Accountant; Attorney; Computer Programmer; Purchasing Agent; Technical Writer/Editor. Principal educational backgrounds sought: Accounting; Business Administration; Computer Science; Economics; Finance; Marketing. Company benefits include: medical and life insurance; pension plan; disability coverage; profit sharing; employee discounts; savings plan. Corporate headquarters location. Operations at this facility include: research/development; administration. International.

ERNST & YOUNG
277 Park Avenue
New York NY 10172
212/407-1500
Contact Aaron Hipscher, Director of Recruiting. A major worldwide certified public accounting organization, with operations in three main areas: Auditing and Accounting; Tax Services; and Management Consulting. Company has approximately 5000 professionals and 600 partners and directors in offices throughout the United States, including Boston, Chicago, Dallas, San Fransisco, Phoenix, and many others; and a substantial presence abroad. Corporate headquarters location.

H&R BLOCK (NYC) INC.
370 Seventh Avenue
New York NY 10001
212/594-5480
Contact District Manager. More than 50 area locations, including Manhattan, the Bronx, Brooklyn, and Queens. Primarily engaged in consumer tax preparation, operating more than 9500 United States offices, and preparing more than 10 million tax returns each year. Also operates more than 800 offices in Canada. H&R Block has established in-store offices in over 750 Sears stores in both the United States and Canada; many offices operate as franchisees, and some operate on a seasonal basis. Company is also engaged in a number of other tax-related activities, including: Group Tax Programs, Executive Tax Service, Tax Training Schools, and Real Estate Tax Awareness Seminars. Operations at this facility include: administration. Corporate headquarters location: Kansas City, MO. New York Stock Exchange. International. Common positions include: Income Tax Preparer; Branch Manager; Management Trainee; Seasonal Bookkeeper; Tax Preparer. Principal educational background sought: Income Tax Preparation. Training programs offered. Company benefits include (for full-time year-round employees only): medical, dental, and life insurance; pension plan; tuition assistance; disability coverage; profit sharing; savings plan.

KPMG PEAT MARWICK
345 Park Avenue
New York NY 10154
212/758-9700
Contact Robert J. Zibelli, Director/Professional Staff Recruiting. Several area locations, including Manhattan and White Plains, NY; Stamford, CT; Short Hills, NJ; and others. One of the largest certified public accounting firms, with offices throughout the United States and the world (approximately 500 international locations in 115 countries). Provides auditing, accounting, management consulting, and tax services. Over 1900 partners and principals in the United States in approximately 135 offices. Common positions include: Accountant. Principal educational backgrounds sought: Accounting. Company benefits include: medical, dental and life insurance; pension plan; disability coverage; savings plan.

PRICE WATERHOUSE
153 East 53rd Street
New York NY 10022
212/371-2000
Contact Steve Butterfield, Recruitment Director. Multiple area locations, including Hackensack, Morristown, NJ; and Stamford, CT; and others. One of the six largest certified public accounting firms, with offices in 90 cities in the United States, and more than 300 other offices in approximately 90 foreign countries. Corporate headquarters location. International. Common positions include: various positions in auditing; tax consulting; and management consulting.

Connecticut

DELOITTE & TOUCHE
P.O. Box 820
Wilton CT 06897-0820
203/761-3000
Contact National Recruiting Director. A CPA firm. Provides accounting, management advisory services, and tax consultation services. Corporate headquarters location. International. Common positions include: Accountant. Educational backgrounds sought: Accounting. Training programs and internships available. Company benefits include: medical insurance; dental insuarnace; life insurance; tuition assistance; disability coverage. Corporate headquarters location.

ADVERTISING, MARKETING, PUBLIC RELATIONS

For more information on professional opportunities in advertising, marketing or public relations, contact the following professional and trade organizations, as listed beginning on page 449:

AMERICAN ADVERTISING FEDERATION
AMERICAN ASSOCIATION OF ADVERTISING AGENCIES
AMERICAN MARKETING ASSOCIATION
BUSINESS-PROFESSIONAL ADVERTISING ASSOCIATION
PUBLIC RELATIONS SOCIETY OF AMERICA
TELEVISION BUREAU OF ADVERTISING

New York

N.W. AYER AND SONS
825 8th Avenue
New York NY 10019
212/474-5000
Contact Joseph Harte, Personnel Director. An area advertising agency employing 1,275 people.

BBDO INTERNATIONAL INC.
1285 Avenue of the Americas
New York NY 10019
212/459-5000
Contact Personnel Department. Operates a worldwide network of advertising agencies with related businesses in public relations, direct marketing, sales promotion, graphic design, graphic arts, and printing. Operates 156 offices in 42 countries and 96 cities. Operates 83 subsidiaries, affiliates, and associates engaged solely in advertising and related operations. The company's largest subsidiary, Batten, Barton, Durstine & Osborn, Inc., is based at this location. TEAM/BBDO GmbH (West Germany) is the largest international subsidiary. Offices and subsidiary offices are located throughout the United States, Latin America, Europe, Middle East/Africa, and Asia/Pacific. Corporate headquarters location. International. Common positions include: Media Planner; Market Researcher; Traffic Trainee; Account Management Trainee; Account Executive; Senior Media Planner; Traffic Coordinator. Principal educational backgrounds sought: Liberal Arts; Marketing. Company benefits include: medical insurance; dental insurance; pension plan; life insurance; disability coverage; profit sharing.

BACKER SPIELVOGEL BATES, INC.
405 Lexington Avenue
New York NY 10174
212/297-7000

Contact Ann Melanson, Director of Personnel. One of the largest advertising/public relations agencies in the United States; operating for more than 40 years. Corporate headquarters location.

BOZELL
40 West 23rd Street
New York NY 10010
212/727-5000
Contact Mary Anne Schiffert, Personnel Manager. One of New York's largest advertising agencies, whose services include marketing, communications, and public relations. International.

CAMPBELL METHUN ESTY
The Chrysler Building
405 Lexington Avenue
New York NY 10174
212/856-4500
Contact Patricia Shores, Manager of Human Resources. A full-service advertising agency. Corporate headquarters location.

D'ARCY MASIUS BENTON & BOWLES, INC.
1675 Broadway
New York NY 10019-5809
212/468-3622
Contact Judith Kemp, Director of Personnel. A multi-national, full-service advertising and communications agency. Company operates 50 offices in 31 countries throughout the world, with clients in many diverse fields, including food, health care, household products, travel, finance, autos, and many others. The company provides innovative marketing and advertising services to its clients. Subsidiaries include Clarion (promotions/corporate communication/direct marketing); and Medicus Intercom International Inc. (health care advertising). Other United States offices are in Los Angeles, St. Louis, Chicago, and Bloomfield Hills. Common positions include: Advertising Worker; Management Trainee; Marketing Specialist. Principal educational backgrounds sought: Art/Design; Business Administration; Communications; Marketing. Training programs offered. Company benefits include: medical, dental, and life insurance; pension plan; disability coverage; savings plan. Corporate headquarters location. Operations at this facility include: research/development; administration; service.

DDB NEEDHAM WORLDWIDE, INC.
437 Madison Avenue
New York NY 10022
212/415-2000
Contact Jud Saviskas, Senior V.P., Dir. of Human Resources. A full service international advertising agency. Common positions include: Advertising Worker. Training programs offered; Internships offered. Company benefits include: medical, dental, and life insurance; tuition assistance; disability coverage; profit sharing. Corporate headquarters location.

REUBEN H. DONNELLEY
287 Bowman Avenue
Purchase NY 10577
914/933-6400
Contact Personnel Section Manager. Firm is engaged in selling advertising space in 500 Yellow Pages directories of more than 58 independent telephone companies. Also provides telemarketing services. Subsidiary of The Dun & Bradstreet Corporation. Corporate headquarters location: Purchase, NY. Common positions include: Accountant; Buyer; Claim Representative; Commercial Artist; Computer Programmer; Credit Manager; Customer Service Representative; Draftsperson; Financial Analyst; Manager; Department Manager; General Manager; Operations/Production Manager; Marketing Specialist; Personnel & Labor Relations Specialist; Purchasing Agent; Sales Representative; Statistician; Systems Analyst. Principal educational backgrounds sought: Accounting; Art/Design; Business Administration; Communications; Computer Science; Economics;

Finance; Liberal Arts; Marketing. Company benefits include: medical insurance; dental insurance; pension plan; life insurance; tuition assistance; disability coverage; profit sharing; savings plan.

FOOTE, CONE & BELDING COMMUNICATIONS INC.
767 5th Avenue
New York NY 10153
212/705-1000
Contact Paula Ordway, Personnel Manager. Second area location in Stamford, CT. One of the 10 largest advertising agencies in the world; services include analyzing the advertising needs of clients, planning and creating advertising, and placing advertising for dissemination through various media. Company also offers additional services, including the design and production of merchandising and sales promotion programs, public relations, and collateral services such as market and product research, package design, and trademark and trade name development. Company operates fully-staffed advertising offices in New York, Stamford, Chicago, San Francisco, Los Angeles, and Philadelphia. International business conducted through subsidiaries of FCB International, with fully-staffed offices throughout Europe, Africa, Australia, Latin America, Canada, and the Far East. Company conducts public relations activities through subsidiary Carl Byoir & Associates (offices nationwide and in several international locations). Recruitment advertising subsidiary, Deutsch, Shea & Evans, operates offices in New York, Los Angeles, Los Altos (CA), San Francisco, Salt Lake City, and Denver. Corporate headquarters location: Chicago, IL. New York Stock Exchange. International.

GREY ADVERTISING INC.
777 Third Avenue
New York NY 10017
212/546-2000
Contact Lisa Welsh, Personnel Manager. A major worldwide advertising agency. Founded in 1917, the company has expertise in such related areas as marketing, consultation, direct response, research, product publicity, public relations, sales promotion, and cooperative advertising. Ten specialized area subsidiaries include: GCI Group, specializing in public relations; Gross Townsend Frank Hoffman, specializing in advertising and promotion of health care products and services; Beaumont-Bennett, a full-service sales promotion company; Rada Recruitment Communications, specializing in recruitment advertising; Grey Direct, specializing in direct response marketing; J. Brown & Associates, specializing in co-op advertising; Font & Vaamonde, providing Hispanic marketing; Grey Directory Marketing, specializing in Yellow Pages advertising; Gindick Productions, a premier producer of audio-visual presentations; and Grey Entertainment and Media, servicing clients in the entertainment and media industries. Grey International, with headquarters in New York, has 223 offices in 34 countries worldwide. Other United States offices in Los Angeles, Orange County, and San Francisco. Common positions include: Media Planner; Account Executive; Research Executive; Copywriter; Art Director. Principal educational backgrounds sought: Business Administration; Communications; Liberal Arts; Marketing. Company benefits include: medical, dental and life insurance; tuition assistance; profit sharing; employee discounts; employee stock ownership plan. Training programs offered; Internships offered. NASDAQ. Corporate headquarters location.

HILL AND KNOWLTON INC
420 Lexington Avenue
New York NY 10017
212/697-5600
Contact Director, Human Resources. One of the largest public relations/public affairs counseling firms in the world, serving more than 1000 clients throughout the world, through more than 60 company offices and through associate arrangements with some 50 leading regional firms worldwide. Besides serving as the firm's worldwide headquarters, the New York office is also the center of the company's wide range of specialized services, and its International Division, the focal point of work done on behalf of foreign-based clients. Operates through several divisions: Research, including survey research and information research; editorial services, creative design and corporate identity, and advertising; and Specialized Public Relations/Public Affairs Services, including financial relations, proxy

solicitation and shareholder list analysis, financial media relations, publicity and marketing, sports development, travel and leisure communications, broadcast services, industrial/high-technology scientific communications, food and nutrition, medical, agribusiness, entertainment, environmental and consumer affairs, energy affairs, public issues and public policy, corporate philanthropy, labor communications, Japanese business, organizational communications, communications audits, communications training, and senior consultants. Affiliated and associated offices are located throughout the United States and the world.

INTERPUBLIC GROUP
1271 Avenue of the Americas
New York NY 10020
212/399-8000
Contact Donna Borseso, Personnel Recruiter. A leading New York advertising agency.

LINTAS: NEW YORK
One Dag Hammarskjold Plaza
New York NY 10017
212/605-8000
Contact Frank A. Ryder, Vice-President, Personnel. A full-service international advertising agency with expertise in the marketing of consumer packaged goods. Common positions include: Accountant; Advertising Worker; Commercial Artist; Computer Programmer; Financial Analyst; Management Trainee; Marketing Specialist; Personnel & Labor Relations Specialist; Public Relations Worker; Copywriter. Principal educational backgrounds sought: Accounting; Art/Design; Business Administration; Communications; Finance; Liberal Arts; Marketing; Psychology; Advertising/Journalism. Company benefits include: medical insurance; dental insurance; pension plan; life insurance; tuition assistance; disability coverage; savings plan. Corporate headquarters location. Parent company: Interpublic Group of Companies. Operations at this facility include: administration. New York Stock Exchange.

McCAFFREY & McCALL INC.
575 Lexington Avenue
Seventh Floor
New York NY 10022
212/421-7500
Contact Director of Personnel. A general advertising agency. Corporate headquarters location.

MEDIA NETWORKS INC.
530 Fifth Avenue
15th Floor
New York NY 10036
212/536-7800
Contact Personnel Department. Provides a variety of specialized marketing, advertising, and media services as a subsidiary of 3M Corporation. Corporate headquarters location.

METRO CREATIVE GRAPHICS
33 West 34th Street
New York NY 10001
212/947-5100
Contact E.R. Zimmerman, CEO. Over 80 years of providing camera ready graphics, editorial and professional production services to the newspaper and graphic communication industries. Common positions include: Commercial Artist; Customer Service Representative; Sales Representative (in Graphics). Educational backgrounds sought include: Art/Design; Communications; Graphic Art Sales. Company benefits include: medical insurance; dental insurance; life insurance; savings plan.

MICKELBERRY CORPORATION
405 Park Avenue
10th Floor
New York NY 10022

Contact Personnel Department. A holding company with a growing communications services business consisting of three advertising agencies, three marketing companies, and a commercial printing group. Each subsidiary operates autonomously, with parent company's relationship confined to financial matters and corporate development. Operating subsidiaries are: Laurence, Charles & Free, Inc., an advertising agency with numerous major national clients; Clavillo, Shevack & Partners, Inc., an advertising agency also with many national clients; Cunningham & Walsh, an advertising/marketing agency with five full-service offices nationwide, including Chicago, San Francisco, Los Angeles, and Dallas; marketing agencies Caribiner, Inc., Direct Marketing Agency, Inc., and Ventura Associates; and Sandy-Alexander, a lithographer specializing in high-quality color reproduction. Companies should be contacted directly. Corporate headquarters location. New York Stock Exchange. Common positions include: Accountant.

JOHN F. MURRAY ADVERTISING AGENCY INC.
685 Third Avenue
New York NY 10017
212/878-5200
Contact Edward Behrendt, Personnel Manager. Operates as a subsidiary of American Home Products (see separate listing); responsible for advertising the parent company's complete line of products. Corporate headquarters location.

THE NPD GROUP OF
CUSTOM & SYNDICATED RESEARCH
900 West Shore Road
Port Washington NY 11050
516/625-2401
Contact Harriet Abrams, Director of Human Resources. A major market research firm, with a comprehensive line of custom and syndicated consumer research services, including Point-of-Sale Computerized Audits, purchase panels, mail panels, telephone research (CRT), mathematical modeling and consulting. Industries covered include: consumer packaged goods, apparel, toys, electronics, automotive, sports, books, food consumption-in home and away from home. Offices are located in New York, Cincinnati, Chicago, Los Angeles, and Houston. Common positions include: Marketing Specialist; Data Processor. Principal educational backgrounds sought: Business Administration; Computer Science; Marketing; Mathematics. Limited internships offered. Company benefits include: medical, dental, and life insurance; tuition assistance; disability coverage; profit sharing; dependent care program. Corporate headquarters location. Operations include: research/development; administration; sales.

OGILVY & MATHER
309 W. 49th Street
New York NY 10019
212/237-4000
Contact Liz Tunkiar, V.P. Head of Personnel Administration or Mary Mahon, Vice-President/Manager Creative Department. One of the nation's largest advertising agencies, with regional offices in Atlanta, Chicago, Houston, Los Angeles, and Honolulu; and in 45 other countries. New York area divisions include: Ogilvy & Mather Direct; Ogilvy & Mather Promotions; Ogilvy & Mather Public Relations. Corporate headquarters location. International. Common positions include: Advertising Worker. Principal educational backgrounds sought: Art/Design; Business Administration; Communications; Liberal Arts; Marketing. Company benefits include: medical insurance; dental insurance; life insurance; tuition assistance; disability coverage; profit sharing; employee discounts.

PUBLISHERS CLEARING HOUSE
382 Channel Drive
Port Washington NY 11050
516/883-5432
Contact Nancy Schwartz, Employment Manager. A major direct-mail marketing company, PCH is the largest single source of new magazine subscribers, offering consumers a wide variety of titles at competitive prices. The company also conducts continuing research to develop effective promotion of other products and services. Has subsidiary magazine,

Campus Subscriptions. Corporate headquarters location. Common positions include: Accountant; Advertising Worker; Computer Programmer; Customer Service Representative; Industrial Engineeer; Financial Analyst; Marketing Specialist; Programmer; Systems Analyst. Principal educational backgrounds sought: Accounting; Business Administration; Computer Science; Marketing. Company benefits include: medical insurance; dental insurance; pension plan; life insurance; tuition assistance; disability coverage.

RUDER FINN
301 East 57th Street
3rd Floor
New York NY 10022
212/593-6400
Contact Personnel Office. One of New York's largest public relations firms. Company offers a wide range of services in the public relations field to clients in the public sector, private industry, and the communications industries. North American offices are located in Chicago, Los Angeles, Washington DC, and Toronto. International affiliates. Corporate headquarters location.

THE SPERRY & HUTCHINSON COMPANY, INC.
315 Park Avenue South
New York NY 10010
212/598-3100
Contact Vicki Reid, Employment Administrator. Engaged in designing and selling promotional marketing services to retailers, principally trading stamps. Diversified corporation with four major divisions: S&H Promotional Services; Furnishings; Insurance Services; and Investment Management. S&H Promotional operates the company's S&H Green Stamp operations. Furnishings Division is one of the largest producers of carpeting and furniture in the United States. Insurance Services provides coverage in more than 50 cities, including New York and London. Investment Management Division manages the company's portfolio and provides operating funds. Common positions include: Accountant. Principal educational backgrounds sought include: Accounting. Company benefits include: medical and life insurance; pension plan; disability coverage; employee savings. Corporate headquarters location. Operations at this facility include: regional headquarters.

SUDLER & HENNESSEY INC.
1633 Broadway
New York NY 10019
212/696-5800
Contact Dorothy Gallagher, Personnel Director. An area advertising agency. Corporate headquarters location.

WELLS RICH GREENE INC.
1740 Broadway
New York NY 10019
212/303-5000
Contact Valerie Church, Personnel Office. A major area advertising agency. Corporate headquarters location.

YOUNG & RUBICAM
285 Madison Avenue
New York NY 10017
212/210-3000
Contact Stephen Nisberg, Personnel Supervisor. A major international advertising agency, with 126 agency offices throughout the world. Operates through three divisions: Young & Rubicam International, with offices throughout the world; Marsteller Inc., a worldwide leader in business-to-business and consumer advertising, with offices throughout the United States and worldwide, with subsidiary Burson-Marsteller providing public relations services throughout the world; and Young & Rubicam USA, with 14 consumer advertising agencies operating through four regional groups (except Young & Rubicam Detroit), and five specialized advertising/marketing agencies. Corporate headquarters location.

AMUSEMENTS, ARTS AND RECREATION

For more information on professional opportunities in the arts, entertainment and leisure industries, contact the following professional and trade organizations, as listed beginning on page 449:

AMERICAN ASSOCIATION OF ZOOLOGICAL PARKS & AQUARIUMS
AMERICAN FEDERATION OF MUSICIANS
AMERICAN FEDERATION OF TELEVISION AND RADIO ARTISTS
NATIONAL ENDOWMENTS FOR THE ARTS
THEATRE COMMUNICATIONS GROUP

New York

AMERICAN MUSEUM OF NATURAL HISTORY
Central Park West at 79th Street
New York NY 10024
212/769-5000
Contact Geraldine Smith, Personnel Manager. Founded in 1869; a preeminent center of basic inquiry in anthropology, astronomy, mineralogy, and zoology. Offers 38 exhibition halls located on four square blocks on the Upper West Side of Manhattan. Besides offering a wide range of innovative programs of exhibition and education, 200 scientists and their assistants are involved in a wide array of research programs into the areas mentioned previously. Also offers a world-renowned research library, and publishes several in-house and nationally-distributed magazines based on its research. Corporate headquarters location.

ARISTA RECORDS, INC.
6 West 57th Street
New York NY 10019
Contact Nancy Composto, Director/Personnel. Provides sales, promotion and A&R activities for Arista Records and contracted artists. Corporate headquarters location. Parent company: BMG Music. Operations at this facility include: administration; sales.

ATLANTIC RECORDING CORPORATION
75 Rockefeller Plaza
New York NY 10019
212/484-6000
Contact Linda Wade, Director of Personnel. An international music recording and publishing organization, whose contracted artists offer a wide variety of musical styles. Corporate headquarters location.

CITY CENTER OF MUSIC AND DRAMA INC.
70 Lincoln Center Plaza
4th Floor
New York NY 10023
212/580-5420
Contact Carla Hunter, Controller. Organizational and management offices for the not-for-profit cultural organization, whose activities include plays, ballets, and operas. Operates the New York State Theater. Programs include the New York City Opera, the New York Ballet, and City Center Special Productions. Corporate headquarters location.

COLUMBIA PICTURES INDUSTRIES INC.
711 Fifth Avenue
New York NY 10022
212/751-4400
Contact Susan Garelli, Vice President/Personnel. A major producer and distributor of motion pictures and television programming. Other operations include involvement in pay-

television, video-cassette, and videodisc markets; coin-operated amusement games; and licensing and distribution operations for its extensive library of filmed entertainment. Corporate headquarters location. International.

MADISON SQUARE GARDEN CORPORATION
3 Penn Plaza
New York NY 10001
212/563-8290
Contact Jon Scheller, Director, Human Resources. Produces and packages sports and entertainment events in its own complex and other sites (professional sports teams include the New York Knickerbockers Basketball Club and the New York Rangers Hockey Club). Madison Square Garden operates the MSG Network (the nation's oldest regional cable television sports network and one of the largest). Other Madison Square Garden operations include Miss Universe Inc., which produces Miss Universe, Miss USA, and Miss Teen USA Pageants. Common positions include: Accountant; Administrator; Attorney; Computer Programmer; Industrial Engineer; Mechanical Engineer; Marketing Specialist; Public Relations Specialist; Sales Representative; Systems Analyst. Principal educational backgrounds sought: Accounting; Art/Design; Business Administration; Communications; Engineering; Finance; Liberal Arts; Marketing. Training programs and internships available. Company benefits include: medical, dental, and life insurance; pension plan; tuition assistance; disability coverage; employee discounts; savings plan; employee stock. Corporate headquarters location. Parent company: Paramount Commmunications. New York Stock Exchange.

THE METROPOLITAN MUSEUM OF ART
Fifth Avenue at 82nd Street
New York NY 10028
212/879-5500, ext. 3283
Contact Paggy Saldak, Employment Services. One of the world's finest and most complete art museums. Permanent exhibitions include major representations of art styles ranging from prehistoric art to modern art. Departments include: Conservation and Catalogue Departments; Education Services; Libraries; Concerts and Lectures; Fellowships; Publications and Reproductions; and Exhibitions. Also operates The Cloisters in Fort Tryon Park. Corporate headquarters location. Common positions include: Accountant; Administrator; Computer Programmer; Researcher; Electrical Engineer; Librarian. Principal educational backgrounds sought: Accounting; Art History; Liberal Arts; Art. Company benefits include: medical insurance; dental insurance; pension plan; life insurance; tuition assistance; disability coverage; employee discounts; savings plan; prescription drug plan.

METROPOLITAN OPERA ASSOCIATION INC.
Lincoln Center
New York NY 10023
212/799-3100
Contact Employment Coordinator. A major opera company, offering operas from September through May. Hires over 150 administrative full-time personnel, and over 300 'behind-the-scenes' people: Singers, Dancers, Orchestra, Stage Hands, Costume, Make-up, etc. Corporate headquarters location. Operations at this facility include: administration; service; sales. Common positions include: Accountant; Administrator; Advertising Worker; Blue-Collar Worker Supervisor; Computer Programmer; Customer Service Representative; Financial Analyst; Department Manager; Management Trainee; Marketing Specialist; Personnel & Labor Relations Specialist; Programmer; Public Relations Worker; Purchasing Agent; Sales Representative; Systems Analyst; Technical Writer/Editor; Performers (Dancers, Singers, Musicians); Stage Hands. Principal educational backgrounds sought: Accounting; Art/Design; Business Administration; Communications; Computer Science; Finance; Liberal Arts; Marketing. Company benefits include: medical insurance; dental insurance; pension plan; life insurance; disability coverage; employee discounts; savings plan.

NASSAU REGIONAL OFF-TRACK BETTING CORPORATION
220 Fulton Avenue
Hempstead NY 11550
516/292-8300
Contact Donald W. Kehoe, Director of Corporate Affairs. A county-established legalized wagering operation, providing informational and administrative services on thoroughbred and harness racing in New York, and on special events (such as the Kentucky Derby) raced out-of-state. Operates 25 branch offices throughout Nassau County. Corporate headquarters location.

NEW YORK BOTANICAL GARDEN
Southern Boulevard at 200th Street
Bronx NY 10458
212/220-8744
Contact Director of Personnel Services. Several area locations, including Millbrook, NY. Founded in 1891; one of the world's leading contributors to basic plant science through its program of exploration, research, and publication. The Garden's Herbarium is one of the world's ten largest collections of preserved plant specimens; its library is the leading plant science library in the country; and its laboratories have the most advanced equipment for conducting basic plant research. The Garden also offers the public a living museum of plants, and an extensive education program serving school children, college students, and professional and general audiences. Also operates the Cary Arboretum (Millbrook, NY 12545; 914/677-5343), a major ecological field research center. Three major areas of concern are Science, Education and Horticulture. The Garden has an active publications department. Operations at this facility include: research/development; administration. Corporate headquarters location. Common positions include: Accountant; Administrator; Blue-Collar Worker; Supervisor; Buyer; Computer Programmer; Financial Analyst; Forester; Personnel & Labor Relations Specialist; Purchasing Agent. Principal educational backgrounds sought: Accounting; Business Administration; Horticulture; Botany; Plant Science. Company benefits include: medical insurance; dental insurance; pension plan; life insurance; tuition assistance; disability coverage; employee discounts; savings plan.

THE NEW YORK RACING ASSOCIATION INC.
P.O. Box 90
Jamaica NY 11417
718/641-4700
Contact Christopher J. Lotito, Manager, Human Resources. A state-established, non-profit agency, responsible for the operation and management of parimutuel wagering at three horse racing tracks: Aqueduct, Belmont Park, and Saratoga. Facilities are the site of some of America's most prestigious stakes races, including the Belmont Stakes, the Travers, the Beldame, the Marlboro Cup, the Jockey Club Gold Cup, the Vosburgh and the Turf Classic Invitational, as well as many others. Common positions include: Accountant; Computer Programmer; Personnel & Labor Relations Specialist; Public Relations Worker; Purchasing Agent; Reporter/Editor; Systems Analyst; Secretarial; Maintenance Workers. Principal educational backgrounds sought: Accounting; Business Administration; Communications; Computer Science. Company benefits include: medical, dental and life insurance; pension plan; tuition assistance; disability coverage; profit sharing; employee discounts; savings plan. Corporate headquarters location: Ozone Park, NY. Operations at this facility include: regional headquarters; divisional headquarters; administration; service; sales.

NEW YORK SHAKESPEARE FESTIVAL
425 Lafayyette Street
New York NY 10003
212/598-7140
Contact Bob McDonald, General Manager. Founded and produced by Joseph Papp; in operation for over 35 years. A not-for-profit organization involved year-round on Broadway, off-Broadway, on tour around the country, television specials of theatrical works, free Shakespearean productions in Central Park each summer, and the development of new works at the Festival's home base, the Public Theater. NYSF shows have won three Pulitzer Prizes, countless Tony Awards, and over a hundred off-Broadway

awards. Core managerial staff of approximately 20 people supervises 75 supportive administrative and technical staff, and hundreds of actors. With the exception of actors, turnover is slow. Corporate headquarters location. Common positions include: Accountant; Department Manager; General manager; Management Trainee; Operations/Production Manager; Marketing Specialist; Public Relations Specialist. Internships available. Company benefits include: medical insurance; dental insurance; pension plan; life insurance. Operations at this facility include: administration; sales.

ORION PICTURES CORPORATION
1325 Avenue of the Americas
New York NY 10019
212/632-5674
Contact Personnel. One of the nation's largest film distribution companies. Common positions include: Administrator; Customer Service Representative. Common positions include: Business Administration. Internships available. Company benefits include: medical insurance; dental insurance; life insurance; tuition assistance; disability coverage; profit sharing; savings plan. Corporate headquarters location. New York Stock Exchange.

RADIO CITY MUSIC HALL PRODUCTIONS
1260 Avenue of the Americas
New York NY 10020
212/632-4125
Contact Carol Curro, Director of Compensation and Benefits. One of the world's largest and best-known production companies. Worldwide productions include stage shows which may include the renowned Rockettes, popular music concerts by leading artists, and special events. Common positions include: Advertising Worker; Attorney; Customer Service Representative; Marketing Specialist; Personnel & Labor Relations Specialist; Public Relations Worker; Purchasing Agent; Sales Representative. Principal educational backgrounds sought: Business Administration; Communications; Liberal Arts; Marketing. Company benefits include: medical, dental, and life insurance; pension plan; tuition assistance; disability coverage; savings plan. Corporate headquarters location. Parent company: The Rockefeller Group. Operations at this facility include: regional headquarters; divisional headquarters; administration; service; sales.

SHUBERT ORGANIZATION, INC.
234 West 44th Street
New York NY 10036
212/944-3700
Contact Elliot H. Greene, Controller. A major theater company. Common positions include: Accountant; Management Trainee; Administrative Assistant. Principal educational backgrounds sought: Accounting; Business Administration; Liberal Arts. Company benefits include: medical, dental, and life insurance; pension plan; disability coverage. Corporate headquarters location. Operations at this facility include: administration; sales.

TIME WARNER, INC.
Time Life Building
Rockefeller Center
New York NY 10020
212/522-1212
Contact Susan Geisenhimer, Snr. Vice President & Personnel Director. A diversified communications corporation with interests in book and magazine publishing, records and film, and cable and pay TV.

TWENTIETH CENTURY FOX
1211 Avenue of the Americas
Third Floor
New York NY 10036
212/556-2400
Contact Personnel Department. A major producer of motion pictures.

YONKERS RACEWAY
Yonkers Avenue
Yonkers NY 10704
914/968-4200
Contact Anita Tripo, Director of Personnel. Operates a major harness racing facility, as well as an off-season convention and meeting facility. Corporate headquarters location. Common positions include: Accountant; Sales Representative; Marketing Research Worker; Public Relations Worker; Food Service Worker.

New Jersey

NEW JERSEY SPORTS & EXPOSITION AUTHORITY
P.O. Box C200
East Rutherford NJ 07073-0200
201/935-8500
Contact Gina Klein, Manager of Personnel. A state-appointed agency responsible for sports and entertainment activities at the Meadowlands Sports Complex, which includes Meadowlands Racetrack (harness and thoroughbred racing, and other events), Giants Stadium (New York Giants, New York Cosmos, concerts and other events), and Meadowlands Arena (New Jersey Nets, New Jersey Devils, tennis, track, concerts, and other events). Corporate headquarters location.

APPAREL & TEXTILE MANUFACTURING

For more information on professional opportunities in the apparel and textile industry, contact the following professional and trade organizations, as listed on page 449:

AMERICAN APPAREL MANUFACTURERS ASSOCIATION
AMERICAN TEXTILE MANUFACTURERES INSTITUTE
NORTHERN TEXTILE ASSOCIATION
TEXTILE RESEARCH INSTITUTE

New York

ABERDEEN MANUFACTURING CORPORATION
One Park Avenue, 9th Floor
New York NY 10016
212/951-7800
Contact Sarah Abramson, Personnel Manager. Engaged in the production and export/import of comforters, curtains, towels, and other textile goods.

ALLIED FIBERS DIVISION/
ALLIED CORPORATION
1411 Broadway
New York NY 10018
201/455-2000
Contact Personnel Department. For information on professional positions, Personnel Department at main headquarters location: P.O. Box 2245-R, Columbia Road/Park Avenue, Morristown NJ 07960. Produces synthetic fibers and yarns as a subsidiary of Allied Corporation.

ARIS ISOTONER GLOVES INC.
417 Fifth Avenue
New York NY 10016
212/532-8627
Contact Personnel Director. Produces a wide range of gloves and related accessories, including nationally-distributed 'Isotoner' products. Corporate headquarters location.

THE ARROW SHIRT COMPANY
530 Fifth Avenue, 8th Floor
New York NY 10036
212/930-2900
Contact Sheila Rossheim, Personnel Administrator. Produces a line of quality men's shirts as a division of Cluett, Peabody & Company (see separate listing).

BELDING HEMINWAY COMPANY INC.
1430 Broadway
New York NY 10018
212/944-6040
Contact Cheryl Goudoras, Personnel Director. Several area locations, including Manhattan; Carlstadt, and Elizabeth, NJ; and Putnam, CT. Operates in two industry segments: Industrial, in which company is a pioneer in the production of high-technology industrial threads and yarns, sold to manufacturers in the apparel, footwear, leather goods, furniture, mattress, and wire and cable industries, and decorative fabrics sold to manufacturers of draperies, luggage, and bedspreads; and Home Sewing, producing a nationally-known line of threads, buttons, notions, zippers, and sewing aids, as well as materials for hand embroidery, knitting, crocheting, and weaving. Area subsidiaries include Belding Hausman, Inc. (synthetic fibers). Company operates nine plants in seven United States locations, and employs more than 1,700 people nationwide. Corporate headquarters location. New York Stock Exchange. International.

BELDOCH INDUSTRIES CORPORATION
44 Cherry Valley Avenue
West Hempstead NY 11552
516/485-4400
Contact Phyllis Sloane, Controller. Several area locations, including West Hempstead, and New York, NY; and South Norwalk, CT. A women's apparel manufacturer. Products include knitwear and sportswear from catalog to designer clothes, including pants, shirts, and sweaters. Supplies products to major department stores and other retailers. Corporate headquarters location.

BIG YANK CORPORATION
350 Fifth Avenue
32nd Floor
New York NY 10118
212/736-9393
Contact Harold Baxter, Personnel Department. Engaged in apparel manufacturing. Parent company, Interco, is a broadly based major manufacturer and retailer of consumer products and services with operations in apparel manufacturing, retailing, footwear manufacturing, and furniture and home furnishings.

BURLINGTON INDUSTRIES INC.
1345 Avenue of the Americas
New York NY 10105
212/621-3000
Contact Janice Jarsky, Personnel Director. Merchandising headquarters for the nation's largest and most diversified manufacturer of textiles and related products for apparel, the home, and industry. The company manufactures and merchandises apparel fabrics, yarns, carpets, rugs, furniture, mattress ticking, draperies, bedspreads, comforters, sheets, pillowcases, towels, and fabrics for industrial uses. Burlington employs 52,000 people worldwide. This facility is responsible for marketing, advertising, and related sales activities for the national organization. Corporate headquarters location: Greensboro, NC. International. New York Stock Exchange.

BUTTERICK COMPANY
161 Avenue of the Americas
New York NY 10013
212/620-2500

Contact Personnel Manager. Produces two well-known lines of clothes patterns for the home sewing market, and five related fashion publications, including Weddings, Butterick Home Catalog, Vogue Patterns Magazine, Vogue Knitting Magazine, and Make It! Common positions include: Customer Service Representative; Department Manager; Personnel and Labor Relations Specialist; Public Relations Specialist; Technical Writer; Fashion Designer; Editorial Assistant. Educational background sought: Art/Design; Business Administration; Communications; Economics; Marketing; Liberal Arts; Fashion; Merchandising. Internships available (if appropriate). Company benefits include: medical insurance; dental insurance; pension plan; life insurance; tuition assistance; disability coverage; employee discounts; savings plan. Corporate headquarters location. Operations at this facility include: development; administration; service; sales.

CALDERON BELTS & BAGS INC.
443 Greenwich Street
New York NY 10013
212/966-4920
Contact Charlotte Schwartz, Personnel Officer. Manufactures Anne Klein ladies' handbags and belts. Corporate headquarters location. Operations at this facility include: manufacturing. Common positions include: Accountant; Credit Manager; Customer Service Representative. Principal educational backgrounds sought: Accounting; Finance. Company benefits include: medical insurance; dental insurance; life insurance; disability coverage; profit sharing; employee discounts.

CARNIVALE BAG COMPANY
544 Park Avenue
Brooklyn NY 11205
718/855-0613
Contact Personnel Department. One of the largest manufacturers of a wide line of bags and other packaging products in the United States. Corporate headquarters location.

CHF INDUSTRIES INC.
1 Park Avenue
New York NY 10016
212/951-7800
Contact Personnel Manager. Several area locations, including Garfield, NJ; Danielson, CT. Company operates in four divisions: Aberdeen Manufacturing Corporation, designers and manufacturers of many different styles of popular-priced curtains, draperies, bedspreads, comforters, shower curtains; Cameo Curtains, designers and manufacturers of draperies, bedspreads, comforters, and shower curtains which are sold in exclusive department stores; Finkel Outdoor Products, designers and manufacturers of a wide variety of quality outdoor and casual furniture, and garden, lawn, and beach umbrellas and related accessories; Lee L. Woodward, manufacturers of a complete line of outdoor aluminum and steel furniture as well as a premium line of wrought iron furniture and accessories. Corporate headquarters location.

LIZ CLAIBORNE
1441 Broadway
New York NY 10018
212/354-4900
Contact Kathy Conners, Personnel Director. An apparel company which designs and manufactures men's and women's clothes, accessories, and cosmetics.

CLUETT, PEABODY & COMPANY
530 Fifth Avenue
New York NY 10036
212/930-3000
Contact Director of Human Resources. A diversified apparel company; operating as a wholly owned subsidiary of West Point Pepperell Company; company is among the leading manufacturers of apparel for men, women, and children. Subsidiary companies include: The Arrow Company (men's shirts, sportswear, and furnishings); Saturdays in California (young men's sportswear); J. Shoeneman (men's clothing; women's suits and sportswear);

and many others. Company also operates an International Division (operations in Canada, Mexico, Venezuela, and Central America); and a Licensing Division, which licenses several of the company's processes and trademarks. Company benefits include: medical, dental and life insurance; pension plan; tuition assistance; disability coverage; employee discounts; savings plan. Corporate headquarters location: West Point, GA. Operations at this facility include: divisional headquarters. New York Stock Exchange. International.

CONCORD FABRICS INC.
1359 Broadway, 4th floor
New York NY 10018
212/760-0300
Contact Leslie J. Spitzer, Director, Personnel. Engaged in the textile converting business; company designs, develops, and styles woven and knitted fabrics of natural and synthetic fibers, in a wide range of colors and styles, for sale to manufacturers and retailers. One of the nation's largest independent textile converters. Manufacturing facilities are located in Georgia and California. Corporate headquarters location houses administration, design, merchandising, and marketing functions. Common positions include: Accountant; Computer Programmer; Credit Analyst; Customer Service Representative; Management Trainee; Operations/Production Manager; Personnel & Labor Relations Specialist; Purchasing Agent; Quality Control Supervisor; Sales Representative. Principal educational backgrounds sought: Accounting; Business Administration; Finance; Liberal Arts; Marketing; Fashion/Design. Company benefits include: medical and life insurance; tuition assistance; disability coverage. Operations at this facility include: divisional headquarters; manufacturing; administration; service; sales. American Stock Exchange.

CONE MILLS MARKETING COMPANY
1440 Broadway
New York NY 10018
212/391-1300
Contact Pamela Maxell, Personnel. Two area locations. Marketing and sales headquarters for the major textile manufacturer. Company is one of the world's leading producers of denims, corduroys, and related fabrics for jeans and casual sportswear. Other products are yarn-dyed and uniform fabrics; greige goods; commission textile dyeing, printing and finishing services; decorative fabrics; polyurethane products; furniture cushions; and hardware distribution. Other sales offices in Chicago, San Francisco, and Los Angeles. Operates 21 plants in North Carolina, South Carolina, and Mississippi. Employs 10,800 people nationwide. Corporate headquarters location: Greensboro, NC. New York Stock Exchange.

CROSCILL CURTAIN COMPANY
261 Fifth Avenue
New York NY 10016
212/689-7222
Contact Personnel Manager. Produces curtains, draperies, and other textile products.

DAMON CREATIONS INC.
1370 Avenue of the Americas
New York NY 10019
212/399-3500
Contact Diane Williams, Director of Personnel. Engaged in the design, production, and marketing of apparel, primarily in two categories: men's furnishings and men's sportswear. Products are of high quality and are sold in the higher retail ranges throughout the United States. Operations located primarily in the New York area. Corporate headquarters location. American Stock Exchange.

DAN RIVER INC.
111 West 40th Street
New York NY 10018
212/554-5531
Contact Otis A. Braithwaite, Personnel Administrator. One of the nation's major textile manufacturers, with 7,000 employees, and operates modern manufacturing facilities in the

states of Virginia, South Carolina, Georgia, and Alabama. The company's line of finished products includes dress goods, shirtings, sportswear fabrics, and knit velours. Home Fashion products, sold directly to consumer, include sheets and pillow cases, comforters, bed ruffles, pillow shams, and draperies. Other important consumer products include piece goods for home sewing and arts and crafts use, and carpeting for home and commercial applications. Corporate headquarters location: Danville, VA.

EXQUISITE FORM INDUSTRIES INC.
14 Pelham Parkway
Pelham Manor NY 10803
914/738-2200
Contact Office Manager. Manufactures and distributes a large line of women's lingerie and undergarments. Corporate headquarters location. International.

THE LESLIE FAY COMPANIES, INC.
1400 Broadway
New York NY 10018
212/221-4145
Contact Personnel Manager. Engaged in the design, manufacture, and sale of a diversified line of women's dresses and sportswear. Products marketed to a varied group of consumers, and cover the moderate to higher-priced range. Company performs all pattern making, grading, cutting, and some sewing operations at several manufacturing facilities. Products are sold to retailers throughout the United States, with sales offices located in major United States cities. Some popular trade names include Leslie Fay, Leslie Fay Sportswear, Outlander, Head Sportswear. Other locations in Wilkesbarre, PA; Columbia, MD; Atlanta, GA; Philadelphia, PA; Cincinnati, OH; and Boston, MA. Common positions include: Administrator; Credit Manager; Industrial Engineer; Department Manager; Operations/Production Manager; Marketing Specialist; Personnel & Labor Relations Specialist; Public Relations Specialist; Sales Representative; Designer/Assistant Designer. Principal educational backgrounds sought: Business Administration; Communications; Marketing; Fashion Design; Merchandising. Company benefits include: medical, dental, and life insurance; pension plan; disability coverage; employee discounts. Corporate headquarters location. Operations at this facility include: administration; sales. New York Stock Exchange.

M. FINE & SONS MANUFACTURING COMPANY
350 Fifth Avenue, Suite 4310
New York NY 10118
212/239-1111
Contact Stephen L. Fine, Co-President. Manufactures and distributes men's work clothes and leisure apparel. Corporate headquarters location. Common positions include: Bookkeeper; Merchandising Specialist; Production Control Specialist; Salesperson.

FOWNES BROTHERS & COMPANY INC.
411 Fifth Avenue
New York NY 10016
212/683-0150
Contact Howard Chaiet, Controller. A manufacturer and distributor of gloves. Manufactures dress gloves for men and women, made of fabric, vinyl, acrylic, leather, and golf gloves. Nationwide direct sales force sells to more than 9000 retail outlets. Manufacturing plants are located in the Philippines and the Peoples Republic of China. This facility houses the company's executive offices, and the principal sales office.

DAVE GOLDBERG INC.
29-10 Thompson Avenue
Long Island City NY 11101
718/786-7477
Contact Personnel Director. Manufactures and distributes loungewear, marketing through wholesalers and retailers throughout the United States. Corporate headquarters location.

HERTLING MANUFACTURING COMPANY
500 Driggs Avenue
Brooklyn NY 11211.
718/782-7059
Contact Gregory Schiemer, Controller. A growing manufacturer of women's and men's apparel; markets include department stores, specialty shops, and diversified retail outlets throughout the country. Corporate headquarters location. Common positions include: Computer Programmer; Credit Manager; Customer Service Representative; Sales Representative. Educational backgrounds sought: Accounting; Business Administration; Finance; Liberal Arts. Company benefits include: medical insurance; dental insurance; life insurance; disability coverage; employee discounts. Operations include: regional headquarters; manufacturing; administration; service; sales.

HOME CURTAIN CORPORATION
295 Fifth Avenue, Room 1414
New York NY 10016
212/686-2080
Contact Gloria Jenkins, Human Resources. Manufactures and distributes curtains, draperies, and related items. Common positions include: Administrator; Credit Manager; Customer Service Representative; Public Relations Specialist; Purchasing Agent; Sales Representative. Principal educational backgrounds sought: Art/Design; Business Administration; Economics; Marketing. Company benefits include: medical, dental, and life insurance; disability coverage; employee discounts; savings plan. Corporate headquarters location. Operations at this facility include: administration; sales.

HARRY IRWIN INC.
116 West 23rd Street
New York NY 10011
212/741-9898
Contact Personnel. Manufactures a broad range of men's clothing. Corporate headquarters location.

JORDACHE ENTERPRISES
220 West 37th Street
New York NY 10018
212/279-7343
Contact Personnel Director. Engaged in the distribution of designer jeans and other fashion apparel products.

KINGS POINT MANUFACTURING COMPANY
280 Northern Boulevard
P.O. Box 798
Great Neck NY 11022
516/466-3800
Contact Charlie Snyder, Personnel Department. Manufactures a broad line of apparel. Corporate headquarters location.

KINNEY SHOE CORPORATION
233 Broadway
New York NY 10279
212/720-3700
Contact John Kozlowski, VP/Human Resources. More than 50 area locations. One of the nation's largest retailers of shoes, accessories, and related apparel items. A subsidiary of F.W. Woolworth Company. Corporate headquarters location.

LEHIGH VALLEY INDUSTRIES INC.
345 Hudson Street, 16th Floor
New York NY 10014
212/337-6600
Contact Office Manager. A highly diversified corporation engaged, through various subsidiaries, in the manufacture and sale of textiles, dredging equipment, and precision

machine castings, as well as producing women's footwear. Subsidiaries and operating divisions include: Mobile Pulley & Machine Works Division; Dori Shoe Company Inc.; Motivational Marketing; and Blue Ridge-Winkler Textiles Division. International subsidiaries in Great Britain, West Germany, and Belgium. Corporate headquarters location. New York Stock Exchange. International.

LIBERTY FABRICS, INC.
295 5th Avenue
New York NY 10016
212/684-3100
Contact Alan Hammer, Director of Administration. A manufacturer of knitted lace and elastic fabrics used by manufacturers of lingerie, sportswear, swimwear, and home furnishings. Manufacturing facilities located in North Bergen, NJ; and Gordonsville, VA. Manufacturing facilities located in North Bergen, NJ; Gordonsville, VA; Jamesville, NC; Woolwine, VA; and Barrington, RI. Common positions include: Accountant; Customer Service Representative. Principal educational backgrounds sought: Accounting; Business Administration; Finance. Company benefits include: medical and life insurance; tuition assistance; disability coverage; profit sharing. Corporate headquarters location. Operations at this facility include: administration; sales

MAIDENFORM INC.
90 Park Avenue
New York NY 10016
212/953-1400
Contact Geri Bull, Office Manager. A nationally-recognized apparel manufacturer, producing a large line of quality women's undergarments, swimwear, and sleepwear. Corporate headquarters location.

J.B. MARTIN CO.
10 East 53rd Street, Suite 3100
New York NY 10022
212/421-2020
Contact David Budd, Personnel Director. Produces velvet for a wide range of end uses. Headquarters location.

MILLIKEN & COMPANY APPAREL FABRIC SALES
1045 Sixth Avenue
New York NY 10018
212/819-4200
Contact Personnel Director. Engaged in the textile manufacturing industry, producing a wide range of textile yarns and fabrics, apparel, and related chemical and packaging products. Products range from tire cord to yarn and fashion fabrics to women's wear and men's wear. Company has also developed several products and industrial processes used in textile products manufacturing, chemicals for use in textile manufacturing, and industrial fabrics for numerous uses. This facility is the company's primary sales facility. Most manufacturing facilities are located in North Carolina, South Carolina, and Georgia. Corporate headquarters location.

MOVIE STAR INC.
136 Madison Avenue, 6th Floor
New York NY 10016
212/679-7260
Contact Yolaine Goldberg, Personnel Director. One of the country's largest and most diversified manufacturers in the loungewear and lingerie industry, producing daywear, sleepwear, and loungewear sold by major department stores, chain stores, and specialty store businesses throughout the United States. Brand names include 'Movie Star', 'Movie Star Loungewear', and 'Cinema Etoile'. Also produces men's work and leisure shirts through subsidiary Irwin B. Schwabe Company, with most products sold to Sears Roebuck & Company. Sales offices are also located in Atlanta, Charlotte (NC), Chicago, Dallas, Denver, Los Angeles, and Miami. International facilities in Costa Rica, Panama, Puerto Rico, Singapore, and South Africa. Corporate headquarters location.

NANTUCKET INDUSTRIES CORPORATION
105 Madison Avenue
New York NY 10016
212/889-5656
Contact Diane Wofford, Vice President of Operations. Manufactures lines of men's and women's underwear as a division of Nantucket Industries. Corporate headquarters location.

NATIONAL SPINNING COMPANY INC.
183 Madison Avenue
New York NY 10016
212/889-3800
Contact Personnel Director. Engaged in the manufacture, marketing, and distribution of yarn products to knitwear manufacturers. Also produces hand-knitting yarn and rug kits for distribution to retail chains throughout the United States. Corporate headquarters location.

NATIVE TEXTILES INC.
16 East 34th Street
New York NY 10016
212/951-5100
Contact Virginia Korz, Personnel Department. Manufactures lace and other quality fabrics for distribution throughout the United States. Corporate headquarters location.

PHILLIPS-VAN HEUSEN CORPORATION
1290 Avenue of the Americas
New York NY 10104
212/541-5200
Contact Personnel Director. Engaged in the manufacture and procurement for sale of a broad range of men's apparel, and in the operation of retail stores selling apparel. The manufacturing operation includes products manufactured, imported, and sold by the following divisions and subsidiaries of the company: The Van Heusen Company; The Joseph & Feiss Company; PVH Somerset Company; PVH Sportswear; Somerset Knitting Mills Inc.; Men's Wear International Inc.; and the Outlet Store Division. Products include a wide variety of low to higher-priced items, including men's dress shirts, sport shirts, pajamas, robes, sweaters, slacks, sportswear, outerwear, suits, sportcoats, and women's tailored clothing. Name brands include: 'Van Heusen', 'Hennessy', 'Cricketeer', 'Crestmark', and others. Company also markets products under the designer names 'Halston', 'Geoffrey Beene', and 'Cacharel'. Products are also sold to national chains and discounters under the 'McGregor' and 'Windbreaker' labels, and under private labels. The Retail Division sells men's, women's, and children's apparel in specialty and junior department stores located in the Middle Atlantic, Northeastern, Midwestern, and Western United States. Other area facilities in Waldwick, NJ (Research & Development Center), and Piscataway, NJ (Administrative Center). Corporate headquarters location. New York Stock Exchange.

ROSSINI FOOTWEAR INC.
1795 Express Drive North
Smithtown NY 11787
516/582-3230
Contact Kathryn Donahue, Executive Secretary. Operates through three divisions: Footwear (manufactures dancing shoes, leotards, and tights); Art Stone Dance and Gymnastics (retailer of Rossini Footwear Products); and Statler Records (records popular music for dancing and gymnastics). Corporate headquarters location.

RUSS TOGGS INC.
1411 Broadway, 2nd Floor
New York NY 10018
212/642-8500
Contact Personnel Director. Several area locations, including Queens. Operates more than 15 separate divisions, each with a complete apparel line. Products include coordinated

sportswear, dresses, and separates for men and women. Sales for all divisions are handled through more than 30 regional sales offices throughout the United States. Products are sold under company brand name and under private label.

SALANT CORPORATION
11155 Avenue of the Americas, 18th Floor
New York NY 10036
212/221-7500
Contact Miriam Rightbart, Personnel Manager. Operates a group of companies engaged in the manufacture and marketing of a broad variety of apparel products in the popular to higher-priced range for the entire family. The company's apparel is sold principally throughout the United States and Canada in all channels of distribution. Operates through the following subsidiary companies: United Pioneer Company (New York, NY); Thomson Company (New York, NY); Obion Company (New York, NY); Campbell's Inc. (Paris, TN); and Salant Canada Ltd. (Toronto, Canada). Corporate headquarters location. New York Stock Exchange. International.

SANMARK-STARDUST INC.
145 Madison Avenue
New York NY 10016
212/684-3400
Contact Personnel Manager. One of the nation's largest sleepwear and loungewear manufacturers, designing, manufacturing, and distributing products that include slips, pajamas, nightgowns, baby dolls, and loungewear, both under company labels, and as a contract manufacturer. Company also operates two Manhattan showrooms where products are displayed and sold. Corporate headquarters location. American Stock Exchange.

ABE SCHRADER CORPORATION
530 Seventh Avenue
New York NY 10018
212/840-7733
Contact Personnel Director. Engaged in apparel manufacturing. Parent company, Interco, is a broadly based major manufacturer and retailer of consumer products and services with operations in apparel manufacturing, retailing, footwear manufacturing, and furniture and home furnishings.

F. SCHUMACHER & COMPANY
79 Madison Avenue
New York NY 10016
212/213-7900
Contact Nino Orfeo, Personnel Director. A textile wholesaler, with offices in all 50 states, and brokers throughout the world. Specializes in rugs and fabrics trading. Corporate headquarters location. International.

SPRINGS INDUSTRIES INC.
104 West 40th Street
New York NY 10018
212/556-6214
Contact Roy Cureton, Human Resources Director. Five area locations. Produces a wide range of finished apparel fabrics, consumer fashion fabrics, and retail and specialty fabrics. Nationally, company is a major international manufacturer of finished fabrics and home furnishings products. Company operates 43 manufacturing plants, 10 distribution centers, and 29 sales and administrative offices in 19 states, England, Japan, and Belgium. Employs 23,500 worldwide. This facility is administrative headquarters. New York Stock Exchange. International. Common positions include: Marketing Specialist; Sales Representative; Business Administration; Marketing. Company benefits include: medical insurance; dental insurance; pension plan; life insurance; tuition assistance; disability coverage; profit sharing; employee discounts; savings plan. Corporate headquarters location: Ft. Mill, SC. Operations include: regional and divisional headquarters; sales.

STUFFED SHIRT INC.
1407 Broadway, Room 505
New York NY 10018
212/997-1000
Contact Personnel Department. Engaged in apparel manufacturing. Parent company, Interco, is a broadly based major manufacturer and retailer of consumer products and services with operations in apparel manufacturing, retailing, footwear manufacturing, and furniture and home furnishings group.

WARNER-RICHTER LABEL COMPANY
32 West 39th Street
New York NY 10018
800 962-9683
Contact Personnel Administrator. A manufacturer of woven and printed fabric labels for use by the apparel industry. Corporate headquarters location.

WEST MILL CLOTHES INC.
57-07 31st Avenue
Woodside NY 11377
718/204-6640
Contact Clifford Goodman, Personnel Officer. One of the nation's leading manufacturers of formal wear. Corporate headquarters location.

WEST POINT PEPPERELL, INC.
1185 Avenue of the Americas
New York NY 10036
212/930-2050
Contact Linda Harris, Personnel. A major worldwide marketing and manufacturing organization. Its core products are fabrics made from both natural and man-made fibers and yarns for a broad range of end uses, including apparel and products for the home and industry. New York Stock Exchange.

Connecticut

BROWNELL & COMPANY, INC.
P.O. Box 362
Moodus CT 0646
203/873-8625
Contact Cindy Stackowitz, Secretary of Accounts Payable. A producer of textiles. Principal products include: twine and cordage, fishing nets, sport nets, air cargo restraint systems, archery bowstrings, camouflage netting, and helicopter nets. Operations include: manufacturing. Common positions include: Accountant; Administrator; Blue-Collar Worker Supervisor; Buyer; Credit Manager; Customer Service Representative; Engineer; Electrical Engineer; Industrial Engineer; Financial Analyst; Manager; Department Manager; President; Operations/Production Manager; Quality Control Supervisor; Sales Representative. Principal educational backgrounds sought: Accounting; Finance. Company benefits include: medical insurance; life insurance; tuition assistance; disability coverage.

THE WILLIAM CARTER CO.
100 Bridgeport Avenue
Shelton CT 06484
203/926-5000
Contact Janine McManus, Manager of Human Resources. Sells nationally-advertised apparel, primarily for children, under the 'Carter's label to approximately 7,000 retailers, including leading department and specialty stores. Operates 48 retail outlet stores across the country. Regional sales offices in New York, Chicago, and Los Angeles. Common postions include: Accountant; Buyer; Computer Programmer;

<u>New Jersey</u>

ABERDEEN SPORTWEAR, INC.
P.O. Box 8413
Trenton NJ 08650
609/587-2309
Contact Personnel. A major manufacturer of quality sportswear.

BEACON LOOMS, INC.
411 Alfred Avenue
Teaneck NJ 07666
201/833-1600
Contact Personnel Manager. Produces a wide range of textiles, primarily for sale and to major retailers throughout the country. Corporate headquarters location. Several area locations, including Englewood, NJ.

BURLINGTON COAT FACTORY
1830 Route 130
Burlington NJ 08016
609/387-7800
Contact Sara Orleck, Recruiter. A manufacturer and wholesale dealer of a wide variety of a wide variety of coats.

COOPER SPORTSWEAR MANUFACTURING COMPANY
720 Frelinghuysen Avenue
Newark NJ 07114
201/824-3400
Contact John Bell, Controller. An importer and manufacturer of men's and boys' leather and cloth coats and jackets in the moderate-to high price range. Sells to fine department stores and private label distributors. Distributes products throughout the world, including the Far East, South America, and Europe. Common positions include: Accountant; Buyer; Credit Manager; Customer Service Representative; Sewing Machine Mechanic. Principal educational backgrounds sought: Accounting; Business Administration; Finance. Company benefits include: medical and life insurance; pension plan. Corporate headquarters location. Operations at this facility include: manufacturing; administration.

FABRICAN
375 Diamond Bridge Avenue
Hawthorne NJ 07506
201/423-4800
Contact Josie Giovinazzo, Personnel Director. Manufactures curtains for retailers and chain stores. Corporate headquarters location. Common positions include: Accountant; Administrator; Computer Programmer; Customer Service Representative; Financial Analyst. Principal educational backgrounds sought: Accounting; Business Administration; Computer Science. Company benefits include: medical insurance; dental insurance; life insurance; disability coverage; employee discounts. Operations at this facility include: administration.

S. GOLDBERG & CO. INC.
20 East Broadway
Hackensack NJ 07601
201/342-1200
Contact Personnel Manager. Manufactures house slippers. Common positions include: Industrial Engineer. Company benefits include: medical and life insurance; pension plan; tuition assistance; disability coverage; profit sharing; employee discounts; profit sharing bonus. Corporate headquarters location. Operations at this facility include: manufacturing.

ELLEN HART INC.
25 New Market Street
Salem NJ 08079
609/935-3650

Contact Personnel Department. A leading producer of women's apparel.

LORD JEFF KNITTING COMPANY, INC.
10 Maple Street
Norwood NJ 07648
201/767-8800
Contact Diane E. Gucene, Personnel Manager. Several area locations, including New York, NY; and Williamstown, NJ. A manufacturer and distributor of quality sportswear, knitwear, accessories, and related items. Engaged in wholesale trade to retailers nationwide, including better department stores and specialty shops. Primary products are men's and ladies' knit sweaters, shirts, pants, and shorts. Main sales office and showroom located in New York City. Other showrooms in major cities across the United States. Distribution center and general offices at headquarters location. Corporate headquarters location. Common positions include: Accountant; Administrator; Computer Programmer; Credit Manager; Customer Service Representative; Department Manager; General Manager; Personnel & Labor Relations Specialist; Purchasing Agent; Quality Control Supervisor; Sales Representative. Principal educational backgrounds sought: Accounting; Business Administration; Finance; Communications; Computer Science; Liberal Arts. Company benefits include: medical insurance; dental insurance; pension plan; life insurance; tuition assistance; disability coverage; employee discounts. Corporate headquarters location. Operations at this facility include: administration; service; sales.

MAGLA PRODUCTS INC.
700 Shunpike Road
Chatham NJ 07928-2199
Contact Controller. A manufacturer of kitchen and domestic household textiles, including ironing-board covers, dish towels, oven mitts, rubber gloves, disposable wipe cloths, and cling sheets. Principal customers are department store chains. Corporate headquarters location.

MEGASTAR APPAREL
Mack Centre Drive
Paramus NJ 07653
201/262-9100
Contact Personnel Director. Engaged in apparel manufacturing. Parent company, Interco, is a broadly-based major manufacturer and retailer of consumer products and services, with operations in apparel manufacturing, retailing, footwear manufacturing, and furniture and home furnishings.

MORLEY SHIRT CO.
402-412 Route 23
Franklin NJ 07416
201-827-9135
Contact Mrs. Pat Ward, Personnel Manager. Produces men's shirts. Employs over 500 people. Corporate headquarters location.

OLD DEERFIELD FABRICS INC.
30 Canfield Road
Cedar Grove NJ 07009
201/239-6600
Contact Personnel Department. Produces decorative fabrics and other household decorations. Corporate headquarters location.

PHILLIPS-VAN HEUSEN CORPORATION
281 Centennial Avenue
Piscataway NJ 08854
201/885-5000
Contact Personnel Director. Engaged in the manufacture and procurement for sale of a broad range of men's and women's apparel, and in the operation of retail stores selling apparel. The manufacturing operation includes products manufactured, imported, and sold by the following divisions and subsidiaries of the company: The Van Heusen Company;

PVH Somerset Company; PVH Sportswear; Somerset Knitting Mills Inc.; and the Retail Store Division. Products include a wide variety of low to higher-priced items, including men's dress shirts, sport shirts, sweaters, slacks, sportswear, outerwear, suits, sportcoats, and women's clothing. Name brands include: 'Van Heusen', 'Hennessy', 'Crown & Cross' '417', and others. Company also markets products under the designer names 'Halston', 'Geoffrey Beene', and 'Cacharel'. The Retail Division sells men's, and women's apparel in specialty department stores located in the Middle Atlantic, Northeastern, Midwestern, and Western United States. Facilities in Piscataway, NJ (Administrative Center). Common positions include: Accountant; Computer Programmer; Credit Manager; Customer Service Representative; Department Manager; Marketing Specialist; Personnel & Labor Relations Specialist; Purchasing Agent; Clerical Accounting Positions. Principal educational backgrounds sought: Accounting; Business Administration; Communications; Finance; Liberal Arts; Marketing. Company benefits include: medical insurance; pension plan; life insurance; tuition assistance; disability coverage; profit sharing; employee discounts; savings plan. Corporate headquarters location: New York, NY. Operations at this facility include: administration. New York Stock Exchange.

UNITED MERCHANTS & MANUFACTURERS INC.
1650 Palisade Avenue
Teaneck NJ 07666
201/837-1700
Contact Stanley Siegel, Director of Personnel. Can also contact Claire Langella, Personnel Manager. A Fortune 500 textile and apparel corporation producing apparel and accessories, apparel fabrics, home furnishing fabrics and products, and yarns. Common positions include: Accountant; Attorney; Auditor; Commercial Artist; Computer Programmer; Financial Analyst; Sales Representative; Systems Analyst. Principal educational backgrounds sought: Accounting; Art/Design; Business Administration; Computer Science; Liberal Arts; Marketing. Company benefits include: medical, dental, and life insurance; pension plan; tuition assistance; disability coverage; employee discounts. Corporate headquarters location: New York, NY. Operations at this facility include: administration; service. New York Stock Exchange.

WELLMAN INC.
1040 Broad Street, Suite 302
Shrewsbury NJ 07702
201/542-7300
Contact Personnel Department. Corporate office for a textile manufacturing company.

BANKING/SAVINGS & LOAN

For more information on professional opportunities in the banking industry, contact the following professional and trade organizations, as listed beginning on page 449:

AMERICAN BANKERS ASSOCIATION
BANK ADMINISTRATION INSTITUTE
INDEPENDENT BANKERS ASSOCIATION OF AMERICA
INSTITUTE OF FINANCIAL EDUCATION
INSTITUTE OF FINANCIAL EDUCATION/CHAPTER 18
NATIONAL COUNCIL OF SAVINGS INSTITUTIONS

New York

APPLE BANK FOR SAVINGS
205 East 42nd Street
New York NY 10017
212/573-8000
Contact Joyce Wynn, Assistant Vice-President/Personnel. Operates a full-service savings bank, serving Manhattan, the Bronx, and Long Island. Operates 11 Manhattan branches; three branches in Nassau County (Manhasset, Massapequa, and Syosset); and two in

Suffolk County (Greenlawn and Smithtown). Operates through the following divisions: Accounting and Control; Auditing; Banking Operations; Business Development; Consumer and Installment Loans; Data Processing; Legal; Marketing; Office Services; Personnel; and Real Estate and Mortgage. Assets exceed $1.5 billion. Corporate headquarters location.

ASTORIA FEDERAL SAVINGS & LOAN ASSOCIATION
75-20 Astoria Boulevard
Jackson Heights NY 11370
718/397-6714
Contact Carol Cappellino, Manager of Recruiting. Multiple area locations. Offers a wide range of traditional banking and financial services, operating 30 branch offices in Queens, Nassau, Suffolk, Westchester, Chenango and Otsego counties. Assets exceed $3 billion. Corporate headquarters location. Common positions include: Accountant; Computer Programmer; Customer Service Representative; Branch Manager; Management Trainee; Systems Analyst; Underwriter; Teller; Loan Representative; Auditor. Principal educational backgrounds sought include: Accounting; Business Administration; Computer Science. Training programs offerred. Company benefits include: medical, dental, and life insurance; pension plan; tuition assistance; disability coverage; 401K. Corporate headquarters location.

BANK OF AMERICA
335 Madison Avenue
New York NY 10017
212/503-7498
Contact Human Resource Services Department. Area management offices for the bank holding company, whose subsidiaries are engaged in general banking and trust services (through Bank of America NT&SA), with more than 1200 domestic and foreign branches and 27 corporate banking and representative offices in 77 nations. The corporation's major non-bank subsidiaries are engaged in consumer finance; commercial lending; mortgage banking; computer equipment leasing and data processing; marketing and distribution services for travelers checks issued by BankAmerica; credit-related life and disability insurance; investment advisory services; securities processing, paying, clearing, and transfer agency services; and venture capital advisory services. Corporate headquarters location: San Francisco, CA. New York Stock Exchange. International.

BANK LEUMI TRUST COMPANY OF NEW YORK
139 Center Street, First Floor
New York NY 10013
212/382-4000
Contact Herbert Small, Manager of Employment. Provides a wide range of banking services, including complete commercial and personal banking services, domestic and international banking, foreign exchange transactions, and financing operations. Corporate headquarters location. Operates a Management Development Program for a variety of fields, including Credit and Bank Operations. Common positions include: Data Processing Specialist; Programmer; Accountant; Internal Auditor; Loan Officer.

BANK OF MONTREAL
430 Park Avenue
New York NY 10022
Contact Manager, Recruitment Office. Operates the New York City area branch bank for the Canadian-based international bank. Also engaged in corporate and government banking and international loan syndication activities. Overall, parent company is one of the largest banks in North America (assets exceed $87 billion), with operations throughout Canada, the United States (including Chicago, Houston, and Los Angeles), Latin America, The Bahamas, Europe, Asia, and Australia. Employs 33,000 people worldwide. Important U.S. subsidiary is Harris Bank of Chicago.

BANK OF NEW YORK
1401 Franklin Avenue
Garden City NY 11530
516/294-2424

Contact Personnel Manager. A bank holding company, operating primarily through subsidiary Long Island Trust Company; operates banking offices in Manhattan; Nassau County (25 locations, including Hicksville, Jericho, Levittown, Mineola, and Syosset); Queens County (Maspeth and Queens Village); Suffolk County (19 locations, including Farmingdale, Hauppauge, Huntington, Melville, Patchogue, and Port Jefferson); and one overseas office in Nassau, The Bahamas. Services include commercial banking, consumer banking trust services, data processing, and international services. Corporate headquarters location. International.

BANK OF NEW YORK
48 Wall Street, 16th Floor
New York NY 10286
212/495-1509
Contact Personnel Department. The Bank of New York is a money center commercial bank employing over 10,000 people. Common positions include: Bank Officer/Manager. Principal educational backgrounds sought: Economics; Finance. Corporate headquarters location.

THE BANK OF NEW YORK
One Wall Street
College Relations, 13th Floor
New York NY 10015
Contact Manager/College Relations. A principal subsidiary of Irving Bank Corporation. A New York money center bank with extensive national and international business. Serves individuals, corporations, foreign and domestic banks, governments and other institutions through banking offices in New York City and foreign branches, representative offices, subsidiaries and affiliates. Corporate headquarters location. New York Stock Exchange. Common positions include: Accountant; Bank Officer/Manager; Computer Programmer; Financial Analyst. Principal educational backgrounds sought: Accounting; Business Administration; Computer Science; Economics; Finance; Liberal Arts. Company benefits include: medical insurance; dental insurance; pension plan; tuition assistance; life insurance; disability coverage; profit sharing; savings plan.

THE BANK OF NEW YORK
101 Barkley, 1st Floor
New York NY 10007
212/815-4984
Contact Personnel Department. Operates as a bank holding company, providing banking and trust services through subsidiaries The Bank of New York and The Bank of New York Trust Company (123 Main Street, White Plains NY 10602), with offices located throughout the state of New York; overseas offices in London, Singapore, and the Cayman Islands; an international banking subsidiary and an investment representative office (both in Miami, FL); and an International Banking Facility in New York City. Non-banking subsidiary companies include: ARCS Mortgage, Inc. (Canoga Park, CA); The Bank of New York Life Insurance Company (Phoenix, AZ); BNY Financial Corporation (New York, NY); BNY Leasing (New York, NY); and the Bank of New York International and BNY International Investments (Miami, FL). Corporate headquarters location. New York Stock Exchange. International. Operations at this facility include: service. Common positions include: Accountant; Administrator; Attorney; Bank Officer/Manager; Computer Programmer; Credit Manager; Customer Service Representative; Financial Analyst; Operations/Production Manager; Personnel & Labor Relations Specialist; Systems Analyst; Auditor; Securities Administrator. Principal educational backgrounds sought: Accounting; Business Administration; Computer Science; Finance. Company benefits include: medical insurance; pension plan; life insurance; tuition assistance; disability coverage; profit sharing; employee discounts; stock purchase.

THE BANK OF TOKYO TRUST COMPANY
100 Broadway
New York NY 10005
212/766-3400

Contact Personnel. One of the fifty largest commercial banks in the United States; operates five offices throughout the New York metropolitan area, as well as in London and The Bahamas. Offers a wide range of traditional banking services, financial advisory services, international banking services, and trust services. A major operating subsidiary of The Bank of Tokyo Ltd. (Tokyo, Japan), which operates offices throughout the world. Corporate headquarters location.

BANKERS TRUST
1 Bankers Trust Plaza
New York NY 10006
212/250-2500
Contact Personnel. Corporate office of a chain of state banks and financiers.

BANKERS TRUST NEW YORK CORPORATION
280 Park Avenue
New York NY 10017
Mailed inquiries only
Contact Management Recruiting Department. Corporation operates the sixth largest commercial bank in New York City, and the eighth largest in the United States, with assets of more than $39 billion. Primarily engaged in wholesale banking for corporations, governments, financial institutions, and high-net-worth individuals. Operates in four core businesses: commercial banking, the money securities markets business, the corporate finance business, and the fiduciary business. Commercial banking function is carried out through three departments: World Corporate, United States, and International. Other major line departments are Resource Management (money and securities markets), and Corporate Finance and Fiduciary (trust and investment services). Company has domestic representative offices in Los Angeles, San Francisco, Palm Beach (FL), Atlanta, Chicago, Houston, and Dallas. International branches are located throughout the world. Corporate headquarters location. New York Stock Exchange.

BARCLAYS INTERNATIONAL
75 Wall Street, 34th Floor
New York NY 10265
212/412-4000
Contact Pam Boyle, Vice-President/Personnel. A major international banking institution, with more than 5000 offices in 70 countries, including most international trade centers. Maintains an extensive network of correspondent banks in virtually every region in the world. International banking services include commercial loans, foreign exchange services, drafts and money transfers, foreign collections, leasing, stock and security custodial services, and economic information and publications. Corporate headquarters location.

THE BOWERY SAVINGS BANK
110 East 42nd Street
New York NY 10017
212/953-8000
Contact Gail Anderson, Personnel Manager. Operates a full-service retail banking institution, offering a wide range of traditional banking services. Branch offices are located in Manhattan (10 locations); Brooklyn (five locations); Queens (three locations); and Long Island (six locations). Corporate headquarters location.

CHASE MANHATTAN BANK
31 Mamaroneck Avenue
White Plains NY 10601
914/328-8058
Contact Manager of Personnel Administration. A division of Chase Manhattan Bank, N.A., a leading financial institution worldwide. Chase NBW is a full-service bank operating in Westchester, Rockland, Orange, Duchess and Putnam Counties, New York. The company employs approximately 950 people in 54 branches, with assets of $2 billion. Corporate headquarters location: New York, NY. New York Stock Exchange. Common positions include: Accountant; Advertising Worker; Bank Officer/Manager; Credit Manager; Customer Service Representative; Financial Analyst; Branch Manager; Department

Manager; Management Trainee; Marketing Specialist; Personnel & Labor Relations Specialist; Public Relations Worker; Purchasing Agent. Principal educational backgrounds sought: Accounting; Business Administration; Communications; Economics; Finance; Liberal Arts; Marketing. Training programs offered. Company benefits include: medical insurance; pension plan; life insurance; tuition assistance; disability coverage; savings plan

THE CHASE MANHATTAN CORPORATION
1 Chase Manhattan Plaza, 27th floor
New York NY 10081
212//676-6000
Contact Ms. Christie Hanfman, Director/Professional Recruiting. Christie Hanfman can be reached at the following number: 552-3374. Multiple area locations. Operates through The Chase Manhattan Bank and numerous other subsidiaries, with assets of more than $77 billion and operations in more than 100 countries. Company provides a comprehensive range of financial services to corporations, individuals, financial institutions, and governments around the world. The Chase Manhattan Bank is one of the five largest commercial banks in the United States. Company operates through numerous subsidiaries, many of them based in the New York metropolitan area. Some area subsidiaries include: Chase Commercial Corporation (Englewood Cliffs, NJ); Chase Home Mortgage Corporation (Montvale, NJ); Chase Manhattan Financial Services, Chase Investors Management Corporation, Chase Manhattan Capital Markets Corporation, Chase Manhattan Government Securities, Chase Manhattan Service Corporation (New York, NY); and many others. Corporate headquarters location. New York Stock Exchange. International.

CHEMICAL BANK CORP.
277 Park Avenue
New York NY 10172
212/310-6161
Contact Personnel. Corporate headquarters location of the full service banking corporation.

CITICORP/CITIBANK
575 Lexington Avenue
12th Floor
Long Island City NY 10043
800/248-4636
Contact University Relations. Multiple area locations throughout New York City, Brooklyn, Queens, Nassau County. Company is a multinational financial services organization, with a worldwide staff of 60,000 people serving the financial needs of individuals, businesses, governments, and financial institutions in approximately 2400 locations, including branch banks, representative offices, and affiliate offices in 40 states and the District of Columbia, and in 94 countries throughout the world. Operates in several units: Institutional Banking; Individual Banking; Capital Markets Group; The Financial and Information Services Group; and The Legal and External Affairs Group. Corporate headquarters location.

CONTINENTAL BANK INTERNATIONAL CORP.
520 Madison Avenue
New York NY 10022
212/308-1000
Contact Personnel Director. An international bank specializing in corporate and international banking. Subsidiaries, affiliates, and joint-venture companies are located in more than 70 countries. Corporate headquarters location: Chicago, IL. International.

COLUMBIA FEDERAL SAVINGS BANK
80-31 Jamaica Avenue
Woodhaven NY 11421
718/296-2927

Contact Eleanor Reed, Vice President, Personnel. Offers a full range of traditional banking services. Operates branch offices in Forest Hills, Amityville, Rockaway Beach, Howard Beach, Bellerose, Manhattan, Forest Parkway, Ozone Park, and Snug Harbor. Assets exceed $750 million. Common positions include: Bank Officer/Manager; Customer Service Representative; Branch Manager; Department Manager; Management Trainee. Principal educational backgrounds sought: Accounting; Business Administration; Finance; Marketing. Company benefits include: medical, dental, and life insurance; pension plan; disability coverage; profit sharing; employee discounts; savings plan. Corporate headquarters location: Woodhaven, NY. Operations at this facility include: administration.

CROSS LAND SAVINGS BANK
211 Montague Street
Brooklyn NY 11201
718/780-0400
Contact Karen Jones, Personnel Director. Multiple area locations, including Westchester and Nassau counties. Operates a full-service mutual savings bank with 11 banking offices serving the New York area. Corporate headquarters location.

THE DIME SAVINGS BANK, FSB
EAB Plaza, 10th Floor, East Tower
Uniondale NY 11556-0128
516/745-2400
Contact Anthony M. Micolo, Vice President, Human Resources. A full service New York area savings bank. Common positions include: Accountant; Bank Officer/Manager; Computer Programmer; Credit Manager; Customer Service Representative; Financial Analyst; Branch Manager; Sales Representative; Systems Analyst. Educational backgrounds sought: Computer Science; Finance. Company benefits include: medical, dental, and life insurance; pension plan; tuition assistance; disability coverage; employee discounts; savings plan; stock purchase plan. Corporate headquarters location. Operations at this facility include: administration; service; sales. New York Stock Exchange.

DOLLAR DRY DOCK BANK
50 Main Street
White Plains NY 10606
914/397-2017
Contact Linda Monzi, Recruitment Manager. A leading financial institution with 23 locations throughout New York City and Westchester County. Common positions include: Accountant; Bank Officer/Manager; Computer Programmer; Customer Service Representative; Financial Analyst; Insurance Agent/Broker; Branch Manager; Management Trainee; Systems Analyst; Underwriter. Principal educational backgrounds sought: Accounting; Business Administration; Computer Science; Finance; Marketing. Company benefits include: medical, dental and life insurance; pension plan; tuition assistance; savings plan. Corporate headquarters location.

THE EAST NEW YORK SAVINGS BANK
41 West 42nd Street, 8th Floor
New York NY 10036
212/382-4700
Contact David Palmer, Assistant Vice President. A full-service savings bank, providing services that include co-op apartment loans, home improvement loans, mortgage loans, pension plans, retirement accounts, life insurance, student loans, and other traditional banking services. Corporate headquarters location. Common positions include: Accountant; Attorney; Bank Officer/Manager; Credit Manager; Customer Service Representative; Financial Analyst; Insurance Agent/Broker; Manager; Branch Manager; Department Manager; Management Trainee; Operations/Production Manager; Marketing Specialist; Personnel & Labor Relations Specialist; Public Relations Worker; Purchasing Agent; Sales Representative; Systems Analyst. Principal educational backgrounds sought: Accounting; Finance; Marketing. Company benefits include: medical insurance; pension plan; life insurance; tuition assistance; disability coverage; savings plan.

EMMIGRANT SAVINGS BANK
5 East 42nd Street, Level C
New York NY 10017
212/883-5800
Contact Edward Tully, Director of Personnel. Multiple area locations, including Manhattan, Brooklyn, Queens, and Nassau, Suffolk, and Westchester counties. Offers a wide range of traditional banking services. Assets exceed $2.9 billion. Corporate headquarters location.

EUROPEAN AMERICAN BANK
EAB Plaza
Uniondale NY 11555
516/296-5779
Contact Glenn Roman, Vice-President. A full service commercial bank offering a range of services and products through more than 80 branch banking offices in metropolitan New York and Long Island. Opportunities include: Management Training for Commercial Loan Officers; Branch Banking; Operations; Automation. Principal educational backgrounds sought: Business Administration; Finance; Liberal Arts. Company benefits include: medical insurance; tuition assistance; disability coverage; incentive savings plan.

FEDERAL RESERVE BANK OF NEW YORK
59 Maiden Lane
New York NY 10045
212/720-6557
Contact Regina Fredericks, Professional Recruiter. One of 12 regional Federal Reserve banks which, together with the Board of Governors in Washington DC, comprise the Federal Reserve System: the nation's central bank. The New York Federal Reserve Bank serves the Second Federal Reserve District, encompassing New York State, the 12 northern and central counties in New Jersey, and Fairfield County, CT. Conducts domestic open market operations on behalf of the entire Federal Reserve System, primarily the buying and selling of U.S. Government securities. All foreign exchange trading for the Federal Reserve System is done through this office, which buys and sells foreign currencies in the New York exchange market at the direction of the Federal Open Market Committee. Also responsible for storing 'official' gold owned by approximately 80 foreign nations, central banks, and international organizations. New York Fed also operates a branch office in Buffalo, as well as five regional check processing centers. Three major responsibilities include formulating and executing monetary policy, maintaining a safe, sound, and competitive banking system, and ensuring the safety, solvency, and certainty of the nation's payment mechanism. Principal educational backgrounds sought: Accounting; Computer Science; Economics; Finance; Liberal Arts; Mathematics. Major organizational units include: Monetary Policy, Bank Supervision, Domestic and International Research, Operations, and Management Planning and Support. Headquarters location.

FIDELITY NEW YORK F.S.B.
1000 Franklin Avenue
Garden City NY 11530
516/746-8500
Contact Joanne Scoppa, First Vice President, Personnel. Provides a full range of banking and related financial services. Common positions include: Accountant; Customer Service Representative; Branch Manager; Management Trainee; Teller. Principal educational backgrounds sought: Accounting; Business Administration; Economics; Finance. Company benefits include: medical, dental, and life insurance; pension plan; tuition assistance; disability coverage; employee discounts; savings plan. Operations at this facility include: administration.

GREATER NEW YORK SAVINGS BANK
One Penn Plaza
New York NY 10119
212/613-4150
Contact Susan Siegel, Personnel Representative. A mutual savings bank offering a complete range of traditional banking and mortgage services through 14 offices in the

metropolitan New York area. Common positions include: Accountant; Bank Officer/Manager; Buyer; Financial Analyst; Branch Manager; Department Manager; Management Trainee; Personnel & Labor Relations Specialist; Purchasing Agent; Systems Analyst (manual methods & procedures); Auditor; Securities Analyst; Personnel-related; Mortgage/Real Estate-related. Principal educational backgrounds sought: Accounting; Business Administration; Finance; Liberal Arts. Company benefits include: medical insurance; dental insurance; pension plan; life insurance; tuition assistance; disability coverage; savings plan-401K; vision care. Corporate headquarters location. Operations at this facility include: administration.

HOME SAVINGS BANK
21111 Northern Boulevard
Bayside NY 11361
718/423-6500
Contact Paul LaRosa, Personnel Officer. Operates a multi-branch full service savings bank, offering a wide range of banking and financial services. Offices are located throughout Brooklyn (two branch locations), Kew Gardens, Ridgewood, Sunnyside, Albertson, Great Neck, and Hicksville. Assets exceed $694 million. Corporate headquarters location.

HONG KONG & SHANGHAI BANKING CORPORATION
140 Broadway, 4th Floor
New York NY 10015
212/658-2888
Contact Personnel. A major international banking institution; provides a wide range of individual and institutional services. Corporate headquarters location.

INDEPENDENCE SAVINGS BANK
130 Court Street
Brooklyn NY 11201
718/624-6620
Contact Vice-President/Personnel. A savings bank established in 1850; offers a wide range of traditional banking services, as well as specialized financial services, loans, and insurance services. Offices are located in Brooklyn (four offices); Manhattan; Queens/Bayside; Nassau County (New Hyde Park and Manhasset); and Huntington Station. Assets exceed $1.08 billion. Corporate headquarters location.

JAMAICA SAVINGS BANK
303 Merrick Road
Lynbrook NY 11563
516/887-7000
Contact Personnel Interviewer. Multiple area locations, including Manhattan, Queens, Suffolk. A full-service commercial bank, offering a wide range of traditional banking services, including savings, checking, and retirement accounts; home improvement and other consumer loans; student loans; 24-hour banking; direct deposit services; and other financial and banking services. Corporate headquarters location.

LONG ISLAND SAVINGS BANK
201 Old Country Road
Melville NY 11747
516/547-2579
Contact Linda Blume, Recruiter. Operates a full-service area savings bank, with a wide range of traditional banking and financial services. Common positions include: Accountant; Bank Officer/Manager; Computer Programmer; Customer Service Representative; Branch Manager; Department Manager; Teller; Clerical Worker. Principal educational backgrounds sought: Accounting; Business Administration; Computer Science; Economics; Finance; Liberal Arts; Marketing. Company benefits include: medical, dental, and life insurance; pension plan; tuition assistance; disability coverage; employee discounts; savings plan. Corporate headquarters location: Melville, NY. Operations at this facility include: administration; service; sales.

MANUFACTURERS HANOVER TRUST COMPANY
P.O. Box 3732
Grand Central Station
New York NY 10163
212/270-6000
Contact Assistant Vice-President. A diverse banking organization offering services to individuals, small businesses, major industries, institutions, and financial and governmental customers. The corporation is divided into five business sectors. The Retail Banking Sector includes: the Branch Banking Division, covering 215 full-service branches in New York State; the Personal Loan Department, including the automobile leasing subsidiary, Wheelease; Retail Card Services Division; Manufacturers Hanover Mortgage Corporation, which has the third largest mortgage servicing portfolio in the nation. The Asset Based Financing Sector includes: the Real Estate Division; Manufacturers Hanover Leasing Company; and CIT Financial Corporation, offering small to mid-sized businesses a variety of products including leasing and equipment finance, factoring, commercial finance and industrial finance. The Banking and International Sector includes: the International Corporate and Government Division, which handles all business with governments, major corporations, and middle market firms outside North America; and the Global Financial Institutions Division, responsible for all correspondent banking relationships in the U.S. and overseas. The Corporate Banking Sector includes: North American Divisions I and II, serving major corporate customers throughout the United States and Canada, and middle market customers in the metropolitan New York area; the Energy Division; the Private Banking and Securities Industry Division; the Institutional Trust and Agency Division; Manufacturers Hanover Bank (Delaware); and Manufacturers Hanover Bank of Canada. The Investment Banking Sector includes: the Treasury Division; the Foreign Exchange Division; Manufacturers Hanover Ltd., a London-based merchant bank; Manufacturers Hanover Investment Corporation; Manufacturers Hanover Venture Capital Corporation; and the Special Financing Division. Common positions include: Bank Officer/Manager. (Trainees are hired for a specific sector and division within the corporation.) Principal educational backgrounds sought: all majors will be considered. Company benefits include: medical insurance; dental insurance; pension plan; life insurance; tuition assistance; disability coverage; profit sharing; employee discounts; savings plan. Corporate headquarters location.

MARINE MIDLAND BANKS, NA
140 Broadway
New York NY 10015
212/658-1000
Contact College Relations. Multiple area locations. A financial services institution, operating primarily through subsidiary Marine Midland Bank, N.A., a major United States international bank with assets of more than $20 billion. Operates the most extensive retail and commercial banking system in New York State, serving 200 communities through 293 branch offices and a network of electronic banking terminals. Provides banking, financial market, and investment services to corporations, institutions, governments, and individuals. Bank operates worldwide through a network of branches, other offices, and correspondent banks. Operates in partnership with The Hong Kong and Shanghai Banking Corporation (see separate listing). Area subsidiaries include Marine Midland Leasing Corporation, Marine Midland Realty Credit Corporation, and others. Common positions include: Accountant; Bank Officer/Manager; Credit Manager; Customer Service Representative; Financial Analyst; Branch Manager; Department Manager; Management Trainee. Principal educational backgrounds sought: Accounting; Business Administration; Communications; Economics; Finance; Liberal Arts; Marketing; Mathematics. Company benefits include: medical, dental, and life insurance; pension plan; tuition assistance; disability coverage; employee discounts; savings plan. Corporate headquarters location. Operations at this facility include: regional headquarters; administration; service; sales.

**MERCHANTS NATIONAL BANK AND TRUST
COMPANY OF SYRACUSE**
216 South Warren Street
P.O. Box 4950
Syracuse NY 13221
315/472-5561
Contact Joseph B. McGraw, Assistant Vice President. Mid-sized commercial bank operating primarily in the retail market. Common positions include: Accountant; Bank Officer/Manager; Credit Manager; Financial Analyst; Branch Manager; Management Trainee. Training programs and internships available. Principal educational backgrounds sought: Accounting; Economics; Finance; Liberal Arts. Company benefits include: medical insurance; dental insurance; pension plan; life insurance; tuition assistance; disability coverage; employee discounts.

J.P. MORGAN & CO.
23 Wall Street
New York NY 10015
212/483-2323
Contact Personnel. A commercial banker.

NATIONAL WESTMINSTER BANK USA
175 Water Street
New York NY 10038
212/602-1000
Contact John Finnerty, Senior Vice-President/Human Resources. Multiple area locations. A full-service money center bank offering a wide range of products to commercial and retail customers. Bank also provides commercial, corporate trust, treasury, and correspondent banking services for customers in all parts of the United States and abroad. Company operates 140 retail branches in the metropolitan New York service area, serving hundreds of thousands of individual customers and small businesses in New York City and its environs, through its New York City Regional and Community Banking Groups, while the company's United States Group concentrates on major corporations and correspondent banking relationships in the rest of the United States (regional offices in Chicago, Denver, Dallas, Los Angeles, and San Francisco). The International Banking Group's customers include foreign corporations, banks and governments, and domestic companies with international banking requirements. Representative offices for this segment are located in London, Rio de Janeiro, Hong Kong, and Miami. Company is a wholly-owned subsidiary of National Westminster Bank (London, England), an international banking and financial services organization with more than $85 billion in assets and more than 85,000 employees worldwide. Corporate headquarters location. International.

NORSTAR
56 East 42nd Street
New York NY 10017
212/682-5000
Contact Director of Personnel. Engaged in a wide range of commercial and consumer banking services, through 18 branch offices located in New York City and Yonkers. Operates in three divisions: Commercial Banking; Consumer Banking; and Operations. Branch office locations include Manhattan, The Bronx, Brooklyn, Queens, and Westchester-Yonkers. A subsidiary of First American Bankshares, Inc. Corporate headquarters location.

NORSTAR BANK
300 Broadhollow Road
Melville NY 11747
516/560-2000
Contact Mary Sinatra, Vice-President of Human Resources. Personnel should be contacted at 300 Broad Hollow Road, Melville, NY 11747. Operates a full-service commercial bank, offering a wide range of traditional banking services. Several area branch locations. Corporate headquarters location: Garden City, NY.

NORSTAR BANK, N.A.
10 Fountain Plaza
Rochester NY 14638
716/849-2200
Contact Lynne Jakubowski, Vice President. A commercial bank, serving the commercial and consumer banking needs of individuals, corporations, institutions, and governments of the Genesee, Finger Lakes, Southern Tier, and western regions of upstate New York. Affiliated with Fleet/Norstar Financial Group. Operations at this facility include: service. Common positions include: Accountant; Administrator; Bank Officer/Manager; Customer Service Representative; Financial Analyst; Manager; Branch Manager; Department Manager; Management Trainee; Operations/Production Manager; Marketing Specialist; Personnel & Labor Relations Specialist; Public Relations Worker. Principal educcational backgrounds sought: Accounting; Business Administration; Economics; Liberal Arts. Company benefits include: medical, dental, and life insurance; pension plan; tuition assistance; disability coverage; employee discounts; savings plan.

NORTH SIDE SAVINGS BANK
170 Tulip Avenue
Floral Park NY 11001
516/488-6900
Contact Vice President and Personnel Officer. Operates a full-service savings bank, with several area locations. Offers the complete range of traditional banking services. Corporate headquarters location.

PEOPLES WESTCHESTER SAVINGS BANK
3 Skyline Drive
Hawthorne NY 10532
914/347-3800
Contact June Mascioli, Vice President of Human Resources. Multiple area locations. Operates a full-service savings bank with 28 branch locations throughout the area. Locations include Armonk, Briarcliff Manor, Dobbs Ferry, Fishkill, Hartsdale, Ossining, Peekskill, Tarrytown, Tuckahoe, Yonkers, and others. Assets exceed $1.1 billion. Corporate headquarters location.

QUEENS COUNTY SAVINGS BANK
38-25 Main Street
Flushing NY 11354
718/359-6400
Contact Jeanenne Gorman, Assistant Vice-President/Personnel. Multiple area locations. Operates a mutual savings bank, offering a wide range of traditional banking services. Assets exceed $747 million. Maintains seven offices, with branch locations in Corona, Little Neck, Kew Gardens Hills, Plainview, and Lawrence. Established 1859. Corporate headquarters location.

REPUBLIC NEW YORK CORP.
452 Fifth Avenue
New York NY 10018
212/525-5000
Contact Personnel. A major area banker.

RIDGEWOOD SAVINGS BANK
7102 Forest Avenue
Ridgewood NY 11385
718/240-4800
Contact Norman McNamee, Personnel Director. Operates a full-service area savings bank. Corporate headquarters location.

ROOSEVELT SAVINGS BANK
1122 Franklin Avenue
Garden City NY 11530
516/742-9300
Contact Elaine Cordiello, V.P./Personnel. Multiple area locations. Operates a full-service mutual savings bank; founded in 1895. Offers the full range of commercial and savings bank services through 12 offices, including locations in Brooklyn, Queens, Deer Park, and several locations in Nassau County. Assets exceed $850 million. Corporate headquarters location.

THE ROYAL BANK OF CANADA
One Financial Square
New York NY 10055
212/428-6200
Contact Richard Clark, Personnel Director. United States headquarters for Canada's largest bank and one of North America's four largest banks, with assets exceeding $88.5 billion. Company's international network of branches, subsidiaries, and affiliates has more than 200 operating units in nearly 50 countries, with more than 1400 branches across Canada. Banking services include a wide range of retail, international commercial, and wholesale banking services. Specialized groups within the bank have particular expertise in energy, mining and trade finance, merchant banking and project financing, money markets, foreign exchange, and agricultural financing. Employs 40,000 people worldwide. Corporate headquarters location: Montreal, PQ, Canada. International.

STANDARD CHARTERED BANK
160 Water Street
New York NY 10038
212/612-0246
Contact Mary Weisinger, Personnel Officer. New York area offices for a major London-based international bank. Common positions include: Bank Officer/Manager; Credit Manager; Customer Service Representative; Financial Analyst; Branch Manager; Operations/Production Manager; Marketing Specialist; Personnel and Labor Relations Specialist; Public Relations Specialist; Systems Analyst. Principal educational backgrounds sought include: Accounting; Business Administration; Communications; Finance; Marketing. Company benefits include: medical insurance; dental insurance; pension plan; life insurance; tuition assistance; disability coverage; savings plan. Corporate headquarters location. Operations include: divisional headquarters location; administration; sales.

STERLING NATIONAL BANK & TRUST COMPANY
355 Lexington Avenue
New York NY 10017
212/490-9809
Contact Roger Maglio, Personnel Department. Several area locations. A full-service commercial bank, offering a complete range of corporate and individual services. Corporate headquarters location.

UNITED STATES TRUST COMPANY OF NEW YORK
114 West 47th Street
New York NY 10036
Contact Human Resources. Four area locations. A premier investment management, private banking and securities services firm. Service categories include: Investment Management; Estate and Trust Administration; Financial Planning; Corporate Trust and Agency; Unit Investment Trust; Mutual Funds. Common positions include: Accountant; Administrator; Computer Programmer; Customer Service Representative; Financial Analyst; Department Manager; Operations/Production Manager; Systems Analyst. Principal educational backgrounds sought: Accounting; Communications; Computer Science; Economics; Finance; Liberal Arts; Marketing. Company benefits include: medical, dental, and life insurance; tuition assistance; disability coverage; profit sharing; employee discounts; savings plan. Corporate headquarters location. New York Stock Exchange. International.

THE WILLIAMSBURGH SAVINGS BANK
452 5th Avenue
New York NY 10018
212/525-6000
Contact Evelyn Hansen, Assistant Vice President/Personnel. Operates a full-service savings bank, with branch offices in Brooklyn (four locations); Manhattan (two locations); Queens (three offices); Nassau County (two locations); and Suffolk County (two locations). Corporate headquarters location.

Connecticut

THE BANK MART
948 Main Street
Bridgeport CT 06604
203/579-5484
Contact Sheila Smith, Vice-President of Human Resources. A major area financial services organization offering deposit and mortgage services, with assets of $680 million and 200 employees. Corporate headquarters location. Common positions include: Accountant; Bank Officer/Manager. Principal educational backgrounds sought: Accounting; Business Administration; Liberal Arts; Marketing. Company benefits include: medical, dental, and life insurance; pension plan; tuition assistance; disability coverage; profit sharing; savings plan (401K); reimbursement account. Operations at this facility include: regional headquarters; administration.

CENTERBANK
60 North Main Street
Waterbury CT 06720
203/573-7861
Contact Philip Murphy, Employment Representative. A billion-dollar, full-service financial institution. Operations include: administration. Corporate headquarters location. Common positions include: Accountant; Bank Officer/Manager; Computer Programmer; Credit Manager; Customer Service Representative; Financial Analyst; Branch Manager; Department Manager; Management Trainee; Marketing Specialist; Personnel & Labor Relations Specialist; Sales Representative; Systems Analyst; Underwriter. Principal educational backgrounds sought: Accounting; Business Administration; Computer Science; Finance; Liberal Arts; Marketing. Company benefits include: medical insurance; dental insurance; pension plan; life insurance; tuition assistance; disability coverage; employee discounts; savings plan.

CONNECTICUT BANK & TRUST
One Constitution Plaza
Hartford CT 06115
203/244-4903
Contact Recruiters. Multiple statewide locations, including southwestern Connecticut (Stamford, Greenwich, Bridgeport, others). A major commercial bank, offering a wide range of traditional and specialized banking and investment services. Corporate headquarters: Bank of New England Corporation, Boston, MA. Common positions include: Accountant; Financial Analyst; Branch Manager; Management Trainee. Principal educational backgrounds sought: Accounting; Business Administration; Computer Science; Finance; Liberal Arts. Company benefits include: medical, dental, and life insurance; tuition assistance; disability coverage; savings plan.

THE PUTNAM TRUST COMPANY
10 Mason Street
Greenwich CT 06830
203/869-3000
Contact Gregory S. Hannigan, Vice President. Six area locations. Operates a full-service bank, providing traditional general banking and trust services for individuals, business, and industry. All six offices are located in the Town of Greenwich. Operations include Ten Mason Realty Corporation, which operates bank properties. Assets exceed $300 million. Corporate headquarters location.

New Jersey

ANCHOR SAVINGS BANK
1460 Valley Road
Wayne NJ 07470
201/628-9400
Contact John Coughlin, Personnel Director. Operates a full-service savings and loan institution, with 27 branch locations, including Bayonne, Elmwood Park, Hackettstown, Morris Plains, Nutley, Paramus, Piscataway, Ridgefield, Somerset, Toms River, and others. Assets exceed $2.08 billion. Subsidiary Suburban Coastal Corporation provides a wide range of mortgage services through Wayne headquarters facility, and through regional offices in Rolling Meadows, IL; Rockville, MD; Orlando, FL; Dallas, TX; and Newport Beach, CA. Corporate headquarters location.

BROADWAY BANK & TRUST COMPANY
100 Hamilton Plaza
Paterson NJ 07505
201/742-6000
Contact Bill Hugaboom, Personnel Director. A full-service commercial bank, operating through the following departments: Accounting; Auditing; Branch Administration; Commercial Loan; Consumer Credit; Data Processing; Brokerage Operations; and Marketing. Operates several branch offices, located in Wayne, Midland Park, Little Falls, Park Ridge, Montauk, Teaneck, Fairfield, and Kinnelon, NJ. Assets exceed $375 million. Corporate headquarters location. NASDAQ.

CARTERET SAVINGS BANK
10 Waterview Boulevard
Parsippany NJ 07054
201/263-3011
Contact Laura Valvano, Human Resources. Provides retail banking services as well as mortgage, consumer and commercial loans.

FIRST FIDELITY BANK, HQ
765 Broad Street
Newark NJ 07102.
Contact Employment Office. Headquarters offices for the major area banking institution. Common positions include: Accountant; Bank Officer/Manager; Computer Programmer; Credit Manager; Financial Analyst; Manager; Management Trainee; Personnel & Labor Relations Specialist. Principal educational backgrounds sought include: Accounting; Business Administration; Communications; Computer Science; Economics; Finance; Liberal Arts; Mathematics. Company benefits include: medical insurance; dental insurance; pension plan; life insurance; tuition assistance; disability coverage; profit sharing; employee discounts; savings plan. Corporate headquarters location. New York Stock Exchange.

FIRST FIDELITY BANK, N.A.
SOUTH JERSEY
Liberty Square Shopping Center
Route 541
Burlington NJ 08016
609/387-6883
Contact Employment Administrator. Member of one of the East Coast's Super Regional Bancorporations--A leading Southern New Jersey Affiliate Bank. Common positions include: Administrator; Bank Officer/Manager; Credit Manager; Customer Service Representative; Financial Analyst; Department Manager; Personnel and Labor Relations Specialist. Principal educational backgrounds sought: Accounting; Business Administration; Economics; Finance; Liberal Arts. Company benefits include: medical insurance; dental insurance; pension plan; life insurance; tuition assistance; disability coverage; profit sharing; employee discounts; free checking account. Corporate headquarters location: Lawrenceville, NJ. Operations at this facility include: regional

headquarters location: administration. New York Stock Exchange. American Stock Exchange.

THE HOWARD SAVINGS BANK
200 South Orange Avenue
Livingston NJ 07039
201/533-7475
Contact Henry Thorne, Human Resources Director. A full-service savings institution, operating 64 offices in 14 New Jersey counties. Services include traditional banking services such as full-service banking, commercial services, loan services, discount brokerage services, and trust services, as well as offering money market accounts and other financial services, and through subsidiary Howco Investment Corporation, a commercial real estate development operation. Assets exceed $3.6 billion. Operations include: administration; service; sales. Corporate headquarters location: Newark NJ. Common positions include: Accountant; Administrator; Attorney; Bank Officer/Manager; Computer Programmer; Customer Service Representative; Financial Analyst; Branch Manager; Department Manager; Management Trainee; Programmer; Sales Representative; Technical Writer/Editor. Principal educational backgrounds sought: Accounting; Business Administration; Computer Science; Finance. Company benefits include: medical insurance; dental insurance; pension plan; tuition assistance; life insurance; disability coverage; profit sharing; employee discounts; savings plan.

HUDSON CITY SAVINGS BANK
West 80 Century Road
Paramus NJ 07652
201/967-1900
Contact Ernest Hellren, Vice President/Personnel. Operates a full-service mutual savings bank, with 55 branches in Bergen, Burlington, Camden, Essex, Gloucester, Hudson, Middlesex, Monmouth, Morris, Ocean, Passaic, and Union counties. Services include a wide range of traditional banking services, as well as other financial services, including IRA's, Keogh plans, and special time deposit accounts. Assets exceed $1.8 billion. Corporate headquarters location.

MIDLANTIC BANK NORTH
P.O. Box 2177
Paterson NJ 07509
201/881-5000
Contact Karen Dunne, Human Resources. Operates a full-service commercial bank.

MIDLANTIC NATIONAL BANK
Metro Park Plaza, P.O. Box 600
Edison NJ 08818
201/321-8554
Contact Human Resources. Company is a $11+ billion holding company. Entry level positions in auditing, finance, corporate planning departments. Operates over 300 banking offices through the following subsidiary banks: Midlantic National Bank, Midlantic National Bank/North, Midlantic National Bank/South. Midlantic National Bank/Merchants, Midlantic National Bank/Sussex & Merchants, Midlantic National Bank/Union Trust. For Midlantic National Bank Gil Sager, Vice-President (Edison) (201) 321-8560 or Joan Monahan, Vice-President (West Orange) (201) 266-8322. Full range of services (personal & Corporate banking, international banking, mortgage & trust services) offered through these banks and the following bank-related affiliates: Midlantic Commercial Company, Midlantic Home Mortgage Corporation, Midlantic Commercial Leasing Corporation, Midlantic Brokerage Services, Inc. Management Training programs available to college graduates- Dorine Nicol, Vice-President (MNB/North) (201) 881-5488 or Gordon Carrigan, Vice-President (MNB/South) (609) 778-2500. International: Overseas facilities in Grand Cayman, Hong Kong, London. Common positions include: Accountant; Attorney; Bank Officer/Manager; Credit Manager; Economist; Branch Manager; Management Trainee;Marketing Specialist; Personnel & Labor Relations Specialist. Principal educational backgrounds sought: Accounting; Business Administration; Economics; Finance; Liberal Arts; Marketing. Company benefits include:

medical insurance; dental insurance; pension plan; life insurance; tuition assistance; disability coverage; profit sharing; employee discounts; savings plan.

MORRIS SAVINGS BANK
21 South Street
Morristown NJ 07960
201/539-0500
Contact Personnel Director. Operates a mutual savings bank, offering a broad spectrum of savings accounts, investment accounts, and checking accounts. The bank also provides a full range of loan programs for individuals and business. Offices are in Morris, Warren, Sussex, and Somerset counties. Assets exceed $797 million. Corporate headquarters location.

NATIONAL COMMUNITY BANK
113 West Essex Street
Maywood NJ 07607
201/845-1603
Contact Michael Bryan, Personnel Officer. Operates one of New Jersey's largest commercial banks, with more than 100 offices and more than 2000 employees statewide. Company operates through nine banking regions centered in Secaucus, Rutherford, Teaneck, Ridgewood, Cedar Knolls, Franklin, Edison, Wall Townships, and Linwood, NJ. Corporate headquarters location: Maywood, NJ. Common positions include: Management Trainee. Principal educational backgrounds sought: Business Management; Finance; Marketing. Company benefits include: medical insurance; dental insurance; pension plan; life insurance; tuition assistance; disability coverage; 401K savings plan.

THE NATIONAL STATE BANK
68 Broad Street
Elizabeth NJ 07207
201/354-3400, ext. 2601
Contact Personnel Department. One of the largest commercial banks in New Jersey, with 44 branches and three automated teller locations throughout the state, primarily in Union, Middlesex, Mercer, and Hunterdon counties. Offers a wide range of traditional banking and related financial and trust services, as well as international banking services. Office locations include Belmar, Woodbridge, Trenton, Edison, Iselin, Newark, Plainfield, Rahway, Summit, Perth Amboy, and others. Assets exceed $1.04 billion. Corporate headquarters location.

NATWEST
200 East State Street
Trenton NJ 08608
Contact Isabella Isitoro, Branch Manager. A leading Trenton full-service bank.

RTC
300 Davidson
Somerset NJ 08875.
Contact Personnel Recruiter. A 100-year old financial institution which provides a broad range of consumer financial services; operates 100+ full-service banking facilities in New Jersey and Florida. While the bank serves as a financial intermediary accepting deposits and originating property-related and other loans, an expanding range of additional consumer financial services has been developed through a network of wholly-owned subsidiaries engaged in mortagae banking, real estate development, and property management, insurance brokerage, stock brokerage services, and trust and other fiduciary services.

UNITED JERSEY BANKS
P.O. Box 2066
Princeton NJ 08543
609/987-3200
Contact James N. Ferrier, Manpower Planning/Staffing Manager. A multi-bank holding company with 115 branch banking offices located throughout the state. Corporate headquarters location.

UNITED NATIONAL BANK
P.O. Box 632
Plainfield NJ 07061
908/756-5000
Contact Jean Carr, Vice-President/Human Resources. Operates a full-service area commercial bank, offering a wide range of traditional banking, trust, and other financial services. Branch offices located in Plainfield (3 offices); South Plainfield, Branchburg, Bridgewater, Fanwood, Green Brook, Warren, Annandale, Bunnvale, Califon, Belvidere, Harmony, Blairstown (2), Knowlton Township and Oldwick. Assets exceed $600 million. Corporate headquarters location

VALLEY NATIONAL BANK
615 Main Avenue
Passaic NJ 07055
201/777-1800 ext. 479
Contact Peter Verbout, Director Human Resources. Multiple area locations. Operates a commercial bank with a wide range of traditional banking services. Common positions include: Bank Officer/Manager; Computer Programmer; Credit Manager; Customer Service Representative; Financial Analyst; Branch Manager; Department Manager; General Manager; Management Trainee; Personnel & Labor Relations Specialist. Principal educational backgrounds sought: Accounting; Business Administration; Computer Science; Economics; Finance; Mathematics. Company benefits include: medical, dental, and life insurance; pension plan; tuition assistance; disability coverage; profit sharing. Corporate headquarters location. Parent company: Valley National Bancorp. Operations at this facility include: administration. New York Stock Exchange.

WESTMINSTER CORPORATION
Ten Exchange Place Center, 26th Floor
Jersey City NJ 07302
201/547-7003
Contact Human Resources. Multiple area locations. A multibank holding company, providing a broad range of corporate and consumer financial services through its four banking subsidiaries: The First Jersey National Bank; The First Jersey National Bank/Central (Perth Amboy, NJ); The First Jersey National Bank/South (Beach Haven, NJ); and The First Jersey National Bank/Delaware Valley (Turnersville, NJ). Areas of operation include Retail Banking; Corporate Banking; Financial Services; and Trust and Investment Management. Overall, the company operates 52 banking offices in 11 New Jersey counties. Corporate headquarters location.

BOOK AND MAGAZINE PUBLISHING

For more information on professional opportunities in the book and magazine publishing industries, contact the following professional and trade organizations, as listed beginning on page 449:

AMERICAN BOOKSELLERS ASSOCIATION
ASSOCIATION OF AMERICAN PUBLISHERS
MAGAZINE PUBLISHERS ASSOCIATION
WRITERS GUILD OF AMERICA EAST, INC.

New York

AMERICAN BANKER INC.
One State Street Plaza
New York NY 10004
212/943-8200
Contact Personnel Director. A financial publishing firm whose publications include 'Bond Buyer,' 'Money Manager,' and others.

AMERICAN BIBLE SOCIETY
1865 Broadway
New York NY 10023
212/581-7400
Contact Catherine DeJaneiro, Personnel Administrator. Founded in 1816; goal is to translate, publish, and distribute the Bible and portions of the Scriptures, without doctrinal note or comment, in more than 180 nations. Corporate headquarters location. International. Common positions include: Accountant; Administrator; Customer Service Representative; Financial Analyst; Department Manager; General Manager; Operations/Production Manager; Public Relations Worker; Purchasing Agent; Editor; Sales Representative; Systems Analyst; Secretary. Principal educational backgrounds sought: Theology; Accounting; Business Administration; Communications; Finance; Liberal Arts; Mathematics. Company benefits include: medical insurance; dental insurance; pension plan; life insurance; disability coverage; employee discounts; savings plan.

AMERICAN HERITAGE PUBLISHING
60 5th Avenue
New York NY 10011
212/206-5500
Contact Personnel Director. Publishes a wide range of historical and reference works.

AMERICAN JOURNAL OF NURSING
555 West 57th Street
New York NY 10019
Contact Human Resources. A magazine publisher; activities include editing, art layout, subscriptions, advertising sales, promotion, and related operations. Also sells and rents nursing videos, books and pamphlets; and gives nursing reviews and seminars. Corporate headquarters location. Common positions include: Accountant; Advertising Representative; Commercial Artist; Customer Service Representative; Department Manager; Personnel & Labor Relations Specialist; Public Relations Worker; Reporter/Editor; Sales Representative; Technical Writer/Editor. Principal educational backgrounds sought: Accounting; Art/Design; Business Administration; Liberal Arts; Registered Nursing. Company benefits include: medical insurance; dental insurance; pension plan; life insurance; tuition assistance; disability coverage.

AVERY PUBLISHING GROUP
350 Thorens Avenue
Garden City Park NY 11040
Contact Rudy Shur, Managing Editor. Publisher of a wide range of titles, including non-fiction, natural food cookbooks, and special interest titles.

BANTAM DOUBLEDAY DELL PUBLISHING GROUP, INC.
666 Fifth Avenue
New York NY 10103
212/765-6500
Contact Robert J. Defendorf, Personnel Director. One of the largest book publishing companies in the USA, Bantam Doubleday Dell has a leading position in mass market, trade, and hardcover publishing of general books. With sales over $400 million, the company is a broad-based publisher with strengths in adult fiction and non-fiction, children's books, and category books (western, science fiction, romance, computer books, etc.). The company is an autonomously run subsidiary of Bertelsmann, a $6 billion diversified media company, based in West Germany. Common positions include: Accountant; Computer Programmer; Credit Manager; Financial Analyst; Production Manager; Marketing Specialist; Systems Analyst; Editor; Publicist. Principal educational backgrounds sought: Accounting; Art/Design; Business Administration; Communications; Computer Science; Finance; Liberal Arts; Marketing. Company benefits include: medical, dental, and life insurance; pension plan; tuition assistance; disability coverage; savings plan; 401 K. Corporate headquarters location. Operations at this facility include: regional headquarters; divisional headquarters; research/development; administration; service.

MATTHEW BENDER
11 Penn Plaza
New York NY 10001
212/967-7707
Contact Sylvia Layne, Human Resources Director. A publisher of technical and reference books for law firms, real estate organizations, and industry. Recent titles include books covering modern estate planning, banking law, deposition practice, advocacy, bankruptcy, courtroom science, criminal law, natural resources, and taxes. Also offers an on-line interactive legal practice data system, as well as other electronic publishing services. A subsidiary of The Times Mirror Company (Los Angeles, CA; Eastern Corporate offices are located at 280 Park Avenue, New York NY 10017). Corporate headquarters location.

THE BERKLEY PUBLISHING GROUP
200 Madison Avenue
New York NY 10016
212/951-8400
Contact Grace Schlemm, Personnel Recruiter. A major mass market paperback publishing company specializing in a variety of fiction and non-fiction titles. Major imprints include Berkley, Jove, Ace (science fiction), Charter, and Second Chance at Love (romance). Corporate headquarters location. Common positions (entry level) include: Operations/Production Assistant; Marketing Assistant; Public Relations Worker; Sales Representative. Principal educational backgrounds sought: Art/Design; Business Administration; Communications; Liberal Arts; Marketing. Company benefits include: medical insurance; life insurance; tuition assistance; disability coverage; profit sharing; employee discounts; summer hours.

BILLBOARD PUBLICATIONS, INC.
1515 Broadway
New York NY 10036
212/764-7300
Contact Deborah Kahlstrom, Personnel Manager. Publishes 'Billboard' magazine and other related books and periodicals. Common positions include: Accountant, Administrator; Credit Manager; Reporter/Editor; Sales Representative. Principal educational backgrounds sought: Accounting; Business Administration; Communications; Liberal Arts; Marketing. Company benefits include: medical, dental and life insurance; disability coverage; employee discounts; savings plan. Corporate headquarters location. Operations at this facility include: administration; service; sales.

BOOKAZINE COMPANY INC.
303 West 10th Street
New York NY 10014
212/675-8877
Contact Personnel Director. A general trade book jobber serving retail bookstores with a full line of quality titles. Operating for more than 50 years. Corporate headquarters location.

CAHNERS PUBLISHING COMPANY/
R.R. BOWKER
245 West 17th Street
New York NY 10011
212/463-6629
Contact Personnel Department. Cahners publishes close to 60 magazines in specialized business and consumer fields. Publications include 'Variety', 'Publishers Weekly', 'Interior Design', 'Datamation', 'American Journal of Surgery,' American Journal of Cardiology', 'Modern Bride', and 'American Baby'. Cahners Publishing Company is a division of Reed Publishing, USA (Newton, MA). R.R. Bowker is an international publisher and distributor of reference material, directories and related media in a wide range of subject areas. Titles include Books In Print, Literary Marketplace and Who's Who in American Art. R.R. Bowker is also the official ISBN agency in the US. R.R Bowker is a division of Reed Publishing, USA (Newton, MA). Common positions include: Accountant; Advertising Worker; Commercial Artist; Customer Service Representative; Financial Analyst;

Marketing Specialist; Public Relations Worker; Reporter/Editor; Sales Representative; Systems Analyst; Technical Writer/Editor; Copy Editor; Proofreader; Editorial Production; Atex Specialist; Research Specialists. Principal educational backgrounds sought: Accounting; Art/Design; Business Administration; Communications; Finance; Liberal Arts; Marketing; Journalism; Library Science. Company benefits include: medical, dental, and life insurance; pension plan; tuition assistance; disability coverage; profit sharing; employee discounts; saving plan. Corporate headquarters location: Newton, MA. Operations at this facility include: regional headquarters; service; sales.

CONDE NAST PUBLICATIONS INC.
350 Madison Avenue
New York NY 10017
Contact Personnel Director. Publishes a broad range of nationally-distributed magazines, including Mademoiselle, Glamour, House & Garden, Vogue, Self, Gentleman's Quarterly, Vanity Fair, and Gourmet. Corporate headquarters location.

DAVIS PUBLICATIONS, INC.
380 Lexington Avenue, 14th Floor
New York NY 10017
212/557-9100
Contact Phyllis Cohen, Personnel. A magazine publishing company.

DOW JONES & COMPANY INC.
200 Liberty Street
New York NY 10281
212/416-2000
Contact Corporate Recruiting. A highly diversified publishing/communications firm. Publishing operations include: The Wall Street Journal, the world's premier business daily newspaper, with a circulation of more than two million; Barron's; The Asian Wall Street Journal; The Wall Street Journal/Europe; the National Business Employment Weekly; and others. Communications products and services include: The Wall Street Journal Report; Dow Jones Telephone Report; Dow Jones News Services; and other divisions in radio and cable television broadcasting; and Dow Jones News/Retrieval, a computerized delivery system for news and information. Through wholly-owned Ottaway Newspapers, Inc. subsidiary, the company publishes daily and Sunday newspapers in 20 communities from California to Massachusetts. Through Richard D. Irwin, Inc., another wholly-owned subsidiary, the company publishes college texts and professional books. Also, the company has equity investments in Continental Cablevision, the country's 10th largest cable TV systems operator. A Fortune 500 company. Other national operations in South Brunswick, NJ; Chicopee, MA; and Palo Alto, CA. Corporate headquarters location. New York Stock Exchange. Common positions include: Accountant; Administrator; Computer Programmer; Customer Service Representative; Electrical Engineer; Public Relations Worker; Purchasing Agent; Reporter/Editor; Sales Representative; Statistician. Principal educational backgrounds sought: Accounting; Business Administration; Communications; Computer Science; Economics; Liberal Arts; Marketing.

EDITOR & PUBLISHER MAGAZINE
11 West 19th Street
New York NY 10011
212/691-7210
Contact John Consoli, Managing Editor. Publishes a weekly trade periodical covering newspapers and an annual yearbook for the newspaper industry. Corporate headquarters location. Common positions include: Reporter

ENCYCLOPAEDIA BRITANNICA USA
One Suffolk Square
Islandia NY 11722
516/232-1260
Contact Regional Vice President. Encyclopaedia Britannica USA, a division of Encyclopaedia Britannica, Inc. an international publisher of reference books and educational materials, is responsible for sales of EB products in the U.S. and its territories.

Principal products include: The New Encyclopaedia Britannica, Great Books of the Western World, Annals of America, and the Britannica Atlas. Products are sold in the home, at over-the-counter site locations and by mail. Corporate headquarters location: Chicago, IL. International. Common positions include: Sales Representative; Marketing Representative.

FORBES MAGAZINE
60 Fifth Avenue
New York NY 10011
212/620-2200
Contact Lawrence Minard, Managing Editor. Publishes one of the nation's most respected business magazines, appearing biweekly. Magazine's articles are directed toward corporate officers and other major business executives. Circulation exceeds 700,000. Company is a privately-owned organization. Corporate headquarters location.

SAMUEL FRENCH INC.
45 West 25th Street
New York NY 10010
212/206-8990
Contact Mr. Peter LaBeck, Personnel Director. A publishing firm engaged in the production and distribution of books relating to the theater. A subsidiary of Van Nostrand Reinhold.

GEYER-McALLISTER PUBLICATIONS
51 Madison Avenue
New York NY 10010
212/689-4411
Contact Sue Steffy, Personnel Director. Publishes a number of trade periodicals. Corporate headquarters location.

HARCOURT BRACE JOVANOVICH INC.
111 Fifth Avenue
New York NY 10003
212/614-3000
Contact Personnel Department. Operates through three major divisions. Harcourt Brace Jovanovich, Publishers, is engaged in publishing textbooks and related materials, as well as scientific, medical, and scholarly books and journals, and in conducting courses and seminars for law, accounting, and business. Sea World Enterprises, Inc., owns and operates marine parks and related food and merchandise purveying operations in Orlando, FL, and San Diego, CA, as well as related real estate development activities. HBJ Communications and Services, Inc., is engaged in publishing business professional, and farm periodicals, operating book clubs and television stations, selling accident and health and life insurance to farmers, underwriting and servicing life insurance acting as general insurance brokers and agents in New York City, and furnishing counseling services to business executives. New York Stock Exchange.

HARPERCOLLINS PUBLISHERS
10 East 53rd Street
New York NY 10022
212/207-7224
Contact Delia Mowat, Recruiting Officer. HarperCollins Publishers is one of the largest book publishers in the world. Over 600 employees in New York office. Divisions include: Trade, Children's, Audio, Business, Basic, College, and Paperbacks. Common positions include: Administrator; Customer Service Representative; Financial Analyst; Operations/Production Manager; Marketing Specialist; Personnel and Labor Relations Specialist; Sales Representative; Systems Analyst; Editor/Assistant; Book Designer. Educational backgrounds sought include: Art/Design; Communications; Computer Science; Finance; Liberal Arts; Marketing. Company benefits include: medical insurance; dental insurance; pension plan; life insurance; tuition assistance; disability coverage; employee discounts; savings plan. Corporate headquarters location. Parent company: News America.

THE HEARST CORPORATION
224 West 57th Street
New York NY 10019
212/649-2000
Contact Recruiting Staff. One of the nation's largest and best-known media organizations. Publishes a number of major metropolitan newspapers, as well as numerous national magazines, most based in New York. Magazines include: Cosmopolitan, Harper's Bazaar, Popular Mechanics, Science Digest, Sports Afield, Motor Boating, Town & Country, House Beautiful, American Druggist, and many other general interest and specialized publications. Corporate headquarters location.

ALFRED A. KNOPF INC.
201 East 50th Street
New York NY 10022
212/751-2600
Contact Personnel Department. One of the nation's most respected publishers of fiction and non-fiction titles. A subsidiary of Random House.

LEBHAR-FRIEDMAN INC.
425 Park Avenue
New York NY 10022.
Contact Human Resources Department. A major publisher of retail business publications, including newspapers, magazines, and retail directories. Common positions include: Advertising Space Sales Representative; Tele-marketer; Editor/Reporter; Secretary. Principal educational backgrounds sought: Journalism. Company benefits include: medical, dental, and life insurance; profit sharing. Corporate headquarters location.

MACMILLAN INC.
866 Third Avenue, 2nd Floor
New York NY 10022
212/702-5541
Contact Human Resources. Company's core businesses are educational publishing, instruction, and information services. Operates in five segments: Publishing, including the School Division, which publishes textbooks and instructional materials for elementary and high schools; College Division, which publishes textbooks for both undergraduate and graduate levels of higher education, and which owns the Dellen Publishing Corporation and certain textbook lists of the PennWell Publishing Company; Professional Books Division, which publishes text and reference books for business, medicine, government, and academia; Glencoe Publishing, which publishes textbooks and materials for Catholic education; G. Schirmer, publishers of scores of educational, traditional, and contemporary music; Harper & Row School Text Division, which includes an elementary phonics-based reading program, high school mathematics texts and other textbooks to complement Macmillan's school text programs; Scribner, which publishes college texts, reference works and trade books; Macmillan Educational Company, which supplements other divisions and provides editorial and production services to outside publishers; Macmillan Software Company, which markets ASYST to the scientific community; and General Books Division, which publishes fiction and nonfiction books for adult and juvenile readers, and which incorporates Four Winds Press, a premier juvenile imprint. Instruction segment operates through Berlitz operations (see separate listing), which provide intensive language instruction programs, home self-teaching programs, language reference works, travel guides, dictionaries, and translation services; Katharine Gibbs Schools, which provide office skills training and business education; United Electronics Institute, which offers a two-year vocational program in electronics technology training; and the Stone School, offering business training programs. Information Services segment operates through Standard Rate & Data Service, the nation's leading publisher of advertising reference works; National Register Publishing, a business and institutional directory publisher; Macmillan Professional Journals, which publishes and sells to healthcare advertisers; Business Mailers, managing over 60 commercial mailing lists; and Macmillan Book Clubs, the largest special-interest book club in the country. Home Learning and Reference Materials segment operates through P.F. Collier encyclopedia publishers. Retail and Mail Order

Distribution segment operates through Gump's, which offers fine quality merchandise at retail locations in San Francisco, Houston, Dallas, Beverly Hills and Los Angeles, and through mail order operations. Corporate headquarters location. International. New York Stock Exchange. Common positions include: Accountant; Advertising Worker; Attorney; Customer Service Representative; Financial Analyst; Marketing Specialist; Personnel & Labor Relations Specialist. Principal educational backgrounds sought: Accounting; Art/Design; Business Administration; Communications; Computer Science; Economics; Finance; Liberal Arts; Marketing. Company benefits include: medical insurance; dental insurance; pension plan; life insurance; tuition assistance; disability coverage; employee discounts; savings plan.

MARCEL DEKKER INC.
270 Madison Avenue
New York NY 10016
212/696-9000
Contact Maureen Smith, Personnel Recruiter. A science and technical publishing company of textbooks, encyclopedias, and academic journals, in fields such as chemistry, computer science, physics, library science, engineering, and biology. Distributes to professors, doctors, engineers, book stores and individuals. Corporate headquarters location. Operations at this facility include: administration; service; sales. Common positions include: Accountant; Administrator; Advertising Worker; Commercial Artist; Computer Programmer; Credit Manager; Customer Service Representative; Financial Analyst; Department Manager; Management Trainee; Operations/Production Manager; Marketing Specialist; Personnel & Labor Relations Specialist; Programmer; Public Relations Worker; Purchasing Agent; Quality Control Supervisor; Reporter/Editor; Sales Representative; Systems Analyst; Technical Writer/Editor; Copywriter; Word Processor. Principal educational backgrounds sought: Accounting; Art/Design; Business Administration; Communications; Computer Science; Economics; Finance; Liberal Arts; Marketing; Journalism; English; General Science. Company benefits include: medical insurance; dental insurance; pension plan; life insurance; tuition assistance; disability coverage; profit sharing; employee discounts.

MARCO BOOK COMPANY
P.O. Box 108
Rugby Station
Brooklyn NY 11203
718/773-0005
Contact Personnel Manager. A leading distributor of hardcover and paperback books to schools throughout the metropolitan New York area. Corporate headquarters location.

McGRAW-HILL INC.
1221 Avenue of the Americas
New York NY 10020
212/512-2000
Contact Patrick Pavalski, Vice President of Staffing. Several area locations, including Clifton, Hightstown, and Princeton, NJ. An international information services firm, operating through the following segments: Books and Education Services, through divisions McGraw-Hill Book Company (produces more than 20,000 books, audiovisuals, learning systems, computer software programs, and other materials to educate and inform readers around the world), and McGraw-Hill International Book Company, (publisher and marketer of educational materials, professional information, and training systems, through 17 operating units); Magazines, Newsletters, and Newswires, through McGraw-Hill Publications Company, which publishes nearly 60 business, professional, and technical publications, magazines, newsletters, newswires, and other specialized information services for more than 12 million readers worldwide; Broadcasting Operations, through subsidiary McGraw-Hill Broadcasting Company, which owns and operates four television stations (Denver, Indianapolis, San Diego, and Bakersfield, CA); Information Systems, through the division McGraw-Hill Information Systems Company, which provides essential business information services to a variety of industries (services include Dodge Reports, Sweet's Catalog Files, and others); Financial Services and economic information through subsidiary Standard & Poor's Corporation, one of America's leading sources of authoritative financial

investment, and marketing information for the business and financial communities and the general public. Corporate headquarters location. New York Stock Exchange. International.

MEDIA PROJECTS INCORPORATED
305 Second Avenue
New York NY 10003
Contact Administrative Editor. An independant book producer that performs book editorial work from concept through material turn-over to the printer. Specializing in visual non-fiction (children's, reference, cookery, etc.) Common positions include: Editorial Assistant (50 wpm on word processor and some knowledge of the editorial process required.) Educational backgrounds sought: College graduates preferred. Company benefits include: medical insurance.

NATIONAL REVIEW INC.
150 East 35th Street
New York NY 10016
212/679-7330
Contact Rose Flynn, Personnel Director. Publishes a nationally-distributed magazine of politically conservative thought. Headquarters location.

NEW YORK MAGAZINE
755 Second Avenue
New York NY 10017
212/880-0700
Contact Mary O'Connor, Vice-President of Human Resources. Publishes a features-oriented weekly magazine, with primary emphasis on a wide range of stories of interest to New York City residents. Magazine also contains 'CUE', a complete entertainment guide to the week's activities throughout New York. Corporate headquarters location.

THE NEW YORKER MAGAZINE
20 West 43rd Street
New York NY 10036
212/536-5476
Contact Anthony R. Pisano, Director of Personnel. One of the nation's most honored weekly magazines, noted for its non-fiction articles, short stories, and cartoons. Other operations include subsidiary Boulder Enterprise, Inc. (Boulder, CO), a printing firm manufacturing and selling computer forms, business forms, envelopes, and letters. Common positions include: Administrator; Advertising Worker; Credit Manager; Sales Assistant; Promotion Associate. Principal educational backgrounds sought: Accounting; Communications; Liberal Arts; Marketing. Company benefits include: medical, dental and life insurance; pension plan; tuition assistance; disability coverage; employer contribution plan; employee discounts; vision care. Corporate headquarters location.

NEWSWEEK MAGAZINE
444 Madison Avenue
New York NY 10022
212/350-4000
Contact Personnel Manager. Publishes one of the most comprehensive weekly news magazines in the world. Operates a global network with 85 correspondents and 200 stringers reporting on important developments in politics, international affairs, business, sports, science, and a broad range of other disciplines. Operates 28 bureaus throughout the United States and abroad. A major operating subsidiary of The Washington Post Company (Washington, DC). Newsweek also publishes an international edition. Corporate headquarters location.

OXFORD UNIVERSITY PRESS
200 Madison Avenue, 9th Floor
New York NY 10016
212/679-7300
Contact Nancy O'Conner, Personnel Director. Publishes a diverse line of scholarly books.

PARADE PUBLICATIONS INC.
750 Third Avenue
New York NY 10017
212/573-7000
Contact Barbara Wachtel, Employment Manager. Publishes 'Parade' magazine, a nationally-syndicated general interest weekly magazine distributed as a supplement to Sunday newspapers throughout the country. Circulation exceeds 30 million. Principal educational backgrounds sought: Accounting; Art/Design; Business Administration; Communications; Liberal Arts; Marketing; English. Company benefits include: medical, dental, and life insurance; pension plan; tuition assistance; disability coverage; savings plan. Corporate headquarters location.

PARENTS MAGAZINE
685 Third Avenue
New York NY 10017
212/878-8730
Contact Susan Levy, Personnel Manager. Publishes and distributes 'Parents' and 'Geo' magazines, both distributed nationally. A subsidiary of Bortelsman AG (Hamburg, West Germany). Corporate headquarters location.

PENGUIN USA
375 Hudson Street
New York NY 10014
212/366-2000
Contact Shelly Sadler, Personnel Manager. A publisher of paperback (Signet, Signet Classics, Mentor Meridian, Plume, Onyx, Daw, Vista) and hardcover books (NAL Books and E.P. Dutton). Common positions include: Editor; Sales Manager; Copywriter; Publicist. Principal educational background sought: Liberal Arts. Company benefits include: medical insurance; dental insurance; life insurance; tuition assistance; disability coverage; employee discounts; 401K. Corporate headquarters location. Operations at this facility include: administration; sales.

PUTNAM & GROSSET GROUP
200 Madison Avenue
New York NY 10016
212/951-8700
Contact Grace Schlemm, Personnel Recruiter. A major publishing firm, specializing in juvenile books. A separate paperback division publishes a wide range of fiction and nonfiction titles. Corporate headquarters location. A subsidiary of The Putnam Publishing Group (see separate listing).

THE PUTNAM PUBLISHING GROUP INC.
200 Madison Avenue, 14th Floor
New York NY 10016
212/951-8400
Contact Grace Schlemm, Personnel Manager. A major trade book publishing company, specializing in adult fiction and non-fiction titles as well as juvenile books. Major imprints include G.P. Putnam's Sons, Perigee, and Grosset & Dunlap. Corporate headquarters location. Common positions include: Operations/Production Manager; Marketing Specialist; Public Relations Worker; Writer/Editor; Sales Representative. Principal educational backgrounds sought: Art/Design; Business Administration; Communications; Liberal Arts; Marketing. Company benefits include: medical insurance; life insurance; tuition assistance; disability coverage; profit sharing; employee discounts; summer hours.

RANDOM HOUSE INC.
201 East 50th Street
New York NY 10022
212/572-2698
Contact Patricia Flatz-Ortiz, Personnel Manager. One of the nation's largest and best-known publishers, producing a wide range of fiction, non-fiction, reference, travel guides, juvenile, audio/video, mass market paperbacks, and direct mail marketing. Subsidiary

operations include: Ballantine Books; Alfred A. Knopf Inc.; Pantheon Books; Vintage Books; The New Modern Library; Times Books, Fodor's; Villard; and others. Common positions include: Accountant; Systems Analyst; Editorial Assistant; Secretary; Publicity Assistant; Subsidiary Assistant; Production Trainee. Principal educational backgrounds sought: Accounting; Art/Design; Communications; Finance; Liberal Arts; Marketing. Company benefits include: medical, dental, and life insurance; pension plan; tuition assistance; disability coverage; profit sharing; employee discounts; savings plan. Corporate headquarters location. Operations at this facility include: administration; sales.

THE READER'S DIGEST ASSOCIATION INC.
Pleasantville NY 10570
914/238-1000
Contact Joseph Grecky, Human Resources. Publishes The Reader's Digest, Reader's Digest Condensed Books, general books, educational materials, and tapes and records. Corporate headquarters location. International.

THE RESEARCH INSTITUTE OF AMERICA INC.
90 Fifth Avenue
New York NY 10011
212/337-4100
Contact Hope Hurley, Recruiting Specialist. One of the leading publishers of tax and other professional services and publications designed for attorneys, accountants, and the business community. Founded in 1935. Common positions include: Attorney; Computer Programmer; Credit Manager; Customer Service Representative; Marketing Specialist; Reporter/Editor; Sales Representative; Systems Analyst; Editorial Assistant. Principal educational backgrounds sought: Accounting; Liberal Arts; Law. Company benefits include: medical, dental, and life insurance; tuition assistance; disability coverage; savings plan. Corporate headquarters location. Operations at this facility include: regional headquarters; administration.

WILLIAM H. SADLIER INC.
11 Park Place
New York NY 10007
212/227-2120
Contact Personnel Department. A major international textbook publisher. Headquarters location.

ST. MARTIN'S PRESS
175 Fifth Avenue
New York NY 10010
212/674-5151
Contact Linda Torraco, Personnel Director. A major national book-publishing firm. Common positions include: Accountant; Credit Manager; Book Editor. Company benefits include: medical insurance; pension plan; life insurance; tuition assistance; disability coverage; 401K plan. Corporate headquarters location.

G.S. SCHIRMER
866 Third Avenue
New York NY 10022
212/702-2000
Contact Employment Department. Several area locations, including Woodside, NY. A music publishing firm, engaged in publishing scores of educational, traditional, and contemporary music. A subsidiary of Macmillan, Inc. (see separate listing). Corporate headquarters location.

SCHOLASTIC INC.
730 Broadway
New York NY 10003
212/505-3000

Contact Katherine Ryden, Personnel Director. A publisher of books, magazines, software, film, and video, primarily for the educational market. Corporate headquarters location. International.

SCIENTIFIC AMERICAN, INC.
415 Madison Avenue
New York NY 10017
212/754-0550
Contact Personnel Manager. Publishes a highly respected international monthly magazine dealing with recent scientific research. Headquarters location.

CHARLES SCRIBNER'S SONS
866 Third Avenue
New York NY 10022
212/702-2000
Contact Personnel Manager. A major international book publisher, offering a wide range of fiction/nonfiction titles. Headquarters location.

SIMMONS-BOARDMAN PUBLISHING CORPORATION
345 Hudson Street
New York NY 10014
212/620-7200
Contact Paul Cocheo, Personnel Director. Publishes trade magazines and books. Common positions include: Operations/Production Manager; Reporter/Editor; Sales Representative; Technical Writer/Editor. Principal educational backgrounds sought: Art/Design; Business Administration; Communications; Liberal Arts. Internships available. Company benefits include: medical insurance; life insurance. Corporate headquarters location. Operations at this facility include: administration; sales.

SIMON & SCHUSTER
1230 Avenue of the Americas
New York NY 10020
212/698-7000
Contact Susan Fitzpatrick, Director of Staffing. One of the nation's best-known publishers of trade, paperback, and mass market books, both fiction and nonfiction. A subsidiary of Gulf & Western. Corporate headquarters location.

SIMPLICITY PATTERN COMPANY INC.
200 Madison Avenue
New York NY 10016
212/576-0500
Contact Jane Bowman, Personnel Manager. One of the nation's best-known home dress and apparel pattern manufacturers. Corporate headquarters location. Common positions include: Technical Writer/Editor. Dressmakers; Patternmakers/Checkers. Principal educational backgrounds sought: Art/Design. Internships available. Company benefits include: medical insurance; dental insurance; pension plan; life insurance; tuition assistance. Corporate headquarters location. Operations include: administration.

SPRINGER-VERLAG PUBLISHERS/
NEW YORK, INC.
175 Fifth Avenue
New York NY 10010.
Contact Personnel Department. International publisher of scientific/technical/medical books, journals, and magazines. Common positions include: Accountant; Customer Service Representative; Financial Analyst; Editor; Accounting Clerk; Personnel Associate; Editorial Assistant; Promotion Assistant; Product Manager; Production Assistant; Production Editor. Educational backgrounds sought: Accounting; Art/Design; Biology; Business Administration; Chemistry; Communications; Computer Science; Engineering; Finance; Geology; Liberal Arts; Marketing; Mathematics; Physics. Company benefits include: medical, dental, and life insurance; pension plan; tuition assistance; disability coverage; employee discounts; 401K. Corporate headquarters location.

STANDARD & POOR'S CORP.
25 Broadway, 15th Floor
New York NY 10004
212/208-8000
Contact Human Resources. Publishes internationally known 'Standard & Poor's Register,' and other books dealing with finance and business. Also engaged in electronic publishing. A subsidiary of McGraw-Hill (see separate listing).

STERLING PUBLISHING CO.
387 Park Avenue South
New York NY 10016
212/532-7160
Contact Clyde Braunstein, Controller. Book-publishing firm. Headquarters location.

TIME WARNER, INC.
Time Life Building
Rockefeller Center
New York NY 10020
212/522-1212
Contact Susan Geisenhimer, Snr. Vice President & Personnel Director. A diversified communications corporation with interests in book and magazine publishing, records and film, and cable and pay TV.

WARREN, GORHAM, & LAMONT
One Penn Plaza
New York NY 10119
212/971-5000
Contact Mary A. Semple, Senior Vice-President/Personnel. Company publishes business reference products for professionals in accounting, banking, business, engineering, financial services, law, real estate, and taxation. Common positions include: Accountant; Computer Programmer; Financial Analyst; Personnel and Labor Relations Specialist; Marketing Specialist; Editor; Sales Representative; Systems Analyst; Technical Writer/Editor. Principal educational backgrounds sought: Accounting; Art/Design; Business Administration; Communications; Computer Science; Economics; Engineering; Finance; Liberal Arts; Marketing. Training programs offered; Internships offered. Corporate headquarters location. Parent company: The Thomson Corporation.

JOHN WILEY & SONS INC.
605 Third Avenue
New York NY 10158
212/850-6238
Contact Human Resources. A publicly held, international publishing house with over 1,500 employees in office in the U.S., Canada, England, and Australia. Wiley is a leader in college, scientific, technical, professional, trade books and materials. Wiley currently has 10,000 books in print and serves college, professional and consumer markets. Company benefits include: medical, dental, and life insurance; pension plan; tuition assistance; disability coverage; savings plan. Corporate headquarters location. Operations at this facility include: all divisional headquarters and administration.

THE H.W. WILSON COMPANY
950 University Avenue
Bronx NY 10452
212/588-8400
Contact Harold Regan, Personnel Director. One of the world's leading publishers of indexes and reference works for libraries. Publishes reference materials and indexes for a broad range of the arts and sciences, specialized fields, biography and reference, and librarianship and education. Well-known publications include Reader's Guide to Periodical Literature, Current Biography, Business Periodicals Index, Cumulative Book Index, and many others. Corporate headquarters location.

WORLD BOOK EDUCATIONAL PRODUCTS INC.
43-70 Kissena Boulevard, Lobby I-J
Flushing NY 11355
718/353-4450
Contact Vito Mazza, Zone Manager. World Book Encyclopedia, Childcraft and Early World of Learning products. Corporate headquarters location: Chicago, IL. Common positions include: Management Trainee; Sales Representative. Principal educational backgrounds: education. (PTA, teaching of church work helpful). Offices located nationally.

ZIFF DAVIS PUBLISHING COMPANY
One Park Avenue
New York NY 10016
212/503-3500
Contact Personnel Department. A major magazine publishing organization, whose publications primarily deal with lifestyle and leisure activities. Publications include: Flying; Boating; Runner; Sport Drive; Modern Bride; Psychology Today; Car & Driver; Travel Weekly; Hotel & Travel Index; Cycle; and Unique Homes. Also has minor broadcasting operations. Corporate headquarters location.

Connecticut

GROLIER INCORPORATED
Sherman Turnpike
Danbury CT 06816
203/797-3663
Contact Anne Graves, Director of Employee Relations. A leading Connecticut book publisher, from children's books to encyclopedias. Common positions include: Accountant; Computer Programmer; Customer Service Representative; Financial Analyst; Department Manager; Marketing Specialist; Reporter/Editor; Systems Analyst. Principal educational backgrounds sought include: Accounting; Business Administration; Computer Science; Finance; Liberal Arts; Marketing. Company benefits include: medical, dental, and life insurance; pension plan; tuition assistance; disability coverage; employee discounts; savings plan. Corporate headquarters location. Parent company: Hachette. Operations at this facility include: divisional headquarters.

New Jersey

ALLYN & BACON/SIMON & SCHUSTER
200 Old Tappan Road
Old Tappan NJ 07675
201/767-5000
Contact Human Resources. A major international textbook pubisher.

THE ASBURY PARK PRESS
3601 Highway 66
P.O. Box 1550
Neptune NJ 07754
201/922-6000
Contact Employment Interviewer. A publishing company. Common positions include: Accountant; Advertising Worker; Blue-Collar Worker Supervisor; Commercial Artist; Computer Programmer; Credit Manager; Customer Service Representative; Branch Manager; Department Manager; General Manager; Operations/Production Manager; Marketing Specialist; Personnel & Labor Relations Specialist; Reporter/Editor; Sales Representative; Statistician; Systems Analyst. Principal educational backgrounds sought: Accounting; Art/Design; Business Administration; Communications; Economics; Finance; Liberal Arts; Marketing; Mathematics. Training programs offered; Internships offered. Company benefits include: medical, dental, and life insurance; pension plan; tuition

assistance; disability coverage; savings plan. Corporate headquarters location. Operations at this facility include: regional headquarters; service; sales.

DOW JONES & COMPANY, INC.
P.O. Box 300
Princeton NJ 08540
609/520-4000
Contact Personnel. New Jersey office of the financial news service and publishing company. Publications include: The Wall Street Journal, Baron's Educational Book Services, and many others. Other services include domestic and international wire services (particularly financial news), and a commercial news retrieval system. Corporate headquarters location: New York, NY. New York Stock Exchange.

THE DUN & BRADSTREET CORPORATION
One Diamond Hill Road
Murray Hill NJ 07974-0027
201/665-5139
Contact Human Resource Associate. A leading producer of business information and services through three divisions: Dun & Bradstreet Credit Services (marketing and sales); Dun & Bradstreet Operations (data-gathering); and Dun & Bradstreet Commercial Collections (debt management and collections). These units collect, store, and sell information on over 9,000,000 businesses; information is used by the business community to make decisions on credit, insurance, marketing, financial, merger, and other issues. Divisional headquarters location. Corporate headquarters location: New York, NY. New York Stock Exchange. Common positions include: Accountant; Computer Programmer; Customer Service Representative; Economist; Financial Analyst; Marketing Specialist; Personnel & Labor Relations Specialist; Sales Representative; Systems Analyst; Credit Analyst. Principal educational backgrounds sought: Accounting; Business Administration; Finance; Marketing. Company benefits include: medical insurance; dental insurance; pension plan; life insurance; tuition assistance; disability coverage; profit sharing; employee discounts; savings plan; travel accident insurance, fitness center.

MEDICAL ECONOMICS
680 Kinderkamack Road
Oradell NJ 07649
201/262-3714
Contact Manager of Human Resources. Divisional headquarters for Medical Economics Magazines, which offers 14 publications related to the health-care professions. A subsidiary of Thompson International. Corporate headquarters location. Common positions include: Accountant; Buyer; Commercial Artist; Computer Programmer; Customer Service Representative; Department Manager; Marketing Specialist; Personnel & Labor Relations Specialist; Programmer; Reporter/Editor; Sales Representative; Systems Analyst; Technical Writer/Editor. Company benefits include: medical insurance; dental insurance; pension plan; life insurance; tuition assistance; disability coverage; 401(K).

FLEMING H. REVELL CO.
184 Central Avenue
Old Tappan NJ 07675
201/768-8060
Contact Personnel Director. A publisher of evangelical Christian books. Affiliated with Guideposts Associates, Inc. Common positions include: Accountant; Computer Programmer; Credit Manager; Customer Service Representative; Computer Programmer; Department Manager; Operations/Production Manager; Marketing Specialist; Sales Representative. Company benefits include: medical, dental, and life insurance; tuition assistance; disability coverage; employee discounts. Parent company: Guideposts Associates, Inc. Operations at this facility include: divisional headquarters.

SCOTT, FORESMAN & CO.
99 Bauer Drive
Oakland NJ 07436
201/337-5861

Contact Bonny Trent, Personnel Director. A major international textbook publisher. Common positions include: Customer Service Representative; Sales Representative. Company benefits include: medical insurance; dental insurance; pension plan; life insurance; tuition assistance; disability coverage; profit sharing; savings plan. Parent company: HarperCollins Publishers (New York, NY).

BROADCASTING

For more information on professional opportunities in the broadcasting industry, contact the following professional and trade organizations, as listed beginning on page 449:

BROADCAST EDUCATION ASSOCIATION
CABLE TELEVISION ASSOCIATION
INTERNATIONAL RADIO AND TV SOCIETY
NATIONAL ASSOCIATION OF BROADCASTERS
NATIONAL ASSOCIATION OF BUSINESS AND EDUCATIONAL RADIO
TELEVISION BUREAU OF ADVERTISING
WOMEN IN RADIO AND TV, INC.
WOMEN IN RADIO AND TV, INC./NEW YORK

New York

JOHN BLAIR & COMPANY
1290 Avenue of the Americas
New York NY 10104
212/603-5772
Contact Vyshali Mokadam, Personnel Administrator. A diversified corporation with interests primarily in broadcasting and graphic arts. Broadcasting segment operates through 2 divisions: Blair Television Division offers advertising time sales representation for television clients in 119 markets (Other broadcasting-related activities are now being developed by the company); Blair Entertainment Division. Employs 2,200 people nationwide. Corporate headquarters location. New York Stock Exchange.

CABLEVISION SYSTEMS CORPORATION
One Media Crossways
Woodbury NY 11797
516/496-1192
Contact Diane Savato, Corporate Manager, Human Resources. Corporate office of the cable company. Common positions include: Accountant; Administrator; Advertising Worker; Attorney; Blue-Collar Worker Supervisor; Buyer; Commercial Artist; Computer Programmer; Financial Analyst; Department Manager; General Manager; Personnel & Labor Relations Specialist; Public Relations Worker; Purchasing Agent; Reporter/Editor; Systems Analyst. Principal educational backgrounds sought: Accounting; Art/Design; Business Administration; Communications; Computer Science; Finance; Marketing. Company benefits include: medical, dental, and life insurance; pension plan; tuition assistance; disability coverage; cable TV if in area. Corporate headquarters location. Operations at this facility include: administration. American Stock Exchange.

CAPITAL CITIES/ABC
77 West 66th Street
New York NY 10023
212/456-7777
Contact Personnel Department. Several area locations, including New Haven, CT, and Clifton, NJ. A diversified communications organization; engaged in television and radio broadcasting, providing cable television service to subscribers, and the publishing of newspapers and specialized publications. Operates in three business segments: Broadcasting, Cable Television, and Publishing. Broadcasting operations consist of six network-affiliated television stations, seven AM radio stations, and seven FM radio stations. Cable Television consists of 53 systems providing service to subscribers in 16

states. Publishing operations consist of 10 daily newspapers in eight communities, 26 weekly community newspapers and shopping guides, and 36 business and specialized publications. Area subsidiaries include WTNH-TV (New Haven/Hartford, CT), and WPAT-AM/FM (Paterson, NJ). Area publishing subsidiaries include Fairchild Publications (New York, NY), publishers of Women's Wear Daily, and many other trade and specialty publications; Professional Press Group (New York, NY), publishers of several optometry-related magazines; and American Traveler Group (New York, NY), publishers of several magazines serving the travel industry. Company operates a decentralized management structure. Corporate headquarters location. New York Stock Exchange.

CBS INC.
51 West 52nd Street
New York NY 10019
Contact Placement Department. A broad-based entertainment and communications company which operates one of the country's three commercial television networks and two nationwide radio networks. In addition, CBS owns five television stations and 20 AM and FM radio stations.

KING WORLD PRODUCTIONS
1700 Broadway
New York NY 10019
212/315-4000
Contact Margie Tortoriello, Personnel Manager. A broadcasting company involved in the syndication of programs to affiliate networks.

GROUP W BROADCASTING & CABLE
888 Seventh Avenue
New York NY 10106
212/307-3000
Contact Judy Woods, Employment Representative. One of the nation's leading broadcasting companies and cable television firms.

NBC INC. (NATIONAL BROADCASTING COMPANY)
30 Rockefeller Plaza
New York NY 10112
212/664-4444
Contact Employment Office. One of the nation's three largest broadcasting communications firms, operating in three divisions: Television Network Division, Owned Stations Division, and Radio Division. Develops, produces, and distributes television programming and radio services to owned and affiliated stations throughout the country. Owned television stations include: WNBC-TV; KNBC-TV; WMAQ-TV; WRC-TV; and WKYC-TV. NBC Television Network has 214 affiliated stations; NBC Radio Network has 379 affiliates. Provides a wide range of associated and related services and operations. A major operating subsidiary of RCA Corporation. Corporate headquarters location.

A.C. NIELSEN COMPANY
1290 Avenue of the Americas
New York NY 10104
Contact Caroline Thomas, Personnel Administrator. Operates a major client service office for the international business services firm. Company's principal business is the marketing of a broad and diversified line of services to the international business community. Operates in four business segments: Research Services (through the company's Marketing Research Group, Media Research Group, and subsidiaries Coordinated Management Systems Inc., Dataquest Inc., and Compucon, Inc.); Clearing House Services (through Nielsen Clearing House Group); Petroleum Information Services (through subsidiary Petroleum Information Corporation); and Other Services (through subsidiaries Neodata Services Group, which maintains subscriber lists for publishers, and Compumark, Inc., a professional sales service company serving the packaged goods industry). Company is best known for its Nielsen Television Index, but services extend to a wide range of industries.

Offices are located throughout the United States (more than 20 locations), and in 24 countries abroad. Corporate headquarters location: Northbrook, IL.

REEVES COMMUNICATIONS CORPORATION
708 Third Avenue
8th Floor
New York NY 10017
Contact Personnel Department. A multinational company which supplies programming and production services to the television and film industries. Corporate headquarters location.

VIACOM, INC.
1515 Broadway
New York NY 10036
212/258-6000
Contact Personnel. A major broadcasting and syndication corporation.

New Jersey

IMNET, INC.
34 Maple Avenue
Pine Brook NJ 07058
201/882-2777
Contact Personnel. A major communication and cable television firm.

CHARITABLE/NON-PROFIT/HUMANITARIAN

For more information on professional opportunities in the charitable, non-profit, or humanitarian fields, contact the following professional and trade organizations, as listed beginning on page 449:

NATIONAL ASSOCIATION OF SOCIAL WORKERS
NATIONAL ASSOCIATION OF SOCIAL WORKERS/NEW YORK
NATIONAL ORGANIZATION FOR HUMAN SERVICE EDUCATION

New York

AMERICAN KENNEL CLUB
51 Madison Avenue
New York NY 10010
919/493-7396
Contact Michael Weiser, Personnel Director. An independent, non-profit organization devoted to the advancement of purebred dogs. Purpose is to adopt and enforce rules and regulations governing dog shows, obedience trials and field trials, and to foster and encourage interest in the health and welfare of purebred dogs. Offers a wide range of books and magazines for national distribution. Corporate headquarters location.

AMERICAN SOCIETY FOR THE PREVENTION
OF CRUELTY TO ANIMALS (ASPCA)
441 East 92nd Street
New York NY 10128
212/876-7700
Contact Personnel Director. America's first humane society; founded 1866. Involved in six primary areas: Animals as Pets; Humane Education; Animals for Sport and Entertainment; Experimentation on Animals; Animal Industries; and Protection of Wild Animals and Endangered Species. The ASPCA directly cares for some 200,000 animals every year; operates a fleet of modern rescue ambulances; enforces anti-cruelty laws in New York and

New York State; maintains the nation's largest non-profit animal shelter system; drafts and monitors humane legislation on the local, state and national levels; promotes humane education; finds homes for more than 16,000 animals each year; cares for more than 20,000 animals annually in America's largest veterinary hospital; and operates one of the nation's largest free spay/neuter clinics. Corporate headquarters location.

ASSOCIATED YM-YWHA'S OF GREATER NEW YORK
130 East 59th Street
New York NY 10022
Contact Personnel Director. Administrative offices for the citywide Jewish umbrella philanthropic organization; YM and YWHA facilities located throughout the five boroughs, and in Westchester. Corporate headquarters location. Common positions include: Accountant; Secretary; Bookkeeper. Principal educational backgrounds sought: Accounting; Business School; Secretarial School. Company benefits include: medical insurance; pension plan; life insurance; disability coverage; savings plan; vacation; sick pay; holidays.

BEDFORD STUYVESANT RESTORATION CORP.
1368 Fulton Street
Brooklyn NY 11216
718/636-6900
Contact Judith Anglin, Personnel Manager. The nation's oldest and largest non-profit community development corporation. Goal is to promote the economic revitalization of Bedford Stuyvesant, through a comprehensive program of business, physical, and social redevelopment ventures. Comprised of three operating divisions: Physical Development, including development and construction, rehabilitation, exterior renovation, providing mortgage financing, and weatherization projects; Business Development, including direct loans, equity investments, and the attraction of new business concerns to the area; and Community Development, which provides services that include job placement, the operation of Neighborhood Centers and a theatre (Billie Holiday Theatre), and the operation of the Bedford Stuyvesant Family Health Center. Recent projects include the construction of Restoration Plaza, housing shops, banks, university affiliates, government offices, a health center, and the corporation's general offices. Corporate headquarters location.

CATHOLIC CHARITIES COUNSELING SERVICES/
ARCHDIOCESE OF NEW YORK
1011 First Avenue
New York NY 10022
212/371-1000
Contact Joe Abruzzese, Personnel Director. Multiple area locations. Attempts to fulfill social service needs of the urban community through a wide range of social and counseling services. Services range from counseling and recreation for the young, adolescents, and the elderly. Other programs include alcohol rehabilitation, drug rehabilitation, and job placement. Corporate headquarters location.

CATHOLIC CHARITIES/
DIOCESE OF BROOKLYN & QUEENS
191 Joralemon Street
Brooklyn NY 11201
718/596-5500, ext.133
Contact Thomasine Watson Smith, Employment Relations Specialist. Operates a social service agency for the elderly, the mentally retarded, the psychiatrically disabled, preschool children, and the economically depressed populations of the area. Corporate headquarters location. Common positions include: Accountant; Administrator; Counselor/Direct Service; Program Director; Social Worker; Social Work Supervisor; Case Manager. Principal educational backgrounds sought: Accounting; Business Administration; Counseling, MA; BSW; Liberal Arts; MSW; Psychology; Special Education; Social Work; Psychology; Early Childhood Education. Company benefits include: medical insurance; dental insurance; pension plan; life insurance; 4 wks. vacation. Operations at this facility include: regional headquarters; administration.

CATHOLIC FOREIGN MISSION SOCIETY OF AMERICA
MARYKNOLL FATHERS
Pines Bridge Road
Maryknoll NY 10545
914/941-7590
Contact Arline Lauro, Employment Interviewer. Administrative and fund-raising offices for the international order of religious missionaries. Common positions include: Accountant; Administrator; Blue-Collar Worker Supervisor; Buyer; Claim Representative; Artist; Computer Programmer; Personnel & Labor Relations Specialist; Public Relations Worker; Purchasing Agent; Editor; Sales Representative; Systems Analyst; Technical Writer/Editor. Principal educational backgrounds sought: Accounting; Business Administration; Computer Science; Liberal Arts. Company benefits include: medical, dental and life insurance; pension plan; tuition assistance; disability coverage; employees discounts; savings plan. Corporate headquarters location. Operations at this facility include: administration; service; sales.

CHILDREN'S VILLAGE
Dobbs Ferry NY 10522
914/693-0600
Contact Director of Personnel. Several area locations, including Queens. A non-profit organization, providing a residential treatment center for emotionally disturbed children. Corporate headquarters location.

COMMUNITY SERVICE SOCIETY OF NEW YORK
105 East 22nd Street
New York NY 10010
Contact Jennifer Oladapo, Employment Coordinator. A non-profit social advocacy organization which conducts policy analysis, research and advocacy activities, provides training and technical assistance to strengthen community-based organizations, and develops innovative service programs that effectively respond to the complex problems faced by the poor in New York City. Common positions include: Administrator; Department Manager; Planner; Policy Analyst; Project Manager; Researcher; Training/Technical Assistance Specialist; Community Development Assistant; Project Supervisor; Social Researcher. Principal educational backgrounds sought: Liberal Arts; Social Work; Public Administration; Public Policy; Sociology; Urban Studies; Social Work. Internships offered. Company benefits include: medical insurance; dental insurance; pension plan; life insurance; tuition assistance; disability coverage; day care assistance; savings plan.

ECONOMIC OPPORTUNITY COUNCIL OF SUFFOLK
356 Middle Country Road
3rd Floor, Suite 306
Coram NY 11727
516/696-0900
Contact Catherine Budd, Personnel Department. A county agency responsible for various social programs in Suffolk County. Maintains other satellite agencies. Provides counseling in Energy Conservation; Outreach; Summer Work; Health and Education; Housing; Employment Training. Headquarters location. Human Service Director; Community Advocate. Company benefits include: medical, dental, and life insurance; disability coverage.

FEDERATION OF THE HANDICAPPED
211 West 14th Street
New York NY 10011
212/727-4210
Contact Gail K. Chalcraft, Director of Personnel. A state-chartered organization; provides a wide range of vocational rehabilitation and related support services for adults with physical, emotional, and mental handicaps. Programs and services include: Diagnostic Services; Vocational Training Employment Programs; and Related Support Services. Headquarters location.

THE FORD FOUNDATION
320 East 43rd Street
New York NY 10017
212/573-5000
Contact Manager of Employment. One of the largest and best-known philanthropic organizations in the United States. This private, non-profit institution works primarily by giving funds for educational, developmental, research, and experimental efforts designed to produce significant advances on selected important problems. Company also operates several overseas field offices in Asia; Latin America; the Middle East; and Africa. Has an active publications department. Corporate headquarters location. Common positions include: Accountant; Administrator; Attorney; Economist; Personnel Specialist; Program Officer; Assistant Program Officer; Systems Analyst. Principal educational backgrounds sought (at graduate level): Social Sciences; Anthropology; Agricultural and Resource Economics; International Relations (or area studies); Political Science. Company benefits include: medical insurance; dental insurance; retirement plan; life insurance; tuition assistance; disability coverage; savings plan.

HELEN KELLER SERVICES FOR THE BLIND
57 Willoughby Street
Brooklyn NY 11201
718/522-212/2
Contact Personnel Manager. Other area locations, including Hempstead, Cold Spring Harbor, Sands Point, and other Brooklyn locations. Operates a voluntary non-profit service agency for the legally blind. Services and programs include: Services for Children (braille library, educational placement, early childhood programs, summer day camps, camp placement, pre-school vision screening); Services for Adults (social casework, rehabilitation center, rehabilitation teaching, low vision rehabilitation, vocational guidance, Helen Keller Industries, business enterprises, selective placement, residences, recreation, senior day centers, and special service for deaf-blind persons); and Medical Services (community clinic, medical units, research, public education, professional training, in-service training program, volunteer services, professional library, publications, films, speakers, and college-affiliated training programs). Also operates The Helen Keller National Center for Deaf-Blind Youths and Adults (111 Middle Neck Road, Sands Point NY 11050). Helen Keller Industries, which operates skilled workshops, operates two facilities in Brooklyn. Corporate headquarters location. Common positions include: Accountant; Administrator; Blue-Collar Worker Supervisor; Department Manager; Public Relations Worker; Purchasing Agent; Purchasing Agent; Sales Representative; Technical Writer/Editor. Principal educational backgrounds sought: Accounting; Business Administration; Computer Science; Finance; Marketing. Company benefits include: medical insurance; pension plan; life insurance; tuition assistance; disability coverage; savings plan.

HENRY STREET SETTLEMENT
265 Henry Street
New York NY 10002
212/766-9200 ext. 211
Contact John Chung, Personnel Director. An area civic/social services organization, offering a wide range of programs and activities for children and youths.

HUNT'S POINT MULTI-SERVICE CENTER INC.
630 Jackson Avenue
Bronx NY 10455
212/402-8899
Contact Carmen Bizardi, Personnel Director. A private, non-profit organization which operates a multi-service program center, whose facilities include a health center, six mental health centers, community advocacy organizations, and housing and economic development activities. Corporate headquarters location.

JEWISH CHILD CARE ASSOCIATION
575 Lexington Avenue
New York NY 10022
212/303-4606
Contact Joanne Mack, Personnel Associate. A child care agency. Common positions include: Social Worker; Registered Nurse. Principal educational backgrounds sought: Social Work; Sociology; Psychology; Nursing. Company benefits include: medical, dental, and life insurance; pension plan; tuition assistance; disability coverage. Corporate headquarters location. Operations at this facility include: administration; service.

JEWISH COMMUNITY CENTER ASSOCIATION/
(JCC ASSOCIATION)
15 East 26th Street, 14th Floor
New York NY 10010
212/532-4949
Contact Diane Rogoff, Personnel Manager. More than 50 area locations, including Brooklyn, Queens, and The Bronx. The non-profit, national coordinating body for the Jewish Community Center (JCC) movement in North America. Serves as the central service agency for some 275 JCC's, YM-YWHA's and camps operating at nearly 500 sites in the United States and Canada, and serving more than one million people. Also serves as the principal recruiting and training source for full-time JCC career workers in many United States locations, operates cultural media services, and serves as the service agency for Jewish U.S. military personnel. Publishes several nationally-distributed periodicals. Corporate headquarters location. International.

THE LIGHTHOUSE
800 Second Avenue
New York NY 10017
212/303-6741
Contact Richard Pontone, Personnel Recruiter. Other area locations include: Poughkeepsie, White Plains, Queens, Staten Island, and Suffolk County. A private non-profit organization serving the blind and visually impaired since 1906, through direct Social Services, Rehabilitation, Medical, Low Vision, Recreational, Community Public Education, Vision Research, and Music Instructional Services to infants, youth and adults in the New York area. Serves more than 5000 persons with a staff of 475 paid workers and 1,000 volunteers. Also has Lighthouse Industries in Queens, a light manufacturing and Optical Aids center. Corporate headquarters location: Manhattan. Common positions include: Accountant; Computer Programmer; Public Relations Specialist; Systems Analyst; Director; Personnel & Labor Relations Specialist; Social Worker (MSW/BSW); Special Education/Pre-School/Rehabilitation Teacher (MA/MS/BS); Recreation Instructor/ Therapeutic Recreation Specialist (BA/MS); Adaptive Physical Education/Physical Education Instructor (BS/MS); Music Teacher (MS); Orientation and Mobility Instructor (MA/BA); Registered Nurse; Research Associate (BS/MS); Counselor (BA); Water Safety Instructor/Assistant Lifeguard; Secretary; Word Processor; Accounting Clerk; Switchboard Operator; Food Server; Cook; Porter; Driver; Paraprofessional; Housekeeper; Part Time Teacher. Principal backgrounds include: Special Education; Rehabilitational Teaching; Vocational Counseling; Social Work; Psychology; Orientation & Mobility; Recreation; Physical Education; Vision Research. Internships offered. Company benefits include: paid medical/dental insurance; HMO/HIP; life insurance; tuition assistance; disability coverage; employee discounts; tax deferred annuity, liberal vacation; internal advancement. Corporate headquarters location. Operations at this facility include: administration; service.

LITTLE FLOWER CHILDREN'S SERVICES
P.O. Box 1000
Wading River NY 11792
516/929-6200
Contact Phyllis F. McLaughlin, Personnel Director. Other area location is: 186 Remsen Street, Brooklyn NY 11210. 718/858-1212. Corporate headquarters. Services include foster care, adoption, group homes, residential treatment units, shelter cottages, and intermediate care facilities for the mentally retarded. Cares for more than 1200 children annually.

Common positions include: Accountant; Administrator; Computer Programmer; Social Worker; Child Care Worker, Registered Nurse. Principal educational backgrounds sought: Social Work; Psychology; Sociology. Company benefits include: medical insurance; pension plan; life insurance; tuition assistance; disability coverage; employee discounts; savings plan. Corporate headquarters location: Wading River, NY. Operations include: administration; service.

LOWER WEST SIDE HOUSEHOLD SERVICES CORP.
250 West 57th Street, Suite 814
New York NY 10019
212/307-7107
Contact Director. Provides housekeeping services to the elderly and disabled. Under contract with New York City Social Services. Corporate headquarters location. Common positions include: Home Health Aide. Company benefits include: medical insurance; disability coverage.

MISSION OF THE IMMACULATE VIRGIN
6581 Hylan Boulevard, Mt. Loretto
Staten Island NY 10309
718/317-2754
Contact Personnel Department. Residential treatment center. Provides care to emotionally disturbed, retarded and autistic adolescents. Common positions include: Social Worker (MSW or BSW); Child Care Staff; Nurse; Psychologist. Company benefits include: medical insurance; pension plan; life insurance; disability coverage. Training programs available.

SELFHELP COMMUNITY SERVICES, INC.
440 9th Avenue South
New York NY 10001
212/971-7600
Contact Coleen Cleeve, Human Resources Specialist. Operates a citywide, non-profit social services organization, providing a broad range of housing, homecare, food service, and outreach services, primarily for elderly people. Agency employs more than 200 full-time employees, and has more than 1000 volunteers. Common positions include: Accountant; Administrator; Claim Representative; Computer Programmer; Department Manager; Personnel & Labor Relations Specialist; Social Worker; Nurse; Clerical Worker. Principal educational backgrounds sought: Accounting; Business Administration; Computer Science; Liberal Arts; Social Work; Psychology; Nursing. Company benefits include: medical, dental, and life insurance; pension plan; disability coverage; TDA's. Corporate headquarters location.

UNDERWRITERS LABORATORIES INC.
1285 Walt Whitman Road
Melville NY 11747
516/271-6200
Contact Laura Sorace, Staffing Associate. An independent, not-for-profit corporation established to help reduce or prevent bodily injury, loss of life, and property damage. Organization accomplishes its objectives by scientific investigation of various materials, devices, equipment, constructions, methods and systems, and by the publication of standards, classifications, specifications, and other information. Engineering functions are divided between six departments: Electrical Department; Burglary Protection and Signaling Department; Casualty and Chemical Hazards Department; Fire Protection Department; Heating, Air Conditioning, and Refrigeration Department; and Marine Department. Major inspection facilities are located in Northbrook, IL; this facility; Santa Clara, CA; and Tampa, FL. Also provides a factory inspection service through offices throughout the United States and in 54 other countries. Organization has a worldwide staff of more than 2600 people, with more than 1000 engaged in engineering work. Common positions include: Computer Programmer; Electrical Engineer; Mechanical Engineer; Personnel & Labor Relations Specialist; Principal educational backgrounds sought: Engineering. Training programs offered. Company benefits include: medical, dental, and life insurance; pension plan; tuition assistance; disability coverage; savings plan; flex-time. Corporate headquarters location: Northbrook, IL.

UNITED CEREBRAL PALSY ASSOCIATIONS OF NEW YORK STATE INC.
330 West 34th Street
New York NY 10001
212/947-5770, ext. 153
Contact Joy Benjamin, Personnel Coordinator. Several area locations, including Bronx, Staten Island, Brooklyn, Queens, and Manhattan. A not-for-profit voluntary agency which serves as a central statewide medium through which assistance is provided to local affiliates dealing with problems of cerebral palsy and other developmental disabilities. In addition, the association plans, promotes, and assists in the establishment, maintenance, and operation of training centers, and educational and rehabilitation facilities throughout New York State, and residential facilities in the New York City area. Corporate headquarters location. Common positions include: Health-Care Administration. Principal educational backgrounds sought: Liberal Arts; Health Care. Company benefits include: medical, dental, and life insurance; pension plan; tuition assistance; disability coverage. Corporate headquarters location. Operations at this facility include: administration.

UNITED JEWISH APPEAL INC.
99 Park Avenue
New York NY 10016
212/818-9100
Contact Jeanette Weinstock, Manager, Human Resources. United Jewish Appeal is an American organization that raises funds for humanitarian programs to aid people in Israel through the Jewish Agency and in other countries around the world through the American Jewish Joint Distribution Committee (JDC). In Israel, the funds are allocated for such purposes as absorption and education of new immigrants, social programs for disadvantaged youths, and rural settlements. Through Project Renewal, distressed neighborhoods are revitalized. Established in 1939, the UJA also helps local Jewish communities in the U.S. to strengthen their fundraising campaigns. Common positions include: Accountant; Department Manager; Public Relations Writer; Secretary; Administrative Assistant; Fundraiser. Principal educational backgrounds sought: Accounting; Business Administration; Communications; Social Work; Liberal Arts. Company benefits include: medical, dental and life insurance; pension plan; disability coverage; savings plan; vision care coverage; paid prescription. Operations at this facility include: regional headquarters; administration. Corporate headquarters location.

WESTCHESTER COMMUNITY OPPORTUNITY PROGRAM
172 South Broadway
White Plains NY 10605
914/328-8921
Contact Paulette Warren, Personnel Director. Multiple area locations. A county-sponsored non-profit social services agency, operating through numerous Community Action Programs which provide clinical services, employment training programs, energy programs, and a wide range of other community services. Corporate headquarters location.

YOUNG MEN'S CHRISTIAN ASSOCIATION OF GREATER NEW YORK
422 Ninth Avenue
New York NY 10001
212/564-1300
Contact Diane Simonson, Personnel Recruiter. Multiple area locations, including facilities in all five boroughs, and Pawling, NY. One of the nation's largest and most comprehensive service organizations, operating 21 branch offices and more than 200 program centers and sites throughout the city. The YMCA of Greater New York provides Health & Fitness; Social & Personal Development; Sports & Recreation; Education & Career Development; and Camps and Conferences to children, youths, adults, the elderly, families, the disabled, refugees and foreign nationals, YMCA residents, and community residents through a broad range of specific programs. An equal opportunity employer. Corporate headquarters location. International.

Connecticut

TECHNOSERVE INC.
49 Day Street
Norwalk CT 06854
203/852-0377
Contact Karen Ann Simmons, Director, Human Resources. A private, non-profit development aid organization. Works with low-income people and development institutions in Africa and Latin America to help establish or strengthen self-help enterprises. Corporate headquarters location. Common positions include: Accountant; Administrator; Financial Analyst; Fundraiser; Trainer; Project Advisor; Program Officer. Principal educational backgrounds sought: Accounting; Business Administration; Finance. Company benefits include: medical, dental, and life insurance; pension plan; disability coverage; savings plan.

CHEMICAL & RELATED: PRODUCTION, PROCESSING & DISPOSAL

For more information on professional opportunities in the chemical industry, contact the following professional and trade organizations, as listed beginning on page 449:

AMERICAN CHEMICAL SOCIETY
AMERICAN INSTITUTE OF CHEMICAL ENGINEERING
AMERICAN INSTITUTE OF CHEMISTS
AMERICAN INSTITUTE OF CHEMISTS/NEW YORK
ASSOCIATION OF STATE & INTERSTATE
      WATER POLLUTION CONTROL ADMINISTRATORS
DRUG, CHEMICAL, AND ALLIED TRADES ASSOCIATION
WATER POLLUTION CONTROL FEDERATION

New York

CELANESE CORPORATION
1211 Avenue of the Americas
New York NY 10036
212/719-8000
Contact Personnel Manager. A diversified producer of chemicals, fibers, and specialties products. Corporation and its affiliates operate 75 plants, with 35,000 employees in the United States and 14 foreign countries, including Brazil, Canada, and Mexico. Celanese Chemical Company produces more than 40 basic petrochemicals at four manufacturing complexes in Texas. Company sells a variety of man-made fibers and yarns directly to mills and other intermediate processors. Specialties group produces a variety of products, including engineering resins, water-soluble polymers, structural composites, specialty resins, specialty chemicals, and agricultural products. Company also operates an International Division, with subsidiaries and affiliates throughout the world. Corporate headquarters location. International. New York Stock Exchange.

ELM COATED FABRICS DIVISION/
KALEX CHEMICAL PRODUCTS INC.
235 Gardner Avenue
Brooklyn NY 11211
718/417-8282
Contact Andy Schatz, Personnel Director. Second area facility in Queens. Manufactures calandered vinyl films and pelletized PVC compounds at multiple area locations. Company is one of the largest United States manufacturers of unsupported vinyl films. Other divisions and operations in Yardville, NJ; and Los Angeles, CA. Corporate headquarters location: Fords, NJ.

FRITZSCHE DODGE & OLCOTT/
A UNIT OF BASF K&F CORPORATION
76 Ninth Avenue
New York NY 10011.
Contact Human Resources Department. Several area locations in New Jersey. A manufacturer of flavors, fragrances, essential oil and aromatic chemicals. Common positions include: Cost Accountant; Flavor Chemist; Food Technologist; Flavor Marketing Manager; Customer Service Representative; Purchasing Agent. Principal educational backgrounds sought: Accounting; Business Administration; Chemistry; Finance; Marketing. Company benefits include: medical insurance; dental insurance; pension plan; life insurance; tuition assistance; disability coverage; savings plan. Corporate headquarters location. Parent company: BASF Corporation. Operations at this facility include:research/development; administration; sales. A unit of BASF K&F Corporation. International. European Stock Exchange.

GROW GROUP,INC.
200 Park Avenue
49th Floor
New York NY 10166
212/599-4400
Contact Miss Judith Krupka, Personnel Department. Formulates and produces a diverse line of specialty chemical products, including chemical coatings, thinners and adhesives, and blend solvents. These products are sold to clients in the aviation/aerospace, automotive, construction, appliance, transportation, and marine industries. Other facilities and subsidiary operations are located throughout the United States and abroad. Corporate headquarters location. International. New York Stock Exchange.

W.R. GRACE & COMPANY
1114 Avenue of the Americas
New York NY 10036
212/819-5500
Contact Christine Hilker, Director of Employee Relations. Founded in 1854; today an international company with worldwide interests in chemicals, and natural resources. Operates 260 plants and employs more than 50,000 people worldwide. Company is the world's leading specialty chemical concern, manufacturing more than 85 major specialty chemical product lines, and is the nation's fifth largest chemical company. Natural resource interests include the exploration and production of crude oil and natural gas, coal, contract drilling operations, oil field and offshore oil well services, and rental tools and equipment for the petroleum industry. Common positions include: Accountant; Financial Analyst. Principal educational backgrounds sought: Accounting; Business Administration; Finance; Legal backgrounds. Company benefits include: medical, dental and life insurance; pension plan; tuition assistance; disability coverage; savings plan. Corporate headquarters location. Operations at this facility include: financial administration; legal operations. New York Stock Exchange. International

MEARL CORP.
41 East 42nd Street
Room 708
New York NY 10017
212/573-8500
Contact Personnel Director. Produces industrial pigments. Headquarters location.

NL INDUSTRIES
445 Park Avenue
New York NY 10022
212/421-7200
Contact Personnel. A chemical company.

PALL CORPORATION
2200 Northern Boulevard
East Hills NY 11548
516/484-5400
Contact Robin McConnell, Corporate Employment Manager. Pall Corporation and its subsidiaries are leading suppliers of fine filters and other fluid clarification equipment for the remvoal of solid, liquid, and gaseous contaminants from a wide variety of liquids and gases. The company operates out of three main segments: Health Care; Aeropower; and Fluid Processing. Common positions include: Accountant; Advertising Worker; Biochemist; Biologist; Buyer; Chemist; Computer Programmer; Draftsperson; Biomedical Engineer; Industrial Engineer; Mechanical Engineer; Personnel & Labor Relations Specialist; Public Relation Specialist. Principal educational backgrounds sought: Biology; Chemistry; Computer Science; Engineering; Marketing; Mathematics; Physics. Training programs offered; Internships offered. Corporate headquarters location. Operations at this facility include: manufacturing; administration; service; sales. American Stock Exchange.

QUANTUM CHEMICAL CORPORATION
99 Park Avenue
New York NY 10016
Contact Human Resources Department. Administrative offices for a company which manufactures petrochemicals and markets propane. Common positions include: Accountant; Computer Programmer. Principal educational backgrounds sought: Accounting; Business Administration; Economics; Liberal Arts. Company benefits include: medical, dental, and life insurance; pension plan; tuition assistance; disability coverage; savings plan. Corporate headquarters location. Operations at this facility include: administration. New York Stock Exchange.

WEST SANITATION SERVICES INC.
6600 Long Island Expressway
Maspeth NY 11378
718/457-4447
Contact Diana Furintino, Office Manager. Markets chemical products for odor control in industrial, commercial, etc. washrooms. Available for all plumbing fixtures. Main Office Harbor City, CA. Common positions include: Regional Sales Manager; Office Manager; Secretaries. Company benefits include: medical, dental and life insurance. Corporate headquarters location: Harbor City, CA. Operations at this facility include: regional headquarters; administration; service; sales.

WITCO CHEMICAL CORP.
520 Madison Avenue
New York NY 10022
212/605-3800
Contact Arthur R. Kuhn, V.P. of Industrial Relations. A major worldwide chemical and chemical products manufacturer. Wide range of products and services include specialty chemicals, industrial chemicals, plastics, pigments, chemicals used in construction products, coatings, sealers, engineered industrial materials, plant installation services, and many others. Headquarters location.

Connecticut

UNION CARBIDE
39 Old Ridgebury Road
Danbury CT 06817
203/794-2000
Contact T.J. Neelan, Manager of Professional Placement. A multi-national corporation engaged in the manufacture of petrochemical products, industrial gases, and carbon products. Established in 1876.

New Jersey

ALLIED SIGNAL, INC.
10 North Avenue East
Elizabeth NJ 07201
201/354-3215
Contact Matritza Perez, Personnel Director. An major producer of chemicals, such as genetron/genesolv, muriatric acid, halon, halar, and aclon. Parent company, Allied Signal Corporation, serves a broad spectrum of industries through its more than 40 strategic businesses, which are grouped into five sectors: Aerospace; Automotive; Chemical; Industrial and Technology; and Oil and Gas. Allied Signal is one of the nations's largest industrial organizations, and has 115,000 employees in over 30 countries. Corporate headquarters location: Morristown, NJ.

AMERICAN GAS & CHEMICAL CO. LTD
220 Pegasus Avenue
Northvale NJ 07647
201/767-7300
Contact Melanie Kershaw, Personnel Director. Manufactures chemical and electronic leak detectors. Common positions include: Accountant; Administrator; Blue-Collar Worker Supervisor; Buyer; Chemist; Customer Service Representative; Industrial Engineer; General Manager; Management Trainee; Operations/Production Manager; Purchasing Agent; Quality Control Supervisor. Principal educational backgrounds sought: Accounting; Chemistry; Engineering; Finance; Marketing. Company benefits include: medical and life insurance; disability coverage. Corporate headquarters location. Operations at this facility include: manufacturing.

BASF CORPORATION/
CHEMICALS DIVISION
100 Cherry Hill Road
Parsippany NJ 07054
201/316-3000
Contact Mr. Robert Stein, Human Resources Manager. An international chemical products organization, doing business in five operating groups: Agricultural Chemicals; Chemicals; Colors; and Auxiliaries; Pigments and Organic Specialties; and Polymers. This facility houses United States headquarters and management offices. Area manufacturing plants located in South Brunswick, NJ (produces ethoxylated textile auxiliary intermediates, specialty surfactants, and esters); and Washington, NJ (produces polyether polyols). Employs more than 125,000 people worldwide. Common positions include: Accountant; Computer Programmer; Chemical Engineer; Financial Analyst; Marketing. Company benefits include: medical, dental, and life insurance; pension plan; tuition assistance; disability coverage; savings plan. Corporate headquarters location. Parent company: BASF Corporation. Operations at this facility include: divisional headquarters; administration; sales.

DREW CHEMICAL CORPORATION
One Drew Plaza
Boonton NJ 07005
201/263-7602
Contact Senior Recruiter. A division of Ashland Oil Inc., and a leading supplier of specialty chemicals and services to the international maritime industry and other industrial markets worldwide. Through its industrial chemical division, the company manufactures and markets products for water management and fuel treatment, as well as specialized chemicals for major industries. The Ameroid Marine Division provides chemical and sealing products and applications technology for these products to the maritime industry. Provides shipboard technical service for more than 15,000 vessels in more than 140 ports around the world. Corporate, regional, and divisional headquarters location. Common positions include: Chemist; Computer Programmer; Chemical Engineer; Mechanical Engineer; Marketing Specialist; Sales Representative; Systems Analyst. Principal educational backgrounds sought: Chemistry; Engineering. Company benefits include: medical, dental and life insurance; pension plan; tuition assistance; disability coverage;

profit sharing; savings plan. Operations at this facility include: manufacturing; research/development; administration; service; sales.

GAF CORPORATION
1361 Alps Road
Wayne NJ 07470
201/628-3000
Contact Vice-President/Human Resources. A Fortune 500 manufacturer of speciality chemicals and building materials. Worldwide chemicals include high-pressure acetylene derivatives, industrial organic and inorganic chemicals, surfactants, GAF filter systems, and GAF mineral products. Building materials include prepared roofing, roll roofing, built-up roofing systems,and single-ply roofing. Company maintains active research and development facilities (including Wayne, NJ), and operates WNCN-FM, a New York regional classical music station. Facilities are located throughout the United States and abroad. Employs 4,300 people overall. Corporate headquarters location. New York Stock Exchange.

HERCULES INDUSTRIAL CHEMICALS
P.O. Box 249, Neck Road
Burlington NJ 08016
609/386-1300
Contact Personnel. Manufacturer of synthetic resins.

HULS AMERICA INC.
Turner Place
Piscataway NJ 08855-0365
201/981-5000
Contact W. James Ryan, Manager EEO and Recruitment. Company is engaged in the manufacture and sale of Organic and Intermediate Chemicals. Common positions include: Accountant; Computer Programmer; Credit Manager; Customer Service Representative; Marketing Specialist; Sales Representative; Secretary; Administrative Assistant; Clerk. Principal educational backgrounds sought: Accounting; Business Administration; Computer Science; Marketing; Secretarial/Word Processing. Company benefits include: medical, dental and life insurance; pension plan; tuition assistance; 401K plan. Corporate headquarters location. Parent company: Dynamit Nobel of America. Operations at this facility include: administration; service; sales.

BENJAMIN MOORE & COMPANY INC.
51 Chestnut Ridge Road
Montvale NJ 07645
201/573-9600
Contact Personnel Administrator. A major paint manufacturer, distributing products nationwide. Manufacturing facilities are in Newark; this facility houses executive offices. Common positions include: Accountant; Chemist; Sales Representative. Principal educational backgrounds sought: Accounting; Business Administration; Chemistry. Company benefits include: medical insurance; dental insurance; pension plan; life insurance; tuition assistance; disability coverage; profit sharing; employee discounts; savings plan. Corporate headquarters location. Operations at this facility include: divisional headquarters; administration; service; sales.

NATIONAL STARCH AND CHEMICAL COMPANY
10 Finderne Avenue
Bridgewater NJ 08807
201/685-5033,800/366-4031
Contact Carol Dedrick, Manager of College Relations. An industrial chemical manufacturer producing adhesives, resins, starches and specialty chemicals for the packaging, textile, paper, food, furniture, electronic materials, and automotive markets. Operates 100 facilities worldwide. 1990 annual sales: $1.8 billion. A division of Unilever. Corporate headquarters location. Common positions include: Accountant; Chemist; Business Programmer Analyst; Chemical Engineer; Food Scientist; Sales Representative. Principal educational backgrounds sought: Accounting; Business Administration;

Chemistry; Chemical Engineer; Food Science; Marketing; Computer Information Systems. Company benefits include: medical insurance; dental insurance; pension plan; life insurance; tuition assistance; disability coverage; profit sharing; employee discounts; savings plan.

OAKITE PRODUCTS, INC.
50 Valley Road
Berkeley Heights NJ 07922
201/464-6900
Contact Mr. Juergen H. Schmelzer, Corporate Compensation Manager. Several area locations, including Metuchen. Company is principally engaged in the manufacture and marketing of chemical specialty products used primarily for industrial and institutional cleaning and metal-conditioning. Branch offices and manufacturing facilities are located throughout the United States and Canada. Common positions include: Accountant; Chemist; Marketing Specialist; Sales Representative. Principal educational backgrounds sought: Accounting; Business Administration; Chemistry; Marketing. Company benefits include: medical, dental, and life insurance; tuition assistance; disability coverage; profit sharing. Corporate headquarters location. Operations at this facility include: research/development; administration.

SEQUA CORPORATION
3 University Plaza
Hackensack NJ 07061
201/343-1122
Contact Mr. W.V. Machaver, Vice President. A diversified corporation, offering a wide range of industrial products, including pigments and printing inks; fine chemicals for the papermaking industry; aircraft instrumentation; and automotive products. Headquarters location.

STEPAN CO.
100 West Hunter Avenue
Maywood NJ 07607
201/845-3030
Contact Tim O'Donnell, Office Manager. Produces specialty chemicals and protein derivatives.

COLLEGES AND UNIVERSITIES

For more information on professional opportunities in higher education, contact the following professional and trade organizations, as listed beginning on page 449:

AMERICAN ASSOCIATION OF SCHOOL ADMINISTRATORS
ASSOCIATION OF AMERICAN UNIVERSITIES

New York

ADELPHI UNIVERSITY
Garden City NY 11530
516/877-3000
Contact Personnel. A major university.

BARUCH COLLEGE OF THE CITY UNIVERSITY
OF NEW YORK
155 East 24th
New York NY 10010
212/447-3000
Contact Personnel Department. A major campus of the CUNY system.

CITY COLLEGE
OF THE CITY UNIVERSITY OF NEW YORK
138th Street and Convent Avenue
New York NY 10031
212/650-7000
Contact Personnel Department. A major campus of the CUNY system.

COLLEGE OF STATEN ISLAND
OF THE CITY UNIVERSITY OF NEW YORK
130 Styvesant Place, Building 1-923
Staten Island NY 10301
718/390-7733
Contact Personnel Department. A major campus of the CUNY system.

CORNELL UNIVERSITY
16 Day Hall
Ithaca NY 14853
607/255-2000
Contact Staffing Services. One of the nation's most prestious universities.

FASHION INSTITUTE OF TECHNOLOGY
7th Avenue at 27th Street
New York NY 10001
212/760-7703
Contact Personnel. A major school of fashion and design.

FORDHAM UNIVERSITY
East Fordham Road
New York NY 10458
212/579-2095
Contact Personnel Department. A major university.

HOFSTRA UNIVERSITY
Hempstead NY 11550
516/463-6600
Contact Personnel Department. A major university.

HUNTER COLLEGE OF THE CITY OF NEW YORK
695 Park Avenue
New York NY 10021
212/772-4000
Contact Personnel Department. A major campus of the CUNY system.

IONA COLLEGE
715 North Avenue
New Rochelle NY 10801
914/633-2000
Contact Personnel Department. A major college.

JOHN JAY COLLEGE OF CRIMINAL JUSTICE
OF CITY UNIVERSITY OF NEW YORK
899 Tenth Avenue
New York NY 10019
212/237-8517
Contact Personnel Department. A major campus of the CUNY system, with a focus on criminal justice.

LEHMAN COLLEGE
OF THE CITY UNIVERSITY OF NEW YORK
250 Bedford Park Boulevard West
Room 329
Bronx NY 10468
212/960-8181
Contact Personnel Department. A major campus of the CUNY system.

LONG ISLAND UNIVERSITY/C.W. POST CAMPUS
Brookville NY 11548
516/299-0200
Contact Personnel Department. Long Island location of the major university.

LONG ISLAND UNIVERSITY
1 University Plaza
Brooklyn NY 11201
718/834-6000
Contact Mr. George Sutton, University Director of Personnel & Labor Relations. A major area university.

MERCY COLLEGE
555 Broadway
Dobbs Ferry NY 10522
914/693-4500
Contact Personnel Department. A well known private college.

NEW YORK INSTITUTE OF TECHNOLOGY
Old Westbury NY 11568
516/686-7516
Contact Personnel Department. A major technical university.

NEW YORK UNIVERSITY
246 Greene Street
Room 100
New York NY 10003
212/998-1250
Contact Patrick Keebler, Supervisor of Recruitment. A well-known and highly respected university. Common positions include: Accountant; Administrator; Computer Programmer; Personnel & Labor Relations Specialist; Purchasing Agent; Systems Analyst; Technical Writer/Editor; Secretary; Administrative Assistant. Principal educational backgrounds sought: Accounting; Business Administration; Communications; Computer Science; Education; Finance; Liberal Arts. Company benefits include: medical, dental, and life insurance; pension plan; tuition assistance; disability coverage.

PACE UNIVERSITY
1 Pace Plaza
New York NY 10038
212/346-1200
Contact Personnel Department. Major metropolitan university with three campus locations: New York City, White Plains, and Pleasantville. Common positions include: Accountant; Administrator; Computer Programmer; Mechanical Engineer; Purchasing Agent. Principal educational backgrounds sought: Accounting; Computer Science; Liberal Arts. Company benefits include: medical, dental, and life insurance; pension plan; tuition assistance; disability coverage; employee discounts.

QUEENS COLLEGE OF THE CITY OF NEW YORK
65-30 Casino Boulevard
Flushing NY 11367
718/997-5411
Contact Personnel Department. A major four-year college.

RENSSELAER POLYTECHNIC INSTITUTE
110 8th Street
Troy NY 12180
518/276-6000
Contact Human Resource Department. A major technical college.

ROCHESTER INSTITUTE OF TECHNOLOGY
One Lomb Memorial Drive
Rochester NY 14623
716/475-2424
Contact Personnel Director. Major four-year technical institute offering baccalaureate and masters degrees, as well as a PhD in imaging science. Common positions include: Accountant; Administration; Advertising Worker; Blue Collar Worker Supervisor; Buyer; Chemist; Commercial Artist; Commercial Artist; Computer Programmer; Civil Engineer; Financial Analyst; Department Manager; Marketing Specialist; Personnel and Labor Relations Specialist; Public Relations Specialist; Purchasing Agent; Reporter/Editor; Systems Analyst; Technical Writer/Editor. Educational backgrounds sought include: Accounting; Art/Design; Business Administration; Communications; Computer Science; Economics; Finance; Liberal Arts. Training programs and internships available. Company benefits include: medical insurance; dental insurance; tuition assistance; disability coverage; daycare assistance; employee discounts.

ST. JOHN'S UNIVERSITY
Jamaica NY 11439
718/990-6373
Contact Personnel Department. A major university.

STATE UNIVERSITY OF NEW YORK/ALBANY
Albany NY 12222
518/442-3150
Contact Personnel Department. Albany location of the New York state university system.

STATE UNIVERSITY OF NEW YORK/BINGHAMTON
P.O. Box 6000
Binghamton NY 13902-6000
607/777-2186
Contact Personnel Director. Binghamton campus of the New York state university system.

STATE UNIVERSITY OF NEW YORK/CORTLAND
P.O. Box 2000
Cortland NY 13045
607/753-2001
Contact Personnel Department. Cortland campus of the New York state university system.

STATE UNIVERSITY OF NEW YORK/FREDONIA
Fredonia NY 14063
716/673-3111
Contact Personnel Department. Fredonia campus of the New York state university system.

STATE UNIVERSITY OF NEW YORK/NEW PALTZ
New Paltz NY 12561
914/257-2170
Contact Personnel Department. New Paltz location of the New York state university system.

STATE UNIVERSITY OF NEW YORK COLLEGE/OSWEGO
Oswego NY 13126
315/341-2215
Contact Personnel Department. Oswego location of the New York state university system.

STATE UNIVERSITY OF NEW YORK/STONY BROOK
Stony Brook NY 11794
516/444-2525
Contact Personnel Department. Stony Brook location of the New York state university system.

SYRACUSE UNIVERSITY
Skytop Office Building
Syracuse NY 13244
315/443-2463
Contact Office of Human Resources. A well-known university.

UNIVERSITY OF ROCHESTER
260 Crittenden Boulevard
P.O. Box 636
Rochester NY 14642
716/275-4311
Contact Personnel Director. A major university.

Connecticut

CENTRAL CONNECTICUT STATE UNIVERSITY
1615 Stanley Street
New Britain CT 06050
203/827-7295
Contact Personnel Department. A major state university.

FAIRFIELD UNIVERSITY
North Benson Road
Fairfield CT 06430
203/254-4000
Contact Personnel Department. A major university.

SOUTHERN CONNECTICUT STATE UNIVERSITY
501 Crescent Street
New Haven CT 06515
203/397-4265
Contact Personnel Department. A major state university.

TRINITY COLLEGE
300 Summit Street
Hartford CT 06106
203/297-2000
Contact Personnel Department. A highly regarded private liberal arts college.

UNIVERSITY OF CONNECTICUT
U-75, 28 North Eagleville Road
Storrs CT 06268
203/486-3033
Contact Personnel Services. A major university.

UNIVERSITY OF NEW HAVEN
300 Orange Avenue
West Haven CT 06516
203/932-7240
Contact Personnel. A major university. Benefits include: medical insurance; pension plan; life insurance; tuition assistance; disability coverage. Corporate headquarters location.

WESTERN CONNECTICUT STATE UNIVERSITY
181 White Street
Danbury CT 06810
203/797-4374
Contact Personnel Department. A major state university.

YALE UNIVERSITY
P.O. Box 9168
New Haven CT 06532-0168
203/785-3838
Contact Department of Human Resources. One of the country's oldest and most prestigious universities.

New Jersey

BERLITZ SCHOOL OF LANGUAGES, INC.
293 Wall Street
Research Park
Princeton NJ 08540
609/924-8500
Contact Carmen Zaccaria, Personnel Director. Operates the world's leading foreign-language instruction program, operating 218 schools in 23 countries. Company offers instruction in more than 40 languages, as well as offering a self-teaching course. A subsidiary of Macmillan, Inc. (see separate listing). Corporate headquarters location. Multiple area branches, including Manhattan and other locations.

GLASSBORO STATE COLLEGE
Linden Hall
Glassboro NJ 08208
609/883-5247
Contact Personnel Department. A major state college.

JERSEY CITY STATE COLLEGE
2039 Kennedy Boulevard
Jersey City NJ 07305
201/547-3043
Contact Human Resources. A major state college.

KEAN COLLEGE OF NEW JERSEY
Morris Avenue
Union NJ 07083
908/527-2150
Contact Personnel Department. A major college.

MONTCLAIR STATE COLLEGE
Upper Montclair NJ 07043
201/983-4000
Contact Personnel Department. A major state college.

NEW JERSEY INSTITUTE OF TECHNOLOGY
University Heights
Newark NJ 07102
201/596-3140
Contact Personnel Department. A major university.

PRINCETON UNIVERSITY
Clio Hall
Princeton NJ 08544
609/258-6130
Contact Human Resources. One of the nation's most repected institutes of higher learning.

RUTGERS STATE UNIVERSITY OF NEW JERSEY
Piscataway NJ 08855
908/932-3020
Contact Personnel Services. A major state university.

SETON HALL UNIVERSITY
400 South Orange Avenue
South Orange NJ 07079
201/761-9177
Contact Personnel Department. A major university.

THOMAS EDISON STATE COLLEGE
101 W. State Street
Trenton NJ 08608-1176
609/984-1114
Contact Personnel Department. A major state university.

TRENTON STATE COLLEGE
Hillwood Lakes
P.O. Box 4700
Trenton NJ 08650
609/771-1855
Contact Personnel Department. A major state university.

WILLIAM PATERSON COLLEGE OF NEW JERSEY
300 Pompton Road
Wayne NJ 07470
201/595-212/3
Contact Personnel Director. A well known New Jersey college.   .

COMMUNICATIONS: EQUIPMENT AND SERVICES

For more information on professional opportunities in the communications field, contact the following professional and trade organizations, as listed beginning on page 449:

COMMUNICATIONS WORKERS OF AMERICA
COMMUNICATIONS WORKERS OF AMERICA/NEW JERSEY
COMMUNICATIONS WORKERS OF AMERICA/NEW YORK
UNITED STATES TELEPHONE ASSOCIATION

New York

AT&T
550 Madison Avenue
New York NY 10022
212/644-1000
Contact H.W. Burlingame, Senior Vice President of Human Resources. New York office of the well-known telecommunications corporation.

CCTV CORPORATION
315 Hudson Street, 5th Floor
New York NY 10013
212/989-4433
Contact Ms. Ranzman, Personnel Director. Produces a wide variety of video equipment, including cameras, monitors, and related equipment. Corporate headquarters location.

COMTECH MICROWAVE CORPORATION
63 Oser Avenue
Hauppauge NY 11788
516/435-4646
Contact Irene Webb, Personnel Manager. Other facilities in Port Chester, NY. One of two subsidiaries of Comtech Telecommunications Corporation; company is a telecommunications firm, providing satellite and tropo communications systems for military and commercial use. Common positions include: Accountant; Administrator; Blue-Collar Worker Supervisor; Buyer; Computer Programmer; Customer Service Representative; Draftsperson; Electrical Engineer; Department Manager; General Manager; Marketing Specialist; Personnel & Labor Relations Specialist; Purchasing Agent; Quality Control Supervisor; Technical Writer/Editor; Production Worker; Wirer & Assembler. Principal educational backgrounds sought: Accounting; Business Administration; Engineering; Marketing. Company benefits include: medical, dental and life insurance; tuition assistance; disability coverage; employee discounts. Operations at this facility include: manufacturing research/development; administration; service; sales. Corporate and divisional headquarters location. International.

CONTEL INFORMATION SYSTEMS
130 Steamboat Road
Great Neck NY 11024
516/829-5900)
Contact Personnel Department. A custom designer, integrator, and developer of on-line information systems. A subsidiary of Continental Telecom, Inc.

CONTINENTAL TELEPHONE SYSTEM/
CONTINENTAL TELECOM INC.
24 South William
Johnstown NY 12095
518/773-6531
Contact Bob Selzer, Director of Personnel. Several area locations, including Middletown, Sherburne. New York Division offices for the Continental Telephone System, which operates an affiliated group of companies providing telephone service and equipment to more than two million customers in 37 states and the Caribbean. Overall, company has 41 telephone operating companies. Other Continental Telecom subsidiaries in the area include Contel Information Systems Inc. (130 Steamboat Road, Great Neck NY 11024; 516/829-5900), a custom designer, integrator, and developer of on-line information systems; and Executone Inc. (Two Jericho Plaza, Jericho NY 11753; 516/681-4000), a nationwide business telephone supplier. Corporate headquarters location: Atlanta, GA. New York Stock Exchange. International.

ESQUIRE RADIO & ELECTRONICS INC.
4100 First Avenue
Brooklyn NY 11232
718/499-0020
Contact Lorraine Bryant, Personnel Director. Two other Brooklyn locations (manufacturing, distribution, and receiving operations). Engaged in the research, design and development of telecommunications products. Common positions at this facility include: Accountant; Blue-Collar Worker Supervisor; Customer Service Representative; Electrical Engineer; Quality Control Supervisor; Technical Writer/Editor; Electronic Technicians; Secretaries; Clerk/Typists; Receptionists; Shipping & Receiving Clerks. Principal educational backgounds sought: Accounting; Engineering; hands on experience with key systems and consumer telephone product. Company benefits include: medical insurance; dental insurance; employee discounts. Corporate headquarters location. Operations at this facility include: research/development. American Stock Exchange.

EXECUTONE, INC.
Two Jericho Plaza
Jericho NY 11753
516/681-4000

Contact Personnel Department. A nationwide business telephone supplier. A subsidiary of Continental Telecom, Inc.

NEW YORK TELEPHONE/A NYNEX COMPANY
1095 Avenue of the Americas, Room 3225
New York NY 10036
212/395-5768
Contact Director of Management Employment. Multiple area locations in New York State, predominantly in the metropolitan New York City area. Engaged in the business of furnishing communications services, mainly local and toll telephone service, throughout New York and Greenwich, CT. Other communications services include the distribution of voice, data, graphics, facsimile, and mobile phone service. More than 60,000 employees total. Corporate headquarters location. New York Stock Exchange. Common positions include: Accountant; Computer Programmer; Economist; Engineer; Civil Engineer; Electrical Engineer; Industrial Engineer; Mechanical Engineer; Financial Analyst; Management Trainee; Marketing Specialist; Programmer; Sales Representative; Systems Analyst. Principal educational backgrounds sought: Accounting; Business Administration; Computer Science; Economics; Engineering; Finance; Marketing. Company benefits include: medical insurance; dental insurance; pension plan; life insurance; tuition assistance; disability coverage; employee discounts; savings plan.

NYNEX CORP.
335 Madison Avenue
New York NY 10017
212/370-7400
Contact Personnel. Provides communications systems and services.

PORTA SYSTEMS CORP.
575 Underhill Boulevard
Syosset NY 11791
516/364-9300
Contact J.S. Newlin, Manager, Human Resources. A high-technology designer and manufacturer of telecommunications systems and equipment for sale to telephone operating companies in the United States and foreign countries, and to suppliers and manufacturers of telecommunications systems and equipment. Major products are equipment used to connect lines and trunks entering central offices with central office equipment and to provide electrical protection to switching equipment and office personnel; and computer-based electronic systems for testing and identifying faults with subscriber lines and central office switching equipment. Common positions include: Accountant; Attorney; Buyer; Computer Programmer; Credit Manager; Customer Service Representative; Draftsperson; Electrical Engineer; Industrial Engineer; Mechanical Engineer; Financial Analyst; Industrial Manager; Department Manager; General Manager; Operations/Production Manager; Marketing Specialist; Personnel & Labor Relations Specialist; Purchasing Agent; Quality Control Supervisor; Systems Analyst; Technical Writer/Editor. Principal educational backgrounds sought: Accounting; Business Administration; Computer Science; Engineering; Finance; Liberal Arts; Marketing. Company benefits include: medical, dental, and life insurance; tuition assistance; disability coverage; employee discounts; 401K. Operations at this facility include: manufacturing; research/development; administration; sales. American Stock Exchange.

ROANWELL CORP.
180 Varick Street
New York NY 10014
212/989-1090
Contact Personnel Manager. Manufactures terminal voice communication equipment. Headquarters location.

SIEMENS, INC.
89 Arkay Drive
Hauppauge NY 11788
516/435-4000
Contact Personnel Director. A worldwide supplier of telecommunications networks, switching equipment, and transmission products. Involved in the design, manufacture, sales, installation, and service of these products. Corporate headquarters location. International.

Connecticut

CENTURY COMMUNICATIONS
50 Locust Avenue
New Canaan CT 06840
203/966-8746
Contact Office Manager. Connecticut company engaged in cable communications.

CONTEL IPC
42 Pequot Park Road
Westbrook CT 06498
203/399-5981
Contact Kay Moody, Manager, Human Resources. Designs, manufactures, installs and services telecommunications systems for the financial industry. Operations include: manufacturing; research/development; administration; service; and sales. Corporate headquarters location: Greenwich, CT. Common positions include: Customer Service Representative; Electrical Engineer; Sales Representative. Company benefits include: medical insurance; dental insurance; life insurance; tuition assistance; disability coverage; savings plan.

GTE CORPORATION
One Stamford Forum
Stamford CT 06904
203/965-2000
Contact Ron Meadows, Personnel Manager. Multiple area locations, including Naugatuck, CT; Fairfield, NJ. A worldwide leader in developing, manufacturing, and marketing telecommunications, electrical and electronic products, services and systems, with operations in 43 states, Puerto Rico, and 18 foreign countries. The company is comprised of four principal groups: GTE Telephone Operating Group; GTE Electrical Products, operating through GTE Lighting Products, GTE Precision Materials, and GTE Electrical Equipment divisions; GTE Communications Products Group, which produces a wide range of communications systems, equipment and devices, including electronic digital central office switching equipment, digital private automatic exchanges, transmission equipment, telephone instruments, and electronic systems for defense and aerospace applications; and GTE Telenet Communications Group, which operates public data communications networks and markets specially designed data communications networks for business and government organizations throughout the world. The company is also engaged in advanced research and development work in such high-technology areas as fiber optics communications, satellite communications, digital systems, micro-electronics, precision materials, and packet switching. Corporate headquarters location. New York Stock Exchange. International.

TIE/COMMUNICATIONS INC.
4 Progress Avenue
Seymour CT 06483
203/888-8145
Contact Barry Schumaker, Vice President, Corporate Administration. Develops, manufactures, and markets key telephone systems for the business and residential markets. Corporate headquarters location. Common positions include: Accountant; Advertising Worker; Attorney; Blue-Collar Worker Supervisor; Buyer; Commercial Artist; Computer Programmer; Customer Service Representative; Draftsperson; Electrical Engineer;

Industrial Engineer; Financial Analyst; Personnel & Labor Relations Specialist; Public Relations Worker; Quality Control Supervisor; Sales Representative; Systems Analyst; Technical Writer/Editor. Principal educational backgrounds sought: Communications; Engineering. Company benefits include: medical, dental, and life insurance; tuition assistance.

New Jersey

AT&T NETWORK SYSTEMS PERSONNEL
475 South Street, Room 1W4
Morristown NJ 07962-1976
201/606-2129
Contact Clara Vecchione, Personnel Services Supervisor. Multiple area locations. A wholly-owned subisidiary of AT&T Corporation. Operates one industry: communications products and services. Company is organized primarily to serve independent telephone companies and AT&T Communications as a manufacturing and supply unit. Product sements include: Business And Residence Products (including telephones and components, keyboard display units, data transmission products, PBX switching systems, and many other telecommunications products); Electronic Components (including silicon integrated circuits, memory devices, power supplies, and many other components); Network Systems (electronic systems, digital and analog carrier systems, and other associated business systems); Lightwave Communications (lightguied fibers, fiber-optics systems, and related products); U.S. Navy Applications in submarine, surface ship, and land-based systems, and many other products); and International, which distributes company's telecommunications products worldwide. Corporate headquarters location. Common positions include: Accountant; Electrical Engineer; Industrial Engineer; Mechanical Engineer; Financial Analyst; Marketing Specialist; Personnel & Labor Relations Specialist; Sales Representative; Systems Analyst; Secretary; Clerk; Typists. Principal educational backgrounds sought: Accounting; Business Administration; Communications; Computer Science; Engineering; Finance; Liberal Arts; Marketing; Mathematics. Company benefits include: medical, dental, and life insurance; pension plan; tuition assistance; disability coverage; employee discounts; savings plan. Operations at this facility include: regional headquarters.

CAP GEMINI AMERICA
960 Holmdel Road
Holmdel NJ 07733
908/946-8900
Contact Joanna Ellis, Director of Human Resources. GCA is a leader in information technology services. Forty-five branches located nationwide provide technical assistance and project management services in systems development, systems conversion, systems integration, training and documentation. Other areas of specialization include: manufacturing; telecommunications, financc, and database management. Common positions include: Computer Programmer; Electrical Engineer; Branch Manager; Systems Analyst; Technical Writer/Editor. Principal educational backgrounds sought: Computer Science; Engineering; Mathematics. Training programs offered. Company benefits include: medical insurance; dental insurance; life insurance; tuition assistance; disability coverage. Corporate headquarters location. Operations at this facility include: administration.

DOWTY CONTROL TECHNOLOGIES
Powerville Road
Boonton NJ 07005
201/334-3100
Contact Marge Samuelson, Personnel Director. Manufactures a wide range of products: Telecommunications, including powerline carrier, protective relaying tones, AM, FSU, FDM, and TDM supervisory control and data acquisition, voice frequency carriers for telephone and telegraph applications; Mobile Data Communications; Instrumentation, with products for calibration. Customers include electric, water, sewage, gas and telephone utilities; railroads; mines; pipelines; airlines; oil drilling and refining firms; private contractors; OEM's; and many government agencies. Corporate and divisional

headquarters location. International. Common positions include: Accountant; Draftsperson; Electrical Engineer (R&D); Industrial Engineer; Sales Engineer; Applications Engineer; Electronic Technician; Assembler. Principal educational backgrounds sought: Accounting; Computer Science; Engineering. Company benefits include: medical, dental and life insurance; tuition assistance; disability coverage; profit sharing; employee discounts; savings plan. Parent company: Dowty Group. Operations at this facility include: manufacturing; research/development; administration; service; sales. London Exchange.

GRAPHIC SCANNING CORP.
25 Rockwood Place
Englewood NJ 07631
201/894-8000
Contact Camille Tritto, Director/Personnel & Employee Relations. A leading telecommunications service company, providing a wide variety of specialized data and message-processing and communications services. Operates a nationwide computer-controlled network which electronically receives, processes, and transmits record and data communications, and operates the nation's largest radio paging business. Corporate headquarters location: Teaneck, NJ. New York Stock Exchange. Common positions include: Accountant; Computer Programmer; Electrical Engineer; Systems Analyst. Principal educational backgrounds sought: Communications; Computer Science. Company benefits include: tuition assistance; 401K retirement savings plan; flexible benefits plan.

WESTERN UNION CORPORATION
One Lake Street
Upper Saddle River NJ 07458
201/818/5000
Contact Human Resources Department. Multiple area locations. Provides telecommunications systems and services to business, government, and the public. Operates a nationwide communications network that includes 'Westar' satellites in orbit, a transcontinental microwave system, electronic switching centers, and local transmission lines in major metropolitan areas. Company also operates computer centers which complement this network with message-switching and processing capabilities, and three Central Telephone Bureaus which afford convenient nationwide access to its consumer services. Most of the corporation's services are provided through principal subsidiary Western Union Telegraph Company, a leading carrier of record message and data traffic. Services include: teletypewriter and other office message services; communications systems and services tailored to the special needs of business and government users; public message services such as electronic funds transfer, telegram, mailgram, and cablegram messages; priority mail services; 'MetroFone,' a long-distance telephone service; and other services that utilize the company's service capability, primarily contract maintenance of communications-related equipment. Specialized information and communications services are provided by several smaller subsidiaries of Western Union Corporation; Western Union Electronic Mail, Inc.; Telstat Systems, Inc.; and Distronics Corporation. Corporation also has two equipment manufacturing subsidiaries: Western Union Teleprocessing, Inc. produces microprocessor-based data communications equipment; and E.F. Johnson Company is a manufacturer of mobile telecommunications equipment and electronic components. Corporate headquarters location. New York Stock Exchange. International.

COMPUTER-RELATED: HARDWARE, SOFTWARE, AND SERVICES/ INFORMATION SYSTEMS

For more information on professional opportunities in the computer industry, contact the following professional and trade organizations, as listed beginning on page 449:

ADAPSO/THE COMPUTER SOFTWARE AND SERVICES INDUSTRY ASSOCIATION
ASSOCIATION FOR COMPUTER SCIENCE
ASSOCIATION FOR COMPUTING MACHINERY

IEEE COMPUTER SOCIETY
SEMICONDUCTOR INDUSTRY ASSOCIATION

<u>New York</u>

APPLIED DIGITAL DATA SYSTEMS, INC.
SUBSIDIARY OF NCR CORP.
100 Marcus Boulevard
Hauppauge NY 11788
516/231-5400
Contact Stephen Green, Director, Personnel Resources. Manufactures and markets a broad line of general purpose computer video-display terminals and small business computers. A subsidiary of NCR Corporation (Dayton, OH). Corporate headquarters location. Common positions include: Computer Programmer; Electrical Engineer; Sales Representative; Systems Analyst. Principal educational backgrounds sought: Computer Science; Engineering. Company benefits include: medical insurance; dental insurance; pension plan; life insurance; tuition assistance; disability coverage; profit sharing; savings plan. Operations at this facility include: manufacturing; research/development; administration; service; sales.

COMPUTER ASSOCIATES INTERNATIONAL INC.
711 Stewart Avenue
Garden City NY 11530
516/227-3300
Contact Lisa Breiman, Manager of Recruitment. A leading independent software company. Develop, market, and support systems management, information management, and business applications software products for a broad range of mainframe, midrange and desktop microcomputers. Common positions include: Accountant; Administrator; Commercial Artist; Computer Programmer; Customer Service Representative; Personnel & Labor Relations Specialist; Sales Representative; Systems Analyst; Technical Writer/Editor. Principal educational backgrounds sought: Accounting; Art/Design; Business Administration; Computer Science; Finance. Training programs offered; Internships offered. Company benefits include: medical, dental, and life insurance; tuition assistance; disability coverage; profit sharing. Corporate headquarters location. Operations at this facility include: research/development; administration; sales. New York Stock Exchange.

DIGITAL EQUIPMENT CORPORATION
One Penn Plaza, 3rd Floor
New York NY 10119
212/714-6293
Contact Colleen Kenny, Senior Personnel Specialist. Designs, manufactures, sells, and services computers and associated peripheral equipment and related software and supplies. Applications and programs include scientific research, computation, communications, education, data analysis, industrial control, time sharing, commercial data processing, graphic arts, word processing, health care, instrumentation, engineering, and simulation. Employs 100,000 people in the United States and 37 foreign countries. Common positions include: Accountant; Administrator; Computer Programmer; Credit Manager; Financial Analyst; Personnel & Labor Relations Specialist; Sales Representative; Systems Analyst. Principal educational backgrounds sought: Accounting; Business Administration; Computer Science; Finance; Marketing. Company benefits include: medical, dental and life insurance; pension plan; tuition assistance; disability coverage; employee discounts; savings plan. Operations at this facility include: regional headquarters; administration; service; sales. Corporate headquarters location: Maynard, MA. New York Stock Exchange. International.

IBM CORP.
Old Orchard Road
Armonk NY 10504
914/765-1900

Contact Personnel. Corporate headquarters location of one of the leaders in information technology.

IMS INTERNATIONAL
800 Third Avenue
New York NY 10022
212/371-2310
Contact Personnel Department. A business and information services company which provides medical information and data services to the health care industry.

NCR CORPORATION
1290 Avenue of the Americas
New York NY 10104
Contact Jim March, District Manager of Administration. Company develops, manufactures, markets, installs, and services business information processing systems for worldwide markets. Generally, company's products and services may be grouped in the following categories: general-purpose computer systems, which range from small business systems to large, mainframe processors; industry-specific occupational workstations, which include word-processing workstations, as well as application-specific workstations for retail, financial, manufacturing, and other markets; general-purpose workstations, which include personal computers and data entry/inquiry workstations; software at both the operating system and application levels; support services, which include hardware and software maintenance, consulting services, customer training, and documentation; data processing and telecommunications services, including a worldwide network of data processing centers; components, including semiconductor products and component sub-assemblies marketed to other manufacturers; and business forms and supplies, marketed to both NCR and non-NCR users. Operates through the following divisions: Direct Marketing and Customer Support; Systemedia Group; Office Systems Division; Independent Marketing Organization; Development and Production Group; NCR Comten, Inc.; and Applied Digital Data Systems Inc. Corporate headquarters location: Dayton, OH. New York Stock Exchange. International. Common positions include: Salesperson; Software Engineers; Programmers.

NORTH ATLANTIC INDUSTRIES INC.
60 Plant Avenue
Hauppauge NY 11788-3890
516/582-6500
Contact Len Stanton, Director, Personnel and Facilities. For over 35 years, North Atlantic Industries has been in the business of designing, manufacturing, and marketing computers, computer peripherals, communications, and electronic test and measurement products, and in serving government, aerospace and industrial custoemrs. North Atlantic Industries is a leading supplier of TEMPEST printers, MIL-SPEC teleprinters, tape storage systems, and electronic test and measurement instruments. Common positions include: Accountant; Administrator; Buyer; Draftsperson; Electrical Engineer; Industrial Engineer; Mechanical Engineer; Operations/Production Manager; Marketing Specialist; Personnel and Labor Relations Specialist; Purchasing Agent; Quality Control Supervisor; Systems Analyst; Technical Writer/Editor; Software Engineers. Principal educational backgrounds sought: Accounting; Computer Science; Engineering; Finance. Company benefits include: medical insurance; dental insurance; pension plan; life insurance; tuition assistance; disability coverage; savings plan. Corporate headquarters location. Operations include: manufacturing; research/development; administration; service; sales.

PHOENIX SERVICE TECHNOLOGIES, INC.
40 Rector Street
New York NY 10004
212/693-6617
Contact Delia Marchese, Human Resources. Provides third party computer maintenance. Sixty offices throughout the country. Corporate headquarters location: Valley Forge, PA. Parent company: Phoenix Technologies.

SUPREME EQUIPMENT & SYSTEMS CORPORATION
4901 First Avenue
Brooklyn NY 11232-4210
718/965-0100
Contact Robert DiSalvo, Personnel Department. A manufacturer of information storage and retrieval systems. Products include manual filing systems, primarily metal filing cabinets, as well as electro-optical storage and retrieval systems. Corporate headquarters location.

Connecticut

COMPUTER ASSISTANCE INC.
200 Park Road
West Hartford CT 06119
203/233-9848
Contact Mike Bianca, Personnel Manager. A leading area consulting firm, providing advisory services, systems analysis and design, programming services, various software packages, and government services. 16 branch offices and divisions nationwide. Corporate headquarters location. Operations include: administration; service; sales. Common positions include: Computer Programmer; Systems Analyst. Principal educational background sought: Computer Science. Company benefits include: medical insurance; dental insurance; pension plan; life insurance; tuition assistance; disability coverage.

DATA SWITCH CORPORATION
One Enterprise Drive
Shelton CT 06484
203/926-1801 ext. 245
Contact Dorothy Leary, Manager of Employment. Several area locations, including Stamford, Shelton, Milford, and our subsidiary, Channel Net, in Shelton. A high-technology company producing proprietary switching and control equipment used to increase the performance of on-line data communications, data processing, and information systems. Company's products help anticipate failures, isolate hardware and software problems, diagnose reasons for failure, and restore failed service in customer's data communications and data processing networks. Products are marketed worldwide. Common positions include: Accountant; Administrator; Computer Programmer; Customer Service Representative; Draftsperson; Electrical Engineer; Department Manager; Management Trainee; Marketing Specialist; Personnel & Labor Relations Specialist; Public Relations Specialist; Sales Representative; Systems Analyst; Technical Writer/Editor. Principal educational backgrounds sought: Accounting; Business Administration; Communications; Computer Science; Economics; Engineering; Finance; Liberal Arts; Marketing; Mathematics. Company benefits include: medical, dental, and life insurance; tuition assistance; disability coverage; savings plan; fitness center. Corporate headquarters location. Operations at this facility include: regional headquarters; divisional headquarters; administration; service; sales. NASDAQ.

XEROX
P.O. Box 1600
800 Long Ridge Road
Stamford CT 06904
Contact Personnel Department. Corporate office of the manufacturers of copiers and office machinery. Develops, manufactures, and markets information-processing products, including copiers and duplicators, electronic printing systems, word-processing systems, personal computers, and computer peripherals.

<u>New Jersey</u>

ADP, INC.
1 ADP Boulevard
Roseland NJ 07068
201/994-5554
Contact Fred Schmitz, Manager of H.R. & College Relations. ADP is the largest, independent company dedicated exclusively to providing computerized transaction processing, record keeping, data communications, and information services. Sales training programs and internships available throughout the U.S. at 40 regional offices. Common positions include: Sales Representative. Principal educational backgrounds sought: Accounting; Business Administration; Marketing. Training programs offered; Internships offered. Company benefits include: medical, dental, and life insurance; pension plan; tuition assistance; disability coverage; employee discounts; savings plan; stock plan. Operations at this facility include: divisional headquarters; research/development. New York Stock Exchange.

AW COMPUTER SYSTEMS INC.
9000A Commerce Parkway
Mount Laurel NJ 08054
609/234-3939
Contact Bradford Smith III, Treasurer. A designer developer and marketer of high performance computer based point of sale systems for major retail chains. Common positions include: Computer Programmer; Electrical Engineer; Systems Analyst. Principal educational backgrounds sought: Computer Science; Engineering; Liberal Arts. Company benefits include: medical, dental, and life insurance; disability coverage; employee stock options. Corporate headquarters location. Operations at this facility include: research/development; administration; service; sales.

GLOBAL TURNKEY SYSTEMS
4 North Street
Waldwick NJ 07463
201/445-5050
Contact Barbara Cullen, Personnel Director. Operates in the sales and service of computer software/hardware. Headquarters location. Company benefits include: medical, dental, and life insurance; tuition assistance; disability coverage; profit sharing; savings plan.

HEWLETT PACKARD/
NEW JERSEY DIVISION
150 Green Pond Road
Rockaway NJ 07866
Contact Personnel Department. Produces computer-controlled data acquisition, test and control systems and system components and DC systems and laboratory power supplies. Parent company, Hewlett Packard, is engaged in the design and manufacture of measurement and computation products and systems used in business, industry, engineering, science, health care, and education; principal products are integrated instrument and computer systems (including hardware and software), computer systems and peripheral products, and medical electronic equipment and systems.

KULITE SEMICONDUCTOR PRODUCTS
One Willow Tree Road
Leonia NJ 07605
201/461-0900
Contact Personnel Manager. Produces computerized metering systems for medical applications and for use in aircraft. Sales offices throughout the United States. Also produces tungsten and tungsten-based products. Headquarters location.

NCR CORPORATION
14 Walsh Drive
Parsippany NJ 07054
201/402-4621

Contact Joseph H. Steward, Region Personnel Manager. Company develops, manufactures, markets, installs, and services business information processing systems for worldwide markets. Generally, company's products and services may be grouped in the following categories: general-purpose computer systems, which range from small business systems to large, mainframe processors; industry-specific occupational workstations, which include word-processing workstations, as well as application-specific workstations for retail, financial, manufacturing, and other markets; general-purpose workstations, which include personal computers and data entry/inquiry workstations; software at both the operating system and application levels; support services, which include hardware and software maintenance, consulting services, customer training, and documentation; data-processing and telecommunications services, including a worldwide network of data processing centers; components, including semiconductor products and component sub-assemblies marketed to other manufacturers; and business forms and supplies, marketed to both NCR and non-NCR users. Operates through the following divisions: Direct Marketing and Customer Support; Systemedia Group; Office Systems Division; Independent Marketing Organization; Development and Production Group; NCR Comten, Inc.; and Applied Digital Data Systems Inc. International. Common positions include: Sales Representative. Principal educational backgrounds sought: Accounting; Business Administration; Economics; Finance; Marketing. Company benefits include: medical, dental, and life insurance; pension plan; tuition assistance; disability coverage; profit sharing; savings plan. Corporate headquarters location: Dayton, OH. Operations at this facility include: regional headquarters; sales. New York Stock Exchange.

SCIENCE MANAGEMENT CORPORATION
P.O. Box 0600
Basking Ridge NJ 07920
201/647-7000
Contact Virginia Brandt, Director of Human Resources. A professional services firm. Also provides management and technological services, as well as developing and marketing package computer software and small business computer systems. Corporate headquarters location. American Stock Exchange. Common positions include: Accounting; Computer Programmer; Industrial Engineer; Financial Analyst; Manager; General Manager; Personnel Specialist; Systems Analyst. Principal educational backgrounds sought: Accouting; Business Administration; Computer Science; Engineering; Finance; Liberal Arts; Marketing. Company benefits include: medical insurance; dental insurance; pension plan; life insurance; tuition assistance; disability coverage; profit sharing; savings plan.

CONSTRUCTION: SERVICES, MATERIALS AND RELATED

For more information on professional opportunities in the construction industry, contact the following professional and trade organizations, as listed beginning on page 449:

ASSOCIATION OF BUILDERS & OWNERS OF GREATER NEW YORK
BUILDING OFFICIALS AND CODE ADMINISTRATORS INTL., INC.
CONSTRUCTION INDUSTRY MANUFACTURERS ASSOCIATION
INTERNATIONAL CONFERENCE OF BUILDING OFFICIALS
NATIONAL ASSOCIATION OF HOME BUILDERS

New York

CENTRAL INTERNATIONAL ELEVATOR COMPANY
460 West 34th Street
New York NY 10001
212/268-9988
Contact Personnel Director. Provides maintenance, repair, rebuilding, and construction services for commercial customers. A division of Prudential Building Maintenance Corporation. Corporate headquarters location.

HUDSON-SHATZ PAINTING COMPANY INC.
429 West 53rd Street
New York NY 10019
212/757-6363
Contact Bob Cafarella, Personnel Office. A major area painting contractor. Corporate headquarters location.

MORSE DIESEL INTERNATIONAL
1515 Broadway
New York NY 10036
212/642-0575
Contact Irwin R. Wecker, Vice President, Human Resources. One of the largest construction management companies in the world. With 10 offices across the United States and one in the United Kingdom, the firm offers a wide range of services which include construction management, program management, consulting and design/build. Morse Diesel International is a 50-50 partnership of AMEC Projects, Inc., a wholly-owned subsidiary of AMEC p.l.c., the publicly-quoted United Kingdom construction, engineering and development group, and Morse/Diesel, Inc., a major U.S. based construction management consulting firm. Founded in 1936, Morse Diesel pioneered the concept of construction management. Company involved in the planning and construction of some of the nation's largest and most prestigious building projects, including numerous corporate headquarters facilities, industrial facilities, correctional facilities, health care facilities, hotels, offices, institutions, commercial structures, residential structures, and renovation projects. Specific projects include The Sears Tower (Chicago); Pan Am Building (New York); National Gallery of Art (Washington, DC); Avery Fisher Hall (New York); and many others. Common positions include: Accountant; Project Manager; Field Superintendent; Computer Programmer; Civil Engineer; Electrical Engineer; Mechanical Engineer; Marketing Specialist; Personnel & Labor Relations Specialist; Public Relations Worker; Purchasing Agent. Principal educational background sought: Accounting; Business Administration; Construction Management; Computer Science; Engineering; Finance; Marketing. Company benefits include: medical, dental and life insurance; pension plan; tuition assistance; disability coverage; savings plan; bonus program. Operations at this facility include: regional headquarters.

J.D. POSILLICO INC.
1610 New Highway
Farmingdale NY 11735
516/249-1872
Contact Anne M. Seeley, Secretary. Several area locations. A major heavy construction firm whose projects include sewage systems, drainage, road work, and other projects. Corporate headquarters location.

SLATTERY ASSOCIATES INC.
46-36 54th Road
P.O. Box 7806
Maspeth NY 11378
718/392-2400
Contact Timothy J. Klein, Director/Employee Benefits. A member of the Skanska Group, operating primarily in the New York Metropolitan area. A major heavy construction firm engaged in large scale projects such as mass transit, sewage treatment plants, highways, bridges, and tunnels. Common positions include: Draftsperson; Civil Engineer; Mechanical Engineer; Superintendent. Principal educational background sought: Engineering. Company benefits include: medical, dental and life insurance; pension plan; disability coverage; 401K plan; incentive bonus plan. Corporate headquarters location.

TURNER CONSTRUCTION CO.
633 Third Avenue
New York NY 10017
212/878-0400

Contact Personnel Manager. One of the world's largest general contracting and construction management firms, with operations throughout the world. Headquarters location.

Connecticut

THE LEAKE & NELSON COMPANY
P.O. Box 3036, Barnum Station
Bridgeport CT 06605
203/366-7747
Contact Terry Nelson, Vice President. Engaged in steel erection and fabrication and related construction services. Corporate headquarters location.

LONE STAR INDUSTRIES
300 First Stamford Place
Stamford CT 06912-0014
203/969-8500
Contact Tom Curtin, Personnel Representative. Manufactures cement, concrete products, and construction materials. Common positions include: Accountant; Administrator; Blue-Collar Worker Supervisor; Computer Programmer; Industrial Engineer; Mining Engineer; Industrial Manager; Operations/Production Manager; Personnel & Labor Relations Specialist; Sales Representative. Principal educational backgrounds sought: Accounting; Business Administration; Computer Science; Engineering; Finance; Liberal Arts. Training programs offered. Company benefits include: medical, dental, and life insurance; pension plan; tuition assistance; disability coverage; savings plan; stock purchase. Corporate headquarters location. Operations at this facility include: regional headquarters; administration. New York Stock Exchange.

New Jersey

ARVEY CORPORATION
20 Sand Park Road
Cedar Grove NJ 07009
201/239-8100
Contact Tom Curcio, Personnel Director. Engaged in the laminating of a wide range of builder's material; metals and fabrication. Nationally, company manufactures products such as flexible films, paper converting products, medical packaging materials, numerical control tabs, food and drug packaging, graphic arts, lamination products, paper, and printing supplies. Corporate headquarters location: Chicago, IL.

CONCRETE PLANK P.J.R. INDUSTRIES
Two Porete Avenue
North Arlington NJ 07032
201/998-7600
Contact Personnel Director. Engaged in precast concrete panel construction and installation.

CONGOLEUM CORPORATION/TRENTON PLANT
861 Sloan Avenue
Trenton NJ 08619
609/584-3000
Contact Plant Personnel Manager. Distributes vinyl floor products to wholesalers nationwide and internationally. Parent company (Portsmouth, NH) is a diversified manufacturer/distributor, operating in the areas of home furnishings, shipbuilding, and automotive/industrial distribution. Common positions include: Accountant; Blue-Collar Worker Supervisor; Chemist; Computer Programmer; Electrical Engineer; Industrial Engineer; Mechanical Engineer; Department Manager; Operations/Production Manager; Personnel & Labor Relations Specialist; Quality Control Supervisor; Systems Analyst; Transportation & Traffic Specialist. Principal educational backgrounds sought: Accounting;

Business Administration; Chemistry; Computer Science; Engineering; Finance; Liberal Arts. Company benefits include: medical insurance; pension plan; life insurance; tuition assistance; disability coverage. Corporate headquarters location: Lawrenceville, NJ. Operations at this facility include: manufacturing; research/development.

CONSTRUCTION SPECIALTIES, INC.
55 Winans Avenue
Cranford NJ 07016
201/272-5200
Contact Lee Dirubbo, Human Resources Manager. A manufacturer of aluminum architectural products.

HOBOKEN WOOD FLOORING CORPORATION
70 Demerest Drive
Wayne NJ 07470
201/694-2888
Contact Vice President. Produces hardwood flooring for use in construction. Headquarters location.

C-E LUMMUS/THE LUMMUS COMPANY
1515 Broad Street
Bloomfield NJ 07003
201/893-1515
Contact Human Resources. One of the largest process industry engineering and construction industries in the world. Services include planning, engineering, procurement, and construction. An international contractor, and a wholly-owned subsidiary of Combustion Engineering Inc., company serves the petroleum, petrochemical, chemical, pharmaceutical, metallurgical, energy, and other processing industries worldwide. This facility is the firm's international headquarters, and houses the Lummus Technical Center, Engineering Development Center, Computer Systems Center, Heat Transfer Division, and Bloomfield Division. Company also operates a New York Office: 277 Park Avenue, New York NY 10017. Other international engineering and construction centers are located in Houston, Toronto, Calgary, Mexico City, Sao Paulo, London, The Hague, and Wiesbaden. Corporate headquarters location.

SCHIAVONE CONSTRUCTION COMPANY INC.
1600 Paterson Plank Road
Secaucus NJ 07096
201/867-5070
Contact Personnel Department. Several area locations. A major heavy construction firm, engaged in large-scale projects such as highways, tunnels, and bridges. Clients include city, state, and federal government. Corporate headquarters location.

DEFENSE-RELATED: RESEARCH AND PRODUCTION

New York

SLIGHTLINE ELECTRONICS
7500 Main Street
P.O. Box 750
Fishers NY 14453
716/924-4000
Contact Manager of Human Resources. A defense contractor involved in the design, development and manufacture of military airborne communications equipment. Operations at this facility include: manufacturing; development. Corporate headquarters location: Grand Rapids, MI. Common positions include: Accountant; Blue-Collar Worker Supervisor; Buyer; Commercial Artist; Computer Programmer; Draftsperson; Electrical Engineer; Industrial Engineer; Mechanical Engineer; Financial Analyst; Department Manager; Personnel & Labor Relations Specialist; Quality Control Supervisor; Technical Writer/Editor. Principal educational backgrounds sought: Computer Science; Engineering.

Company benefits include: medical insurance; dental insurance; pension plan; life insurance; tuition assistance; disability coverage; profit sharing; savings plan.

Connecticut

UNITED TECHNOLOGIES CORPORATION/ NORDEN SYSTEMS
Norden Place
P.O. Box 5300
Norwalk CT 06856
203/852-5000
Contact Joseph Laczko, Personnel Director. A design, development, and manufacturing firm. Products include advanced command, control and communications systems, avionic systems, and data processing systems for military applications. Corporate headquarters location.

New Jersey

ALLIED-SIGNAL AEROSPACE CO. BENDIX FLIGHT SYSTEMS DIVISION
Route 46
Teterboro NJ 07608
201/393-2176
Contact W. Randall Fuchs, Administrator, Employee Relations. A major manufacturer of aircraft avionics systems, including: automatic flight control systems, guidance, and navigation systems, map readers, and instrumentation systems, primarily for military aircraft. Also produces automated test equipment at this site. A major subsidiary of Allied Corporation (see separate listing). Divisional headquarters location. New York Stock Exchange. Company benefits include: medical, dental, and life insurance; pension plan; tuition assistance; disability coverage; savings plan.

CURTISS-WRIGHT CORPORATION
1200 Wall Street West
Lyndhurst NJ 07071
201/896-8400
Contact Mr. Cap W. Orr, Corporate Director of Labor Relations. A diversified multinational manufacturing concern. The corporation manufactures and markets products and provides services to industrial customers and under Government contracts in four broad areas: Aerospace; Flow Control and Marine; Industrial; and Electrical Generating. Aerospace segment produces jet engine and reciprocating engine parts, control and actuation components and systems, shot-peening and peen-forming services, and custom extruded shapes and shafts, for U.S. Government agencies, foreign governments, commercial/military/general aviation airframe manufacturers, commercial/military helicopter manufacturers, jet aircraft engine manufacturers, and commercial airlines. Flow Control and Marine segment produces globe, gate, solenoid and safety relief valves, and custom extruded shapes and seamless alloy pipe for U.S. Navy propulsion systems, commercial power systems, and U.S. Navy shipbuilders. Industrial segment produces precision spring clutches, manual impact wrenches, and aircraft windshield wiper systems for the office machine, industrial/military hand tool and general aviation markets, custom extruded shapes and seamless alloy pipe for the shipbuilding, oil/petrochemical/chemical construction industries, shot-peening and heat treating for the general metal working, and oil and gas drilling and exploration industries. The industrial compressor industry, and U.S. Government agencies, and Canadian operations, which manufactures air compressors and distributes small reciprocating engines for commercial/industrial, and lawn and garden uses. Area subsidiaries include Curtiss-Wright Flight Systems, Inc., a manufacturer of aerospace control and actuation components and systems (300 Fairfield Road, Fairfield NJ 07006); Metal Improvement Company, which performs shot-peening, peen-forming, and heat-treating services (10 Forest Avenue, Paramus NJ 07652); and Target Rock Corporation, a manufacturer of flow control valves. (East Farmingdale NY 11735).

Common positions include: Accountant; Administrator; Attorney; Computer Programmer; Draftsperson; Aerospace Engineer; Electrical Engineer; Industrial Engineer; Mechanical Engineer; Metallurgical Engineer; Financial Analyst; Operations/Production Manager; Personnel & Labor Relations Specialist; Quality Control Supervisor; Systems Analyst. Principal educational backgrounds sought: Accounting; Business Administration; Engineering; Finance. Company benefits include: medical, dental, and life insurance; pension plan; tuitin assistance; disability coverage; savings plan. Corporate headquarters location. New York Stock Exchange.

MERRIMAC INDUSTRIES INC.
41 Fairfield Place
West Caldwell NJ 07006
201/575-1300
Contact David Palumbo, Manager, Human Resources, Information Systems. A world leader in high-reliability signal-processing components. Products include IF-baseband components (used by the electronics and military electronics OEM's); RF-microwave components (military electronics and fiber-optics users); high-reliability space and missile products (electronic components used in major military satellite and missile programs); integrated microwave products (for the military and commercial communications markets); satellite reception products (products for the CATV and satellite master antenna systems); and others. International. Common positions include: Accountant; Buyer; Computer Programmer; Customer Service Representative; Draftsperson; Electrical Engineer; Industrial Engineer; Mechanical Engineer; Metallurgical Engineer; Operations/Production Manager; Purchasing Agent; Quality Control Supervisor; Sales Representative (Engineer); Technical Writer/Editor. Principal educational backgrounds sought: Business Administration; Computer Science; Engineering; Marketing. Company benefits include: medical insurance; dental insurance; life insurance; tuition assistance; disability coverage; profit sharing; savings plan (401K). Corporate headquarters location. Operations at this facility include: manufacturing; research/development; administration; sales.

NAVAL AIR ENGINEERING CENTER (NAEC)
Human Resources
Lakehurst NJ 08733-5056
201/323-2695
Contact Charles E. Adler Jr., Personnel Staffing Specialist. Involved in the research, development, and test of innovative technologies and equipment needed to support the world's most sophisticated aircraft, both shipboard and landbased, from takeoff to touchdown. NAEC engineers are responsible for the following aircraft systems: guidance and recovery, handling, electronics maintenance and repair, mechanical maintenance and repair, servicing and armament, and launching systems. Operations include: research/ development. Common positions include: Aerospace Engineer; Ceramics Engineer; Chemical Engineer; Electrical Engineer; Industrial Engineer; Mechanical Engineer; Metallurgical Engineer. Principal educational backgrounds sought: Engineering. Company benefits include: medical insurance; dental insurance; pension plan; life insurance; tuition assistance; disability coverage.

SMITHS INDUSTRIES
7-11 Vreeland Road
Florham Park NJ 07932
Contact Christine Leonhardt, Human Resources. The company engineers, designs and manufactures weapon management systems, communication control systems, and flight data recorders for military aircraft. Also engineers computer systems for space shuttle. Common positions include: Accountant; Buyer; Draftsperson; Aerospace Engineer; Electrical Engineer; Industrial Engineer; Mechanical Engineer; Systems Analyst; Technical Writer/Editor. Principal educational backgrounds sought: Computer Science; Engineering. Company benefits include: medical insurance; dental insurance; pension plan; life insurance; tuition assistance; disability coverage; savings plan.

THOMAS ELECTRONICS, INC.
100 River View Drive
Wayne NJ 07470
201/696-5200
Contact Personnel Department. Manufactures cathode-ray tubes for use by military/industrial OEM's. Corporate headquarters location.

ELECTRICAL & ELECTRONIC: MANUFACTURING & DISTRIBUTION

For more information on professional opportunities in the electronics and electrical industry, contact the following professional and trade organizations, as listed beginning on page 449:

AMERICAN ELECTROPLATERS AND SURFACE FINISHERS SOCIETY
ELECTROCHEMICAL SOCIETY
ELECTRONIC INDUSTRIES ASSOCIATION
ELECTRONICS TECHNICIANS ASSOCIATION
INSTITUTE OF ELECTRICAL AND ELECTRONICS ENGINEERS
INT'L BROTHERHOOD OF ELECTRICAL WORKERS/LOCAL 3
INTERNATIONAL BROTHERHOOD OF ELECTRICAL WORKERS
INT'L SOCIETY OF CERTIFIED ELECTRONICS TECHNICIANS
NATIONAL ELECTRICAL MANUFACTURERS ASSOCIATION
NATIONAL ELECTRONICS SALES AND SERVICES ASSOCIATION

New York

ADEMCO
(ALARM DEVICE MANUFACTURING COMPANY)
178 Michael Drive
Syosset NY 11791
516/921-2075
Contact Employment Manager. An electronic security/fire equipment firm. A subsidiary of Pittway Corporation. Divisional headquarters location. Corporate headquarters location: Northbrook, IL. American Stock Exchange. Common positions include: Electrical Engineer; Industrial Engineer; Mechanical Engineer. Principal educational backgrounds sought: Computer Science; Engineering. Company benefits include: medical insurance; dental insurance; pension plan; life insurance; tuition assistance; disability coverage.

AIL SYSTEMS INC./
SUBSIDIARY OF EATON CORPORATION
Commack Road
Deer Park NY 11729
516/595-5000
Contact Gregg Russo, Personnel Administrator. Five company locations: Deer Park, Melville, Farmingdale, Hauppauge, and Ronkonkoma. This division is engaged in the engineering and manufacture of electronic systems, including defensive avionics, ATC radar, satellite communications systems, and components. International. New York Stock Exchange. Common positions include: Electrical Engineer; Industrial Engineer; Mechanical Engineer; Programmer. Principal educational backgrounds sought: Computer Science; Engineering; Physics. Company benefits include: medical insurance; dental insurance; pension plan; life insurance; tuition assistance; disability coverage; profit sharing; savings plan. Corporate headquarters location: Cleveland, OH. Operations at this facility include: manufacturing; research/development; administration; service. New York Stock Exchange.

AVNET INC.
80 Cutter Mill Road
Great Neck NY 11021
516/466-7000

Contact Mrs. Phyllis Bosselli, Office Manager. The world's largest distributor of electronic components and computer products for industrial and military customers. Components are shipped either as received from suppliers, or with assembly or other value added. Also produces or distributes other electronic, electrical, electro-automotive, and video communications products. Operates in the following groups: Electronic Marketing Group-engaged in the distribution of electronic components, connectors, and computer products to retailers and end users through Hamilton/Avnet Computer and Avnet Computer Technologies divisions. Electrical and Industrial Group-engaged in the electrical and electronic industrial distribution industry of trophy parts, plastic molding, and zinc diecasting through its Freeman Products division; and the manufacture of industrial shop supplies, hydraulic/pneumatic components and electrical wire/cable/terminals through its Mechanics Choice division. Video Communications Group-engaged in manufacture of TV antennas and hardware, satellite TV receiving equipment and cable TV signal processing equipment through its Channel Master Division and manufacture of TV signal processing products, compact disc products, and turntables through its Avnet International (Taiwan) and Avnet Industries (Malaysia) divisions. New York Stock Exchange. International.

AVX CORPORATION
750 Lexington
New York NY 10022
212/935-6363
Contact Susan Nicosia, Office Manager. Leading manufacturer of multilayer ceramic capacitors (MLC's), electronic components used extensively in conjunction with integrated circuits in a wide variety of applications. Also manufactures tantalum, glass, microwave capacitors, filters, and sells a wide range of other passive components. Operates manufacturing and/or sales operations in the United States, Europe, Japan and Southeast Asia. Primarily serves the data processing, telecommunications, military, consumer, and instrumentation markets. Employs more than 7,500 people worldwide. Corporate headquarters location. Became part of the Kyocera Group in January 1990. Common positions include: Accountant; Financial Analyst; Insurance Agent/Broker; Public Relations Specialist. Principal educational backgrounds sought: Accounting; Business Administration; Communications; Computer Science; Economics; Finance; Marketing. Company benefits include: medical insurance; dental insurance; pension plan; life insurance; tuition assistance; disability coverage; profit sharing; employee discounts. Corporate headquarters location. Parent company: Kyocera Corporation. Operations at this facility include: administration.

BROADWAY MAINTENANCE CORPORATION
1941 42nd Street
Astoria NY 11105
718/274-4200
Contact Fred Goodman, Personnel Department. Several area locations, including Manhattan, Queens, NY; Newark, NJ: Nassau County. An electrical construction/electrical maintenance firm, specializing in the following product areas: steel lighting, traffic lighting, fluorescent and neon lighting. Clients include private industry and government. In business for more than 50 years. Corporate headquarters location.

CECO/RICHARDSON ELECTRONICS
2115 Avenue X
Brooklyn NY 11235
718/646-6300
Contact Division Manager. An electronics products manufacturer.

CONCORD ELECTRONICS CORPORATION
30 Great Jones Street
New York NY 10012
212/777-6571
Contact Josie Wheaton, Personnel Director. An electronics manufacturing firm, producing computer terminals, chassis hardware, and related accessories.

CONTINENTAL CONNECTOR CORPORATION
34-63 56th Street
Woodside NY 11377
718/899-4422
Contact Personnel Department. Engaged in the development, manufacture, and sale of a broad line of multi-precision rack and panel circuit connectors. Manufacturing operations consist primarily of the processing and assembly of plated metals, receptacles, and plugs of various types designed and molded from thermosetting molding compounds, and other precision connector parts. Connector facilities at this location. Other company subsidiaries own and operate the Dunes Hotel and Country Club (Las Vegas, NV), and own and develop land in Atlantic City, NJ. Corporate headquarters location: Las Vegas, NV. American Stock Exchange.

DEUTSCH RELAYS INC.
65 Daly Road
East Northport NY 11731
516/499-6000
Contact Personnel. Manufactures miniature relays. Corporate headquarters location.

EAGLE ELECTRIC MANUFACTURING COMPANY INC.
45-31 Court Square
Long Island City NY 11101
718/937-8000
Contact Jerry Rocker, Personnel Director. Manufactures electrical wiring devices. Corporate headquarters location. Common positions include: Administrator; Advertising Worker; Blue-Collar Worker Supervisor; Commercial Artist; Computer Programmer; Credit Manager; Customer Service Representative; Draftsperson; Engineer; Electrical Engineer; Industrial Engineer; Mechanical Engineer; Personnel & Labor Relations Specialist; Purchasing Agent; Quality Control Supervisor; Sales Representative; Transportation & Traffic Specialist. Principal educational backgrounds sought: Art/Design; Computer Science; Engineering. Company benefits include: medical insurance; dental insurance; pension plan; life insurance; tuition assistance; disability coverage; employee discounts; savings plan.

EATON CORPORATION/
AIL DIVISION
Commack Road
Deer Park NY 11729
516/595-5000
Contact John Menechino, Director of Personnel. Five company locations: Deer Park, Melville, Farmingdale, Happauge, and Rokonkoma. This division is engaged in the engineering and manufacture of electronic systems, including defensive avionics, ATC radar, satellite communications systems, and components. International. New York Stock Exchange. Common positions include: Electrical Engineer; Industrial Engineer; Mechanical Engineer; Programmer. Principal educational backgrounds sought: Computer Science; Engineering; Physics. Company benefits include: medical insurance; dental insurance; pension plan; life insurance; tuition assistance; disability coverage; profit sharing; savings plan. Corporate headquarters location: Cleveland, OH. Operations at this facility include: manufacturing; research/development; administration; service. New York Stock Exchange.

GEM ELECTRIC MANUFACTURING COMPANY INC.
390 Vanderbilt Motor Parkway
Hauppauge NY 11788
516/273-2230
Contact Bob Becker, Plant Manager. Manufactures electrical wiring devices, fuses, extension cords, and consumer electric products such as Christmas tree light packages. Corporate headquarters location.

HADCO CORPORATION
1160 Taylor Road
Oswego NY 13827-1160
607/687-3425
Contact Jim Sullivan, Human Resources Manager. A manufacturer of high-grade printed wiring boards. Divisional headquarters. Operations at this facility include: manufacturing; research/development; administration; sales. Corporate headquarters location: Salem, NH. Common positions include: Accountant; Blue-Collar Worker Supervisor; Buyer; Chemist; Computer Programmer; Chemical Engineer; Civil Engineer; Industrial Engineer; Mechanical Engineer; Financial Analyst; General Manager; Operations/Production Manager; Personnel & Labor Relations Specialist; Quality Control Supervisor; Statistician; Technical Writer/Editor. Principal educational backgrounds sought: Accounting; Business Administration; Chemistry; Computer Science; Engineering; Finance; Marketing. Company benefits include: medical, dental and life insurance; tuition assistance; disability coverage; profit sharing; employee discounts; savings plan.

HAZELTINE CORPORATION
MS 1-66, 450 East Pulaski Road
Greenlawn NY 11740
516/261-7000
Contact Ron Davis, Employment Manager. A world leader in information electronics, designing, developing, and producing advanced systems that acquire, protect, enhance, communicate, and display information, operating primarily in the defense and technically-related areas. Operates in four areas of business: Computer Systems, producing advanced systems and products to process and display image, alphanumeric and graphic data for analysis and command-and-control decision making; Communications Systems, producing radio transmission/reception systems and products for military voice and data communications networks, interconnecting sensors, computers, and command posts, with emphasis on protection of information against interference. Electronic Identification, producing electronic systems and products to automatically provide 'identification friend or foe' information for airborne and ground defense systems and air traffic control systems; Anti-Submarine Warfare, producing systems and expendable sensors for detecting and locating submarines, and related acoustic transducers, tracking, and communications devices and jam resistant radio communications systems. Division of Esco Electronics. Common positions at this facility include: Accountant; Buyer; Computer Programmer; Draftsperson; Electrical Engineer; Industrial Engineer; Mechanical Engineer; Operations/Production Manager; Personnel/Labor Relations Specialist; Quality Control Supervisor; Systems Analyst; Technical Writer/Editor; Principal educational backgrounds sought: Business Administration; Computer Science; Engineering; Finance. Company benefits include: medical insurance; dental insurance; pension plan; life insurance; tuition assistance; savings plan. Corporate headquarters location: St. Louis, MO. Operations at this facility include: divisional headquarters.

INDUSTRIAL ELECTRONIC HARDWARE CORPORATION
109 Prince Street
New York NY 10012
212/677-1881
Contact Miss Ana Romero, Personnel Manager. An industrial electronics firm, manufacturing a varied line of sophisticated high performance electronic connectors and specialized interconnection devices. Corporate headquarters location.

ITT CORPORATION
1313 Avenue of the Americas
New York NY 10019
212/258-1000
Contact Personnel Manager. Multiple area locations. Engaged principally in the businesses of Telecommunications and Electronics; Engineered Products; Consumer Products and Services; Natural Resources; and Insurance and Finance. Company maintains manufacturing or sales operations in approximately 100 countries. Telecommunications and Electronics Group operations include managing the largest international record carrier through land, undersea, and satellite networks, and the design and manufacture of

navigation and marine electronics systems for commercial and military customers worldwide, as well as operating and maintaining support services at major NASA facilities through defense and avionics unit. Engineered Products Group produces automotive products (through subsidiaries Teves, Koni, and SWF); pumps, valves, and fluid-handling products; and electronic memories, and distribution of electrical and electronic connectors, controls and other instrumentation. Consumer Products and Services includes operations through 'Sheraton' hotels and inns subsidiary, lawn care and gardening products through Scotts and Burpee subsidiaries, and publishing through the 'Marquis Who's Who' directories. Natural Resources Group produces forest products (including the production of wood pulps and other wood products through subsidiary ITT Rayonier and others); and energy and mineral products through subsidiary Eason Oil Company, involved in oil and gas exploration, and in the mining, preparation, and sale of metallurgical and steam coal, silica, and attapulgite. Insurance and Finance Group writes a broad range of life, property, and casualty insurance through subsidiary The Hartford Insurance Group (New York, NY); and makes consumer and commercial loans, and provides financing to ITT customers through ITT Financial Corporation. Area subsidiaries include Federal Electric Corporation (Paramus, NJ). Subsidiaries operate independently. Corporate headquarters location. International. New York Stock Exchange.

KINGS ELECTRONICS COMPANY INC.
40 Marbledale Road
Tuckahoe NY 10707
914/793-5000
Contact Bruce Munson, Director of Human Resources/Personnel. Manufactures, sells, and distributes a large line of specialized RF coaxial connectors for various electronics and aerospace industry applications. Common positions include: Accountant; Blue-Collar Worker Supervisor; Chemist; Computer Programmer; Credit Manager; Customer Service Representative; Draftsperson; Electrical Engineer; Industrial Engineer; Mechanical Engineer; Operations/Production Manager; Personnel & Labor Relations Specialist; Purchasing Agent; Quality Control Supervisor; Sales Representative. Principal educational backgrounds sought: Business Administration; Computer Science; Engineering. Company benefits include: medical, dental, and life insurance; pension plan; disability coverage; savings plan. Corporate headquarters location. Operations at this facility include: manufacturing; research/development; administration; service; sales.

LEECRAFT MANUFACTURING INC.
21-02 44th Road
Long Island City NY 11101
718/392-8800
Contact Personnel Director. A manufacturer of pre-wired electrical devices, indicator lights, and lamp holders for small appliances. Corporate headquarters location.

LEVITON MANUFACTURING COMPANY INC.
59-25 Little Neck Parkway
Little Neck NY 11362
718/229-4040
Contact Personnel Administrator. Several area locations, including: Brooklyn, Maspeth, and Melville. A major manufacturer of electrical wiring devices. Company produces more than 80,000 variations of light switches, sockets, and plugs, for both consumers and industry. Products are typically used in small appliances, lamps, and similar products.

LORAL CORPORATION
600 Third Avenue
New York NY 10016
212/697-1105
Contact Administration Department. Several area locations, including Yonkers, NY; Garwood, NJ. An international high-technology company, which primarily designs, develops, and produces electronic systems and microwave devices used in defense electronics and communications. In its principal activity, electronic warfare, company makes state-of-the-art defense electronic systems that protect military aircraft; provide surveillance for long-range reconnaissance, airborne early warning, and command and

control aircraft; assist in target acquisition; and serve as telemetry, tracking, and control data links which monitor and control missiles and space vehicles. In the field of information and graphic display systems, company produces advanced systems that display both data-based and real-time sensor information with computer graphics for military applications. Company's instrumentation products also support electronic warfare activities with equipment that monitors and analyzes telemetry, tracking and control data streams in real-time, analyzes avionic computers, tests advanced equipment in the field, and simulates electronic environments for mission planning and pilot training. Company is also a leader in the development and manufacture of solid-state microwave sources, control devices, specialized semi-conductors, and integrated assemblies supporting the electronic warfare, communications, telemetry, space, radar, and missile guidance markets. In communications, company is a leading producer of portable microwave radios and multiplex equipment used by commercial and private communications networks to transmit and receive voice, video, facsimile, and digital data. Also makes portable transceivers and teletypewriters for overseas military and other governmental markets. Operates two additional businesses: the precision fabrication of exotic metals for optical, navigational, and structural aerospace assemblies; and the molding and custom-decorating of plastic packaging for pharmaceutical and consumer products. Area subsidiaries include Loral Electronic Systems (Yonkers); and Loral Packaging (Garwood, NJ). Other subsidiaries in Massachusetts, California (eight locations), Florida, and Georgia; international facility in London. Corporate headquarters location. New York Stock Exchange. International.

LORAL MICROWAVE-NARDA
435 Moreland Road
Hauppauge NY 11788
516/231-1700
Contact Kathy Joyce, Director, Human Resources. Manufactures and distributes microwave communications equipment and components. Common positions include: RF/Microwave Engineer; Technician. Principal educational backgrounds sought: Business Administration; Engineering. Company benefits include: medical, dental, and life insurance; pension plan; tuition assistance; disability coverage; profit sharing; employee discounts; savings plan. Corporate headquarters location: Manhattan, NY. Parent company: Loral Corp. Operations at this facility include: divisional headquarters; manufacturing; administration; sales.

LORD ELECTRIC COMPANY INC.
230 Park Avenue
New York NY 10169
212/943-6999
Contact Vice-President/Administration. A major area electrical contractor. Corporate headquarters location.

MARCONI CIRCUIT TECHNOLOGY CORPORATION
160 Smith Street
Farmingdale NY 11735
516/293-8686
Contact Dennis McGuire, Vice President, Human Resources. A manufacturer of custom-designed hybrid microcircuits for use in applications including electrical systems used in aircraft maintenance, flight and navigational systems, sonar systems, satellite experimentation systems, missile firing systems, power supply systems, computer testing systems, television camera and radio receiver systems, and other applications using miniaturized components. Corporate headquarters location.

MATERIALS RESEARCH CORPORATION
560 Route 303
Orangeburg NY 10962
914/359-4200
Contact Maryann Fabian, Personnel Director. Several area locations, including Pearl River and Congers, NY. Primarily engaged in the design and manufacture of thin film coating and etching systems, which are utilized in the manufacture of integrated circuits, for sale principally to the semi-conductor, computer, and telecommunications industries. Also

processes and fabricates ultra-high purity metals, metal alloys, and ceramics, principally for thin film purposes. Company's thin-film technology products are also used in non-electronic applications such as protective coatings for corrosion and wear-resistance in razor blades and various automotive products. Operates in three segments: Sputtering Equipment and Associated Target Materials; Other High Purity Materials; and Ceramics. Company operates five sales offices in the United States; sales or manufacturing facilities located throughout the world, including South America, Europe, Asia, Australia, and the Middle East. Common positions include: Accountant; Administrator; Buyer; Chemist; Ceramics Engineer; Customer Service Representative; Draftsperson; Chemical Engineer; Electrical Engineer; Mechanical Engineer; Metallurgical Engineer; Software Engineer; Financial Analyst; Materials Scientist; Department Manager; General Manager; Operations/Production Manager; Marketing Specialist; Personnel & Labor Relations Specialist; Physicist; Purchasing Agent; Quality Control Supervisor; Systems Analyst; Trainer. Principal educational backgrounds sought: Accounting; Chemistry; Engineering; Finance; Physics. Training programs offered. Company benefits include: medical, dental, and life insurance; pension plan; tuition assistance; disability coverage; employee discounts; savings plan. Corporate headquarters location. Parent company: Sony USA. Operations at this facility include: manufacturing; research/development; administration; service; sales.

PARAMOUNT ELECTRONICS COMPANY
57 Willoughby Street
Brooklyn NY 11201-5211
718/237-8730
Contact Personnel Manager. Provides contract drafting services. Corporate headquarters location.

PARK ELECTROCHEMICAL CORPORATION
5 Dakota Drive
Lake Success NY 11042
516/354-4100
Contact Alan Lesh, Personnnel Manager. Several area locations, including Flushing, and Farmingdale. Operates in two business segments: Decorative Materials, and Circuitry Materials. Company and eight operating subsidiaries are engaged in manufacturing advanced electronic circuit materials; unique plumbing products; decorative hardware for consumer goods; electronic instrument panels; and special purpose bonding films. Area subsidiaries include: Park Nameplate Company; Hallmark Nameplate, Inc. (Farmingdale, NY); and Closed Loop Environmental and Recovery Corporation (Great Neck, NY). Corporate headquarters location. American Stock Exchange.

PASS & SEYMOUR/LEGRAND
45 Sea Cliff Avenue
Glen Cove NY 11542
516/671-7000
Contact John Lito, Personnel Director. Manufactures and sells wiring devices for use primarily in residential, institutional, industrial, and commercial buildings. Products include switches, electrical outlets, connectors, wallplates, weather resistant boxes and covers, plastic outlet boxes, wire mesh cable grips, group fault interrupter receptacles, and various lighting products. Products are sold to electrical distributors in the United States and Canada through independent sales representative organizations. Corporate headquarters location.

PHILIPS COMPONENTS
5083 Kings Highway
Saugerties NY 12477
914/246-2811
Contact Don Putman, Employment Recruiter. Products include linear ferrites (power transformers, switching systems) and machined ferrites (digital recording products). Both are electronic ceramic components. Operations at this facility include: manufacturing. Corporate headquarters location. Common positions include: Accountant; Blue-Collar Worker Supervisor; Buyer; Chemist; Computer Programmer; Engineer; Ceramics Engineer; Electrical Engineer; Industrial Engineer; Mechanical Engineer;

Operations/Production Manager. Principal educational backgrounds sought: Engineering. Company benefits include: medical insurance; dental insurance; pension plan; life insurance; tuition assistance; disability coverage; employee discounts; savings plan; relocation; credit union.

PICKERING & COMPANY INC.
200 Terminal Drive
Plainview NY 11803
516/349-0200
Contact Virginia Rumpler, Personnel Manager. Produces a variety of electronics and electro-magnetic products primarily for sale to the consumer markets. Products include stereo cartridges and others. A division of Stanton Magnetics, Inc. Corporate headquarters location.

SEMI-ALLOYS
888 South Columbus Avenue
Mount Vernon NY 10550
914/664-2800
Contact Yolanda Vitalo, Personnel Director. Manufactures ceramic/glass alloy products for use in semiconductor manufacturing, and related glass, plastic, and ceramic materials.

SIGNAL TRANSFORMER/
DIVISION OF INSILICA
500 Bayview Avenue
Inwood NY 11696
516/239-5777
Contact John Bisci, Engineering Manager. Manufactures and distributes transformers for a range of applications, from printed circuit board requirements to rectifiers and chokes. Common positions include: Accountant; Blue-Collar Worker Supervisor; Buyer; Credit Manager; Customer Service Representative; Electrical Engineer; Industrial Engineer; Mechanical Engineer; General Manager; Operations/Production Manager; Purchasing Agent; Quality Control Supervisor. Principal educational backgrounds sought: Accounting; Business Administration; Engineering; Finance; Mathematics. Company benefits include: medical, dental, and life insurance; pension plan; tuition assistance. Corporate headquarters location: Menden, CT. Operations at this facility include: manufacturing; sales. New York Stock Exchange.

WELSBACH ELECTRIC CORPORATION
1941 42nd Street
Astoria NY 11105
718/274-4200
Contact Fred Goodman, Vice-President/Personnel. An electrical contractor engaged primarily in the installation and maintenance of street lights and traffic signals. Currently performing contracts in four states, with the largest contracts being performed in the metropolitan New York area. A subsidiary of Jamaica Water Properties (see separate listing). Corporate headquarters location.

WESTINGHOUSE ELECTRIC CORPORATION
805 Third Avenue
New York NY 10022
212/715-0400
Contact Personnel Director. Several area locations, including Randolph, Newark, Bloomfield, NJ. Engaged principally in the manufacture, sale, and service of equipment and components for the generation, transmission, distribution, utilization, and control of electricity. Its businesses also include a wide range of products and services which are unrelated to electrical manufacturing, such as broadcasting and cable television operations, land development, bottling and distribution of beverage products, transport refrigeration, and financial services. Operates in four segments: Power Systems; Industry Products; Public Systems; and Broadcasting and Cable. Area subsidiaries are located in Randolph, NJ (elevators); Bloomfield, NJ (light bulbs); Manhattan (Group W Broadcasting operations); Stamford, CT (Satellite News Channels, a joint venture with ABC); and other

locations. Corporate headquarters location: Pittsburgh, PA. New York Stock Exchange. International.

WITTENBERG DISTRIBUTORS/
NORTHEAST DIVISION
620 Erie Boulevard West
Syracuse NY 13204
800/347-4300
Contact Personnel. A major distributor of Tappan and Zenith products.

Connecticut

AMPHENOL RF/MICROWAVE OPERATIONS
1 Kennedy Avenue
Danbury CT 06810
203/743-9272
Contact Hilary Weiss, Specialist, Human Resources. Amphenol RF/Microwave Operations is the world's largest manufacturer of coaxial connectors and cable assemblies for use in radio frequency (RF), microwave, and data transmission systems applications. Common positions include: Accountant; Blue-Collar Worker Supervisor; Mechanical Engineer. Principal educational backgrounds sought: Engineering. Company benefits include: medical insurance; dental insurance; pension plan; life insurance; tuition assistance; disability coverage; savings plan. Corporate headquarters location: Wallingford, CT. Parent company: LPL Technologies Inc. Operations at this facility include: divisional headquarters; manufacturing; research/development; administration; service; sales.

B&J ELECTRIC MOTOR REPAIR COMPANY
30 Maple Street
Ansonia CT 06401
203/734-1695
Contact Alan Johns, President. Services electrical equipment; also provides wiring supplies and related construction materials.

BERKSHIRE TRANSFORMER CORPORATION
3 Segar Mountain Road
P.O. Box 129
Kent CT 06757
203/927-3541
Contact Deena-Marie Adams, Office Administrator. Designs and manufactures electronic transformers. Divisional headquarters location. Operations include: manufacturing; research/development; administration; sales. Corporate headquarters location: Wallingford, CT. Common positions include: Accountant; Administrator; Electrical Engineer; General Manager; Operations/Production Manager; Personnel & Labor Relations Specialist; Purchasing Agent; Quality Control Supervisor; Sales Representative. Principal educational backgrounds sought: Accounting; Business Administration; Engineering; Electronics. Company benefits include: medical insurance; life insurance; disability coverage; savings plan. Corporate headquarters location: Westfield, MA. Parent company: Preferred Electronics, Inc. Operations at this facility include: divisional headquarters; manufacturing; research/development; administration.

BRAND-REX COMPANY
1600 West Main Street
Willimantic CT 06226
203/456-8000
Contact Kevin Toomey, Manager of Human Relations. Brand-Rex is a division of BICC Cables, manufacturing wire and cables for military, commercial, data communications, and computer products. Corporate headquarters location. Common positions include: Accountant; Administrator; Blue-Collar Worker Supervisor; Buyer; Chemist; Computer Programmer; Credit Manager; Customer Service Representative; Draftsperson; Engineer; Electrical Engineer; Industrial Engineer; Mechanical Engineer; Financial Analyst;

Industrial Manager; Department Manager; General Manager; Management Trainee; Operations/Production Manager; Marketing Specialist; Personnel & Labor Relations Specialist; Programmer; Public Relations Worker; Purchasing Agent; Quality Control Supervisor; Sales Representative; Statistician; Systems Analyst; Transportation & Traffic Specialist. Principal educational backgrounds sought: Accounting; Business Administration; Chemistry; Communications; Computer Science; Economics; Engineering; Finance; Liberal Arts; Marketing; Physics. Training programs offered; Internships offered. Company benefits include: medical insurance; dental insurance; pension plan; life insurance; tuition assistance; disability coverage; savings plan; profit sharing. Operations at this facility include: divisional headquarters; manufacturing; research/development; administration; sales.

BURNDY CORPORATION
51 Richards Avenue
Norwalk CT 06856
203/838-4444
Contact Personnel Director. Founded in 1924; a multi-national corporation serving virtually every segment of industry through the design, manufacture, and sale of one of the world's broadest lines of electrical and electronic connectors and allied products. Products are employed to join, splice, tap, or terminate conductors, wires, and circuits utilizing electrical energy or signals. Company products range in size from microminiature components for use in sophisticated electronic equipment to very large electrical connectors used by utilities in the generation, transmission, and distribution of electrical power. Markets include OEM's in the electronics industries, and the power industries. Also operates plants in Canada, Belgium, France, Germany, Italy, Spain, Mexico, Brazil, Japan, and Australia. Employs 4000 people worldwide. Corporate headquarters location. New York Stock Exchange.

FOOD AUTOMATION-SERVICE TECHNIQUES
905 Honeyspot Rd.
Stratford CT 06497
203/377-4414
Contact Sandra H. Chandler, Personnel Administrator. A manufacturer of electronic control systems devoted to the food service industry. Operations include: manufacturing; research/development; service. Corporate headquarters location. Common positions include: Accountant; Administrator; Credit Manager; Customer Service Representative; Draftsperson; Electrical Engineer; Food Technologist; Department Manager; Management Trainee; Operations/Production Manager; Marketing Specialist; Personnel Specialist; Programmer; Purchasing Agent. Principal educational backgrounds sought: Accounting; Business Administration; Engineering; Marketing. Company benefits include: medical insurance;life insurance; tuition assistance; disability coverage.

GENERAL ELECTRIC COMPANY
3135 Easton Turnpike
Fairfield CT 06431
203/373-2211
Contact Jack Peiffer, Senior Vice President for Corporate Human Resources. Researches, develops, manufactures, and markets electrical, electronic, chemical, microelectronic products for business, industry, and home use. Employs 330,000.

HUBBELL INCORPORATED
584 Derby Milford Road
Orange CT 06477-4024
203/799-4255
Contact George D. Zurman, Director of Management Staffing. An international manufacturer of quality electrical and electronic products serving a broad range of industrial, commercial, telecommunications, and utility markets. The company operate facilities in the United States, Canada, Puerto Rico, and the United Kingdom. Common positions include: Accountant; Computer Programmer; Electrical Engineer; Industrial Engineer; Mechanical Engineer; Metallurgical Engineer; Sales Representative; Systems Analyst. Principal educational backgrounds sought: Accounting; Business Administration;

Computer Science; Engineering; Finance; Marketing. Training programs offered. Company benefits include: medical, dental, and life insurance; pension plan; tuition assistance; disability coverage; daycare assistance; savings plan. Corporate headquarters location. American Stock Exchange.

KOLLMORGEN COMPANY
10 Mill Pond Lane
Simsbury CT 06070
203/651-3757
Contact Director of Human Resources. Several area locations, including Hartford, CT; Hicksville, Melville, Commack, Riverhead, and Newburgh, NY. A diversified technology company with proprietary positions in discrete segments of a large number of growing markets, most related to the electronics industry. Operates in three business segments: printed circuitry and associated interconnection technology, special purpose servo motors and controls, and electro-optical instruments. Area subsidiaries include Additive Products Division (Riverhead, NY), which manufactures additive printed circuit boards for automotive electronics, cable TV equipment, consumer electronics, home and personal computer systems, industrial electronics, and mobile and telecommunications applications; PCK Technology Division (Melville, NY), which produces hybrid circuits, and advanced-technology circuit boards, and is engaged in the licensing of patented products, processes, and proprietary manufacturing techniques, and equipment, chemicals, and materials used by these licensees, for international interconnection boards manufacturers, the electronics industry, and chemical suppliers to these industries; Multiwire Division (Hicksville NY), which manufactures multiwire interconnection boards, and is engaged in computer-aided circuit design, for business and office equipment, CAD/CAM systems, computers and peripheral equipment, data and telecommunications, military electronics, and seismic and geophysical instrument manufacturers; PMI Motors Division (Commack, NY), which produces disc-armature, DC servo motors, electronic servo drive amplifiers, servo feedback components, and digital positioning systems for business and office equipment, computer peripheral equipment, high-performance industrial machinery, medical equipment, robotics, and test and measuring products; Macbeth Division (Newburgh, NY), which produces photometers, spectroradiometers, spectral scanning systems, and light meters for commercial photography, graphic arts, papermaking, photofinishing, plastics manufacturing, and textiles applications. Administrative offices located in Simsbury, CT. Corporate headquarters location. New York Stock Exchange. International. Common positions (for NY and CT locations) include: Accountant; Blue-Collar Worker Supervisor; Buyer; Chemist; Computer Programmer; Draftsperson; Chemical Engineer; Electrical Engineer; Mechanical Engineer; Financial Analyst; Operations/Production Manager; Marketing Specialist; Personnel & Labor Relations Specialist; Physicist; Programmer; Purchasing Agent; Quality Control Supervisor; Systems Analyst. Principal educational backgrounds sought: Chemistry; Computer Science; Engineering; Marketing. Company benefits include: medical insurance; dental insurance; pension plan; life insurance; tuition assistance; disability coverage; profit sharing; savings plan.

NEW HAVEN MANUFACTURING CORPORATION
446 Blake St.
New Haven CT 06515
203/387-2572
Contact E.R. Calistro, V.P. Human Resources. Develops, manufactures, and markets time equipment, hydraulic control valves, and electronic hardware. Common positions include: Accountant; Administrator; Advertising Worker; Blue-Collar Worker Supervisor; Buyer; Computer Programmer; Credit Manager; Customer Service Representative; Draftsperson; Electrical Engineer; Industrial Engineer; Mechanical Engineer; Industrial Designer; Branch Manager; Department Manager; General Manager; Management Trainee; Operations/Production Manager; Marketing Specialist; Personnel & Labor Relations Specialist; Purchasing Agent; Quality Control Supervisor; Sales Representative; Systems Analyst; Techncial Writer/Editor; Transportation & Traffic Specialist. Principal educational backgrounds sought include: Accounting; Business Administration; Computer Science; Engineering; Finance; Liberal Arts; Marketing. Company benefits include: medical, dental, and life insurance; pension plan; tuition assistance; disability coverage;

credit union. Corporate headquarters location. Operations at this facility include: divisional headquarters; manufacturing; research/development; administration; service; sales.

PERKIN ELMER/
PLASMA SYSTEMS DIVISION
761 Main Avenue
Norwalk CT 06859
203/762-4210
Contact Isabelle Kalmanides, Director of Human Resources. Develops, manufactures and markets high technology semiconductor processing equipment, specifically, plasma etching and sputter deposition machines. Corporate headquarters location. Operations include: manufacturing; research/development; administration; service; sales. New York Stock Exchange. Common positions include: Accountant; Administrator; Blue-Collar Worker Supervisor; Computer Programmer; Customer Service Representative; Draftsperson; Chemical Engineer; Electrical Engineer; Mechanical Engineer; Financial Analyst; Marketing Specialist; Personnel & Labor Relations Specialist; Physicist; Purchasing Agent; Sales Representative; Electronic Technician; Electrical Technician; Vacuum Technician. Principal educational backgrounds sought: Accounting; Chemistry; Computer Science; Engineering; Marketing; Physics; Material Science. Company benefits include: medical, dental, and life insurance; pension plan; tuition assistance; disability coverage; profit sharing; savings plan; relocation assistance; stock purchase.

PITNEY-BOWES
Walter H. Wheeler Jr. Drive
Stamford CT 06926
203/356-5000
Contact Micki Lemieux, Employment Manager. Corporate office of the well-known office equipment distributing company.

POWER SYSTEMS INC.
45 Griffin Road South
Bloomfield CT 06002
203/726-1300
Contact Joan Davidson, Personnel Manager. Firm designs and manufactures switchmode power supplies. Operations include: manufacturing; research/development; administration; service; sales. Corporate headquarters location. Common positions include: Accountant; Blue-Collar Worker Supervisor; Buyer; Draftsperson; Electrical Engineer; Industrial Engineer; Mechanical Engineer; Personnel & Labor Relations Specialist; Programmer; Quality Control Supervisor; Sales Representative; Systems Analyst. Principal educational backgrounds sought: Accounting; Art/Design; Business Administration; Computer Science; Engineering; Finance; Marketing; Mathematics. Company benefits include: medical, dental, and life insurance; pension plan; tuition assistance; disability coverage; profit sharing; employee discounts; savings plan. Operations at this facility include: regional headquarters; manufacturing; administration; service; sales.

ROGERS CORPORATION
One Technology Drive
Rogers CT 06263
203/774-9605
Contact Employment Manager. Operates in two business segments: Interconnection Products, and Polymer Products. Interconnection Products include 'MEKTRON' components, a family of products including flexible circuits, keyboards, bus bars, and microwave circuits used for transmitting, distributing, and controlling electrical signals in electronic equipment and data entry in digital devices; 'DUROID' and 'R/FLEX' circuit materials are either fiber-reinforced polymer structures or resin-coated films and composites designed for use in microwave devices and digital equipment. Polymer Products include 'ENDUR' elastomer parts and assemblies which are principally used as components in paper transport systems in office equipment; 'NITROPHYL' floats for liquid level sensing in automotive carburetors and fuel tanks; 'ENVEX' high-performance parts of reinforced PTFE and polymide materials used in bearings, bushings, and other high-temperature applications; 'RT/DUROID' ablative radomes for hypersonic missiles;

Molding Materials, which are fiber-reinforced thermosetting engineered plastics used in electronics, automotive, electrical, and printing industries; and 'PORON' high-density microcellular polyurethane and breathable polyvinyl products for industrial and footwear applications. Founded in 1832; now employs 2800 people in 15 plants in five states and three foreign countries. Serves international markets, principally in Western Europe and Japan, through its subsidiaries and licensees. Corporate headquarters location. American Stock Exchange. Common positions include: R&D Engineer: BS, MS, or PhD in chemical engineering, materials, or related areas to conduct experimental work on polymer-based composite materials, products, and process development and improvement; Manufacturing and Process Engineer: BS in chemical or mechanical engineering to provide support through trouble-shooting, quality assurance, process development and improvement; Sales Specialist: BS in electrical or mechanical engineering for technical sales openings nationwide, solving customers' design or application problems; Division Controller: BS, BA or MBA, responsible for cost accounting, systems, and related business operating analysis and problem-solving; Internal Auditor: BS or BA, responsible for financial and operational audits and recommendations for improvement.

SEALECTRO CORPORATION
585 East Main Street
New Britain CT 06051
203/223-2700
Contact Linda Heisler, Personnel Supervisor. Engaged in the manufacture of cable assemblies and coaxial connectors. Common positions include: Blue-Collar Worker Supervisor; Buyer; Claim Representative; Electrical Engineer; Industrial Engineer; Mechanical Engineer; Department Manager; Operations/Production Manager; Quality Control Supervisor. Principal educational backgrounds sought: Engineering. Company benefits include: medical, dental, and life insurance; tuition assistance; disability coverage; profit sharing. Corporate headquarters location: Trumbull, CT. Operations at this facility include: manufacturing.

THE SUPERIOR ELECTRIC COMPANY
383 Middle Street
Bristol CT 06010
203/582-9561
Contact Mark Roseman, Personnel Manager. Manufactures electronic and electrical control equipment, incremental motion devices, including voltage regulators and voltage conditioning equipment, and synchronous/stepping motors. International. Corporate headquarters location. Operations include: manufacturing. Common positions include: Electrical Engineer; Mechanical Engineer. Principal educational background sought: Engineering. Company benefits include: medical insurance; dental insurance; pension plan; life insurance; tuition assistance; disability coverage; savings plan.

New Jersey

ALPHA METALS, INC.
600 Route 440
Jersey City NJ 07304
201/434-6778
Contact Employment Manager. Manufactures specialized alloys, chemicals, and instrumentation for soldering applications for electronics OEM's throughout the world. Consumer division manufactures solders for plumbing and hobbyists. Operations located in Chicago and Atlanta, and international facilities in England, Italy, France, Germany, Hong Kong, and U.S. (NJ). Corporate headquarters location, also houses research and development activities.

ALPHA WIRE CORPORATION
711 Lidgerwood Avenue
Elizabeth NJ 07207
201/925-8000

Contact Human Resources Department. An international manufacturer and distributor of high technology/reliability wire, cable, tubing, and connector products. Products include: communication and control cables, shrinkable and non-shrinkable tubing and insulation, instrumentation cables, flat cable and connectors, coaxial and data cables, plenum cable, hook-up wire, as well as many others used for both electrical and electronic equipment and installations. Products are sold to a network of distributors and OEM's, primarily in the aerospace, communications, and computer manufacturing industries. Common positions include: Accountant; Administrator; Blue-Collar Worker Supervisor; Buyer; Computer Programmer; Credit Manager; Customer Service Representative; Draftsperson; Industrial Engineer; Financial Analyst; Department Manager; General Manager; Management Trainee; Operations/Production Manager; Marketing Specialist; Personnel & Labor Relations Specialist; Purchasing Agent; Quality Control Supervisor; Sales Representative; Systems Analyst. Principal educational backgrounds sought: Accounting; Business Administration; Communications; Computer Science; Engineering; Finance; Liberal Arts; Marketing; Mathematics. Training programs offered. Company benefits include: medical, dental, and life insurance; tuition assistance; disability coverage; employee discounts; savings plan; 401 K. Corporate headquarters location. Operations at this facility include: manufacturing; research/development; administration; service; sales.

ASEA, BROWN, BOVERI, INC.
1460 Livingston Avenue
North Brunswick NJ 08902
201/932-6000
Contact Personnel Assistant. Produces a broad range of industrial electric power equipment and related products. A subsidiary of BBC Brown, Boveri & Company, LTD. (Baden, Switzerland), a major international manufacturer of industrial products, including power generation products, power distribution apparati and systems, information and telecommunications products, power electronics products, traction drive products, and turbocharger products for ships, commerical vehicles, and trucks. Second area facility in Manhattan.

CHECKPOINT SYSTEMS, INC.
550 Grove Road
P.O. Box 188
Thorefare NJ 08086
609/848-1800
Contact Joanne Nacucchio, Manager of Personnel. A manufacturer of article-surveillance systems.

THE DEWEY ELECTRONICS CORP.
27 Muller Road
Oakland NJ 07436
201/337-4700
Contact Personnel Manager. A systems-oriented civilian and military electronics development, design, engineering, and manufacturing firm. Operations include: manufacturing; research/development; administration; sales. Common positions include: Buyer; Draftsperson; Electrical Engineer; Industrial Engineer; Mechanical Engineer; Quality Control Supervisor. Principal educational background sought: Engineering. Company benefits include: medical insurance; pension plan; life insurance; tuition assistance; disability coverage. Equal opportunity employer. Corporate headquarters location.

DIALIGHT CORPORATION
1913 Atlantic Avenue
Manasquan NJ 08736
201/223-9400
Contact Patricia O'Neill, Personnel Manager. A division of North American Philips Corporation, a multi-market company ranking in the top 150 on the 'Fortune 500' list, with operations in consumer products and services, electrical/electronic components, and professional equipment. Dialight manufactures, develops/researches, and markets electronic components. Although Dialight is still noted for its indicator lights, newer

products have been introduced to meet the needs of the aerospace and computer industries, medical electronics, the military, industrial controls, telecommunications, and consumers. Common positions include: Accountant; Administrator; Advertising Worker; Blue-Collar Worker Supervisor; Buyer; Computer Programmer; Credit Manager; Customer Service Representative; Draftsperson; Chemical Engineer; Electrical Engineer; Industrial Engineer; Mechanical Engineer; Financial Analyst; Industrial Designer; Operations/Production Manager; Marketing Specialist; Personnel & Labor Relations Specialist; Programmer; Quality Control Supervisor; Sales Representative; Systems Analyst. Principal educational backgrounds sought: Accounting; Business Administration; Engineering; Finance; Liberal Arts; Marketing. Company benefits include: medical insurance; dental insurance; pension plan; life insurance; tuition assistance; disability coverage; employee discounts; savings plan; credit union; family survivors.

EG & G INSTRUMENTS
375 Phillips Boulevard
Trenton NJ 08618
609/530-1000
Contact Warren Davis, Manager. Manufacturer of a variety electronic instruments for scientific use. Common postions include: Chemist; Electrical Engineer. Company benefits include: medical, dental, and life insurance; pension plan; tuition assistance; disability coverage; savings plan. Corporate headquarters location: Wellesley, MA. Parent company: EGG. Operations at this facility include: research/development; administration; service; sales. New York Stock Exchange.

ESC ELECTRONICS CORP.
534 Bergen Boulevard
Palisades Park NJ 07650
201/947-0400
Contact Personnel Manager. An electronics manufacturer and distributor whose products include filters and specialty transformers. Sales offices throughout the U.S. Corporate headquarters location.

ELECTRO-SCAN INC.
P.O. Box 368
Garfield NJ 07026-0368
201/478-6800
Contact Judy Bowen, Personnel Department. Produces electronic scanning products, including electron guns and stems. Headquarters location.

ELECTRONIC ASSOCIATES, INC.
185 Monmouth Parkway
West Long Branch NJ 07764
908/229-1100
Contact Manager, Human Resources. EAI is engaged in three service businesses, serving users and producers of electronic products and systems. In Contract Manufacturing, EAI provides manufacturing services for products designed and marketed by customers. In Field Service, the company offers independent maintenance of electronic equipment. In Product Engineering, EAI provides SIMSTAR and VISIDAQ products plus design and engineering services to private industry and government agencies. Common positions include: Accountant; Administrator; Blue-Collar Worker Supervisor; Buyer; Computer Programmer; Aerospace Engineer; Electrical Engineer; Industrial Engineer; Department Manager; Operations/Production Manager; Personnel and Labor Relations Specialist; Sales Representative; Systems Analyst. Principal educational backgrounds sought: Accounting; Business Administration; Computer Science; Engineering. Company benefits include: medical, dental, and life insurance; tuition assistance; disability coverage; employee discounts; 401K plan. Corporate headquarters location. Operations at this facility include: divisional headquarters; manufacturing; administration; service; sales. New York Stock Exchange.

ELECTRONIC MEASUREMENTS INC.
405 Essex Road
Neptune NJ 07753
201/922-9300
Contact Mary Ann Schulz, Personnel Manager. Manufacturer of DC power supplies. Corporate headquarters location. Operations include: manufacturing; research/development; administration; sales. Common positions include: Administrator; Blue-Collar Worker Supervisor; Buyer; Draftperson; Electrical Engineer; Industrial Engineer; Purchasing Agent. Principal educational backgrounds sought: Business Administration; Engineering. Company benefits include: medical insurance; dental insurance; Matching 401(K)plan; life insurance; tuition assistance; savings plan; vision insurance.

FORMATION, INC.
121 Wittendale
Morristown NJ 08057
609/234-5020
Contact Kathy Hellyer, Administrator of Human Resources. Designs, produces, markets, installs, and services electronic data processing equipment. Develops high-volume manufacturing of turnkey systems for the small-to-moderate-sized business marketplace. Also develops software product for manufacturing operations and provides support for these operations. International. Operations include: manufacturing; research/development; administration; service; and sales. Corporate headquarters location. Common positions include: Electrical Engineer (Digital/Computer); Systems Analyst. Principal educational backgrounds sought: Computer Science; Engineering (Electrical/Computer). Company benefits include: medical insurance; dental insurance; life insurance; tuition assistance; disability coverage; profit sharing; 401K plan; employee stock ownership.

GIORDANO ASSOCIATES INC.
5 Century Drive
Parsippany NJ 07054
201/292-0079
Contact Personnel Director. Bonnie Heinvelman can be contacted at 21 White Deer Plaza, Sparta NJ 07871. 201/729-5888. Produces computer-controlled electronic test systems for varied applications. Headquarters location. Common positions include: Aerospace Engineer; Electrical Engineer. Principal educational backgrounds sought: Computer Science; Electrical Engineering. Company benefits include: medical insurance; dental insurance; pension plan; life insurance; tuition assistance; disability coverage.

GOULD INC.
405 Murryhill Parkway
East Rutherford NJ 07073
201/935-1717
Contact Barbara Meyer, Office Manager. Region sales offices for a major integrated manufacturer and developer of electronic, electrical, battery, and industrial products. Worldwide, company operates nearly 100 plants in more than 25 states, and more than 30 other plants in 13 foreign countries. Corporate headquarters location: Rolling Meadows, IL. New York Stock Exchange. International.

HEINEMANN ELECTRIC COMPANY
P.O. Box 6800
Lawrenceville NJ 08648-0800
609/882-4800
Contact Dennis Richardson, Human Resources Manager. A manufacturer of circuit breakers and circuit protection devices, 'Time Delay' and 'Solid State' relays. Operations include: manufacturing. Common positions include: Accountant; Administrator; Blue-Collar Worker Supervisor; Buyer; Computer Operator; Customer Service Representative; Draftsperson; Electrical Engineer; Industrial Engineer; Manufacturing Engineer; Department Manager; Quality Control Supervisor; Sales Representative. Principal educational backgrounds sought: Business Administration; Computer Science; Engineering; Marketing. Company benefits include: medical insurance; dental insurance;

pension plan; life insurance; tuition assistance; disability coverage; profit sharing. Corporate headquarters location. Operations at this facility include: manufacturing; adminstration; sales.

JOHANSON MANUFACTURING CORPORATION
Rockaway Valley Road
Boonton NJ 07005
201/334-2676
Contact Personnel Director. A world leader in the design and manufacture of variable capacitors, sold to a wide range of OEM's in the electronics manufacturing, aerospace, defense, and other markets. Products include air dielectric variable capacitors; several proprietary capacitor products; microwave tuning elements; microwave diode holders; variable ceramic capacitors; tuning tools, taps, and hardware; and prototyping kits. Corporate headquarters location. Common positions include: Electronic Technician; Electrical Engineer.

McBEE SYSTEMS
299 Cherry Hill Road
Parsippany NJ 07054
201/263-3225
Contact Personnel Office. Produces 'one-write' bookkeeping systems designed to save accounting time. Parent company, Litton Industries, is a major electronics company serving worldwide markets with high-technology products and services designed for commercial, industrial, and defense-related applications. More than 14,000 Litton scientists, engineers, and technicians work to provide for defense markets, to produce sophisticated industrial automation systems, and to provide seismic exploration services and products.

MITA COPYSTAR AMERICA
777 Terrace Avenue
Hasbrouck Heights NJ 07604
201/288-6900
Contact Carl Hyszczak, Vice-President/Personnel. Imports and distributes a large line of copier machines and related supplies. Second regional facility in Clifton, NJ.

MONROE SYSTEMS FOR BUSINESS INC.
The American Road
Morris Plains NJ 07950
201/993-2510
Contact Maureen Morse, Assistant Manager of Employee Relations. Manufactures and markets a wide range of large- and small-scale electronic calculators, programmable calculators, electronic accounting machines, microcomputers, and copy machines. Products are used in a wide range of business, governmental, medical, and educational applications. International operations reach 70 countries, with facilities in Venezuela, Puerto Rico, Hong Kong, and Zurich. Products are sold through more than 250 company-owned branches in the United States and Canada. Common positions include: Accountant; Administrator; Advertising Worker; Attorney; Computer Programmer; Credit Manager; Customer Service Representative; Draftsperson; Economist; Mechanical Engineer; Financial Analyst; Branch Manager; Department Manager; General Manager; Personnel & Labor Relations Specialist; Purchasing Agent; Quality Control Supervisor; Sales Representative; Systems Analyst. Principal educational backgrounds sought: Accounting; Business Administration; Communications; Economics; Engineering; Finance; Liberal Arts; Marketing. Company benefits include: medical, dental, and life insurance; pension plan; tuition assistance; disability coverage. Corporate headquarters location. Operations at this facility include: regional headquarters; divisional headquarters location; administration.

OLIVETTI CORPORATION OF AMERICA
765 U.S. Highway 202
Bridgewater NJ 08807
201/526-8200
Contact Director of Personnel. Part of an international corporation which manufactures and distributes a broad line of electronic office products, including typewriters, calculators,

word processors, cash registers, copiers, personal and small computers, business computers, complete data-processing systems, teleprinters, video terminals, telephone-switching systems, minicomputers, automatic tellers, and associated equipment. Parent corporation is an Italian-based firm. United States corporate headquarters location.

PANASONIC INDUSTRIAL COMPANY
2 Panasonic Way, 7C-5
Secaucus NJ 07094
201/348-7000
Contact Howard Arden, Senior Recruiter. Several area locations. One of the world's largest manufacturers of consumer electronic equipment and components. Company produces 'Panasonic' radios, TV's, video tape products, audio tape recorders, tape decks, portable cameras for videotape recording, VCR's, and components such as speakers, audio accessories, circuit components, home appliances, push-button telephones, broadcasting equipment, CATV systems, electric motors for industrial products and lighting equipment, and batteries. Corporate headquarters location. International. Common positions include: Accountant; Electrical Engineer; Marketing Specialist; Sales Representative. Educational backgrounds sought: Accounting; Engineering; Marketing. Company benefits include: medical, dental, and life insurance; pension plan; tuition assistance; disability coverage; profit sharing; employee discounts; savings plan. Corporate headquarters location. Parent company: Mutshushita Electronics Inc. Operations at this facility include: regional headquarters; divisional headquarters; research/development; service; sales. New York Stock Exchange.

PLESSEY DYNAMICS CORPORATION
110 Algonquin Parkway
Whippany NJ 07981
201/428-9898
Contact John Culish, Personnel Manager. Manufactures electronics equipment for aviation users. Corporate headquarters location.

SIEMENS CORPORATION
186 Wood Avenue South
Iselin NJ 08830
201/321-3400
Contact Personnel Office. United States distribution headquarters for one of the world's leading companies in the electrical and electronics industry. Operates internationally through the following groups: Power Engineering and Automation; Electrical Installations; Communications; Medical Engineering; Data Systems; and Components. Company's manufacturing and sales organization is well established in more than 100 countries. Corporate headquarters location (Siemens AG): Munich, West Germany. International.

SONY CORPORATION OF AMERICA
Sony Drive
Park Ridge NJ 07656
201/930-1000
Contact Human Resources Department. Several area branches, including Paramus, Moonachie, and Teaneck, NJ; and New York, NY. United States headquarters for the international electronics manufacturer. Products are classified into eight divisions; Consumer Display Products; Consumer Video Products; Consumer Audio Products; Consumer Sales; Video Communication Products Division; Information Products; and Professional Audio Products. Its operating structure includes three marketing companies: Sony Broadcast Products; Sony Magnetic Products Company; and Sony Service Company. The company's manufacturing, distribution, and sales operations are conducted throughout the world. Parent company is based in Tokyo, Japan. Corporate headquarters location. International. New York Stock Exchange.

SYMTRON SYSTEMS, INC.
17-01 Pollitt Drive
Fair Lawn NJ 07410
201/794-0200

Contact Janet Sondak, Personnel Manager. Designs, develops, manufactures, and installs large-scale electro-mechanical training devices for military and commercial markets. Common positions include: Accountant; Administrator; Blue-Collar Worker Supervisor; Buyer; Draftsperson; Electrical Engineer; Industrial Engineer; Mechanical Engineer; Department Manager; Operations/Production Manager; Purchasing Agent; Quality Control Supervisor; Sales Representative; Technical Writer/Editor; Program Manager. Principal educational backgrounds sought: Accounting; Engineering. Company benefits include: medical, dental, and life insurance; pension plan; tuition assistance; disability coverage; savings plan. Corporate headquarters location. Operations at this facility include: manufacturing; research/development; administration; service; sales.

TRW/CUSTOMER SERVICE DIVISION
15 Law Drive
Fairfield NJ 07006
201/575-7110
Contact Personnel Director. Provides nationwide maintenance service for electronic equipment. Parent company, TRW, is a diversifed technology firm with operations in electronics and space systems, car and truck equipment for both original equipment manufacturers and the replacement market, and a wide variety of industrial and energy components, including aircraft parts, welding systems, and electromechanical assemblies. New York Stock Exchange. Corporate headquarters location: Cleveland, OH.

THERMO ELECTRIC COMPANY INC.
109 North Fifth Street
Saddle Brook NJ 07662
201/843-5800
Contact Joanne Corroccio, Personnel Director. A fully-integrated leader in the temperature control industry. Company's diverse products are designed to measure, control, and connect temperature control systems. Company's three major product lines -- sensors, instruments, and connectors (wire and cable) -- are sold to customers in the petrochemical, metals, processing, aircraft and aerospace, transport, power, engineering contracting and architecture, government, and military industries. Facilities in Canada and The Netherlands. Common positions include: Accountant; Blue-Collar Worker Supervisor; Buyer; Draftsperson; Ceramics Engineer; Electrical Engineer; Industrial Engineer; Mechanical Engineer; Metallurgical Engineer; Industrial Designer; Marketing Specialist; Personnel & Labor Relations Specialist; Sales Representative; Systems Analyst. Principal educational background sought: Accounting; Business Administration; Computer Science; Engineering; Finance; Marketing. Company benefits include: medical, dental, and life insurance; pension plan; tuition assistance; savings plan. Corporate headquarters location. Operations at this facility include: manufacturing; research/development; administration; service; sales.

THOMAS & BETTS CORPORATION
36 Butler Street
Elizabeth NJ 07207
201/351-8800
Contact Jon Schierer, Personnel Director. A designer, manufacturer, and marketer of electrical and electronic components and related systems. Components and systems include connectors, terminals, fittings, application tools, cable ties, flat cables, and wire makers. Products are sold through distributors to the construction, maintenance and repair, electronic and electrical equipment, electric utility, transportation, and telecommunications industries. Corporate headquarters location: Raritan, NJ. International.

TIMEPLEX INC.
400 Chestnut Ridge Road
Woodcliff Lake NJ 07675
201/391-1111
Contact Human Resources. Several area locations, including Rochelle Park and Hackensack. Engaged in the design, manufacture, sale, and servicing of communications networking systems and equipment, and is the world's leading producer and distributor of high performance T-1 and T-3 networking systems, FDDI, Ethernet and token ring

LAN/WAN and LAN/WAN connectivity packet switching and network management systems. Company's products are used to increase the capacity and efficiency of communications facilities by employing advanced, high-speed, real time data processing techniques to collect and combine digital voice, image and data for transmission at high speeds over communications circuits. They also provide network management, statistical and diagnostic information, supervisory capabilities for users. Corporate headquarters location: Woodcliff Lake, NJ. Field Service location: Clearwater, Fl. International. Sales Offices: Langley England, Brussels, Hong Kong, Sydney, and Toronto. Common positions include: Electrical Engineer; Branch Manager; Marketing Specialist. Principal educational backgrounds sought: Communications; Computer Science; Engineering. Training programs offered. Company benefits include: medical, dental, and life insurance; tuition assistance; disability coverage; savings plan. Corporate headquarters location. Parent company: Unisys. Operations at this facility include: divisional headquarters; research/development; administration; sales.

TRIUMPH-ADLER-ROYAL, INC.
P.O. Box 1038
200 Sheffield Street
Mountainside NJ 07092
908/526-8200
Contact Mary Kay Carter, Personnel Administrator. A wholly owned subsidiary of Triumph Adler AG of West Germany. The company distributes and services typewriters, word processors and other office equipment in the US. It also manufactures supplies. Company sales are approximately $200 million. Common positions include: Accountant; Administrator; Advertising Worker; Computer Programmer; Credit Manager; Customer Service Representative; Financial Analyst; Department Manager; Marketing Specialist; Personnel & Labor Relations Specialist; Sales Representative; Systems Analyst. Principal educational backgrounds sought: Accounting; Business Administration; Computer Science; Finance; Marketing. Company benefits include: medical, dental and life insurance; tuition assistance, disability coverage; savings plan; 401K pension and savings. Parent Company: Olivetti. Corporate, regional and divisional headquarters location. Operations at this facility include: administration; service; sales.

U.S. JVC CORPORATION
41 Slatter Drive
Elmwood Park NJ 07407
201/794-3900
Contact Steve Matsuzaki, Personnel Manager. Distributes a wide range of consumer audio and video products.

ENGINEERING AND ARCHITECTURE

For more information on professional opportunities in the engineering and architectural industries, contact the following professional and trade organizations, as listed beginning on page 449:

AMERICAN INSTITUTE OF ARCHITECTS
AMERICAN SOCIETY FOR ENGINEERING EDUCATION
AMERICAN SOCIETY OF CIVIL ENGINEERS
AMERICAN SOCIETY OF HEATING, REFRIGERATING
        AND AIR CONDITIONING ENGINEERS
AMERICAN SOCIETY OF LANDSCAPE ARCHITECTS
AMERICAN SOCIETY OF NAVAL ENGINEERS
AMERICAN SOCIETY OF PLUMBING ENGINEERS
AMERICAN SOCIETY SAFETY ENGINEERS
ILLUMINATING ENGINEERING SOCIETY OF NORTH AMERICA
INSTITUTE OF INDUSTRIAL ENGINEERS
NATIONAL ACADEMY OF ENGINEERING
NATIONAL SOCIETY OF PROFESSIONAL ENGINEERS

SOCIETY OF FIRE PROTECTION ENGINEERS
UNITED ENGINEERING TRUSTEES

New York

BIENSTOCK, LUCCHESI & ASSOCIATES, P.C.
134 Broadway
Amityville NY 11701
516/691-2020
Contact Frank M. Russo, Associate Personnel Manager. Regional offices located in Parsippany, NJ; and Wallingford, CT. Top ten Long Island consulting engineers specializing in sanitary, water, electrical, mechanical, and architectural consulting. Common positions include: Architect; Draftsperson; Civil Engineer; Electrical Engineer; Mechanical Engineer. Principal educational backgrounds sought: Chemistry; Engineering. Internships offered. Company benefits include: medical, dental, and life insurance; tuition assistance. Corporate headquarters location. Operations at this facility include: regional headquarters.

PARSONS BRINCKERHOFF INC.
One Penn Plaza
New York NY 10019
212/465-5000
Contact Ed Swartz, Recruiter of Personnel. Provides total engineering and construction management services from project conception through completion, through a worldwide staff of more than 1400 professionals and support personnel. Services include the development of major bridges, tunnels, highways, marine facilities, buildings, industrial complexes, and railroads. Numerous domestic and international subsidiaries include: Parsons Brinckerhoff Quade & Douglas; Parsons Brinckerhoff Development Corporation; Parsons Brinckerhoff Construction Services; Parsons Brinckerhoff International; and others. United States offices are in 21 other locations. Corporate headquarters location. International.

New Jersey

EMR PHOTOELECTRIC/SCHLUMBERGER
20 Wallace Road
Princeton Junction NJ 08550
609/799-1000
Contact Rebecca Millard, Personnel Manager. A research, development, and manufacturing facility for Schlumberger, Ltd.; engaged in engineering and manufacturing of critical, high-reliability transducers and transducer systems: nuclear sources and detectors for oilfield services, and sensors/transducers for high-value measurement and control. Corporate, divisional headquarters. Operations include: manufacturing; research/development; administration. Common positions include: Accountant; Administrator; Buyer; Chemist; Computer Programmer; Draftsperson; Engineer; Ceramics Engineer; Electrical Engineer; Mechanical Engineer; Manager; Department Manager; General Manager; Operations/Production Manager; Marketing Specialist; Personnel & Labor Relations Specialist; Physicist; Purchasing Agent; Quality Control Supervisor; Systems Analyst; Quality Engineer; Manufacturing Engineer; Production Supervisor; Materials Manager; Inventory/Production Control Specialist. Principal educational backgrounds sought: Accounting; Business Administration; Chemistry; Computer Science; Engineering; Finance; Liberal Arts; Physics. Company benefits include: medical insurance; dental insurance; pension plan; life insurance; tuition assistance; disability coverage; profit sharing; employee discounts; savings plan; paid vacation; paid holidays; sick days.

EDWARDS AND KELCEY ORGANIZATION
70 South Orange Avenue
Livingston NJ 07039
201/994-4520

Contact George Steidle, V.P. - Human Resources. A consulting engineering and planning organization whose range of services includes location and economic feasibility studies, valuations and appraisals, cost analyses, computer technology, marketing studies, traffic and transportation studies, soils and foundation analyses, environmental impact studies, master planning, structural surveys, preliminary and final designs, and preparation of contract documents and observation of construction operations for the public transit systems, terminals, railroads, stations, bus depots, parking garages, airports, ports, highways, streets, bridges, tunnels, traffic control systems, military facilities, communications systems, storm and sanitary sewers, water supply and distribution, flood control, and land development. Regional offices located in New York City, Boston, Minneapolis, and Anaheim, CA. Common positions include: Accountant; Architect; Biologist; Draftsperson; Civil Engineer; Electrical Engineer; Forester; Geographer; Geologist; Technical Writer; Writer; Transportation & Traffic Specialist; Traffic & Transportation Engineer. Principal educational backgrounds sought: Accounting; Biology; Communications; Engineering; Finance; Geology; Marketing; Mathematics. Company benefits include: medical, dental, and life insurance; pension plan; tuition assistance; disability coverage; profit sharing; savings plan. Corporate headquarters location. Operations at this facility include: service.

FACTORY MUTUAL ENGINEERING AND RESEARCH
30 Vreeland Road, Suite 60
Florham Park NJ 07932
Contact Personnel Department. A loss-prevention service. Services include the inspection of properties to help pinpoint hazards or conditions that could cause fires or explosions and result in damage to property and lost production. Corporate headquarters location: Norwood, MA.

KILLAM ASSOCIATES
P.O. Box 1008
27 Bleeker Street
Millburn NJ 07041
201/379-3400
Contact Cheryl Wilkinson, Personnel Coordinator. Over the years, Killam has greatly expanded its technical capabilities, and currently provides consulting services in the following areas: Wastewater Management, Water Supply Management, Stormwater Management, Industrial Waste Management, Solid Waste Management, Hazardous Waste Management, Environmental Site Assessments, Groundwater/UST Management, Air Quality/Asbestos Management, Wetlands & Coastal Management, Site Development Engineering, Municipal Engineering, Construction Services, Infrastructure Evaluation, Mining Services, and Operations & Maintenance. Corporation founded in 1937 and currently employs 400. Operations are headquartered in Millburn, NJ. Branch locations in Randolph, NJ; Whitehouse, NJ; Freehold, NJ; Cape May Court House, NJ; Trevose, PA; Warredale, PA, Somerset, PA; Dublin, OH; and Indiana, PA. Common positions include: Chemist; Draftsperson; Civil Engineer; Geologist; Branch Manager; Environment Scientist; Environmental Engineer. Principal educational backgrounds sought: Geology; Civil/Environmental Engineering. Company benefits include: medical, dental, and life insurance; pension plan; tuition assistance; disability coverage; profit sharing; savings plan. Corporate headquarters location.

MORETRENCH AMERICAN CORPORATION
P.O. Box 316
Rockaway NJ 07866
201/627-2100
Contact Personnel Manager. A nationwide engineering/contracting firm specializing in groundwater control & hazardous waste removal. Operations include: manufacturing; administration; service; sales. Corporate headquarters location. Common positions include: Accountant; Draftsperson; Civil Engineer; Geologist; Personnel & Labor Relations Specialist; Purchasing Agent; Sales Representative. Principal educational backgrounds sought: Civil Engineering. Company benefits include: medical insurance; pension plan; life insurance; tuition assistance; disability coverage; profit sharing.

SCHAEVITZ ENGINEERING
7905 North Route 130
Pennsauken NJ 08110-1489
609/662-8000
Contact Patricia Cannon, Personnel. Firm involved in the design, application, and manufacture of transducer-based measurement and control systems and devices. Customers are those requiring transducers for the measurement of displacement, position, dimension, pressure, force, weight, angle, level, acceleration, velocity, or other physical parameters. Operations include: manufacturing; sales. Corporate headquarters location. Common positions include: Accountant; Buyer; Computer Programmer; Customer Service Representative; Draftsperson; Aerospace Engineer; Electrical Engineer; Industrial Engineer; Mechanical Engineer; Marketing Specialist; Personnel & Labor Relations Specialist; Purchasing Agent; Quality Control Supervisor; Technical Writer/Editor; Design Engineer; Application Engineer. Principal educational backgrounds sought: Accounting; Engineering; Mathematics; Physics. Company benefits include: medical insurance; pension plan; life insurance; tuition assistance; disability coverage.

FABRICATED METAL PRODUCTS/PRIMARY METALS

For more information on professional opportunities in the fabricated and primary metals industries, contact the following professional and trade organizations, as listed beginning on page 449:

AMERICAN CASTE METALS ASSOCIATION
AMERICAN POWDER METALLURGY INSTITUTE
ASSOCIATION OF IRON AND STEEL ENGINEERS
MASTERS ASOCIATION OF METAL FINISHERS
NATIONAL ASSOCIATION OF METAL FINISHERS

New York

AT&T NASSAU METALS CORPORATION
286 Richmond Valley Road
Staten Island NY 10307
718/317-4400
Contact Mrs. Gail Todd, Personnel Administration. A recycling firm specializing in precious metals recovery. Operations at this facility include: manufacturing. Corporate headquarters location: Gaston, SC. Common positions include: Accountant; Administrator; Blue-Collar Worker Supervisor; Customer Service Representative; Draftsperson; Engineer; Chemical Engineer; Electrical Engineer; Industrial Engineer; Mechanical Engineer; Metallurgical Engineer; General Manager; Operations/Production Manager; Personnel & Labor Relations Specialist; Sales Representative. Principal educational backgrounds sought: Accounting; Business Administration; Chemistry; Engineering. Company benefits include: medical insurance; dental insurance; pension plan; life insurance; tuition assistance; disability coverage; employee discounts; savings plan.

AL TECH SPECIALTY STEEL CORPORATION
Willowbrook Avenue
Dunkirk NY 14048
716/366-1000
Contact Philip J. Kleeberger, Manager, Employment & Training. Manufacturer of specialty steel bar, wire, rod, extrusions. Common positions include: Accountant; Blue-Collar Worker Supervisor; Claim Representative; Computer Programmer; Credit Manager; Customer Service Representative; Civil Engineer; Electrical Engineer; Industrial Engineer; Mechanical Engineer; Metallurgical Engineer; Financial Analyst; Industrial Designer; Department Manager; General Manager; Management Trainee; Operations/Production Manager; Marketing Specialist; Personnel & Labor Relations Specialist; Quality Control Supervisor; Reporter/Editor; Sales Representative; Systems Analyst; Transportation & Traffic Specialist. Principal educational backgrounds sought:

Engineering; Accounting; Business Administration; Computer Science; Finance; Marketing. Training programs offered; Internships offered. Company benefits include: medical insurance; pension plan; life insurance; tuition assistance; disability coverage; profit sharing; employee discounts. Corporate headquarters location. Parent Company: Sammi Steel Co. of South Korea. Operations at this facility include: divisional headquarters; manufacturing; administration; service; and sales.

ASARCO INC.
180 Maiden Lane
New York NY 10038
212/510-2000
Contact Madeline Fotopulos, Supervisor of Employment. One of the world's leading producers of non-ferrous metals, principally silver, copper, lead, and zinc. Operates in industry segments including: primary precious metals, limestone, and coal. Company operates mines in the United States, with subsidiaries in Canada, Australia, South America, Europe, and Asia. In addition to mining and treating ore from its own mines, company is a custom smelter and refiner of nonferrous metal ores mined by others. Company also produces nonmetallic minerals, such as coal and limestone, from United States mines. Company operates in four divisions: Mines; Smelter and Refineries; Specialty Chemicals and Manufacturing; and Associated Companies. Corporate headquarters location. International. New York Stock Exchange. Company benefits include: medical, dental, and life insurance; pension plan; tuition assistance; disability coverage; savings plan; optical plan. Operations at this facility include: administration; sales.

DAYTON T. BROWN INC.
555 Church Street
Bohemia NY 11716
516/589-6300
Contact Bob Single, Director/Personnel & Corporate Service. Engaged in sheet metal fabrication, Engineering and Testing Services, Technical Communications, and job-shopping. Common positions include: Accountant; Administrator; Attorney; Blue-Collar Worker Supervisor; Buyer; Computer Programmer; Credit Manager; Customer Service Representative; Draftsperson; Electrical Engineer; Mechanical Engineerl; Operations/Production Manager; Personnel & Labor Relations Specialist; Purchasing Agent; Technical Writer/Editor. Principal educational backgrounds sought: Accounting; Engineering. Company benefits include: medical, dental, and life insurance; pension plan; tuition assistance; disability coverage; profit sharing; employee discounts. Corporate headquarters location. Operations at this facility include: manufacturing; research/development.

BUILDEX INC.
100 Jericho Quadrangle
Jericho NY 11753
516/938-5544
Contact Susan Reilly, Personnel Director. A diversified manufacturer, operating in two divisions: Fabricated Structural Metal Products, in which company is a leading designer and fabricator of architectural metal work, including curtain wall facades, thermal-break windows, stairways, doors, and innovative aluminum windows and doors for both residential and commercial buildings, as well as pipe support systems and control devices; and Specialty Hardware, in which the company manufactures a wide variety of industrial hardware products, including metal slides and tracks for such diverse applications as closet doors, furniture, electronic cabinetry, hospital curtain systems, and other products such as stainless steel hardware for institutional and refrigeration equipment. Corporate headquarters location. American Stock Exchange.

GENERAL BEARING CORPORATION
304 Route 303
Blauvelt NY 10913
914/358-6000
Contact Sandra Masilotti, Personnel Manager. A manufacturer of ball bearings. Corporate headquarters location. Operations include: manufacturing; sales. Common positions at this

facility include: Accountant; Administrator; Advertising Worker; Computer Programmer; Credit Manager; Customer Service Representative; Draftsperson; Engineer; Industrial Engineer; Mechanical Engineer; General Manager; Management Trainee; Quality Control Supervisor. Company benefits include: medical insurance; dental insurance; life insurance; pension plan; tuition assistance; disability coverage; profit sharing; savings plan.

LABORATORY FURNITURE INC.
174 Glen Cove Road
Carle Place NY 11514
516/484-2027
Contact Charles Mehlich, Personnel Director. Several area locations, including Brooklyn and The Bronx. Manufactures, designs, and installs steel laboratory furniture. A major supplier to large research, chemical, and pharmaceutical companies, hospitals, schools and universities, and other institutional customers. Corporate headquarters location.

MARUBENI AMERICA CORPORATION
200 Park Avenue
New York NY 10166-0199
212/599-3737
Contact Personnel Director. A major international trading firm; a subsidiary of Maruoeni Corporation (Tokyo and Osaka, Japan). Operations conducted through seven groups: Metals and Minerals Group; Machinery Group; Petroleum Group; General Merchandise Group; Chemical & Plastics Group; Textile Group; and Grain, Marine, and Other Products Group. New York and New Jersey operations are involved in all groups, offering a wide range of products. Area subsidiaries include Don Juan Sportswear Inc., and It Fabrics Inc. Common positions include: Attorney; Computer Programmer; Credit Manager; Chemical Engineer; Metallurgical Engineer; Mechanical Engineer; Petroleum Engineer; Department Manager; General Manager; Management Trainee; Marketing Specialist; Personnel & Labor Relations Specialist; Sales Representative. Principal educational backgrounds sought: Business Administration; Engineering; Marketing. Company benefits include: medical, dental and life insurance; pension plan; disability coverage. Corporate headquarters location. Branch offices located in principal cities in the U.S. Parent company has operations in every continent throughout the world. Operations at this facility include: regional headquarters; research/development; administration; service; sales. D & B Stock Exchange.

Connecticut

TELEDYNE ANSONIA
One Riverside Drive
Ansonia CT 06401
203/735-9311
Contact Personnel Department. Produces copper products through three divisions: Screw Machine Products, Plumbing Products, and Solderless Connector Products. Parent company is a high-technology, multi-product corporation consisting of 130 individual companies employing 50,000 people nationwide. Nationally, company operates in four industrial areas: Aviation and Electronics; Machines and Metals; Engines, Energy, and Power; and Commercial and Consumer. Corporate headquarters location: Los Angeles, CA. New York Stock Exchange.

TORRINGTON COMPANY
59 Field Street
Torrington CT 06790
Contact Manager/Professional Recruiting. Firm designs, develops, manufactures, and markets anti-friction bearings. Also produces universal joints and precision metal components and assemblies. Locations throughout the U.S., Germany, Australia, Brazil, Canada, England, and Japan. A subsidiary of Ingersoll-Rand. Common positions include: Accountant; Electrical Engineer; Industrial Engineer; Mechanical Engineer; Metallurgical Engineer. Principal educational backgrounds sought: Accounting; Engineering. Training programs offered. Company benefits include: medical, dental, and life insurance; pension

plan; tuition assistance; disability coverage; savings plan. Corporate headquarters location. Parent company: Ingersoll-Rand. Operations at this facility include: divisional headquarters location; research/development; administration; sales.

New Jersey

ALLIED METGLAS PRODUCTS
6 Eastmans Road
Parsippany NJ 07054
201/581-7550
Contact George Kereke, Manager of Employee Relations. Producer of rapidly solidified metals for the electrical power and metal joining industries. Applications include transformer cores and brazing and soldering alloys. Parent company, Allied Signal Corporation, serves a broad spectrum of industries through its more than 40 strategic businesses, which are grouped into five sectors: Aerospace; Automotive; Chemical; Industrial and Technology; and Oil and Gas. Allied Signal is one of the nation's largest industrial organizations, and has over 115,000 employees in over 30 countries. Common positions include: Ceramics Engineer; Electrical Engineer; Mechanical Engineer. Principal educational backgrounds sought: Engineering; Materials Science/Metallurgy. Company benefits include: medical, dental, and life insurance; pension plan; tuition assistance; disability coverage; savings plan. Corporate headquarters location: Morristown, NJ. Operations at this facility include: manufacturing; research/development; administration; service; sales. New York Stock Exchange.

ARMCO
300 Interpace Parkway
Parsippany NJ 07054
201/316-5200
Contact John Bilich, Director of Human Resources. A leading New Jersey steel company.

ARROW GROUP INDUSTRIES, INC.
Third Avenue
Haskell NJ 07420
201/839-4888
Contact Diane Flynn, Director of Industrial Relations. A sheet metal products manufacturer, producing items such as steel storage buidlings and many other sheet metal products. Second manufacturing facility in Breese, IL. General offices located in Pompton Plains, NJ. Corporate headquarters location. Several area locations.

ATHLONE INDUSTRIES, INC.
200 Webro Road
Parsippany NJ 07054
201/887-9100
Contact Evelyn Corcoran, Office Manager. Primarily a manufacturer and distributor of specialty steels and industrial fasteners. Operations consist of Green River Steel, a major producer of alloy and specialty carbon steel bars and semifinished steel product lines; Jessop Steel, a major producer of specialty metals, primarily stainless steels, tool steels, an nickel alloys; and Reynolds Fasteners, a manufacturer of industrial fasteners and one of the largest distributors of imported industrial fasteners in the United States. Company also manufactures and distributes consumer products. Consumer products group includes Dudley Sports, the largest manufacturer of top-grade softballs in the United States; Gelfo Manufacturing and Sea Fashions of California, producers of women's, children's, and junior swimwear; Henschel Shoe, a manufacturer of hand-sewn and machine sewn casual shoes; and Lee Mar, a manufacturer of women's blouses, shirts, and tops. Corporate headquarters location. International. New York Stock Exchange.

ATLANTIC CHEINCO
William Street
Burlington NJ 08016
609/386-2800

Contact Mr. Massimi, Labor Relations. Manufacturers of a variety of metalware, including waste baskets.

ATLANTIC METAL PRODUCTS, INC.
21 Fadem Road
Springfield NJ 07081
201/379-6200
Contact Cheryl Garcia, Personnel Director. Manufactures a custom sheet metal parts (precision only), serving the computer and office equipment industries. Corporate headquarters location. Second area facility in Hillside.

THE C/S GROUP
55 Winans Avenue
Cranford NJ 07016
201/272-5200
Contact Lee Dirubbo, Jr., Manager, Human Resources. A manufacturer of aluminum architectural products. Principal products include louvers, solar controls, grilles, curtain wall systems, floor mats, railing systems, and raised flooring. Common positions include: Accountant; Computer Programmer; Credit Manager; Draftsperson; Industrial Engineer; Mechanical Engineer; Financial Analyst; Management Trainee; Operations/Production Manager; Personnel & Labor Relations Specialist; Purchasing Agent. Principal educational backgrounds sought: Accounting; Business Administration; Computer Science; Marketing. Company benefits include: medical, dental, and life insurance; tuition assistance; disability coverage; profit sharing; savings plan. Corporate headquarters location. Operations at this facility include: divisional headquarters; manufacturing; research/development; administration; sales. International.

CARPENTER TECHNOLOGY CORPORATION
P.O. Box 1267
West Caldwell NJ 07006
201/227-5400
Contact Charlie Bigelow, Branch Manager. Nationally, company manufactures, fabricates, and markets a wide range of specialty metals for a variety of end-use markets. Produces stainless steels, tool steels, high-temperature and electronic alloys, and other special purpose metals.

DOOLAN STEEL CORPORATION
2 Eves Drive, Suite 220
Marltown NJ 08053
609/988-8100
Contact Pat O'Neil, Personnel. A major South Jersey steel service center.

FEIN CONTAINER CORPORATION
106 Kenney Place
Saddle Brook NJ 07662
201/843-1800
Contact James Barr, Personnel Director. Manufactures a wide range of steel container products. Principal clients include the paint and ink manufacturing industries. Corporate headquarters location. Common positions include: Accountant; Blue-Collar Worker Supervisor; Buyer; Computer Programmer; Customer Service Representative; Electrical Engineer; Purchasing Agent; Sales Representative. Educational backgrounds sought: Accounting; Computer Science; Engineering. Company benefits include: medical insurance; pension plan; life insurance; disability coverage; savings plan; 401k. Corporate headquarters location. Operations at this facility include: manufacturing.

PEERLESS TUBE COMPANY
58 Locust Avenue
Bloomfield NJ 07003
201/743-5100
Contact Bob Miceli, Personnel Director. Second area location in Freehold Township, NJ. Manufactures collapsible metal tubes, plastic tubes, and one-piece extruded aluminum

aerosol containers for the pharmaceutical, drug, cosmetic, toiletries, and household product industries. The company also manufactures and sells extruded aluminum shells for marking pens and aluminum blanks or slugs for other producers of containers, and markets a variety of plastic caps for metal and plastic tubes. The company also operates a wholly-owned subsidiary in Puerto Rico which manufactures collapsible metal tubes. Corporate headquarters location. American Stock Exchange. Common positions include: Blue-Collar Worker Supervisor; Computer Programmer; Engineer; Mechanical Engineer; Quality Control Supervisor; Sales Representative. Company benefits include: medical insurance; pension plan; life insurance; disability coverage. International.

PIONEER INDUSTRIES
401 Washington Avenue
Carlstadt NJ 07072
201/933-1900
Contact Mary Albaugh, Personnel Director. Produces industrial doors, fireproof and theftproof doors, and other sheet metal specialties. A division of Core Industries. Headquarters location.

SCHIAVONE-BONOMO CORPORATION
One Jersey Avenue
Jersey City NJ 07302
201/333-4300
Contact John Doddy, Personnel Office. Several area locations. A metals-recycling firm, engaged primarily in the purchase, sale, and export of scrap metal. Customers include firms throughout the world. In operation for more than 90 years. Corporate headquarters location.

SHELLCAST CORPORATION
201 Sweetland Avenue
Hillside NJ 07205
201/688-4120
Contact Personnel Department. Engaged in the production of shell-molded stainless steel, carbon steel, nickel, monel, and high-alloy steels. A subsidiary of Cooper Alloy Corporation. Corporate headquarters location.

TELEDYNE POWDER ALLOYS
350 Allwood Road
Clifton NJ 07012
201/773-4850
Contact Personnel Director. A major manufacturer of machinable tungsten alloys. Also a leading producer of tungsten products, marketing machinable tungsten alloys under the 'Densalloy' trademark. Parent company, Teledyne, Inc., is a high-technology, multi-product corporation consisting of 130 individual companies employing 50,000 people nationwide. Nationally, company operates in four industrial areas: Aviation and Electronics; Machines and Metals; Engines, Energy, and Power; and Commercial and Consumer. Corporate headquarters location.

FINANCIAL SERVICES/MANAGEMENT CONSULTING

For more information on profesional opportunities in the financial services and management consulting industry, contact the following professional and trade organizations, as listed beginning on page 449:

AMERICAN FINANCIAL SERVICES ASSOCIATION
AMERICAN MANAGEMENT ASSOCIATION
AMERICAN SOCIETY OF APPRAISERS
ASSOCIATION OF MANAGEMENT CONSULTING FIRMS
COUNCIL OF CONSULTANT ORGANIZATIONS
FEDERATION OF TAX ADMINISTRATORS
FINANCIAL ANALYSTS FEDERATION

FINANCIAL EXECUTIVES INSTITUTE
INSTITUTE OF FINANCIAL EDUCATION
NATIONAL ASSOCIATION OF CREDIT MANAGEMENT
NATIONAL ASSOCIATION OF REAL ESTATE INVESTMENT TRUSTS
NATIONAL CORPORATE CASH MANAGEMENT ASSOCIATION
NEW YORK CREDIT AND FINANCIAL MANAGEMENT ASSOCIATION
SECURITIES INDUSTRY ASSOCIATION

New York

AMERICAN EXPRESS TRAVEL RELATED SERVICES
American Express Tower
World Financial Center
New York NY 10285
212/640-2000
Contact Director of Personnel. A travel, financial and communications product and service company.

AMERICAN MANAGEMENT ASSOCIATION
135 West 50th Street
New York NY 10020
212/903-8018
Contact George B. Harmon, Director, Human Resources & Development. An international educational organization -- membership based and not for profit -- dedicated to broadening the management knowledge and skills of people, and, by doing so, strengthening their organizations. Company's educational programs, products, services serve international management needs through meetings, practical instruction provided by other practicing managers, books, video and audio cassettes, periodicals, and special reports. Corporate headquarters location. International. Common positions include: Administrator; Advertising - copywriters; Commercial Artist; Computer Programmer; Customer Service Representative; Manager; Marketing Specialist; Personnel Specialist; Editorial Assistant; Publishing; Public Relations; Purchasing Agent; Reporter/Editor; Sales Representative; Systems Analyst; Market Researcher; Seminar Leader; Program Assistant; Direct Mail Specialist. Principal educational backgrounds sought: Business Administration; Communications; Computer Science; Liberal Arts; Marketing; Organizational Development; Human Resources/Personnel Administration. Company benefits include: medical, dental, and life insurance; pension plan; tuition assistance; disability coverage; employee discounts; savings plan; tax shelter annuity; gratis attendance at company seminars. Operations at this facility include: research/development; administration; service; sales.

AMERICAN STOCK EXCHANGE
86 Trinity Place
New York NY 10006
212/306-1210
Contact Janice Marcketta, Employment Manager. The nation's second largest stock exchange, providing a market for stocks and bonds of generally mid-range growth companies. Conducts trading in a wide range of securities, including common stocks, preferred stocks, warrants, put and call options, corporate bonds, and U.S. Government and government agency securities. Founded in 1849 as the New York Curb Exchange; moving inside in 1921; and adopting its present name in 1953. Corporate headquarters location. Common positions include: Accountant; Attorney; Administrative Assistant; Engineer; Mechanical Engineer; Financial Analyst; Operations Manager; Marketing Specialist; Personnel & Labor Relations Specialist; Public Relations Worker; Secretary; Sales Representative; Systems Analyst; Trading Analyst. Principal educational backgrounds sought: Accounting; Art/Design; Business Administration; Communications; Economics; Finance; Liberal Arts; Marketing. Company benefits include: medical, dental, and life insurance; pension plan; tuition assistance; disability coverage; savings plan

BEAR STEARNS & COMPANY, INC.
245 Park Avenue, 13th Floor
New York NY 10167
212/272-2000
Contact Steven Lacoff, Managing Director. A leading investment banking and brokerage firm, headquartered in New York City. Company is engaged in corporate finance and mergers and acquisitions, institutional equities and fixed income sales and trading, individual investor services, asset management and correspondent clearing. Also have a large operational facility located in Manhattan. Subsidiary is Custodial Trust Company, which is engaged in securities lending and custody services. Employs approximately 5,000 in 13 offices worldwide. Common positions include: Accountant; Computer Programmer; Management Trainee. Principal educational background sought: Accounting; Business Administration. Company benefits include: medical, dental, and life insurance; pension plan; tuition assistance; disability coverage; profit sharing; 401K. New York Stock Exchange.

BOOZ-ALLEN & HAMILTON INC.
101 Park Avenue
New York NY 10178.
Contact Michael Massey, Director, Executive Recruiting. A diversified, international management consulting organization, offering services in both the commercial and public sectors. Areas of expertise include technology, strategy and planning, and other areas such as social research and many other technical fields. Specific services include: corporate strategy and long-range planning, organization design, human resources management, financial management and control, acquisitions and divestiture, information systems and automation, manufacturing and inventory and distribution control, qualitative and quantitative market research, attitudinal and demographic trend research, marketing strategy and positioning, venture management, transportation and environmental systems, technology research, new products and process development, government programs, and regulatory compliance. Staff includes 185 partners and 1,600 professionals nationally. Operates 15 regional offices in the United States, eight in Europe, North Africa, and Latin America, all offering a full range of services. Corporate headquarters location. Common positions include: Consultant. Principal educational backgrounds sought: Business Administration; Computer Science; Economics; Engineering; Finance; Marketing. Training programs. Corporate headquarters location.

BUCK CONSULTANTS INC.
Two Pennsylvania Plaza
New York NY 10121
212/330-1000
Contact Personnel Department. One of the nation's oldest and largest actuarial and employee benefits consulting organizations. Corporate headquarters location. International. Operations at this facility include: research/development; administration; service. Common positions include: Accountant; Actuary; Attorney; Computer Programmer; Personnel & Labor Relations Specialist; Programmer. Principal educational backgrounds sought: Actuarial Science; Business Administration; Economics; Finance; Marketing. Company benefits include: bonus; medical insurance; pension plan; life insurance; disability coverage; employee discounts; savings plan; 401K.

CIT GROUP FACTORING/
DIVISION OF MANUFACTURES HANOVER
1211 Avenue of the Americas
College Relations, New York NY 10036
212//382-7000
Contact Melissa Harris, Personnel Officer. Resumes should be sent to Personnel at 135 West 50th Street, New York NY 10020. Provides factoring services to a wide range of customers, as a subsidiary of CIT Financial Services. Corporate headquarters location. International

COWEN & COMPANY
Financial Square
New York NY 10005-3597
Contact Personnel Manager. A major stock brokerage firm. Corporate headquarters location. New York Stock Exchange and American Stock Exchange. Common positions include: Accountant; Financial Analyst; Sales Representative; Statistician; Systems Analyst. Principal educational backgrounds sought: Accounting; Business Administration; Computer Science; Finance; Liberal Arts. Company benefits include: medical insurance; life insurance; tuition assistance; disability coverage; profit sharing.

DEAN WITTER REYNOLDS INC.
2 World Trade Center, 44th Floor
New York NY 10048
212/524-3500
Contact Employment Division. The nucleus of the Financial Services Group of Sears, Roebuck and Company. Offers diversified financial services including equities, fixed income securities, commodities, money market instruments, and investment banking services. Operates in four groups: Dean Witter Reynolds, Inc.; Dean Witter Reynolds Capital Markets Group; Dean Witter Reynolds InterCapital Inc.; and Dean Witter Reynolds International Group. Corporate headquarters location. International.

DONALDSON, LUFKIN & JENRETTE INC.
140 Broadway
New York NY 10005
212/504-3000
Contact Gerald Rigg, Personnel Director. A leading independent investment banking and securities firm with total assets exceeding $5 billion and capital funds of $250 million. Services are directed primarily to professional markets: corporations, institutions, other securities firms, and substantial individual investors. Provides a full range of capital raising, merger and acquisition, and related financial advisory services to corporations and public entities. The Sprout Group is one of the nation's leading venture capital investors. Provides research, trading and order equities to large institutional investors. Autranet subsidiary is also a leading factor in marketing investment services originated by independent research groups. Through two investment management subsidiaries, Alliance Capital Management, and Wood, Struthers & Winthrop, it ranks as one of the nation's largest institutional investors, with more than $16 billion of assets under investment supervision. The Pershing Division provides correspondent services, including order execution, clearance and communications for a unique network of more than 200 independent regional securities firms. ACLI International, also a subsidiary, is a leader in international traded commodities. Corporate headquarters location.

DREXEL BURNHAM LAMBERT INC.
60 Broad Street, 18th Floor
New York NY 10004
212/232-5000
Contact Jack English, Employment Manager. An investment banking and brokerage firm. Members of the New York Stock Exchange and other leading financial exchanges. Corporate headquarters location. Common positions include: Accountant; Administrator; Architect; Attorney; Bank Officer/Manager; Draftsperson; Economist; Financial Analyst; Industrial Designer; Branch Manager; Management Trainee; Operations/Production Manager; Marketing Specialist; Personnel & Labor Relations Specialist; Public Relations Worker; Purchasing Agent; Sales Representative; Systems Analyst; Technical Writer/Editor. Principal educational backgrounds sought: Accounting; Business Administration; Economics; Finance; Marketing. Company benefits include: medical insurance; dental insurance; pension plan; life insurance; tuition assistance; disability coverage; profit sharing; savings plan.

DREYFUS
200 Park Avenue
New York NY 10166
212/922-6000

Contact Ms. Linda Nielsen, Personnel Director. An investment corporation.

DUN & BRADSTREET CORPORATION
299 Park Avenue
New York NY 10171
212/593-6800
Contact Rosalind Frykberg, Personnel Director. The world's premier supplier of information and services to businesses; utilizes computer technology to develop and deliver nearly 2000 products and services to more than two million customers worldwide. Operates in three business segments: Business Information Services, Publishing, and Marketing Services. Many of the units are well-known business names, such as Moody's Investors Service, Reuben H. Donnelley, Official Airline Guides, and Dun & Bradstreet Credit Services. Customers use D&B's resources in making credit, marketing, investment, data processing, insurance, and general management decisions. Corporate headquarters location. New York Stock Exchange. Common positions include: Accountant; Attorney; Computer Programmer; Financial Analyst; Marketing Specialist; Personnel & Labor Relations Specialist; Public Relations Worker; Systems Analyst. Principal educational backgrounds sought: Accounting; Business Administration; Computer Science; Finance; Liberal Arts; Marketing; Mathematics. Company benefits include: medical insurance; dental insurance; pension plan; life insurance; tuition assistance; disability coverage; profit sharing; savings plan.

EBASCO SERVICES INC.
Two World Trade Center, 78th Floor
New York NY 10048
212/839-1881
Contact Human Resources, Employment. Several area locations. Performs professional, technical, and management consulting services for the electric utility and other energy-intensive industries in the United States and overseas. A subsidiary of Enserch Corporation (Dallas, TX), an energy exploration and production firm. Corporate headquarters location. International. New York Stock Exchange. Common positions include: Civil Engineer; Electrical Engineer; Industrial Engineer; Mechanical Engineer. Principal educational background sought: Engineering. Company benefits include: medical insurance; pension plan; life insurance; dental insurance; tuition assistance; disability coverage; savings plan.

FIRST BOSTON, INC.
Park Avenue Plaza
55 East 52nd Street
New York, NY 10055
212/444-1000
Contact Personnel. An investment brokerage firm.

FIRST DATA RESOURCES
3 Dakota Drive
Lake Success NY 11042
516/358-5800
Contact Barbara Tomitz, Technical Recruiter. Provides extensive bank card data processing and support services for member financial institutions, with more than 400 major financial institution members nationwide. Services include cardholder and merchant accounting services, online database service and design, credit authorizations and transaction processing. Common positions include: Accountant; Blue-Collar Worker Supervisor; Computer Programmer; Customer Service Representative; Draftsperson; Financial Analyst; Department Manager; Operations/Production Manager; Marketing Specialist; Personnel & Labor Relations Specialist; Public Relations Worker; Purchasing Agent; Quality Control Supervisor; Sales Representative; Statistician; Systems Analyst; Technical Writer/Editor; Data Entry Operator; Computer Operator; Telemarketing Representative; Media Technician. Principal educational backgrounds sought: Accounting; Business Administration; Communications; Computer Science; Finance; Liberal Arts; Marketing. Company benefits include: medical, dental, and life insurance; pension plan; tuition assistance; disability coverage; profit sharing; employee discounts; job-posting.

FIRST INVESTORS CORPORATION
95 Wall Street, 23rd Floor
New York NY 10005
212/858-8000
Contact Karen Nelson, Personnel Director. Several area locations in Westchester County, New Jersey, and Long Island. Specializes in the distribution and management of investment programs for individuals and corporations, as well as retirement plans. Operating for more than 50 years. Corporate headquarters location. Common positions include: Accountant; Attorney; Computer Programmer; Customer Service Representative; Financial Analyst; Management Trainee; Sales Representative. Principal educational backgrounds sought: Accounting; Computer Science; Finance; Mathematics. Company benefits include: medical insurance; life insurance; tuition assistance; disability coverage; profit sharing.

INTEGRATED RESOURCES, INC.
10 Union Square East
New York NY 10003
212/353-7000
Contact Personnel. A financial services firm.

C. ITOH & COMPANY (AMERICA) INC.
335 Madison Avenue
New York NY 10017
212/818-8000
Contact Steven Blankenship, Recruitment Manager. An international, multi-business trading and investment company. Specializes in developing and sponsoring profitable opportunities in international and domestic commerce, industry and finance, either as a principal or agent. Company's services are designed to enhance virtually all aspects of business, including exporting, importing, domestic, or offshore trading. Company also participates in joint ventures in the United States and abroad. Company operates 16 offices coast-to-coast, with almost 500 professional staffers. Also operates 13 subsidiaries and affiliates with more than 1100 employees. Markets include textiles, motor vehicles, machinery, steel and raw materials, non-ferrous and light metals, grains, provisions, general merchandise, chemicals, and energy. A subsidiary of C. Itoh & Company, Ltd. (Tokyo, Japan), with 167 offices worldwide. Other United States facilities in Los Angeles; San Francisco; Houston, Chicago, Detroit, Seattle. Corporate headquarters location. International. Common positions include: Accountant; Administrator; Attorney; Electrical Engineer; Financial Analyst; Management Trainee; Marketing Specialist; Sales Representative; Transportation and Traffic Specialist. Educational backgrounds sought include: Accounting; Business Administration; Economics; Engineering; Finance; Liberal Arts. Training programs and internships available. Company benefits include: medical insurance; dental insurance; pension plan; life insurance; disability coverage. Operations include: regional headquarters; administration; sales.

JESUP, JOSEPHTHAL & CO., INC.
61 Broadway, Suite 1901
New York NY 10006
212/952-6287
Contact Martin Katz, Personnel. A securities clearinghouse.

MANAGISTICS INC.
P.O. Box 699
32-31 57th Street
Woodside NY 11377
718/545-6200
Contact Shirley Parris, Personnel Manager. A data processing payroll service bureau. Corporate headquarters location.

WILLIAM M. MERCER, INCORPORATED
1166 Avenue of the Americas
New York NY 10036-2708
212/345-7000
Contact Alison L. Rutter, National Recruiting Coordinator. An employee benefits and compensation consulting company, providing advice to organizations on almost all aspects of employee/management relationships. Services include: pension, profit sharing, thrift and savings, survivors' income, life insurance, accidental death and dismemberment, disability income, hospital/surgical/major medical, dental, and legal. Operates 80 offices in the United States, Canada, and other international locations. A Marsh & McLennan Company (see separate listing). Common positions include: Accountant; Actuary; Attorney; Personnel and Labor Relations Specialist; Benefits Consultant. Principal educational backgrounds sought: Accounting; Business Administration; Communications; Computer Science; Economics; Engineering; Finance; Liberal Arts; Mathematics. Internships offered. Company benefits include: medical, dental, and life insurance; pension plan; tuition assistance; disability coverage; daycare assistance; employee discounts; savings plan; flex savings account. Corporate headquarters location. Parent company: Marsh & McLennan Los, Inc. Operations at this facility include: regional headquarters; divisional headquarters; administration. New York Stock Exchange.

MERRILL LYNCH & CO.
225 Liberty
New York NY 10080
212/449-1000
Contact Personnel. A major financial services firm.

MITSUI & COMPANY (USA)
200 Park Avenue
New York NY 10166
212/878-4000
Contact Personnel Director. A major international trading firm, engaged in a wide range of import/export activities. Parent company, Mitsui Group, is a major Tokyo-based industrial corporation, operating in the following areas: Cement; Chemicals; Commerce; Construction; Energy; Engineering; Finance and Insurance; Food; Machinery; Mining; Nonferrous Metals; Paper; Real Estate; Steel; Synthetic Fibers & Plastics; Transportation; Warehousing; and Other Services. Offices are located throughout the United States, including Washington DC, Cleveland, Miami, Chicago, Detroit, Houston, Dallas-Fort Worth, Atlanta, San Francisco, Los Angeles, and others. Parent company has numerous subsidiaries operating throughout the world. Corporate headquarters location.

J.P. MORGAN & COMPANY/
MORGAN GUARANTY TRUST COMPANY
23 Wall Street
New York NY 10015
212/483-2323
Contact Personnel. A bank holding company, operating primarily through subsidiary Morgan Guaranty Trust Company of New York. Also owns Morgan Bank/Delaware (Wilmington, DE), and numerous United States and international subsidiaries. Morgan Guaranty has four New York City banking offices. Subsidiaries, associated companies, and representative offices are located throughout the world. Many subsidiaries are located in New York City. Corporate headquarters location. New York Stock Exchange. International.

MORGAN STANLEY
1251 Avenue of the Americas
New York NY 10020
212/703-4000
Contact Human Resources Department. One of the largest investment banking firms in the United States. Services include: Financing Services; Financial Advisory Services; Real Estate Services; Corporate Bond Services; Equity Services; Government and Money

Market Services; Mergers and Acquisitions Services; Investment Research Services; Investment Management Services; and Individual Investors Services. Offices are located throughout the United States and abroad. Common positions include: Financial Analyst. Principal educational backgrounds sought: Economics; Finance; Liberal Arts. Company benefits include: medical, dental and life insurance; pension plan; tuition assistance; disability coverage; profit sharing. Corporate headquarters location. Operations at this facility include: research/development; administration. International. New York Stock Exchange.

NEW YORK STOCK EXCHANGE
Eleven Wall Street, 16th Floor
New York NY 10005
212/656-3000
Contact Recruiting Manager. The principal securities trading marketplace in the United States, serving a broad range of industries within and outside of the securities industry. More than 1600 corporations, accounting for approximately 40 percent of American corporate revenues, are listed on the exchange, making it the largest securities trading organization in the nation. Also operates the New York Futures Exchange, a major international futures trading center. Engaged in a wide range of public affairs and economic research programs, aimed at broadening the dialogue between the public and private sectors. Corporate headquarters location.

NISSHO IWAI AMERICAN CORPORATION
1211 Avenue of the Americas
New York NY 10036
212/704-6536
Contact Manager, Human Resources. A leading international trading company with 10 different product divisions. Together with parent company, Nissho Iwai Corporation (Toyko, Japan), company ranks among the world's largest businesses. Operates in the following divisions: Machinery (general machinery, machinery product development, marine, aircraft, electronics); Ferrous Metal Products; Ferrous Materials (coal, scrap metal, ferro-alloys, other materials); Non-Ferrous Metals (copper, aluminum, titanium, silver, platinum, palladium); Textiles; Fuel; General Merchandise (hides and skins, paper and pulp, clay and kaolin, Nike athletic shoes, and many other consumer products); Lumber; Chemicals (including organic and inorganic chemicals, specialty chemicals, plastics, and petrochemicals); and Foodstuffs. Parent company and subsidiaries employ 7800 people worldwide, through a global network of 47 Japanese and 130 overseas offices. Corporate headquarters location (United States operations). International.

OPPENHEIMER & COMPANY INC.
200 Liberty Street, Oppenheimer Tower
One World Financial Center
New York NY 10281
212/667-7000
Contact Personnel Manager. Engaged in the nationwide management, financing, and operation of cattle ranches and farms; as well as conducting real estate brokerage operations in more than 15 states. Offices in New York, Chicago, Fort Lauderdale, Houston, Los Angeles, and London. Corporate headquarters location.

PAINEWEBBER INC.
1285 Avenue of the Americas
New York NY 10019
212/713-4012
Contact Employment Manager, Human Resources Dept. A holding company that, together with operating subsidiaries, forms one of the world's largest investment services firm. Services are conducted through subsidiaries Paine, Webber, Jackson & Curtis Inc., one of the largest securities firms in the United States, engaged primarily in providing investment services to individual and institutional clients; Blyth Eastman Paine Webber Inc., a leading investment banking firm, providing financial advice to, and raising capital for, a broad range of clients, including both corporations and governmental entities; Paine Webber Mitchell Hutchins Inc., which provides institutional equity sales, trading, and

research and investment advisory and portfolio management services to domestic and foreign institutions and to money market funds; and Paine Webber Real Estate Securities Inc., which concentrates its trading activities in government-guaranteed securities. Employs more than 9500 people worldwide. Regional offices are located throughout the United States and internationally. Branch offices are located throughout the world. Corporate headquarters location. New York Stock Exchange. International.

PRESCOTT BALL & TURBEN
One World Trade Center, 56th Floor
New York NY 10048
212/938-7000
Contact Tina Karathomas, Personnel Director. A major national investment banking and stock brokerage firm; offices in several major United States cities. Corporate headquarters location: Cleveland, OH.

PRUDENTIAL-BACHE SECURITIES INC.
100 Gold Street
New York NY 10292
212/776-1000
Contact Paul Rumely, Director of Personnel. Multiple area locations. A major international securities brokerage and investment firm (formerly operating as Bache Halsey Stuart Shields Inc.). Offers clients more than 70 different investment products, including stocks, options, bonds, commodities, tax-favored investments, and insurance, as well as several specialized financial services. Currently operates more than 240 offices in 17 countries. A major operating subsidiary of Prudential Insurance Company. Corporate headquarters location. International.

QUOTRON SYSTEMS, INC.
77 Water Street
New York NY 10005
212/344-0400
Contact Human Resource Department. Provides computerized financial information services, primarily to the investment management and banking industries. Headquarters location: Los Angeles, CA.

RELIANCE GROUP HOLDINGS, INC.
Park Avenue Plaza
New York NY 10055
212/909-1100
Contact Ann Colleran, Human Resources Analyst. A New York holding company whose subsidiaries operate primarily in the areas of insurance and financial services. Common positions include: Accountant; Attorney; Financial Analyst. Principal educational backgrounds sought: Accounting; Business Administration; Economics; Finance. Company benefits include: medical, dental, and life insurance; pension plan; tuition assistance; disability coverage; savings plan. Corporate headquarters location. New York Stock Exchange.

SALOMON BROTHERS
Two New York Plaza, 33rd Floor
New York NY 10004
212/747-7000
Contact Personnel Manager. An international investment banking, market making, and research firm, serving corporations, state and local governments, sovereign and provincial governments and their agencies, supranational organizations, central banks, and other financial institutions. A major operating subsidiary of Salomon Inc. Common positions include: Accountant; Attorney; Computer Programmer; Economist; Financial Analyst; Operations/Production Manager; Personnel & Labor Relations Specialist; Public Relations Specialist; Statistician; Systems Analyst; Underwriter. Principal educational backgrounds sought: Accounting; Business Administration; Computer Science; Economics; Finance; Marketing; Mathematics. Company benefits include: medical, dental, and life insurance; tuition assistance; disability coverage; profit sharing; savings plan. Corporate

headquarters location. Operations at this facility include: research/development; administration; sales. New York Stock Exchange.

SHEARSON LEHMAN BROS.
2 World Trade Center, 101 Floor
New York NY 10048
212/528-7000
Contact Professional Recruiting Office. One of the nation's largest and best-known investment banking and securities brokers; also provides related financial services. Operations in the securities industry include: agency transactions, principal transactions, and investment banking. Operations in the life insurance industry include: the sale of life insurance and annuities. Leasing and credit operations include: leasing, time sales contracts, and general purpose commercial loans. Operating divisions include: Retail Marketing; Asset Management; Commodity Division; Equity Division; Operations; Public Finance; Corporate Finance; Administrative Services; Control and Planning; and subsidiary operations E.F. Hutton Life Insurance Company and E.F. Hutton Credit Corporation. Operates more than 250 offices nationwide. Corporate headquarters location. New York Stock Exchange. International.

SHEARSON LEHMAN BROTHERS, INC.
American Expressway Tower
World Financial Center, Lobby Level
New York NY 10285-0250
212/640-2000
Contact Employment Manager. A full service brokerage firm. Common positions include: Accountant; Sales Assistant; Administrative Assistant; Research Assistant; Secretary; Computer Programmer; Customer Service Representative; Financial Analyst; Broker; Branch Manager; Operations/Production Manager; Marketing Specialist; Systems Analyst; Underwriter. Principal educational backgrounds sought: Accounting; Business Administration; Computer Science; Finance; Liberal Arts; Marketing. Company benefits include: medical, dental, and life insurance; pension plan; tuition assistance; disability coverage; profit sharing; employee discounts; savings plan. Corporate headquarters location. New York Stock Exchange.

SMITH BARNEY
1345 Avenue of the Americas
New York NY 10105
212/603-8800
Contact Laurie Richman, Employment Recruiter. A major international investment banking firm, offering a wide range of financial services through more than 100 locations worldwide. Corporate headquarters location. International.

STONE & WEBSTER MANAGEMENT CONSULTANTS
250 West 34th Street
New York NY 10119
212/290-7196
Contact Darleen Lucas, Personnel Specialist. Provides a wide range of financial, marketing, economic, and management consulting services, including financial forecasting and feasibility studies; acquisitions and merger analysis; plant maintenance studies; new market potential analysis; market research, planning, operations, and organizational studies; site selection and land use; materials handling; transportation management; plant layout; computer systems planning and design; rate analysis; and depreciation studies. Corporate headquarters location. New York Stock Exchange. Common consulting positions include: Accountant; Computer Programmer; Economist; Electrical Engineer; Industrial Engineer; Mechanical Engineer; Petroleum Engineer; Marketing Specialist; Systems Analyst. Principal educational backgrounds sought: Accounting; Business Administration; Computer Science; Economics; Engineering; Finance; Marketing; Mathematics. Company benefits include: medical insurance; dental insurance; pension plan; life insurance; tuition assistance; disability coverage; stock plan; investment plan.

238/*The Metropolitan New York JobBank*

TPF&C
245 Park Avenue
New York NY 10167
212/309-3807
Contact Coordinator, College Recruiting. A management consulting firm. Corporate and regional headquarters. Common positions include: Actuary. Principal educational backgrounds sought: Mathematics; Actuarial Science. Company benefits include: medical insurance; dental insurance; pension plan; life insurance; tuition assistance; disability coverage; profit sharing. Parent company: Towers Perrin.

WERTHEIM SCHRODER & CO.
787 Seventh Avenue, 6th Floor
New York NY 10019
212/492-6000
Contact Veronica K. Baard, Associate Managing Director. A leading international investment banking, asset management and securities firm. Domestic branch offices in Boston, Dallas, Houston, Philadelphia and Los Angeles. International offices in Amsterdam, Geneva, Paris, and London. Corporate headquarters location: New York.

New Jersey

C.I.T. GROUP, INC.
650 C.I.T. Drive
Livingston NJ 07039.
Contact Assistant V.P. of Employment. A diversified financial services organization with more than 2,500 employees in operating companies throughout the United States. Founded in 1908, C.I.T. provides flexible funding alternatives, secured business lending and financial advisory services for corporations, manufacturers and dealers. Owned 60% by Dai-Ichi Kangyo Bank, Limited, the World's Largest bank, and 40% by Manufacturers Hanover Corporation. Common positions include: Accountant, Financial Analyst, Computer Programmer, Auditor, Systems Analyst. Principal educational backgrounds sought: Accounting; Computer Science; Finance. Company benefits include: medical, dental and life insurance; disability coverage; savings and pension plans; tuition reimbursement.

CRUM & FORSTER, INC.
305 Madison Avenue
Morristown NJ 07962
201/285-7000
Contact Vicki B. Carter, Chief Estimator. A major New Jersey financial services company, employing 11, 800.

KEPNER-TREGOE, INC.
P.O. Box 704, Research Road
Princeton NJ 08542
609/921-2806
Contact Human Resources. A worldwide management consulting firm with headquarters in Princeton, NJ. Product categories include Strategy Formulation, Systems Improvement, Skill Development, and Specific Issue Resolution. Industry markets are Automotive, Information Technology, Chemical, Financial Services, and Natural Resources. Operating in 44 countries and 14 languages, Kepner-Tregoe is unique in its markets and exceptional role with nearly all of the Fortune 100. Common positions include: Accountant; Administrator; Operations/Production Manager; Marketing Sales Representative; Process Consultant; Strategic Planner. Principal educational backgrounds sought: Business Administration; Finance; Liberal Arts; Marketing; Education. Company benefits include: medical insurance; dental insurance; pension plan; life insurance; tuition assistance; disability coverage; profit sharing; employee discounts; savings plan. Corporate headquarters location. Parent company: USF & G. Operations at this facility include: administration; service; sales. New York Stock Exchange

PRUDENTIAL CAPITAL & INVESTMENT SERVICES
56 North Livingston Avenue
Roseland NJ 07068
201/716-8306
Contact Personnel Office. A major division of The Prudential, the diversified insurance and financial services company. The division operate primarily through Prudential Bach Securities, Inc.

TELERATE SYSTEMS
Harborside Financial Center
600 Plaza 2
Jersey City NJ 07311
201/309-1390
Contact Susan Phipps, Personnel. Personnel can be contacted at Harborside Financial Center, 600 Plaza Two, Jersey City NJ 07311. Producers of computerizes financial market data information systems.

YEGEN ASSOCIATES, INC.
Mack Centre Drive
Paramus NJ 07652
201/262-7400
Contact Eleanor Loveland, Vice-President of Human Resources. A highly diversified corporation established as a financial services firm. Company develops installment lending portfolios or banks throughout the United States, specializing in automobile, mobile home, aircraft, marine, and recreation land loan programs. Corporate headquarters location. Common positions include: Accountant; Claim Representat ive; Computer Programmer; Credit Manager; Financial Analyst; Insurance Agent/Broker; Branch Manager; Department Manager; General Manager; Management Trainee; Programmer; Purchasing Agent; Sales Representative; Systems Analyst; Underwriter. Principal educational backgrounds sought: Accounting; Business Administration; Computer Science; Finance; Liberal Arts. Company benefits include: medical insurance; pension plan; life insurance; tuition assistance.

FOOD AND BEVERAGE RELATED: PROCESSING & DISTRIBUTION

For more information on professional opportunities in the food processing and production industries, contact the following professional and trade organizations, as listed on page 449:

AMERICAN ASSOCIATION OF CEREAL CHEMISTS
AMERICAN ASSOCIATION OF CEREAL CHEMISTS/NEW YORK
AMERICAN SOCIETY OF AGRICULTURAL ENGINEERS
AMERICAN SOCIETY OF BREWING CHEMISTS
DAIRY AND FOOD INDUSTRIES SUPPLY ASSOCIATION
NATIONAL AGRICULTURAL CHEMICALS ASSOCIATION
NATIONAL DAIRY COUNCIL
PESTICIDE ASSOCIATION OF NEW YORK STATE
UNITED FOOD AND COMMERCIAL WORKERS INTERNATIONAL
    UNION

New York

AMSTAR SUGAR CORPORATION
49 South Second Street
Brooklyn NY 11211
718/387-6800
Contact Employee Relations Department. A major area sugar refinery. Refines Domino brand sugar, and distributes it to grocery and industrial customers. A subsidiary of Tate & Lyle, PLC, the world's largest producer of nutritive sweeteners. Common positions include:

Blue-Collar Worker Supervisor; Engineer (entry level); Chemist; Customer Service Representative; Food Technologist. Principal educational backgrounds sought: Business Administration; Chemistry; Engineering; Food Science. Company benefits include: medical, dental, and life insurance; vision plan; pension plan; tuition assistance; disability coverage; savings plan. Corporate headquarters location: New York City. Operations at this facility include: manufacturing; customer service; sales. Other manufacturing facilities located in Baltimore, MD and New Orleans, LA.

BOAR'S HEAD
PROVISION COMPANY INC.
24 Rock Street
Brooklyn NY 11206
718/456-3600
Contact Leo Hafner, Personnel Department. A wholesale packer and distributor of smoked meat and delicatessen products. Corporate headquarters location.

BORDEN INC.
277 Park Avenue
New York NY 10172
212/573-4000
Contact Director of Employee Relations. Operates in two major industry segments (foods and chemicals), through four operating divisions: Borden Grocery Products; Borden Chemical; Borden Dairy; and Borden Snacks and International Consumer Products. Company offers hundreds of well-known name brands, including 'Borden' dairy products, 'Wise' potato chips, 'Wyler's' drink mixes, 'Old London' snack foods, 'Creamette' pasta products, 'Krylon' spray paints, 'Elmer's' glue products and many others. New York Stock Exchange. International.

CPC INTERNATIONAL/BEST FOODS BAKING GROUP
1776 Eastchester Road
Bronx NY 10461
212/518-2726
Contact Paul C. O'Brien, Manager, Human Resources. Major producer of a wide range of snacks, including Melba Toast, Croutons Bread Crubs and others. Products are distributed through wholesalers and retailers. International. Common positions include: Accountant; Administrator; Blue-Collar Worker Supervisor; Computer Programmer; Credit Manager; Customer Service Representative; Electrical Engineer; Industrial Engineer; Mechanical Engineer; Food Technologist; Department Manager; General Manager; Marketing Specialist; Personnel & Labor Relations Specialist. Principal educational backgrounds sought: Accounting; Business Administration; Computer Science; Economics; Engineering; Finance; Liberal Arts. Company benefits include: medical, dental, and life insurance; pension plan; tuition assistance; disability coverage; profit sharing; employee discounts; savings plan. Corporate headquarters location: Englewood Cliffs, NJ. Parent company: CPC International. Operations at this facility include: manufacturing. New York Stock Exchange.

CARROLS CORPORATION
968 James Street
Syracuse NY 13203
315/424-0513
Contact Jerry DiGenova, Region Personnel Manager. World's largest operators of Burger King Restaurants. Common positions include: Assistant Manager. Principal educational backgrounds sought: Accounting; Business Administration. Company benefits include: medical insurance; dental insurance; life insurance; disability coverage; savings plan.

CARVEL CORPORATION
201 Saw Mill River Road
Yonkers NY 10701
914/969-7200

Contact Georgine Murray, Personnel Department. Engaged in ice cream products manufacturing and franchising operations for the chain of Carvel Ice Cream outlets. Corporate headquarters location.

CHOCK FULL O' NUTS CORPORATION
370 Lexington Avenue, 11th Floor
New York NY 10017
212/532-0300
Contact Peter Baer, Vice President, Labor Relations. Produces a nationally-distributed brand of premium coffee. Common positions include: Accountant.

CULBRO CORPORATION
387 Park Avenue South
New York NY 10016
212/561-8700
Contact Robert Grimaldi, Personnel Manager. Produces a variety of well-known consumer products, including snack foods and tobaccos. Corporate headquarters location.

ENTENMANN'S INC.
1724 Fifth Avenue
Bayshore NY 11706
516/273-6000
Contact Human Resources Manager. A nationwide bakery products firm, manufacturing and distributing a wide line of cakes, cookies, doughnuts, and similar baked products. Products are distributed through retailers nationwide. A subsidiary of General Foods Corporation. Corporate headquarters location.

FINK BAKING CORPORATION
535 54th Avenue
Long Island City NY 11101
718/392-8300
Contact Norman Mast, Controller. Produces a full line of bakery products. Supplies bread and rolls to airlines, restaurants, steamship operators, hotels, and other institutional customers. Corporate headquarters location.

HORN & HARDART COMPANY
730 5th Avenue
New York NY 10019
212/582-4210
Contact Rose Kalatzis, Secretary. A national food service company with over 400 restaurants, which include Burger Kings, Arby's, and Bojangles', as well as some full-service restaurants. Horn & Hardart also owns Hanover House Industries -- a large mail-order firm in Hanover, PA. Corporate headquarters location. Common Positions include: Restaurant Managers (Unit and above).

JAMAICA WATER PROPERTIES INC.
410 Lakeville Road
Lake Success NY 11042
516/488-4600
Contact Janice Varley, Personnel Recruiter. Several area locations, including Westbury, and Long Island City, NY. A holding company, engaged in the following businesses: Supply and Distribution of Water, whose operations are conducted through Jamaica Water Supply Company, and Sea Cliff Water Company, which supply water primarily for residential and commercial use in parts of Queens, and parts of western Nassau County, with an aggregate service population of approximately 670,000; Trailer Rental Sales (through subsidiary A to Z Equipment Corporation; Westbury, NY), engaged primarily in the rental and sale of trailers to the construction industry for temporary office and storage use; and Specialized Electrical Contracting (through subsidiary Welsbach Electric Corporation; Long Island City, NY; see separate listing), an electrical contractor. Company also holds majority shares of Orbit International, Inc., a Puerto Rico-based firm, engaged primarily in the

manufacture of kitchen cabinets for use in housing developments in Puerto Rico. Corporate headquarters location.

KRASDALE FOODS INC.
400 Food Center Drive
Bronx NY 10474
212/378-1100
Contact Personnel Department. Engaged in the wholesale distribution of canned goods and other processed food products. Corporate headquarters location.

LEVER BROTHERS CO.
390 Park Avenue
New York NY 10022
212/688-6000
Contact Personnel Manager. A major international consumer products firm, providing a wide range of well-known soaps, toiletries and foods. A subsidiary of Unilever NV (Netherlands). U.S. headquarters location.

PHILIP MORRIS INC.
120 Park Avenue
New York NY 10017
212/880-5000
Contact Manager/Employee Relations. A leading company operating in the manufacture and sales of consumer products. Wholly-owned subsidiaries include: Philip Morris Incorporated, Philip Morris International, Inc, Kraft General Foods, Inc. (Glenview, Il) and Miller Brewing Company (Milwaukee, WI). Philip Morris Capital Corporation (New York, NY) engages in various financing and investment activities and owns a real-estate subsidiary, the Mission Viejo Company (Mission Viejo, CA). New York Stock Exchange. International. Areas include: Finance; Marketing; Planning; Human Resources; Corporate Affairs; Headquarters Services; Information Services. Comprehensive benefits package. An equal Employment/Affirmative Action Employer. Minority/ Female/ Handicapped/ Veterans.

NATIONAL FOODS INC.
600 Food Center Drive
Bronx NY 10474
212/842-5000
Contact Connie Petillo, Personnel Director. One of the nation's leading manufacturers and distributors of high-quality kosher foods since 1939. Products and services include Hebrew National hot dogs, salami, bologna, other luncheon meats, poultry and pickles. Common positions include: Accountant; Blue-Collar Worker Supervisor; Computer Programmer; Customer Service Representative; Financial Analyst; Marketing Specialist; Purchasing Agent; Sales Representative; Systems Analyst. Company benefits include: medical, dental and life insurance; pension plan; tuition assistance; long term disability coverage; employee discounts; savings plan. Corporate headquarters location. Operations at this facility include: manufacturing; administration; sales.

NESTLE COMPANY INC.
100 Manhattanville Road
Purchase NY 10577
914/251-3000
Contact Corporate Employment Department. One of the nation's best-known manufacturers of a wide range of food products. Popular consumer products include Nestle's wide line of food products: 'Nestle' chocolates, 'Taster's Choice', 'Nescafe', and 'Decaf' instant coffees, 'Nestle' soups, 'Deer Park' bottled water, and many others. Also produces a wide range of ingredients for the food-processing and beverage industries. A wholly-owned subsidiary of Nestle SA (Vevey, Switzerland), a major international food products firm. Corporate headquarters location.

PEPCOM INDUSTRIES, INC.
800 East Gate Boulevard
Garden City NY 11530
516/228-8200
Contact Rich Poche, Sales Manager. A major area soft drink bottler and distributor. Products include a wide range of nationally-advertised soft drinks, including 'Pepsi-Cola', 'Diet Pepsi', 'Teem', 'Mountain Dew', 'Orange Crush', 'Schweppes' flavors, and others. Company operates under franchise agreements with PepsiCo, Inc.; Crush International, Inc.; Schweppes USA Ltd.; The Seven Up Company; Dr. Pepper Company; and other soft drink manufacturers from whom it purchases syrup concentrates. Other facilities in North Carolina.

PEPSI, INC.
800 East Gate Boulevard
Garden City NY 11530
516/228-8200
Contact Tom Fay, Sales Manager. A major area soft drink bottler and distributor. Products include a wide range of nationally-advertised soft drinks, including 'Pepsi-Cola', 'Teem', 'Mountain Dew', 'Orange Crush', 'Schweppes' flavors and others. Company operates under franchise agreements with PepsiCo, Inc.; Crush International, Inc; Schweppes USA Ltd.; The Seven Up Company; Dr. Pepper Company; and other soft drink manufacturers from whom it purchases syrup concentrates. Other facilities in North Carolina.

PEPSICO INC.
700 Anderson Hill Road
Purchase NY 10577
914/253-2755
Contact Manager/Staffing. Operates nationally in four business segments: beverages, food products, food service, and sporting goods. Products include a wide range of nationally-known consumer items. Corporate headquarters location. New York Stock Exchange. Common positions include: Accountant; Attorney; Computer Programmer; Financial Analyst; Department Manager; General Manager; Personnel & Labor Relations Specialist; Public Relations Worker. Principal educational backgrounds sought: Accounting; Business Administration; Communications; Economics; Finance. Company benefits include: medical insurance; dental insurance; pension plan; life insurance; tuition assistance; disability coverage; profit sharing; employee discounts; savings plan.

POLLIO DAIRY PRODUCTS CORPORATION
120 Mineola Boulevard
Mineola NY 11501
516/741-8000
Contact Eileen A. Ferringno, Human Resources Assistant. Engaged in the manufacturing and distribution of Italian-style soft cheeses and food products, primarily throughout the northeastern United States. Corporate headquarters location. Common positions include: Accountant; Computer Programmer; Credit Manager; Financial Analyst; Marketing Specialist; Sales Representative. Principal educational backgrounds sought: Accounting; Business Administration; Computer Science; Finance; Liberal Arts; Marketing; Mathematics. Company benefits include: medical insurance; dental insurance; pension plan; life insurance; tuition assistance; disability coverage; profit sharing; employee discounts; savings plan. Corporate headquarters location. Parent company: Kraft General Foods. Operations at this facility include: regional headquarters; administration; service; sales.

REFINED SUGARS INC.
One Federal Street
Yonkers NY 10702
914/963-2400
Contact Robert Jandovitz, Assistant Manager, Human Resources. A major area sugar refinery. Refines raw sugar, and distributes it to major national clients in the soft drink, confectionery, and baking industries. Corporate headquarters location. International. Operations at this facility include: manufacturing; administration; service; sales. Common

positions include: Accountant; Administrator; Blue-Collar Worker Supervisor; Chemist; Computer Programmer; Credit Manager; Customer Service Representative; Chemical Engineer; Electrical Engineer; Food Technologist; Department Manager; Operations/Production Manager; Marketing Specialist; Personnel & Labor Relations Specialist; Programmer; Purchasing Agent; Quality Control Supervisor; Sales Representative; Systems Analyst. Principal educational backgrounds sought: Accounting; Biology; Business Administration; Chemistry; Computer Science; Engineering. Company benefits include: medical insurance; dental insurance; pension plan; life insurance; tuition assistance; disability coverage; profit sharing; employee discounts; savings plan.

RONZONI FOODS CORPORATION
50-02 Northern Boulevard
Long Island City NY 11101
718/204-3000
Contact Personnel Manager. A nationally-known manufacturer and distributor of pasta products, including spaghetti, macaroni, egg noodles, and pastina, as well as other Italian-style specialty foods and sauces. Common positions include: Accountant; Blue-Collar Worker Supervisor; Chemical Engineer; Electrical Engineer; Mechanical Engineer; Quality Control Supervisor. Principal educational backgrounds sought: Engineering. Company benefits include: medical insurance; pension plan; life insurance; disability coverage. Corporate headquarters location: White Plains, NY. Parent Company: General Foods. Operations at this facility include: manufacturing.

JOSEPH E. SEAGRAM & SONS, INC./
THE SEAGRAM COMPANY LTD.
800 Third Avenue
New York NY 10022
212/572-1254
Contact Helan Wong, Supervisor of Staffing. The world's largest producer of distilled spirits and wines, with subsidiaries and affiliates in 29 countries on six continents, with international sales exceeding $2.9 billion. Divisions include Seagram Distillers Company. The Gold Seal Wine Company; Paul Masson Vineyards, B&G Vineyards, Mumms Champagnes, Wilson Distillers Ltd., and others. Other company operations include ownership of significant portion (approximately one-fifth) of E.I. Du Pont de Nemours & Company, the international chemical products manufacturer; and oil exploration and drilling subsidiary Texas Pacific. Company is based in Montreal, Canada. Company headquarters location for U.S. International. Several area locations.

STELLA D'ORO BISCUIT COMPANY INC.
184 West 237th Street
Bronx NY 10463
212/549-3700
Contact James V. Perduto, Sr., Vice-President/Industrial Relations. Produces a well-known line of bakery specialties, including bread sticks, cookies, and biscuits, for sale to supermarket and specialty store wholesalers. Corporate headquarters location.

TASTY BAKING COMPANY
131-33 Avery Avenue
Flushing NY 11355
718/670-7700
Contact Tony Napodano, Personnel Director. A nationwide food processor, primarily engaged in the production and distribution of bakery products. Operates more than 25 bakeries nationally which produce items such as bread, buns, rolls, donuts, and other bakery products, for sale to retailers, restaurants, and institutions, as well as the company's 200-plus thrift stores. Company markets products under the following brand names: Taystee (Northeast and Midwest); Langendorf (California); Merita (Southeast); Cookbook (Texas); and Mickey snack cakes and Dressel's frozen baked goods nationwide. Corporate headquarters location: Chicago, IL. New York Stock Exchange.

WHITE ROSE FOOD CORPORATION
150 Price Parkway
Farmingdale NY 11735
516/293-9600
Contact Selma Silverman, Personnel Director. A major area distributor of a wide range of food products. A subsidiary of DiGiorgio Corporation (San Francisco, CA). Corporate headquarters location.

Connecticut

BEST FOODS BAKING GROUP
10 Hamilton Avenue
Greenwich CT 06830
203/531-2000
Contact Regional Personnel Director. A major wholesale baker and food processor of bread, rolls, stuffing, croutons and other food products. Corporate headquarters location. Operations include: manufacturing; research/development; administration; sales. Common positions include: Accountant; Blue-Collar Worker Supervisor; Buyer; Electrical Engineer; Industrial Engineer; Mechanical Engineer; Financial Analyst; Food Technologist; Branch Manager; Department Manager; General Manager; Operations/Production Manager; Marketing Specialist; Personnel & Labor Relations Specialist; Programmer; Purchasing Agent; Quality Control Supervisor; Sales Representative; Systems Analyst; Transportation & Traffic Specialist; Technical Services-Baking. Principal educational backgrounds sought: Accounting; Business Administration; Chemistry; Computer Science; Engineering; Finance; Marketing. Company benefits include: medical insurance; dental insurance; pension plan; life insurance; tuition assistance; disability coverage; employee discounts; savings plan.

CADBURY BEVERAGES, INC.
P.O. Box 3800, High Ridge Park
Stanford CT 06905-0800
203/968-5600
Contact Human Resources. A major franchiser selling soft drinks

PEPPERIDGE FARM INC.
595 Westport Avenue
Norwalk CT 06851
203/846-7265
Contact Patricia M. Denne, Corporate Manager Human Resources. Manufactures and distributes a range of fresh and frozen baked goods and confections. A subsidiary of Campbell Soup Company (Camden, NJ). Operations include: research/development; administration. Corporate headquarters location. Common positions include: Accountant; Chemist; Computer Programmer; Credit Specialist; Draftsperson; Electrical Engineer; Financial Analyst; Food Technologist; Marketing Specialist; Personnel & Labor Relations Specialist; Public Relations; Systems Analyst. Principal educational backgrounds sought: Accounting; Business Administration; Chemistry; Computer Science; Engineering; Finance; Liberal Arts; Marketing. Company benefits include: medical insurance; dental insurance; pension plan; life insurance; tuition assistance; disability coverage; employee discounts; savings plan; including 401K option; flexible spending accounts for healthcare and dependent care.

PETER PAUL
P.O. Box 310
Naugatuck CT 06770
203/729-0221
Contact Paul M. Russo, Manger of Human Resources. Manufactures and markets confectionery products. Common positions include: Accountant; Administrator; Biochemist; Blue-Collar Worker Supervisor; Chemist; Computer Programmer; Chemical Engineer; Electrical Engineer; Industrial Engineer; Mechanical Engineer; Food Technologist; General Manager; Management Trainee; Operations/Production Manager;

Personnel & Labor Relations Specialist; Quality Control Supervisor; Statistician; Systems Analyst. Principal educational backgrounds sought: Accounting; Business Administration; Chemistry; Computer Science; Engineering; Marketing. Company benefits include: medical, dental, and life insurance; tuition assistance; disability coverage; profit sharing; employee discounts; savings plan. Corporate headquarters location. Operations at this facility include: divisional headquarters; manufacturing; research/development.

SERVICE AMERICA CORPORATION
88 Gate House Road
P.O. Box 10203
Stamford CT 06904
203/964-5000
Contact Human Resources Department. Engaged in the business of vending machine operators, food, and refreshment services, industrial and institutional food services and concessions.

TETLEY INC.
100 Commerce Drive
Shelton CT 06484-0856
203/929-9200
Contact Kathryn K. Cantore, Manager of Staffing, HQ Personnel. Manufactures and distributes fine beverage and food products under Tetley, Martinson, Bustelo, Savarin, Medaglia D'Oro, Brown Gold and El Pico trade names. Common positions include: Accountant; Administrator; Computer Programmer; Financial Analyst. Principal educational backgrounds sought include: Accounting; Business Administration; Computer Science; Finance; Marketing. Company benefits include: medical, dental, and life insurance; pension plan; tuition assistance; disability coverage; employee discounts; savings plan. Corporate headquarters location. Parent company: J. Lyons Ltd. Operations at this facility include: administration.

New Jersey

AMBROSIA CHOCOLATE COMPANY
364 North Fifth Street
Newark NJ 07107
201/485-5385
Contact Personnel Department. Produces chocolate and compound coatings, ice cream coatings, cookie drops, cocoa powders, and chocolate liquors. Parent company, W. R. Grace & Co., is a diversified worldwide enterprise consisting of specialty and agricultural chemicals, energy production and services, retailing, restaurants, and other businesses. The firm operates over 2,500 facilities in 47 states and 42 foreign countries and employes 80,000 people. Corporate headquarters location: New York, NY.

ANHEUSER-BUSCH, INC.
200 U.S. Highway 1
Newark NJ 07101
Contact Paul Charrier, Personnel Director. Operates a major brewery facility producing nearly five million barrels of beer annually. Well-known family of beers include: Budweiser, Michelob, Mechelob Light, Busch, Natural Light, Classic Dark, and bottling operations for Wurzburger Hofbrau (brewed in West Germany). Nationally, company operates 11 breweries, including operations in St. Louis, Los Angeles, Tampa, Houston, Columbus (OH), Jacksonville (FL), Merrimack (NH), Williamburg (VA), Fairfield (CA), and Baldwinsville (NY). Corporate headquarters location: St. Louis, MO. International. New York Stock Exchange.

AUNT MILLIE SAUCES, INC./PRINCE FOODS
BORDEN, INC.
P.O. Box 555
Pennsauken NJ 08110
609/488-7100

Contact Cathi DeMarco, Employee Relations Manager. Manufacturers of spaghetti sauce. Common positions include: Accountant; Blue-Collar Worker Supervisor; Industrial Engineer; Mechanical Engineer; Financial Analyst; Food Technologist; Department Manager; General Manager; Operations/Production Manager; Personnel and Labor Relations Specialist; Purchasing Agent; Quality Control Supervisor; Distribution Manager. Principal educational backgrounds sought: Accounting; Biology; Business Administration; Chemistry; Engineering; Finance; Liberal Arts. Training programs offered. Company benefits include: medical insurance; dental insurance; pension plan; life insurance; tuition assistance; disability coverage; profit sharing; employee discounts; savings plan. Corporate headquarters location: Columbus, OH. Parent company: Borden, Inc. Operations at this facility include: manufacturing; administration. New York Stock Exchange.

BEST FOODS
180 Baldwin Avenue
Jersey City NJ 07306
201/653-3800
Contact Jeff Willard, Manager of Human Resources. Engaged in food-processing operations; products include entire line of Mueller quality food products. Common positions include: Accountant; Blue-Collar Worker Supervisor; Chemicst; Chemical Engineer; Electrical Engineer; Mechanical Engineer; Food Technologist; General Manager; Operations/Production Manager; Personnel & Labor Relations Specialist; Purchasing Agent; Quality Control Supervisor. Principal educational backgrounds sought: Accounting; Biology; Engineering; Finance. Company benefits include: medical, dental, and life insurance; pension plan; tuition assistance; disability coverage; profit sharing; employee discounts; savings plan. Corporate headquarters location: Englewood Cliffs, NJ. Operations at this facility include: manufacturing.

BEST FOODS BAKING
Greenbrook Corporate Center
100 Passaic Avenue
Fairfield NJ 07006
201/256-8200
Contact Alison Vagasky, Personnel Recruiter. Bakes, packages, and distributes complete line of Thomas' English Muffins. A subsidiary of CPC International. Corporate headquarters location.

BEST FOODS/
DIVISION OF CPC INTERNATIONAL
P.O. Box 8000
Englewood Cliffs NJ 07632.
Contact Manager of Staffing. Food manufacturer whose products include 'Hellman's/Best Foods Mayonnaise', 'Mazola' corn oil, 'Muellers' pasta, 'Knorr'soups, 'Skippy' peanut butter, and 'Arnold' breads. Common positions include: Accountant; Financial Analyst; Marketing Specialist; Personnel & Labor Relations Specialist; Purchasing Agent; Systems Analyst; Transportation & Traffic Specialist. Principal educational backgrounds sought: Accounting; Business Administration; Computer Science; Finance; Liberal Arts; Marketing. Company benefits include: medical, dental, and life insurance; tuition assistance; disability coverage; savings plan. Corporate, regional, and divisional headquarters location. Operations at this facility include: divisional headquarters; administration; service. New York Stock Exchange.

CPC INTERNATIONAL, INC.
P.O. Box 8000
Englewood Cliffs NJ 07632
201/894-4000
Contact John Jordan, Director of Management. A worldwide group of businesses, principally engaged in two major industry sectors: grocery products and corn wet milling.

CANTEEN CORPORATION
495 River Road
Clifton NJ 07014
201/779-0600
Contact Ms. Pat Allegretto, Comptroller. Company is one of the largest food service companies in the nation. Sales are primarily through food and vending operations, serving more than 800 manual food accounts nationwide, inboth office and manufacturing facilities. Concessions Division serves major accounts, including Yankee Stadium and Yellowstone National Park. Hospital Host Division services school districts, hospitals, and nursing homes, universities, and other major institutional customers. Also has some restaurant operations.

CLOFINE DAIRY PRODUCTS
1407 New Road
P.O. Box 335
Linwood NJ 08221
609/653-1000
Contact Marie Losco, Personnel. A brokerage services company for dairy and other food products.

HENRY COLT ENTERPRISE, INC.
Sykes Lane
Williamstown NJ 08094
609/629-4081
Contact Betsy Rosa, Personnel. A leading turkey processing plant.

DEALS SEAFOOD COMPANY INC.
212 East Madison Avenue
Magnolia NJ 08049
609/783-8700
Contact Mr. Jacobs, Personnel. A leading seafood packing company.

DRAKE BAKERIES
75 Demarest Drive
Wayne NJ 07470.
Contact Branch Manager. A small sales office for this national distributor and processor of bakery goods. Corporate headquarters location.

EL JAY POULTRY CORPORATION
P.O. Box 778
Voorhees NJ 08043
609/435-0900
Contact Julia O'Connor, Personnel. A major poultry processing company.

GOOD HUMOR CORPORATION
710 Route 46 East
Fairfield NJ 07004
201/227-6450
Contact Mary Ann Nordman, Personnel. A leading distributor of premium ice cream and frozen desserts. Sales offices located in Fairfield, N.J, Hartford, CT, Cincinnati, OH, Detroit, MI, Maywood, IL, and Hyattsville, MD. Corporate headquarters location. Common Positions include: Accountant; Operations/Production Manager; Sales Representative; Product Manager. Company benefits include: medical, dental and life insurance; pension plan; tuition assistance; disability coverage; profit sharing; savings plan. Parent company: Thomas J. Lipton, Inc. Operations at this facility include: administration; sales.

GREAT BEAR SPRING COMPANY
Great Bear Plaza
Teterboro NJ 07608
201/288-6550

Contact Kevin Flaherty, Human Resources Manager. A major distributor of bottled spring and distilled drinking water for home and industrial use. Also provides water coolers, microwave ovens, and similar equipment for installation in commercial and industrial locations. Corporate headquarters location. Common positions include: Accountant; Blue-Collar Worker Supervisor; Customer Service Representative; Branch Manager; Department Manager; General Manager; Management Trainee; Operations/Production Manager; Sales Representative. Principal educational backgrounds sought: Accounting; Computer Science; Finance; Liberal Arts; Marketing; Sales; Labor; Operations. Company benefits include: medical insurance; dental insurance; life insurance; tuition assistance; disability coverage; 401K plan. A subsidiary of the Perrier Group of America, (Greenwich, CT).

GREENWICH MILLS
520 Secaucus Road
Secaucus NJ 07094
201/865-0200
Contact Lorraine Sadowski, Office Manager. Produces and distributes coffee used in institutional, commercial, restaurant, food service, and similar operations. Corporate headquarters location.

S. GUMPERT COMPANY INC.
812 Jersey Avenue
Jersey City NJ 07303
201/652-3497
Contact Bob Breitman, Office Manager. Howard Janover, Vice President, can also be contacted. Manufactures and distributes specialty food products for institutions, bakeries, and ice-cream manufacturers. Corporate headquarters location.

INTERNATIONAL PROTEINS CORPORATION
P.O. Box 1169
Fairfield NJ 07007
201/227-2710
Contact Personnel Office. Company's operations are in the fishing industry, primarily in the production and distribution of fishmeal and fishoil, and frozen seafood, principally shrimp. In addition, the company is engaged in the trading of fishmeal and fishoil on a worldwide basis, and imports frozen seafood for distribution within the United States. Fishmeal products are used as a feed additive for poultry and livestock, and in the aquaculture industry. Fishoil is principally exported, to be used in the production of margarine or shortening, and to a lesser extent, in the manufacture of paints and cosmetics. International facilities include operations in Panama, Canada, Ecuador, and Chile. Corporate headquarters location. American Stock Exchange. International.

J & J SNACK FOODS CORPORATION
6000 Central Highway
Pennsauken NJ 08109
609/665-9533
Contact Diane Radcliff, Personnel. A major New Jersey manufacturer of a variety of snack foods.

LAIRD & COMPANY
1 Laird Road
Scobeyville (Monmouth County) NJ 07724
Contact Personnel Director. A distiller, importer, exporter and contract bottler of alcoholic beverages. Common positions include: Accountant; Administrator; Buyer; Computer Programmer; Customer Service Representative; Aerospace Engineer; Civil Engineer; Electrical Engineer; Mechanical Engineer; Financial Analyst; Industrial Designer; Marketing Specialist; Personnel & Labor Relations Specialist; Quality Control Supervisor; Sales Representative; Systems Analyst; Technical Writer/Editor. Principal educational backgrounds sought: Accounting; Computer Science; Engineering. Company benefits include: medical, dental, and life insurance; tuition assistance; disability coverage;

employee discounts. Corporate headquarters location: London, England. Operations at this facility include: manufacturing.

THOMAS J. LIPTON COMPANY
800 Sylvan Avenue
Englewood Cliffs NJ 07632
201/894-7585
Contact Personnel Administrator. Several area plants, including Flemington, NJ. A nationally-recognized manufacturer of quality food and beverage products. Divisions include: Beverage Division, which produces and distributes tea bags, herbal teas, flavored teas, iced tea mixes, and instant tea; Foods Division, whose products include soup mixes, 'Cup-a-Soup' products, 'Wish-Bone' dressings, 'Noodles and Sauce,' and 'Knox' gelatine, as well as other products; and General Management Group which has a foodservice division, 'Kind' and 'Knox' specialty gelatine products for the pharmaceutical and photographic markets, and a Continental markets division. Corporate headquarters location

MARATHON ENTERPRISES INC.
66 East Union Avenue
East Rutherford NJ 07073
201/935-3330
Contact Personnel Manager. Company is a manufacturer of provisions and baked goods. Corporate headquarters location.

MAXWELL HOUSE COFFEE
1125 Hudson Street
Hoboken NJ 07030
201/420-3414
Contact Cathy McSorley, Personnel Manager. Manufacturing facility for coffee products, including 'Maxwell House,' 'Sanka,' 'Yuban, and 'Brim.' A subsidiary of General Foods Corporation (White Plains, NY). Corporate headquarters location. Common positions include: Accountant; Blue-Collor Worker Supervisor; Computer Programmer; Engineer; Chemical Engineer; Electrical Engineer; Industrial Engineer; Mechanical Engineer; Financial Analyst; Department Manager; Operations/Production Manager; Personnel and Labor Relations Specialist; Purchasing Agent; Quality Control Supervisor; Transportation and Traffic Specialist. Principal educational backgrounds sought: Accounting; Engineering; Finance. Company benefits include: medical insurance; dental insurance; pension plan; life insurance; tuition assistanc; disability coverage; profit sharing; employee discounts; savings plan.

NABISCO BISCUIT COMPANY
100 DeForest Avenue
East Hanover NJ 07936
201/503-2000
Contact Personnel Center. One of the largest consumer foods operations in the country with annual sales of almost $3.0 billion. The company markets a broad line of high quality cookie and cracker products with popular brand names like Oreo, Ritz, Premium, Teddy Grahams, Chips Ahoy!, and Wheat Thins. The company operates nine bakeries, a flour mill and a cheese plant. The bakeries produce over one billion pounds of finished product each year in 80 ovens, each the length of a football field. These eleven facilities are in the following locations: Atlanta, GA; Buena Park, CA; Chicago, IL; Fair Lawn, NJ; Houston, TX; Philadelphia, PA; Pittsurgh, PA; Portland, OR; Richmond, VA; Toldeo, OH (flour plant); and Wrightstown, WI (cheese plant). Over 150 Biscuit brands reach the consumer via the industry's largest distribution network. The company has nine distribution centers, one at each of the bakeries. From these distribution centers the company delivers products to 140 warehouses located in each of six sales regions. Company market share stands at 44% of the cookie and cracker category. Common positions include: Chemist; Computer

assistance; disability coverage; employee discounts; savings plan. Operations at this facility include: research/development;administration. RJR Nabisco.

REITMAN INDUSTRIES, INC.
10 Patton Drive
West Caldwell NJ 07006
201/228-5100
Contact Personnel. Engaged in the wholesale importation and distribution of liquors and wines. Corporate headquarters location.

TUSCAN FARM PRODUCTS
750 Union Avenue
Union NJ 07083
201/686-1500
Contact Corporate Personnel Office. A major area dairy products firm, producing and distributing milk and related products throughout northern New Jersey and adjacent areas. Corporate headquarters location.

VENICE MAID COMPANY, INC.
P.O. Box 1505
Vineland NJ 08360
609/691-2100, ext. 255
Contact Personnel Manager. A food products firm. Produces a line of private-label canned Italian specialities, including: ravioli, spaghetti, soups, chilies, corned beef hash. Also produces a line of syrups (pancake and table type) and mayonnaise. Operations include: manufacturing; research/development; administration; sales. Corporate headquarters location: Bala Cynwyd, PA (Connelly Containers, Inc.). Common positions include: Accountant; Blue-Collar Worker Supervisor; Buyer; Chemist; Credit Manager; Customer Service Representative; Dietician; Electrical Engineer; Mechanical Engineer; Food Technologist; General Manager; Operations/Production Manager; Personnel & Labor Relations Specialist; Purchasing Agent; Quality Control Supervisor; Sales Representative; Transportation & Traffic Specialist. Principal educational backgrounds sought: Accounting; Business Administration; Chemistry; Engineering; Finance. Company benefits include: medical insurance; pension plan; life insurance; disability coverage.

FOOD/TRADE

New York

BIG V SUPERMARKETS INC.
176 North Main Street
Florida NY 10921
914/651-4411
Contact Erwin J. Fox, Vice-President/Industrial Relations. Engaged primarily in the business of operating and managing a chain of supermarkets primarily in the Mid-Hudson Valley of New York State. Operates 30 supermarkets, carrying a full line of grocery items and other non-grocery items. Offers both nationally-advertised brand names, and a wide variety of 'ShopRite' private label products. Corporate headquarters location.

D'AGOSTINO SUPERMARKETS INC.
2525 Palmer Avenue
New Rochelle NY 10801
914/576-1820
Contact Roi R. Tucker, Vice President, Human Resources. A major area supermarket chain, offering a full line of grocery, produce, and meats; in operation for more than 50 years. Operates more than 15 stores serving Westchester County, Brooklyn, Riverdale, and Manhattan. Common positions include: Department Manager; Management Trainee; Operations/Production Manager. Principal educational backgrounds sought: Business Administration. Training programs offered; Internships offered. Company benefits include:

medical, dental, and life insurance; disability coverage; savings plan. Corporate headquarters location. Operations at this facility include: administration.

DAIRY BARN STORES INC.
544 Elwood Road
East Northport NY 11731
516/368-8050
Contact John J. Konrad, Vice-President. A chain of 59 drive-in, convenience dairy stores, selling such products as milk, juice, bread, rolls, cakes, and ice cream. Common positions include: Management Trainee; Store Manager. Principal educational backgrounds sought: Business Adminstration. Company benefits include: medical, dental, and life insurance; pension plan; disability coverage.

FOOD CITY MARKETS INC.
57 East Burnside Avenue
Bronx NY 10453
212/295-4900
Contact Barry Schwartz, Supervisor of Store Operations. Multiple area locations in Manhattan, Queens, and Brooklyn. A major area supermarket chain, serving the five boroughs. Stores located primarily in the Bronx and Manhattan. Corporate headquarters location.

H.F.M. SUPERMARKETS, INC.
24 West 135th Street
New York NY 10037
212/368-0090
Contact Marco Regal, Comptroller. Several area locations. Produces a wide range of food products. Corporate headquarters location.

KEY FOOD STORES CO-OPERATIVE INC.
8925 Avenue D
Brooklyn NY 11236
718/451-1000
Contact Ronald Phillips, Assistant Controller. Operates a major area chain of food stores. Corporate headquarters location.

KING KULLEN GROCERY COMPANY INC.
1194 Prospect Avenue
Westbury NY 11590
516/333-7100
Contact Tom Nagle, Personnel Director. A pioneer in the development of the self-service, high volume, retail food supermarket; in the retail food distribution business, operating 55 supermarkets in Suffolk, Nassau, Queens, and Brooklyn, and maintaining its own grocery, meat, and produce warehouses, and a fleet of delivery vehicles. Corporate headquarters location.

PICK QUICK FOODS INC.
83-10 Rockaway Boulevard
Ozone Park NY 11416
718/296-9100
Contact Krish Malik, Controller. A major area grocery retailer. Corporate headquarters location.

SHELL MAR FOODS, INC.
425 Northern Boulevard
Great Neck NY 11021
516/487-6341
Contact Anthony Nisi, Personnel Director. A supermarket retailing chain. Corporate headquarters location.

TWIN COUNTY GROCERS
145 Talmadge Road
Edison NJ 08818
201/287-4600
Contact Ron Kuboski, Communications/Training Manager. Can also contact Joseph Casamento, Vice-President of Human Resources. Operates the sixth-largest food cooperative in the United States, providing member stores with grocery, dairy, deli, meat, frozen foods, produce, bakery goods, health and beauty aids, as well as other services, including insurance, training, food merchandising, equipment purchase, and sign-making. Company services more than 60 members, who own and operates almost 180 stores in New York, New Jersey, and Connecticut. Approximately 140 stores operate under the 'Foodtown' name, with about 40 others operating under different names. Subsidiary Twinco Graphics, which provides printing, binding, silkscreening, and other creative services to member stores, is located in Piscataway.

Connecticut

SHOP RITE SUPERMARKETS INC.
P.O. Box 641
Hartford CT 06142
203/291-9912
Contact Kathy Morrome, Human Resource Manager. Corporate headquarters of the well-known chain of retail food stores. Common positions include: Accountant; Administrator; Customer Service Representative; Department Manager; General Manager; Management Trainee; Retail Manager; Pharmacist. Principal educational backgrounds sought: Accounting; Business Administration; Finance; Liberal Arts; Marketing. Training programs available. Company benefits include: medical benefits include: medical insurance; dental insurance; pension plan; life insurance; tuition assistance; 401K plan; vision insurance. Corporate headquarters location: Edison, NJ. Parent company: Wakefern Food Corporation.

New Jersey

AGRICOL CORPORATION, INC.
Plaza 1000 at Main Street, Suite 404
Voorhees NJ 08043
609/665-7733
Contact Gamil Shab, Personnel. A wholesale grain trading company. Subsidiary of Conagra Company.

FOODARAMA SUPERMARKETS
P.O. Box 592
Freehold NJ 07728
201/462-4700
Contact John J. McAteer, Vice President of Personnel. A member of the ShopRite group; operates 24 supermarkets in three states, with 15 New Jersey locations, 5 in Long Island, and 5 in Pennsylvania. Corporate and regional headquarters location. American Stock Exchange. Common positions include: Accountant; Management Trainee. Principal educational backgrounds sought: Accounting. Company benefits include: medical, dental and life insurance; pension plan; disability coverage.

THE GREAT ATLANTIC & PACIFIC TEA CO.
(A&P)
2 Paragon Drive
Montvale NJ 07645
201/930-4416
Contact Corinne Blake, Manager of Personnel and Employment. Administrative offices for one of the nation's largest supermarket retailers. Company maintains more than 1400 supermarkets throughout the east coast and mid-atlantic states and Canada. Corporate

headquarters location. New York Stock Exchange. Common positions include: Accountant; Attorney; Buyer; Computer Programmer; Customer Service Representative; Draftsperson; Mechanical Engineer; Financial Analyst; Department Manager; General Manager; Store Management Trainee; Personnel & Labor Relations Specialist; Programmer; Purchasing Agent; Systems Analyst. Principal educational backgrounds sought: Accounting; Business Administration; Computer Science; Finance. Company benefits include: medical insurance; dental insurance; life insurance; disability coverage; savings plan; vision care; prescription drugs.

SUPERMARKETS GENERAL CORPORATION
301 Blair Road
Woodbridge NJ 07095
201/499-4019
Contact Manager/Selection & Placement. A diversified retailer engaged primarily in the operation of large supermarket-drug stores. Founded 27 years ago, the company is the 21st largest retailer in the country and is ranked as the 8th largest supermarket retailer. Its Rickel Home Center division is the 9th largest do-it-yourself home center chain in the nation. The company's retail stores are located in the Middle Atlantic and New England areas, with the most significant concentrations in the New York, Philadelphia and Boston metropolitan areas. The company's operations are divided as follows: Pathmark supermarket/drug stores, with 133 stores in New Jersey, New York, Connecticut, Delaware, and Pennsylvania; Purity Supreme and Heartland, 42 supermarkets and super warehouse stores in Massachusetts, New Hampshire and Connecticut; Pathmark, Pharmacity and Heartland, 49 conventional and deep discount drug stores in New York, Massachusetts, New Hampshire, Connecticut, Maryland, and New Jersey; Rickel, 40 'do-it-yourself home centers' in New Jersey, New York, Pennsylvania, Connecticut, Deleware and Maryland; Howland, Steinbach, Hochschild, Kohn, 29 department stores operating in New York, New Jersey, Maryland, and in New England; and Purity Supreme Supermarkets. Corporate headquarters location. New York Stock Exchange. Common positions include: Accountant; Attorney; Retail Buyer; Computer Programmer; Draftsperson; Industrial Engineer; Financial Analyst; Marketing Specialist; Programmer; Systems Analyst; Auditor; Night Store Manager. Principal educational backgrounds sought: Accounting; Business Administration; Computer Science; Engineering; Finance; Marketing. Company benefits include: medical insurance; dental insurance; pension plan; life insurance; tuition assistance; disability coverage; employee discounts; savings plan.

VILLAGE SUPER MARKET, INC.
733 Mountain Avenue
Springfield NJ 07081
201/467-2200
Contact Vic D'Ann, Personnel Director. Multiple area stores, in The Oranges, Livingston, Bernardsville, Florham Park, Union, Morristown, and Chester. Operates 20 supermarkets, 17 in north central New Jersey, and three in eastern Pennsylvania. Stores offer traditional grocery, meat, produce, dairy, frozen food, bakery, and delicatessen departments, as well as health and beauty aids, housewares, stationery, and automotive and paint supplies. Six stores contain prescription pharmacy departments, and the company also owns and operates two retail package liquor stores and one variety store. A member of Wakefern Food Corporation. Corporate headquarters location.

WAKEFERN FOOD CORPORATION
600 York Street
Elizabeth NJ 07207
201/527-3300
Contact Bill Britton, Manager of Recruiting. Operates a retailer-owned, non-profit food cooperative. Provides purchasing, warehousing, and distribution services to various grocery retailers throughout the metropolitan area. Many products are distributed under the 'ShopRite' name. Company also provides a wide range of support services to member firms. Principal educational backgrounds sought: Accounting; Liberal Arts. Internships offered. Company benefits include: medical, dental, and life insurance; pension plan; tuition assistance; disability coverage; savings plan. Operations at this facility include: regional headquarters; divisional headquarters; administration.

ZALLIE ENTERPRISES
1230 Blackwood-Clementon Road
Clementon NJ 08021
609/627-6501
Contact Personnel Department. Corporate offices for a chain of six Shop-Rite supermarkets.

GENERAL MERCHANDISE/TRADE

For more information on professional opportunities in the retail and wholesale industries, contact the following trade organization, as listed beginning on page 449:

NATIONAL RETAIL MERCHANTS ASSOCIATION

<u>New York</u>

ABRAHAM AND STRAUS
420 Fulton Street
Brooklyn NY 11201
718/802-7500
Contact Recruitment Director. Multiple area locations, New York, New Jersey Metropolitan Area. Operates a chain of full-line department stores with multiple branches throughout the region. Caters to a broad customer base ranging from traditional apparel to designer fashions. Employs 15,000 people in 15 stores, including seven on Long Island, four in New Jersey, and locations in Manhatten, Brooklyn, Queens, and White Plains. A major subsidiary of Federated Department Stores (Cincinnati, OH). Common positions include: Buyer; Department Manager; Management Trainee; Operations/Production Manager; Operations/Finance. Training programs offered; Internships offered.

ALEXANDER'S INC.
31 West 34th Street
New York NY 10001
212/560-2121
Contact Miss Annette Palazzolo, Personnel Director. A retailing complex of promotional department stores serving New York City and surrounding areas in Nassau and Westchester counties (NY), Connecticut, and New Jersey. Merchandise mix ranges from a wide assortment of apparel and accessories for the entire family, to housewares and small appliances. Operates 16 department stores total. Corporate headquarters location. New York Stock Exchange.

AMES CORPORATION
500 Seventh Avenue
New York NY 10018
212/536-9300
Contact Harold Goldstein, Personnel Office. One of the nation's largest and best-known merchandisers; maintains and operates over 250 general merchandise stores under the 'Zayre' name, offering a full line of hard and soft goods at discount prices. Also operates more than 240 ladies' and general apparel stores under the names 'Hit or Miss' and 'T.J. Maxx'. Corporate headquarters location: Framingham, MA. New York Stock Exchange.

AUDIOVOX CORPORATION
150 Marcus Boulevard
Hauppauge NY 11788
516/231-7750
Contact Mary Macedonia, Manager of Personnel. Engaged in the dealer distribution level sale of a variety of electronic components, including a wide range of auto radios, small screen televisions, video, home phones and cellular telephones, and many other items. Corporate headquarters location. Common positions include: Accountant; Advertising

Worker; Computer Programmer; Credit Manager; Customer Service Representative; Electrical Engineer; Financial Analyst; Department Manager: Operations/Production Manager; Marketing Specialist; Personnel & Labor Relations Specialist; Purchasing Agent; Quality Control Supervisor; Sales Representaive; Systems Analyst; Transportation & Traffic Specialist. Company benefits include: medical insurance; life insurance; disability coverage; profit sharing; employee discounts; savings plan; 401k; vacation; sicktime; holidays. Operations at this facility include: administration; service; sales. American Stock Exchange.

BARNES & NOBLE BOOKSTORES INC.
105 Fifth Avenue
New York NY 10003
212/633-3300
Contact Susan Comple, Human Resource Manager. A major discount bookstore chain, operating throughout the Northeast. Stores are concentrated in the metropolitan New York area, greater Boston, in Connecticut, and in many other locations. Comprehensive book departments cover a wide range of subjects. Corporate headquarters location. Common positions include: Accountant; Advertising Worker; Retail Buyer; Commercial Artist; Customer Service Representative; Financial Analyst; Branch Manager; Department Manager; Management Trainee. Principal educational backgrounds sought: Accounting; Business Administration; Liberal Arts. Company benefits include: medical insurance; dental insurance; life insurance; disability coverage; employee discounts; savings plan.

BARNEYS NEW YORK
106 Seventh Avenue
New York NY 10011
212/929-9000
Contact Mary Cooke, Personnel Director. A national specialty retailer, offering primarily men's and women's apparel collections from noted American and international designers. Common positions include: Accountant; Administrator; Advertising; Buyer; Customer Service Representative; Manage.; Department Manager; Personnel & Labor Relations Specialist; Purchasing Agent; Assistant Buyer; Assistant Manager; Operations Worker; Public Relations Specialist; Sales Associate. Company benefits include: medical insurance; dental insurance; pension plan; life insurance; disability coverage; employee discounts; savings plan. Corporate headquarters location. Operations at this facility include: administration; sales; service.

BERGDORF GOODMAN INC.
754 Fifth Avenue
New York NY 10019
212/753-7300
Contact Miss Marita O'Dea, Personnel Director. One of the world's foremost high fashion specialty stores; a division of Carter Hawley Hale Stores, Inc. (Los Angeles, CA), a diversified retailer. Corporate headquarters location.

BLOOMINGDALE'S
1000 Third Avenue
Executive Placement
New York NY 10022
212/705-2383
Contact Erika Garfield, Manager of Executive Recruiting. A leading department store with locations in the New York metropolitan area, Boston, Philadelphia, suburban Washington DC, Dallas and Miami. Stores are planned for entry into Palm Beach, Florida and Minniapolis, Minnesota. Company image stresses quality, innovation, customer service and trend-setting merchandise. A subsidiary of Federated Stores Inc. Common positions include: Administrator; Advertising Worker; Architect; Blue-Collar Worker Supervisor; Buyer; Commercial Artist; Computer Programmer; Customer Service Representative; Draftsperson; Branch Manager; Department Manager; General Manager; Management Trainee; Operations/Production Manager; Public Relations Worker; Purchasing Agent; Quality Control Supervisor; Systems Analyst. Principal educational backgrounds sought: Accounting; Business Administration; Communications; Computer Science; Economics;

Finance; Liberal Arts; Marketing; Mathematics. Company benefits include: medical insurance; dental insurance; pension plan; life insurance; tuition assistance; disability coverage; profit sharing; employee discounts. Corporate headquarters location. Parent company: Federated Department Stores. Regional headquarters. Operations at this facility include: research/development; administration; service; sales. New York Stock Exchange

BONWIT TELLER
1120 Avenue of the Americas
New York NY 10036
212/764-3651
Contact Director of Executive Recruitment. Women's specialty store carrying women's, men's and children's merchandise. Operates 15 stores nationwide. Common positions include: Accountant; Administrator; Customer Service Representative; Financial Analyst; Department Manager; General Manager. Principal educational backgrounds sought: Accounting; Art/Design. Company benefits include: medical insurance; pension plan; dental insurance; employee discounts. Corporate headquarters location.

BROOKS BROTHERS
346 Madison Avenue
New York NY 10017
212/682-8800
Contact John Irvin, Sr. Vice President/Human Resources. Operates one of the foremost specialty store retailing chains in the United States; a well-known name in high-quality, traditionally-styled apparel. Overall, operates 52 stores in the United States, and 25 in Japan, with further expansion planned. A subsidiary of Marks and Spencer, London. Common positions include: Advertising Worker; Architect; Buyer; Claim Representative; Computer Programmer; Customer Service Representative; Draftsperson; Branch Manager; Department Manager; Management Trainee; Operations/Production Manager; Personnel & Labor Relations Specialist; Purchasing Agent; Reporter/Editor; Sales Representative; Technical Writer/Editor. Principal educational backgrounds sought: Business Administration; Communications; Computer Science; Marketing. Training programs offered. Company benefits include: medical, dental and life insurance; pension plan; tuition assistance; disability coverage; profit sharing; employee discounts; savings plan. Corporate headquarters location. International.

FORTUNOFF
1300 Old Country Road
Westbury NY 11590
516/832-1520
Contact Robyn Ornstein, Executive Recruiter. Manages and operates home furnishings department stores, offering a wide range of quality of merchandise, including fine jewelry and silver. Corporate headquarters location. Common positions include: Accountant; Assistant Buyer; Buyer; Computer Programmer; Customer Service Representative; Department Manager; Management Trainee; Warehouse Executive Management. Principal educational backgrounds sought: Accounting; Business Administration; Communications; Economics; Finance; Liberal Arts; Marketing & Retailing. Company benefits include: medical insurance; dental insurance; pension plan; life insurance; disability coverage; employee discounts; savings plan; wellness plan.

FOXMOOR SPECIALTY STORES CORPORATION
393 Seventh Avenue
11 Penn Plaza
New York NY 10001
Contact Personnel Department. One of the nation's largest chains of specialty stores with over 600 stores and a division of B.R. Investors, Inc. Common positions include: Buyer; Associate Buyer; Assistant Buyer; Merchandise Planner, Distributor, and Clerk; Secretary; Visual Merchandise Manager; Marketing Manager. Principal educational backgrounds sought: Accounting; Business Administration; Computer Science; Marketing. Company benefits include: medical, dental and life insurance; tuition assistance; pension plan; disability coverage; profit sharing; employee discounts; savings plan. Fashion office location. Corporate headquarters: Brockton, MA.

LERNER STORES
460 West 33rd Street
New York NY 10001
212/736-1222
Contact Tom Bennett, Vice President of Personnel. Multiple area locations. Operates a national chain of women's and children's moderately-priced fashion apparel outlets. Nationally, company operates almost 800 stores coast-to-coast. Stores are located in 45 states, Washington DC, Puerto Rico, and the Virgin Islands. Corporate headquarters location.

THE LIMITED STORES INC.
1450 Broadway, 4th Floor
New York NY 10018
212/221-0030
Contact Personnel Department. Area management offices for a nationwide fashion retailer. Stores specialize in the sale of medium-priced fashion apparel for women aged 20-40. Fashion merchandise includes shirts and blouses, sweaters, skirts, pants, coats, suits, dresses, and accessories. Company operates 500 Limited Stores nationwide; 17 in New York; 15 in New Jersey; and three in Connecticut. Fashion stores are located in White Plains and New York, NY; Meriden and Hartford, CT. Subsidiaries include Mast Industries (office in New York, NY), an international contract manufacturer. Corporate headquarters location: Columbus, OH. International. New York Stock Exchange.

LORD AND TAYLOR
424 Fifth Avenue
New York NY 10018
212/391-3784
Contact Director of Recruitment. Multiple area locations, including Westchester, Manhasset, and Garden City, NY; Milburn, and Paramus-Ridgewood, NJ. An upscale, full-line department store, offering high-quality clothing, accessories, home furnishings, and many other retail items. Stores located throughout the country, including metropolitan Washington DC, Virginia, Massachusetts, Pennsylvania, Connecticut (Stamford and West Hartford), Illinois, Texas, Georgia, Michigan, and Florida. A division of the May Department Stores Company. Common positions include: Buyer; Credit Manager; Branch Manager; Department Manager; Management Trainee. Principal educational backgrounds sought: Business Administration; Communications; Economics; Finance; Liberal Arts; Marketing; Mathematics. Company benefits include: medical, dental and life insurance; pension plan; employee discounts; savings plan. Corporate headquarters location. Operations at this facility include: divisional headquarters; research/development; administration; service; sales.

MBI, INC.
47 Richards Avenue
Norwalk CT 06857
203/853-2000
Contact W.J. McEnery Jr., Personnel Manager. Engaged in direct marketing of commemorative/collectible items. Corporate headquarters location. Common positions include: Product Manager. Principal educational backgrounds sought: Business Administration; Finance; Marketing. Company benefits include: medical insurance; dental insurance; pension plan; life insurance; tuition assistance; disability coverage; employee discounts; profit sharing; vacation; holiday; year-end bonus; personal days.

R.H. MACY & CO. INC.
151 West 34th Street, Room 1303
New York NY 10001
212/560-4048
Contact Administrator/Executive Development. One of the nation's largest retailing firms. Conducts its department store business through four operating divisions: Macy's New York, Bamberger's, Macy's California, and Macy's Atlanta. The stores carry primarily medium-and higher-priced lines in a wide variety of merchandise, including apparel and

accessories, furniture, home furnishings, housewares, and electronics. The corporation wholly owns a financing subsidiary, operates six regional shopping centers, and has significant interest in five others. Also has a corporate buying division which is responsible for new product development, primarily via foreign markets, and is responsible for sales of over $1 billion per year in private label business. Each division recruits, hires, and trains its own professionals. Most divisions feature two entry-level executive training programs, one for merchandise executives, and one for executives in the areas of control, operations, personnel, and sales promotion. Maintains a strong policy of hiring from within, but also recruits experienced executives. Corporate headquarters location. New York Stock Exchange. Common positions include: Accountant; Advertising Worker; Buyer; Computer Programmer; Customer Service Representative; Food Technologist; Department Manager; Management Trainee; Personnel & Labor Relations Specialist; Systems Analyst. Principal educational backgrounds sought: Accounting; Art/Design; Business Administration; Finance; Liberal Arts; Marketing. Company benefits include: medical insurance; dental insurance; pension plan; life insurance; tuition assistance; disability coverage; employee discounts; savings plan.

MAY MERCHANDISING
1120 Avenue of the Americas
New York NY 10036
212/704-2600
Contact Ron Devine, Personnel Manager. One of the nation's leading retail companies, operating 6 quality department store divisions in 24 states and Washington DC, and a specialty store division operating in five midwestern states. Overall, the company operates more than 160 department stores and 30 specialty stores, with the majority of sales in women's apparel and related accessories. Subsidiary stores include Lord & Taylor; Goldwaters (primarily western United States); J.W. Robinson (primarily Southern California); Hahne & Company; The William Hengerer Company; Sibley; Lindsay & Curr Company; and others. Most hiring is performed through specific store divisions. Corporate headquarters location. New York Stock Exchange.

J.W. MAYS INC.
9 Bond Street
Brooklyn NY 11201
718/624-7400
Contact Pearl Small, Personnel Director. Multiple area locations throughout Brooklyn, Queens, and Manhattan. Operates a general department store through four retail department stores, all located in metropolitan New York. Specializes in the volume distribution of apparel for men, women, and children, in the popular and higher price ranges, and also sells a wide assortment of other general retail merchandise. Corporate headquarters location.

McCRORY
725 Fifth Avenue
New York NY 10022
212/735-9500
Contact Personnel. Company operates general merchandise stores.

MELVILLE CORP.
1 Theall Road
Rye NY 10580
914/925-4000
Contact Personnel. Corporation operates specialty chain stores.

MERCANTILE STORES COMPANY INC.
128 West 31st Street
New York NY 10001
212/560-0500
Contact Nancy Cates, Employment Manager. Engaged in general merchandise department store retailing. Company operates 84 department stores, with 81 located in the United

States. None of the department store chains operate in the New York metropolitan area, but central buying and administrative offices are centered here. Stores operate under 15 different chain names, including Bacons, Root's, Hennessy's, Glass Block, de Lendrecie's, Castner Knott Company, Gayfers, The Jones Store Company, Joslins, The People's Store, Gayfers/Montgomery Fair, Lion, McAlpin's, The Right House, and J. B. White. The stores operate in 17 states and in Ontario, Canada, with most United States stores located in the South, Midwest, and North Central states. Corporate headquarters location: Wilmington, DE. New York Stock Exchange. International.

POTAMKIN CADILLAC CORPORATION
787 54th & Eleventh
New York NY 10019
212/603-7200
Contact Vice-President. Operates the nation's largest Cadillac dealership, with complete sales and service facilities. Two Manhattan locations. Corporate headquarters location.

ROCK BOTTOM STORES, INC.
83 Harbor Road
Port Washington NY 11050
516/944-9000
Contact Kathryn Tenenholz, VP/Human Resources. A major area retail drug store chain, specializing in health and beauty aids. Corporate headquarters location. Common positions include: Buyer; Management Trainee; Purchasing Agent; Store Managers; Bookkeepers. Educational backgrounds sought include: Liberal Arts. Training programs available. Company benefits include: medical insurance; dental insurance; disability coverage; savings plan. Corporate headquarters location.

SAKS FIFTH AVENUE
611 Fifth Avenue
New York NY 10021
212/753-4000
Contact Mary Jean Basileo, Employment Manager. One of the nation's leading high-quality specialty retail chains. Company operates 46 fashion specialty stores located in Arizona, California, Florida, Georgia, Illinois, Louisiana, Oklahoma, Oregon, Colorado, Minnesota, Maryland, Massachusetts, Michigan, Missouri, Nevada, New Jersey, New York, Ohio, Pennsylvania, and Texas. Company employs more than 10,000 people nationwide. Emphasis is on fashion-forward, high-quality soft goods, primarily apparel. Common positions include: Administrator; Blue-Collar Worker Supervisor; Department Manager; Management Trainee; Operations/Production Manager; Personnel & Labor Relation Specialist; Quality Control Supervisor; Sales Representative; Statistician. Principal educational backgrounds sought: Business Administration; Liberal Arts; Marketing. Training programs offered; Internships offered. Company benefits include: medical, dental, and life insurance; pension plan; tuition assistance; disability coverage; employee discounts; savings plan; credit union. Operations at this facility include: service; sales.

F.W. WOOLWORTH COMPANY
233 Broadway
New York NY 10279
212/553-2000
Contact William Forcht, Personnel Administrator. Multiple area locations. A multinational retailer, distributing a broad range of variety, footwear, apparel, and department store merchandise through more than 6900 stores and leased departments throughout the world. The company operates retail units under the following names: Woolworth, Woolco, Kinney, Richman, Anderson-Little, J. Brannam, Shirt Closet, Susie's Casuals, Foot Locker, Lewis, Mankind, Fredelle, Williams the Shoeman, Frugal Frank's Shoe Outlet, Woolco Catalogue Stores, Shoppers World, B&Q (Retail) Ltd., Dodge City, Burgermaster, and Furnishing World. Corporate headquarters location. New York Stock Exchange. International.

WORLD-WIDE VOLKSWAGEN CORPORATION
Greenbush Road
Orangeburg NY 10962
914/578-5000
Contact Carolyn Heerlein, Personnel Director. The area's largest distributor of Volkswagen, Porsche, and Audi automobiles and parts, serving New York, New Jersey, and Connecticut. An independent, privately-owned firm. Corporate headquarters location.

Connecticut

AMES DEPARTMENT STORES
2418 Main Street
Rocky Hill CT 06067
203/257-2167
Contact Human Resources Department. Nationally known chain of discount stores with 17 locations in Connecticut. Corporate headquarters location.

CALDOR INC.
20 Glover Avenue
Norwalk CT 06850-1299
203/846-1641
Contact Personnel Department. A division of Associated Dry Goods Corporation, Caldor operates 109 full-line upscale discount department stores in Connecticut, Massachusetts, Rhode Island, New Hampshire, Maryland, Virginia, and Pennsylvania. Expansion is planned at the rate of 8-14 stores per year. Corporate headquarters location. Common positions include: Accountant; Advertising Worker; Buyer; Computer Programmer; Data Processing Specialist; Draftsperson; Department Manager; Assistant Store Manager; Personnel & Labor Relations Specialist; Programmer; Purchasing Agent. Principal educational backgrounds sought include: Computer Science. Company benefits include: medical insurance; pension plan; life insurance; tuition assistance; disability coverage; employee discounts.

DRESS BARN, INC.
P.O. Box 10220
Stamford CT 06904
203/327-4242
Contact Lori Tiani, Personnel. Operates a chain of over 430 women's speciality, fashion apparel stores in 31 states. Opening an average of 1 store every 4 days, they offer store management opportunities in most major metro markets. Common positions include: Department Manager; Management Trainee; Store Manager. Principal educational backgrounds sought: Retailing. Company benefits include: medical, dental, and life insurance; disability coverage; profit sharing; employee discounts.

WALDENBOOKS
201 High Ridge Road
Stamford CT 06904
203/352-2066
Contact Maryellyn R. Haffner, Manager, Human Resources. Established in 1933, the company is now the nation's largest retail bookselling chain, with more than 1,400 stores across the country. Common positions include: Entry-level, Intermediate, and Senior Accountant; Computer Operator; Computer Programmer; Programmer Analyst; Systems Analyst; Financial Analyst; various Marketing Specialists; Human Resources Specialists, and a variety of entry-level positions. Principal educational backgrounds sought: Accounting; Business Administration; Finance; Economics; Computer Science; Liberal Arts; Marketing. Company benefits include: medical, dental, and life insurance; short-term disability; long-term disability; employee discounts; savings plan; pension plan; tuition reimbursement; matching gift company. Corporate headquarters location. A subsidiary of Kmart Corporation.

New Jersey

CHANNEL HOME CENTERS
945 Route 10
Whippany NJ 07981
201/887-7000
Contact Marc Hettinger, V.P. Personnel. Operates a chain of home improvement centers. Parent company: W.R. Grace & Co., is a diversified worldwide enterprise consisting of specialty and agricultural chemicals, energy production, and services, and retailing, restaurants, and other businesses; the firm operates over 2,500 facilities in 47 states and 42 foreign countries and employs 80,000 people.

S.P. DUNHAM & COMPANY INC.
Route 1 and Texas Avenue
Trenton NJ 08648
609/989-7777
Contact Karen Vegotsky, Personnel Director. A leading Trenton department store.

EDMUND SCIENTIFIC COMPANY
101 East Gloucester Pike
Barrington NJ 08007
609/573-6279
Contact Virginia Lamelas, Personnel Director. A major southern New Jersey mail order house.

M. EPSTEIN, INC.
32 Park Place
Morristown NJ 07960
201/538-5000
Contact David R. Pollio, Personnel Manager. Other area facilities in Bridgewater, Princeton, and Shrewsbury. A family-owned specialty customer-service oriented department store, offering a wide range of quality fashions and other soft and hard goods. Common positions include: Accountant; Administrator; Advertising Worker; Credit Manager; Department Manager; General Manager. Principal educational backgrounds sought: Business Administration; Marketing. Company benefits include: medical and life insurance; disability coverage; employee discounts. Corporate headquarters location: Cedar Knolls, NJ. Operations at this facility include: sales.

HERMAN'S WORLD OF SPORTING GOODS
2 Germak Drive
Carteret NJ 07008
201/541-1550
Contact Personnel Department. Engaged in sporting goods equipment and apparel retailing. Common positions include: Accountant; Buyer; Computer Programmer; Financial Analyst; Management Trainee; Systems Analyst, Retail Managers; Retail Sales. Principal educational backgrounds sought: Accounting; Business Administration; Finance; Marketing. Company benefits include: medical insurance; life insurance; tuition assistance; disability coverage; profit sharing; employee discounts; savings plan. Corporate headquarters location. Parent company: Isosceles PLC (United Kingdom). Over 200 stores in operation nationwide

JACOBS DEPARTMENT STORE
190 Main Street
Paterson NJ 07505
201/684-8100
Contact Personnel Department. An area department store; features designer labels and a complete traditional department store selection of merchandise at discount prices as well as substantial close-out inventories. Specializing in women's and men's fashion apparel, domestics, shoes, children's toys, and children's clothing and housewares. Corporate headquarters location.

JAMESWAY CORPORATION
40 Hartz Way
Secaucus NJ 07096
201/330-6000
Contact Executive Placement. A leading regional discount Department store chain, currently operating stores in seven Mid-Atlantic states. Stores average approximately 60,000 square feet in size, and incorporate the latest and most innovative concepts in the discount retail industry. Common positions include: Management Trainee. Principal educational backgrounds sought: all majors. Training programs offered. Company benefits include: medical and life insurance; tuition assistance; disability coverage; profit sharing; employee discounts. Corporate headquarters location. New York Stock Exchange.

K-MART APPAREL CORPORATION
7373 West Side Avenue
North Bergen NJ 07047
201/861-9100
Contact Personnel Director. One of the largest non-food retailers in the United States. Operates stores nationwide under the K-Mart, Kresge, and Jupiter names, with more than 50 K-Mart stores located in the New York metropolitan area. All stores offer a broad range of discounted general merchandise, both soft and hard goods. Overall, company operates more than 2,000 stores. Corporate headquarters location. New York Stock Exchange. International.

LINENS 'N THINGS
6 Brighton Road
Clifton NJ 07015
201/778-1300
Contact Director of Personnel. A national retail specialty chain with 130 stores with anticipated growth of at least 15 new stores this year. Common positions include: Assistant Store Manger. Principal educational backgrounds sought: Business Administration; Liberal Arts; Marketing. Company benefits include: medical insurance; dental insurance; pension plan; life insurance; disability coverage; employee discounts; stock purchase plan. Corporate headquarters location: Clifton, NJ. Parent company: Subsidiary of HuMelville Corp. New York Stock Exchange.

T.H.MANDY
1 Ellisburg Circle
Cherry Hill NJ 08034
609/429-1912
Contact City Manager. Women's specialty retailer. Common positions include: Management Trainee; Store Management; Sales Associates. Company benefits include: medical, dental and life insurance; tuition assistance; disability coverage; profit sharing; employee discounts; savings plan. Corporate headquarters location: Merrifield, VA. Parent company: U.S. Shoe Corporation. Operations at this facility include: sales. New York Stock Exchange.

ORMOND SHOPS INC.
7300 West Side Avenue
North Bergen NJ 07047
201/861-5800
Contact Isabella Spiegel, Personnel Manager. Several area locations. Operates a retail specialty store chain, specializing in women's apparel. This facility houses administrative, buying, distribution, and accounting departments. Management training program. Corporate headquarters location. Common positions include: Management Trainee; Warehouse Supervisor; Associate Buyer; Store Manager; Distribution/Planning Director; Accountant. Principal educational backgrounds sought: Accounting; Business Administration; Liberal Arts; Retail. Company benefits include: medical insurance; life insurance; profit sharing; employee discounts; savings plan.

PETRIE STORES CORPORATION
70 Enterprise Avenue
Secaucus NJ 07094
201/866-3600
Contact Patricia Hughes, Personnel Manager. Multiple area locations. Operates a chain of approximately 1400 women's specialty stores in 49 states, Puerto Rico, the Virgin Islands, and the District of Columbia, selling apparel at moderate prices to teen, junior, and contemporary miss customers. The principal tradenames are 'Petrie's,' 'Stuart's,' 'Marianne,' 'David's,' 'G&G,' 'Franklin's,' 'Hartfield's,' 'Jean Nicole,''Diana Marco,' and 'Three Sisters.' Corporate headquarters location. New York Stock Exchange. Common positions include: Attorney; Buyer; Computer Programmer; Draftsperson; Management Trainee; Programmer; Buyer Trainee; Merchandise Distributor; Accounts Payable. Principal educational backgrounds sought: Accounting; Business Administration; Marketing; Retail Fashion and Merchandising. Company benefits include: medical insurance; pension plan; life insurance; disablity coverage; employee discounts.

PITMAN COMPANY
721 Union Boulevard
Totowa NJ 07512
201/812-0400
Contact Bob Schmidt, National Marketing Manager. A major area distributor for Kodak, 3-M, BisMarch, and others.

STERN'S
Executive Placement Office
Route 4, Bergen Mall
Paramus NJ 07652
201/845-2378
Contact Ernest Buffalino, Director of Executive Placement & Development. Seventeen area branches, including Paramus, Woodbridge, NJ; Flushing, and Hicksville, NY. Operates a chain of full-line department stores located in New Jersey, Queens, and Long Island. A unit of Allied Stores Corporation. Corporate headquarters location.

TOYS R' US
461 From Road
Paramus NJ 07652
201/262-7800
Contact Manager of Human Resources Planning. Operates over 450 retail toy stores throughout the USA with sales approaching $5 billion. Diversifying internationally with over 100 stores in nine countries currently. Continued expansion estimated at 15-20% per year. Primary recruiting needs for retail management trainees. Over 1000 candidates hired annually in the U.S. Common positions include: Retail Manager. Principal educational backgrounds sought: Business Administration; Computer Science; Liberal Arts; Marketing; Retail Management, Logistics. Training programs offered; Internships offered. Company benefits include: medical, dental, and life insurance; pension plan; disability coverage; profit sharing; savings plan; stock options; bonus plan. Corporate headquarters location.

HEALTH CARE & PHARMACEUTICALS: PRODUCTS AND SERVICES

For more information on professional opportunities in the health care and pharmaceutical industries, contact the following professional and trade organizations, as listed beginning on page 449:

AMERICAN ACADEMY OF PHYSICIAN ASSISTANTS
AMERICAN COLLEGE OF HEALTHCARE EXECUTIVES
AMERICAN DENTAL ASSOCIATION
AMERICAN HEALTH CARE ASSOCIATION
AMERICAN MEDICAL ASSOCIATION
AMERICAN OCCUPATIONAL THERAPY ASSOCIATION
AMERICAN PHARMACEUTICAL ASSOCATION

AMERICAN PHYSICAL THERAPY ASSOCIATION
AMERICAN SOCIETY FOR BIOCHEMISTRY
    AND MOLECULAR BIOLOGY
AMERICAN SOCIETY OF HOSPITAL PHARMACISTS
AMERICAN VETERINARY MEDICAL ASSOCIATION
CARDIOVASCULAR CREDENTIALING INTERNATIONAL
MEDICAL GROUP MANAGEMENT ASSOCIATION
NATIONAL HEALTH COUNCIL
NATIONAL MEDICAL ASSOCIATION
NEW YORK DENTAL SOCIETY
NEW YORK COUNTY MEDICAL SOCIETY
PHARMACEUTICAL SOCIETY OF THE STATE OF NEW YORK

New York

AMERICAN HOME PRODUCTS CORPORATION
685 Third Avenue
New York NY 10017
212/986-1000
Contact Employment Specialist. A leading manufacturer and marketer of prescription drugs and medical supplies, packaged medicines, food products, and household products and housewares. Prescription Drugs and Medical Supplies segment operates through the following subsidiaries: Wyeth Laboratories (produces ethical pharmaceuticals, biologicals, and nutritional products); Ayerst Laboratories (produces ethical pharmaceuticals, over-the-counter antacids, vitamins, and sunburn remedies); Ives Laboratories (ethical pharmaceuticals); Fort Dodge Laboratories (veterinary pharmaceuticals and biologicals); Sherwood Medical (medical devices, diagnostic instruments, test kits, bacteria identification systems); and Corometrics Medical Systems (medical electronic instrumentation for obstetrics and neonatology). Packaged Medicines segment operates through subsidiary Whitehall Laboratories (produces analgesics, cold remedies, and other packaged medicines). Food Products segment operates through subsidiaries American Home Foods (canned pasta, canned vegetables, specialty foods, mustard, popcorn); and E.J. Brach & Sons (assorted chocolates, novelties, and other general line candies). Household Products and Housewares segment operates through subsidiaries Boyle-Midway (cleaners, insecticides, air fresheners, waxes, polishes, and other items for home, appliance, and apparel care); Dupli - Color Products (touch-up, refinishing, and other car-care and shop-use products); Ekco Products (food containers, commercial baking pans, industrial coatings, food handling systems, foilware, plasticware); Ekco Housewares (cookware, cutlery, kitchen tools, tableware and accessories, padlocks); and Prestige Group (cookware, cutlery, kitchen tools, carpet sweepers, pressure cookers). Corporate headquarters location. International.

AMERICAN WHITE CROSS LABORATORIES INC.
40 Nardozi Place
New Rochelle NY 10802
914/632-3045
Contact Kaare Numme, Controller. Manufactures and distributes a complete range of hospital and surgical supplies, including bandages, ointments, and many other products. Products are distributed at the consumer level to drugstores, supermarkets, and other mass marketers; and to hospitals, clinics, and other medical institutions. Corporate headquarters location.

BOLAR PHARMACEUTICAL
33 Ralph Avenue
Copiague NY 11726-1297
516/842-8383
Contact Fran Herman, Personnel Director. A medicine/pharmaceutical manufacturer.

CMP INDUSTRIES INC.
413 North Pearl Street
Albany NY 12207
518/434-3147
Contact Robert J. Briggs, Director of Administration. A manufacturer of dental metals, dental equipment and other dental supplies. Operations at this facility include: manufacturing. Corporate headquarters location. Common positions include: Accountant; Administrator; Blue-Collar Worker Supervisor; Credit Manager; Customer Service Representative; Engineer; Electrical Engineer; General Manager; Operations/Production Manager; Marketing Specialist; Personnel & Labor Relations Specialist; Purchasing Agent; Sales Representative. Principal educational backgrounds sought: Accounting; Business Administration; Engineering; Finance; Marketing. Company benefits include: medical insurance; dental insurance; pension plan; life insurance; tuition assistance; disability coverage; profit sharing; employee discounts.

CARTER WALLACE INC.
1345 Avenue of the Americas
New York NY 10105
212/339-5000
Contact Personnel Manager. Several area locations, including Cranbury, East Windsor, and Princeton, NJ; and Winstead, CT. Produces and markets toiletries, pharmaceuticals, diagnostic specialties, proprietary drugs, and pet products. Well-known consumer products include 'Arrid Extra-Dry' deodorants, 'Pearl Drops' tooth polish, 'Nair' depilatories, and many others. Health care products include brand names such as 'Miltown', 'Soma', 'Carter's Little Pills', and 'Jordan' toothbrushes, sold primarily to physicians, hospitals, laboratories, and clinics. Divisions include: Carter Products (consumer products); Lambert Kay (pet products); Wallace Laboratories (health care products), and Wampole Laboratories (health care products). Employs more than 3500 people worldwide. International facilities located in England, Mexico, France, Italy, and Puerto Rico. Corporate headquarters location. New York Stock Exchange. International.

CORNELL UNIVERSITY MEDICAL COLLEGE
445 East 69th Street
New York NY 10021
212/746-1036
Contact Janet Garber, Manager, Employment. A teaching and research institution. Operations include: research/development; administration. Common positions: Accountant; Administrator; Biologist; Computer Programmer; Financial Analyst; Personnel & Labor Relations Specialist; Research Technician. Principal educational backgrounds sought: Accounting; Biology; Business Administration; Chemistry; Computer Science; Finance; Liberal Arts. Company benefits include: medical insurance; dental insurance; pension plan; life insurance; tuition assistance; disability coverage; employee discounts; savings plan.

DARBY DRUGS COMPANY INC.
100 Banks Avenue
Rockville Center NY 11570
516/536-3000
Contact Diane Weinstien, Personnel Director. A manufacturer and distributor of pharmaceuticals, over-the-counter drugs, and vitamins. Corporate headquarters location.

DEL LABORATORIES INC.
565 Broadhollow Road
Farmingdale NY 11735
516/752-2061
Contact Laura Segovia, Recruiter. A fully integrated marketing and manufacturing company of packaged consumer products consisting of cosmetics, toiletries, beauty aids, and proprietary pharmaceuticals. Products reach the consumer through overall channels of distribution to chain and independent drug stores, mass merchandisers, and supermarkets. Divisions include: Commerce Drug Company; Flame Glo Division; La Cross Division; La Salle Laboratories Division; Nutri-Tonic Division; Parfums Schiaparelli Division; Rejuvia;

Sally Hansen Division; Del International. Common positions include: Accountant; Advertising Worker; Biochenist; Biologist; Buyer; Chemist; Computer Programmer; Customer Service Representative; Industrial Engineer; Purchasing Agent; Sales Representative; Principal educational backgrounds sought: Accounting; Business Administration; Chemistry; Computer Science; Engineering; Finance; Liberal Arts; Marketing. Company benefits include: medical and life insurance; pension plan; tuition assistance; disability coverage; ESOP. Corporate headquarters location. Operations at this facility include: regional and divisional headquarters; manufacturing; research/development; administration; service. American Stock Exchange. International.

IMS AMERICA
100 Campus Road
Totowa NJ 07512
201/790-0870
Contact Personnel Manager. Provides data processing services for the pharmaceutical industry. Corporate headquarters location.

KIMBERLY QUALITY CARE INC. OF LONG ISLAND
77 North Centre Avenue, Suite 315
Rockville Centre NY 11570
516/678-4100
Contact Director. Operates one of the nation's largest independent home care services, providing care for the infirm and handicapped in more than 25 separate locations in the metropolitan New York area. Overall, company operates 104 wholly-owned and 55 franchised offices in 43 states and Canada. Each facility provides a full range of health care services to meet the needs of its patients, including registered nurses, licensed practical/vocational nurses, nurses' aides, homemakers, and companions. Corporate headquarters location. International.

LEDERLE LABORATORIES
401 North Middletown Road
Pearl River NY 10965
914/732-5000
Contact Personnel Director. Manufactures both prescription and non-prescription pharmaceutical products and hospital products. Products include pharmaceuticals for the treatment of infectious diseases, mental illness, cancer, arthritis, skin disorders, glaucoma, tuberculosis and other diseases; adult and pediatric vaccines; vitamin, multivitamin, and mineral products; Davis & Geck surgical sutures, wound closure devices, and other hospital products. A major operating subsidiary of American Cyanamid Company (see separate listing). Corporate headquarters location.

LUMEX INC.
100 Spence Street
Bay Shore NY 11706
516/273-2200
Contact George E. Lobo, Personnel Director. A manufacturer of health-care products for home care and institutionalized settings. Operations at this facility include: manufacturing; research/development; administration; service; sales. Corporate headquarters location. American Stock Exchange. Common positions include: Accountant; Blue-Collar Worker Supervisor; Claim Representative; Computer Programmer; Credit Manager; Customer Service Representative; Draftsperson; Engineer; Industrial Engineer; Mechanical Engineer; Industrial Designer; Department Manager; Marketing Specialist; Personnel & Labor Relations Specialist; Purchasing Agent; Quality Control Supervisor; Sales Representative. Principal educational backgrounds sought: Accounting; Business Administration; Communications; Engineering; Marketing; Mathematics. Company benefits include: medical insurance; dental insurance; pension plan; life insurance; tuition assistance; disability coverage; profit sharing; employee discounts; savings plan.

PFIZER HOSPITAL PRODUCTS GROUP
235 East 42nd Street
New York NY 10017
212/573-7496
Contact Ann B. Conway, Manager, Personnel Services. Second area location in Rutherford, NJ. A medical specialty products firm, operating through the following divisions: Deknatel (Fall River, MA and Coventry, CT), which manufactures surgical supplies for the operating room and intensive care units of hospitals throughout the world, including surgical sutures and chest drainage devices; Orthopaedic Products (Rutherford, NJ), including total hip and knee systems, trauma products, and endoprosthetic devices; Shiley Division (Irvine, CA), a medical products organization manufacturing cardiovascular, cardiopulmonary, and respiratory care devices, including embolectomy catheters, tracheostomy tubes, endotracheal tubes, oxygenators, and ancillary devices; Valleylab (Boulder, CO) manufacturing electro surgical equipment and infusion pumps; and American Medical Systems Inc. (Minnetonka, MN) engaged in the production of such items as urological implants. Company has diverse international operations, including facilities in Central America, South America, Europe, Australia, and Asia. Company is a major operating subsidiary of Pfizer Inc. Common positions include: Accountant; Biochemist; Buyer; Customer Service Representative; Engineer; Biomedical Engineer; Mechanical Engineer; Financial Analyst; Marketing Specialist; Personnel & Labor Relations Specialist; Programmer; Purchasing Agent; Quality Control Supervisor; Sales Representative; Statistician; Systems Analyst. Principal educational backgrounds sought include: Accounting; Biology; Business Administration; Engineering; Finance; Marketing. Company benefits include: medical insurance; dental insurance; pension plan; life insurance; tuition assistance; disability coverage; employee discounts; savings plan. Corporate headquarters location. International. Operations at this facility include: divisional headquarters. New York Stock Exchange.

STERLING DRUG INC.
90 Park Avenue
New York NY 10016
212/907-2342
Contact Mr. Gil Smith, Personnel Administrator. Multiple area locations, including Montvale, NJ. A diversified transnational company engaged in the manufacture and sale of prescription and over-the-counter health-care medicines, household and personal products, specialty chemicals and pigments. Operates 77 manufacturing facilities in 47 countries, employing 22,500 people. Subsidiary operations include: Sterling Pharmaceutical Group (New York, NY); Lehn & Fink Products Group (Montvale, NJ); Sterling Chemical Group (New York, NY). Sterling International Group (New York, NY); Sterling Research Group (Rensselaer, NY); and several international subsidiaries, based in Switzerland, Canada, and Australia. Well-known company products include 'Bayer' aspirin and others. Common positions include: Accountant; Computer Programmer; Customer Service Representative; Engineer; Financial Analyst; Marketing Specialist; Sales Representative; Systems Analyst. Principal educational backgrounds sought: Accounting; Finance. Company benefits include: medical insurance; dental insurance; pension plan; life insurance; tuition assistance; disability coverage; employee discounts; savings plan. Corporate headquarters location. New York Stock Exchange. International.

TART OPTICAL MANUFACTURING
135 West 27th Street
New York NY 10001
212/675-1986
Contact Elaine Ricciardo, Personnnel Director. Produces optical supplies, including lenses and frames. Headquarters location.

WHITEHALL LABORATORIES
685 Third Avenue
New York NY 10017
212/878-5500
Contact Edward Behrendt, Corporate Personnel Manager. A pharmaceutical manufacturer. Subsidiary of American Home Projects Inc.

WYETH-AYERST LABORATORIES
64 Maple Street
Rouses Point NY 12979
518/297-8265
Contact Gary D. Wagoner, Supervisor, Executive Recruitment. Engaged in the research and manufacture of ethical and over-the-counter pharmaceuticals. A subsidiary of American Home Products Inc. Operations at this facility include: manufacturing; research/development. Corporate headquarters location: Philadelophia, PA. Parent company: American Home Products. New York Stock Exchange. Common positions include: Biochemist; Chemist; Computer Programmer; Chemical Engineer; Electrical Engineer; Mechanical Engineer; Operations/Production Manager; Personnel & Labor Relations Specialist; Statistician; Systems Analyst; Pharmacist; Pathologist (PhD); Toxicologist (PhD). Principal educational backgrounds sought: Chemistry; Computer Science; Engineering; Pharmaceutical (BS/MS/PhD); Statistics (MS). Training programs offered. Company benefits include: medical, dental, and life insurance; pension plan; tuition assistance; disability coverage; employee discounts

Connecticut

BERGEN BRUNSWIG CORPORATION
225 Howard Avenue
Bridgeport CT 06605
203/367-8601
Contact Division Manager. Provides ethical and over-the-counter pharmaceuticals, druggists supplies, and similar products.

CONAIR CORPORATION
1 Cummings Point Road
Stamford CT 06904
203/351-9000
Contact Ann Marie Cioffi, Corporate Director. Manufactures and distributes a large line of personal and health care appliances.

MOORE MEDICAL CORP.
389 John Downey Drive
New Britain CT 06050
203/225-4621
Contact Linda J. Roy, Human Resource Specialist. A leading national distributor of pharmaceuticals and allied health products, as well as a successful business-to-business direct mail company. Common positions include: Accountant; Advertising Worker; Buyer; Computer Programmer; Customer Service Representative; Management Trainee; Department Manager; Sales Representative. Principal educational backgrounds sought: Accounting; Art/Design; Business Administration; Communications; Finance; Marketing; Administration; Clerical. Company benefits include: medical, dental, and life insurance; pension plan; disability coverage; employee discounts. Corporate headquarters location. Operations at this facility include: administration; sales. American Stock Exchange.

NATIONAL PATENT MEDICAL
P.O. Box 419, Lake Road
Dayville CT 06241
203/774-8541
Contact Personnel Director. Manufactures disposable medical and healthcare products, disposable electro-surgical instruments, and industrial cotton (cosmetic, jeweler's industry). Markets products to consumer, industrial/OEM, hospital, and government accounts. Corporate headquarters location: New York, NY. Common positions include: Accountant; Computer Programmer; Credit Manager; Customer Service Representative; Electrical Engineer; Industrial Engineer; Mechanical Engineer; Operations/Production Manager; Marketing Specialist; Personnel & Labor Relations Specialist; Purchasing Agent; Quality Control Supervisor; Sales Representative; Systems Analyst; Transportation and Traffic

Specialist. Principal educational backgrounds sought: Accounting; Business Administration; Engineering; Finance; Marketing. Company benefits include: medical insurance; pension plan; life insurance; tuition assistance; disability coverage.

U.S. SURGICAL
150 Glover Avenue
Norwalk CT 06856
203/866-5050
Contact Human Resources Department. Manufacturers of surgical operating instruments.

New Jersey

BECTON, DICKINSON
1 Becton Drive
Franklin Lakes NJ 07417
201/848-6800
Contact James Wessel, Vice President of Human Resources. Corporate office of a medical and pharmaceutical company engaged in the manufacture of health-care products, medical instrumentation, and industrial safety equipment.

BLESSINGS CORPORATION
645 Martinsville Road
Liberty Corner NJ 07938
201/647-7980
Contact Trudy Kelly, Personnel Director. A diversified manufacturer of products oriented principally toward the health-care field. The Edison Plastics Film Division produces extruded polyethylene and polypropylene films for use in a variety of disposable hygiene products as well as in numerous other industrial and agricultural end uses. The Geri-Care Products Division manufactures and markets an expanding family of reusable and disposable products designed to promote the health and comfort of those in need of incontinence care in nursing homes, hospitals, and at home. Common positions include: Accounting Clerk; Receptionist; Executive Secretary. Principal educational backgrounds sought: Accounting; Engineering; Finance. Company benefits include: medical and life insurance; pension plan; tuition assistance; disability coverage; 401K. Corporate headquarters location. American Stock Exchange.

BLOCK DRUG COMPANY
275 Cornelison Avenue
Jersey City NJ 07302
201/434-3000 ext. 224
Contact Nancy A. Sharko, Personnel Director. Develops, manufactures, and sells products in four general categories: denture, dental care, oral hygiene, and professional dental products; proprietary products; ethical pharmaceutical products; and household products. Dental-related products include 'Polident' denture cleansers, 'Dentu-Creme' toothpaste, 'Poli-Grip' and 'Super Poli-Grip' denture adhesive creams, 'Pycopay' toothbrushes, and many others. Proprietary products include 'BC' headache powders, 'Nytol' sleep-aid products, 'Tegrin' medicated shampoo, and others. Ethical Pharmaceuticals manufactures a wide range of products through the company's Reed & Carnrick Division. Household products include a number of specialty cleaning products. Common positions include: Scientist; Marketing; Sales Representative. Principal educational backgrounds sought: Biology; Chemistry; Marketing. Company benefits include: medical, dental, and life insurance; pension plan; tuition assistance; disability coverage; savings plan.

BRISTOL-MYERS SQUIBB COMPANY
P.O. Box 4000
Princeton NJ 08543-4000
609/921-4000
Contact Corporate Personnel Recruiter. Several area locations, including New Brunswick. A diversified health and personal-care products firm. The corporation's major segment, pharmaceutical products, is engaged in the research and development, manufacture, and

sale of pharmaceuticals for human and veterinary use, and diagnostic agents which include contrast agents and radiopharmaceuticals. The specialty health products and medical systems segment is engaged in the development, manufacture, and sale of surgical and opthalmic instruments, ostomy care products, sterilization-monitoring systems, diagnostic imaging systems, and patient monitoring systems. The corporation's personal care products segment manufactures and sells a variety of fragrances and cosmetics; fragrances are distributed principally under the names 'Yves Saint Laurent,' 'Yves Saint Laurent Opium,' 'Gianni Versace,' 'Senchal,' 'Kouros,' 'Enjoli,' and 'Jean Nate'. Also included in this segment is a wide range of cosmetics sold primarily under the 'Yves Saint Laurent,' 'Charles of the Ritz,' 'Revenescence,' and 'Alexandra de Markoff' brand names, and 'Bain de Soleil' suntan preparations. Several area subsidiaries are operated autonomously. Squibb Medical Systems is based in Bellevue, WA. All other operations are based in Princeton. Corporate headquarters location. New York Stock Exchange. International.

DATASCOPE CORPORATION
580 Winters Avenue
P.O. Box 5
Paramus NJ 07653-0005
201/265-8800, ext. 310
Contact Anthony W. Perlingieri, Personnel Manager. A medical manufacturer of medical instrumentation and disposable products. Products are cardiac arrest systems and numerous physiological monitoring units. Company has a worldwide marketing organization and a second facility in Oakland, NJ International operations include: manufacturing. Common positions include: Accountant; Computer Programmer; Credit Manager; Customer Service Representative; Draftsperson; Biomedical Engineer; Electrical Engineer; Industrial Engineer; Mechanical Engineer; Financial Analyst; Department Manager; Operations/Production Manager; Marketing Specialist; Personnel & Labor Relations Specialist; Programmer; Purchasing Agent; Quality Control Supervisor; Sales Representative; Systems Analyst; Technical Writer/Editor. Principal educational backgrounds sought: Accounting; Computer Science; Engineering; Finance; Marketing. Company benefits include: medical insurance; dental insurance; pension plan; life insurance; tuition assistance; disability coverage. Benefits are non-contributory.

HAUSMANN INDUSTRIES
130 Union Street
Northvale NJ 07647
201/767-0255
Contact Personnel. Produces health-care-related and physical therapy equipment. Headquarters location.

HOFFMANN-LA ROCHE, INC.
340 Kingsland Street
Nutley NJ 07110
201/235-4201
Contact A.L. Vinson, Asst. VP/Dir., Staffing/Emp. Services. Multiple area locations, including Belleville, Clifton, Montclair, Raritan, Somerville, Totowa, and other New Jersey locations. A major international health-care company, producing a wide range of products based on intensive research in biology and chemistry. Operates through the following divisions: Pharmaceuticals; Diagnostic Products; and Chemical Division. Subsidiary companies include Roche Diagnostics (ethical pharmaceuticals); Roche Analytical Instruments; Roche Biomedical Laboratories; Medi-Physics Inc.; Roche Fine Chemicals Department; Agriculture and Animal Health Department; and Maag Agrochemicals, an affiliate. Facilities are located throughout the United States. A subsidiary of Roche SA, a major international Swiss-based health products firm. Operations include: manufacturing; research/development; administration. Corporate headquarters location. Common positions include: Accountant; Attorney; Biochemist; Biologist; Blue-Collar Worker Supervisor; Biologist; Buyer; Chemist; Computer Programmer; Engineer; Biomedical Engineer; Chemical Engineer; Electrical Engineer; Industrial Engineer; Mechanical Engineer; Financial Analyst; Food Technologist; Operations/Production Specialist; Marketing Specialist; Purchasing Agent; Quality Control Supervisor; Sales Representative; Statistician; Systems Analyst; Technical Writer/Editor. Principal educational background

sought: Accounting; Biology; Chemistry; Computer Science; Engineering; Finance; Marketing. Company benifits include: medical, dental, and life insurance; pension plan; tuition assistance; disability coverage; savings plan. Corporate headquarters location. Operations at this facility include: manufacturing; research/development; administration.

INTERBAKE FOODS, INC.
891 Newark Avenue
Elizabeth NJ 07207
908/527-7000
Contact Rita Palacios, Supervisor/Personnel Administration. Operates nationally in four business segments: Food Service; Grocery Products; Dairy Products; and Girl Scout Products. Food Service segment offers a line of more than 160 items, including crackers, cookies, tart shells, and other products to institutional customers, including health-care institutions, schools and colleges, and commercial establishments; Dairy Products segment produces wafers for ice-cream manufacturers; Grocery Products include a wide range of cookies and crackers; Girl Scout Products segment manufactures those products. A subsidiary of General Biscuits of America, Inc., the American subsidiary of General Biscuit, S.A., a French corporation. Corporate headquarters location. International.

JEROME MEDICAL
102 Gaither Drive
Mount Laurel NJ 08054
609/234-8600
Contact President. A leading manufacturer of orthopedic products.

JOHNSON & JOHNSON
1 J&J Plaza
New Brunswick NJ 08933
201/524-0400
Contact Personnel. A well-known company which manufactures a wide variety of health care products and medical supplies.

MEDCO CONTAINMENT SERVICES
491 Edward H. Ross Drive
Elmwood Park NJ 07407
201/794-1000
Contact Edward Pisani, Director of Human Resources. A leading mail order prescription company.

MERCK & COMPANY INC.
P.O. Box 2000
Rahway NJ 07065
201/574-4324
Contact Manager of Corporate Personnel. Several area locations. A worldwide organization engaged primarily in the business of discovering, developing, producing and marketing products and services for the maintenance or restoration of health and environment. Company's business is divided into two industry segments: Human and Animal Health Products, and Specialty Chemicals and Environmental Products. Subsidiaries include: Merck Sharp & Dohme Division (manufactures human-health products); Merck Sharp & Dohme International (human-health products manufacturing in 24 countries, and distribution in nearly 200); MSD Agvet (animal and plant health products); Merck Chemical Manufacturing Division (produces bulk chemicals used by other company divisions); Merck Sharp & Dohme Research Laboratories; and Specialty Chemical and Environmental Products, operating through subsidiaries Kelco Division (produces food additives), Baltimore Aircoil Company (cooling towers and other industrial evaporative cooling products), and Calgon Corporation (water purification products). Corporate headquarters location. New York Stock Exchange. International.

NAPP CHEMICALS
199 Main Street,
Lodi NJ 07644
201/773-3900
Contact Personnel Department. Produces medicinal chemicals and bulk pharmaceuticals.
Headquarters location.

ORGANON INC.
375 Mount Pleasant Avenue
West Orange NJ 07052
201/325-4546
Contact Human Resources. Manufactures ethical pharmaceuticals. Corporate
headquarters location. International. Common positions include: Accountant; Chemist;
Computer Programmer; Industrial Engineer; Mechanical Engineer; Programmer; Sales
Representative. Principal educational backgrounds sought: Chemistry; Marketing.
Company benefits include: medical insurance; dental insurance; pension plan; life
insurance; tuition assistance; disability coverage; profit sharing; employee discounts;
savings plan.

PHARMACY DIAGNOSTICS, INC.
350 Passaic Avenue
Fairfield NJ 07004
201/227-6700
Contact R. Rivera, Personnel Representative. A firm which designs, manufactures, sells
and services biomedical instrumentation (blood analyzers), disposable products and
immunodiagnostic reagents. Serves the hospital and independent clinical laboratory
markets, physicians and international markets. Five separate locations in Fairfield, NJ.
Operations include: manufacturing; research/development; administration; service;
marketing and sales. Corporate headquarters location. Parent company: Pharmacia
Diagnostics; Common positions include: Accountant; Administrator; Advertising Worker;
Biochemist; Blue-Collar Worker Supervisor (Quality Control, Machine Shop, Assembly,
Repair/Test, Design); Buyer; Chemist; Computer Programmer; Credit Manager;
Customer Service Representative; Draftsperson; Engineer; Electrical Engineer; Industrial
Engineer; Mechanical Engineer; Financial Analyst; Department Manager;
Operations/Production Manager; Marketing Specialist; Personnel; Programmer; Public
Relations Worker; Purchasing Agent; Quality Control Supervisor; Sales Representative;
Systems Analyst; Technical Writer. Principal educational backgrounds sought: Accounting;
Biology; Business Administration; Chemistry; Computer Science; Electronic Technology;
Engineering; Marketing; Medical Technology. Company benefits include: medical
insurance; dental insurance; pension plan; life insurance; tuition assistance; disability
coverage; employee discounts; savings plan; 401K.

REED & CARNRICK
One New England Avenue
Piscataway NJ 08854
201/981-0070
Contact Meg Weiss, Director of Personnel. Produces a broad range of ethical
pharmaceuticals as a division of Block Drug Company. Common positions include:
Chemist; Sales Representative. Principal educational backgrounds sought: Biology;
Chemistry. Company benefits include: medical, dental, and life insurance; pension plan;
tuition assistance; savings plan. Corporate headquarters location. Parent company: Block
Drug Company. Operations at this facility include: divisional headquarters; manufacturing;
administration

SANDOZ INC.
59 Route 10
East Hanover NJ 07936
201/503-7500
Contact Director of Personnel. Several area locations. A major international producer of
ethical pharmaceutical products. Corporate headquarters location.

SCHERING-PLOUGH CORPORATION
2000 Galloping Hill Road
Kenilworth NJ 07033
201/298-4373
Contact Personnel Operations Manager. Several area locations, including Kenilworth. A worldwide company primarily engaged in the discovery, development, manufacturing, and marketing of pharmaceutical and consumer products. Pharmaceutical products include prescription drugs, over-the-counter medicines, eye-care products, and animal-health products promoted to the medical and allied professions. The consumer products group consists of proprietary medicines, toiletries, cosmetics, and foot-care products marketed directly to the public. Well-known products include 'Coricidin' cough/cold medicines; 'Maybelline' eye, face, lip, skin-care, and nail-color products; 'Wesley-Jessen' vision-care products; 'Coppertone' sun care products; 'Dr. Scholl' foot-care products; and 'St. Joseph' line of children's over-the-counter analgesics. Corporate headquarters location: Madison, NJ. New York Stock Exchange. International. Operations include: manufacturing; research/development; administration; service;

VICTORY ENGINEERING CORPORATION
P.O. Box 559, Victory Road, Springfield NJ 07081
201/379-5900
Contact Christine Toth, Personnel Manager. Manufactures and distributes quick reducers and catheters for the medical industry. Corporate headquarters location.

WARNER-LAMBERT/
PARKE-DAVIS DIVISION
170 Tabor Road
Morris Plains NJ 07950
201/540-3003
Contact Betty Kuncewitch, Human Resources Supervisor. A major worldwide provider of healthcare and consumer products. The company conducts its business in more than 130 countries, employing approximately 42,000 people and operating more than 100 manufacturing facilities and 4 major research centers. The largest portion of the company's business relates to health care. Ethical health care lines include ethical pharmaceuticals. Other health care products include non-prescription pharmaceuticals and personal care products. Company is also a major producer and marketer of chewing gums, breath mints, shaving products, and pet care items. Well-known name brands include 'Parke-Davis' ethical pharmaceuticals, 'Listerine' mouthwash products, 'Bubblicious,' 'Chewels,' and 'Trident' chewing gums; 'Certs' breath mints; and 'Schick' shaving products. Common positions include: Biochemist; Chemist; Scientist. Principal educational backgrounds sought: Chemistry; Pharmaceutics; Other Sciences. Company benefits include: medical, dental, and life insurance; pension plan; tuition assistance; disability coverage; savings plan. Corporate headquarters location. Operations at this facility include: research/development. New York Stock Exchange.

ZENITH LABORATORIES
140 LeGrand Avenue
Northvale NJ 07647
201/767-1700
Contact Winifred Stavros, Personnel Director. Produces ethical pharmaceuticals for cardiovascular, nervous, digestive and respiratory systems. Headquarters location.

HIGHLY DIVERSIFIED

New York

CIBA-GEIGY CORPORATION
444 Saw Mill River Road
Ardsley NY 10502-2699
914/479-5000

Contact Loretta Alaburta, Employment Manager. "A highly diversified multibillion-dollar corporation that offers 'cutting edge' opportunities for entry-level and experienced scientific, technical, and business professionals at locations nationwide. We provide a highly supportive environment emphasizing corporate ethics while fostering career advancement and personal accomplishment. Many of our positions call for general or specialized backgrounds in Chemistry, Biology, Engineering, the Pharmaceutical Sciences, and related fields. Others require education/experience in Computer Science, Marketing & Sales, Finance & Accounting, or Human Resources." Corporate headquarter location: Ardsley, NY. Principal divisional operations include: Additives, Pigments & Plastics (Hawthorne, NY); Agricultural (Greensboro, NC) and Pharmaceuticals (Summit, NJ). Benefits include: medical, dental, and life insurance; retirement plan; liberal vacation plan; savings plan. Principal educational backgrounds sought: Accounting; Biology; Chemistry; Communications; Computer Science; Finance; Pharmacology; Polymer Science. Company benefits include: medical insurance; dental insurance; pension plan; life insurance; tuition assistance; disability coverage; employee discounts; savings plan.

DELAWARE NORTH COMPANIES, INC.
1 Delaware North Place
438 Main Street
Buffalo NY 14202
716/858-5000
Contact Jean Moran, Manager of Recruiting. Corporate headquarters location of a privately-owned, highly diversified international holding company. The corporation is engaged in a broad and expanding range of industries, including food services, metals, metals processing, parimutuel operations, parking, management, typography, and publishing. Among the company's subsidiaries are the following: Aluminum Smelting & Refining Co., Inc, which is engaged in the recycle of aluminum; Boston Professional Hockey Association, Inc., which owns and manages the National Hockey League's Boston Bruins; Concession Air, which is in the business of providing airport and in-flight foodservice operations; The Boston Garden, a major sports arena which houses Boston's professional hockey and basketball teams; Spectrum Multilanguage Communications, a typography company that produces foreign language typography; Syracuse Mile, a harness racing facility in Syracuse, NY; and Touchdown Publications, a publisher of sports programs and magazines.

DOVER CORPORATION
280 Park Avenue
New York NY 10017
212/922-1640
Contact Personnel Department. A highly diverse corporation with four operating segments, each of which hires independently. The building segment manufactures hydraulic, geared traction and gearless traction elevators for buildings in the United States, Canada, and Great Britain. The petroleum production segment, under the name of the Norris Division, manufactures sucker rods, subsurface pumps, valves, controls and tubular products for the petroleum production industry. The petroleum marketing segment manufactures equipment for automotive service and repair, fuel and propane transportation, and natural gas compressors. The general industry segment provides a variety of equipment to heavy industry, electronics manufacturers, refineries and utilities in the United States and abroad. A Fortune 500 firm. Corporate headquarters location. New York Stock Exchange.

HOTELS AND RESTAURANTS

For more information on professional opportunities in the hotel or restaurant industries, contact the following professional and trade organizations, as listed beginning on page 449:

THE AMERICAN HOTEL AND MOTEL ASSOCIATION
THE EDUCATION FOUNDATION OF THE
NATIONAL RESTAURANT ASSOCATION
NEW YORK STATE RESTAURANT ASSOCIATION

COUNCIL ON HOTEL, RESTAURANT
AND INSTITUTIONAL EDUCATION

<u>New York</u>

BURGER KING CORPORATION
35 Pinelawn Road, Suite 201 W
Melville NY 11757
516/454-1730
Contact Victoria McLaughlin, Human Resources Manager. Multiple area locations. New York area management offices for the world's second largest restaurant chain, specializing in convenience foods. Worldwide, the company operates more than 6,000 restaurants (more than 4,500 in the United States). A subsidiary of Grand Metropolitan, PLC. Corporate headquarters location: Miami, FL. International.

THE CARLYLE
Madison Avenue at 76th Street
New York NY 10021
212/744-1600
Contact Dan Kamp, General Manager. Provides the full range of services through its internationally-renowned hotel and three on-premises restaurants. Also offers banquet and meeting facilities. Corporate headquarters location.

CASCADE LINEN SERVICES
835 Myrtle Avenue
Brooklyn NY 11206
718/963-9660
Contact Tom Hogan, Vice President of Industrial Operations. Provides a major commercial linen supply/rental service for hotels, restaurants, medical institutions, and many other institutional customers. Corporate headquarters location.

ESSEX HOUSE/
NIKKO INTERNATIONAL
1700 Broadway
New York NY 10019
212/247-0300
Contact David Lloyd, Corporate Director of Personnel. Operates a major area hotel facility as a unit of Nikko International Corporation.

THE HELMSLEY PALACE
212 East 42nd Street
New York NY 10017
212/490-8900
Contact Carol Sullivan, Corporate Personnel Director. Operates one of New York City's newest, largest, and most complete hotel/entertainment facilities. Facilities include 1100 rooms, and a wide range of dining, lounge, and meeting facilities. Together with Harley Hotel, parent company (Helmsley-Spear) operates more hotel rooms in New York City than any other firm. Corporate headquarters location.

HELMSLEY PARK LANE HOTEL
36 Central Park South
New York NY 10019
212/371-4000
Contact Lisa Lichtenspein, Recruiter-Human Resources. Operation of a 650-room, 4-star Central Park South luxury hotel with a wide range of lodging, lounge, dining, and meeting rooms. Common positions include: Accountant; Blue-Collar Worker Supervisor; Credit Manager; Customer Service Representative; Hotel Manager/Assistant Manager; Department/General Manager; Personnel/Labor Relations Specialist; Purchasing Agent; Sales Representative; Hotel Management; Food & Beverage Management. Principal educational backgrounds sought: Accounting; Hotel Management; Food and Banquet Management; Business Administration; Communications; Finance; Marketing. Company

benefits include: medical, dental and life insurance; pension plan; disability coverage. Parent company: Helmsley Hotels. Operations at this facility: administration; service; sales. Corporate headquarters location.

HOTEL INTER-CONTINENTAL NEW YORK
111 East 48th Street
New York NY 10017
212/755-5900
Contact James G. Woods, Director, Human Resources. A major New York Hotel. Common positions include: Hotel Manger/Assistant Manager.

HUNTINGTON TOWN HOUSE INC.
124 East Jericho Turnpike
Huntington Station NY 11746
516/427-8485
Contact Vito Buccelato, Controller. Over 25 area locations, including Brooklyn, Queens, the Bronx, and Manhattan. A general service catering company specializing in service to weddings, organizational functions, bar-mitzvahs, anniversaries, and special parties. Corporate headquarters location.

INTER-CONTINENTAL NEW YORK
111 East Forty-Eighth Street
New York NY 10017
212/755-5900
Contact Mr. James Woods, Personnel Director. Operates a luxury, full-service hotel, centrally located in mid-town Manhattan. Services include 767 rooms, complete dining and lounging facilities, and meeting facilities, equipment, and services. Worldwide Intercontinental Hotels Corporation operates hotels in 51 countries in Europe, Latin America, Asia, the Middle East, Africa, the Pacific Islands, the United States, and Canada, with 87 operating as Inter-Continental Hotels, and 12 operating as moderate-priced Forum Hotels. A subsidiary of Grand Metropolitan Ltd., a diversified consumer products and services firm operating throughout the world. Corporate headquarters location: Cheshire, England.

JBA NATIONAL INC.
1600 Deer Park Avenue
Deer Park NY 11729
516/586-6610
Contact John Frohnhoefer, Vice-President/Operations. Thirty-eight area locations, including Queens, the Bronx, and Nassau and Suffolk counties. Owns, operates, and manages Arby's Roast Beef Restaurants and Jack's Restaurants throughout the region. Corporate headquarters location.

KENTUCKY FRIED CHICKEN OF LONG ISLAND
135 West Merrick Road
Merrick NY 11566
516/867-6600
Contact Vice President of Operations. Part of a large corporation which owns and operates another fast food chain, an advertising agency, and a construction corporation headquartered in Detroit, MI. Kentucky Fried Chicken of Long Island is also the Franchisee of Kentucky Fried Chicken Corporation for all territories in Nassau, Suffolk, and Richmond Counties. KFC of Long Island currently owns and operates 26 Kentucky Fried Chicken Restaurants. The company also has a District Office, which houses the Catering, Human Resources, Public Affairs, Maintenance, Training, and Administrative Departments. Corporate headquarters location. Operations include: administration; sales. Common positions at this facility include: Food Technologist; Assistant Manager; Management Trainee. Principal educational background sought: Business Administration. Company benefits include: medical insurance; life insurance.

MARRIOTT EASTSIDE
525 Lexington Avenue
New York NY 10017
212/755-4000, ext. 3402
Contact Andrew Halper, Director of Personnel. Operates a centrally-located, luxury hotel facility, with 652 guest rooms, and complete dining, meeting, and sales function facilities. Corporate headquarters location.

MARRIOTT HOST SERVICES OF NEW YORK
Marriott Host Intl.
Laguardia, CTB
Flushing NY 11371
718/476-0098
Contact Maggie Calabrese, Manager, Human Resources. Engaged in retail food and beverage concessions services in greater New York airports. Nationally, company is a diversified food service, retail merchandising, and hospitality company, doing business in more than 25 United States airports, as well as operating restaurants under various names throughout the United States. Common positions include: Customer Service Representative; Food Technologist; F & B Manager; Administrative Assistant; Foodserver; Cook; Waiter; Assistant Manager; Management Trainee; Purchasing Agent; Cashier; Waitress. Principal educational backgrounds sought: Restaurant; Food/Hospitality. Company benefits include: medical, dental, and life insurance; pension plan; tuition assistance; disability coverage; profit sharing; employee discounts; savings plans; salary continuation insurance; travel insurance. Corporate headquarters location: Santa Monica, CA. Washington, DC. Parent company: Marriott. Operations at this facility include: divisional headquarters; administration; service; sales. American Stock Exchange.

THE NEW YORK HELMSLEY HOTEL
212 East 42nd Street
New York NY 10017
212/490-8900, ext. 7080
Contact Personnel Director. Operates a 793-room luxury hotel facility, with a wide range of lodging, dining, meeting, and other facilities. Part of Helmsley Hotels Group, which has six hotels in New York City and a total of 26 hotels nationwide. Common positions include: Accountant; Hotel Manager/Assistant Manager; Manager; Department Manager; Management Trainee; Sales Manager; Restaurant Manager. Principal educational backgrounds sought: Accounting; Business Administration; Liberal Arts; Marketing; Hotel/Restaurant Management. Company benefits include: medical insurance; dental insurance; pension plan; disability coverage; free meals.

OMNI PARK CENTRAL HOTEL
870 Seventh Avenue
New York NY 10019
212/484-3330
Contact Mary Goodwin, Personnel Manager. Large midtown property, part of Omni/Donley Hotel Group, with 1260 rooms, restaurant, lounge, banquet, convention and meeting facilities. Common positions include: Accountant; Computer Programmer; Credit Manager; Customer Service Representative; Electrical Engineer; Mechanical Engineer; Hotel Manager/Assistant Manager; Personnel & Labor Relations Specialist; Purchasing Agent; Sales Representative. Principal educational backgrounds sought: Accounting; Communications; Computer Science; Engineering; Liberal Arts; Marketing; Hotel and Restaurant Management. Training programs available. Company benefits include: medical, dental and life insurance; pension plan; tuition assistance; disability coverage; employee discounts; savings plan; union positions also available. Corporate headquarters location: Hampton, NH. Operations at this facility include: sales; service.

RESTAURANT ASSOCIATES CORPORATION
36 West 44th Street, 5th Floor
New York NY 10036
212/642-1500

Contact Manager of Recruitment. Several area locations. A broad-based company in the hospitality industry which operates 60 restaurants in major cities, at cultural centers, and leisure attractions along the East Coast. Private foodservice facilities are also managed for clients such as corporations, institutions, and clubs. Common postions include: Chefs; Restaurant Managers. Principal educational backgrounds sought: Culinary; Restaurant Management. Training programs and internships available. Company benefits include: medical insurance; life insurance; tuition assistance; disability coverage; savings plan. Corporate headquarters location. Operations at this facility include: divisional headquarters location.

ST. MORITZ HOTEL INC.
50 Central Park South
New York NY 10019
212/755-5800
Contact Frances Mecca, Director of Personnel. Operates a full-service, quality hotel, with numerous meeting and banquet facilities, restaurants, and lounges. Corporate headquarters location.

TW SERVICES, INC.
605 Third Avenue
New York NY 10158
212/972-4700
Contact Personnel. A restaurant and food services company.

TAVERN ON THE GREEN
Central Park at West 67th Street
New York NY 10023
212/873-6748
Contact Thomas Manetti, Managing Director. Operates one of New York's oldest and best-known restaurants.

THE '21' CLUB INC.
21 West 52nd Street
New York NY 10019
212/582-7200
Contact Personnel. An internationally-recognized restaurant, offering fine cuisine to a primarily business and professional clientele. Corporate headquarters location. Operations at this facility include: administration; service. Common positions include: Accountant; Administrator; Credit Manager; Restaurant Manager/Assistant Manager; Department Manager; Operations/Production Manager; Personnel & Labor Relations Specialist; Purchasing Agent; Sales Representative (catering). Principal educational background sought: Business Administration. Company benefits include: medical insurance; pension plan; life insurance.

New Jersey

PRIME MOTOR INNS, INC.
700 Route 46 East
Fairfield NJ 07007
Contact Personnel Department. A New Jersey based company which owns, manages and operates approximately 100 hotels nationwide. Common positions include: Accountant; Attorney; Hotel Manager/Assistant Manager; Food and Beverage Manager/Assistant Manager. Company benefits include: medical, dental, and life insurance; 401K; employee discounts; prescription. Corporate headquarters location: Northern NJ. New York Stock Exchange.

SHERATON HASBROUCK HEIGHTS HOTEL
650 Terrace Avenue
Hasbrouck Heights NJ 07604
201/288-6100
Contact Cynthia Schalabba, Human Resources Manager. Provides a wide range of lodging, restaurant, lounge, meeting, and banquet facilities as part of the international Sheraton Hotels Corporation chain. Common positions include: Customer Service Representative; Food & Beverage Server; Room Attendant; Front Desk Guest Service Agent. Company benefits include: medical insurance; employee discounts. Corporate headquarters location: Boston, MA. Parent company: Sheraton. Operations at this facility include: administration.

INSURANCE

For more information on professional opportunities in the insurance industries, contact the following professional and trade organizations, as listed beginning on page 449:

ACTUARIAL SOCIETY OF GREATER NEW YORK
ALLIANCE OF AMERICAN INSURERS
AMERICAN COUNCIL OF LIFE INSURANCE
AMERICAN COUNCIL OF LIFE INSURANCE/NEW YORK
AMERICAN INSURANCE ASSOCIATION
INSURANCE INFORMATION INSTITUTE
NATIONAL ASSOCIATION OF LIFE UNDERWRITERS
SOCIETY OF ACTUARIES

New York

ALEXANDER & ALEXANDER OF NEW YORK INC.
1185 Avenue of the Americas
New York NY 10036
212/575-8000
Contact Employment & Recruiting Manager. Several area locations. An international insurance brokerage firm. Common positions include: Claim Representative; Industrial Engineer; Insurance Agent/Broker. Principal educational backgrounds sought: Business Administration; Economics; Engineering; Finance; Liberal Arts; Mathematics; Risk Management. Company benefits include: medical, dental, and life insurance; pension plan; tuition assistance; disability coverage. Corporate headquarters location. Operations at this facility include: regional headquarters. New York Stock Exchange.

AMALGAMATED LIFE INSURANCE COMPANY
770 Broadway
New York NY 10003
212/473-5700
Contact Jeanette C. Galletta, Human Resources Manager. A non-profit insurance firm handling claims service and group medical, life, and health maintenance policies for the national textile workers union. Common job positions include: Accountant; Computer Programmer; Technical Writer/Editor. Company benefits include: medical insurance; dental insurance; pension plan; life insurance; tuition assistance; disability coverage; savings plan. Corporate headquarters location.

AMERICAN INTERNATIONAL GROUP
72 Wall Street
New York NY 10270
212/770-7000
Contact Patricia Weil, Manager/College Relations. Several area locations. A major international insurance firm, providing primarily property and casualty coverages in 50 states, and 130 jurisdictions throughout the world. Corporate headquarters location: 70 Pine Street, New York NY 10270. Other major national offices in Philadelphia, PA; and Wilmington, DE. International.

AMERICAN INTERNATIONAL GROUP
70 Pine Street
New York NY 10270
212/770-7000
Contact Axel Freudmann, Vice President of Human Resources. A leading New York area insurance company.

ATLANTIC COMPANIES
45 Wall Street
New York NY 10005
Contact Senior Personnel Representative. Several area locations including Short Hills, NJ; and Woodbury, NY. Operates two multiple line insurance companies, writing property, liability, and marine insurance. The Atlantic Companies consist of the Atlantic Mutual Insurance Company, and its wholly-owned subsidiary, the Centennial Insurance Company, which share the same offices and staff. Services are sold primarily through independent insurance agents and brokers. Other subsidiaries include Atlantic Lloyd's Insurance Company of Texas. Corporate headquarters location.

CORROON & BLACK
Wall Street Plaza
New York NY 10005
212/363-4100
Contact Maureen Heeley, Personnel Director. A leading New York area insurance brokerage company.

EMPIRE BLUE CROSS AND BLUE SHIELD
622 Third Avenue
New York NY 10017
212/476-1000
Contact Linda Tufo, Director of Employment. The nation's largest private not-for-profit health insurance company, serving over 10 million policy holders under various programs providing hospital and/or basic medical, major medical, dental, prescription drug, Health Maintenance Organization and Medicare Supplemental benefits. The Corporation serves the 28 eastern counties of New York State. Common positions include: Accountant; Actuary; Customer Service Representative; Department Manager; Sales Representative; Statistician; Systems Analyst; Underwriter. Principal educational backgrounds sought: Accounting; Business Administration; Computer Science; Mathematics. Company benefits include: medical, dental and life insurance; pension plan; tuition assistance; disability coverage. Corporate headquarters location. Operations at this facility include: research/development; administration; service; sales.

FIREMAN'S FUND INSURANCE COMPANIES
One Liberty Plaza
New York NY 10006-1404
212/553-0736
Contact Linda Scott, Human Resources Manager. The umbrella company for the group of property/liability insurance companies, operating primarily in the United States. Common positions include: Attorney; Claim Representative; Underwriter. Principal educational backgrounds sought: Accounting; Business Administration. Company benefits include: medical, dental, and life insurance; pension plan; savings plan; tuition assistance; disability coverage; profit sharing; employee discounts; savings plan. Corporate headquarters location: Novato, CA. New York Stock Exchange.

GOVERNMENT EMPLOYEES INSURANCE COMPANY
(GEICO)
750 Woodbury Road
Woodbury NY 11797
516/496-5000
Contact John Thorne, Manager of Human Resources. An insurance and financial services organization whose principal subsidiary is a multiple line property and casualty insurer

offering private passenger automobile, homeowners, fire and extended coverage, professional and comprehensive personal liability, and boatowners insurance. Operated throughout the United States. Also, the subsidiary Resolute Group, Inc. is Government Employees' property/casualty reinsurance company, with offices in New York. Corporate headquarters location: Washington, DC. New York Stock Exchange. Common positions include: Attorney; Claim Representative; Credit Manager; Customer Service Representative; Department Manager; Sales Representative; Underwriter. Principal educational backgrounds sought: Accounting; Business Administration; Economics; Finance; Liberal Arts; Marketing. Company benefits include: medical insurance; dental insurance; pension plan; life insurance; tuition assistance; disability coverage; profit sharing; savings plan.

GROUP HEALTH INCORPORATED
330 West 42nd Street
New York NY 10036
212/760-6700
Contact Tom Nemeth, AVP, Human Resources. Provides medical, hospital, dental, optical and prescription drug insurance coverage for small, medium and large corporations. Regional offices are located in Albany, Syracuse, Rochester, Buffalo Garden City, Long Island, and Tarrytown. Corporate headquarters location. Operations at this facility include: administration; service; sales. Common positions at this facility include: Claim Representative; Customer Service Representative; Quality Control Supervisor. Principal educational backgrounds sought: Accounting; Business Administration; Computer Science; Finance; Liberal Arts; Marketing; Mathematics. Company benefits include: medical insurance; dental insurance; pension plan; life insurance; tuition assistance; disability coverage; savings plan; optical; prescription drugs.

HEALTH INSURANCE PLAN
OF GREATER NEW YORK
220 West 58th Street
New York NY 10019
212/373-5665˙
Contact Wes McMillan, Human Resource Associate. A large health maintenance organization marketing a comprehensive pre-paid health plan with care delivered by independent medical groups and coverage provided for hospitalization. H.I.P. employs 900 people. Corporate headquarters location. Common positions include: Accountant; Architect; Buyer; Claim Representative; Computer Programmer; Customer Service Manager; Financial Analyst; Department Manager; Marketing Specialist; Sales Representative; Statistician; Systems Analyst; Secretary; Health Care Administrator. Company benefits include: medical insurance; dental insurance; pension plan; life insurance; tuition assistance; disability coverage. Educational backgrounds sought: Accounting; Business Administration; Computer Science; Finance; Marketing; Nursing.

INSURANCE SERVICES OFFICE INC.
7 World Trade Center
New York NY 10048
212/898-6084
Contact Nancie L. Merritt, Asst. Manager Recruitment. ISO is a non-profit organization that serves the property/casualty insurance industry. The company gathers and analyzes data to develop advisory loss costs; conducts research to predict future economic and social trends; and develops model programs for the company's insurer clients. Common position: Actuary. Principal educational background sought: Economics; Mathematics. Company benefits include: medical insurance; dental insurance; pension plan; life insurance; 100% tuition assistance; disability coverage; employee discounts; savings plan; flexible hours. Corporate headquarters location. Operations at this facility include: research/development and actuarial service.

KEMPER NATIONAL INSURANCE COMPANY
2 World Trade Center, 31st Floor
New York NY 10048
212/313-4281

Contact Helene Schwartz, Human Resources Manager. A major national/international insurance corporation. Engaged in a wide range of insurance, financial, and related activities. Provides property, casualty, and life insurance, as well as reinsurance, and a wide range of diversified financial services. Corporate headquarters location: Long Grove, IL.

LIBERTY MUTUAL INSURANCE COMPANY
10 Rockefeller Plaza
New York NY 10020
212/489-8500
Contact Administration Manager. A full line insurance firm, offering life, medical, and business insurance, as well as investment and retirement plans. Corporate headquarters location: Boston, MA.

MBIA
113 King Street
Armonk NY 10504
914/273-4545
Contact Alan Pearlman, Human Resources Administrator. A company engaged in the insurance of municipal bonds. Common positions include: Accountant; Administrator; Computer Programmer; Financial Analyst; Marketing Specialist; Public Relations Worker; Underwriter. Principal educational backgrounds sought: Accounting; Business Administration; Economics; Finance; Marketing. Corporate headquarters location. New York Stock Exchange.

MANHATTAN LIFE INSURANCE COMPANY
111 West 57th Street
New York NY 10019
212/484-9300
Contact Alfred B. Tenreiro, Senior Vice President. Company is primarily engaged in the sale of individual life insurance, and is licensed in all 50 states. Common positions include: Accountant; Administrator; Claim Representative; Customer Service Representative; Department Manager; General Manager; Purchasing Agent; Underwriter. Training programs offered. Company benefits include: medical, dental, and life insurance; pension plan; tuition assistance; disability coverage; savings plan. Corporate headquarters location: Cincinnati, OH.

MARSH & McLENNAN COMPANIES
1166 Avenue of the Americas
New York NY 10036
212/345-6000
Contact Richard Mikulak, AVP/Administration. A leading professional firm which provides advice and services worldwide through an insurance brokerage and risk management firm, reinsurance intermediary facilities, and a consulting and financial services group, to clients concerned with the management of assets and risks. Specific services include: Insurance and Risk Management Services, Reinsurance, Consulting and Financial Services, Consulting, Merchandising, and Investment Management. Company has subsidiaries and affiliates in 57 countries, and correspondents in 20 more. Corporate headquarters location. New York Stock Exchange. International.

MUTUAL OF AMERICA
666 Fifth Avenue
New York NY 10103
212/399-0262
Contact Vivian Giacini, Senior Vice-President/Human Resources. One of the nation's leading insurance companies measured by assets, with field offices throughout the United States. Services include: Actuarial (annual valuations, cost proposals, reports to auditors); Administrative (preparation of documents, preparation of monthly billings, maintenance of employee records, benefit payment services, development of administrative manuals, calculation of benefit estimates, annual participant benefit statements); Assistance with Government Filings (preparation and release of ERISA Information Bulletins, distribution of employer kits for qualifying pension plans); Communications (Mutual of America

Report, audio/visual presentations, annual report); Investment (5 investment funds); and Field Consulting (a complete range of professional services to clients). Products include pension plans, tax-deferred annuity plans, IRA plans, deferred compensation plans, individual insurance and annuity thrift plans, funding agreements, guaranteed interest contracts, group life insurance and group long-term disability income insurance to employees of not-for-profit tax-exempt employers such as voluntary hospitals, religious groups, government agencies and educational and human service agencies. Common positions include: Accountant; Actuary; Claim Representative; Computer Programmer; Customer Service Representative; Department Manager; Personnel & Labor Relations Specialist; Underwriter. Principal educational backgrounds sought: Accounting; Business Administration; Computer Science; Mathematics. Company benefits include: medical, dental and life insurance; pension plan; life insurance; disabilty coverage; savings plan; 401K plan; ER Match @ 50% of 1 at 6%. Corporate, regional, and divisional headquarters location. Operations at this facility include: administration; service; sales.

MUTUAL LIFE INSURANCE COMPANY
1740 Broadway
New York NY 10019
212/708-2000
Contact College Relations. A major insurance/financial services firm, offering a broad line of life and health insurance policies, pension plans, and annuities. Company also operates an investment subsidiary engaged in the management of mutual funds.Corporate headquarters location. International.

NASD, INC.
33 Whitehall Street
New York NY 10004
212/858-4409
Contact Louise A. Santilli, Human Resources Assistant. Organization (NASD) is the self-regulatory organization of the securities industry, which oversees the over-the-counter market. Through its subsidiary, NASDAQ, Inc., it owns and operates the nationwide, electronic NASDAQ system which serves the fastest growing and second largest securities market in the United States. Working closely with the Securities and Exchange Commission, NASD sets the standards for NASDAQ securities and market makers, and provides ongoing surveillance of trading activities. The NASD also provides key services for its membership and NASDAQ companies, particularly through its cooperative efforts with governmental and other agencies on policies and legislation which affect the investment banking and securities business. Corporate headquarters location: Washington, DC. Common positions include: Accountant; Attorney (Securities); Customer Service Representative; Financial Analyst; Systems Analyst. Principal educational backgrounds sought: Accounting; Business Admimistration; Computer Science; Financial Analysis; Experience in the securities industry. Training programs offered. Company benefits include: medical insurance; dental insurance; pension plan; life insurance; tuition assistance; disability coverage; savings plan. Operations at this facility include: divisional headquarters. NASDAQ.

NATIONAL BENEFIT LIFE INSURANCE COMPANY
Two Park Avenue
New York NY 10016
212/684-6565
Contact Personnel Administrator. A nationally-licensed insurance firm, dealing primarily in health and life insurance. Corporate headquarters location. New York Stock Exchange.

NEW YORK LIFE INSURANCE COMPANY
51 Madison Avenue, Room 151
New York NY 10010
212/576-5417
Contact Yvonne Harmon, Employment Consultant. Offers a wide range of insurance and financial services; present activities are in the areas of life, health, and disability insurance; annuities; and a wide range of new products and services combining investment and term life insurance protection in one package. Services are provided to individuals, families, and

businesses. Corporate headquarters location. Common positions include: Accountant; Actuary; Attorney; Claim Representative; Customer Service Representative; Financial Analyst; Underwriter. Educational backgrounds sought include: Accounting; Business Administration; Communications; Economics; Finance; Liberal Arts; Marketing; Mathematics. Training programs available. Company benefits include: medical insurance; dental insurance; pension plan; life insurance; tuition assistance; disability coverage; profit sharing; savings plan. Corporate headquarters location. Operations at this facility: administration; service.

PUBLIC SERVICE MUTUAL INSURANCE COMPANY
132 West 31st Street
New York NY 10001-3406
212/560-5100
Contact Steven Z. Desner, Vice-President of Human Resources. An insurance firm, dealing in property, casualty, and automobile insurance. Corporate headquarters location.

ROYAL INSURANCE COMPANY
150 William Street
New York NY 10038
212/553-3304
Contact Personnel Manager. An insurance holding company, operating nationwide through the following subsidiaries: Royal Insurance Company of America; Royal Indemnity Company; Globe Indemnity Company; Safeguard Insurance Company; Newark Insurance Company; American & Foreign Insurance Company; Royal Life Insurance Company of America; and Royal Life Insurance Company of New York. Companies offer a wide range of property, liability, fidelity, surety, marine, and life insurance coverages, distributed exclusively through almost 5000 insurance agents and brokers located throughout the United States. Operates through three divisions: Commercial Lines, which provides property and liability protection services; Personal Lines, which provides insurance coverages for homeowners, tenants, automobile owners, and others; and Specialty Lines, which provides insurance coverage for boiler and machine operators, inland marine, and commercial floater customers. Also provides marine and aviation insurance services. Parent company is a London-based insurance firm with more than 500 offices and 22,000 employees worldwide. Corporate headquarters location (United States operations). International.

TEACHERS INSURANCE & ANNUITY ASSOCIATION/ COLLEGE RETIREMENT EQUITY FUND
730 Third Avenue
New York NY 10017
212/490-9000
Contact Martina S. Horner, Personnel Director. Operates non-profit service organizations that provide retirement and group insurance plans for employees of college, universities, independent schools, and related non-profit research organizations and educational associations. TIAA retirement annuities are based on broadly diversified investments in publicly traded bonds, direct loans to business and industry, commercial and industrial mortgages, and income-producing real estate. CREF was established to provide variable annuities to retirement and annuity plans; TIAA also offers group coverages providing life, major medical, and total disability benefits insurance. Company also provides benefit counseling services for non-profit educational institutions. Corporate headquarters location.

THE TRAVELERS INSURANCE COMPANY
80 John Street
New York NY 10038
212/574-2000
Contact Tony Archibald, Personnel Director. Multiple area locations. One of the world's largest investor-owned financial service organizations. Operating groups and services include: Group, in which company is one of the nation's largest group insurance companies, providing life, accident, and health benefits for more than eight million employees and their families in 76,000 organizations; Individual Life, Health, and Financial

Services, in which company provides a full spectrum of life and health insurance products and financial services to more than four million individuals and small business owners; Casualty-Property Commercial Lines, in which company provides more than 300,000 clients with protection against business-related financial risks, with products such as workers' compensation, auto, general liability, and property insurance; Casualty-Property Personal Lines, which is a major insurer of personal property for more than five million customers, including automobile, home, boat, and other assets; and Investments. Corporate headquarters location: Hartford, CT. New York Stock Exchange.

U.S. LIFE CORP.
125 Maiden Lane
New York NY 10038
212/709-6000
Contact Personnel. A life insurance company.

ZURICH-AMERICAN INSURANCE COMPANIES
20 Exchange Place, 10th Floor
New York NY 10005
212/509-9500
Contact Herb Tanneberger, Personnel Supervisor. Provides a full spectrum of insurance products and services in the United States, including commercial and personal lines, and excess and surplus coverages. Other area offices are located in Woodbury, NY; and Pinebrook, NJ. Other offices are located throughout the country. Parent company (Zurich Corporation) is a major Swiss-based international insurance firm, with operations in 31 countries worldwide. Clients include major firms in virtually every industry category. Corporate headquarters location: Schaumburg, IL.

Connecticut

AETNA LIFE AND CASUALTY
151 Farmington Avenue
Hartford CT 06156-3400
203/273-1349
Contact Manager, College Programs. One of the nation's largest investor-owned insurance and financial services organizations. Based on assets of more than $46 billion, Aetna ranks among the 15 largest corporations in the United States. Company markets all types of business and personal insurance and pension products. Common positions include: Accountant; Actuary; Architect; Claim Representative; Computer Programmer; Branch Manager; Department Manager; General Manager; Management Trainee; Operations/Production Manager; Marketing Specialist; Systems Analyst; Technical Writer/Editor; Underwriter. Principal educational backgrounds sought: Accounting; Business Administration; Computer Science; Economics; Finance; Liberal Arts; Marketing; Mathematics. Company benefits include: medical insurance; dental insurance; pension plan; life insurance; tuition assistance; disability coverage; employee discounts; savings plan. Corporate headquarters location. New York Stock Exchange.

CIGNA COMPANIES
900 Cottage Grove Road
Employment A-11
Bloomfield CT 06002
Contact Employment Director. Provides insurance and financial services to individuals and corporations worldwide. Common positions include: Accountant; Actuary; Attorney; Claim Representative; Computer Programmer; Customer Service Representative; Economist; Financial Analyst; General Manager; Management Trainee; Operations/Production Manager; Sales Representative; Systems Analyst; Technical Writer/Editor; Underwriter. Principal educational backgrounds sought: Accounting; Business Administration; Communications; Computer Science; Economics; Finance; Liberal Arts; Marketing; Mathematics. Company benefits include: medical insurance; dental insurance; pension plan; life insurance; tuition asssistance; disability coverage; employee discounts; savings

plan. Corporate headquarters location: Philadelphia, PA. Parent company: CIGNA Corporation. Operations at this facility include: regional headquarters; divisional headquarters. New York Stock Exchange.

GENERAL RE SERVICES CORPORATION/ FINANCIAL CENTRE
P.O. Box 10353
Stamford CT 06904-2353
203/328-5000
Contact Mr. Theron Hoffman, Jr., Director of Personnel. A reinsurance company involved with insuring life and casualty insurance companies.

HARTFORD STEAM BOILER INSPECTION & INCURANCE CO.
1 State Street
Hartford CT 06102
203/722-1866
Contact Ray Ford, Assistant Vice President. An insurance company specializing in the areas of property and casualty.

PHOENIX MUTUAL LIFE INSURANCE COMPANY
100 Bright Meadow Boulevard
Enfield CT 06083-1900
203/253-1000
Contact Jan Bellinger, Manager, Human Resources. The twelfth largest mutual life insurance company in the United States, with assets exceeding $5 billion. Branch operations located at 100 Bright Meadow Boulevard, Enfield, CT (Group Operations), and Box 810, Greenfield, MA (Customer Service Operations). Common positions include: Accountant; Actuary; Administrator; Attorney; Buyer; Claim Representative; Computer Programmer; Customer Service Representative; Financial Analyst; Insurance Agent/Broker; Manager; Branch Manager; Department Manager; General Manager; Management Trainee; Operations Manager; Personnel & Labor Relations Specialist; Public Relations Worker; Purchasing Agent; Reporter/Editor; Sales Representative; Statistician; Systems Analyst; Technical Writer/Editor; Underwriter. Principal educational backgrounds sought: Accounting; Business Administration; Communications; Computer Science; Finance; Marketing; Mathematics; Law; Human Resources Development. Company benefits include: medical, dental, and life insurance; pension plan; tuition assistance; disability coverage; employee discounts; savings plan; 401K; flexible hours; YMCA subsidy; credit union; dental cleanings.

New Jersey

ADMIRAL INSURANCE COMPANY
1255 Caldwell Road
Cherry Hill NJ 08034
609/429-9200
Contact Personnel. A major suburban Philadelphia insurance agency.

ALLSTATE INSURANCE COMPANIES
721 U.S. Route 202/206 South
Bridgewater NJ 08807
908/704-7500
Contact Human Resources Manager. One of the nation's largest insurance companies; primarily dealing with life insurance.

AMERICAN RE-INSURANCE COMPANY
555 College Road East
Princeton NJ 08543
609/243-4648
Contact Lisa Bronstein, Senior Employment Representative. Primarily offers re-insurance covers to property/casualty insurance firms. World recognized leader in the re-insurance

industry. Branches throughout the U.S. and the world. Subsidiary of the Aetna Life and Casualty Company. Common positions include: Accountant; Actuary; Administrator; Claim Representative; Financial Analyst; Department Manager; Personnel and Labor Relations Specialist; Statistician; Systems Analyst. Principal educational backgrounds sought: Accounting; Business Administration; Communications; Computer Science; Finance; Marketing. Company benefits include: medical insurance; dental insurance; pension plan; life insurance; tuition assistance; disability coverage; savings plan. Corporate headquarters location. Operations at this facility include: divisional headquarters; administration. American Stock Exchange (listed under AETNA).

CHUBB & SON, INC.
15 Mountain View Road
Warren NJ 07059
201/580-2000
Contact Human Resources. An insurance company.

CONTROL DATA CORPORATION/
COMMERCIAL CREDIT MANAGEMENT
Raritan Plaza 1, Raritan Center
Edison NJ 08837
908/417-4830
Contact Personnel. A wholly-owned subsidiary of Control Data Corporation; provides financing and insurance services through a large network of business centers and offices.

GAB BUSINESS SERVICES
Linden Plaza, 9 Campus Drive
Parsippany NJ 07054
201/993-3594
Contact Patricia Sarpa, Manager of Human Resources. Multiple locations. Provides adjustment, inspection, appraisal, and claims management services to 15,000 insurance industry customers, employing 3,400 professionals in over 550 branch offices. Specific services include the settlement of claims following major disasters, appraisal, investigation, and adjustment of auto insurance claims, casualty claims, and fire, marine, life, accident, health, and disability claims. The parent company is SGS North America. Corporate headquarters location. Common positions include: Accountant; Claim Representative; Computer Programmer; Customer Service Representative; Personnel Specialist; Principal educational backgrounds sought: Accounting; Business Administration; Liberal Arts. Company benefits include: medical insurance; dental insurance; pension plan; life insurance; disability coverage; savings plan; tuition reimbursement.

HOME LIFE INSURANCE COMPANY
One Centennial Avenue
Piscataway NJ 08855
908/980-4070
Contact Paul Neill, Director, Staffing/Employee Relations. Primarily a life insurance carrier, providing a wide range of coverages to individuals and groups. Corporate headquarters location: New York, NY. Common positions at this facility: Accountant; Actuary; Administrator; Claim Representative; Computer Programmer; Underwriter. Educational backgrounds sought: Accounting; Business Administration; Finance; Mathematics; Statistics. Training programs available. Company benefits include: medical insurance; dental insurance; pension plan; life insurance; tuition assistance; disability coverage; employee discounts.

PRUDENTIAL INSURANCE COMPANY OF AMERICA
213 Washington Street
Newark NJ 07101
201/802-7863
Contact Mary Podolak, Manager/Personnel Admin. & Employment. Multiple area locations, including Roseland, Parsippany, and South Plainfield, NJ. The largest multi-line financial services organization in the world, with offices throughout the United States and Canada. Provides a wide range of financial services for individuals and groups, including:

individual insurance; personal investments; group insurance; reinsurance; institutional Investments; group pensions; and health-care programs. Regional home offices are located throughout the United States, including South Plainfield, NJ; metropolitan Philadelphia; Boston, MA; Chicago, IL; Houston, TX; Jacksonville, FL; Minneapolis, MN; and Westlake Village, CA. Canadian operations are based in Toronto, Ontario. Corporate headquarters location: 745 Broad Street, Newark NJ 07101. International.

LEGAL SERVICES

For more information on professional opportunities in legal services, contact the following professional and trade organizations, as listed beginning on page 449:

AMERICAN BAR ASSOCIATION
FEDERAL BAR ASSOCIATION
FEDERAL BAR ASSOCIATION/EMPIRE STATE CHAPTER
NATIONAL ASSOCIATION FOR LAW PLACEMENT
NATIONAL ASSOCIATION OF LEGAL ASSISTANTS
NATIONAL FEDERATION OF PARALEGAL ASSISTANTS
NATIONAL FEDERATION OF PARALEGAL ASSOCIATIONS
NATIONAL PARALEGAL ASSOCIATIONS

New York

CADWALADER WICKERSHAM & TAFT
100 Maiden Lane
New York NY 10038
212/504-6000
Contact Madeline Castellotti, Administrative Recruiter. Large Wall Street law firm specializing in corporate law, litigation, tax, real estate, and trusts and estates. Other offices located in Washington DC, and Palm Beach, FL. Corporate headquarters location. Common positions include: Accountant; Administrator; Attorney; Blue-Collar Worker Supervisor; Computer Programmer; General Manager; Personnel & Labor Relations Specialist; Legal Secretary; Law Clerk; Library Clerk. Company benefits include: medical insurance; pension plan; life insurance; disability coverage; profit sharing; employee discounts.

CAHILL GORDON & REINDEL
80 Pine Street
New York NY 10005
212/701-3000
Contact Mr. Nawal Gupta, Personnel Manager. An area corporate law firm, also specializing in real estate, trusts, and estates. Corporate headquarters location.

CHADBOURNE & PARKE
30 Rockefeller Plaza
New York NY 10112
212/408-5100
Contact Sylvia Moss, Director of Services. Can also contact Malcolm E. Martin, Partner. A major area law firm. Corporate headquarters location. Common positions include: Legal Assistant; Staff Specialist.

CLEARY GOTTLIEB STEEN & HAMILTON
One Liberty Plaza
New York NY 10006
212/255-2000
Contact Norma F. Cirincione, Legal Personnel Coordinator. An international law firm, with other offices in Washington DC, Paris, Brussels, London, and Hong Kong. Areas of specialty include corporate, securities, and financial matters; all areas of civil commercial litigation; public and administrative law; antitrust law; real estate law; estate planning; and

probate law. A significant portion of practice involves international financial and business transactions throughout the world, including South America, Europe, Asia, Africa, and the Middle East. Corporate headquarters location.

COUDERT BROTHERS
200 Park Avenue
New York NY 10166
212/880-4400
Contact Mary Simpson, Personnel Manager. A major area law firm. Corporate headquarters location.

CRAVATH, SWAINE & MOORE
Worldwide Plaza
825 Eighth Avenue
New York NY 10019-7415
Contact Personnel Division. A major Wall Street law firm, specializing in corporate, litigation, trusts and estates, and real estate. Common positions include: Legal Assistant (entry-level college graduates). Principal educational backgrounds sought: Communications; Computer Science; Economics; Engineering; Liberal Arts. Company benefits include: medical insurance; dental insurance; pension plan; life insurance; disability coverage; profit sharing; savings plan.

DEBEVOISE & PLIMPTON
875 Third Avenue
New York NY 10022
212/909-6000
Contact Rachel Kagan, Personnel Manager. A major area law firm. Corporate headquarters location.

DEWEY BALLANTINE
1301 Avenue of the Americas
New York NY 10019
212/259-7328
Contact Evelyn M. Scoville, Recruiting Coordinator. An international law firm specializing in corporate, litigation, tax, ERISA/pension, bankruptcy and real estate. Other locations include: DC, LA, Florida, and London. Common positions include: Attorney; Paralegal. Educational backgrounds sought: Law. Corporate headquarters location.

DONOVAN, LEISURE, NEWTON, AND IRVINE
30 Rockefeller Plaza
New York NY 10112
212/632-3000
Contact Personnel. Law firm. Corporate headquarters location.

FRIED, FRANK, HARRIS, SHRIVER & JACOBSON
One New York Plaza, 23rd Floor
New York NY 10004
212/820-8305
Contact Ms. Ronnie Grabon, Personnel Director. A major Wall Street law firm with offices in New York, Washington DC, and London. Practice is centered around sophisticated domestic and international financial transactions. Specific areas include: corporate law, litigation, real estate, estates, trusts and pension. Corporate headquarters location. International. Common positions include: Attorney; Paralegal. Principal educational backgrounds sought: Business Administration; Finance; Liberal Arts; Pre-law; History. Company benefits include: medical insurance; dental insurance; pension plan; life insurance; disability coverage.

KAYE, SCHOLER, FIERMAN, HAYS & HANDLER
425 Park Avenue
New York NY 10022
212/836-8000

Contact Hiring Partner. Operates a major area law firm·

LORD DAY & LORD, BARRETT & SMITH
1675 Broadway
New York NY 10019
212/969-6000
Contact Linda Sheer, Recruitment Coordinator. A law firm with a diversified, multinational practice, specializing in corporate, banking, insurance, admiralty, litigation, antitrust, tax, trusts and estates and real estate. Corporate headquarters location.

MILBANK, TWEED, HADLEY & McCLOY
One Chase Manhattan Plaza
New York NY 10005
212/530-5000
Contact Manager. A major area law firm, specializing in litigation, corporate, trusts and estates, and tax law. Corporate headquarters location. International.

PAUL WEISS RIFKIND WHARTON & GARRISON
1285 Avenue of the Americas
New York NY 10019-6064
212/373-3000
Contact Miss Sally Spink, Personnel Director. One of New York's largest law firms, with a broadly-based practice.

SIMPSON THACHER & BARTLETT
425 Lexington Avenue
New York NY 10017
212/455-2000
Contact Eric Edelson, Manager, Human Resources. One of the nation's largest corporate law firms. Corporate headquarters location. International.

WEIL GOTSHAL & MANGES
767 Fifth Avenue
New York NY 10153
212/310-8000
Contact Human Resources. A major area law firm.

WHITE & CASE
1155 Avenue of the Americas
New York NY 10036
212/819-8200
Contact Richard Piotrowicz, Controller. A major area law firm.

WINTHROP STIMSON PUTNAM & ROBERTS
1 Battery Park Plaza
New York NY 10004-1490
212/858-1000
Contact Valerie Grosso, Office Manager. An international law firm with a broad-based practice, including corporate law, litigation, real estate, and tax law. Corporate headquarters location. International.

MANUFACTURING: MISCELLANEOUS CONSUMER

For more information on professional opportunities in the manufacturing industry, contact the following professional and trade organizations, as listed beginning on page 449:

NATIONAL ASSOCIATION OF MANUFACTURERS
NATIONAL MACHINE TOOL BUILDERS
NATIONAL SCREW MACHINE PRODUCTS ASSOCIATION

NATIONAL TOOLING AND MACHINING ASSOCIATION
NATIONAL TOOLING AND MACHINING ASSOCIATION/NEW YORK
THE TOOLING AND MANUFACTURING ASSOCIATION

New York

AMERICAN TACK & HARDWARE COMPANY INC.
25 Robert Pitt Drive
Monsey NY 10952
914/352-2400
Contact Ms. Pat McDonnell, Personnel Manager. Manufactures a broad range of decorative hardware items; distributed nationally for more than 50 years. Common positions include: Accountant; Blue-Collar Worker Supervisor; Buyer; Claim Representative; Commercial Artist; Computer Programmer; Credit Manager; Customer Service Representative; Industrial Engineer; Mechanical Engineer; Financial Analyst; Department Manager; Operations/Production Manager; Purchasing Agent; Quality Control Supervisor; Sales Representative; Transporation & Traffic Specialist. Principal educational backgrounds sought: Accounting; Marketing. Company benefits include: medical, dental, and life insurance; pension plan; tuition assistance; disability coverage; employee discounts; savings plan; 401 K. Corporate headquarters location.

ELIZABETH ARDEN INC.
1345 Avenue of the Americas
New York NY 10105
212/261-1000
Contact Personnel Director. One of the world's best-known manufacturers and distributors of a wide range of nationally-distributed cosmetics and toiletries. Corporate headquarters location.

ARROW FASTENER COMPANY
271 Mayhill Street
Saddle Brook NJ 07662
201/843-6900
Contact Martin Fischer, Controller. Produces stapling machines, tackers, and similar products.

AVON PRODUCTS INC
9 West 57th Street
New York NY 10019
212/546-6015
Contact Personnel Director. Operates through the following divisions: Avon Division, in which company is the world's leading manufacturer and distributor of cosmetics, fragrances, and fashion jewelry, operating in 32 countries; Mallinckrodt, Inc., which develops, manufactures, and markets health-care products, specialty chemicals, and food ingredients, flavors, and fragrances; Tiffany & Company, a jeweler and silversmith which sells its merchandise to retail, corporate, and direct mail customers, and which designs and manufactures many of its exclusive products; and Direct Mail Division, which is engaged primarily in the sale of popularly-priced high-quality women's apparel, as well as operations in men's apparel and magazine subscriptions. Corporate headquarters location. New York Stock Exchange.

BULOVA CORPORATION
1 Bulova Avenue
Woodside NY 11377
718/204-3384
Contact Personnel. Engaged principally in the manufacture and sale of a wide variety of watches and clocks for the consumer market, and non-consumer products for defense and industrial uses (through subsidiary Bulova Systems & Instruments Corporation; P.O. Box 189, Valley Stream NY 11582; 516/561-2600; Eleanor Smith, Personnel Manager). Corporate headquarters location.

CASTRO CONVERTIBLE CORPORATION
1990 Jericho Turnpike
New Hyde Park NY 11040
516/488-3000
Contact Carol Fitzgerald, Personnel Department. One of the world's largest and best-known manufacturers and distributors of high-quality convertible furniture. Products include convertible couches, loveseats, sectionals, modulars, chairs, and many other furniture items and accessories. Sells directly to the public through showrooms located throughout the country (including Manhattan and Long Island). Corporate headquarters location.

CLINIQUE LABORATORIES INC.
767 Fifth Avenue
New York NY 10153
212/572-3800
Contact Human Resources. Manufactures and distributes a wide line of fine non-allergenic cosmetics, skin care products, hairsprays, deodorants, and other personal care products. Corporate headquarters location.

COLGATE-PALMOLIVE COMPANY
300 Park Avenue
New York NY 10022
212/310-2000
Contact Matt Rohsler, Corporate Employment Relations. Several locations, including Piscataway, NJ; Jeffersonville, IN; Kansas City, KS; Cambridge, OH. Markets a variety of consumer products globally with 62 worldwide subsidiaries serving over 160 countries. Focused on five core businesses: Oral, Fabric and Body care, Household Product and and Animal Dietary. New York City corporate headquarters. Large multinational consumer products company. New York Stock Exchange. Common positions include: Accountant; Administrator; Advertising Worker; Attorney; Computer Programmer; Financial Analyst; Industrial Manager; Management Trainee; Marketing Specialist; Personnel and Labor Relations; Specialist; Public Relations Specialist; Transportation & Traffic Specialist. Principal educational backgrounds sought: Accounting; Chemistry; Computer Science; Finance; Marketing. Training programs and internships available. Company benefits include: medical insurance; pension plan; life insurance; tuition assistance; disability coverage; daycare assistance; profit sharing; employee discounts; savings plan. Corporate headquarters location. Operations at this facility include: divisional headquarters; administration; service; sales. New York Stock Exchange.

DAUMAN DISPLAYS INC.
527 West 34th Street
New York NY 10001
212/947-7030
Contact Stella Wyatt, Office Manager. Manufacturer of display units used for lipsticks, stockings, and various other small consumer products. Corporate headquarters location. International.

EASTMAN KODAK COMPANY
343 State Street
Rochester NY 14650
Contact Manager of Professional Recruitment. Manufactures photographic equipment and supplies, medical products; information storage and retrieval systems, copiers/duplicators; and business systems. Corporate headquarters location. Operations at this facility include: manufacturing; research/development. New York Stock Exchange. Common positions include: Accountant; Biomedical Engineer; Chemical Engineer; Chemist; Electrical Engineer; Industrial Engineer; Mechanical Engineer; Financial Analyst; Marketing Specialist; Programmer; Sales Representative; Systems Analyst. Principal educational backgrounds sought: Accounting; Chemistry; Computer Science; Engineering; Marketing. Company benefits include: medical insurance; dental insurance; pension plan; tuition

assistance; life insurance; disability coverage; profit sharing; employee discounts; savings plan.

EFFANBEE DOLL CORPORATION
200 Fifth Avenue, Suite 420
New York NY 10010-3389
212/675-5650
Contact Miss Brooks, Personnel Director. Manufactures dolls. Corporate headquarters location.

EMPIRE SCIENTIFIC CORPORATION
P.O. Box EEE
Deer Park NY 11729
800/645-7220
Contact Jeff English, Personnel Supervisor. Manufactures and distributes a line of sophisticated recording products and systems, and stereo components. Principal customers include retail stores throughout the world. Corporate headquarters location. International.

EX-CELL HOME FASHIONS INC.
261 Fifth Avenue
New York NY 10016
212/679-4597
Contact Dotty Angermann, Director of Field Sales for sales positions only. Manufactures and distributes home furnishing products, including shower curtains, pillows, table cloths, bathroom accessories, and similar items. Corporate headquarters location.

FARBERWARE, INC.
1500 Bassett Avenue
Bronx NY 10461
212/863-8000
Contact Eli Bresinger, Manager Human Resources/Administration. A leading manufacturer and distributor of a complete line of housewares, including quality cookware and electric appliances marketed through retailers nationwide. A Hanson Industries, Co. Common positions at this facility include: Accountant; Advertising Worker; Buyer; Computer Programmer; Credit Manager; Customer Service Representative; Draftsperson; Industrial Engineer; Purchasing Agent; Transportation & Traffic Specialist. Principal educational backgrounds sought: Accounting; Computer Science; Engineering; Finance; Marketing. Company benefits include: medical insurance; dental insurance; pension plan; life insurance; disability coverage; savings plan. Corporate headquarters location. Operations at this facility: administration; service; sales. Parent company: Hanson Industries.

FORWARD INDUSTRIES INC.
106-15 Foster Avenue
Brooklyn NY 11236-2297
718/257-7700
Contact Director of Personnel. One of the nation's three largest manufacturers of designer-look, leather-style business gifts, including portfolios, desk sets, and attache cases. The company also produces and markets commercial loose-leaf binders not sold in stores, but designed to customer requirements. Second facility located in El Segundo, CA. Customers include national department store chains, large corporations, and governments. Common positions include: Accountant; Blue-Collar Worker Supervisor; Buyer; Computer Programmer; Credit Manager; Customer Service Representative; General Manager; Management Trainee; Operations/Production Manager; Marketing Specialist; Personnel & Labor Relations Specialist; Purchasing Agent; Quality Control Supervisor; Sales Representative. Principal educational backgrounds sought: Accounting; Business Administration; Computer Science; Marketing. Company benefits include: medical, dental and life insurance; pension plan; disability coverage. Corporate headquarters location. Operations at this facility include: regional headquarters; divisional headquarters; manufacturing; research/development; administration; service; sales. New York Stock Exchange.

GENERAL CIGAR COMPANY
387 Park Avenue South
New York NY 10016
212/561-8700
Contact Robert Grimaldi, Personnel Manager. Produces a wide variety of well-known cigars. Corporate headquarters location.

GRABER INDUSTRIES
295 Fifth Avenue, Suite 218
New York NY 10016
212/532-9060
Contact Personnel Department. A manufacturer of custom-made shades, vertical blinds, draperies and related hardware, trimmings, and tassels. Corporate headquarters location: Middleton, WI.

GREAT NECK SAW MANUFACTURERS INC.
165 East Second Street
Mineola NY 11501
516/746-5352
Contact Sydney Jacuff, President. Manufacturers of a wide range of consumer and shop-quality hand tools. Corporate headquarters location.

IMPERIAL SCHRADE
99 Madison Avenue, Suite 1500,
New York NY 10016
212/889-5700
Contact Burt Hines, Office Manager. Produces a large line of pocket knives and hunting knives.

INSTRUMENT SYSTEMS CORPORATION
100 Jericho Quadrangle
Jericho NY 11753
516/938-5544
Contact Susan Reilly, Personnel Manager. Company operates through four business segments: Home Furnishings and Furniture-Related Products (production and sale of bedding products, drapery hardware, and synthetic batting); Specialty Hardware (production and sale of industrial hardware and related components); Electronic Communications Equipment (production and sale of communication, control, service, and entertainment systems for the aerospace industry); and Other Products (production and sale of commercial lighting, truck bodies, postal lock boxes, torque converters, and special purpose clutches). Subsidiaries include: Telephonics Corporation (electronic communications equipment); Buildex Inc. (specialty hardware); Lightron Corporation (home furnishing and furniture-related products). Corporate headquarters location. American Stock Exchange.

INTERNATIONAL FLAVORS & FRAGRANCES INC.
521 West 57th Street
New York NY 10019
212/765-5500
Contact Sheila A. Darken, Employee Relations Manager. Several area locations, including Union Beach, and South Brunswick, NJ. A leading creator and manufacturer of flavors and fragrances used by other manufacturers to impart flavor or fragrance in a wide variety of consumer products. Fragrance products are sold principally to manufacturers of perfumes, cosmetics and personal care items, soaps, detergents, other household products, as well as air fresheners. Flavor products are sold principally to manufacturers of dairy, meat, and other processed foods, beverages, pharmaceuticals, snacks and baked goods, confectioneries, tobacco, oral care products, and animal foods. Research and Development Center is located in Hazlet, NJ. Common positions include: Chemist; Computer Programmer; Marketing Specialist; Personnel Specialist; Systems Analyst. Principal educational backgrounds sought: Business Administration; Chemistry; Computer Science;

Marketing. Company benefits include: medical, dental, and life insurance; pension plan; tuition assistance; disability coverage; profit sharing; 401K; Christmas Bonus. Corporate headquarters location. Operations at this facility include: regional headquarters; administration; service; sales.

KITTINGER COMPANY
1893 Elmwood Avenue
Buffalo NY 14207
716/876-1000
Contact Kelly Julius, Personnel Manager. A manufacturer of casegoods and upholstered furniture. Corporate headquarters location. Operations at this facility include: manufacturing; administration. Common positions include: Blue-Collar Worker Supervisor; Credit Manager; Customer Service Representative; Draftsperson; Operations/Production Manager; Personnel & Labor Relations Specialist; Purchasing Agent; Quality Control Supervisor; Sales Representative. Principal educational backgrounds sought: Accounting; Art/Design; Business Administration; Engineering; Finance; Marketing. Company benefits include: medical insurance; dental insurance; life insurance; disability coverage; employee discounts.

ESTEE LAUDER INC.
350 South Service Road
Melville NY 11747
516/454-7000
Contact Employee Relations Department. Several area locations, including Manhattan, Queens, and The Bronx. A manufacturer and distributor of fine fashion cosmetics and skin care products. Company's worldwide sales, marketing, and international divisions are located in New York City; research and development, manufacturing operations, finance, and data processing centers are located at Long Island facilities. Corporate headquarters location.

LOEWS CORPORATION
1 Park Avenue
New York NY 10016
212/545-2000
Contact Laurie Ferro, Employment Manager. Company, through its subsidiaries, is engaged primarily in insurance (property, casualty, and life); the production and sale of cigarettes; of watches and other timing devices; the operation of hotels, and consumer finance. Operations are carried out through the following subsidiaries: Lorillard (produces a number of popular cigarette brands, including 'Kent', 'Newport', and others); CNA Financial Corporation (insurance operations); Loews Hotel Division; and Bulova Watch Company. Corporate headquarters location. New York Stock Exchange. International.

LONGINES - WITTNAUER WATCH COMPANY
145 Huguenot Street
New Rochelle NY 10802
914/576-1000
Contact Janet Carter, Personnel Manager. Engaged in the assembly and distribution of a large line of internationally-recognized watches and timepieces. Products are sold to quality retail stores throughout the United States. Corporate headquarters location. International.

ARTHUR MATNEY COMPANY INC.
4014 First Avenue
Brooklyn NY 11232
718/788-3200
Contact Bob Krischner, Personnel Department. A cosmetics manufacturer. Corporate headquarters location.

MITSUBISHI INTERNATIONAL CORPORATION
520 Madison Avenue
New York NY 10022
212/605-2000
Contact Mr. Ohno, Manager of Recruiting. An integrated trading company for one of Japan's largest and most diversified corporations. Operates through 10 trading divisions and a related support division. Divisions include: Petroleum; Steel; Foods; Chemicals; Machinery; Textiles; Non-Ferrous Metals; Ferrous Raw Materials; Lumber & Pulp; and General Merchandise. Regional offices are located throughout the United States, including Philadelphia, Pittsburgh, Washington DC, Chicago, Atlanta, Detroit, St. Louis, Houston, Denver, Los Angeles, Palo Alto, San Francisco, Portland (OR), and Seattle. Corporate headquarters location.

MONARCH LUGGAGE COMPANY INC.
5 Delavan Street
Brooklyn NY 11231
718/858-6900
Contact Personnel Department. Manufactures and distributes a wide range of luggage products, including briefcases, tote bags, athletic bags, attache cases, and related accessories. Corporate headquarters location.

MR. CHRISTMAS INC.
41 Madison Avenue
New York NY 10010
212/889-7220
Contact Joan Gilford, Office Manager. Manufacturer and importer of Christmas items, light sets, artificial Christmas trees, and many other Christmas novelties. Corporate headquarters location.

NIKON INC.
1300 Walt Whitman Road
Melville NY 11747
516/547-4259
Contact Carmen G. Estrada/Manager of H.R. or, Diane M. Pfadenhauer, Asst. Manager, H.R. A major importer of a full line of precision photographic and optical supplies, primarily from Japan, for distribution to retailers throughout the United States. Common positions include: Accountant; Administrator; Advertising Worker; Attorney; Blue-Collar Worker Supervisor; Claim Representative; Computer Programmer; Credit Manager; Customer Service Representative; Biomedical Engineer; Electrical Engineer; Industrial Engineer; Financial Analyst; Department Manager; General Manager; Operations/Production Manager; Personnel & Labor Relations Specialist; Purchasing Agent; Quality Control Supervisor; Sales Representative; Systems Analyst. Principal educational backgrounds sought: Accounting; Biology; Business Administration; Communications; Computer Science; Finance; Liberal Arts; Marketing. Training programs offered. Company benefits include: medical, dental, and life insurance; tuition assistance; employee discounts; savings plan; 401 K. Corporate headquarters location. Operations at this facility include: administration; service; sales.

NORTH AMERICAN PHILIPS CORPORATION
100 East 42nd Street
New York NY 10017
212/850-5000
Contact Marlene Weiss, Supervisor. Multiple area locations, including Stamford, CT; Murray Hill, Morristown, NJ; Woodbury and Briarcliff Manor, NY. One of the 100 largest industrial companies in the United States; a multi-market manufacturing organization with more than 40,000 employees in the United States. Company concentrates its efforts primarily in the fields of consumer products and services; electrical and electronic components and professional equipment, with a large number of well-known brand names. Some well-known products include 'Magnavox', 'Philco', and 'Sylvania' home entertainment products, 'Norelco' electric razors and coffee makers, 'Philips' lamps, and 'Philips' medical systems and electronic instruments. Owned by N.V. Philips, a major

Dutch-based industrial organization. Operates in the following divisions: Consumer Products/Services; Electrical and Electronic Components; Professonal Equipment; and Research. Area subsidiaries and divisions include Norelco (Stamford, CT); Philips Lighting Company (Somerset, NJ); Philips Business Systems (Woodbury, NY); Philips Electronic Instruments, Inc. (Mahwah, NJ); Philips Laboratories (Briarcliff Manor, NY). Corporate headquarters location. New York Stock Exchange. Common positions include: Accountant; Attorney; Computer Programmer. Principal educational backgrounds sought: Accounting; Computer Science; Finance. Company benefits include: medical insurance; dental insurance; pension plan; life insurance; tuition assistance; disability coverage; employee discounts; savings plan

ONEIDA LIMITED
Kenwood Avenue
Oneida NY 13421
315/361-3000
Contact Michael Reilly, Manager of Employment. Oneida Ltd.'s tree business units--consumer, food service and industrial--serve a diversified customer base including many of America's leading retailers, food service operators, and manufacturing companies. Through these divisions, the company specializes in the production of quality tableware, commercial china, and industrial wire and cable products.

PHILIPS BUSINESS SYSTEMS INC.
810 Woodbury Road
Woodbury NY 11797
516/921-9310
Contact Denise Morris, Personnel Director. Engaged in the manufacture and sale of a line of dictating machines, including desk-top and hand-held machines. A subsidiary of North American Philips Corporation. Corporate headquarters location.

POLYCHROME CORPORATION
137 Alexander Street
P.O. Box 817
Yonkers NY 10702
914/378-4383
Contact Linda Roskosky, Employee Services Representative. Several area locations, including Clark, NJ. Manufactures a wide range of graphic arts supplies and equipment. Common positions include: Accountant; Administrator; Blue-Collar Worker Supervisor; Chemist; Computer Programmer; Chemical Engineer; Mechanical Engineer; Financial Analyst; Branch Manager; Operations/Production Manager; Sales Representative; Systems Analyst. Principal educational backgrounds sought: Accounting; Business Administration; Chemistry; Computer Science; Engineering; Finance; Marketing. Company benefits include: medical, dental, and life insurance; pension plan; tuition assistance; disability coverage; employee discounts; savings plan; Flex Plus. Corporate headquarters location. Parent company: DICA. Operations at this facility include: manufacturing; research/development; administration; service.

REVLON, INC.
625 Madison Avenue, 3rd Floor
New York NY 10022
212/527-4000
Contact JoAnn Grillo, Personnel Department. Manufactures and distributes a line of high-quality skin care products, fragrances, and other cosmetics. Corporate headquarters location. International.

ROSS BICYCLE
51 Executive Boulevard
Farmingdale NY 11735
516/249-6000
Contact Personnel Director. Manufactures a complete line of bicycles, from three-wheelers to racing bikes, for international distribution. Corporate headquarters location.

SANBORN MAPPING & GEOGRAPHIC INFORMATION SERVICE
629 Fifth Avenue
Pelham NY 10803
914/738-1649
Contact Joseph Cirillo, President. Publishes a wide variety of maps. Corporate headquarters location.

STEINWAY & SONS
1 Steinway Place
Long Island City NY 11105
718/721-2600 ext. 108
Contact Michael Anesta, Director of Personnel. One of the world's largest and most respected manufacturers and distributors of pianos, including a wide range of grand and vertical pianos. Company's products are used by many of the world's best-known concert pianists, as well as other professional and amateur musicians throughout the world. Common positions include: Accountant; Blue-Collar Worker Supervisor; Buyer; Computer Programmer; Credit Manager; Customer Service Representative; Industrial Engineer; Mechanical Engineer; Department Manager; Operations/Production Manager; Personnel & Labor Relation Specialist; Public Relations Worker; Purchasing Agent; Quality Control Supervisor; Systems Analyst. Principal educational backgrounds sought: Accouting; Business Administration; Computer Science; Engineering; Finance; Liberal Arts; Marketing. Company benefits include: medical, dental, and life insurance; pension plan; tuition assistance; disability coverage; employee discounts; savings plan. Corporate headquarters location: Waltham, MA. Parent company: Steinway Musical Properties, Inc. Operations at this facility include: manufacturing; research/development; administration; service.

SWANK INC.
90 Park Avenue
New York NY 10016
212/867-2600
Contact Mel Goldfeder, Senior Vice-President. Executive and national/international sales headquarters for the leading United States manufacturer and distributor of men's and women's jewelry, personal leather goods, belts, fragrances, gifts, and personal accessory items. Brand names include Swank, Prince Gardner, Princess Gardner, Royal Copenhagen, Flora Danica, Pierre Cardin, L'Aiglon, Anne Klein, Etienne Aigner, and Biagi. Company operates six production and distribution facilities: two in Massachusetts, two in Arkansas, and one each in Connecticut and Missouri. Corporate headquarters location. Administrative offices are located in Attleboro, MA.

TOPPS CHEWING GUM INC.
254 36th Street
Brooklyn NY 11232
718/768-8900
Contact Bill O'Connor, Personnel Office. Manufactures and markets, in the United States and abroad, a variety of chewing gum, candy, and other products which primarily appeal to young consumers. Company also licenses its technology and trademarks and sells its chewing gum base and flavors to other overseas manufacturers. Company is best known for its internationally registered trademark Bazooka, and its perenial Topps Baseball Bubble Gum picture cards. The company is the leading marketer, under exclusive licenses, of collectible picture cards, albums, and stickers for baseball, football, and hockey; also a leading producer and distributor of cards and stickers containing pictures of popular motion picture, television and cartoon characters, also under exclusive licenses. Primary United States manufacturing facility located in Duryea, PA; international facilities in Ireland. Corporate headquarters location. American Stock Exchange.

TRIFARI, KRUSSMAN & FISHEL INC.
404 5th Avenue
New York NY 10018
212/643-8030

Contact Diane McLoone, Office Manager. Produces fashion and costume jewelry. Headquarters location.

VICTORIA CREATIONS
385 Fifth Avenue
New York NY 10016
212/725-0600
Contact Personnel Director. Produces costume jewelry. Headquarters location.

WILL & BAUMER INC.
P.O. Box 4880
Syracuse NY 13221
Contact Executive Vice President. Firm develops, manufactures and sells candles and wax goods. Sells primarily to dealers and distributors. Operations at this facility include: manufacturing; research/development; administration; sales. Corporate headquarters location. Common positions include: Accountant; Blue-Collar Worker Supervisor; Buyer; Computer Programmer; Credit Manager; Customer Service Representative; Engineer; Management Trainee; Operations/Production Manager; Purchasing Agent; Sales Representative. Principal educational backgrounds sought: Accounting; Business Administration; Computer Science; Engineering; Marketing. Company benefits include: medical insurance; dental insurance; pension plan; life insurance; tuition assistance; disability coverage; employee discounts; savings plan.

HARRY WINSTON INC.
718 Fifth Avenue
New York NY 10019
212/245-2000
Contact Mindy Berk, Assistant Controller. Engaged manufacturing and sales of rare jewels and precious stones. Corporate headquarters location. International.

YVES SAINT - LAURENT PARFUMS CORPORATION
40 West 57th Street
New York NY 10019
212/621-7300
Contact Director of Personnel. A well-known name in the personal care business, specializing in fine cosmetics, perfumes, and skin care products.

Connecticut

AMERICAN BRANDS
1700 East Putnam Avenue
Old Greenwich CT 06870
203/698-5000
Contact Mr. Dennis Doherty, Personnel Director. Corporate headquarters of a Connecticut area holding company.

BIC CORPORATION
500 Bic Drive
Milford CT 06460
203/783-2144
Contact Paul Moyher, Manager, Personnel Administration. Manufactures such consumer items as pens, lighters, shavers, and perfume. Common positions include: Electrical Engineer; Mechanical Engineer; Sales Representative. Principal educational backgrounds sought: Business Administration; Computer Science; Engineering. Company benefits include: medical, dental, and life insurance; pension plan; tuition assistance; disability coverage; profit sharing; employee discounts; savings plan. Corporate headquarters location. Operations at this facility include: manufacturing; research/development. American Stock Exchange.

CLAIROL INC.
One Blachley Road
Stamford CT 06922
203/357-5000
Contact Director of Human Resources. Manufactures and markets a full range of hair coloring and hair care products for home and salon use, and is a worldwide marketer and manufacturer of hair care, beauty care, and personal care appliances. A major operating subsidiary of Bristol-Myers Company. Corporate headquarters location. International.

THE FORSCHNER GROUP, INC.
151 Longhill Cross Roads
Shelton CT 06484
203/929-6391
Contact Lesley Olsen, Director of Personnel. An importer and marketer of Forschner Cutlery, Swiss Army knives. Corporate headquarters location. Common positions include: Accountant; Commercial Artist; Customer Service Representative; Programmer; Sales Representative; Secretary. Principal educational backgrounds sought: Accounting; Business Administration; Communications; Computer Science. Company benefits include: medical insurance; dental insurance; pension plan; life insurance; tuition assistance; disability coverage; employee discounts; 401K; physical fitness reimbursement.

C.R. GIBSON COMPANY
32 Knight Street
Norwalk CT 06856
203/847-4543
Contact Ruth Eckert, Personnel. Manufactures photo albums, wedding albums, desk accessories, stationery, note paper, greeting cards, wrapping paper, paper table wear and candles. Corporate headquarters location. Common positions include: Accountant; Administrator; Advertising Worker; Blue-Collar Worker Supervisor; Buyer; Commercial Artist; Credit Manager; Customer Service Representative; Operations/Production Manager; Marketing Specialist; Personnel & Labor Relations Specialist; Programmer; Public Relations Worker; Purchasing Agent; Systems Analyst. Principal educational background sought: Business Administration. Company benefits include: medical insurance; pension plan; life insurance; disability coverage; profit sharing; employee discounts; savings plan.

LOCTITE
705 North Mountain Road
Newington CT 06111
203/278-1280
Contact Don Atencio, Human Resources Director. A manufacturer of adhesives.

RICHARDSON-VICKS INC.
P.O. Box 854
Shelton CT 06484-0925
203/925-6000
Contact John Chasmar, Personnel Manager. Several area locations, including Westport, Shelton, CT; Phillipsburg, NJ. A leading worldwide marketer of branded consumer products in four major areas: Personal Care; Health Care; Home Care; and Natural/Nutritional Care. The company also produces specialty chemicals, laboratory reagents, and diagnostic instruments. Well-known brands include 'Vicks' cold and cough relief products, 'Oil of Olay' and 'Clearasil' skin care products, 'Pantene' and 'Vidal Sasson' hair care products, 'Formby's' wood care products, 'Mill Creek' natural hair and skin care products, and others. Corporate headquarters location. New York Stock Exchange. International.

THE STANLEY WORKS
P.O. Box 7000
New Britain CT 06050
203/225-5111

Contact Ann Bernard, Corporate Personnel Manager. Several area locations, including Farmington, and New Britain, CT. A worldwide marketer and manufacturer of quality tools for do-it-yourselfers and professionals, including carpenters, mechanics, electricians, plumbers, and industrial maintenance engineers. Manufactures hardware and complementary products for the home, the factory, and the building industry. Its industry segments are: Consumer Products, including hand tools, fasteners, home hardware, garage door openers, and residential entry doors for the do-it-yourself market; Builders Products, which provides products to the professional construction industry, including architectural and residential hardware, pedestrian power-operated doors, insulated steel entry doors, garage doors and openers, automatic parking gates and commercial doors, and Industrial products; which include products sold to industrial and automotive customers, including professional hand tools, 'MAC' mechanics tools, air tools, hydraulic tools, industrial storage systems, steel and plastic strapping, industrial hardware and stampings. Plants are located throughout the United States (significant Connecticut operations), and in more than 30 foreign countries. Corporate headquarters location. New York Stock Exchange. International.

UST
100 West Putnam Avenue
Greenwich CT 06830
203/661-1100
Contact Nella Viesta, Manager of Corporate Human Resources. A Fortune 500 company and leading producer and marketer of moist smokeless tobacco products. Common positions include: Accountant; Administrator; Attorney; Buyer; Computer Programmer; Credit Manager; Customer Service Representative; Financial Analyst; Purchasing Agent; Systems Analyst. Principal educational backgrounds sought include: Accounting; Finance; Marketing. Internships available. Company benefits: medical insurance; dental insurance; pension plan; life insurance; tuition assistance; disability coverage; savings plan. Corporate headquarters location. New York Stock Exchange.

<u>New Jersey</u>

AGFA-GEVAERT, INC.
100 Challenger Road
Richfield Park NJ 07660
201/440-2500
Contact Personnel Manager. Originally an international photographic products firm; now a diversified international corporation operating in several divisions: Photographic Division, which produces films, printing papers, cameras, and film projectors, lenses, and other related products used in X-ray and non-destructive testing applications; Office Systems Division, including office duplicators and printers, a wide range of microfiche and microfilm products, and related supplies; and the Magnetic Tape Division, which produces professional audio products and amateur video cassette products. United States production facilities are located in West Caldwell, NJ; and Shoreham, NY. This facility is United States headquarters, and also houses marketing and distribution functions. Corporate headquarters location: Mortsel, Belgium.

RUSS BERRIE & COMPANY, INC.
111 Bauer Drive
Oakland NJ 07436
201/337-9000 Ext. 221
Contact Gloria Fleischman, Personnel Manager. A distributor of toys, stuffed animals, novelties, cards, and similar items. Common positions include: Accountant; Commercial Artist; Customer Service Representative; Financial Analyst; Management Trainee; Marketing Specialist; Sales Representative. Principal educational backgrounds sought: Accounting; Art/Design; Business Administration; Finance; Liberal Arts; Marketing. Company benefits include: medical, dental, and life insurance; tuition assistance; profit sharing; employee discounts. Corporate headquarters location: Oakland,NJ. Operations at this facility include: administration. New York Stock Exchange.

CHARLES BESELER COMPANY
1600 Lower Road
Linden NJ 07036
201/862-7999
Contact Personnel Administrator. A manufacturer and distributor of photographic products. These consist mainly of darkroom equipment used by amateurs and professionals, including enlargers, color analyzers, and photo color printing equipment and accessories, as well as photo chemistry products and color printing materials and supplies. Products are sold primarily to retail photographic shops. The company has recently entered the field of computer graphics generation systems with the introduction of a line of graphics film recorders. These products are sold through computer equipment dealers and distributors. The company also produces shrink film packaging equipment, primarily sealers and tunnels, sold to packaging equipment dealers and film distributors. Common positions include: Accountant; Buyer; Credit Manager; Data Processing Specialist; Draftsperson; Electrical Engineer; Mechanical Engineer; Operations/Production Manager; Marketing Research Worker; Marketing Specialist; Programmer; Purchasing Agent; Quality Control Supervisor; Systems Analyst; Design Engineer; Quality Control Supervisor; Quality Control Technician.

COLORITE PLASTICS DIVISION/
PLASTIC SPECIALTIES & TECHNOLOGY
101 Railroad Avenue
Ridgefield NJ 07657
201/941-2900
Contact Manuel Aneiros, Personnel Manager. Manufactures garden hoses and PVC compounds.

EMERSON RADIO CORPORATION
One Emerson Lane
North Bergen NJ 07047
201/854-6600
Contact Lori Milat, Assistant Personnel Manager. Designs and markets a line of home entertainment equipment for the consumer market. The company's products include VCR's, televisions, radios, tape players and player/recorders, clock radios, and compact stereos. Cardiac Resuscitator Corporation, a 71 percent-owned subsidiary, is engaged in the development, manufacture, and sale of automatic heart defibrillator-pacemaker devices. Imatron, Inc., an 18 percent-owned affiliate, has developed a high-speed computerized axial tomographic X-ray scanner system. Corporate headquarters location. International. New York Stock Exchange. Common positions include: Accountant; Administrator; Customer Service Representative. Principal educational backgrounds sought: Accounting; Communications; Engineering; Finance. Company benefits include: medical insurance; dental insurance; life insurance; disability coverage; profit sharing; employee discounts.

GOODY PRODUCTS INC.
969 Newark Turnpike
Kearny NJ 07032
201/997-3000
Contact Personnel Office. A manufacturer of hair accessories, including combs, brushes, curlers, and other products.

M. GRUMBACHER, INC.
30 Englehard Drive
Cranbury NJ 08512
609/655-8282
Contact James Preston, III, Director, Human Resources. A manufacturer of artists' supplies, including paints, brushes, and many other products. Common positions include: Accountant; Blue-Collar Worker Supervisor; Buyer; Chemist; Computer Programmer; Customer Service Representative; Financial Analyst; Department Manager; General Manager; Operations/Production Manager; Marketing Specialist; Personnel & Labor Relations Specialist; Purchasing Agent; Quality Control Supervisor; Sales Representative;

Transportation & Traffic Specialist. Training programs offered. Company benefits include: medical, dental, and life insurance; pension plan; tuition assistance; disability coverage; profit sharing; employee discounts; savings plan. Corporate headquarters location: Brentwood, TN. Parent company: Berol Corporation. Operations at this facility include: divisional headquarters; manufacturing; research/development; administration; service; sales.

HARTZ MOUNTAIN CORPORATION
700 Frank E. Rodgers Boulevard South
Harrison NJ 07029-9987
201/481-4800
Contact Corporate Personnel Office. Engaged in the manufacture, packaging, and distribution of consumer products, including pet foods, pet accessories, livestock feed and products, chemical products, home carpet-cleaning products, and equipment rentals. Second area manufacturing facility located in Bloomfield, NJ. Other area subsidiaries include Cooper Pet Supply, Permaline Manufacturing Corporation, Sternco-Dominion Real Estate Corporation, and The Pet Library Ltd. Corporate headquarters location. American Stock Exchange.

HAYWARD INDUSTRIES
900 Fairmount Avenue
Elizabeth NJ 07207
201/351-5400
Contact Evan Zimmerman, Manager of Employment. Second Elizabeth facility. A leading manufacturer of swimming pool equipment. Company is engaged in all aspects of production, including design and sales. Principal clients use equipment in construction, repair, and maintenance of private and commercial swimming pools. The company also manufactures and distributes a standard line of industrial pipeline strainers and valves. Operates an international subsidiary located in Belgium. Principal educational backgrounds sought: Accounting; Business Administration; Communications; Computer Science; Economics; Engineering; Finance; Liberal Arts; Marketing. Company benefits include: medical, dental, and life insurance; pension plan; tuition assistance; disability coverage; employee discounts; savings plan; 401 K. Corporate headquarters location: Elizabeth, NJ. Operations at this facility include: manufacturing; research/development; administration; service; sales.

HOUBIGANT INC.
1135 Pleasant View Terrace West
P.O. Box 299
Ridgefield NJ 07657-0299
201/941-3400
Contact Ralph De Padua, Personnel Office. Other area locations in North Bergen, NJ; and Staten Island, NY. A major international manufacturer of fine perfumes and cosmetics, and other personal care products. Corporate headquarters location. International.

JACLYN INC.
635 59th Street
West New York NJ 07093
201/868-9400
Contact Benjamin Fleischauer, Vice President/Personnel. Company and its subsidiaries are involved in the design, manufacture, distribution, and sale of handbags and related products, including luggage (carry-on bags and backpacks), and active wear carrying bags. Common positions include: Accountant; Administrator; Blue-Collar Worker Supervisor; Buyer; Computer Programmer; Credit Manager; Industrial Engineer; Financial Analyst; Department Manager; General Manager; Operations/Production Manager; Personnel & Labor Relations Specialist; Purchasing Agent; Quality Control Supervisor; Sales Representative; Transportation & Traffic Specialist. Principal educational backgrounds sought: Accounting; Business Administration; Economics; Engineering; Finance. Company benefits include: medical, dental, and life insurance; pension plan; disability coverage; profit sharing; employee discounts; savings plan. Corporate headquarters location.

Operations at this facility include: manufacturing; research/development; administration; service; sales. American Stock Exchange.

JACOBSON MANUFACTURING COMPANY INC.
1 Mark Road
Kenilworth NJ 07033
201/686-0200
Contact Christine Sapienza, Personnel. Manufactures and distributes a broad line of nationally-distributed consumer home-maintenance equipment, including lawn mowers and other lawn care products, tractors, snow blowers, and similar items. A subsidiary of Textron Inc.'s (Providence, RI) Consumer Products Group. Corporate headquarters location.

KAYSAM CORPORATION OF AMERICA
27 Kentucky Avenue
Paterson NJ 07503
201/684-5700
Contact Tony Rowe, Personnel Manager. Two area facilities. Manufactures vinyl compounds, vinyl footwear, vinyl toys, meteorological balloons, and other miscellaneous soft goods. Corporate headquarters location.

KREMENTZ & COMPANY
375 McCarter Highway
Newark NJ 07114
201/621-8300
Contact Personnel Director. An internationally-recognized manufacturer and distributor of fine jewelry and related items.

L & F PRODUCTS
225 Summit Avenue
Montvale NJ 07645
201/573-5222
Contact Betty Harden, Director of Staffing. Operates through eleven manufacturing and six marketing units. Divisions include: Staffing Household for cleaner-disinfectants and other household products (includes 'Lysol' products, 'Chubs/Wet Ones,' 'Mop & Glo,' 'Perk,' 'Love My Carpet' and many other well-known products); The Minwax Company and the Thompson Formby Division for 'do-it-yourself' wood finishing products; the National Laboratories for cleaning and maintenance products for institutions and industry; the Personal Products Division, for personal care products sold under the 'Tussy,' 'Ogilvie,' and 'Dorothy Gray' names. A wholly owned subsidiary of Eastman Kodak. New York Stock Exchange. Common positions include: Accountant; Biologist; Chemist; Computer Programmer; Credit Manager; Customer Service Representative; Chemical Engineer; Industrial Engineer; Systems Analyst. Principal educational backgrounds sought include: Accounting; Business Administration; Computer Science; Engineering; Marketing. Company benefits include: medical insurance; dental insurance; pension plan; life insurance; tuition assistance; disability coverage; employee discounts; savngs plan. Corporate headquarters location.

LETRASET
40 Eisenhower Drive
Paramus NJ 07653
201/845-6100
Contact Janet Krusche, Personnel Manager. Produces and distributes graphic arts products, including transferrable lettering and markers, color products, framing products, and software products. Common positions include: Accountant; Administrator; Customer Service Representative; Sales Representative. Principal educational backgrounds sought: Accounting; Computer Science; Finance; Marketing. Training programs offered. Company benefits include: medical, dental, and life insurance; disability coverage; 401K. Parent company: Esselte. Operations at this facility include: divisional headquarters; administration; service.

MELARD MANUFACTURING CORPORATION
153 Linden Street
P.O. Box 58
Passaic NJ 07055
201/472-8888
Contact Marlene Reiter, Office Manager. Manufactures a broad range of hardware products. Corporate headquarters location.

MEM COMPANY INC.
Union Street Extension
Northvale NJ 07647
201/767-0100
Contact Director of Personnel. Operates in three business segments: the production and distribution of toiletries for men, women and children; the manufacture and sale of leather products. Primary business is the manufacture, sale and distribution of a diversified line of men's toiletries in six fragrance groups under the 'English Leather' line. Other products include 'Tinkerbell' children's cosmetics (sold through subsidiary Tom Fields Ltd.), 'Heaven Sent' and 'Loves' lines of women's fragrance items, and others. Products are manufactured in company-licensed facilities and distributed throughout the world. Corporate headquarters location. American Stock Exchange. International.

MINOLTA CORPORATION
101 Williams Drive
Ramsey NJ 07446
201/825-4000
Contact Linda A. Loveland, Employment Manager. A wholly-owned subsidiary of Minolta Camera Company, Ltd. (Osaka, Japan). Markets, sells and distributes parent company's extensive line of cameras, lenses (for photographic and industrial optics uses), meters, business machines (primarily copiers), and other specialized equipment (includes microphotographic equipment, color-analyzing instruments, optico-medical equipment, scientific measuring and analyzing instruments, and other equipment). Other area facilities located in Mahwah, NJ (Minolta Business Systems); and New York, NY (Minolta Copier Corporation of New York). Parent company has facilities throughout the world. Corporate headquarters location. Other facilities located in Ramsey, NJ (Minolta Business Systems).

P.P.I. ENTERTAINMENT GROUP
88 St. Francis Street
Newark NJ 07105
201/344-4214
Contact Personnel Department. Several area locations, including Lakewood. A manufacturer of children's phonograph records. Corporate headquarters location.

PRESTO LOCK CORPORATION
100 Outwater Lane
Garfield NJ 07026
201/340-1000
Contact Personnel Manager. A major manufacturer and distributor of builder's hardware, including locks and other security devices. Corporate headquarters location.

PULEO'S MANUFACTURING COMPANY
435 Division Street
Elizabeth NJ 07201
201/965-1500
Contact Personnel Department. Manufactures a diverse line of Christmas products, primarily artificial Christmas trees, for sale to wholesalers, general merchandise retailers, and specialty retailers throughout the country. Other products include Christmas wreaths, ornaments, and decorations. Corporate headquarters location.

REVLON INC./
IMPELEMENT DIVSION
196 Coit Street
Irvington NJ 07111
201/373-5803
Contact Personnel Manager. Manufactures nail files, scissors, tweezers, and other manicure and pedicure products. A subsidiary of Revlon, Inc. Corporate headquarters location: New York, NY. New York Stock Exchange. Common positions include: Accountant; Blue-Collar Worker Supervisor; Industrial Engineer; Mechanical Engineer; Department Manager; General Manager; Operations/Production Manager; Personnel & Labor Relations Specialist; Purchasing Agent; Quality Control Supervisor. Principal educational backgrounds sought: Accounting; Business Administration; Engineering; Finance; Liberal Arts. Company benefits include: medical insurance; pension plan; life insurance; tuition assistance; disability coverage; profit sharing; employee discounts; savings plan.

RIVIERA TRADING CORPORATION
80 Seaview Drive
Secaucus NJ 07096
201/864-8686
Contact Melvin Urfirer, Director of Industrial Relations. Imports and distributes hair ornaments and sunglasses. Corporate headquarters location: New York, NY. Operations include: manufacturing; service. Common positions include: Accountant; Administrator; Customer Service Representative; Branch Manager; Department Manager; General Manager; Management Trainee; Operations/Production Manager; Marketing Specialist; Personnel & Labor Relations Specialist; Purchasing Agent. Principal educational backgrounds sought: Accounting; Business Administration. Company benefits include: medical insurance; dental insurance; pension plan; life insurance; disability coverage; profit sharing.

VARITYPER INC.
11 Mt. Pleasant Avenue
East Hanover NJ 07936
201/887-8000
Contact Employment Department. Varityper is one of the world's leading suppliers of high resolution, professional quality systems for both in house and commercial imagesetting applications. Common positions include: Accountant; Electrical Engineer; Industrial Engineer. Principal educational backgrounds sought: Accounting; Computer Science; Engineering; Marketing. Company benefits include: medical insurance; dental insurance; pension plan; life insurance; tuition assistance; disability coverage; profit sharing. Corporate headquarters location. Parent company: Tegra, Inc. Operations at this facility include: manufacturing.

THE WELLA CORPORATION
524 Grand Avenue
Englewood NJ 07631
201/569-1020
Contact Personnel Manager. Produces a complete line of hair cosmetics, including hair colors, permanent waves, hair conditioners, shampoos, and other products. Corporate headquarters location. International.

WELLINGTON HOME PRODUCTS
52 Courtland Street
Paterson NJ 07503
201/278-6300
Contact Cathy Smith, Personnel Supervisor. Manufactures a line of outdoor consumer products, including patio furniture, vinyl screening, and tablecloths. Corporate headquarters location. Corporate headquarters location: Accountant; Administrator; Computer Programmer; Credit Manager; Customer Service Representative; Sales Representative. Educational backgrounds sought include: Accounting; Business Administration; Computer Science; Finance; Marketing. Company benefits include:

medical insurance; dental insurance; pension plan; life insurance; disability coverage; employee discounts. Corporate headquarters location.

MANUFACTURING: MISCELLANEOUS INDUSTRIAL

New York

R.P. ADAMS COMPANY INC.
P.O. Box 963
Buffalo NY 14240
716/877-2608
Contact David R. Henning, Vice President/Personnel Management. A manufacturer of heat exchange and strainer/filtration equipment. Operations include: manufacturing. Corporate headquarters location. Common positions at this facility include: Buyer; Draftsperson; Chemical Engineer; Industrial Engineer; Mechanical Engineer; Metallurgical Engineer; Department Manager; Operations/Production Manager; Programmer; Purchasing Agent; Quality Control Supervisor; Sales Engineer. Principal educational backgrounds sought: Business Administration; Engineering. Internships offered. Company benefits include: medical insurance; dental insurance; pension plan; life insurance; tuition assistance; disability coverage; profit sharing; 401 K; flexible spending account. Operations at this facility include: manufacturing; administration; sales.

ALLOY TECHNOLOGY INTERNATIONAL INC.
169 Western Highway
West Nyack NY 10994
914/358-5900
Contact Personnel Department. Several area locations. A division of the multi-industry products and services firm; produces proprietary machinable carbide products, as well as providing sales and distribution services for company products. Nationally, the firm is a large multi-industry business which produces and sells a complete range of products and services. Operating companies are in the following business segments: Metal Fabrication; Transportation; Petroleum Services; Apparel; and Financial Services. Corporate headquarters location: St. Louis, MO. New York Stock Exchange. International.

AMERICAN FELT & FILTER COMPANY
Walsh Avenue
New Windsor NY 12553
914/561-3560
Contact Richard E. Price, Director of Personnel. Manufactures a complete line of filter products, including filter bags, filter cartridges, pressure filters, molded filter media, and non-woven filter media for air, gas, and liquid filtration. Company's technical service staff, with experience in more than 200 different types of industrial and water process applications, provides market and applications expertise. Some typical products include wool and synthetic felts used for filtration media, decorative felts, industrial felts, piano hammer felt, and many others. Principal customers include the appliance industry, manufacturers of paint and chemicals, and the piano industry. Corporate headquarters location. Operations at this facility include: manufacturing; research/development; administration. Common positions include: Accountant; Blue-Collar Worker Supervisor; Buyer; Chemist; Computer Programmer; Credit Manager; Customer Service Representative; Industrial Engineer; Mechanical Engineer; Operations/Production Manager; Personnel & Labor Relations Specialist; Programmer; Purchasing Agent; Quality Control Supervisor; Sales Representative. Principal educational backgrounds sought: Accounting; Engineering. Company benefits include: medical insurance; pension plan; life insurance; tuition assistance; disability coverage; profit sharing.

AMERICAN STANDARD INC.
1114 6th Avenue
New York NY 10036
212/840-5100

Contact Sophia Stratis, Director of Personnel. A major worldwide manufacturer; operates in four diversified areas: Transportation Products; Building Products; Security and Graphic Products; and Construction and Mining Equipment. Conducts manufacturing operations in more than 20 countries. Corporate headquarters location. New York Stock Exchange.

AMPHENOL-BENDIX
40-60 Delaware Street
Sidney NY 13838
607/563-5011
Contact Personnel Director. An area producer of connectors. Parent company, Allied Signal Corporation, serves a broad spectrum of industries through its more than 40 strategic businesses, which are grouped into five sectors: Aerospace; Automotive; Chemical; Industrial and Technology; and Oil and Gas. Allied Signal is one of the nation's largest industrial organizations, and has 115,000 employees in over 30 countries. Corporate headquarters location: Morristown, NJ.

ARKWIN INDUSTRIES
686 Main Street
Westbury NY 11590
516/333-2640
Contact Thomas Malloy, Director of Administration. Designs and manufacutures fluid power control components for the aerospace and other high tech industries. Common positions include: Blue-Collar Worker Supervisor; Buyer; Computer Programmer; Draftsperson; Aerospace Engineer; Industrial Engineer; Mechanical Engineer; Department Manager; Management Trainee; Operations/Production Manager; Marketing Specialist; Personnel & Labor Relations Specialist; Purchasing Agent; Sales Representative; Statistician; Systems Analyst; Technical Writer/Editor. Principal educational backgrounds sought: Business Administration; Computer Science; Engineering; Liberal Arts. Company benefits include: medical insurance; dental insurance; pension plan; life insurance; tuition assistance; disability coverage; profit sharing. Corporate headquarters location. Operations at this facility include: manufacturing; research/development; administration; service; sales.

BERGER INDUSTRIES INC.
74-16 Grand Avenue
Maspeth NY 11378
718/335-8000
Contact Bernie Bender, Personnel Manager. Several area locations, including Queens. Original manufacturer and recognized leader in the development of lamp parts. Also manufactures steel and electronic tubing. Corporate headquarters location.

CHRIS CRAFT INDUSTRIES/
INDUSTRIAL DIVISION
600 Madison Avenue
New York NY 10022
212/421-0200
Contact Personnel Director. Produces industrial chemicals, plastics, and foams for automobile and other OEMs.

CRANE COMPANY
757 Third Avenue
New York NY 10017
212/415-7300
Contact Richard Phillips, Vice President/Human Resources. Crane is a diversified manufacturer of engineered products for industry, aerospace and defense, as well as a distributor of industrial and building products. Operations at this facility include: administration. Corporate headquarters location. New York Stock Exchange.

COX & CO. INC.
200 Varick Street
New York NY 10014
212/366-0200
Contact John Matuzsa, Personnel Director. Produces temperature control systems: heating and cooling. Corporate headquarters location.

DRESSER-RAND
P.O. Box 560
Olean NY 14760
716/375-3000
Contact John Snyder, Director, Human Resources. Provides compressors and gas turbines to customers in the energy processing and conversion market. Parent company, Dresser Industries, Inc., is one of the world's leading suppliers of technology, products and services to worldwide energy, natural resource and industrial markets; operations include petroleum, energy processing and conversion, mining and construction, and general industry. The company markets its products and services in more than 100 countries. Common positions include: Industrial Engineer; Mechanical Engineer. Principal educational backgrounds sought: Engineering. Company benefits include: medical, dental, and life insurance; pension plan; tuition assistance; disability coverage; savings plan. Divisional headquarters.

EMBASSY/
P&F INDUSTRIES INC.
300 Smith Street
Farmingdale NY 11735
516/694-1800
Contact Leon D. Feldman, Executive Vice President. Several locations, including Farmingdale, New Hyde Park, NY and Boynton Beach, Florida. A manufacturing firm specializing in the production of portable pneumatic tools, baseboard heating equipment, hardware, and sheet metal contracting. Corporate headquarters location.

ESSELTE PENDAFLEX CORPORATION
71 Clinton Road
Garden City NY 11530
516/741-3200
Contact Andres Anderson, Director of Human Resources. Other area facilities in New York City; Moonachie, NJ. Manufactures and distributes filing and marking systems, storage furniture, and other office materials. Primary products are paper-based filing products, mainly suspension filing systems. Operates production and sales facilities in the United States and Canada. Parent company, Esselte AB, is a Swedish-based firm engaged in industrial production, trade, and services, primarily in the fields of office equipment, stationery and price marking, custom printing and binding, consumer and transport packaging, textbooks and instructional materials, cartography, publishing, and bookstores. Employs 15,000 people in 22 countries. Corporate headquarters location. International. Operations at this facility include: manufacturing; research/development; administration; sales. New York Stock Exchange. Common positions include: Accountant; Blue-Collar Worker Supervisor; Buyer; Claim Representative; Computer Programmer; Draftsperson; Industrial Engineer; Mechanical Engineer; Industrial Designer; Operations/Production Manager; Marketing Specialist; Personnel & Labor Relations Specialist; Sales Representative. Principal educational backgrounds sought: Accounting; Business Administration; Engineering; Finance; Liberal Arts; Marketing. Company benefits include: medical insurance; dental insurance; pension plan; life insurance; tuition assistance; disability coverage; employee discounts; savings plan. Training programs offered; Internships offered.

EUTECTIC CORPORATION
40-40 172nd Street
Flushing NY 11358
718/358-4000

Contact Marietta Fleming, Director of Administration. A worldwide organization engaged in the development, manufacture, distribution, and sale of special products, processes, and services for maintenance and repair welding, designed to increase industrial productivity and prevent production stoppages by making critical machine parts and tools last longer. Overall, company is one of the world's largest manufacturers of special alloys for protective maintenance and repair. Also offers extensive support and consulting services for company products. Eutectic & Castolin Institute (above location) provides extensive instructional programs in company technology. Common positions include: Accountant; Administrator; Blue-Collar Worker Supervisor; Buyer; Chemist; Computer Programmer; Credit Manager; Draftsperson; Electrical Engineer; Mechanical Engineer; Metallurgical Engineer; Financial Analyst; Industrial Designer; Operations/Production Manager; Marketing Specialist; Personnel & Labor Relations Specialist; Purchasing Agent; Quality Control Supervisor; Sales Representative; Systems Analyst; Transportation & Traffic Specialist. Principal educational backgrounds sought: Accounting; Business Administration; Chemistry; Communications; Computer Science; Engineering; Finance; Liberal Arts; Marketing. Company benefits include: medical and life insurance; tuition assistance; disability coverage; 401K plan; savings plan. Corporate headquarters location. Operations at this facility include: regional headquarters; divisional headquarters; manufacturing; research/development; administration; service; sales.

GOULDS PUMPS INC.
240 Fall Street
Seneca Falls NY 13148
315/568-2811
Contact Tracey L. Barto, Supervisor of Employee Relations. Manufacturer of centrifugal pumps for industrial, commercial and residential uses. Common positions include: Accountant; Attorney; Blue-Collar Worker Supervisor; Buyer; Chemist; Computer Programmer; Credit Manager; Customer Service Representative; Draftsperson; Chemical Engineer; Mechanical Engineer; Metallurgical Engineer; Financial Analyst; Industrial Designer; Branch Manager; Department Manager; General Manager; Marketing Specialist; Personnel & Labor Relations Specialist; Public Relations Worker; Purchasing Agent. Principal educational backgrounds sought: Accounting; Business Administration; Chemistry; Computer Science; Economics; Engineering; Finance; Liberal Arts; Marketing; Mathematics. Company benefits include: medical and dental insurance; pension plan; tuition assistance; disability coverage; employee discounts; savings plan. Operations at this facility include: manufacturing; research/development; administration; service; sales. American Stock Exchange.

GREENWALK INDUSTRIES
1340 Metropolitan Avenue
Brooklyn NY 11237
718/456-6900
Contact Angie Sacristan, Personnel Director. A leading designer and manufacturer of coin meter systems. A subsidiary of Kidde, Inc. Corporate headquarters location.

GUSSCO MANUFACTURING INC.
5112 Second Avenue
Brooklyn NY 11232
718/492-7900
Contact Diane Crosby, Personnel Manager. A manufacturer of office filing supplies and filing cabinets and systems. Corporate headquarters location.

GEORGE HANTSCHO COMPANY
30 Warren Place
Mount Vernon NY 10550
914/664-7100
Contact Cathy Maye, Manager/Employee Relations. The world's second largest manufacturer of web offset presses, offering a wide line of printing capabilities to book, magazine, atlas, textbook, catalog, and directory publishers. Maintains sales and service offices in Chicago, Los Angeles, and West Germany. Company's research and development facilities are located in Stamford, CT. Corporate headquarters location.

INDUSTRIAL ACOUSTICS COMPANY INC.
1160 Commerce Avenue
Bronx NY 10462
212/931-8000
Contact Ray Svana, Personnel. A major company engaged exclusively in the development, manufacture, and installation of engineered noise control and acoustical conditioning products and systems. Company's extensive product line serves multiple applications in industry, architecture, building services, power plants, aerospace, medical/life sciences, research, and testing. Some specific markets served and product applications include: manufacturing and process industries; architectural; medical life sciences; air conditioning systems; research and development laboratories; construction equipment; noise control for utilities and oil industries; jet engine, test cells, and aircraft run-up silencers; and traffic noise control systems. Also produces acoustic test environments for research and development, and quality control. Corporate headquarters location. International.

JAMECO INDUSTRIES
248 Wyandanch Avenue
Wyandanch NY 11798
516/643-5300
Contact Carl Pituskin, Personnel Manager. A plumbing and heating supply manufacturer. Operating as a family-owned business for more than 50 years. Markets products throughout the United States. Corporate headquarters location.

KENTILE FLOORS INC.
58 Second Avenue
Brooklyn NY 11215
718/768-9500
Contact Tom Deasy, Payroll Manager. Manufactures a wide range of flooring products, including vinyl and products made from other materials. The company maintains three production plants and a nationwide sales force. Develops, manufactures and markets to the wholesale trade a variety of resilient floorings, adhesives, and related materials (for commercial and residential use). Corporate headquarters location. Operations at this facility include: manufacturing; research/development; administration; and sales. Common positions include: Accountant; Blue-Collar Worker Supervisor; Buyer; Chemist; Commercial Artist; Computer Programmer; Customer Service Representative; Draftsperson; Electrical Engineer; Industrial Engineer; Mechanical Engineer; Operations/Production Manager; Purchasing Agent; Quality Control Supervisor; Sales Representative; Transportation & Traffic Specialist. Principal educational backgrounds sought: Accounting; Art/Design; Business Administration; Chemistry; Communications; Computer Science; Engineering; Marketing. Company benefits include: medical insurance; life insurance; disability coverage; profit sharing; employee discounts.

KERBY SAUNDERS-WORKOL INC.
37-16 23rd Street
Long Island City NY 10101
718/361-6500
Contact Personnel Office. A mechanical contracting firm, engaged in the installation of heating, ventilation, and air conditioning systems in commercial buildings. Corporate headquarters location.

LEEDALL PRODUCTS INC.
351 West 35th Street
New York NY 10001
212/563-5280
Contact Personnel Department. Produces perforating and duplicating machinery. Headquarters location.

LUCAS AEROSPACE POWER TRANSMISSION CORPORATION
211 Seward Avenue
Utica NY 13503
315/793-1200
Contact Diane Garafalo, Manager/Human Resources. Engaged in the research, engineering and manufacture of control valves, turbine fluid pumps, hydraulic pumps, flexible shafts and couplings, de-icing systems, turbine driven generators, flexural pivots and gimbal systems, ground support equipment, electromechanical components, harnesses, hydraulic motors, and valves for numerical control equipment. Operations at this facility include: manufacturing. Corporate headquarters location: Reston, VA. Parent company is Lucas Inc. Common positions include: Accountant; Chemical Engineer; Electrical Engineer; Industrial Engineer; Mechanical Engineer; Metallurgical Engineer; Systems Analyst; Sales Representative. Principal educational backgrounds sought: Computer Science; Engineering. Company benefits include: medical, dental, and life insurance; pension plan; tuition assistance; disability coverage; savings plan

METCO INC./DIVISION OF PERKIN-ELMER
1101 Prospect Avenue
P.O. Box 10006
Westbury NY 11590-0201
516/334-1300
Contact Personnel Director. Several area locations. A world leader in thermal spray technology. Company's thermal spraying process coats industrial surfaces with special materials to improve resistance to wear, heat, or corrosion. Process has many applications, ranging from aircraft and automotive engines to petroleum drilling equipment and utility boilers. A major operating subsidiary of Perkin-Elmer Corporation. Corporate headquarters location. International.

MOOG INC.
East Aurora NY 14052
Contact Jerry Irving, Employment Manager. A manufacturer of high-precision motion control components and systems for aerospace and industrial applications. Operations include: manufacturing; research/development; administration; service; sales. Corporate headquarters location. American Stock Exchange. Common positions at this facility include: Accountant; Buyer; Commercial Artist; Computer Programmer; Draftsperson; Electrical Engineer; Mechanical Engineer; Financial Analyst; Programmer; Purchasing Agent; Manufacturing Engineer; Quality Control Supervisor; Technical Writer/Editor. Principal educational background sought: Engineering. Company benefits include: medical insurance; dental insurance; pension plan; life insurance; tuition assistance; disability coverage; profit sharing; savings plan.

NEW YORK TWIST DRILL INC.
25 Howard Place
Ronkonkoma NY 11779
516/588-8800
Contact Debra Kraft, Personnel/Payroll. A manufacturer and distributor of industrial quality rotary cutting tools made of cobalt, high speed steels, and solid carbide. Firm features a significant finished goods inventory of special purpose tooling manufactured for specific applications, and then standardized to fit customers' needs in specific industries such as aircraft, automotive, machine tool builders, farm machinery, railroad, bus and truck manufacturing, electronics, screw machine products, and fastener companies. Sells through distributors and directly to the industrial consumer through a factory-trained force of sales engineers located throughout the United States. Sales agents are located worldwide. A subsidiary of the Regal-Beloit Corp., (Beloit, IL) a leading manufacturer of cutting tools & power transmissions. Common positions include: Accountant; Blue-Collar Worker Supervisor; Credit Manager; Industrial Engineer; Metallurgical Engineer; Operations/Production Manager; Personnel & Labor Relations Specialist; Quality Control Supervisor; Sales Representative. Principal educational backgrounds sought: Accounting; Business Administration; Marketing. Training programs offered. Company benefits include: medical, dental, and life insurance; pension plan; tuition assistance; disability coverage; profit sharing; savings plan; 401K. Corporate headquarters location: Beloit, IL.

Parent company: Beloit Corp. Operations at this facility include: divisional headquarters; manufacturing; research/development; service; sales. American Stock Exchange.

OTIS ELEVATOR CO.
521 Third Avenue
New York NY 10175
212/557-5700
Contact Personnel Department. Produces and distributes major line of elevators and escalators for commercial and industrial use. Headquarters location.

OZONE INDUSTRIES INC.
101-32 101st Street
Ozone Park NY 11416
718/845-5200, ext 253
Contact Personnel Department. Specializes in the design, development, and manufacture of hydraulics for the aerospace and industrial markets. Manufacturing, engineering, quality control, marketing, and administration functions are all housed at this facility. Principal products are landing gear, aircraft steering systems, and a variety of hydraulic power, control, and storage devices. A subsidiary of BBA Group, PLC. Operations at this facility include: manufacturing. Common positions include: Accountant; Buyer; Draftsperson; Industrial Engineer; Mechanical Engineer; Metallurgical Engineer; Department Manager; Operations/Production Manager; Marketing Specialist; Personnel & Labor Relations Specialist; Programmer; Quality Control Supervisor; Sales Representative; Systems Analyst; Production Planner. Principal educational backgrounds sought: Business Administration; Engineering; Finance; Marketing. Company benefits include: medical insurance; dental insurance; pension plan; life insurance; disability coverage; savings plan.

PRECISION VALVE CORPORATION
700 Nepperhan Avenue
Yonkers NY 10701
914/969-6500
Contact Tom Harrington, Personnel/Industrial Relations Manager. Manufactures aerosol valves for a wide variety of consumer products OEM's. Corporate headquarters location.

SKAN-A-MATIC CORPORATION
4914 W. Genessee Street
Camillus NY 13031
315/488-5737
Contact Bob Harroum, Personnel Administrator. Manufactures, markets, and services a wide range of fiber-optic scanners, photoelectric sensors, and related products. Operations at this facility include: manufacturing; research/development; administration; sales. Corporate headquarters location: Boca Raton, FL. Common positions include: Administrator; Advertising Worker; Buyer; Draftsperson; Electrical Engineer; Mechanical Engineer; Operations/Production Manager; Purchasing Agent; Quality Control Supervisor. Principal educational backgrounds sought: Engineering. Company benefits include: medical insurance; pension plan; life insurance; tuition assistance; disability coverage.

SLANT/FIN CORPORATION
100 Forest Drive at East Hills
Greenvale NY 11548
516/484-2600
Contact Personnel Director. Company and its subsidiaries are engaged in the manufacture and sale of heating and cooling equipment in both domestic and foreign markets. Corporate headquarters location.

STAR EXPANSION COMPANY
Pleasant Hill Road
Mountainville NY 10953
914/534-3665

Contact Mr. D. Bruce Kerr, Personnel Manager. Manufactures a wide range of fasteners. Common positions include: Accountant; Administrator; Blue-Collar Worker Supervisor; Buyer; Computer Programmer; Credit Manager; Customer Service Representative; Draftsperson; Electrical Engineer; Industrial Engineer; Mechanical Engineer; Metallurgical Engineer; Financial Analyst; Industrial Manager; Department Manager; General Manager; Operations/Production Manager; Personnel & Labor Relations Specialist; Purchasing Agent; Quality Control Supervisor; Sales Representative; Systems Analyst. Principal educational backgrounds sought: Accounting; Business Administration; Chemistry; Computer Science; Economics; Engineering; Finance; Liberal Arts; Marketing; Mathematics; Physics. Training programs offered. Company benefits include: medical and life insurance; tuition assistance; disability coverage; savings plan. Corporate headquarters location. Operations at this facility include: regional headquarters; manufacturing; research/development; administration; service; sales.

TECHNICON INSTRUMENTS CORPORATION
511 Benedict Avenue
Tarrytown NY 10591
914/631-8000
Contact Donna Fitzgerald, Manager of Personnel Services. Several area locations. A world leader in the field of automated analytical instrumentation. Major divisions include research and development, marketing, manufacturing, and finance. Clients include hospital laboratories, clinics, research institutions, physicians' laboratories, and universities. Common positions include: Accountant; Attorney; Biochemist; Blue-Collar Worker Supervisor; Buyer; Chemist; Computer Programmer; Draftsperson; Biomedical Engineer; Chemical Engineer; Electrical Engineer; Industrial Engineer; Mechanical Engineer; Financial Analyst; Industrial Designer; Marketing Specialist; Programmer; Purchasing Agent; Quality Control Supervisor; Statistician; Systems Analyst; Technical Writer/Editor. Principal educational backgrounds sought: Accounting; Chemistry; Engineering; Finance; Marketing. Company benefits include: medical, dental and life insurance; retirement plan; tuition assistance; disability coverage; savings plan; employee discounts; spending accounts.

TELEDYNE HYDRA-POWER
10-12 Pine Court
New Rochelle NY 10801
914/632-2200
Contact Personnel Director. Designs, develops, and manufactures hydraulic and pneumatic components for aircraft, helicopters, ground-support equipment, and industrial use. Also provides products for subsea petroleum exploration and production, and power generating steam and gas turbines. Parent company is a high-technology, multi-product corporation consisting of 130 individual companies employing 50,000 people nationwide. Nationally, company operates in five industrial areas: Aviation and Electronics; Machines and Metals; Engines, Energy, and Power; Commercial and Consumer; and Insurance and Finance. Corporate headquarters location: Los Angeles, CA. New York Stock Exchange.

TESSA TUCK, INC.
1 LeFevre Lane
New Rochelle NY 10801
914/235-1000
Contact Raymond L. Maseman, VP, Human Resources Director. Three area locations, including Middletown, NY. Engaged in the production and sale of an extensive line of masking, cellophane, electrical, cloth, and other pressure-sensitive tape products for business, industrial, and household use. Other facilities located in Carbondale, IL (industrial and retail tapes); and Los Angeles, CA (industrial and retail tapes). Two facilities in England. Corporate headquarters location. Common postions include: Accountant; Buyer; Chemist; Claim Representative; Computer Programmer; Credit Manager; Chemical Engineer; Industrial Engineer; Mechanical Engineer; Financial Analyst; Department Manager; Personnel & Labor Relations Specialist; Public Relations Worker; Sales Representative. Principal educational backgrounds sought: Accounting; Business Administration; Chemistry; Engineering; Finance; Marketing. Company benefits include: medical and life insurance; disability coverage. Corporate headquarters location. Operations at this facility include: regional headquarters.

TRAULSEN & COMPANY INC.
114-02 15th Avenue
College Point NY 11356
718/463-9000
Contact Cookie McLeod, Personnel Office. Manufactures an extensive line of commercial refrigerators and freezers. Corporate headquarters location.

WEKSLER INSTRUMENTS CORPORATION
80 Mill Road, Box 808
Freeport NY 11520
516/623-0100
Contact Grace Tozzi, Office Manager. Manufactures and distributes precision instruments for indicating and recording temperature, pressure, and humidity. Common positions include: Blue-Collar Worker Supervisor; Buyer; Draftsperson; Mechanical Engineer; Sales Representative. Company benefits include: medical and life insurance; profit sharing. Corporate headquarters location. Operations at this facility include: regional headquarters; divisional headquarters; manufacturing; research/development; administration; service; sales.

Connecticut

AMPHENOL/HAMDEN
720 Sherman Avenue
Hamden CT 06514
203/281-3200
Contact Personnel Director. An area producer of flat ribbon cable. Parent company, Allied Signal Corporation, serves a broad spectrum of industries through its more than 40 strategic businesses, which are grouped into five sectors: Aerospace; Automotive; Chemical; Industrial and Technology; and Oil and Gas. Allied Signal is one of the nation's largest industrial organizations, and has 115,000 employees in over 30 countries. Corporate headquarters location: Morristown, NJ.

ASEA BROWN BOVARI, INC.
900 Long Ridge Road
P.O. Box 9308
Stamford CT 06904
203/329-8771
Contact Personnel. Supplier of industrial equipment and services for the basic industries such as electric power generation, oil and gas exploration and production and chemical refinement processing. Employs 35,500.

CROMPTON & KNOWLES CORPORATION
1 Station Place, Metrocenter
Stamford CT 06902
203/353-5400
Contact Esther Mattson, Personnel Director. A major manufacturer of specialty chemicals, plastics, and related products. Corporate headquarters location.

DORR-OLIVER INC.
612 Wheeler's Farm Road
Milford CT 06460
203/876-5400
Contact Employment Manager. Manufacturer of heavy process equipment for handling liquid, solid and fluid bed technology; machinery for CPI and environmental industries, minerals and food processing. Corporate headquarters location. New York Stock Exchange. International.

**DRESSER INDUSTRIES/
INSTRUMENT DIVISION**
250 East Main Street
Stratford CT 06497
203/378-8281
Contact Personnel Department. Supplies pressure and temperature instruments and controls to a variety of customers. Parent company, Dresser Industries, Inc., is one of the world's leading suppliers of technology, products and services to worldwide energy, natural resource and industrial markets; operations include petroleum, energy processing and conversion, mining and construction, and general industry. The company markets its products and services in more than 100 countries.

GENERAL SIGNAL CORPORATION
Box 10010
Stamford CT 06904
203/357-8800
Contact Mrs. Eileen Joyce, Manager of Personnel. A worldwide leader in the fields of instrumentation and control for a broad range of industrial markets. Operates in four industry groups: Energy Control products for the electric utilities, electrical construction, process, semiconductor, and telecommunications industries; Fluid Process Control products for the chemical, petrochemical, petroleum, food and beverage, primary and fabricated metals, pulp and paper, and other process industries, agriculture, construction, and industrial and municipal water and wastewater processing industries; Transportation Control products, including products for mainline railroads and rail mass transit systems, civil and defense air traffic control and navigation, shipboard communications systems and propulsion controls to the marine industry, and products for the heavy-duty mobile construction, mining, materials-handling, agricultural, and auto and truck markets; and Consumer Products, a major producer of electric appliances, and electric motors for portable appliances, power tool, automotive, pump, and garden equipment markets. Area subsidiaries include: Bishop Electric (Cedar Grove, NJ); Edwards (Farmington, CT); Warren/Dielectric (Livingston, NJ); Axel Electronics (Jamaica, NY); Cardion Electronics (Woodbury, NY); and Regina (Rahway, NJ). Manufacturing facilities are located throughout the United States, Canada, and Mexico. Corporate headquarters location. New York Stock Exchange.

GERBER SCIENTIFIC
83 Gerber Road West
South Windsor CT 06074
203/644-1551
Contact Anthony Pagliuco, Personnel Manager. A company engaged in the manufacture of high tech drafting equipment such as photo plotters.

THE NASH ENGINEERING COMPANY
P.O. Box 5130
310 Wilson Avenue
South Norwalk CT 06856-5130
203/852-3900
Contact Tom Kelly, Employment Manager. Manufactures, distributes, and services compressed air and vacuum systems for industrial use. Corporate headquarters location. International. Operations include: manufacturing; research/development; administration; service; sales. Common positions include: Accountant; Administrator; Blue-Collar Worker Supervisor; Buyer; Computer Programmer; Credit Manager; Customer Service Representative; Draftsperson; Chemical Engineer; Industrial Engineer; Mechanical Engineer: Petroleum Engineer; Programmer Analyst-HP3000. Personnel & Labor Relations Specialist; Programmer; Systems Analyst. Principal educational backgrounds sought: Accounting; Computer Science; Engineering; Finance. Company benefits include: medical insurance; dental insurance; pension plan; life insurance; tuition assistance; disability coverage.

NEW HERMES INC.
28 Cross Street
Norwalk CT 06851
Contact Director of Human Resources. Produces computerized and mechanical machinery for engraving, marking and profiling; and plastics and adhesives used in signs, displays, and manufacturing. Corporate headquarters location. Operations at this facility include: manufacturing; research/development; administration; service; sales. Common positions include: Accountant; Administrator; Blue-Collar Worker Supervisor; Buyer; Credit Manager; Customer Service Representative; Electrical Engineer; Financial Analyst; Branch Manager; Department Manager; General Manager; Management Trainee; Operations/Production Manager; Marketing Specialist; Personnel & Labor Relations Specialist; Quality Control Supervisor; Sales Representative; Systems Analyst; Transportation & Traffic Specialist. Principal educational backgrounds sought: Accounting; Business Administration; Computer Science; Economics; Engineering; Finance; Liberal Arts. Company benefits include: medical insurance; dental insurance; pension plan; life insurance; tuition assistance; disability coverage; profit sharing; savings plan.

OLIN CORPORATION
120 Long Ridge Road
Stamford CT 06904-1355
203/356-2315
Contact Deloris Ennico, Manager of College Relations. A Fortune 200 Company, Olin produces primarily in the areas of Chemicals, Metals and Ammunitions, with expanding interests in Electronic Materials, Defense/Aerospace and Water Management. International operations include plants and offices in 20 countries, with customers in approximately 120 countries. Operations include: regional and divisional headquarters; manufacturing; research/development; administration; service; sales. Corporate headquarters location. Common positions include: Accountant; Biochemist; Biologist; Chemist; Computer Programmer; Customer Service Representative; Chemical Engineer; Electrical Engineer; Industrial Engineer; Mechanical Engineer; Metallurgical Engineer; Financial Analyst; Marketing Specialist; Personnel & Labor Relations Specialist; Programmer; Sales Representative; Researcher; Systems Analyst; Transportation & Traffic Specialist. Prinicipal educational backgrounds sought: Accounting; Business Administration; Chemistry; Computer Science; Engineering; Finance; Marketing; Mathematics; Molecular Biology; Biochemistry; Synthetic Polymers Chemistry; Material Polymer Science. Company benefits include: medical, dental, and life insurance; pension plan; tuition assistance; disability coverage; employee discounts; savings plan. New York Stock Exchange.

OMEGA ENGINEERING, INC.:
OMEGA GROUP/OMEGA PROCESS CONTROL
One Omega Drive
P.O. Box 4047
Stamford CT 06907-0047
203/359-1660
Contact Employment Department. Additional manufacturing facility: Pureland Industrial Complex, Bridgeport, NJ. A leading manufacturer and worldwide distributor of process measurement and control instrumentation. Products include an extensive selection of temperature, pressure, strain and flow devices (everything from connectors to computer interface equipment), pH equipment, as well as a large selection of instrument and control tools. Also provides related consulting and manufacturing engineering services. Corporate headquarters location. Operations include: manufacturing; research/development; sales. Common positions include: Accountant; Advertising Worker; Blue-Collar Worker Supervisor; Buyer; Computer Programmer; Credit Manager; Customer Service Representative; Draftsperson; Engineer; Electrical Engineer; Mechanical Engineer; Operations/Production Manager; Marketing Specialist; Personnel & Labor Relations Specialist; Purchasing Agent; Sales Representative; Technical Writer/Editor; Transportation & Traffic Specialist. Principal educational backgrounds sought: Accounting; Business Administration; Engineering; Marketing; Physics. Company benefits include: medical and dental insurance; tuition assistance.

OTIS ELEVATOR COMPANY
10 Farm Springs
Farmington CT 06032
203/678-2000
Contact Manager/Professional Recruitment. Operates several area facilities, including New York, NY; Montvale, NJ. The world's largest producer of elevators and escalators. The company is engaged in the manufacture, installation, and servicing of elevators and escalators. A subsidiary of United Technologies Corporation (Hartford, CT). Common positions include: Computer Programmer; Customer Service Representative; Electrical Engineer; Mechanical Engineer; Financial Analyst; Personnel & Labor Relations Specialist; Software Engineer. Principal educational backgrounds sought: Accounting; Business Administration; Computer Science; Engineering; Finance. Company benefits include: medical, dental, and life insurance; pension plan; tuition assistance; disability coverage; employee discounts; savings plan. Corporate headquarters location: Farmington, CT. Parent company: United Technologies Corp. New York Stock Exchange.

UNITED TECHNOLOGIES CORPORATION/
INTERNATIONAL FUEL CELLS
195 Governors Highway
South Windsor CT 06074
203/727-2203
Contact James J. Zapatka, Supervisor of Professional Employment. Engaged in the research, design, marketing, and manufacturing of energy conversion systems. Corporate headquarters location.

New Jersey

ADAMAS CARBIDE CORPORATION
141 Market Street
Kenilworth NJ 07033
201/241-1000
Contact Julie Vasile, Personnel Manager. Manufactures carbide inserts, blanks, tools, holders, and related products, distributed both nationally and internationally. Primary market is the metal-cutting industry. A wholly-owned subsidiary of BTR Inc., a multinational worldwide supplier of industrial products. Corporate headquarters location. International.

AIRCO GASES
575 Mountain Avenue
Murray Hill NJ 07974
201/464-8100
Contact Director of Recruiting. Manufactures and markets industrial gases and related equipment, and provides full engineering and technical service capabilities. Manufacturing and sales locations nationwide.

AIRTRON
200 East Hanover Avenue
Morris Plains NJ 07950
201/539-5500
Contact Bob Chapman, Personnel Director. Operates the largest crystal growing facility of its kind in the world, producting single crystal rods for solid state lasers. Principal uses include target designators and rangefinders for military applications; welding, cutting, drilling, and scribing in commercial markets; and precision optics and dielectric coatings used in laser systems. Company is also one of the nation's leading suppliers of microwave waveguide transmission lines and components, used primarily as weather radar for commercial airlines. Other uses include counter-measure systems for the military, and relay towers and satellite ground systems for the military and for communications. Company also manufactures and distributes simulated diamonds through its DIAMONAIR subdivision. Parent company, Litton Industries, is a major electronics company serving worldwide markets with high-technology products and services designed

for commercial, industrial, and defense-related applications. More than 14,000 Litton scientists, engineers, and technicians are working to enhance the company's advanced electronics leadership capability for defense markets, for sophisticated industrial automation systems, and for seismic exploration services and products.

ALLIED SIGNAL, INC.
101 Columbia Road
Morristown NJ 07962
201/455-2000
Contact Employee Relations. A diversified manufacturer of products used by other manufacturers in the production or processing of industrial and consumer items. The corporation's businesses are manged by subsidiaries: Allied Chemical Company; Allied Fibers & Plastics Company; Union Texas Petroleum Corporation; Eltra Corporation; Allied Health & Scientific Products Company, and Bendix Corporation. Operates in six business segments: Chemicals; Fibers and Plastics; Oil and Gas; Electric and Electronic; Health & Scientific Products; and Other Operations. Chemical Division produces soda ash, industrial acids; chrome, electronic water treatment, and fine chemicals; specialty oximes, tar products, fluorocarbons, uranium hexafluoride, and nitrogen and phosphate fertilizers. Primary markets are the glass, aluminum, refrigeration, metal finishing, semiconductor, chemical, nuclear, water treatment, wood treatment, pulp and paper, and agricultural industries. Fibers and Plastics Division produces nylon filament and staple fibers, polyester industrial fiber, nylon and fluoropolymer engineered plastics, high-density polyethylene, low molecular weight polyethylenes, phenol, ammonium, sulfate, and acetone. Principal markets are the floor-covering, apparel, automotive cordage packaging, electrical, and container industries. Oil and Gas Division produces a crude oil and condensate, natural gas, liquified natural gas, liquified petroleum gases, antrual gasoline, residue gas, and ethylene. Markets are the oil-refining, gas pipelines, chemical feedstocks, and home, farm, utility and industrial fuels industries. Electrical and Electronic Division produces batteries, motors, ignition systems, alternators, wire and cable, chargers, telephone cable, electrical and electronic connectors components, phototypesetting equipment, and electronic informations systems. Marekts include transportation, communications, publishing, electronics, electric utility, computer aerospace, military, and materials handling industries. Health and Scientific Products Division produces analytical and measuring instruments and apparatus, glassware, reagent chemicals, diagnostic reagents, and laboratory furniture. Markets include industrial, hospital, and medical laboratories, educational institutions, and government agencies. Other Operations Division produces refractory brick, zinc, and aluminum die castings and fittings, automotive safety restraints, and athletic footwear. Other subsidiaries include: Bedix Corporation (Southfield, MI), which is engaged in the automotive, aerospace-electronics, and industrial energy businesses in the United States and abroad; Bunker Ramo Corporation; Prestolite Battery Corporation; Mergenthaler Group; Fisher Scientific Company; North American Refractories Company; and Converse Rubber Company. Corporate headquarters location.

ALLIED-SIGNAL AEROSPACE COMPANY/
BENDIX TEST SYSTEMS DIVISION
Route 46
Teterboro NJ 07608
201/288-2000
Contact Human Resources Department. A major manufacturer of automatic test equipment, primarily for the aerospace industry. Divisional headquarters location. Common positions include: Accountant; Administrator; Buyer; Computer Programmer; Draftsperson; Electrical Engineer; Quality Control Supervisor. Principal educational backgrounds sought: Accounting; Computer Science; Engineering; Mathematics; Physics. Company benefits include: medical, dental, and life insurance; pension plan; tuition assistance; disability coverage; savings plan; vision; hearing. Corporate headquarters location: Morristown, NJ. Operations at this facility include: manufacturing; research/development; administration. New York Stock Exchange.

AMERICAN CYANAMID COMPANY
One Cyanamid Plaza
Wayne NJ 07470
201/831-2000
Contact Robert Koegel, Director, Personnel Resources. A diversified multinational organization, engaged in the research, development, manufacture, and marketing of agricultural, chemical, and medical products. Operates 17 research laboratories and nearly 100 plants nationwide; offers 2,500 products in more than 135 countries. Medical business consists of both prescription and nonprescription pharmaceutical products and hospital products, made and marketed by Lederle Laboratories Division (in U.S.). Agricultural business consists of animal feed and health products; insecticides, fungicides, herbicides, and plant regulators. Chemical business consists of more than 5,000 organic and inorganic chemicals and related products in two operating divisions: Chemical Products and Industrial and Performance Products. Common positions include: Biochemist; Chemist; Engineer; Engineer; Agricultural Engineer; Chemical Engineer; Industrial Engineer; Mechanical Engineer; Metallurgical Engineer; Mining Engineer; Petroleum Engineer; Marketing Specialist; Statistician; Systems Analyst. Principal educational backgrounds sought: Business Administration; Chemistry; Computer Science; Engineering; Marketing. Corporate headquarters location. International. New York Stock Exchange. Company benefits include: medical insurance; dental insurance; pension plan; life insurance; tuition assistance; disability coverage; savings plan. Corporate headquarters location. Operations at this facility include: divisional headquarters; administration.

AMERICAN DISTRICT TELEGRAPH (ADT)
290 Veterans Boulevard
Rutherford NJ 07070
201/804-8600
Contact Gerry Prudden, General Manager. Services more than 15,000 burglar, fire, and other alarm systems in several area locations, including Newark, Parsippany, and Trenton, NJ; other offices located in Tampa, Orlando, and St. Petersburg, FL; Baltimore and Rockville, MD; and Atlanta, GA. A variety of alarms and monitoring equipment is manufactured both for use in alarm service operations and for sale to commercial and industrial users. Corporate headquarters location: Parsippany, NJ.

AUTOMATIC SWITCH COMPANY/
A SUBSIDIARY OF EMERSON
50 Hanover Road
Florham Park NJ 07932
201/966-2595
Contact John Casciano, Manager of Personnel. A major international manufacturer of an extensive line of control equipment used for the automation of machinery, equipment, and industrial processes and the control of electric power. Operates manufacturing facilities at this location, in Elk Grove, IL; Aiken, SC; and Stockton, CA (Delta Controls); with warehousing facilities in Elk Grove and Los Angeles. Operates three wholly-owned United States manufacturing subsidiaries in the area: A& M Ludwig Corporation (Parsippany, NJ), which manufactures screw machine parts; ASCO Electrical Products Company (second location in Parsippany, NJ, which makes metal enclosures and electrical distribution equipment; and Auger Scientific (Cedar Knolls, NJ), which makes miniature and microminiature solenoid valves and controls for medical, analytical, and pharmaceutical uses. Company has manufacturing and marketing subsidiaries throughout the world. Other domestic subsidiaries include ADCO Sisc INC. (Dover, DE); ASCO Investment Corporation; and ASCO Services INC. (this facility). Common positions include: Accountant; Electrical Engineer; Industrial Engineer; Mechanical Engineer; Management Trainee; Operations/Production Manager. Principal educational backgrounds sought: Accounting; Engineering; Finance; Liberal Arts; Marketing. Company benefits include: medical, dental, and life insurance; pension plan; tuition assistance; disability coverage; profit sharing; employee discounts; savings plan.

BELCO TECHNOLOGIES, INC.
7 Entin Road
Parsippany NJ 07054
201/884-4700
Contact Personnel. A worldwide manufacturer of processes and equipment for the removal of air and water pollutants. Pollution control equipment includes electrostatic precipitators, baghouses, and related components, used in pollution control and manufacture of pollution control equipment. Common positions include: Accountant; Administrator; Blue-Collar Worker Supervisor; Draftsperson; Engineer; Chemical Engineer; Electrical Engineer; Mechanical Engineer; Department Manager; General Manager; Operations/Production Manager; Personnel & Labor Relations Specialist; Purchasing Agent; Quality Control Supervisor; Sales Representative. Principal educational backgrounds sought: Accounting; Engineering. Company benefits include: medical and life insurance; tuition assistance; disability coverage; credit union. Corporate headquarters location.

BOBST GROUP, INC.
146 Harrison Avenue
Roseland NJ 07068
201/226-8000
Contact Personnel Manager. Produces a line of equipment for the converting, printing, and publishing industries. Operates in the United States through three groups: Bobst, Bobst Champlain, and Bobst Registron. Products include diecutter/creasers, folder/gluers, flexo and gravure presses, electronic controls, and other sheet and seb-fed equipment for the paper and paper-converting and printing industries. A subsidiary of Bobst SA (Launsanne, Swizerland), the world's leading manufacturer of converting equipment for the folding carton corrugated industries. Common positions include: Accountant; Administrator; Advertising Worker; Buyer; Credit Manager; Customer Service Representative; Draftsperson; Engineer; Electrical Engineer; Mechanical Engineer; Manager; Department Manager; Operations/Production Manager; Marketing Specialist; Personnel & Labor Relations Specialist; Programmer; Purchasing Agent; Quality Control Supervisor; Sales Representative; Systems Analyst; Transportation & Traffic Specialist. Principal educational backgrounds sought: Accounting; Business Administration; Computer Science; Engineering; Finance; Marketing. Company benefits include: medical, dental, and life insurance; tuition assistance; disability coverage; savings plan. Corporate headquarters location. Operations at this facility include: manufacturing; administration; sales.

BREEZE-EASTERN/
DIVISION OF TRANSTECHNOLOGY GROUP
700 Liberty Avenue
Union NJ 07083
908/686-4000
Contact Human Resources Director. Manufactures helicopter rescue hoists, winches, electro-mechanical and hydromechanical components and systems. Common positions include: Accountant; Mechnical Worker; Assembly Worker; Electrical Worker; Supervisor; Buyer; Computer Programmer; Credit Manager; Customer Service Representative; Draftsperson; Aerospace Engineer; Electrical Engineer; Industrial Engineer; Mechanical Engineer; Operations/Production Manager; Human Resources Administrator; Programmer; Purchasing Agent; Quality Control Supervisor; Sales Representative; Systems Analyst. Principal educational backgrounds sought: Accounting; Business Administration; Computer Science; Engineering; Finance; Marketing; Physics. Company benefits include: medical, dental, and life insurance; pension plan; tuition assistance; disability coverage; savings plan.

BRIGHT STAR INDUSTRIES, INC.
9 Brighton Road
P.O. Box 1909
Clifton NJ 07015-1909
201/772-3200
Contact Alfred Catania, Personnel Manager. Send resumes to Alfred Catania at 380 Stewart Road, Wilkes-Barre, PA 18706. Manufactures and distributes industrial batteries and dry cell batteries, as well as related lighting products. A subsidiary of Kidde, Inc.

Corporate headquarters location. International. Other area locations in Passaic and Paterson.

CONSARC CORPORATION
100 Indel Avenue
Rancocas NJ 08073
609/267-8000
Contact Pat Vogel, Executive Administrator. Consarc sells, designs and manufactures industrial melting furnaces. Common positions include: Buyer; Computer Programmer; Draftsperson; Electrical Engineer; Mechanical Engineer; Operations/Production Manager. Principal educational backgrounds sought: Computer Science; Engineering. Company benefits include: medical insurance; life insurance; tuition assistance; disability coverage; profit sharing. Corporate headquarters location. Parent company: Inducto Therm Industries. Operations at this facility include: administration.

COOPER ALLOY CORPORATION
201 Sweetland Avenue
Hillside NJ 07205
201/688-4120
Contact Estelle Barone, Personnel Director. Manufactures and distributes a line of plastic pumps to OEM's. Company also operates a stainless steel foundry in Montgomery, AL. Common positions include: Accountant; Blue-Collar Worker Supervisor; Customer Service Representative; Mechanical Engineer; Metallurgical Engineer; Operations/Production Manager; Purchasing Agent. Principal educational backgrounds sought: Business Administration; Engineering. Company benefits include: medical, dental, and life insurance; 401 K. Corporate headquarters location.

CROWN CORK & SEAL COMPANY INC.
7101 Tonnelle Avenue
North Bergen NJ 07047
201/854-5800
Contact Personnel. A major worldwide manufacturer and distributor of a wide range of crowns, seals, and aluminum/steel cans including aerosol and beverage cans; as well as manufacturer of bottling equipment. Corporate headquarters location: Philadelphia, PA. New York Stock Exchange. International. Common positions include: Blue-Collar Worker Supervisor; Mechanical Engineer; Operations/Production Specialist; Mechanical Supervisors. Principal educational backgrounds sought: Engineering; Manufacturing. Operations at this facility include: manufacturing. This plant facility manufactures two piece aluminum soda cans and three piece steel coffee cans.

DURO-TEST CORPORATION
9 Law Drive
Fairfield NJ 07004
201/808-1800
Contact Shirley Benson, Employment Manager. One of the nation's largest exclusive manufacturers of light bulbs. Products include incandescent, fluorescent, xenon, mercury vapor, fluomeric, carbon filament, and neon glow lamps, primarily for industrial and commercial use. Products are marketed throughout the world. Operations at this facility include: manufacturing; research/development; administration; service. Corporate headquarters location. International. Common positions include: Accountant; Blue-Collar Worker Supervisor; Computer Programmer; Credit Manager; Customer Service Representative; Draftsperson; Chemical Engineer; Civil Engineer; Electrical Engineer; Industrial Engineer; Mechanical Engineer; Financial Analyst; Operations/Production Manager; Marketing Specialist; Personnel & Employee Benefits & Compensation Specialists; Purchasing Agent; Quality Control Supervisor; Sales Representative; Technical Writer/Editor. Principal educational backgrounds sought: Accounting; Business Administration; Computer Science; Engineering; Finance; Marketing. Company benefits include: medical insurance; pension plan; life insurance; disability coverage; employee discounts; savings plan.

JOHN DUSENBERY COMPANY INC.
220 Franklin Road
Randolph NJ 07869
201/366-7500
Contact Alfred Guber, Controller. A manufacturer of machinery for the paper, film, and foil industries. Corporate headquarters location.

EDWARDS ENGINEERING CORPORATION
101 Alexander Avenue
P.O. Box 487
Pompton Plains NJ 07444-0487
201/835-2800
Contact David Edwards, Vice President of Production Engineering. Manufactures and distributes a wide range of heating and cooling products, as well as related items, for comfort and industrial applications. Products include: air pollution control systems; hydrocarbon and solvent vapor recovery systems; solar energy components; packaged water and liquid chillers to -165; valance heating/cooling; baseboard and fin-pipe radiation; control valves; coaxial heat exchangers; centrifugal pumps; and boilers and liquid heaters. Common positions include: Programmer; Draftsperson; Systems Analyst; Chemical Engineer; Electrical Engineer; Mechanical Engineer; Marketing Specialist; Physicist; Accountant. Principal educational backgrounds sought: Chemistry; Engineering; Marketing; Physics; Accounting. Company benefits include: medical, dental, and life insurance; vision insurance; employee discounts. Corporate headquarters location. Operations at this facility include: manufacturing; research/development; administration; service; sales. International. Employs 165.

ELASTIMOLD
Route 24
Hackettstown NJ 07840
201/852-1122
Contact Kay Hedges, Personnel Manager. A leading manufacturer of products and components for industrial and consumer markets. Products are classified in the following three segments: Fluid Power and Metal Components; Electrical Components and Controls; and Consumer and Safety Products. Fluid Power and Metal Components include hose and tubing, flexible hose assemblies, metal fastener products, and high-precision metal molds; markets include automotive, industrial equipment, aerospace and plastics manufacturers. Electrical Components and Controls include a variety of molded rubber connectors and distribution systems components marketed under the Elastimold trademark. These products are used predominantly by electrical power distribution companies, primarily for the underground installation of power lines serving residential, commercial, and industrial customers. Also manufactures electromechanical and solid state time delay relays and swiches, controls, and motors; and other products including battery separators, aviation lighting transformers, splice caps, terminal blocks, electronic packaging components, crimping tools used in electronic installation, switch gear, and other industrial, electrical, and electronic equipment. Comsumer and Safety Products include molded plastic key products for typewriters and telephones, and components for the automotive, appliance, computer, business machine and hardware fields. Corporate headquarters location. New York Stock Exchange.

ENGELHARD CORPORATION
33 Wood Avenue South
Edison NJ 08818
201/632-6000
Contact Placement Office. Several area locations, including Newark, East Newark, Carteret, and Menlo Park, NJ. A diversified firm, manufacturing catalysts, paper coatings, and fillers, precious metal components and mill products, products for the electronics industry, products for dental and medical requirements, sorbents, suspension agents, lime and industrial extenders, precious metals supply/management/refining, research and developing process technology, catalyst products, and new metallurgical specialties. Company operates 25 plants and eight principal mines throughout the United States and internationally. Corporate headquarters location. New York Stock Exchange. International.

ENGINE DISTRICTS INC.
332 South 17th Street
Camden NJ 08105
609/365-8631
Contact Glen Cummins, Jr., Vice President. Distributors for industrial engines. Common positions include: Branch Manager; General Manager; Operations/Production Manager; Sales Representative.

FIFTH DIMENSION INC.
801 New York Avenue
Trenton NJ 08638
609/393-8350
Contact Elaine Caine, Secretary-Treasurer. Manufacturer of Mercury and tilt switches.

FISHER SCIENTIFIC
1 Reagent Lane
Fair Lawn NJ 07410
201/796-7100
Contact Deb Fenton, Manager of Employee Relations. Manufactures, distributes, and sells a wide range of products used in laboratories; company is a leading supplier to industrial labs and the second largest supplier to medical labs. Products include analytical and measuring instruments, apparatus, and appliances; reagent chemicals and diagnostics; glassware and plasticware; and laboratory furniture. Customers are primarily industrial laboratories, medical and hospital laboratories serving the health care industry, and educational and research laboratories. Manufacturing operations are carried out by six operating divisions in 11 United States locations. A subsidiary of Henley Group (La Jolla, CA). Operations include: manufacturing; research/development; administration. Corporate headquarters location: Pittsburgh, PA. Common positions include: Accountant; Administrator; Biochemist; Blue-Collar Worker Supervisor; Buyer; Chemist; Computer Programmer; Customer Service Representative; Draftsperson; Biomedical Engineer; Chemical Engineer; Electrical Engineer; Industrial Engineer; Mechanical Engineer; Financial Analyst; Department Manager; General Manager; Operations/Production Manager; Personnel & Labor Relations Specialist; Programmer; Purchasing Agent; Quality Control Supervisor; Systems Analyst; Materials Manager. Principal educational backgrounds sought: Accounting; Chemistry; Engineering; Finance; Liberal Arts; Marketing. Company benefits include: medical insurance; dental insurance; pension plan; life insurance; tuition assistance; disability; profit sharing; savings plan.

FLEXITALLIC GASKET COMPANY
8440 Remington Avenue
P.O. Box 286
Pennsauken NJ 08110
609/486-4400
Contact Ray Parker, Personnel. A leading Philadelphia-area manufacturer of spiral gaskets.

FOSTER WHEELER CORPORATION
Perryville Corporate Park
Clinton NJ 08809-4000.
Contact James Schesser, Personnel Manager. Engaged primarily in three business segments: process plants segment, consisting primarily of the design, engineering, and construction of process plants and fired heaters for oil refiners and chemical producers; a utility and engine segment, consisting primarily of the design and fabrication of steam generators, condensers, feedwater heaters, electrostatic precipitators, and other pollution abatement equipment; and an industrial segment that supplies pressure vessels and internals, electrical copper products, industrial insulation, welding wire, and electrodes. Locations throughout the United States and abroad. Common positions include: Accountant; Computer Programmer; Draftsperson; Chemical Engineer, Civil Engineer; Electrical Engineer; Mechanical Engineer; Financial Analyst; Industrial Designer. Principal educational backgrounds sought: Accounting; Computer Science; Engineering;

Finance. Company benefits include: medical insurance; pension plan; life insurance; tuition assistance; disability coverage; profit sharing; employee discounts. Corporate headquarters location. New York Stock Exchange.

GENERAL ENGINES COMPANY INC.
Route 130
Thorofare NJ 08086
609/845-5400
Contact Personnel Manager. Manufacturing company for trailers and asphalt rollers.

GENERAL HOSE PRODUCTS INC.
30 Sherwood Lane
Fairfield NJ 07004
201/228-0500
Contact Personnel Department. Manufactures heavy-duty hose products, used primarily by auto manufacturers in air conditioning systems, etc. Corporate headquarters location.

THE GENLYTE GROUP, INC.
100 Lighting Way
Secaucus NJ 07096-1508
201/864-3000
Contact Donna Ratliff, Director of Human Resources. A leading designer/manufacturer of broad-line of lighting fixtures and controls for commercial, industrial and residential markets. Extensive sales/distribution network. Manufacturing facilities located throughout the United States, Canada, Mexico. Genlyte companies include: Lightolier, Stonco, Crescent, KLP, Wide-Lite, Craftlite, Diamond F/Timely Sarama, and Canlyte. Corporate headquarters location. International. Common positions include: Accountant; Administrator; Blue-Collar Worker Supervisor; Computer Programmer; Credit Manager; Customer Service Representative; Electrical Engineer; Industrial Engineer; Mechanical Engineer; Industrial Designer; General Manager; Management Trainee; Operations/Production Manager; Marketing Specialist; Personnel & Labor Relations Specialist; Purchasing Agent; Quality Control Supervisor; Sales Representative; Transportation & Traffic Specialist. Principal educational backgrounds sought: Accounting; Business Administration; Computer Science; Engineering; Finance; Marketing; Design; Distribution; Materials. Company benefits include: medical and life insurance; pension plan; tuition assistance; disability coverage; savings plan; Employee discounts. Operations at this facility include: research/development; administration; service; sales. NASDAQ.

GUYON GENERAL PIPING INC.
900 Rodgers Boulevard South
Harrison NJ 07029
201/485-5600
Contact Joseph Barry, Personnel Relations. A distributor of pipes, valves, and fittings, serving both domestic and overseas customers. Corporate headquarters location.

HANOVIA LAMP, INC./
A SUBSIDIARY OF CANRAD, INC.
100 Chestnut Street
Newark NJ 07105
201/589-4300
Contact W. Nolan, Director of Human Resources. Designs, develops, manufactures, and markets a variety of products used in theatrical, restaurant, consumer, industrial, scientific, and graphic arts applications. Operates through three divisions: Hanovia (this facility), which designs, develops, produces, and markets plasma arc lamps and related equipment, including commercial and industrial ultraviolet products and accessories, and various phosphorescent pigments, compounds, and films; Strong Electric Corporation (Toledo, OH), which designs, develops, manufactures, assembles and markets high-intensity lighting equipment; and Ballatyne of Omaha (Omaha, NE), which designs, develops, manufactures, assembles, and distributes motion picture projection equipment, and a line of restaurant equipment and supplies. Common positions Electrical Engineer; Mechanical Engineer; Metallurgical Engineer. Principal educational backgrounds sought: Engineering; Physics.

Company benefits include: medical, dental, and life insurance; tuition assistance; disability coverage; savings plan. Corporate headquarters location. Operations at this facility include: manufacturing; research/development.

HOWE RICHARDSON SCALE COMPANY
435 Hamburg Turnpike
Wayne NJ 07470
201/471-3400
Contact Director of Personnel. A manufacturer and distributor of industrial weighing equipment, electronic bulk-packagers, and vehicles for specialized industrial uses. A subsidiary of GenCorp (Akron, OH), the diversified rubber and industrial products, and broadcasting organization. Corporate headquarters location. International.

IMO INDUSTRIES INC.
TURNER & COMPRESSOR DIVISION
P.O. Box 8788
Trenton NJ 08650
609/890-5324
Contact Cheryl Tattler-Peterson, Human Resources Administrator. Manufactures steam turbines, compressors, pumps, and marine gears. Divisional headquarters location. Corporate headquarters location: Lawrenceville, NJ. Operations include: manufacturing; sales. Common positions include: Accountant; Buyer; Computer Programmer; Credit Manager; Customer Service Representative; Draftsperson; Engineer; Electrical Engineer; Industrial Engineer; Mechanical Engineer; Metallurgical Engineer; Financial Analyst; General Manager; Operations/Production Supervisor; Marketing Specialist; Personnel & Labor Relations Specialist; Purchasing Agent; Quality Control Supervisor; Systems Analyst; Technical Writer; Transportation & Traffic Specialist. Principal educational backgrounds sought: Accounting; Business Administration; Computer Science; Engineering; Finance; Marketing. Company benefits include: medical insurance; dental insurance; pension plan; life insurance; tuition assistance; disability coverage; savings plan.

INGERSOLL-RAND COMPANY
200 Chestnut Ridge Road
Woodcliff Lake NJ 07675
201/573-0123
Contact Paula Prusko, Personnel Recruiter. A leading international manufacturer of industrial machinery, contruction equipment, mining machinery, pumps, bearings, door hardware and security systems. Through joint ventures, it is a leading supplier of hydrocarbon processing equipment and services. The company has three worldwide business segments: Standard Machinery; Engineered Equipment; and Bearings, Locks and Tools. The Standard Machinery Segment has three groups: Air Compressor; Construction Equipment; and Mining Machinery. The Engineered Equipment Segment has two groups: Pumps and Process Systems. The Bearings, Locks and Tools Segment has three groups: Bearings and Components; Door Hardware and Production Equipment. The company markets products under the brand name Ingersoll-Rand and also under the names Aro, Centac, ChargeAir Pro, CPM, CPM, Fafnir, Impco, Kilian, LCN, Sclage, Torrington, Von Duprin and others. Operates manufacturing plants around the world. Employs 33,700 worldwide. Corporate headquarters location. New York, Amsterdam, and London Stock Exchanges.

ITT MARLOW PUMPS
P.O. Box 200
445 Godwin Avenue
Midland Park NJ 07432
201/444-6900
Contact Personnel Manager. Produces centrifugal and self-priming pumps. A subsidiary of ITT Corp.

KESTER SOLDER
88 Ferguson Street
Newark NJ 07105
201/589-0246
Contact Walter Major, Office Manager. Manufactures a full line of solders and soldering chemicals, serving the electronic components, consumer electronics, telecommunications, business machines, automotive, and transport industries, as well as the home hobbyist. Parent company, Litton Industries, is a major electronics company serving worldwide markets with high-technology products and services designed for commercial, industrial, and defense-related applications. More than 14,000 Litton scientists, engineers, and technicians are working to enhance the company's advanced electronics leadership capability for defense markets, for sophisticated industrial automation systems, and for seismic exploration services and products.

MAGNATEK MANUFACTURING
29 East Sixth Street
Paterson NJ 07509
201/684-1400
Contact Director of Personnel. Produces fluorescent and H.I.D. lamp ballasts. Corporate headquarters location: Paramus, NJ. Operations include: manufacturing; research/development. Common positions include: Blue-Collar Worker Supervisor; Buyer; Electrical Engineer; Industrial Engineer; Metallurgical Engineer; Personnel & Labor Relations Specialist; Purchasing Agent. Principal educational backgrounds sought: Engineering. Company benefits include: medical insurance; dental insurance; pension plan; life insurance; tuition assistance; disability coverage; profit sharing; savings plan.

MAROTTA SCIENTIFIC CONTROLS INC.
78 Boonton Avenue, Box 427
Montville NJ 07045
201/334-7800
Contact Robert Cooper, Personnel Manager. Manufacturer of high-pressure valves for high-pressure pneumatic and hydraulic equipment. Company is also a custom manufacturer of fluid control products. Principal clients are various industries and government agencies. Corporate headquarters location.

McMASTER-CARR SUPPLY COMPANY
P.O. Box 440
New Brunswick NJ 08903
201/329-6666
Contact Mark Samartino, Personnel Manager. A distributor of industrial products and supplies primarily through catalog sales. Products are sold worldwide. Operations include: service. Corporate headquarters location: Elmhurst, IL. Common positions include: Management Trainee. Principal educational backgrounds sought: Business Administration; Communications; Computer Science; Economics; Engineering; Finance; Liberal Arts; Marketing. Company benefits include: medical, dental, and life insurance; pension plan; tuition assistance; disability coverage; profit sharing; employee discounts.

MELNOR INDUSTRIES
One Carol Place
Moonachie NJ 07074
201/641-5000
Contact Bob Slimowicz, Personnel Manager. Manufactures a broad range of lawn sprinklers for both the consumer and professional markets. Products include both over and underground sprinklers, automatic sprinklers, sprinkler systems, specialty sprinklers, associated nozzle, valve, and connector products, sprayers, and many other related lawn and garden products. Clients include retailers and hardware stores across the country. Corporate headquarters location.

METEX CORP.
970 New Durham Road
Edison NJ 08818
201/287-0800
Contact Linda J. Morgan, Human Resources Manager. Engaged in the manufacture and sale of knitted wire mesh and products made from these materials. Company designs and manufactures knitted wire products and components through its Technical Products Division. Products are used in applications that include adverse environment protective materials used primarily as high-temperature gaskets, seals, shock and vibration isolators, noise reduction elements and shrouds; phase separation devices used as air, liquid, and solid filtering devices. Company is also an OEM for the automobile industry, supplying automobile manufacturers with exhaust seals and components for use in exhaust emission control devices. Common positions include: Accountant; Blue-Collar Worker Supervisor; Buyer; Computer Programmer; Customer Service Representative; Draftsperson; Industrial Engineer; Industrial Designer; General Manager; Operations/Production Manager; Mechanical Engineer; Personnel & Labor Relations Specialist; Purchasing Agent; Quality Control Supervisor; Sales Representative; Systems Analyst. Principal educational backgrounds sought: Accounting; Business Administration; Engineering; Finance; Marketing. Company benefits include: medical insurance; dental insurance; pension plan; life insurance; tuition assistance; profit sharing; savings plan. Corporate headquarters location: South Plainfield, NJ. Parent company: Metex Corp. Operations at this facility include: divisional headquarters; administration; service; sales. American Stock Exchange.

MICRON POWDER SYSTEMS
10 Chatham Road
Summit NJ 07901
201/273-6360
Contact Human Resources Administrator. A leader in the development of air pollution control and process equipment technology, offering a wide range of equipment. Products are used by the primary metals, non-metallic minerals, powder, protective coatings, paper, fertilizer, chemical, pharmaceutical, and food processing industries. Company is a division of Hosokawa Micron Ltd. Common positions include: Accountant; Administrator; Buyer; Computer Programmer; Draftsperson; Electrical Engineer; Mechanical Engineer; Department Manager; Operations/Production Manager; Personnel & Labor Relations Specialist; Purchasing Agent; Quality Control Supervisor; Sales Representative. Principal educational backgrounds sought: Accounting; Business Administration; Chemistry; Computer Science; Engineering; Finance; Marketing. Company benefits include: medical, dental and life insurance; pension plan; tuition assistance; disability coverage; employee discounts; savings plan. Corporate, regional, and divisional headquarters location: New York, NY. Parent company: Hosokawa Micron USA. Operations at this facility include: manufacturing; research/development; administration; service; sales.

NATIONAL TOOL & MANUFACTURING COMPANY
100-124 North 12th Street
Kenilworth NJ 07033
201/276-1600
Contact Personnel Department. Manufactures molding products.

OHAUS CORPORATION
29 Hanover Road
Florham Park NJ 07932
201/377-9000
Contact George Farndell, Human Resources Manager. Several area locations. One of the world's largest suppliers of precision balances and scales for use in laboratory and other medical, industrial, and consumer uses. Corporate headquarters location. International. Common positions include: Accountant; Blue-Collar Worker Supervisor; Buyer; Computer Programmer; Credit Manager; Customer Service Representative; Draftsperson; Electrical Engineer; Industrial Engineer; Mechanical Engineer; Department Manager; General Manager; Operations/Production Manager; Personnel and Labor Relations Specialist; Purchasing Agent; Quality Control Supervisor; Sales Representative; Systems Analyst; Technical Writer/Editor. Educational backgrounds sought: Accounting; Business

Administration; Computer Science; Engineering; Marketing. Internships available. Company benefits include: medical insurance; pension plan; dental insurance; life insurance; tuition assistance; disability coverage; profit sharing; savings plan. Corporate headquarters location. Operations at this facility include: manufacturing; research/development; service.

OKONITE COMPANY
P.O. Box 340
Ramsey NJ 07446
201/825-0300
Contact Kathy Cuomo, Personnel Department. Several area locations, including North Brunswick, Passaic, and Paterson. Manufactures power cable for large-scale users. Corporate headquarters location.

PANTONE
55 Knickerbocker Road
Moonachie NJ 07074
201/935-5500
Contact Patricia Cirincion, Assistant Manager of Human Resources. Produces color charts and color specification materials for use by the printing and publishing industries. Corporate headquarters location. Common positions include: Accountant; Administrator; Blue-Collar Worker Supervisor; Chemist; Credit Manager; Customer Service Representative; Operations/Production Manager; Personnel; Quality Control Supervisor; Sales Representative; Secretary/Administrative Assistant. Principal educational backgrounds sought: Accounting; Chemistry; Finance; Marketing. Training programs available. Company benefits include: medical insurance; dental insurance; pension plan; life insurance; tuition assistance; savings plan. Corporate headquarters location.

PERMACEL/
A NITTO DENKO COMPANY
U.S. Highway 1
P.O. Box 671
New Brunswick NJ 08903
201/418-2550
Contact Leigh R. Isleib, Manager of Labor Relations & Personnel. Manufacturer of pressure-sensitive tape. Common postions include: Accountant; Administrator; Blue-Collar Worker Supervisor; Chemist; Customer Service Representative; Chemical Engineer; Electrical Engineer; Industrial Engineer; Mechanical Engineer; Financial Analyst; Department Manager; General Manager; Operations/Production Manager; Marketing Specialist; Personnel & Labor Relations Specialist; Quality Control Supervisor; Sales Representative; Transportation & Traffic Specialist. Principal educational backgrounds sought: Accounting; Business Administration; Chemistry; Computer Science; Engineering Finance; Liberal Arts; Marketing. Company benefits include: medical, dental, and life insurance; pension plan; tuition assistance; disability coverage; savings plan. Operations at this facility include: divisional headquarters; manufacturing; research/development; administration; service; sales.

THE PERMUTIT COMPANY, INC.
30 Technology Drive, CN 4920
Warren NJ 07059-0920
908/668-1700
Contact Adriane Bailey Summers, Personnel Administrator. Manufactures waste and wastewater systems and equipment for suspended solids removal (filters, clarifiers, etc.) and dissolved solids removal (ion exchange, reverse osmosis, ultrafiltration). A subsidiary of Zurn Industries (Erie, PA). Corporate headquarters location. Common positions include: Chemist; Civil, Electrical, and Mechanical Engineers. Educational backgrounds sought: Chemistry; Engineering. Principal educational backgrounds sought include: medical insurance; dental insurance; pension plan; life insurance; tuition assistance; disability coverage; savings plan. Operations at their facilities include: divisional headquarters; research/development; administration; service; sales. New York Stock Exchange.

PIRELLI CABLE CORPORATION
325 Columbia Turnpike
Florham Park NJ 07932
201/377-7004
Contact John Pruitz, Manager, Human Resources. Manufacturer of wire, cable, and optical cable. Also installs cable systems. Operations include: research/development, administration; sales. Common positions include: Accountant; Advertising Worker; Buyer; Claim Representative; Computer Programmer; Customer Service Representative; Draftsperson; Chemical Engineer; Electrical Engineer; Industrial Engineer; Mechancial Engineer; General Manager; Marketing Specialist; Personnel & Labor Relations Specialist; Purchasing Agent; Sales Representative; Systems Analyst; Programmer. Principal educational backgrounds sought: Accounting; Business Administration; Computer Science; Engineering; Finance; Marketing; Mathematics; Physics. Company benefits include: medical, dental, and life insurance; pension plan; tuition assistance; disability coverage.

RED DEVIL, INC.
2400 Vauxhall Road
Union NJ 07083
201/688-6900
Contact Fran Hondo, Administrator of Employment. Manufactures and distributes paint sundries, hand tools, paint conditioners, and masonry and glazier tools. Corporate headquarters location.

ROWE INTERNATIONAL, INC.
75 Troy Hills Road
Whippany NJ 07981
201/887-0400
Contact Personnel Manager. Engaged in the manufacture and sale of coin operated vending equipment, coin operated phonographs and currency changers. The company is also a major distributor of coin-operated amusement games.

SETON COMPANY
349 Oraton Street
Newark NJ 07104
201/485-4800
Contact Personnel Manager. Company operations are conducted primarily through two business segments: Leather, whose operations include tanning, finishing and distribution of whole hide cattle hide leathers for the automotive and furniture upholstery industries, cattle hide side leathers for footwear, handbag, and other markets, and cattle hide products for collagen, rawhide pet items, and other applications; and Chemicals and Coated Products, engaged in the manufacture and distribution of epoxy and urethane chemicals, specialty leather finishes, industrial and medical tapes, foams, films, and laminates. Area production facilities are engaged in the tanning and finishing of cattle hide leathers (Seton Leather Company/Radel Leather Manufacturing Company); other manufacturing facilities in Wilmington, DE (epoxy, urethane chemicals, leather finishes); Toledo, OH (cattle hide processing); Malvern, PA (industrial coated products); and Saxton, PA (cutting of finished leathers). Corporate headquarters location. American Stock Exchange.

SIER-BATH GEAR COMPANY, INC.
9252 Kennedy Boulevard
North Bergen NJ 07047
201/854-5500
Contact Robert Williams, Personnel Officer. Produces a broad range of industrial gears and couplings. A subsidiary of Ingersoll-Rand. Corporate headquarters location.

SPRINGFIELD INSTRUMENT COMPANY
76 Passaic Street
Woodridge NJ 07075
201/777-2900

Contact Alan Liebeskind, Personnel Director. Manufactures a wide range of weather instruments, as a division of Sunbeam Corporation. Corporate headquarters location. International.

TELEDYNE FERRIS ENGINEERING
400 Commercial Avenue
Palisades Park NJ 07650
201/944-6300
Contact Personnel Director. World leader in design and manufacture of pressure relief valves. Manufacturing facilities located in U.S., Canada, Brazil, England, France, India, and Australia. Parent company, Teledyne, Inc., is a high-technology, multi-product corporation consisting of 130 individual companies employing 50,000 people nationwide. Nationally, company operates in four industrial areas: Aviation and Electronics; Machines and Metals; Engines, Energy, and Power; and Commercial and Consumer. Common positions include: Accountant; Draftsperson; Aerospace Engineer; Industrial Engineer; Mechanical Engineer; Management Trainee; Marketing Specialist; Sales Representative. Principal educational backgrounds sought: Business Administration; Engineering. Company benefits include: medical, dental, and life insurance; pension plan; tuition assistance; disability coverage employee discounts; savings plan. Corporate headquarters location: Los Angeles, CA. Operations at this facility include: manufacturing; research/development. Parent company is listed on New York Stock Exchange.

TUNGSTEN PRODUCTS CORPORATION
9 Law Drive
Fairfield NJ 07004
201/808-1800
Contact Al Anderson, Personnel Director. Manufactures and distributes fluorescent and other specialized lamps. Corporate headquarters location.

VANTON PUMP - EQUIPMENT CORP. DIVISION/
COOPER ALLOY CORP.
201 Sweatland Avenue
Hillside NJ 07205
201/688-4120
Contact Estelle S. Barone, Personnel Director. Manufactures and distributes a line of plastic pumps to OEM's. Company also operates a stainless steel foundry in Montgomery, AL. Corporate headquarters location. International. Common positions include: Accountant; Mechanical Engineer. Principal educational backgrounds sought: Accounting; Business Administration; Engineering; Marketing. Company benefits include: medical, dental, and life insurance; savings plan. Operations at this facility include: manufacturing; administration; sales.

WALLACE & TIERNAN
P.O. Box 178
Newark NJ 07101
201/759-8000, ext. 594
Contact Michael Layton, Personnel Administrator. One of the world's leading manufacturers of chlorinators for water and wastewater treatment, and a major producer of dry chemicals feeders, flow meters, metering pumps, and process control instruments for the power, food, pulp and paper, and chemical process industries. A subsidiary of Pennwalt Corporation (Philadelphia, PA), which operates in the chemical, health, and precision equipment industries. Corporate headquarters location.

WEISS-AUG COMPANY INC.
P.O. Box 520
3 Merry Lane
East Hanover NJ 07936
201/887-7600
Contact Dianne Johnson, Personnel Administrator. Engaged in the manufacture of stampings, assemblies, and moldings. Produces a wide variety of parts, from simple stamping to the most complex connectors, terminals, springs, semiconductor leadframes,

heat sinks, and transistor clips used by the electronic/electrical connector and semi-conductor industry. Services include design, tooling, production, and quality control. Corporate headquarters location. Common positions include: Accountant; Blue-Collar Worker Supervisor; Computer Programmer; Customer Service Representative; Draftsperson; Industrial Engineer; Mechanical Engineer; Department Manager; Operations/Production Manager; Purchasing Agent; Quality Control Supervisor; Sales Representative. Principal educational background sought: Accounting; Computer Science; Engineering; Finance; Liberal Arts. Company benefits include: medical, dental, and life insurance; tuition assistance; disability coverage; profit sharing; savings plan; 401 K. Corporate headquarters location. Operations at this facility include: regional headquarters; divisional headquarters; administration; service; sales.

WILD LEITZ USA INC.
24 Link Drive
Rockleigh NJ 07647
201/767-1100
Contact Paul H. Brown Jr., Personnel Manager. Engaged in United States distribution operations for the 'E. Leitz' and 'Wild Heerbrugg' lines of optical, high-precision mechanical and opto-electronic instruments. Products include: microscopes, microtomes, macroscopes, stereo microscopes, devices for photomicrography and photomacrography, microscope photometers, instruments for electronic image analysis, scanning electron microscopes, metrology instruments, 35-mm. rangefinder and SLR cameras, repro devices, and instruments for surveying and photogrammetry. This facility serves as the company's United States headquarters location. International. Common positions include: Accountant; Administrator; Blue-Collar Worker Supervisor; Buyer; Computer Programmer; Credit Manager; Customer Service Representative; Electrical Engineer; Mechanical Engineer; Department Manager; General Manager; Management Trainee; Personnel & Labor Relations Specialist; Purchasing Agent; Quality Control Supervisor; Sales Representative. Principal educational backgrounds sought: Accounting; Business Administration; Computer Science; Engineering; Liberal Arts; Marketing. Company benefits include: medical insurance; dental insurance; pension plan; life insurance; tuition assistance; disability coverage; employee discounts; savings plan. Corporate headquarters location. Operations at this facility include: administration; service; sales.

MISCELLANEOUS SERVICES

New York

AFS INTERCULTURAL PROGRAMS, INC.
313 East 43rd Street
New York NY 10017
Contact Recruiting Specialist. An international exchange organization which provides intercultural learning experiences to high school students, families, and teachers. AFS operates its programs in approximately 55 countries via an international network of volunteers. Common positions include: Marketing Worker; Recruiter; Communications Worker; Public Relations Worker; Accountant; Fundraiser; Computer Programmer; Admissions Worker; Program Services Worker. Educational backgrounds sought include: Liberal Arts; International Relations; Communications. Company benefits include: health, dental, and life insurance; disability coverage; pension plan; employee assistance program.

**AMERICAN SOCIETY OF COMPOSERS,
AUTHORS & PUBLISHERS (ASCAP)**
1 Lincoln Plaza
New York NY 10023
212/595-3050
Contact Debra Hawkes, Personnel Director. An international service organization serving the music, publishing, and other creative industries. Provides a wide range of services to members, including supervision and enforcement of copyrights. Corporate headquarters location.

AMERICAN STANDARDS TESTING BUREAU INC.
40 Water Street
New York NY 10004
212/943-3156
Contact John Zimmerman, Professional Staffing Director. Offers comprehensive technical and management consulting services, including R&D for government and industry, regulatory compliance studies, lab/field testing for industry and forensic services to the legal and insurance professions through expert teams of senior-level scientists and engineers (over 75% with doctoral degrees). Corporate headquarters location. Operations at this facility include: research/development; administration; service; sales. Common positions include: Accountant; Administrator; Advertising Worker; Architect; Attorney; Biochemist; Biologist; Chemist; Computer Programmer; Customer Service Representative; Engineer; Aerospace Engineer; Agricultural Engineer; Biomedical Engineer; Ceramics Engineer; Chemical Engineer; Civil Engineer; Electrical Engineer; Industrial Engineer; Mechanical Engineer; Mining Engineer; Petroleum Engineer; Financial Analyst; Food Technologist; Forester; Geographer; Geologist; Geophysicist; Manager; Branch Manager; Department Manager; General Manager; Management Trainee; Operations/Production Manager; Marketing Specialist; Physicist; Public Relations Worker; Sales Representative; Statistician; Systems Analyst; Technical Writer/Editor; Transportation & Traffic Specialist. Principal educational backgrounds sought: Accounting; Biology; Business Administration; Chemistry; Communications; Computer Science; Economics; Engineering; Finance; Geology; Liberal Arts; Marketing; Mathematics; Physics. Company benefits include: medical insurance; pension plan; life insurance; tuition assistance.

ANDAL
560 Lexington Avenue
New York NY 10022
212/688-4440
Contact Personnel Department. Owns and operates approximately 175 parking services located throughout the New York metropolitan area. Corporate headquarters location. American Stock Exchange.

ARCADE CLEANING CONTRACTORS, INC
350 West 51st Street
New York NY 10019
212/246-2310
Contact Steve Guiglotto, Personnel Manager. Provides a wide range of cleaning and maintenance services for commercial customers. Maintains refrigeration and air conditioning units, boilers, and plumbing. Major clients include banks, office buildings, and others. Corporate headquarters location. Common positions include: Accountant; Administrator; Blue-Collar Worker Supervisor; Buyer; Claim Representative; Customer Service Representative; Electrical Engineer; Mechanical Engineer; Operations/Production Manager; Personnel & Labor Relations Specialist; Sales Representative. Principal educational backgrounds sought: Accounting; Business Administration; Engineering; Finance. Company benefits include: medical insurance; life insurance; disability coverage. Corporate headquarters location: New York, NY. Operations at this facility include: administration; sales.

COLIN SERVICE SYSTEMS INC.
1 Brockway Place
White Plains NY 10601
914/328-0800
Contact Personnel Department. Several area locations, including the Bronx. An area maintenance firm, specializing in commercial cleaning services. Corporate headquarters location.

EFFECTIVE SECURITY SYSTEMS INC.
1 Brockway Place
White Plains NY 10601
914/328-0700

Contact John Zannis, Personnel Manager. Several area locations, including Manhattan, and Westchester County; Fairfield, CT; and Bergen, NJ. A full-service corporate security firm. Provides contract guard services, electronic security, and investigations. Corporate headquarters location.

EMPIRE STATE MESSENGER SERVICE
216 West 22nd
New York NY 10011
212/581-5312
Contact Personnel. More than 20 locations citywide. Provides pick-up and delivery services throughout New York City. Corporate headquarters location.

KATHARINE GIBBS SCHOOLS INC.
200 Park Avenue, 3rd Floor
New York NY 10166
212/867-9300
Contact Mary Jo Greco, Director. One of the nation's foremost business instruction schools, operating seven schools in the northeast with more than 4,000 graduates annually. Gibbs Consulting Group provides office skills consultation services. A subsidiary of Macmillan Inc. (see separate listing). Corporate headquarters location.

GUARDIAN CLEANING INDUSTRIES
170 Varick Street
New York NY 10013
212/645-9500
Contact Mr. Herzfeld, President. An industrial/commercial maintenance firm, providing cleaning and exterminating services. In business for more than 75 years. Corporate headquarters location.

KINNEY SYSTEMS INC.
60 Madison Avenue
New York NY 10010
212/889-4444
Contact Personnel Director. Operates parking garages and lots throughout New York. Other operations in Massachusetts and Florida. Corporate headquarters location.

JOHN C. MANDEL SECURITY
100 Water Street
9th Floor
Brooklyn NY 11201
718/237-4000
Contact Personnel Director. More than 50 area locations, including Brooklyn, The Bronx, and Staten Island. Provides security services through armed and unarmed guards, on an around-the-clock basis. Clients range from private housing developments and projects, to a wide range of commercial and industrial customers. Corporate headquarters location.

MILLAR ELEVATOR INDUSTRIES
620 12th Avenue
New York NY 10036
212/708-1000
Contact Adrean Morales, Executive Secretary. A firm specializing in the repair, servicing, and renovation of office and apartment building elevators. Corporate headquarters location.

NASSAU LIBRARY SYSTEM
900 Jerusalem Avenue
Uniondale NY 11553
516/292-8920
Contact Paula Freund, Personnel Administrator. Operates as an association of autonomous local public libraries and a central Service Center, with 54 libraries in the system. System office supports local library service through a wide range of supplementary

and complementary services, collections, specialized staff and professional programming; provides more effective and economical centralized services; initiates legislation beneficial to library service; and develops, promotes, and maintains standards of library service within the county. Also provides extensive technical services to member libraries. Corporate headquarters location. Common positions include: Purchasing Agent; Librarian; Clerk; Data Entry Clerk. Principal educational backgrounds sought: Computer Science; Liberal Arts. Company benefits include: medical, dental and life insurance; pension plan; disability coverage; savings plan. Operations at this facility include: administration; service.

NATIONAL COUNCIL OF THE CHURCES OF CHRIST
475 Riverside Drive
New York NY 10115
212/870-2088
Contact Mr. Emilio F. Carillo, Jr., Associate General Secretary of Personnel. One of the largest ecumenical organizations in the United States, composed of 31 Protestant and Orthodox member communions. The program units include three divisions (Overseas Ministries; Education and Ministry; Church and Society); five commissions (Communications; Stewardship; Faith and Order; Local and Regional Ecumenism; and Justice and Liberation); four functional offices (Research, Evaluation and Planning; Information; Finance and Services; and Personnel); and the Office of the General Secretary including the Washington Office.

ROYAL PRUDENTIAL INDUSTRIES INC.
111 Eighth Avenue
New York NY 10011
212/255-4000
Contact Michael T. Powers, Administrator of Human Resources. Multiple area locations. Operates a maintenance and cleaning services firm, primarily serving commercial and office buildings. Common positions include: Accountant; Claim Representative; Computer Programmer; Customer Service Representative; Personnel & Labor Relations Specialist; Sales Representative. Principal educational backgrounds sought: Accounting; Business Administration; Computer Science; Finance. Company benefits include: medical and life insurance; disability coverage; paid vacations and sick days. Corporate headquarters location. Operations at this facility include: administration; service; sales.

SUFFOLK COOPERATIVE LIBRARY SYSTEM
627 North Sunrise Service Road
Bellport NY 11713
516/286-1600
Contact Annette Hauser, Personnel Officer. A county-chartered library association which provides a variety of support services to the 52 libraries comprising the county library system. Corporate headquarters location.

TEMCO SERVICE INDUSTRIES INC.
One Park Avenue
New York NY 10016
212/889-6353
Contact Karen Wagner, Manager, Human Resources. Offers a wide variety of maintenance, security, and related services through a work force directed by a network of experienced managers. Operates in the following areas: Building Maintenance Services; Engineering Maintenance Services; Extermination and Security Services; and Incineration and Heat Recovery Systems. International operations in Belgium. Common positions include: Accountant; Blue-Collar Worker Supervisor; Computer Programmer; Mechanical Engineer; Financial Analyst; Branch Manager; General Manager; Operations Manager; Sales Representative. Principal educational backgrounds sought: Accounting; Business Administration; Computer Science; Engineering; Finance; Marketing. Company benefits include: medical and life insurance; tuition assistance; disability coverage; savings plan. Corporate headquarters location. Operations at this facility include: administration; service; sales. American Stock Exchange.

WEIGHT WATCHERS INTERNATIONAL INC.
500 North Broadway
Jericho NY 11753-2196
516/939-0400
Contact Brian Powers, General Manager/Human Resources. The world's largest company in the weight reduction and weight maintenance field. Company conducts and supervises franchised weight control classes in 21 countries; markets packaged products through its food licensees; publishes the Weight Watchers Magazine in three countries, as well as cookbooks; and operates camps for overweight children and adults through licensees. Common positions include: Accountant; Computer Programmer; Dietician; Food Technologist; Management Trainee; Marketing Specialist; Personnel & Labor Relations Specialist; Public Relations Worker; Systems Analyst. Principal educational backgrounds sought: Accounting; Business Administration; Communications; Marketing. Company benefits include: medical, dental and life insurance; pension plan; tuition assistance; disability coverage; savings plan. A wholly-owned subsidiary of H.J. Heinz Company (Pittsburgh, PA). Corporate headquarters location. International.

WESTCHESTER LIBRARY SYSTEM
8 Westchester Plaza
Elmsford NY 10523
914/592-8214
Contact Ellen Goldstein, Personnel Director. Provides a wide range of buying, distribution, and other support services to the 38 member libraries in the county system. Corporate headquarters location.

WINFIELD SECURITY
201 East 34th Street
New York NY 10016
212/532-1177
Contact Personnel Manager. Several area locations, including The Bronx, Queens, Brooklyn. Provides security guard services for office buildings, schools, businesses, and manufacturers. Corporate headquarters location.

Connecticut

BRINK'S INC.
28 Thorndal Circle
Darien CT 06820
203/655-8781
Contact Mr. Charles Tischer, Vice-President/Employee Relations. Multiple locations throughout United States. A major international security service firm. Primarily engaged in the transportation of money and valuables by way of armored vehicle, and air and sea transport, both domestically and internationally. Common positions include: Accountant; Computer Programmer; Branch Manager; General Manager; Sales Representative. Principal educational backgrounds sought: Accounting; Business Administration; Computer Science; Finance; Marketing. Company benefits include: medical insurance; dental insurance; pension plan; life insurance; tuition assistance; disability coverage; 401K savings plan. Corporate headquarters location. Parent company: The Pittston Co. Operations at this facility include: research/development; administration.

CUC INTERNATIONAL
707 Summer Street
Stamford CT 06901
203/324-9261
Contact Fran Johnson, Vice President, Human Resources. A company providing consumers with a variety of membership services, including home-shopping.

New Jersey

BAKER INDUSTRIES, INC.
1633 Littleton Road
Parsippany NJ 07054
201/267-5300
Contact Director of Human Resources. Company, through its Wells Fargo Armored Service, Wells Fargo Alarm Services, Wells Fargo Guard Services, and Pony Express Courier operations, offers armored transport, courier security guard, and alarm services and products in more than 35 states, the District of Columbia, Canada, Spain, and Puerto Rico. Subsidiary Pytronics Division markets smoke, fire, and security protection products and systems. The Pyro Chem Division produces fire-extinguishing chemicals. A division of Borg-Warner, Inc. Several area locations in Morris, Sussex, Essex, and Bergen counties. Corporate headquarters location. International.

POPULAR SERVICES, INC.
22 Lincoln Place
Garfield NJ 07026
201/471-4300
Contact Director of Employee Relations. Operates a full service mail-order catalog operation. Corporate headquarters location.

NEWSPAPER PUBLISHERS

For more information on professional opportunities in newspaper journalism, contact the following professional and trade organizations, as listed beginning on page 449:

AMERICAN SOCIETY OF NEWSPAPER EDITORS
AMERICAN NEWSPAPER PUBLISHERS ASSOCIATION
THE DOW JONES NEWSPAPER FUND
THE DOW JONES NEWSPAPER FUND/NEW YORK
INTERNATIONAL CIRCULATION MANAGERS ASSOCIATION
NATIONAL NEWSPAPER ASSOCIATION
NATIONAL PRESS CLUB
THE NEWSPAPER GUILD

New York

ADVANCE PUBLICATIONS INC.
950 Fingerboard Road
Staten Island NY 10305
718/981-1234
Contact Personnel Office. Publishes the Staten Island Advance, a local general interest newspaper. Part of the Newhouse Newspapers Group. Corporate headquarters location.

THE ASSOCIATED PRESS
50 Rockefeller Plaza
New York NY 10020
212/621-1500
Contact Caroline Turolla, Personnel Executive. The largest independent news-gathering organization in the world; maintains offices throughout the United States and the world. Corporate headquarters location. International.

BINGHAMTON PRESS COMPANY
P.O. Box 1270
Binghamton NY 13902
607/798-1107
Contact Dorothy Petrulis, Employee Relations Director. A newspaper publisher and cable TV firm. Corporate headquarters location (Gannett, Inc.): Rochester, NY. New York

Stock Exchange. Common positions include: Administrator; Advertising Worker; Computer Programmer; Credit Manager; Customer Service Representative; Department Manager; Operations/Production Manager; Marketing Specialist; Personnel & Labor Relations Specialist; Programmer; Public Relations Worker; Purchasing Agent; Reporter/Editor; Sales Representative; Systems Analyst. Principal educational background sought: Journalism. Company benefits include: medical insurance; dental insurance; pension plan; life insurance; tuition assistance; disability coverage; profit sharing; employee discounts; savings plan.

DAILY CHALLENGE
1360 Fulton Street
Brooklyn NY 11216
718/636-9500
Contact Dawad Phillip, Managing Editor. Publishes a daily newspaper. Corporate headquarters location.

HOME REPORTER & SUNSET NEWS INC.
8723 Third Avenue
Brooklyn NY 11209
718/238-6600
Contact Sarah Otey, Editor. Publishes several weekly community newspapers: Brooklyn Home Reporter & Sunset News, Brookly, Bensonhurst News, and Brooklyn Park Slope News. Corporate headquarters location.

MARKS-ROILAND COMMUNICATIONS, INC.
26 Jericho Turnpike
Jericho NY 11753
516/333-7400
Contact Rose A. Koch, Personnel Manager. A regional publisher involved in publishing, printing and distribution of weekly free circulation newspapers, as well as circulars and other promotional and printed material. Common positions include: Accountant; Account Executive; Advertising Worker; Blue-Collar Worker Supervisor; Commercial Artist; Computer Programmer; Customer Service Representative; Department Manager; General Manager; Management Trainee; Operations/Productions Manager; Marketing Specialist; Public Relations Worker; Sales Representative; Telemarketer; Printing Press Operator. Principal educational backgrounds sought: Accounting; Art/Design; Business Administration; Communications; Marketing. Company benefits include: medical insurance; dental insurance; life insurance; disability coverage; profit sharing; savings plan; 401 K. Corporate headquarters location. Operations at this facility include: manufacturing; administration; service; sales.

THE NEW AMERICAN
310 11th Avenue, Room 304
New York NY 10027
212/427-3880
Contact Arlene Wilson, Publisher/Editor In Chief. Publishes a nationally-distributed weekly newspaper (circulation: 130,000), primarily covering cultural, political, and social news of interest to Black Americans. Distributes widely throughout the New York City metropolitan area, and in other cities, including Washington DC, Boston, Baltimore, Philadelphia, Chicago, Cincinnati, Atlanta, and Los Angeles, among others. Common positions include: Accountant; Administrator; Advertising Worker; Computer Programmer; Management Trainee; Operations/Production Manager; Marketing Specialist; Personnel & Labor Relations Specialist; Public Relations Specialist; Reporter/Editor; Sales Representative. Principal educational backgrounds sought: Accounting; Art/Design; Business Administration; Communications; Computer Science. Internships offered. Corporate headquarters location. Operations at this facility include: regional headquarters; divisional headquarters; research/development; administration; service; sales.

NEW YORK NEWS INC.
220 East 42nd Street
New York NY 10017
212/210-6335
Contact Ms. Robin Hill, Human Resources Department. Publishes a daily and Sunday tabloid format newspaper (New York Daily News); daily circulation is 1.3 million. Common positions include: Computer Programmer; Reporter/Editor; Sales Representative. Principal educational backgrounds sought: Accounting; Communications; Computer Science; Finance; Marketing. Company benefits include: medical insurance; dental insurance; pension plan; life insurance; tuition assistance; disability coverage; savings plan. Corporate headquarters location.

NEW YORK POST
210 South Street
New York NY 10002
212/815-8613
Contact Lucy Lambert, Personnel Director. Publishes a tabloid format daily newspaper, with a weekday circulation of more than 770,000.

NEW YORK TIMES COMPANY
229 West 43rd Street
New York NY 10036
212/556-1234
Contact Personnel Department. Publishes The New York Times, one of the most distinguished and honored newspapers in the world (daily circulation exceeds 887,000 weekdays; more than 1.4 million on Sunday). In addition to the New York Times, this diversified, publicly-owned communications firm publishes 30 smaller-city dailies and weeklies; publishes three leading national magazines; and owns and operates three television stations, two radio stations, and a cable television system. The company also publishes syndicated news and features worldwide. Also has interests in paper and newsprint manufacturing mills, and a partial interest in the International Herald Tribune. Newspaper subsidiaries are located throughout the country, with a significant presence in Florida, and have an average daily circulation of 272,000; Magazines segment operates through 'Family Circle' (see separate listing), 'Golf Digest', and 'Tennis' magazines; Television Broadcasting segment operates television stations WREG (Memphis, TN), WHNT (Huntsville, AL), KSFM (Fort Smith, AR), and Radio Broadcasting operations are conducted through New York City station WQXR-AM & FM, one of the country's leading classical music stations. Subsidiary NYT Cable TV, which operates primarily in the metropolitan Philadelphia area, provides service to more than 100,000 subscribers. Corporate headquarters location. New York Stock Exchange.

NEWS WORLD COMMUNICATIONS INC.
401 Fifth Avenue
New York NY 10016
212/532-8300
Contact Kathy Vornbrock, Personnel Director. Publishes one area newspaper (New York City Tribune) and one national newspaper (Noticias del Mundo). Common positions include: Accountant; Administrator; Advertising Worker; Attorney; Commercial Artist; Computer Programmer; Customer Service Representative; General Manager; Operations/Production Manager; Marketing Specialist; Personnel & Labor Relations Specialist; Public Relations Worker; Purchasing Agent; Reporter/Editor; Sales Representative; Librarian; Telecommunicator. Principal educational backgrounds sought: Accounting; Art/Design; Business Administration; Communications; Computer Science; Liberal Arts; Marketing. Company benefits include: medical insurance; dental insurance; life insurance; tuition assistance; disability coverage. Corporate headquarters location. Operations at this facility include: administration; sales.

THE STAR
660 White Plains Road
Tarrytown NY 10591
914/332-5000

Contact Personnel Department. Publishes a mass-market weekly general interest tabloid newspaper, distributed primarily through supermarkets throughout the United States.

THE TIMES-HERALD RECORD
40 Mulberry Street
Middletown NY 10940
914/343-2181
Contact Debra A. Sherman, Personnel Director. Several area locations, including New Paltz, Newburgh, and Port Jervis. Publishes a daily newspaper, with a circulation of more than 80,000. Common positions include: Advertising Worker; Credit Manager; Customer Service Representative; Management Trainee; Operations/Production Manager; Personnel & Labor Relations Specialist; Reporter/Editor; Sales Representative. Principal educational backgrounds sought: Accounting; Art/Design; Communications; Computer Science; Liberal Arts; Journalism. Company benefits include: medical, dental, and life insurance; pension plan; tuition assistance; disability coverage. Corporate headquarters location.

UNITED PRESS INTERNATIONAL
5 Penn Plaza, 16th Floor
New York NY 10001
212/560-1100
Contact Personnel Officer. One of the largest independent news gathering organizations in the world, with news bureaus located throughout the world. Corporate headquarters location: Brentwood, TN.

USA WEEKEND/GANNETT
535 Madison Avenue
New York NY 10022
212/715-2015
Contact Maggie Giraud, Personnel Manager. Publishes a general interest national weekly magazine, sold in syndication as a Sunday newspaper supplement throughout the country. 31.6 million readers every weekend. Features include national affairs, sports, personal care, and other areas. Corporate headquarters location: Arlington, VA. Parent company: Gannett Co., Inc. Common positions include: Accountant; Advertising Worker; Credit Manager; Marketing Specialist; Sales Representative. Principal educational backgrounds sought: Accounting; Art/Design; Business Administration; Communications; Computer Science; Finance; Liberal Arts; Marketing. Training programs and internships available. Company benefits include: medical, dental, life insurance; tuition assistance; pension plan; disability coverage; profit sharing; savings plan.

WESTCHESTER-ROCKLAND NEWSPAPER GROUP
One Gannett Drive
White Plains NY 10604
914/694-9300
Contact Patricia Nagle, Vice President of Personnel. A division of the Gannett Newspapers Group (Rosslyn, NY). Publishes ten daily and two weekly papers; Westminster (20 editions), Rockland, Putnam, and Fairfield (CT) Counties. Corporate headquarters location.

New Jersey

THE HERALD & NEWS
P.O. Box 1019
Passaic NJ 07055
201/365-3000
Contact Charles McDermott, Personnel Manager. Publishes an independent daily evening newspaper, distributed throughout northern New Jersey. Circulation exceeds 75,000 daily. Corporate headquarters location.

THE HUDSON DISPATCH COMPANY
409 39th Street
Union City NJ 07087
201/863-2000
Contact Richard Vezza, Publisher or David Levine, Editor. A local daily serving south Bergen and north Hudson Counties with a circulation of 35,000. Operations include: manufacturing; administration; service; sales. Corporate headquarters location. Common positions include: Reporter; Copy Editor; Photographer. Principal educational background sought: Communications. Company benefits include: medical insurance; life insurance.

THE JERSEY JOURNAL
30 Journal Square
Jersey City NJ 07306
201/653-1000
Contact Managing Editor for editorial positions. Circulation Manager and Advertising Manager can also be contacted. Publishes a daily evening newspaper, with a circulation of more than 64,000. Part of the Newhouse Newspapers group.

MORRISTOWN DAILY RECORD INC.
629 Parsippany Road
Parsippany NJ 07054
201/428-6200
Contact Tracey Reinholdt, Director of Personnel. Publishes a daily morning newspaper (Daily Record), serving all of Morris County and the greater northwest New Jersey area. Circulation is approximately 63,000 daily, and 72,000 Sunday. Corporate headquarters location. Common positions include: Advertising Worker; Computer Programmer; Credit Manager; Customer Service Representative; Department Manager; Personnel & Labor Relations Specialist; Programmer; Public Relations Worker; Purchasing Agent; Reporter/Editor; Sales Representative. Principal educational backgrounds sought: Business Administration; Communications; Computer Science; Journalism; Marketing. Company benefits include: medical insurance; dental insurance; pension plan; life insurance; tuition assistance; disability coverage; profit sharing; employee discounts; savings plan.

NEWARK STAR-LEDGER
Star Ledger Plaza
Newark NJ 07101
201/877-4141
Contact Personnel Department. Publishes New Jersey's largest circulation daily newspaper (daily circulation exceeds 409,000; Sunday circulation is more than 584,000). Part of the Newhouse Newspapers Group.

THE NEWS TRIBUNE
1 Hoover Way
Woodbridge NJ 07095
201/442-0400
Contact Personnel Department. Publishes a daily newspaper, with a weekday circulation of more than 51,000. Independently owned. Corporate headquarters location.

THE RECORD
150 River Street
Hackensack NJ 07601
201/646-4455
Contact Helen B. Moore, Personnel/Employment. A newspaper-publishing organization, whose primary publication is The Record, New Jersey's largest evening newspaper, distributed throughout Passaic County and northern New Jersey. Circulation more than 156,000 daily; 222,000 on Sunday. Corporate headquarters location. Common positions include: Billing Contracts Clerk; Computer Programmer; Customer Service Representative; Systems Engineer; Support Engineer, Electronic Technician/Magnetics; Customer Service Manager; District Manager of Circulation Department; Production; Offset Stripper/Camera Person; Journeyman/woman Offset Pressperson; Programmer;

Programmer Analyst; Reporter/Editor; Sales Representative/Advertising. Principal educational backgrounds sought: Accounting; Business Administration; Communications; Computer Science; Engineering; Finance; Marketing. Company benefits include: credit union; matching gifts; medical insurance; dental insurance; pension plan; life insurance; scholarships; tuition assistance; disability coverage; profit sharing; savings plan.

**RIDGEWOOD NEWSPAPERS/
RIDGEWOOD NEWS**
75 North Maple
Ridgewood NJ 07452
201/445-6400
Contact Rich Sokirka, Personnel. Publishes several area newspapers, including The Ridgewood News/Ridgewood Sunday News, an area weekly with a circulation of more than 19,000. Corporate headquarters location.

**PAPER, PACKAGING & FOREST PRODUCTS/
CONTAINERS & GLASS PRODUCTS**

For more information on professional opportunities in the paper and packaging industries, contact the following professional and trade organizations, as listed beginning on page 449:

**AMERICAN PAPER INSTITUTE
TECHNICAL ASSOCIATION OF THE PULP AND PAPER INDUSTRY**

New York

CORNING
Houghton Park, C-1-8
Corning NY 14831
Mailed inquiries only
Contact George Brewster, Manager of External Staffing. Manufacturer of speciality glass and glass ceramic products in Specialty materials, Consumer Products, Telecommunications and Lab Services. Corning employs 22,000 in their world wide businesses. Common positions include: Ceramics Engineer; Electrical Engineer; Mechanical Engineer; Metallurgical Engineer; Statistician; Systems Analyst. Educational backgrounds sought: Computer Science; Engineering. Training programs and internships offered. Company benefits include: medical insurnace; dental insurance; pension plan; life insurance; tuition assistance; disability coverage; daycare assistance; profit sharing; employee discounts; savings plan. Corporate headquarters location. Parent company: divisional headquarters; manufacturing; research/development; administration; service; sales. New York Stock Exchange.

FOLD-PAK CORPORATION
P.O. Box 269
Newark NY 14513
315/331-3200
Contact Jack D. Slawson, Corporate Personnel Director. Engaged in the manufacture of folding cartons. Corporate headquarters location. Common positions include: Accountant; Administrator; Blue-Collar Worker Supervisor; Buyer; Commercial Artist; Computer Programmer; Credit Manager; Customer Service Representative; Draftsperson; Electrical Engineer; Industrial Engineer; Mechanical Engineer; Financial Analyst; General Manager; Department Manager; Management Trainee; Operations/Production Manager; Purchasing Agent; Marketing Specialist; Quality Control Supervisor; Sales Representative. Principal educational backgrounds sought: Accounting; Art/Design; Business Administration; Computer Science; Engineering; Finance; Marketing. Company benefits include: medical insurance; dental insurance; life insurance; tuition assistance; disability coverage; profit sharing; savings plan. Operations at this facility: divisional headquarters; manufacturing; research/development; administration; service; sales.

GILMAN PAPER COMPANY
111 West 50th Street, 2nd Floor
New York NY 10018
212/246-3300
Contact John Faiella, Treasurer. A privately-owned, major manufacturer of paper, pulp, paper bags, and lumber. Products are marketed throughout the United States. Operations at this facility include: sales. Corporate headquarters location. Common positions include: Accountant; Customer Service Representative; Computer Programmer; Sales Representative. Principal educational backgrounds sought: Accounting; Business Administration; Liberal Arts. Company benefits include: medical insurance; pension plan; life insurance; tuition assistance; disability coverage; savings plan.

IMPERIAL PAPER BOX CORPORATION
252 Newport
Brooklyn NY 11212
718/346-6100
Contact Personnel Office. A manufacturer of paper containers, including boxes and packaging materials. Corporate headquarters location.

INTERNATIONAL PAPER CO.
Two Manhattanville Road
Purchase NY 10577
914/397-1500
Contact Personnel. A manufacturer of paper, paperboard, and other paper products.

KENT PAPER COMPANY INC.
1710 Flushing Avenue
Ridgewood NY 11385
718/366-7100
Contact Personnel Office. Manufactures paper products, primarily envelopes. Corporate headquarters location.

NEW YORK ENVELOPE CORPORATION
29-10 Hunters Point Avenue
Long Island City NY 11101
718/786-0300
Contact Personnel Director. Manufactures a wide range of envelopes for distribution to wholesalers. Corporate headquarters location.

RHEEM MANUFACTURING COMPANY
405 Lexington Avenue
New York NY 10174
212/916-8116
Contact Henry O. Porter, Director, Corporate Personnel. Manufactures water heating and air conditioning equipment. Several locations nationwide. Common positions include: Accountant; Administrator; Attorney; Buyer; Computer Programmer; Credit Manager; Financial Analyst; Insurance Agent/Broker; Department Manager; Management Trainee; Marketing Specialist; Personnel & Labor Relations Specialist; Public Relations Specialist; Purchasing Agent. Principal educational backgrounds sought: Accounting; Business Administration; Computer Science; Economics; Finance. Training programs offered. Company benefits include: medical, dental, and life insurance; pension plan; tuition assistance; disability coverage; profit sharing; employee discounts; savings plan. Parent company: Poloma Industries Inc.

SOMERVILLE PACKAGING
439 Central Avenue
Rochester NY 14605
716/232-4284

Contact Alice Curry, Personnel Director. A manufacturer of ice cream carton packaging. Operations at this facility include: manufacturing; administration; sales. Corporate headquarters location. Common positions include: Accountant; Administrator; Blue-Collar Worker Supervisor; Buyer; Commercial Artist; Computer Programmer; Credit Manager; Customer Service Representative; Engineer; Industrial Engineer; Mechanical Engineer; Financial Analyst; Department Manager; General Manager; Management Trainee; Operations/Production Manager; Personnel & Labor Relations Specialist; Purchasing Agent; Quality Control Supervisor; Sales Representative; Transportation & Traffic Specialist. Principal educational backgrounds sought: Accounting; Art/Design; Business Administration; Engineering; Finance; Marketing. Company benefits include: medical insurance; dental insurance; pension plan; life insurance; disability coverage; profit sharing; savings plan.

STANDARD FOLDING CARTONS
85th Street and 24th Avenue
Jackson Heights NY 11370
718/335-5500
Contact Personnel Department. A major area manufacturer of folding boxes for more than 50 years. Corporate headquarters location.

STUDLEY PAPER COMPANY INC.
95 Inip Drive
Inwood NY 11696
516/239-4000
Contact Bob Amato, Personnel Director. Manufactures and distributes filter and specialty bags for a wide range of applications. A subsidiary of Ply*Gem Company. Corporate headquarters location.

THYSSEN-BORNEMISZA INC.
1211 Avenue of the Americas
New York NY 10036
212/556-8500
Contact Eugene Gross, Vice President of Human Resources. A diversified manufacturer, producing glass and metal container products, automotive products, and other metal products. Facilities are located throughout the United States. Employs more than 10,000 people nationwide. Corporate headquarters location.

WESTVACO CORPORATION
299 Park Avenue
New York NY 10171
212/688-5000
Contact Manager, College Relations. Westvaco is a producer of paper packaging and specialty chemicals. Annual sales exceed $2 billion, placing in the top half of the Fortune 500. Company employs 15,000 nationally and internationally in 50 major facilities. These facilities include paper and paperboard mills, converting plants, chemical plants, lumber mills, research and development laboratories and real estate operations. Common positions include: Accountant; Financial Analyst; Sales Representative. Principal educational backgrounds sought: Business Administration; Engineering; Liberal Arts; Marketing. Training programs offered. Company benefits include: medical, dental, and life insurance; tuition assistance; disability coverage; savings plan. Corporate headquarters location. Operations at this facility include: administration; sales. American Stock Exchange.

Connecticut

CHAMPION INTERNATIONAL
1 Champion Plaza
Stamford CT 06921
203/358-7000
Contact Leslie Forrest, Staffing Manager. A major Connecticut paper products company.

DEXTER NONWOVENS DIVISION/
THE DEXTER CORPORATION
2 Elm Street
Windsor Locks CT 06096
203/623-9801
Contact John Kliska, Professional Recruiting. A paper nonwovens manufacturing division. Common positions include: Accountant; Buyer; Chemist; Computer Programmer; Credit Manager; Customer Service Representative; Draftsperson; Chemical Engineer; Electrical Engineer; Industrial Engineer; Mechanical Engineer; Financial Analyst; Industrial Designer; Marketing Specialist; Purchasing Agent; Statistician; Systems Analyst. Principal educational backgrounds sought: Accounting; Business Administration; Chemistry; Computer Science; Engineering; Finance; Marketing. Company benefits include: medical, dental, and life insurance; pension plan; tuition assistance; disability coverage; profit sharing. Corporate headquarters location. Operations at this facility include: divisional headquarters; manufacturing; research/development; administration; service; sales. New York Stock Exchange.

KEYES FIBRE COMPANY
301 Merit #7
P.O. Box 5317
Norwalk CT 06856
203/846-1499
Contact R.W. Holowiak, Vice President of Human Resources. A leading manufacturer of molded pulp. Manufactures more than 600 different packaging and consumer products. Products include 'Chinet' brand paper plates, and disposable tableware and other products for the fast food market. Corporate headquarters location. International.

New Jersey

ALFORD PACKAGING
Industrial Avenue
Ridgefield Park NJ 07660
201/440-3000
Contact John Sands, Personnel Director. Produces a variety of packaging products, including folding cartons, plastics thermoforming, and others. Also produces paper and labels, and injection-molded plastics.

ANCHOR GLASS CONTAINER CORPORATION
83 Griffith Street
Salem NJ 08079
609/935-4000
Contact Ken Owens, Personnel Manager. Manufacturers of a variety of container products.

BERLIN & JONES COMPANY, INC.
2 East Union Avenue
East Rutherford NJ 07070
201/933-5900
Contact Treasurer. Manufactures envelopes. Corporate headquarters location.

BOSCH PACKAGING MACHINERY DIVISION
121 Corporate Boulevard
South Plainfield NJ 07080
908/753-3700
Contact Barry Greenwood, President. A worldwide leader in the packaging technology. Products include a wide range of equipment used in the packaging of pharmaceuticals and drugs, foods, and beverages, confectionery products, cosmetics, and toiletries, and industrial and chemical products. A subsidiary of the Bosch Group (Stuttgart, West Germany), a manufacturer of automotive components, household appliances, cine camera

technology, medical technology, heating technology, and assembly line technology. Divisional headquarters location. International.

CENTRAL PRODUCTS
531 North Stiles Street
Linden NJ 07036
201/925-0900
Contact Alice Borden, Personnel Director. Produces reinforcement tape used on cartons and other packaging products. Major clients are paperbox/container manufacturers. Corporate headquarters location.

EQUITABLE BAG COMPANY INC.
37-11 35th Avenue
Long Island City NY 11101
718/786-0620
Contact Office Manager. An integrated manufacturer of paper and plastic bags, sold primarily to the retail industry and other users of specialty bags. Corporate headquarters location.

FEDERAL PAPER BOARD COMPANY INC.
75 Chestnut Ridge Road
Montvale NJ 07645
201/391-1776
Contact Personnel Department. Operates nationally in three business segments: Forest Products, including bleached paperboard and pulp, the operation of woodlands, and the operation of lumber plants; Recycled Paperboard, primarily used for folding cartons (company operates three mills); and Folding Cartons, in which company produces specially designed packaging for individual customers (nine plants overall). Clients include a wide range of nationally-known consumer goods manufacturers. Corporate headquarters location. New York Stock Exchange.

GEORGIA PACIFIC/DELAIR
P.O. Box 338
Delair NJ 08110
609/663-6015
Contact Ms. Dana Murray, Personnel Director. Area office of the well-known national paper products manufacturer.

STEPHEN GOULD PAPER COMPANY INC.
35 South Jefferson Road
Whippany NJ 07981
201/428-1500
Contact Personnel Director. Several area locations. Designers, producers, and suppliers of packaging for industry. 26 national locations. Corporate headquarters location

LEONE INDUSTRIES
443 Southeast Avenue
Bridgeton NJ 08302
609/455-2000
Contact Personnel. Manufactures flint or clear glass containers. Operations include: manufacturing. Corporate headquarters location. Common positions include: Accountant; Buyer; Customer Service Representative; Draftsperson; Engineer; Electrical Engineer; Industrial Engineer; Mechanical Engineer; Manager; General Manager; Management Trainee; Operations/Production Manager; Purchasing Agent; Quality Control Supervisor. Principal educational backgrounds sought: Accounting; Business Administration; Engineering; Finance; Marketing. Company benefits include: medical insurance; dental insurance; pension plan; life insurance; tuition assistance.

LOWE PAPER COMPANY
P.O. Box 239
Ridgefield NJ 07657
201/945-4900
Contact Marie Flores, Personnel/Safety Manager. Produces recycled boxboard, clay-coated and specialty boxboard, including extrusion boxboards and specialties. Clients include food, cosmetic, pharmaceutical, and hardware manufacturers and distributors. A subsidiary of Simkins Industries, Inc. Corporate headquarters location. Common positions include: Accountant; Administrator; Customer Service Representative; Mechanical Engineer; General Manager; Management Trainee; Operations/Production Manager; Personnel and Labor Relations Specialist; Purchasing Agent; Quality Control Supervisor; Transportation & Traffic Specialist. Principal educational backgrounds sought: Engineering; Paper Science. Company benefits include: medical insurance; dental insurance; pension plan; life insurance; disability coverage. Corporate headquarters: New Haven, CT. Parent company: Simkins Industries. Operations include: manufacturing; administration; service; sales.

MANNKRAFT CORPORATION
1000 U.S. Highway 1
Newark NJ 07114
201/589-7400
Contact Marcia Maslo, Personnel Director. Second area facility in Irvington, NJ. Manufactures and sells corrugated cartons and displays. Design done on premises at Newark facility. Corporate headquarters location.

MARCAL PAPER MILLS, INC.
1 Market Street
Elmwood Park NJ 07407
201/796-4000
Contact Personnel Dept./Employment Manager. Manufactures and distributes a broad range of nationally-advertised paper products. Common positions include: Accountant; Computer Programmer; Customer Service Representative; Chemical Engineer; Mechanical Engineer; Operations/Production Manager; Sales Representative. Principal educational backgrounds sought: Accounting; Business Admiministration; Computer Science; Engineering. Company benefits include: medical, dental, and life insurance; tuition assistance; disability coverage; employee discounts; savings plan; 401K. Corporate headquarters location. Operations at this facility include: regional headquarters; manufacturing; research/development; administration; sales.

POTTERS INDUSTRIES, INC.
Waterview Corporate Center
20 Waterview Boulevard
Parsippany NJ 07054
201/299-2900
Contact James W. Brinkerhoff, Director of Human Resources. Manufactures a wide range of glass products, including reflective glass for automotive and highway safety use, decorative glass, and industrial glass products. Corporate headquarters location.

SCHIFFENHAUS PACKAGING CORPORATION
2013 McCarter Highway
Newark NJ 07104
201/484-5000
Contact Terry Cmielewskil, Personnel Department. A manufacturer of corrugated boxes and related products. Corporate headquarters location.

SEALED AIR CORPORATION
Park 80 Plaza East
Saddle Brook NJ 07662
201/791-7600
Contact Personnel Department. Several area locations, including Fair Lawn, and Totowa, NJ; Danbury, CT; Holyoke, MA. A producer of specialized protective packaging materials

and systems which reduce or eliminate the damage to products that may occur during shipment. Company operates over 20 sales offices in the United States, and six plants and nine sales offices in foreign countries. The company also has fully-staffed packaging and testing laboratories around the world, and major technical facilities in Fair Lawn (Technical Center), and Danbury, CT. Corporate headquarters location. International.

TENSION ENVELOPE CORPORATION
19 Wesley Street
South Hackensack NJ 07606-1508
201/487-1880
Contact Personnel Manager. A manufacturer of specialty envelopes. Operations include: manufacturing. Common positions include: Sales Administrator; Blue-Collar Worker Supervisor; Commercial Artist; Department Manager; Sales Representative. Principal educational backgrounds sought include: Business Administration; Marketing. Company benefits include: medical, dental, and life insurance; pension plan; tuition assistance; disability coverage. Corporate headquarters location: Kansas City, MO. Operations at this facility include: manufacturing; administration; sales.

UNION CAMP CORPORATION
1600 Valley Road
Wayne NJ 07470
201/628-2000
Contact Jane DelMastro, Personnel Manager. A leading manufacturer of forest-based products; other fields of operation include minerals, land development, chemicals, school supplies, retail building supplies, printing machinery, packaging machinery and systems, plastic products, and cartons and containers. United States facilities include pulp and paper mills, lumber mills, plywood and particleboard plants, and chemical plants. Company's research and development activities are centered in Princeton, NJ. Corporate headquarters location. New York Stock Exchange. International.

PETROLEUM AND ENERGY RELATED/MINING & DRILLING

For more information on professional opportunities in the petroleum or mining industries, contact the following professional and trade organizations, as listed beginning on page 449:

AMERICAN ASSOCIATION OF PETROLEUM GEOLOGISTS
AMERICAN GAS ASSOCIATION
AMERICAN GEOLOGICAL INSTITUTE
AMERICAN INSTITUTE OF MINING,
        METALLURGICAL AND PETROLEUM
AMERICAN NUCLEAR SOCIETY
AMERICAN PETROLEUM INSTITUTE
AMERICAN SOCIETY OF TRIBOLOGISTS
        AND LUBRICATION ENGINEERS
CLEAN ENERGY RESEARCH INSTITUTE
GEOLOGICAL SOCIETY OF AMERICA
SOCIETY OF EXPLORATION GEOPHYSICISTS

New York

AMERADA HESS CORPORATION
1185 Avenue of the Americas, 39th Floor
New York NY 10036
212/536-8167
Contact Larry Fox, Manager of Employee Relations. Several local locations including: Woodbridge, NJ. A Fortune 50 fully integrated company engaged in every phase of the petroleum business from the exploration for and development and production of crude oil and natural gas to the refining and marketing of petroleum products. Amerada Hess's

exploration and production activities are conducted in the U.S., Canada, the Norwegian and United Kingdom sectors of the North Sea, Abu Dhabi, Libya, and other areas of the world. Its refineries produce residual fuel oil, heating oil, gasoline, other petroleum products and petrochemicals, all of which are marketed principally in the United States. Approximately 8,000 employees. Corporate headquarters location. New York Stock Exchange. American Stock Exchange. International. Common positions include: Accountant; Chemical Engineer; Mechanical Engineer; Petroleum Engineer; Geologist; Geophysicist; Programmer. Principal educational backgrounds sought: Accounting; Computer Science; Engineering. Company benefits include: medical insurance; dental insurance; pension plan; life insurance; tuition assistance; disability coverage; profit sharing; savings plan.

CIBRO PETROLEUM COMPANY INC.
1066 Zerega Avenue
Bronx NY 10462
212/824-5000
Contact Dionne Faillace, Personnel Manager. One of the largest independent fuel oil companies in the Northeast, with more than 10 terminals, and a refinery located in Albany, NY. Corporate headquarters location.

GETTY PETROLEUM CORP.
125 Jericho Turnpike
Jericho, NY 11753
516/338-6000
Contact Personnel. One of the nation's leading petroleum companies.

GENERAL ABRASIVE DIVISION/
DRESSER INDUSTRIES
2000 College Avenue
Box 1438
Niagara Falls NY 14302
716/286-1234
Contact Personnel Department. Supplies abrasive grains to a variety of customers. Parent company, Dresser Industries, Inc., is one of the world's leading suppliers of technology, products and services to worldwide energy, natural resource and industrial markets; operations include petroleum, energy processing and conversion, mining and construction, and general industry. The company markets its products and services in more than 100 countries.

GREAT LAKES CARBON CORPORATION
320 Old Briarcliff Road
Briarcliff Manor NY 10510
914/941-7800
Contact Sylveta Bromfield, Personnel Associate. The world's largest calciner of petroleum coke; supplies more than 21 percent of the calcined coke used by the world's aluminum industry. Company is one of the world's largest producers of graphite electrodes for the electric arc steel smelting industry, supplying approximately 20 percent of the graphite electrode market. Other activities include shipping, in which the company is a leading trader and shipper of bulk carbon-related materials. Other activities include the buying and selling of raw petroleum coke. Conducts extensive research and development operations. Manufacturing and sales facilities are located throughout the United States and the world. Other major national facilities include: Niagara, NY; Morganton, NC; Elizabethton, TN; and Ozark, AR. Corporate headquarters location. International.

PHELPS DODGE CORPORATION
300 Park Avenue
New York NY 10022
212/940-6400
Contact John Donovan, Sales Director. Several area locations, including Greenwich, and Norwich, CT; Yonkers, NY; and others. A copper mining and copper products

manufacturing firm, with diversified operations. Company mines approximately 20 percent of the copper produced in the United States, and fabricates a portion of that copper and copper purchased from others into a wide variety of copper and copper alloy products. Also produces silver, gold, and molybdenum as by-products of copper operations. Western Nuclear, Inc., a wholly-owned subsidiary, mines and mills uranium ore. Company also explores for metals and minerals in the United States and abroad, and for oil and gas domestically. Has substantial investments in international mining properties in Peru, South Africa, and Australia; and maintains various interests in companies which manufacture wire and cable products in 14 foreign countries. Area subsidiaries include: Phelps Dodge Exploration (New York, NY); Phelps Dodge Copper Products Company (Norwich, CT); Phelps Dodge Refining Corporation (Laurel Hill, NY); Phelps Dodge Industries (Greenwich, CT), which includes area subsidiaries Phelps Dodge Cable and Wire Company, Phelps Dodge Communications Company, and other divisions operating outside of the metropolitan area. Other subsidiaries are located throughout the United States and internationally. Significant U.S. operations in Arizona, primarily related to copper mining and refining. Corporate headquarters location. New York Stock Exchange. International.

TEXACO
2000 Westchester Avenue
White Plains NY 10650
914/253-4000
Contact Personnel. Engaged in crude petroleum and natural gas exploration, production, refining, and marketing.

Connecticut

AMAX INC.
Amax Center
Greenwich CT 06836-1700
203/629-6369
Contact Joe Pereira, Supervisor Employee Relations. A diversified minerals and energy development company with worldwide operations. The company explores for, mines, refines, and sells a wide variety of minerals and metals, and has interests in coal, petroleum, and natural gas. Principal products are molybdenum, coal, zinc, petroleum and natural gas, potash, tungsten, silver, gold, and magnesium. Through Alumax, Inc., company is also involved in the production of aluminum and the fabrication and marketing of aluminum products. Common positions include: Accountant; Computer Programmer; Financial Analyst. Principal educational backgrounds sought: Accounting; Finance. Company benefits include: medical, dental, and life insurance; pension plan; tuition assistance; disability coverage; profit sharing; savings plan. Corporate headquarters location. Operations at this facility include: administration; sales. New York Stock Exchange.

THE PITTSTON COMPANY
One Pickwick Plaza
P.O. Box 8900
Greenwich CT 06836-8900
203/622-0900
Contact Ed Cox, Personnel Director. Several area locations, including Darien, CT. A diversified world leader in the following areas: the mining and world marketing of premium-quality metallurgical and steam coal through its major affiliated coal companies in Virginia, West Virginia, and eastern Kentucky, and domestic and export sales subsidiaries; and worldwide security transportation services through Brink's, Inc., which also provides warehousing, distribution, and vehicle leasing services through its subsidiaries. Corporate headquarters location. New York Stock Exchange. International.

SOUTHERN CONNECTICUT GAS COMPANY
880 Broad Street
Bridgeport CT 06604
203/382-8141
Contact David McGill, Human Resources Coordinator. Services include oil and gas exploration and development, and natural gas distribution. Common positions include: Accountant; Blue-Collar Worker Supervisor; Computer Programmer; Customer Service Representative; Draftsperson; Civil Engineer; Financial Analyst; Management Trainee; Marketing Specialist; Public Relations Worker; Sales Representative; Systems Analyst; Technical Writer/Editor. Principal educational backgrounds sought: Business Administration; Communications; Computer Science; Engineering; Finance; Liberal Arts; Marketing. Company benefits include: medical, dental, and life insurance; pension plan; tuition assistance; disability coverage; savings plan. Corporate headquarters location. Operations at this facility include: administration.

TELECO OILFIELD SERVICES INC.
105 Pondview Drive
Meriden CT 06450
203/237-9655
Contact Steve Mordecai, Employee Relations Supervisor. Firm develops and manufactures directional and interpretational sensing equipment for the oil and gas industry. Operations include: manufacturing; research/development; administration. Corporate headquarters location (Sonat Inc.): Birmingham, AL. New York Stock Exchange. Common positions include: Electrical Engineer; Mechanical Engineer; Petroleum Engineer; Geologist; Software Engineer; Q.A. Engineer. Principal educational backgrounds sought: Computer Science; Engineering; Geology. Company benefits include: medical insurance; dental insurance; pension plan; life insurance; tuition assistance; disability coverage; savings plan.

UNC-NAVAL PRODUCTS
67 Sandy Desert Road
P.O. Box 981
Uncasville CT 06382-0981
203/848-1511
Contact Mr. Robert Bonito, Vice-President of Human Resources. Manufacturer of nuclear propulsion units for the Department of Energy. Common positions include: Accountant; Administrator; Blue-Collar Worker Supervisor; Buyer; Chemist; Computer Programmer; Draftsperson; Aerospace Engineer; Civil Engineer; Electrical Engineer; Industrial Engineer; Mechanical Engineer; Metallurgical Engineer; Financial Analyst; Industrial Manager; Department Manager; General Manager; Management Trainee; Operations/Production Manager; Marketing Specialist; Personnel & Labor Relations Specialist; Purchasing Agent; Statistician; Systems Analyst; Technical Writer/Editor; Transportation/Traffic Specialist. Principal educational backgrounds sought: Accounting; Business Administration; Chemistry; Communications; Computer Science; Engineering; Finance; Liberal Arts; Mathematics. Company benefits include: medical, dental, and life insurance; tuition assistance; disability coverage; profit sharing. Corporate headquarters location: Annapolis, MD. Parent company: UNC Incorporated. Operations at this facility include: divisional headquarters; manufacturing. New York Stock Exchange.

New Jersey

CHRONER CORPORATION
P.O. Box 177
Princeton NJ 08542
609/799-7586
Contact Personnel Director. A manufacturer of solar panels and other solar products. Products include: walk lites; patio lites; runway and billboard lighting.

J.M. HUBER CORPORATION
333 Thornall Street
Edison NJ 08818
201/549-8600
Contact Personnel Manager. A diversified company, producing oil and natural gas, carbon black, kaolin (china) clay, synthetic inorganic pigments, printing inks and equipment for the petroleum and pipeline industries, timber and plywood, calcium carbonate, and trace minerals. Products are sold to oil refineries and pipelines, and to the rubber, paper, printing, paint, adhesives, plastics, insecticides, ceramics, animal feed, packaging, home construction, and wood-consuming industries. Edison facilities house the company's administrative offices, headquarters and research operations for the company's Ink Division and International Department. The Ink Division is a leading supplier of black and color inks to newspapers, and the packaging and commercial printing industries; International Department exports these inks to many countries, as well as operating an ink manufacturing plant in Venezuela. Corporate headquarters location. International.

NUI CORPORATION
One Elizabethtown Plaza
Union NJ 07083
201/289-5000
Contact Robert Kenney, Vice-President. Several area locations. Engaged primarily in energy discovery and distribution through subsidiaries and investments in joint ventures. Company has two subsidiaries engaged in oil and gas exploration and production in western New York, Pennsylvania, Texas and New Mexico. Also owns Elizabethtown Gas, serving more than 200,000 customers; Utility Propane, a retail and wholesale distributor; Energy Marketing Exchange, which buys and sells 'spot market' gas; Computil, a data-processing firm serving municipalities and utilities; and PIM, which provides equipment for the replacement of underground utility pipelines. Other main office locations in Whitehouse Station, NJ (Utility Propane); Batavia, NY (The Lenape Resources Corporation). Corporate headquarters location: Bridgewater, NJ. New York Stock Exchange. Common positions include: Accountant; Administrator; Attorney; Blue-Collar Worker Supervisor; Buyer; Claim Representative; Computer Programmer; Credit Manager; Customer Service Representative; Draftsperson; Economist; Civil Engineer; Mechanical Engineer; Mining Engineer; Petroleum Engineer; Financial Analyst; Branch Manager; Department Manager; General Manager; Personnel Manager; Management Trainee; Operations/Production Manager; Marketing Specialist; Personnel & Labor Relations Specialist; Programmer; Public Relations Worker; Purchasing Agent; Sales Representative; Statisician; Systems Analyst; Tax Specialist; Transportation & Traffic Specialist. Principal educational backgrounds sought: Accounting; Business Administration; Communications; Computer Science; Engineering; Finance; Liberal Arts; Marketing; Mathematics. Company benefits include: medical insurance; dental insurance; pension plan; life insurance; tuition assistance; disability coverage; profit sharing; employee discounts; savings plan.

PRINTING/GRAPHIC ARTS/PHOTOGRAPHIC SERVICES

For more information on professional opportunities in the printing and graphic arts industries, contact the following professional and trade organizations, as listed beginning on page 449:

ASSOCIATION OF GRAPHIC ARTS
BINDING INDUSTRIES OF AMERICA
NATIONAL ASSOCIATION OF PRINTERS AND LITHOGRAPHERS
PRINTING INDUSTRIES OF AMERICA
TECHNICAL ASSOCIATION OF THE GRAPHIC ARTS

New York

AMERICAN BANK NOTE COMPANY
345 Hudson, 17th Floor
New York NY 10014
212/425-5100
Contact Personnel Department. One of the world's leading printers of securities. Products include currency printed for governments throughout the world; travel documents such as travelers checks, airline tickets, and passports; stocks, bonds, and other security documents for the financial community; and commercial security documents. In-house support departments include the manufacture of inks used in company documents; design; research and development; engineering; and platemaking. Local affiliates include ABN Securities Systems Inc. (230 Park Avenue, New York NY 10169). Offices are located throughout the United States, including Atlanta, Boston, Chicago, Cleveland, Dallas, Detroit, Houston, Los Angeles, Milwaukee, Philadelphia, and San Francisco. International offices located in England and New Zealand. Corporate headquarters location.

BOWNE & COMPANY INC.
345 Hudson Street, 10th Floor
New York NY 10014
212/924-5500
Contact Personnel Department. Founded in 1775; engaged in providing nationwide information management and compliance documentation services through principal business segments: financial printing. Printing activities are divided into three categories: financial, corporate, and commercial and legal printing. Services in this segment include the typesetting and printing of compliance documentation relating to corporate and municipal financings, mergers, and acquisitions; the dissemination of information by companies through annual and interim reports and proxy material; and the printing of materials unrelated to compliance, such as business forms and reports, newsletters, promotion aids, market letters, and sales literature, and legal printing products such as briefs and records used by attorneys. Clients include architects and engineers, attorneys, and governmental agencies. Operates through subsidiary companies in Atlanta; Boston; Chicago; Cincinnati; Cleveland; Dallas; Denver; Detroit; Houston; Irvine; Los Angeles; Minneapolis; Montreal; New Orleans; N.Y.C.; Oklahoma City; Philadelphia; Phoenix; St. Louis; San Francisco; Seattle; Toronto; Washington, DC. New York-based subsidiaries include Legal Systems Inc. (provides computer-based document preparation services in New York); Garber-Pollack Company (pamphlet binders, printers, and mailers); and Intergraphic Technology, Inc. (corporate, textbook, and commercial printers). Corporate headquarters location. International. American Stock Exchange.

CHARLES COMMUNICATIONS
1290 Avenue of the Americas
New York NY 10104
212/924-7551
Contact Personnel Director. Provides a complete range of offset, lithography, and other printing services.

EMPIRE COLOR LITHOGRAPHY INC.
200 Varick Street
New York NY 10014
212/924-7866
Contact Personnel. Provides full service printing and lithography. Corporate headquarters location.

INDEPENDENT PRINTING COMPANY
5-15 49th Avenue
Long Island City NY 11101
Contact Jesse Mapias, Personnel Director. Provides a full range of commercial and specialized printing services. Corporate headquarters location.

LATHAM PROCESS CORPORATION
200 Hudson Street
New York NY 10013
212/966-4500
Contact Mr. George Stern, Personnel Director. Engaged in printing and lithography.

MASTER EAGLE GRAPHIC SERVICES
40 West 25th Street, 8th Floor
New York NY 10010
212/924-8277
Contact Clarence Baylis, Personnel Director. Provides offset printing and color separation services.

MICKELBERRY CORPORATION
405 Park Avenue
10th Floor
New York NY 10022
Contact Personnel Department. A holding company with a growing communications services business consisting of three advertising agencies, three marketing companies, and a commercial printing group. Each subsidiary operates autonomously, with parent company's relationship confined to financial matters and corporate development. Operating subsidiaries are: Laurence, Charles & Free, Inc., an advertising agency with numerous major national clients; Clavillo, Shevack & Partners, Inc., an advertising agency also with many national clients; Cunningham & Walsh, an advertising/marketing agency with five full-service offices nationwide, including Chicago, San Francisco, Los Angeles, and Dallas; marketing agencies Caribiner, Inc., Direct Marketing Agency, Inc., and Ventura Associates; and Sandy-Alexander, a lithographer specializing in high-quality color reproduction. Companies should be contacted directly. Corporate headquarters location. New York Stock Exchange. Common positions include: Accountant.

POTOMAC GRAPHICS
508 West 26th Street
New York NY 10001
212/924-4880
Contact Rose Foley, Personnel Director. A full service printing and graphic arts firm. Other branch locations in Boston and Detroit. Corporate headquarters location.

REILLY NEW YORK GRAPHICS
508 West 26th Street, 8th Floor
New York NY 10001
212/463-0058
Contact Personnel Director. Provides complete range of graphics services. Headquarters location.

SORG PRINTING COMPANY INC.
345 Hudson Street, 10th Floor Mail Room
New York NY 10014
212/741-6600
Contact Personnel Manager. A nationwide printing services firm, specializing in services to the financial industry. Corporate headquarters location.

SUPERIOR PRINTING INK CO. INC.
70 Bethune Street
New York NY 10014
212/741-3600
Contact Hal Rubin, Office Manager. Manufactures inks and pigments used in lithographic and other printing processes. Headquarters location.

Connecticut

IMPRINT NEWSPAPERS
P.O. Box 270002
West Hartford CT 06127-0002
203/236-3571
Contact Personnel Administrator. A printing and publishing firm. Operations include: printing; administration; and sales. Corporate headquarters location. Common positions include: Accountant; Administrator; Advertising Worker; Customer Service Representative; Department Manager; Management Trainee; Programmer; Reporter/Editor; Sales Representative; Systems Analyst; Press Operator; Offset Stripper; Typesetter. Principal educational backgrounds sought: Accounting; Art/Design; Business Administration; Communications; Computer Science; Finance; Liberal Arts; Marketing. Company benefits include: medical insurance; dental insurance; life insurance; disability coverage; employee discounts (newspaper); savings plan.

SWAN COLOR GRAPHICS
31 Wardin Avenue
Bridgeport CT 06605
203/366-4308
Contact Lou LaCroce, Personnel Director. Provides commercial photography and graphics services.

New Jersey

CERAGRAPHIC/CERAGLASS, INC.
171 South Newman Street
Hackensack NJ 07601
201/489-8260
Contact Personnel. A graphic arts firm engaged in silkscreen printing on glass.

DELUXE CHECK PRINTERS, INC.
5 Henderson Drive
West Caldwell NJ 07006
201/575-0900
Contact Russ Perry, Personnel. Engaged in printing and selling a variety of checks, deposit tickets, and related forms to banks and other financial institutions. Also manufactures documents imprinted in magnetic ink. Printing operations are carried out in more than 50 plants throughout the United States.

FAULKNER TECHNICAL REPORTS
114 Cooper Center
7905 Browning Road
Pennsauken NJ 08109-4319
609/662-2070
Contact Betsey Radcliffe, Personnel Administrator. A leading Southern New Jersey technical publisher.

KODALEX PROCESSING SERVICES/QUALEX, INC.
16-31 Route 208
Fair Lawn NJ 07410
201/797-0600
Contact Karen Mergenthaler, Plant Personnel Manager. A major photofinishing company in the United States providing processing services for print and reversal type films. Common positions include: Customer Relations Specialist; Maintentance Mechanic; Electronic Technician; Photo Processor; Printer; Clerical Worker. Principal educational backgrounds sought: Photography; Electronic Technician. Company benefits include: medical, dental, and life insurance; pension plan; tuition assistance; profit sharing; employee discounts; savings plan. Corporate headquarters location: Durham, NC. Parent

companies: Eastman Kodak Co. & Fuqua Industries. Operations at this facility include: film processing and printing; administration; service; sales; customer relations.

KOHL & MADDEN PRINTING INK CORP.
222 Bridge Plaza South, Suite 701
Fort Lee NJ 07024
201/886-1203
Contact Nick Aselta, Controller. Produces printing inks, compounds, and varnishes. Sales offices located throughout the United States. Headquarters location.

MACNAUGHTON EINSON GRAPHICS
20-10 Maple Avenue
P.O. Box 344
FairLawn NJ 07410
201/423-1900
Contact Personnel. Provides a full range of commercial printing services.

MEEHAN-TOOKER, INC
55 Madison Circle Drive
East Rutherford NJ 07073
201/933-9600
Contact Linda Scarry, Personnel Manager. Provides a complete range of commercial printing services. Common positions include: Customer Service Representative (Production Co-ordinator); Sales Representative; Estimator. Principal educational backgrounds sought: Graphic Arts. Company benefits include: medical, dental and life insurance; disability coverage; profit sharing. Corporate location headquarters. Operations at this facility include: manufacturing; administration; sales. Privately held stock.

PAVEY ENVELOPE & TAG CORPORATION
25 Linden Avenue East
Jersey City NJ 07305
212/962-0440
Contact Ralph Pepe, Personnel Manager. Manufactures and prints envelopes and tags. Primary customers are publishing and insurance companies, banks, direct mail and pharmaceutical companies, brokers and jobbers. Operations include: manufacturing; research/development; administration service; sales. Corporate headquarters location. Common positions include: Customer Service Representative; Marketing Specialist; Sales Representative. Principal educational backgrounds sought: College education, preferrably some sales experience calling on above markets or industrial accounts. Some knowledge of paper and/or printing will be an advantage. Company benefits include: dental insurance; disability coverage; savings plan.

SEQUA CORPORATION
3 University Plaza
Hackensack NJ 07061
201/343-1122
Contact Mr. W.V. Machaver, Vice President. A diversified corporation, offering a wide range of industrial products, including pigments and printing inks; fine chemicals for the papermaking industry; aircraft instrumentation; and automotive products. Headquarters location.

REAL ESTATE: SERVICES, MANAGEMENT, AND DEVELOPMENT

For more information on professional opportunities in the real estate industry, contact the following professional and trade organizations, as listed beginning on page 449:

APARTMENT OWNERS AND MANAGERS ASSOCIATION
BROOKLYN BOARD OF REALTORS
BUILDING OWNERS AND MANAGERS ASSOCIATION
INSTITUTE OF REAL ESTATE MANAGEMENT

INTERNATIONAL ASSOCATION OF CORPORATE REAL ESTATE EXECUTIVES
INTERNATIONAL REAL ESTATE INSTITUTE
NATIONAL ASSOCIATION OF REAL ESTATE INVESTMENT TRUSTS
NATIONAL ASSOCIATION OF REALTORS

New York

CUSHMAN AND WAKEFIELD INC.
1166 Avenue of the Americas
New York NY 10036
212/841-7633
Contact Mrs. Grace Ben-Ezra, Employment Manager. Several area locations, including Lyndhurst, NJ; and Stamford and New Haven, CT. A commercial and industrial real estate firm, engaged in the management and leasing of commercial office space, appraisal, project development, and related services. Common positions include: Accountant; Computer Programmer; Financial Analyst; Systems Analyst. Principal educational backgrounds sought: Accounting; Business Administration; Computer Science; Finance; Liberal Arts; Marketing. Limited training programs and internships offered. Company benefits include: medical and life insurance; tuition assistance; disability coverage; 401K plan. Corporate headquarters location. Parent company: Rockefeller Group, Inc. Operations at this facility include: regional headquarters; research; service; sales.

DOUGLAS ELLIMAN GIBBONS & IVES
575 Madison Avenue
New York NY 10022
212/832-4100
Contact Cathy Kleiman, Personnel Recruiter. A major real estate firm engaged in many facets, including property management, consulting on new construction and conversions, apartment sales and rentals, insurance and appraisals. Corporate headquarters location. Most common positions include: Secretary; Clerical Worker. Other common postions include: Accountant (related); Administrator; (related); Computer Programmer; Customer Service Representative (related); Department Manager; Operations/Production Manager; Purchasing Agent. Principal educational backgrounds sought depends on department and position. Company benefits include: medical and life insurance; pension plan; disability coverage. Corporate headquarters location. Operations at this facility: administration; service; sales.

HELMSLEY-SPEAR INC.
60 East 42nd Street, Room 464
New York NY 10165
212/880-0603
Contact Helen Coppola, Personnel Assistant. Multiple area locations in New York, New Jersey, Arizona, California, Texas, and Illinois. One of the largest real estate service companies in the nation, offering the following services through a nationwide network of offices: Leasing (including Industrial Leasing, and Retail and Store Leasing divisions); Sales and Brokerage; Management; Development; Appraisals; Insurance; and Financing. Common positions include: Accountant; Architect; Computer Programmer; Financial Analyst; Personnel & Labor Relations Specialist; Purchasing Agent; Systems Analyst; Salesperson; Real Estate Broker. Principal educational backgrounds sought: Accounting; Business Administration; Computer Science; Finance. Company benefits include: medical insurance; life insurance; tuition assistance; disability coverage; profit sharing; employee discounts. Corporate headquarters location. Operations at this facility include: research/development; administration; sales.

CHARLES F. NOYES COMPANY INC.
22 Courtland Street
New York NY 10007
212/693-4400

Contact Kathy Ruggiero, Corporate Secretary. A commercial real estate agency, engaged in the management of office buildings, and other institutional buildings, from department stores to corporate offices. Corporate headquarters location.

ROCKEFELLER GROUP INC.
1230 Avenue of the Americas
New York NY 10020
212/489-3000
Contact Louise Ippolito, Director of Employment. Owns, manages, and operates Rockefeller Center, one of the city's best-known office complexes, housing Radio City Music Hall, NBC, and other corporate clients, as well as a skating rink, and many fine shops and restaurants. Corporate headquarters location.

New Jersey

JOS. L. MUSCARELLE, INC.
Essex Street & Route 17
Maywood NJ 07607
201/845-8100
Contact Joseph Muscarelle, Jr., President. Engaged in construction and real estate development. Completes more than $100 million in construction projects annually. Common positions include: Corporate Credit Manager; Draftsperson; Civil Engineer; Electrical Engineer; Mechanical Engineer; General Manager; Operations Manager; Personnel & Labor Relations Specialist; Purchasing Agent; Sales Representative; Estimator; Project Manager; Scheduler. Principal educational backgrounds sought: Accounting; Business Administration; Engineering; Finance; Marketing. Company benefits include: medical insurance; dental insurance; life insurance; tuition assistance.

TITAN GROUP, INC.
118 Mill Road
Park Ridge NJ 07656
201/930-0300
Contact Personnel Manager A major area general contracting firm, also engaged in real estate development and specialized construction activities. Corporate headquarters location.

RESEARCH AND DEVELOPMENT

New York

MECHANICAL TECHNOLOGY INC.
968 Albany-Shaker Road
Latham NY 12110
518/785-2879
Contact Steve Ellsworth, Staff Development Coordinator. Founded in 1961, MTI provides technical support to government and industry across a wide spectrum of activities, from contract research and its complementary technologies to prototype development and volume manufacture of products. Company's products are in service across the country, utilizing waste energy, generating power, increasing industrial output and ensuring operating reliability. Common positions include: Computer Programmer; Electrical Engineer; Mechanical Engineer; R&D Program Development Manager; Design Engineer; Controls Engineer; Marketing Engineer; Software Engineer. Principal educational background sought: Engineering. Company benefits include: medical, dental and life insurance; pension plan; tuition assistance; disability coverage; employee discounts; savings plan; retirement plan. Corporate headquarters location. Operations at this facility include: manufacturing; research/development; administration; service; sales. NASDAQ.

Connecticut

UNITED TECHNOLOGIES CORPORATION/
RESEARCH CENTER
400 Main Street (129-37)
East Hartford CT 06108
203/727-7000
Contact Fred Blish, Personnel Director. Provides research in the areas of gas turbine technology, electro-optics, high energy, solid state electronics, microelectronics, microwave physics, manufacturing technology, robotics, optics, computer sciences, computer programming, and instrument research. Corporate headquarters location.

New Jersey

METPATH INC.
1 Malcolm Avenue
Teterboro NJ 07608
201/393-5211
Contact Denise Stephenson, Director of Human Resources. Engaged in clinical and anatomic laboratory testing. Common positions include: Biologist; Chemist; Computer Programmer; Sales Representative; Systems Analyst; Medical Technologist. Principal educational backgrounds sought: Chemistry; Finance. Company benefits include: medical, dental, and life insurance; tuition assistance; disability coverage; profit sharing; employee discounts; savings plan; 401 K. Parent company: Corning Inc. Operations at this facility include: regional headquarters; administration; service; sales. New York Stock Exchange.

TELEDYNE ISOTOPES
50 Van Buren Avenue
Westwood NJ 07675
201/664-7070
Contact Personnel Director. Specializes in the field of isotopic analysis and nuclear technology. Parent company, Teledyne Inc., is a high-technology, multi-product corporation consisting of 130 individual companies employing 50,000 people nationwide. Nationally, company operates in four industrial areas: Aviation and Electronics; Machines and Metals; Engines, Energy, and Power; and Commercial and Consumer. Corporate headquarters location: Los Angeles, CA.

UNITED STATES TESTING COMPANY, INC.
1415 Park Avenue
Hoboken NJ 07030
201/792-2400, ext. 440
Contact Nancy Long, Corporate Employment Manager. An independent laboratory that provides services and products in the field of testing, inspection, research, engineering, product development, and scientific instruments. Common positions include: Accountant; Biologist; Chemist; Credit Manager; Draftsperson; Civil Engineer; Electrical Engineer; Mechanical Engineer; Metallurgical Engineer; Geologist; Branch Manager; Marketing Specialist; Personnel & Labor Relations Specialist. Principal educational backgrounds sought include: Accounting; Biology; Business Administration; Chemistry; Engineering; Geology; Marketing. Company benefits include: medical, dental, and life insurance; pension plan; tuition assistance; disability coverage; savings plan. Corporate headquarters location. Operations at this facility include: administration; service; sales.

RUBBER AND PLASTICS

For more information on professional opportunities in the rubber and plastics industries, contact the following professional and trade organizations, as listed beginning on page 449:

SOCIETY OF PLASTICS ENGINEERS

SOCIETY OF PLASTICS INDUSTRY

New York

ADVANCE INTERNATIONAL INC.
1200 Zerega Avenue
Bronx NY 10462
212/892-3460
Contact Anthony D. Iannuzzo, Assistant Controller. Engaged in the production and import/export of such products as holiday lighting sets, craft items, and other plastic products. Common positions include: Customer Service Representative; Data Entry Operator; Collector. Principal educational backgrounds sought include: Business Administration. Company benefits include: medical and life insurance; disability coverage. Corporate headquarters location. Operations at this facility include: manufacturing; administration; sales.

GARY PLASTIC PACKAGING CORPORATION
770 Garrison Avenue
Bronx NY 10474
212/893-2200
Contact Mark Varella, Personnel Director. Manufactures a wide range of plastic products, sold primarily to retailers. Corporate headquarters location.

REEVES BROTHERS INC.
1271 Avenue of the Americas
New York NY 10020
212/315-2323
Contact Personnel Manager. A major, diversified manufacturer of polyurethane foam and coated fabrics for industrial use, a processor of fabrics, and a manufacturer of consumer goods. Operates in four product groups: Apparel Textile Group, which operates through two divisions: Industrial Coated Fabrics, which processes and manufactures plastic and synthetic rubber coating, urethane transfer coating, fabricating printing blankets, and other coated fabrics; and Consumer Products, which manufactures men's and boy's sport shirts and underwear. Most manufacturing facilities are located in the Southeast. This facility houses the company's principal sales and executive offices. Administrative offices are located in Spartanburg, SC. New York Stock Exchange.

Connecticut

DANCO PRODUCTS, INC.
11 Danco Road
Putnam CT 06260
203/928-7911
Contact Jeanne L. Zesut, Manager, Human Resources. Custom-injected molded plastics manufacturer. Common positions include: Accountant; Customer Service Representative; Industrial Engineer; General Manager; Operations/Production Manager; Purchasing Agent; Quality Control Supervisor; Sales Representative. Principal educational backgrounds sought: Accounting; Business Administration; Engineering; Marketing. Company benefits include: medical insurance; dental insurance; life insurance; disability coverage. Operations at this facility include: manufacturing; administration; sales.

LORD CORP./SEAL DIVISION
Old Stratford Road
Shelton CT 06484
203/929-1461
Contact Sandy D'Alene, Employee Relations Manager. Produces rubber specialty products. Operations include: manufacturing. Corporate headquarters location: Erie, PA. Common positions include: Administrator; Blue-Collar Worker Supervisor; Buyer; Chemist; Customer Service Representative; Draftsperson; Industrial Engineer; Mechanical

Engineer; Operations/Production Manager; Personnel & Labor Relations Specialist; Quality Control Supervisor. Principal educational backgrounds sought: Business Administration; Chemistry; Engineering; Marketing. Company benefits include: medical insurance; dental insurance; pension plan; life insurance; tuition assistance; disability coverage; savings plan.

ROSS AND ROBERTS, INC.
1299 West Broad Street
Stratford CT 06497
203/378-9363
Contact Robert Kinghorn, Industrial Relations Manager. Manufacturer of vinyl products. Operations include: manufacturing. Common positions include: Accountant; Blue-Collar Worker Supervisor; Buyer; Chemist; Engineer; Electrical Engineer; Mechanical Engineer; Purchasing Agent; Quality Control Supervisor; Sales Representative; Transportation & Traffic Specialist. Principal educational backgrounds sought: Accounting; Business Administration; Chemistry. Company benefits include: medical insurance; pension plan; life insurance; disability plan.

New Jersey

AEP INDUSTRIES
125 Philips Avenue
South Hackensack NJ 07606
201/641-6600
Contact Gerald Niemira, Director of Personnel. Produces a wide range of products in the plastics industry. Typical products include trash bags, tubing and sheeting opaque films, printed roll stock, mattress bags, furniture covers, carton liners, and shrink film. Three plants produce 75 million pounds annually. Corporate headquarters location.

ARWIN CORPORATION
301 Westside Avenue
Jersey City NJ 07305
201/432-8032
Contact Mr. Ira Sussman, Personnel Director. Produces a wide range of plastic and molded plastic items.

CREST-FOAM CORP.
100 Carol Place
Moonachie NJ 07074
201/641-9030
Contact Barry Sandler, Director of Personnel. Engaged in the manufacture, fabrication, processing and sale of polyurethane foam for use in a wide variety of products. A large portion of its business consists of the manufacture and fabrication of polyether foam for sale to the bedding, furniture, and carpet underlay markets. Also engaged in the business of manufacturing and selling foam for lamination and bonding of textiles used in home furnishings, automobiles, apparel, shoe linings and innersoles, luggage, leather goods, packaging materials, transportation equipment, novelties, advertising specialties, and toys. Also manufactures a specialized foam for use in air conditioners, humidifiers, stereo speakers, small engines, and other products in which filter material is needed. Corporate headquarters location. American Stock Exchange.

DYNASIL CORPORATION OF AMERICA
Cooper Road
Berlin NJ 08009
609/767-4600
Contact Charlene Menard, Office Manager. Major Southern New Jersey manufacturers of synthetic fused silicon.

GOODALL RUBBER COMPANY
Quaker Bridge Executive Center
Suite 203
Grovers Mill Road
Lawrenceville NJ 08648
609/587-4000
Contact Bonnie Gessner, Manager, Human Resources. A major Trenton rubber manufacturer and distribution and sales company, with 45 US and Canadian sales and service centers. Common positions include: Accountant; Blue-Collar Worker Supervisor; Chemist; Computer Programmer; Customer Service Representative; Chemical Engineer; Industrial Engineer. Principal educational backgrounds sought: Accounting; Business Administration; Chemistry; Engineering; Finance; Marketing. Company benefits include: medical insurance; pension plan; life insurance; tuition assistance; disability coverage; profit sharing; savings plan. Corporate headquarters location. Operations at this facility include: manufacturing; administration; service; sales.

MYRON MANUFACTURING CORP.
205 Maywood Avenue
Maywood NJ 07607
201/843-6464
Contact Eileen M. Yurish, Director, Human Resources. Manufactures a line of vinyl products for the office and business markets. Common positions include: Accountant; Computer Programmer; Customer Service Representative; Department Manager; General Manager; Management Trainee; Marketing Specialist; Purchasing Agent; Quality Control Supervisor; Statistician; Systems Analyst; IBM/38 Programmers. Principal educational backgrounds sought: Accounting; Business Administration; Finance; Marketing. Company benefits include: medical, dental, and life insurance; pension plan; tuition assistance; disability coverage; employee discounts; savings plan. Corporate headquarters location. Operations at this facility include: manufacturing; administration; service; sales.

NORTON CHEMPLAST, INC.
150 Dey Road
Wayne NJ 07470
201/696-4700
Contact Human Resources. Manufactures a wide range of plastic products and shapes, including pipes, rods, rubes, sheet, tape, rectangular stock, insulated wire, coaxial cable core; finished plastic products such as laboratory wire, coaxial cable core; finished plastic products; and nylon products such as rods, tubes, slabs, gear blands, and custom castings. A subsidiary of Norton Company (Worcester, MA), a producer of abrasives, petroleum, and mining products and services, and engineering materals and construction products. Corporate headquarters location.

PERMANENT LABEL
801 Bloomfield Avenue
Clifton NJ 07012
201/471-6617
Contact Personnel Department. Engaged in decorating and labeling of plastic products, primarily bottles. Corporate headquarters location

RAND MCNALLY/KIMBALL
151 Cortland Street
Belleville NJ 07109
201/759-6500
Contact Personnel Officer. A manufacturer of plastic and paper tags and label systems, designed to minimize shrinkage, reduce carrying costs, and facilitate check-out of retail and wholesale inventories.

SHAW PLASTIC CORPORATION
P.O. Box 3004
Middlesex NJ 08846
201/356-3100

Contact Personnel Department. Several area locations. A pioneer in the field of custom molding of plastics for industry. Offers a wide range of services, and is involved in every facet of the molding process from prototype and mold design, to long production runs of a wide range of thermoplastic and thermoset materials. Corporate headquarters location.

STAR-GLO INDUSTRIES, INC.
Two Carlton Avenue
East Rutherford NJ 07073
201/939-6162
Contact Personnel Director. A manufacturer of precision molded rubber and plastic parts, often bonded to metal. Sales are primarily to original equipment manufacturers in the business machine and computer, welding, food packaging equipment, chemical, and aerospace industries. Some major corporate customers include IBM, Pitney Bowes, Itek, Harris Corporation, Visual Graphics, Dorr-Oliver, LCP Chemicals. Corporate headquarters location.

VANGUARD PLASTICS INC.
18 Market Street
Paterson NJ 07501
201/523-5800
Contact Helen Meyersburg, Vice-President/Administration. A manufacturer of blow-molded custom and stock plastic containers. Operations include: manufacturing; research/development; administration; sales. Corporate headquarters location. Common positions include: Blue-Collar Worker Supervisor; Customer Service Representative; Engineer; Industrial Designer; Manager; Department Manager; General Manager; Operations/Production Manager; Marketing Specialist; Purchasing Agent; Quality Control Supervisor; Sales Representative; Machinist. Principal educational backgrounds sought: Accounting; Business Administration; Engineering; Marketing. Company benefits include: medical insurance; dental insurance; pension plan; life insurance; tuition assistance; disability coverage; profit sharing.

TRANSPORTATION: EQUIPMENT AND SERVICES

For more information on professional opportunities in the transportation industry, contact the following professional and trade organizations, as listed beginning on page 449:

AIRLINE EMPLOYEES ASSOCIATION
AIR TRANSPORT ASSOCIATION OF AMERICA
AMERICAN INSTITUTE OF AERONAUTICS AND ASTRONAUTICS
AMERICAN TRUCKING ASSOCIATION
ASSOCIATION OF AMERICAN RAILROADS
AUTOMOTIVE SERVICE ASSOCIATION
AUTOMOTIVE SERVICE INDUSTRY ASSOCIATION
AVIATION MAINTENANCE FOUNDATION
INSTITUTE OF TRANSPORTATION ENGINEERS
MARINE TECHNOLOGY SOCIETY
MOTOR VEHICLE MANUFACTURERS ASSOCIATION
MOTOR VEHICLE MANUFACTURERS ASSOCIATION/NEW YORK
NATIONAL AERONAUTIC ASSOCATION OF USA
NATIONAL AUTOMOTIVE DEALERS ASSOCIATION
NATIONAL INSTITUTE FOR AUTOMOTIVE SERVICE EXCELLENCE
NATIONAL MARINE MANUFACTURERS ASSOCIATION
PROFESSIONAL AVIATION MAINTENANCE ASSOCIATION
SHIPBUILDERS COUNCIL OF AMERICA

New York

AIR INDIA
345 Park Avenue
New York NY 10154
212/407-1300
Contact Mr. Metz, Personnel Administration Manager. A major international airline, with routes in most major cities throughout the world. United States headquarters location.

ALITALIA AIRLINES
666 Fifth Avenue
New York NY 10103
Contact Personnel Department. Mail resumes; Phone calls not accepted. Incorporated in 1946, the company serves as an international airline based in Italy, operating extensive passenger and freight airline routes throughout the world. Destinations include: the Americas, Europe, Africa, the Middle and Far East and Australia. Common U.S. positions include: Accountant; Clerical Support; Telephone Sales Representative; Passenger or Cargo Airport Agent; Sales Representative; Ticket Agent; Customer Service Representative or Specialist in Marketing; Public Relations Specialist; Personnel. Employment for flight crews and other overseas based employees are handled only through Rome Headquarters. Principal educational backgrounds sought: Accounting; Business Administration; Computer Science; Economics; Finance; Italian; Liberal Arts; Marketing; International Business. Company benefits include: medical insurance; dental insurance; pension plan; life insurance; disability coverage; 401K plan; travel discounts. Offices located in many major United States cities. United States corporate headquarters location: New York, NY. Operations at this facility include: regional headquarters; divisional headquarters; administration; service; sales; marketing.

AUBURN TECHNOLOGIES
100 Orchard Street
Auburn NY 13021
315/253-3241
Contact Henry Brown, Manager/Labor Relations. Manufacturer of diesel engines for the rail, marine, and industrial markets. Corporate headquarters location: Montreal, Canada. Operations at this facility include: manufacturing; administration; service; sales. Common positions include: Accountant; Buyer; Computer Programmer; Draftsperson; Industrial Engineer; Mechanical Engineer; Operations/Production Manager; Quality Control Supervisor. Principal educational backgrounds sought: Accounting; Business Administration; Engineering; Finance. Company benefits include: medical insurance; dental insurance; pension plan; life insurance; tuition assistance; disability coverage; employee discounts.

AVIS RENT A CAR SYSTEM, INC.
900 Old Country Road
Garden City NY 11530
516/222-3744
Contact Manager/Equal Opportunity & Employment. Primarily engaged, through its subsidiaries, in the business of renting and selling vehicles through a worldwide system operated by Avis and by independent licensees. Common positions include: Accountant; Administrator; Claim Representative; Computer Programmer; Customer Service Representative; Financial Analyst; Shift Manager; Marketing Specialist; Personnel Specialist; Public Relations Worker; Purchasing Agent; Clerk; Rental Agent; Sales Agent; Vehicle Service Agent. Principal educational backgrounds sought: Accounting; Business Administration; Communications; Computer Science; Finance; Liberal Arts; Marketing; Mathematics. Company benefits include: medical insurance; dental insurance; pension plan; life insurance; tuition assistance; disability coverage; employee discounts; savings plan; ESOP (Avis is employee owned and has an employee stock ownership plan).

CAMP BAUMANN BUSES INC.
107 Lawson Boulevard
Oceanside NY 11572
516/766-6740

Contact Helen Alloco, Personnel Office. Several area locations. A transportation management firm, providing bus service to local school districts, and a range of charter services. Corporate headquarters location.

CARDION ELECTRONICS/GENERAL SIGNAL
Long Island Expressway
Woodbury NY 11797
516/921-7300
Contact Daniel Croucher, Vice-President/Human Resources. Part of General Signal Corporation's Transportation Control segment. Several area locations, including Nassau and Suffolk counties. Designs, develops, and manufactures air traffic control, radar, display, navaid, meteorological equipment, and communications equipment for military, government, and international customers. Corporate headquarters location.

COLT INDUSTRIES
430 Park Avenue
New York NY 10022
212/940-0400
Contact Mr. Matt Martin, Director of Personnel. A diversified industrial firm engaged in the manufacture of aircraft landing gear and engine fuel systems, marine and power diesel engines, and automotive products.

THOMAS COOK TRAVEL
2 Penn Plaza, 18th Floor
New York NY 10121
212/967-4390
Contact James Herb, Human Resource Manager. A major international travel services corporation with over 325 offices in the U.S. (over 1,600 offices worldwide in 145 countries). Primarily, services include arranging travel routes, providing travelers checks and foreign exchange services, and many other travelers' services. Common positions include: Accountant; Financial Analyst; Branch Manager; Purchasing Agent; Sales Representative; Travel Agent. Principal educational backgrounds sought: Accounting; Business Administration; Finance; Liberal Arts; Marketing. Training programs offered; Internships offered. Company benefits include: medical, dental, and life insurance; tuition assistance; disability coverage; profit sharing; employee discounts; savings plan; travel benefits. Corporate headquarters location. Parent company: Maxwell/McMillan. Operations at this facility include: administration; service; sales.

DYNAIR
Dynair Building 150
JFK International Airport
Jamaica NY 11430
718/995-4450
Contact Lawrence Boe, Personnel Manager. Provides a wide range of ground services for airlines and airports. A subsidiary of Dynalectron Corporation. Corporate headquarters location.

EL AL ISRAEL AIRLINES
120 West 45th Street
New York NY 10036-9998
212/768-9200
Contact Personnel Office. An international air carrier, operating an extensive route system that includes major United States cities, and operations in Israel, Europe, and Africa. Corporate headquarters location.

ELLANEF MANUFACTURING CORPORATION
97-11 50th Avenue
Corona NY 11368
718/699-4000
Contact Ernest Contantine, Personnel Manager. Manufactures a wide range of aircraft components for major aerospace OEMs and airlines operating throughout the United

States. Corporate headquarters location. Common positions include: Aerospace Engineer; Quality Control Supervisor; Machinist; Quality Control Supervisors. Educational backgrounds sought: Mathematics. Company benefits include: medical, dental, and life insurance; pension plan; tuition assistance; disability coverage; profit sharing. Corporate headquarters location. Operations include: administration.

FARRELL LINES INCORPORATED
One Whitehall Street
New York NY 10004
212/440-4200
Contact Margaret Nasco, Manager/Human Resources. Several area locations, including Brooklyn, Queens, Manhattan. Operates a steamship service, with extensive shipping routes to West Africa, Australia, New Zealand, Europe, the Mediterranean region, the Middle East, India, and Pakistan. Corporate headquarters location. International. Common positions include: Accountant; Buyer; Claim Representative; Credit Manager; Customer Service Representative; Department Manager; General Manager; Personnel & Labor Relations Specialist; Sales Representative. Principal educational backgrounds sought: Business Administration. Company benefits include: medical, dental, and life insurance; pension plan; tuition assistance; disability coverage. Corporate headquarters. Operations at this facility include: administration. New York Stock Exchange.

FLIGHT SAFETY
Marine Air Terminal
La Guardia Airport
Flushing NY 11371
718/565-4100
Contact Mrs. Gigi Ghear, Director of Personnel. A company engaged in the training of corporate pilots on flight simulators.

GARRETT GENERAL AVIATION/
SERVICES DIVISION
2221 Smithtown Avenue
Ronkonkoma NY 11779-7387
516/585-4700, ext. 227
Contact Martha Screeney, Manager, Human Resources. Parent company, Allied Signal Corporation, serves a broad spectrum of industries through its more than 40 strategic businesses, which are grouped into five sectors: Aerospace; Automotive; Chemical; Industrial and Technology; and Oil and Gas. Allied Signal is one of the nation's largest industrial organizations, and has 115,000 employees in over 30 countries. Common positions include: Blue-Collar Worker; Mechanical & Electrical Craft Trades. Principal educational backgrounds sought: FAA-Licenses. Company benefits include: medical, dental, and life insurance; pension plan; tuition assistance; disability coverage; profit sharing; employee discounts; savings plan. Corporate headquarters location: Phoenix, AZ. Operations at this facility include: service-aircraft maintenance. Parent company is listed on New York Stock Exchange.

GENERAL MOTORS CORPORATION
767 Fifth Avenue, 26th Floor
New York NY 10153
Contact Director/Placement & College Relations. One of the world's largest vertically-integrated manufacturers and distributors of automobiles, trucks, and related parts and accessories. Automobile divisions include: Chevrolet, Buick, Oldsmobile, Pontiac, and Cadillac. Trucks are sold under the GMC name. Subsidiary GMAC (General Motors Acceptance Corporation) provides financing for company products, other financial services, and certain types of automobile insurance to dealers and customers. Company employs more than 650,000 people worldwide. Corporate headquarters location: Detroit, MI. New York Stock Exchange. International.

GREYHOUND CORPORATION
625 Eighth Avenue
New York NY 10018
212/971-6300
Contact Joe Huguley, Personnel Department. Nationally, company is a diversified holding company operating through several subsidiary and affiliated corporations. Subsidiaries operate in four cohesive groups: Greyhound Lines is a common carrier bus firm, with operations throughout the United States with more than 5,000 buses and more than 3,000 stop facilities; Greyhound Manufacturing Group operates in the United States and Canada, and builds bus shells, assembles intercity buses for sale to company and unaffiliated customers, and fabricates and sells bus parts; financial operations consist of companies engaged primarily in equipment financing, computer leasing, and money order and insurance services in the United States and abroad (includes Greyhound Computer Corporation); Armour & Company divisions and subsidiaries are engaged in the slaughter of livestock and poultry, purchases and sells meats and animal products and by-products, and manufactures, processes, and sells other food products including cheese, butter, and food oil products; services subsidiaries provide services directed to business markets, including aircraft ground handling services, temporary help services, convention and exhibition services, and other products and services directed to consumer markets, including hobby craft kits. Corporate headquarters location: Phoenix, AZ. International. New York Stock Exchange.

GULL ELECTRONIC SYSTEMS
300 Marcus Boulevard
P.O. Box 9400
Smithtown NY 11787
516/231-3737
Contact Dan Brennan, Employment Manager. Manufactures and distributes aerospace instrumentation and equipment, including fuel flow instruments. Corporate headquarters location.

**HARRISON RADIATOR DIVISION/
GENERAL MOTORS**
200 Upper Mountain Road
Lockport NY 14094
716/439-2354
Contact Susan Krinock, Salaried Personnel. Manufactures auto components, including radiators, defrosters, heaters, heat exchangers, air conditioners and thermostats. Parent company, General Motors, is a major producer of cars, trucks, and buses sold worldwide; the firm has 152 facilities operating in 26 states and 93 cities in the United States and 13 plants in Canada, and also has assembly, manufacturing, distribution, sales or warehousing operations in 37 other countries.

LIBERTY LINES
P.O. Box 624
Yonkers NY 10703
914/969-6900
Contact Mrs. Carol Terranova, Personnel Manager. One of the largest and most diversified bus services in the Yonkers/Westchester area. Services include commuter bus operations, transit bus operations, and school contracts. Common positions include: Bus Driver; Diesel Mechanic. Company benefits include: medical, dental, and life insurance; disability coverage. Corporate headquarters location. Operations at this facility include: administration; service; sales.

THE LONG ISLAND RAILROAD COMPANY
Jamaica Station
Jamaica NY 11435
718/990-7400
Contact Employment Department. Operates the third oldest active railroad in the United States; now a subsidiary of the Metropolitan Transportation Authority (see separate listing). Operates extensive commuter passenger and freight service railroad operations,

primarily between New York City and numerous points on Long Island. One of the busiest passenger railroad operations in the United States. Corporate headquarters location.

LUFTHANSA GERMAN AIRLINES
1640 Hempstead Turnpike
East Meadow NY 11554
516/794-2020
Contact David Buisch, Personnel Manager. Several area locations. An international air carrier of people and goods, to 85 countries and 174 cities around the world. United States locations include: New York, Boston, Atlanta, Dallas, Miami, Chicago, Philadelphia, Los Angeles, San Francisco, Anchorage, Houston, Washington, San Juan. Common positions include: Accountant; Administrator; Advertising Worker; Attorney; Buyer; Computer Programmer; Credit Manager; Customer Service Representantive; Financial Analyst; Department Manager; Marketing Specialist; Personnel & Labor Relations Specialist; Purchasing Agent; Public Relations Specialist; Sales Representative; Statistician; Systems Analyst; Reservations Agent. Principal educational backgrounds sought: Accounting; Business Administration; Computer Science; Economics; Finance; Liberal Arts; Marketing; Geography; Languages. Company benefits include: medical, dental and life insurance; pension plan; disability coverage; employee discounts; savings plan; flight benefits. Corporate headquarters location: Cologne, West Germany. This facility is headquarters for USA. International. Operations at this facility include: administration; sales. European Stock Exchange.

McALLISTER BROTHERS INC.
17 Battery Place
New York NY 10004
212/269-3200
Contact Jean Brown, Director of Personnel. A major United States marine services firm, providing ship docking, deep-sea and coastwise towing, oil transportation, bulk transportation, special projects such as positioning of tunnel and bridge segments and other services to the transportation industry, and full-service in-house capabilities through a complete packaged transportation service to shippers. Company now operates one of the largest fleets of tugs and barges on the East Coast and in the Caribbean, with ship docking services in New York, Philadelphia, Norfolk (VA), Charleston (SC), Jacksonville (FL), Baltimore (MD) and Puerto Rico. Marine towing and transportation services are operated along the East Coast, in the Caribbean, through the New York State barge canal system, and in the Great Lakes and St. Lawrence River. Common positions include: Accountant; Administrator; Claim Representative; Computer Programmer; Financial Analyst; Department Manager; General Manager; Management Trainee; Operations/Production Manager; Personnel & Labor Relations Specialist; Public Relations Worker; Sales Representative. Principal educational backgrounds sought: Accounting; Business Administration; Communications; Engineering; Finance; Marketing. Company benefits include: medical, dental and life insurance; disability coverage. Corporate headquarters location. Operations at this facility include: service.

METROPOLITAN SUBURBAN BUS AUTHORITY
700 Commercial Avenue
Garden City NY 11530
516/542-0100
Contact Manager of Personnel. Several area locations. A public service transportation agency; operates as part of the Metropolitan Transportation Authority (see following listing). Provides public bus transportation services between various points in Nassau County and New York City. Funding is largely provided by Nassau County through state and federal programs. Common positions include: Accountant; Buyer; Computer Programmer; Financial Analyst; Department Manager; Personnel & Labor Relations Specialist; Transportation Planner. Principal educational backgrounds sought: Accounting; Computer Science: Finance; Liberal Arts; Urban Planning. Company benefits include: medical, dental and life insurance; pension plan; tuition assistance; disability coverage. Corporate headquarters location. Operations at this facility include: administration.

METROPOLITAN TRANSPORTATION AUTHORITY
347 Madison Avenue
New York NY 10017
212/878-7238
Contact Sr. Employment Representative. A public benefit corporation primarily devoted to obtaining funding for mass transportation in the New York City area, as well as serving as the headquarters for the MTA's constituent agencies: New York City Transit Authority; Metro-North Commuter Railroad Company, Long Island Railroad; Triborough Bridge and Tunnel Authority; Staten Island Rapid Transit Operating Authority; and the Manhattan and Bronx Surface Transit Operating Authority. Common positions include: Accountant; Attorney; Computer Programmer; Financial Analyst; Marketing Specialist; Public Relations Worker; Quality Control Supervisor; Systems Analyst; Capital Programs Project Coordinator. Internships available. Principal educational backgrounds sought: Accounting; Art/Design; Business Administration; Computer Science; Economics; Engineering; Finance; Liberal Arts; Marketing. Company benefits include: medical insurance; dental insurance; pension plan; life insurance; tuition assistance; disability coverage; savings plan. Corporate headquarters location

MONITOR AEROSPACE CORPORATION
1000 New Horizons Boulevard
Amityville NY 11701
516/957-2300, ext. 192
Contact Richard P. Dallari, Manager, Human Resources. Manufactures precision structural aerospace parts for commercial and military craft. Common positions include: Mechanical Engineer; Computer Programmer; Manufacturing Engineer; Numerical Control Programmer; Quality Control Inspector. Principal educational backgrounds sought: Computer Science; Mechanical Enineering Technology; Liberal Arts; Technology. Training programs offered. Company benefits include: medical insurance; dental coverage; pension plan; life insurance; tuition assistance; disability coverage (STD/LTD); profit sharing; 401 K; employee discounts; on-site medical/dental facility. Corporate headquarters location. Operations at this facility include: manufacturing; administration.

NEPTUNE WORLD WIDE MOVING INC.
55 Weyman Avenue
New Rochelle NY 10805
914/632-1300
Contact Margaret Frakes, Personnel Director. Several area locations, including New York City, and Long Island City, NY; Danbury, CT; and East Brunswick, and Secaucus, NJ. Operates the largest privately-owned moving firm in the country, with branch offices and affiliates located throughout the country. Moving services provided to households, major commercial and industrial firms, and customers needing specialized handling and moving services, such as electronics manufacturers and others. Company operates 19 offices nationwide, including facilities in Buffalo (Depew), Rochester (West Henrietta), Atlanta, Chicago (Elk Grove Village), San Francisco, Los Angeles, Nashua (NH), St. Louis, Pittsburgh, Alexandria (VA), Durham (NC), Binghamton (NY), and East Syracuse. Over 700 service affiliates are located throughout the United States. Corporate headquarters location.

NEW YORK STATE DEPT. OF TRANSPORTATION
Albany Campus
1220 Washington Avenue
Albany NY 12232
518/457-6195
Contact Greg Montague, Director of Personnel Bureau. Engaged in the planning, design, construction, operation and/or maintenance of public transit modes, railroads, highways, airports, and ports and waterways in New York State. Employs 12,800 people. Eleven Regional Locations involved in design, construction, right of way acquisition, planning, and project management, etc. Corporate headquarters location. Operations at this facility include: research/development; administration. Common positions include: Administrator; Civil Engineer; Transportation & Traffic Specialist. Principal educational backgrounds

sought: Engineering. Company benefits include: medical insurance; dental insurance; pension plan; life insurance; tuition assistance; disability coverage; savings plan.

PAN AMERICAN WORLD AIRWAYS INC.
200 Park Avenue, 9th Floor
New York NY 10166
212/880-1234, ext. 28
Contact Director of Placement. Principal business is the transportation of persons, property, and mail between certain points in the United States, its territories and possessions, and foreign countries. Pan Am's operating routes provide service to 39 cities in the United States and territories and possessions, and to 53 cities in 44 foreign countries and territories. Pan Am World Services, a wholly-owned subsidiary, provides management and technical services for government and commercial projects both in the United States and abroad. Corporate headquarters location. International.

PORT AUTHORITY OF NEW YORK & NEW JERSEY
One World Trade Center
44 North
New York NY 10048
212/775-8700
Contact Julie Bell, Employment Division. Multiple area locations, including Fort Lee and Newark, NJ; and Queens, NY. A government-established transportation agency responsible for the operation, maintenance, and development of public transportation facilities within the New York-New Jersey metropolitan area, and the promotion and protection of commerce of the port of New York-Newark. The Authority operates Kennedy, LaGuardia, and Newark International airports; The Lincoln and Holland tunnels; George Washington Bridge; marine terminals in New York City and Newark; the Port Authority Bus Terminal; The World Trade Center; and the PATH Rapid Transit System. Corporate headquarters location. International.

QUEENS TRANSIT CORPORATION
124-15 28th Avenue
Flushing NY 11354
718/445-3100
Contact Office Manager. A major area public transportation firm providing service throughout Queens. More than 300 buses operate on nearly 20 route lines throughout the area. Corporate headquarters location.

STANDARD MOTOR PRODUCTS INC.
37-18 Northern Boulevard
Long Island City NY 11101
718/392-0200
Contact Mr. Loy Rosner, Employment Manager. Engaged primarily in the manufacture of electrical and fuel system automotive replacement parts. Parts are sold under the Standard Blue Streak, Hygrade, Champ, and Four Seasons brand names throughout the United States and in many foreign countries. The company employs over 3,500 people at its plants and warehouses in the United States, Canada, and Puerto Rico and Hong Kong. Products include ignition products, automotive wire and cable products, carburetor parts and kits, general service auto parts (radio antennas, gasoline cans, brooms and brushes, polishing cloths, fuses, and other auto accessories), and automotive heating and air conditioning systems. Common positions include; Accountant; Buyer; Computer Programmer; Draftsperson; Electrical Engineer; Industrial Engineer; Mechanical Engineer; Financial Analyst; Industrial Designer; Purchasing Agent; Quality Control Supervisor; Statistician; Systems Analyst; Technical Writer/Editor. Principal educational backgrounds sought: Business Administration; Computer Science; Engineering; Finance; Marketing. Company benefits include: medical, dental and life insurance; pension plan; tuition assistance; disability coverage; profit sharing. Corporate headquarters location. Operations at this facility include: manufacturing; research/development; administration. New York Stock Exchange. International.

SUFFOLK TRANSPORTATION SERVICE INC.
10 Moffit Boulevard
Bayshore NY 11706
516/665-3245
Contact Mrs. Tupper, Personnel Department. An area transportation firm, providing bus service primarily to local school districts. Corporate headquarters location.

TRW/BEARINGS DIVISION
402 Chandler Street
Jamestown NY 14701
716/661-2600
Contact Personnel Department. Produces MRC brand ball bearings, roller bearings and speciality steel balls for passenger cars, trucks, tractors, off-the-road machinery, power transmission machinery, office machines, computers, machine tools, electric motors, jet engines, nuclear power and other industrial applications. Parent company, TRW, is a diversifed technology firm with operations in electronics and space systems, car and truck equipment for both original equipment manufacturers and the replacement market, and a wide variety of industrial and energy components, including aircraft parts, welding systems, and electromechanical assemblies. New York Stock Exchange. Corporate headquarters location: Cleveland, OH.

TELEPHONICS
770 Park Avenue
Huntington NY 11743
516/549-6000
Contact Mrs. Wynsome Foulkes, Personnel Director. A leading supplier of advanced engineering products for industrial, military, and aerospace applications. Established in 1933 as a manufacturer of aircraft microphones and headsets, the company has grown into a major worldwide concern with a diversified line of products serving 17 markets in more than 90 countries. Company is the largest supplier of cabin and flight deck avionics for the commercial airline industry, with systems in use by more than 60 different airlines. Company also serves the military and aerospace markets with a complete line of secure communications systems, advanced avionics, and sonar support systems. Also plays a dominant role in the commercial acoustics field, with products ranging from lightweight telephone headsets to highly sensitive earphones used for clinical hearing analysis, as well as company's traditional line of aircraft microphones and headsets. Corporate headquarters location.

TRANS WORLD AIRLINES
100 South Bedford Road
Mount Kisco NY 10549
914/242-3000
Contact Personnel. A major airline.

WE TRANSPORT INC.
42 East Carl Street
Hicksville NY 11801
516/822-5800
Contact Paul Johnston, General Manager. Several area locations. An area school bus and van company, which also operates over-the-road coach buses. Common positions include: Accountant; Administrator; Claim Representative; Customer Service Representative; Industrial Engineer; Financial Analyst; Insurance Agent/Broker; Branch Manager; Department Manager; General Manager; Management Trainee; Operations/Production Manager; Personnel & Labor Relations Specialist; Public Relations Worker; Purchasing Agent; Reporter/Editor; Sales Respresentative; Transportation & Traffic Specialist; Underwriter; Bus Driver; Mechanic. Principal educational backgrounds sought: Accounting; Business Administration; Computer Science; Economics; Finance; Liberal Arts. Company benefits include: medical, dental and life insurance; tuition assistance; disability coverage; profit sharing; employee discounts. Corporate regional and divisional headquarters location. Operations at this facility include: research/development; administration; service; sales.

YELLOW FREIGHT SYSTEMS INC.
149 Leroy
New York NY 10014
212/691-8203
Contact Branch Manager. Operates a major nationwide common carrier trucking firm, operating in more than 40 states with more than 230 terminals. Operates through two divisions: General Freight, which provides transportation of general commodities; and Special Hauling, which provides transportation of commodities requiring special handling, such as temperature-sensitive products and heavy machinery. Corporate headquarters location: Shawnee Mission, KS.

Connecticut

CONSOLIDATED FREIGHT CORPORATION
Old Danbury Road
Wilton CT 06897
203/834-3116
Contact Kelly Copeland, Human Resource Manager. Company provides business to business delivering of ground freight and air cargo. Common positions include: Computer Programmer; Customer Service Representative; Systems Analyst. Principal educational backgrounds sought: Business Administration; Computer Science; Mathematics; Software Engineer. Company benefits include: medical, dental, and life insurance; pension plan; tuition assistance; disability coverage; profit sharing; savings plan; 401 K. Corporate headquarters location: Portland, Oregon. Operations at this facility include: development.

EMERY WORLDWIDE
Old Danbury Rd.
Wilton CT 06897
203/834-3330
Contact Manager of Human Resources. A leader in the air cargo overnight transportation services industry, with over 150 offices. The company offers a controlled lift, closed loop transportation system. Serves all industries. Corporate headquarters location. International. New York Stock Exchange. Common positions include: Accountant; Administrator; Advertising Worker; Attorney; Buyer; Claim Representative; Computer Programmer; Financial Analyst; Department Manager; Marketing Specialist; Personnel & Labor Relations Specialist; Programmer; Public Relations Worker; Purchasing Agent; Software Engineer Systems Analyst; Transporation & Traffic Specialist; Principal educational backgrounds sought: Accounting; Business Administration; Computer Science; Economics; Finance; Liberal Arts; Marketing. Company benefits include: medical insurance; dental insurance; pension plan; life insurance; tuition assistance; disability coverage; savings plan.

UNITED TECHNOLOGIES CORPORATION/
SIKORSKY AIRCRAFT DIVISION
6900 North Main Street
Stratford CT 06601-1381
203/386-6025
Contact Pam O'Neil, Personnel Director. An international leader in the design and manufacture of helicopters for commercial, industrial, and military use. Divisional headquarters location. Operations include: manufacturing; research/development; administration. Corporate headquarters location: Hartford, CT. Common positions include: Accountant; Buyer; Aerospace Engineer; Electrical Engineer; Industrial Engineer; Mechanical Engineer; Metallurgical Engineer; Financial Analyst; Programmer; Systems Analyst. Principal educational backgrounds sought: Engineering. Company benefits include: medical, dental, and life insurance; pension plan; tuition assistance; disability coverage; savings plan.

New Jersey

BMW OF NORTH AMERICA, INC.
P.O. Box 1227
Westwood NJ 07675-1227
201/307-3957
Contact Kevin Clark, Staffing Manager. A wholly-owned subsidiary of BMW (Bayerische Motoren Werke AG), the West German automobile and motorcycle manufacturer. Responsible for United States marketing operations for BMW's extensive line of fine motorcycles and automobiles. United States headquarters location. Corporate headquarters location: Munich, West Germany. Common positions include: Accountant; Administrator; Buyer; Computer Programmer; Credit Manager; Customer Service Representative; Mechanical Engineer; Financial Analyst; Department Manager; General Manager; Management Trainee; Marketing Specialist; Personnel and Labor Relations Specialist; Public Relations Specialist; Purchasing; Sales Representative; Systems Analyst. Principal educational backgrounds sought: Accounting; Business Administration; Communications; Computer Science; Economics; Engineering; Finance; Liberal Arts; Marketing. Training programs offered; Internships offered. Company benefits include: medical insurance; dental insurance; pension plan; life insurance; tuition assistance; disbility coverage; employee discounts; savings plan. Corporate headquarters location. Parent company: BMW AG.

BUTLER INTERNATIONAL, INC.
110 Summitt Avenue
P.O. Box 460
Montvale NJ 07645
201/573-8000
Contact Personnel Manager. A diversified service company with airline and corporate aviation services and contract services. Operates in three divisions: Butler Aviation, the largest aviation service company in the United States, serving 31 airports throughout the United States and Bermuda, and providing fueling and ground handling services for the corporate aviation market, domestic and international air carriers, and commuter airlines and air taxi operators; Butler Service Group, one of the world's leading multi-faceted technical and management services companies, providing technical and management personnel to the aerospace, marine, energy, electronics, communications, and many other industries through a network of 54 branch offices in the United States, Canada, and the United Kingdom, supplying more than 400 active clients with research, engineering, drafting, data processing, and other support services, including consulting, project management and engineering design for central office, outside plant, microwave, satellite and fiber optic systems, in addition to craft services to meet all project requirements. The Telecommunications Group has developed a strong relationship with AT & T and the Bell operating telephone companies. Common positions include: Accountant; Data Processor; Program Analyst; Internal Auditor.

EMERY WORLDWIDE
100 Port Street
Newark NJ 07114
201/985-5656
Contact Personnel Director. Other area location: Rahway, NJ. A diversified corporation operating through the following divisions: Purolator Courier Corporation (Basking Ridge, NJ), which provides overnight delivery of time-sensitive materials by ground and air transportation throughout the United States; Purolator Products Inc. (970 New Brunswick Avenue, Rahway NJ 07065), which manufactures and markets automotive, truck, and off-road vehicle filters and related products in the United States and Canada; Purolator Courier Ltd., which provides identical services to Purolator Courier Corporation in Canada; and Stant, Inc. (Connersville, IN), which manufactures and markets fuel caps, oil caps, radiator caps, and other related automotive products. Corporate headquarters location. New York Stock Exchange. International.

FALCON JET
777 Terrace Avenue
Hasbrouck Heights NJ 07604
201/288-5300
Contact Employment Coordinator. Another office location is: Teterboro Airport, Teterboro NJ 07608. Manufactures and sells a line of two- and three-engine business aircraft, featuring state-of-the-art safety features; and operates an international group of jet aircraft service and maintenance centers (Falcon Jet Service Centers), engaged in a wide range of jet aircraft engine, airframe, avionics, instruments, and accessories service, repair, and maintenance. Service centers in eight United States locations and throughout the world. A subsidiary of Dassault Breguet Aviation, France's largest aircraft manufacturer. Corporate headquarters location (United States operations). Interntional.

FEDERAL EXPRESS CORPORATION
110 Belmont
Somerset NJ 08873
212/777-6500
Contact Personnel Office. Company specializes in the overnight, door-to-door transportation of packages and documents (more than 180,000 shipments daily) through an operating fleet of more than 60 aircraft. Nationwide, company operates a network of 207 full-service stations throughout the United States, providing daily service to 281 major markets and 17,000 smaller communities. Owns and operates its own fleet of aircraft, and more than 4,500 radio-equipped vans which pick up and deliver shipments. Corporate headquarters location: Memphis, TN. New York Stock Exchange.

FORD MOTOR COMPANY
U.S. Highway 46
Teterboro NJ 07608
201/288-9400
Contact Personnel Department. Engaged in the manufacture, assembly, and sale of cars, trucks, and related parts and accessories. Nationally, company operates in four segments: North American Automotive; International Automotive; Diversified Products (includes Ford Aerospace & Communications, a world leader in communications satellites, and Ford Tractor Operations); and Finance and Insurance (primarily operating through subsidiary Ford Motor Credit Company). Corporate headquarters location: Dearborn, MI. New York Stock Exchange. International.

KEM MANUFACTURING COMPANY INC.
River Road
P.O. 351
Fair Lawn NJ 07410
201/427-2800, ext. 231
Contact Lois Blockburger, Personnel Administrator. Manufactures and markets a wide range of products for sale to the automotive aftermarket. Corporate headquarters location. Operations include: manufacturing. Common positions include: Accountant; Administrator; Advertising Worker; Blue-Collar Worker Supervisor; Buyer; Computer Programmer; Credit Manager; Customer Service Representative; Draftsperson; Mechanical Engineer; Department Manager; General Manager; Operations/Production Manager; Marketing Specialist; Personnel & Labor Relations Specialist; Programmer; Purchasing Agent; Quality Control Supervisor; Sales Representative. Principal educational backgrounds sought: Accounting; Business Administration; Computer Science; Engineering; Liberal Arts; Marketing. Company benefits include: medical insurance; pension plan; life insurance; tuition assistance; disability coverage; employee discounts.

WILLIAM McCULLOUGH TRANSPORTATION COMPANY INC.
340 South Stiles Street
Linden NJ 07036
201/353-2300
Contact Personnel Department. A common carrier trucking firm, with operations throughout the Eastern seaboard. Company transports general cargo, bulk liquids, construction materials, and many other products. Corporate headquarters location.

MERCEDES-BENZ OF NORTH AMERICA
1 Mercedes Drive
P.O. Box 350
Montvale NJ 07645
201/573-0600
Contact Staff Recruiter. Several area locations. A major importer of the complete line of Mercedes-Benz automobiles, commercial trucks, and related components. Distributes Mercedes products to dealers throughout the United States. A subsidiary of Daimler-Benz AG (Stuttgart, West Germany). Corporate headquarters location. International.

MOTOR CLUB OF AMERICA COMPANIES
484 Central Avenue
Newark NJ 07107
201/733-4040
Contact Thomas Fastiggi, Vice President. More than 25 area branches. Established in 1926 to serve New Jersey motorists. Now operates through three subsidiaries: Motor Club of America; Motor Club of America Finance Company; and Motor Club of America Insurance Company. Services include traveler's services, towing services, travel facilities, auto, homeowners, and small-business insurance, finance services, and many others. Corporate headquarters location.

NORTON, LILLY & COMPANY, INC.
200 Plaza Drive
Harmon Meadow
Secaucus NJ 07094
Contact Personnel Supervisor. A sea transportation firm, specializing in cargo-hauling in the United States. Handles collection, brokerage, and documentation. Corporate headquarters location.

SANTINI BROTHERS INC.
580 Gotham Parkway
Carlstadt NJ 07072
201/896-4777
Contact Mr. Antonio Galgani, Personnel Manager. Several area locations. A major area moving company, whose services include packing, crating, and shipping of household and commercial goods. Maintains a fleet of vans for inter- and intra-state moving, as well as providing overseas moving services. Corporate headquarters location. International. Common positions include: Accountant; Computer Programmer; Customer Service Representative; Programmer; Sales Representative; Sales Coordinator; Transportation & Traffic Specialist. Principal educational backgrounds sought: Accounting; Business Administration; Finance; Marketing; Transportation. Company benefits include: medical insurance; pension plan; life insurance; disability coverage.

SEATRAN LINES, INC.
270 Sylvan Avenue
Englewood Cliffs NJ 07632
201/871-8900
Contact Israel Farkas, VP/Personnel Director. An international corporation engaged in the container shipping, chartering, and energy industries. Primary operations involve the chartering of vessels for the transport of petroleum products, chemicals, and other commodities; the movement of containerized freight; and; the refining and distribution of petroleum products. International trade routes are principally between the United States and locations in the Caribbean, Europe, the Middle East, and the Far East. Corporate headquarters location. New York Stock Exchange. International.

SEQUA CORPORATION
3 University Plaza
Hackensack NJ 07061
201/343-1122

Contact Mr. W.V. Machaver, Vice President. A diversified corporation, offering a wide range of industrial products, including pigments and printing inks; fine chemicals for the papermaking industry; aircraft instrumentation; and automotive products. Headquarters location.

SUBARU OF AMERICA
Subaru Plaza
P.O. Box 6000
Cherry Hill NJ 08034
609/488-8500
Contact Steve Messana, Personnel Director. Corporate office for the well-known manufacturers for cars and trucks.

UNITED AIR LINES, INC.
Newark International Airport
Newark NJ 07114
201/624-1500
Contact Manager/Professional Employment. Personnel should be contacted at P.O. Box 66140, Chicago, IL 60666. A major air carrier of people and goods; provides more than 1,100 daily scheduled flights at 100 airports in the United States, Canada, and Mexico. New international routes to Japan and Hong Kong are being planned. Parent company (UAL, Inc.; Elk Grove, IL) is a holding company operating through United Air Lines, Westin Hotels (48 locations), and GAB Business Services. Corporate headquarters location: Elk Grove Township, IL. New York Stock Exchange (UAL, Inc.)

VOLVO NORTH AMERICA CORPORATION
P.O. Box 915
Building A
Rockleigh NJ 07647
201/767-4786
Contact Ellen Andretta, Human Resources Services Representative. Several area locations. United States distribution headquarters for the complete range of Volvo products, including automobiles, related components, marine products, and financial products and services. Parent company is a Swedish-based corporation. Corporate headquarters location (United States operations). International.

UTILITIES

For more information on professional opportunities in the utilities industry, contact the following professional and trade organizations, as listed beginning on page 449:

AMERICAN WATER WORKS ASSOCIATION
NEW YORK POWER AUTHORITY

New York

ALLEGHANY CORPORATION
Park Avenue Plaza
55 East 52nd Street, Suite 3300
New York NY 10055
212/752-1356
Contact Eileen Beck, Corporate Secretary. An electric and public utility company.

BROOKLYN UNION GAS
195 Montague Street
Brooklyn NY 11201
718/403-2000
Contact Lenore Puleo, V.P. of Personnel. A utility company which distributes gas to commercial and residential customers.

CENTRAL HUDSON GAS AND ELECTRIC
284 South Avenue
Poughkeepsie NY 12601
914/452-2000
Contact Gary Courtney, Personnel Assistant. Central Hudson is an investor owned utility.

CONSOLIDATED EDISON COMPANY
4 Irving Place
New York NY 10003
212/460-2014
Contact Kevin J. Morgan, Manager-Professional Placement. Multiple area locations, including all five boroughs, and Westchester County. Supplies electric service to all of New York City (except parts of Queens); also supplies natural gas in Manhattan, the Bronx, parts of Queens, and Westchester County; and steam in Manhattan. Corporate headquarters located in the borough of Manhattan. New York Stock Exchange. Common positions include: Accountant; Architect; Attorney; Computer Programmer; Engineer; Civil Engineer; Electrical Engineer; Industrial Engineer; Mechanical Engineer; Metallurgical Engineer; Financial Analyst; Systems Analyst; Nuclear Engineer. Principal educational backgrounds sought: Accounting; Computer Science; Engineering. Company benefits include: medical insurance; dental insurance; pension plan; life insurance; tuition assistance; disability coverage; employee discounts; savings plan

LONG ISLAND LIGHTING COMPANY
175 East Old Country Road
Hicksville NY 11801
516/933-4590
Contact Robert Kelleher, Vice-President/Human Resources. Supplies electric and gas service in Nassau and Suffolk counties, and the Rockaway Peninsula in Queens County. Service area covers 1,230 square miles, with a service area population of 2.7 million persons. Corporate headquarters location: Hicksville, NY. New York Stock Exchange.

NATIONAL FUEL GAS
30 Rockerfeller Plaza
New York NY 10112
212/541-7533
Contact John Solomon, Human Resources. Parent company for natural gas distributing companies, servicing Buffalo and Pennsylvania.

ORANGE & ROCKLAND
1 Blue Hill Plaza
Pearl River NY 10965
914/352-6000
Contact Nicholas Illobra, Personnel. A gas and electric utilites company.

Connecticut

CITIZENS UTILITIES
High Ridge Park
Stamford CT 06905
203/329-8800
Contact Don Owen, Human Resources. Executive headquarters for citizens utilities.

NORTHEAST UTILITIES
100 Corporate Place
Rocky Hill CT 06067
203/665-5000
Contact Mark Francini, Employment Coordinator. An electricity and gas utility company. Provides services to over one million customers. Corporate headquarters location.

UNITED ILLUMINATING CO.
P.O. Box 1564
New Haven CT 06506
203/787-7529
Contact Gerald Gleit, Employment Manager. An investor-owned electric utility system in the Southwestern part of Connecticut. Common positions include: Accountant; Buyer; Computer Programmer; Customer Service Representative; Electrical Engineer; Mechanical Engineer; Financial Analyst; Purchasing Agent. Principal educational backgrounds sought: Accounting; Engineering. Company benefits include: medical, dental, and life insurance; pension plan; tuition assistance; disability coverage. Corporate headquarters location. Operations at this facility include: regional headquarters. New York Stock Exchange.

New Jersey

AMERICAN WATER WORKS
1025 Laurel Oak Road
Voorhees NJ 08043
609/346-8200
Contact Anna M. Michini, Director, Personnel Administration. Acquires, manages, and services water companies across the country.

ATLANTIC ELECTRIC
P.O. Box 1264
Pleasantville NJ 08232
609/645-4100
Contact Bob Pavlocski, Senior Employment Representative. An electric utility company. Common positions include: Accountant; Civil Engineer; Electrical Engineer; Mechanical Engineer; Personnel & Labor Relations Specialist; Systems Analyst. Principal educational background sought: Accounting; Computer Science; Engineering. Company benefits include: medical, dental, and life insurance; pension plan; tuition assistance; disability coverage; savings plan; prescription and vision plan. Parent company: Atlantic Energy. Operations at this facility include: administration. New York Stock Exchange.

ELIZABETHTOWN GAS COMPANY
One Elizabethtown Plaza
Union NJ 07083
201/289-5000
Contact Human Resources Department. Several area locations, including Union, Woodbridge, New Village, and Flemington. A regulated public utility distributing natural gas within a franchised territory consisting of 70 New Jersey municipalities, including Elizabeth, Linden, Perth Amboy, Woodbridge, Union, Phillipsburg, Washington, Hackettstown, Newton, and Flemington. Operates more than 2,000 miles of pipeline. A subsidiary of National Utilities & Investors Corporation. Corporate headquarters location.

GPU SERVICE CORPORATION
100 Interpace Parkway
Parsippany NJ 07054
201/263-6743
Contact Ronald A. Moss, Staff Administrator. A major electric utility holding company, with several operating subsidiaries. Provides administrative services to their three operating companies. Common positions include: Accountant; Administrator; Electrical Engineer; Industrial Engineer; Personnel & Labor Relations Specialist; Systems Analyst. Principal educational backgrounds sought: Accounting. Corporate headquarters location. Operations at this facility include: administration. New York Stock Exchange.

PASSAIC VALLEY WATER COMMISSION
1525 Main Avenue
P.O. Box 230
Clifton NJ 07015
201/340-4300
Contact John Galletta, Personnel Director. Provides water utility service to communities in the area. Corporate headquarters location.

PUBLIC SERVICE ELECTRIC & GAS COMPANY
P.O. Box 570 (2A)
Newark NJ 07101
Contact Manager/Employment & Placement. Multiple area locations. The largest utility in New Jersey, serving approximately 5.4 million people; nearly three-fourths of the state's population. The company's service area, covering some 2,600 square miles, runs diagonally across the state's industrial and commercial corridor, from the New York State border on the north, to south of Camden. The highly diversified and heavily populated areas include six major cities, as well as nearly 300 suburban and rural communities. Common positions include: Computer Programmer; Electrical Engineer; Mechanical Engineer. Principal educational backgrounds sought: Computer Science; Engineering. Company benefits include: medical, dental, and life insurance; pension plan; tuition assistance; disability coverage; savings plan. Corporate headquarters location and field locations. Operations at these facilities include: regional headquarters: electric and gas transmission and distribution operations. New York Stock Exchange.

Professional Employment Services

ABLE PERSONNEL, INC.
280 Madison Avenue
New York NY 10016
Contact Dan Gardner, President. 212/689-5500. Employment agency. Appointment requested. Founded 1955. Member of APCNY, Better Business Bureau, National Employment Association. Specializes in the areas of: Advertising; Architecture; Construction; Engineering; Fashion; Personnel and Human Resources; Printing and Publishing; Real Estate; Sales and Marketing; Transportation; Purchasing. Positions commonly filled include: Accountant; Advertising Worker; Administrative Assistant; Architect; Bookkeeper; Buyer; Civil Engineer; Commercial Artist; Credit Manager; Customer Service Representative; Draftsperson; Electrical Engineer; Financial Analyst; General Manager; Industrial Designer; Industrial Engineer; Marketing Specialist; Mechanical Engineer; Operations/Production Specialist; Personnel and Labor Relations Specialist; Public Relations Worker; Purchasing Agent; Quality Control Supervisor; Reporter/Editor; Sales Representative; Technical Writer/Editor; Word Processing Specialist. Company pays fee.

ABSOLUTE ACTION
420 Lexington Avenue
New York NY 10107
Contact Jane Sanders, Manager. 212/692-9333. Employment agency; temporary help service. No appointment required. Founded 1982. Specializes in the areas of: Accounting and Finance; Banking; Clerical; Fashion; Legal; Manufacturing; Personnel and Human Resources; Sales and Marketing. Positions commonly filled include: Accountant; Advertising Worker; Administrative Assistant; Bookkeeper; Buyer; Clerk; Computer Operator; Computer Programmer; Credit Manager; Customer Service Representative; Data Entry Clerk; EDP Specialist; General Manager; Legal Secretary; Medical Secretary; Model; Office Worker; Operations/Production Specialist; Personnel and Labor Relations Specialist; Purchasing Agent; Quality Control Supervisor; Receptionist; Sales Representative; Secretary; Stenographer; Typist; Word Processing Specialist. Company pays fee. Number of placements per year: 201-500.

ABSOLUTELY PROFESSIONAL TEMPS, INC.
7 Dey Street
New York NY 10007
Contact Jack Talabisco. 212/608-1444. Specializes in the area of: temporary services (secretaries; word processing).

ACCOUNTANTS & AUDITORS AGENCY
310 Madison Avenue Suite 701
New York NY 10017
Contact Walter Murphy. 212/687-5656. FAX: 212/983-3538. Specializes in the areas of: audit; bookkeeping; budgeting; clerical; financial analysis; international; public accounting; tax; temporary services (accounting/bookkeeping).

ACCOUNTANTS UNLIMITED, INC.
2 W. 45th Street, Suite 1508
New York NY 10036
Contact Rosemary Madigan, Placement Manager. 212/840-7137. Employment agency; temporary help service. No appointment required. Founded 1984. Specializes in the areas of: Clerical; Word Processing. Positions commonly filled include: Administrative Assistant; Legal Secretary; Secretary; Typist; Word Processing Specialist. Company pays fee. Number of placements per year: 51-100.

ACCOUNTING AND COMPUTER PERSONNEL
220 Salina Meadows Pkwy. Ste. 220
Syracuse NY 13212
Contact William Winnewisser. 315/457-8000. FAX: 315/457-0029. Specializes in the areas of: audit; bookkeeping; budgeting; computer science (corporate/computer security; consulting; data processing; EDP audit; operations; programming; sales; software engineering; systems; technicians); financial analysis; international; public accounting; tax; sales (computers; services/intangibles).

ACTIVE TECHNICAL PERSONNEL
25 West 14th Street
New York NY 10011
Contact Elliot Elzweig, CPC. 212/924-8100. FAX: 212/924-8107. Specializes in the areas of: distribution (customer service; inventory control; materials handling; operations; planning; traffic); manufacturing/production (plant management; quality control; supervisory; technicians).

ADAM PERSONNEL, INC. & ADAM TEMPORARY SERVICES, INC.
11 E. 44th Street
New York NY 10017
Contact Jill Barry, Vice President. 212/557-9150. Employment agency; temporary help agency. No appointment required. Founded 1979. Aggressive, creative and realistic - Many the agency's client companies are recommended - Over 50 years experience. Specializes in the areas of: Accounting (clerical); Advertising; Banking and Finance; Insurance (clerical); Legal; Nonprofit; Publishing; Real Estate; Secretarial and Clerical. Positions commonly filled include: Administrative Assistant; Bookkeeper; Clerk; Customer Service Representative; Data Entry Clerk; Executive Secretary; Legal Secretary; Medical Secretary; Model/Receptionist; Receptionist; Secretary; Stenographer; Typist; Word Processor. Company pays fee. Number of placements per year: 201-500.

ADIA PERSONNEL SERVICES
41 East 42nd Street, Suite 212
New York NY 10017
Contact Branch Manager. 212/682-5530. Employment agency; temporary help service. Appointment requested. Founded 1957. Nonspecialized. Positions commonly filled include: Administrative Assistant; Advertising Worker; Clerk; Customer Service Representative; Data Entry Clerk; Demonstrator; Legal Secretary; Medical Secretary; Office Worker; Receptionist; Secretary; Stenographer; Typist; Word Processing Specialist. Company pays fee. Number of placements per year: 1000+.

ADVICE PERSONNEL, INC.
230 Park Avenue, Suite 903
New York NY 10169
Contact Shelley Lieff/Alan Schwartz. 212/682-4400. FAX: 212/697-0343. Specializes in the areas of: audit; bookkeeping; budgeting; clerical; financial analysis; public accounting; tax;

legal (paralegals); office administration (administrators; clerks; management; receptionists; secretaries; word processing).

ADWORLD PERSONNEL AGENCY
15 East 40th Street
New York NY 10016
Contact Richard Fuehrer, Owner. 212/889-6532. Employment agency. Appointment required. Founded 1984. One-on-one counseling in selected areas of Advertising. Positions commonly filled include: Administrative Assistant; Advertising Executive; Clerk; Executive Secretary; Media Planner; Public Relations Worker; Receptionist; Secretary; Traffic Coordinator; Word Processor. Company pays fee. Number of placements per year: 50-100.

THE AHRENS AGENCY, INC.
45 John Street, Suite 609
New York NY 10038
Contact Daniel J. Ahrens, President. 212/732-3600. Employment agency. No appointment required. Founded 1978. Specializes in the areas of: Banking; Brokerage; Insurance; Real Estate. Positions commonly filled include: Accountant; Administrative Assistant; Bank Officer/Manager; Credit Manager; Customer Service Representative; Financial Analyst; Office Worker; Receptionist; Secretary; Underwriter. Company pays fee. Number of placements per year: 51-100.

ALL HOME SERVICES AGENCY, LTD
2121 Broadway
New York NY 10023
Contact Nedra J. Kleinman, President. 212/799-9360. Employment agency. Appointment requested. Founded 1983. Specializes in the areas of: Domestic; Elderly; Health and Medical. Positions commonly filled include: Butler; Couple Companion; Driver; Housekeeper; Nanny; Nurse's Aide. Company pays fee. Number of placements per year: 201-500.

PAT ALLEN ASSOCIATES
P.O. Box Q
Golden's Bridge NY 10526
Contact Pat Allen, CPC. 914/232-1545. FAX: 914/232-1726. Specializes in the area of: insurance (actuarial; property/casualty; underwriting).

ALOE PERSONNEL
170 East Post Road
White Plains NY 10601
Contact Edward Aloe, President. 914/761-8900. Employment agency; temporary help service. Specializes in the areas of: Banking; Computer Hardware and Software; Office Personnel; Sales and Marketing. Positions commonly filled include: Administrative Assistant; Bank Officer/Manager; Clerk; Computer Operator; Receptionist; Sales Representative; Secretary; Technical Writer.

ALPHA PERSONNEL OF GARDEN CITY
600 Old Country Road
Garden City NY 11530
Contact Loretta Lynn, CPC. 516/228-9600. Specializes in the areas of: insurance (claims; life/health; property/casualty; rating; reinsurance; sales; underwriting); office administration (administrators; clerks; management; receptionists; secretaries; word processing); temporary services (secretaries; word processing).

ALPHA PERSONNEL OF JERICHO
333 N. Broadway Suite 2008
Jericho NY 11753
Contact Anthony Capece, President. 516/822-6000. Specializes in the areas of: insurance (claims; life/health; pension; property/casualty; rating; reinsurance; sales; underwriting); office administration (administrators; clerks; management; receptionists; secretaries; word processing).

AMERICAN DATA SEARCH & MANAGEMENT CONSULTANTS
160 Broadway, Suite 602
New York NY 10038
Contact H. K. Waldner, President. 212/385-0080. Employment agency. Appointment required. Founded 1979. Strong base in EDP/MIS per diem consulting. Specializes in the areas of: Computer Hardware and Software; MIS/EDP; Technical and Scientific. Positions commonly filled include: Accountant; Administrative Assistant; Computer Programmer; Customer Service Representative; Data Entry Clerk; EDP Specialist; Executive Secretary; Financial Analyst; Management Consultant; Personnel Director; Receptionist; Secretary; Statistician; Technical Writer/Editor; Technician; Word Processor. Company pays fee. Number of placements per year: 1-50.

ANTES ASSOCIATES
3010 Westchester Ave.
Purchase NY 10577
Contact Barbara Antes. 914/694-1977. FAX: 914/694-2935. Specializes in the area of: medical/health care (hospitals; medical secretaries; nurses; nursing homes; paraprofessionals).

TODD ARRO, INC.
232 Delaware Avenue
Buffalo NY 14202
Contact Joseph T. Todaro, CPC. 716/842-1300. FAX: 716/842-1249. Specializes in the area of: sales (consumer products; industrial products; management; medical products).

ASSOCIATION OF PERSONNEL CONSULTANTS OF NEW YORK STATE
322 Eigth Avenue, 12th Floor
New York NY 10001
Contact Joel Dolci, CAE, Executive Director. 212/645-1147. The Association of Personnel consultants of New York State, (APCNY) is a statewide strade organization comprised of 250+ member employment services placing candidates in permanent and temporary positions in the tri-state area (NY, NJ, CT). Members of the Association adhere to a stringent code of ethical business practices, promoting professionalism and the highest degree of ethical standards in the industry. APCNY publishes a comprehensive guide; the "Directory of Personnel Consultants by Specialization". It is an excellent reference tool for the job seeker, listing all current members and their areas of placement specialization. This Directory is available through the Association Headquarters.

AUSTIN EMPLOYMENT AGENCY
71-09 Austin Street
Forest Hills NY 11375
Contact David L. Wexler, Owner. 718/268-2700. Employment agency. Appointment required. Founded 1928. Specializes in Computer/Engineering, Sales/Marketing, top executive nationwide/ international. Specializes in the areas of: Architecture; Computer Hardware and Software; Construction; Engineering; Industrial and Interior Design; Manufacturing; Technical and Scientific. Positions commonly filled include: Architect;

Biomedical Engineer; Ceramics Engineer; Civil Engineer; Computer Programmer; Draftsperson; EDP Specialist; Electrical Engineer; General Manager; Industrial Engineer; Mechanical Engineer; Metallurgical Engineer; Personnel Director; Physicist; Systems Analyst. Number of placements per year: 201-500.

AUTOMOTIVE PERSONNEL AGENCY
271 Madison Avenue, Suite 605
New York NY 10016
Contact Howard Kesten, Manager. 212/922-9800. Employment agency. No appointment required. Founded 1986. Set up to provide placement services nationwide to the automotive industry, from dealers to parts managers. Specializes in the area of: Automotive. Positions commonly filled include: Accountant; Administrative Assistant; Automotive Parts Personnel; Bookkeeper; Clerk; Customer Service Representative; General Manager; Receptionist; Sales Manager; Sales Representative. Company pays fee. Number of placements per year: 1-50.

BAILEY EMPLOYMENT SERVICES
14 Church Street
White Plains NY 10601
Contact Frank DeLigio, CPC. 914/946-1383. Specializes in the area of: insurance (claims; property/casualty; rating; reinsurance; sales; underwriting).

THE BANKERS REGISTER
500 Fifth Avenue Suite 330
New York NY 10110
Contact Gilbert Tucker. 212/840-0800. Specializes in the areas of: asset; credit; international; investment; lending; trainees; trust.

BERMAN & LARSON ASSOC.
275 Madison Ave.
New York NY 10016
Contact Robert Larson. 212/685-7111. FAX: 212/986-3218. Specializes in the areas of: computer science (corporate/computer security; consulting; EDP audit; programming; software engineering; systems).

BI-LINGUAL AGENCY, LTD.
1841 Broadway, Suite 702
New York NY 10023
Contact Michele Morin, Director. 212/246-8568. Employment agency. Appointment required. Founded 1955. Specializes in Bilingual placements on all levels, but particularly Administrative Assistant. Specializes in the areas of: Accounting; Banking and Finance; Legal; Sales and Marketing; Secretarial and Clerical. Positions commonly filled include: Accountant; Administrative Assistant; Bookkeeper; Executive Secretary; Legal Secretary; Marketing Specialist; Receptionist; Sales Representative; Secretary; Typist; Word Processor. Company pays fee.

BIL-LU PERSONNEL AGENCY
60 East 42nd Street
Lincoln Building, Suite 3217
New York NY 10165
Contact Ms. JContact Ms.Jeanine Montas, Licensee/Owner. 212/972-6400. Employment agency. Appointment requested. Founded 1962. International and Bilingual personnel only. Specializes in the areas of: Accounting and Finance; Advertising; Banking; Engineering; Sales and Marketing. Positions commonly filled include: Accountant; Administrative

Assistant; Agricultural Engineer; Bank Officer/Manager; Biomedical Engineer; Bookkeeper; Buyer; Ceramics Engineer; Chemical Engineer; Civil Engineer; Credit Manager; Customer Service Representative; Data Entry Clerk; EDP Specialist; Economist; Electrical Engineer; Financial Analyst; General Manager; Industrial Engineer; Marketing Specialist; Mechanical Engineer; Metallurgical Engineer; Model; Nurse; Office Worker; Purchasing Agent; Sales Representative; Secretary; Statistician; Technical Writer/Editor. Company pays fee. Number of placements per year: 51-100.

BOTAL ASSOCIATES
7 Dey St.
New York NY 10007
Contact Jack Talabisco. 212/227-7370. FAX: 212/964-5033. Specializes in the area of: computer science (data processing).

BROADWAY PERSONNEL AGENCY, INC.
170 Broadway, Suite 3309
New York NY 10038
Contact Patrick Antanelle, C.P.C., President. 212/385-1690. Employment agency. Appointment requested. Founded 1963. Specializes in the areas of: Banking; Clerical; Insurance; Legal; Transportation; Secretarial; Wall Street. Positions commonly filled include: Accountant; Actuary; Administrative Assistant; Bank Officer/Manager; Bookkeeper; Claims Representative; Clerk; Credit Manager; Customer Service Representative; Financial Analyst; Insurance Agent/Broker; Legal Secretary; Loan Officer; Mortgage Officer; Office Worker; Receptionist; Secretary; Statistician; Stenographer; Traffic Specialist; Typist; Underwriter; Wall Street Operations Specialist; Word Processing Specialist. Company pays fee. Number of placements per year: 501-1000.

BROOKE PERSONNEL, INC.
420 Lexington Avenue
New York NY 10170
Contact John Kerr, President. 212/687-8400. Employment agency. Appointment required. Founded 1923. Specializes in the areas of: Accounting; Advertising; Architecture; Banking and Finance; Computer Hardware and Software; Insurance; Legal; Maufacturing; MIS/EDP; Secretarial and Clerical; Transportation. Positions commonly filled include: Accountant; Attorney; Actuary; Administrative Assistant; Bank Officer/Manager; Bookkeeper; Computer Programmer; Credit Manager; Customer Service Representative; Data Entry Clerk; Executive Secretary; Legal Secretary; Marketing Specialist; Medical Secretary; Personnel Director; Receptionist; Secretary; Stenographer; Systems Analyst; Technical Writer/Editor; Typist; Underwriter; Word Processor. Company pays fee. Number of placements per year: 201-500.

BRUCKS CONSULTANTS
300 Main St., Techniplex Center.
East Rochester NY 14445
Contact Murray Brandes. 716/248-9090. FAX: 716/248-5505. Specializes in the area of: engineering (chemical; electrical; environmental/hazardous waste; HVAC; industrial; manufacturing; mechanical; packaging; physics).

BRYANT BUREAU
1321 Central Avenue
Albany NY 12205
Contact Bob Prentiss, CPC. 518/459-4141. FAX: 518/459-5634. Specializes in the areas of: audit; bookkeeping; budgeting; clerical; computer science (corporate/computer security; consulting; data processing; EDP audit; operations; programming; sales; software

engineering; systems; technicians; word processing sales/service); engineering (chemical; civil; electrical; environmental/hazardous waste; HVAC; industrial; manufacturing; mechanical); financial analysis; hospitality/ hotel/ restaurant (food service; hotel; institutional; restaurant; travel); international; public accounting; tax; retailing (buying; management; merchandising; operations; sales).

THELMA BUSH ASSOCIATES
360 Lexington Ave. 20th Floor
New York NY 10017
Contact Thelma Bush, CPC. 212/986-2070. FAX: 212/697-0877. Specializes in the area of: insurance (property/casualty; reinsurance).

CFA GROUP, INC.
5790 Widewaters Parkway
Dewitt NY 13214
Contact Manager. 315/446-8492. FAX: 315/446-4247. Specializes in the areas of: audit; bookkeeping; budgeting; clerical; computer science (corporate/computer security; consulting; data processing; EDP audit; operations; programming; software engineering; systems) financial analysis; international; public accounting; tax; legal (legal administrators; legal secretaries; paralegals); office administration (administrators; clerks; management; receptionists; secretaries; word processing).

CALIBER PERSONNEL, INC.
11 John Street, Third Floor
New York NY 10038
Contact Rita Calvo, President. 212/233-9092. Employment agency. No appointment required. Founded 1982. Nonspecialized. Positions commonly filled include: Administrative Assistant; Legal Secretary; Receptionist; Secretary; Stenographer; Typist; Word Processing Specialist. Company pays fee. Number of placements per year: 201-500.

CAMEO TEMPORARY SERVICES, INC.
507 Fifth Avenue
New York NY 10017
Contact Manager. 212/986-1122. Employment agency; temporary help agency. No appointment required. Founded 1982. Positions commonly filled include: Administrative Assistant; Bank Officer/Manager; Bookkeeper; Clerk; Computer Programmer; Credit Manager; Customer Service Representative; Data Entry Clerk; EDP Specialist; Executive Secretary; Legal Secretary; Medical Secretary; Personnel Director; Receptionist; Sales Representative; Secretary; Stenographer; Typist; Word Processor. Company pays fee. Number of placements per year: 1000+.

J.P. CANON ASSOCIATES
225 Broadway, Suite 3602
New York NY 10007
Contact James E. Rohan. 212/233-3131. FAX: 212/233-0457. Specializes in the areas of: distribution (customer service; inventory control; logistics; materials handling; operations; planning; traffic; transportation); manufacturing/production (factory automation; international; plant management; quality control; robotics; safety; supervisory; technicians); materials management (inventory control [raw/in process]; MRP systems; production control/planning; purchasing); purchasing.

CAREER BLAZERS
590 Fifth Avenue
New York NY 10036
Employment agency; temporary help service. No appointment required. 212/719-3232. Founded 1949. Nonspecialized. Positions commonly filled include: Accountant; Administrative Assistant; Advertising Worker; Bookkeeper; Clerk; Commercial Artist; Computer Operator; Credit Manager; Customer Service Representative; Data Entry Clerk; Demonstrator; Driver; Factory Worker; General Laborer; Legal Secretary; Light Industrial Worker; Medical Secretary; Office Worker; Personnel and Labor Relations Specialist; Public Relations Worker; Receptionist; Sales Representative; Secretary; Stenographer; Technical Writer/Editor; Typist; Word Processing Specialist. Company pays fee. Number of placements per year: 1000+.

CAREER BLAZERS OF WHITE PLAINS
202 Mamaroneck Avenue
White Plains NY 10601
Contact Robert Miller, President. 914/949-1166. Employment agency; temporary help agency. Appointment required. Founded 1949. Offers permanent and temporary positions as well as a nationally accredited business school. Specializes in the areas of: Accounting; Banking and Finance; Legal; Sales and Marketing; Secretarial and Clerical. Positions commonly filled include: Accountant; Administrative Assistant; Bookkeeper; Clerk; Credit Manager; Customer Service Representative; Data Entry Clerk; Executive Secretary; Legal Secretary; Light Industrial Worker; Medical Secretary; Personnel Director; Receptionist; Sales Representative; Secretary; Stenographer; Typist; Word Processor. Company pays fee. Number of placements per year: 1000+.

CAREER PLACEMENTS
One Old Country Rd., Suite 312
Carle Place NY 11514
Contact Steve Gordon, CPC. 516/294-8250. FAX: 516/294-8298. Specializes in the areas of: asset; audit; bookkeeping; budgeting; clerical; computer science (consulting; data processing; EDP audit; operations; programming; sales; word processing sales/service); credit; electronics; engineering (electrical; HVAC; industrial; manufacturing; mechanical); financial analysis; investment; lending; public accounting; tax; insurance (claims; property/casualty; reinsurance; underwriting); office administration (administrators; clerks; receptionists; secretaries; word processing); sales (business products; computers; consumer products; industrial products; medical products; services/intangibles).

IRENE COHEN PERSONNEL SERVICES
475 Fifth Avenue
New York NY 10017
Contact Diane Cohen. 212/725-1666. FAX: 212/889-6746. Specializes in the areas of: audit; bookkeeping; budgeting; clerical; financial analysis; international; public accounting; tax; human resources (benefits; compensation; EEO; labor relations; management; personnel/industrial relations; recruiting/staffing; training/development); legal (legal administration; legal secretaries; paralegals); office administration (administrators; clerks; management; receptionists; secretaries; word processing); temporary services (accounting/bookkeeping; secretaries; word processing).

CONSULTANTS & DESIGNERS, INC.
360 West 31st Street
New York NY 10001
Contact Ray Wesley, Corp. Human Resources Director. 212/563-8400. Temporary help agency. No appointments required. Founded 1950. Long standing Engineering Service firm

with a reputation for service and quality. 31 offices nationally. Specializes in the areas of: Aerospace Technology; Architecture; Computer Hardware and Software; Construction; Electronics; Engineering; Industrial and Interior Design; Manufacturing; Technical and Scientific; Transportation. Positions commonly filled include: Aerospace Engineer; Architect; Biochemist; Civil Engineer; Clerk; Commercial Artist; Computer Programmer; Customer Service Representative; Data Entry Clerk; Draftsperson; EDP Specialist; Electrical Engineer; Industrial Designer; Industrial Engineer; Light Industrial Worker; Mechanical Engineer; Metallurgical Engineer; Statistician; Systems Analyst; Technical Writer/Editor; Technician; Word Processor. Company pays fee. Number of placements per year: 1000+.

CONTEMPORARY, INC.
489 5th Avenue
New York NY 10017
Contact Bill Pendergast, President. 212/765-7905. Employment agency. Appointment requested. Founded 1980. Specializes in the areas of: Accounting and Finance; Advertising; Banking; Clerical; Insurance; Legal; Personnel and Human Resources; Women. Positions commonly filled include: Administrative Assistant; Legal Secretary; Office Worker; Secretary; Stenographer; Typist; Word Processing Specialist. Company pays fee. Number of placements per year: 51-100.

CORPORATE SEARCH
6800 Jericho Turnpike, #203W
Syosset NY 11791
Contact Claire Zukerman, CPC/Harriet Herman. 516/496-3200. FAX: 516/496-3165. Specializes in the areas of: asset; audit; bookkeeping; budgeting; clerical; credit; financial analysis; international; investment; lending; public accounting; tax; trust.

CREATIVE MANAGEMENT STRATEGIES, LTD.
305 Madison Ave.
Suite 2033
New York NY 10165
Contact Ira N. Gottlieb, CPC/John R. Prufeta. 212/697-7207. FAX: 212/697-3509. Specializes in the areas of: human resources (benefits; management; personnel/industrial relations; recruiting/staffing; training/development); insurance (actuarial; claims; life/health; pension; property/casualty; rating; reinsurance; sales; underwriting); management consulting; marketing (consumer products; business products/computers; industrial products; medical products); medical/health care (doctors; hospitals); sales (business products; computers; consumer products; industrial products; management; medical products; services/intangibles).

CROSS PERSONNEL AGENCY
150 Broadway, Suite 902
New York NY 10038
Contact James Zamparelli, President. 212/227-6705. Employment agency; temporary help service. No appointment required. Founded 1968. Specializes in the areas of: Banking; Brokerage; Clerical. Positions commonly filled include: Administrative Assistant; Banking Operations Specialist; Bookkeeper; Brokerage Operations Specialist; Clerk; Data Entry Clerk; Office Worker; Receptionist; Secretary; Stenographer; Typist; Wall Street Trainee; Word Processing Specialist. Company pays fee. Number of placements per year: 1000+.

DAPEXS CONSULTANTS INC.
One Park Place
Syracuse NY 13202
Contact Peter J. Leofsky, CPC. 315/474-2477. FAX: 315/471-5637. Specializes in the areas of: computer science (corporate/computer security; consulting; data processing; EDP audit; operations; programming; sales; software engineering; systems); engineering (chemical; civil; electrical; environmental/hazardous waste; HVAC; industrial; manufacturing; mechanical; nuclear; packaging); medical/health care (doctors; hospitals; nurses).

CAROLYN DAVIS ASSOCIATES INC.
701 Westchester Avenue
White Plains NY 10604
Contact Carolyn Davis, CPC. 914/682-7040. FAX: 914/682-8361. Specializes in the area of: insurance (actuarial; claims; life/health; pension; property/casualty; rating; reinsurance; sales; underwriting).

SETH DIAMOND ASSOC., INC.
25 West 45th Street, Suite 704
New York NY 10036
Contact Seth Diamond, C.P.C., President. 212/944-6190. Employment agency. No appointment required. Founded 1981. Specializes in the areas of: Accounting; Advertising; Banking and Finance; Legal; Manufacturing; Secretarial and Clerical; etc. Positions commonly filled include: Accountant; Administrative Assistant; Bookkeeper; Computer Programmer; Customer Service Representative; Data Entry Clerk; EDP Specialist; Executive Secretary; Financial Analyst; Legal Secretary; Medical Secretary; Personnel Director; Receptionist; Secretary; Stenographer; Typist; Word Processor; etc. Company pays fee. Number of placements per year: 51-100.

DOVER EMPLOYMENT
236 West 72nd Street
New York NY 10023
Contact President. 212/721-4644. Employment agency. Founded 1970. Handling the recent grad to the middle manager with placements in small firms and Fortune 500 companies, introducing the best people to the best companies in New York City, Westchester County, New Jersey, and Long Island. Specializes in the areas of: Accounting; Advertising; Banking and Finance; Insurance; Legal; Manufacturing; MIS/EDP; Publishing; Real Estate; Secretarial and Clerical. Positions commonly filled include: Accountant; Actuary; Administrative Assistant; Bank Officer/Manager; Bookkeeper; Claims Representative; Clerk; Computer Programmer; Credit Manager; Customer Service Representative; Data Entry Clerk; EDP Specialist; Executive Secretary; Financial Analyst; Legal Secretary; Medical Secretary; Personnel Director; Purchasing Agent; Receptionist; Secretary; Statistician; Stenographer; Typist; Underwriter; Word Processor. Company pays fee. Number of placements per year: 1000+.

DUNHILL PERSONNEL AGENCY OF MANHATTAN
47 East 44th Street
New York NY 10017
Contact Bob Morris, President. 212/490-3700. Employment agency. Founded 1979. Specializes in the areas of: Computer Hardware and Software; Sales and Marketing. Positions commonly filled include: Computer Sales Representative; Marketing Specialist.

EDP TEMPS & SERVICES, INC.
2 Penn Plaza, Suite 1190
New York NY 10121
Contact Manager. 212/947-6033. Temporary help service. No appointment required. Founded 1976. Branch offices located in: California, Connecticut, Illinois, Maryland, Massachusetts, Michigan, Ohio, Pennsylvania, and Virginia. Specializes in the areas of: Accounting and Finance; Banking; Computer Hardware and Software; Engineering; Insurance; Manufacturing; MIS/EDP; Nonprofit; Personnel and Human Resources; Printing and Publishing; Technical and Scientific. Positions commonly filled include: Computer Operator; EDP Specialist; MIS Specialist; Systems Analyst; Technical Writer/Editor. Company pays fee. Number of placements per year: 1000+.

ETC SEARCH, INC
226 East 54th Street, Suite 308
New York NY 10022
Contact Marlene Eskenazie. 212/371-3880. Specializes in the area of: computer science (data processing).

ECCO PERSONNEL
One North Broadway
White Plains NY 10601
Contact Joanne Fiala, President. 914/761-4333. Temporary help service. Appointment requested. Founded 1979. Services Westchester and Fairfield counties. Specializes in the areas of: Accounting and Finance; Clerical; Personnel and Human Resources. Positions commonly filled include: Accountant; Clerk; Customer Service Representative; Data Entry Clerk; Driver; Financial Analyst; Legal Secretary; Purchasing Agent; Receptionist; Secretary; Stenographer; Typist; Word Processing Specialist. Company pays fee. Number of placements per year: 1001+.

EDEN PERSONNEL, INC.
280 Madison Avenue, Room 202
New York NY 10016
Contact Jack Scott, General Manager. 212/685-8600. Employment agency; temporary help agency. No appointment required. Founded 1976. Specializes in the areas of: Advertising; Health and Medical; Legal; Nonprofit; Printing and Publishing; Real Estate; Secretarial and Clerical. Positions commonly filled include: Accountant; Administrative Assistant; Bookkeeper; Clerk; Col. Grad. Tr.; Credit Manager; Data Entry Clerk; Executive Secretary; Legal Secretary; Medical Secretary; Nurse; Personnel Director; Public Relations Worker; Receptionist; Sales Representative; Secretary; Stenographer; Typist; Word Processor. Company pays fee. Number of placements per year: 501-1000.

ETHAN ALLEN PERSONNEL OF ALBANY, INC.
404 Troy-Schenectady Road
Latham NY 12110
Contact Harris Metzner. 518/785-7555. FAX: 518/785-8034. Specializes in the area of: human resources (benefits; compensation; labor relations; management; personnel/industrial relations; recruiting/staffing); insurance (claims; life/health; pension; property/casualty; rating; reinsurance; underwriting).

EVANS & JAMES ASSOCIATES, INC.
One North Broadway
White Plains, NY 10601
Contact Arnold Evans, CPC. 914/948-0044. FAX: 914/948-0563. Specializes in the area of: packaging (design; engineering; manufacturing).

FAIRFIELD RESOURCES, LTD.
350 Fifth Avenue
Empire State Building, Suite 7605
New York NY 10118
Contact Bruce Barton, President. 212/268-0220. Fax # 212/268-8849. Employment agency. Appointment required. Founded 1972. Recruit in Manhattan and nationwide for leading Retail and Fashion companies. Positions commonly filled include: Administrative Assistant; Executive Secretary; Model; Secretary; Typist; Word Processor. Company pays fee. Number of placements per year 1000+.

FOCUS CAPITAL
71 Vanderbilt, Suite 200
New York NY 10017
Contact Scott Gerson, President. 212/986-3344. Executive Search Firm. Appointment required. Founded 1976. Pioneered the use of Mathematicians and Physicists on Wall Street. Specializes in the areas of: Computer Hardware and Software; Investment Research; MIS/EDP. Positions commonly filled include: Computer Programmer; Data Entry Clerk; EDP Specialist; Economist. Company pays fee. Number of placements per year: 201-500.

THE FRY GROUP, INC.
18 East 41st Street
New York NY 10017
Contact Mr. John M. Fry, CPC. 212/532-8100. FAX: 212/213-2680. Specializes in the areas of: account management; direct marketing; media; production/traffic; research; sales promotion; public relations (agency; corporate; institutional).

GAMBRILL & ASSOCIATES, INC.
130 North Main Street
Port Chester NY 10573
Contact Lory Gambrill, CPC. 914/939-1919. FAX: 914/939-0545. Specializes in the areas of: office administration (administrators; clerks; management; receptionists; secretaries; word processing); securities/investments (analysts; brokerage; management; operations).

GERRI G. INC.
2795 Richmond Avenue
Pergament Mall
Staten Island NY 10314
Contact Geraldine Gibney, CPC. 718/494-9100. FAX: 718/983-8602. Specializes in the areas of: audit; financial analysis; public accounting; tax; insurance (claims; pension; property/casualty; rating; sales; underwriting); legal (attorneys; legal administrators; legal secretaries; paralegals); office administration (administrators; clerks; management; receptionists; secretaries; word processing); temporary services (accounting/bookkeeping; sales; word processing).

GILDA GRAY PERSONNEL AGENCY, INC.
20 E. 49th, Suite 4G
New York NY 10017
Contact Gilda Gray, President. 212/838-7373. Employment agency. No appointment required. Founded 1969. Specializes in the areas of: Computer Hardware and Software; Legal; MIS/EDP. Positions commonly filled include: Administrative Assistant; Computer Operator; Computer Programmer; Receptionist; Secretary; Systems Analyst; Word Processing Specialist. Company pays fee. Number of placements per year: 50.

GREGORY & GREGORY ASSOC., INC.
19 West 44th Street
Suite 1716
New York NY 10036
Contact Paul Gregory. 212/944-2888. FAX: 212/944-7783. Specializes in the area of: insurance (actuarial; claims; life/health; pension; property/casualty; rating; reinsurance; sales; underwriting); legal (legal administration; legal secretaries; paralegals).

GROUP AGENCY, INC.
1422 Avenue J
Brooklyn NY 11230
Contact Office Manager. 718/258-9202. Employment agency. No appointment required. Founded 1970. Specializes in areas of: Construction; Food Industry; Manufacturing; Transportation. Positions commonly filled include: Driver; Factory Worker; General Laborer; Light Industrial Worker. Individual pays fee. Number of placements per year: 501-1000.

HAMPSHIRE ASSOCIATES, INC.
71 West 23rd Street, Suite 1525
New York NY 10010
Contact Charles A. Winston, President. 212/924-3999. Employment agency. Appointment required; resume required. Founded 1971. Work exclusively in the Electronics industry. Client companies located in New York, New Jersey, Connecticut, and New England. Can place applicants nationwide. Specializes in the areas of: Computer Hardware and Software; Engineering; MIS/EDP; Technical and Scientific. Positions commonly filled include: Aerospace Engineer; Biomedical Engineer; Computer Programmer; EDP Specialist; Electrical Engineer; Industrial Engineer; Marketing Specialist; Mechanical Engineer; Physicist; Technical Writer/Editor. Company pays fee. Number of placements per year 51-100.

T.J. HARBROWE ASSOC., INC.
222 Mamaroneck Avenue
White Plains NY 10605
Contact Judy M. White, President. 914/949-6400. Employment agency. No appointment required. Founded 1972." We are a privately owned, highly selective firm, both in terms of the companies we choose to work with and the candidates that we select to represent our agency." Specializes in the areas of: Banking and Finance; Computer Hardware and Software; Engineering; Food Industry; Health and Medical; Insurance; Legal; MIS/EDP; Sales and Marketing; Secretarial and Clerical. Positions commonly filled include: Accountant; Actuary; Administrative Assistant; Aerospace Engineer; Agricultural Engineer; Bank Officer/Manager; Biologist; Biomedical Engineer; Bookkeeper; Ceramics Engineer; Civil Engineer; Claims Representative; Clerk; Computer Programmer; Credit Manager; Customer Service Representative; Data Entry Clerk; Dietician/Nutritionist; Driver; EDP Specialist; Electrical Engineer; Executive Secretary; Financial Analyst; General Manager; Hotel Manager; Industrial Engineer; Insurance Agent/Broker; Legal Secretary; Light Industrial Worker; Marketing Specialist; Mechanical Engineer; Medical Secretary; Metallurgical Engineer; Mining Engineer; Model; Nurse; Personnel Director; Petroleum Engineer; Public Relations Worker; Purchasing Agent; Receptionist; Sales Representative; Secretary; Statistician; Stenographer; Systems Analyst; Technical Writer/Editor; Technician; Typist; Underwriter; Word Processor. Company pays fee.

HUNT, LTD.
21 W. 38th Street, 11th Floor
New York NY 10018
Contact Alex Metz, C.P.C., President. 212/997-2299. Employment agency. Appointment preferred. Founded 1965. Firm specializes in areas of Traffic/Distribution/Warehousing on the national level. From middle management to senior management. Specializes in the areas of: Food Industry; Health and Medical; Manufacturing; Transportation. Positions commonly filled include: Customer Service Representative; Distribution Manager; Traffic Manager; Warehouse Manager. Company pays fee. Number of placements per year 201-500.

HUNTINGTON PERSONNEL CONSULTANTS
755 New York Avenue, Suite 250
Huntington NY 11743-4240
Contact Jeannette Henry, President. 516/549-8888. Employment agency; temporary help service. No appointment required. Founded 1982. Specializes in the areas of: Clerical; Computer Hardware and Software; MIS/EDP. Positions commonly filled include: Administrative Assistant; Bookkeeper; Clerk; Computer Operator; Computer Programmer; Customer Service Representative; Data Entry Clerk; EDP Specialist; Legal Secretary; Light Industrial Worker; MIS Specialist; Office Worker; Receptionist; Secretary; Systems Analyst; Typist; Word Processing Specialist. Company pays fee. Number of placements per year: 101-200.

INTERIM - NEW YORK
275 Madison Avenue
New York NY 10016
Temporary help service. 212/684-3030. Appointment requested. Founded 1954. A member of Victor Temporary Services, which has over 100 offices throughout the United States. Nonspecialized. Positions commonly filled include: Bookkeeper; Clerk; Computer Operator; Customer Service Representative; Data Entry Clerk; Demonstrator; Draftsperson; Electronic Assembler; Factory Worker; General Laborer; Legal Secretary; Light Industrial Worker; Medical Secretary; Office Worker; Receptionist; Secretary; Stenographer; Technician; Typist; Word Processing Specialist. Company pays fee. Number of placements per year: 1000+.

INTERIM - NEW YORK
39 Broadway, 5th Floor
New York NY 10006
Contact Joan Riddle, Office Manager. 212/269-3030. Temporary help service. Appointment requested. Founded 1954. A member of Victor Temporary Services, which has over 100 offices throughout the United States. Nonspecialized. Positions commonly filled include: Bookkeeper; Clerk; Computer Operator; Customer Service Representative; Data Entry Clerk; Demonstrator; Draftsperson; Electronic Assembler; Factory Worker; General Laborer; Legal Secretary; Light Industrial Worker; Medical Secretary; Office Worker; Receptionist; Secretary; Stenographer; Technician; Typist; Word Processing Specialist. Company pays fee. Number of placements per year: 1000+.

JDC ASSOCIATES
330 Vanderbilt Motor Parkway
Suite 101
Hauppauge NY 11788
Contact Joanne Coraci. 516/231-8581. FAX: 516/231-8011. Specializes in the areas of: bilingual; bookkeeping; clerical; credit & collection (commercial; consumer); manufacturing/production (plant management; quality control; supervisory); office

administration (administrators; clerks; management; receptionists; word processing); pharmaceuticals (sales); sales (business products; computers; medical products; services/intangibles).

JOHN-DAVID PERSONNEL AGENCY, INC.
841 Broadway, Suite 504
New York NY 10003
Contact John Dean, President. 212/475-1800. Employment agency; temporary help service. No appointment required. Founded 1983. Specializes in the areas of: Accounting and Finance; Banking; Clerical; Fashion; Legal; Nonprofit; Personnel and Human Resources. Positions commonly filled include: Accountant; Administrative Assistant; Advertising Worker; Bookkeeper; Clerk; Computer Operator; Credit Manager; Customer Service Representative; Data Entry Clerk; General Manager; Legal Secretary; Medical Secretary; Office Worker; Personnel and Labor Relations Specialist; Public Relations Worker; Receptionist; Secretary; Stenographer; Typist; Word Processing Specialist. Company pays fee. Number of placements per year: 201-500.

JUST ONE BREAK, INC.
373 Park Avenue South
New York NY 10016
Contact Mikki Lam, Executive Director. 212/725-2500. Employment agency. Appointment requested. Founded 1947. Provides counseling and placement for applicants with a physical, developmental or emotional disability. Nonprofit. Specializes in the areas of: Personnel and Human Resources. No fees. Number of placements per year: 201-500.

KAUFMAN ASSOCIATES LTD.
450 Seventh Avenue 9th Fl.
New York NY 10123
Contact Eugene A. Kaufman, CPC. 212/643-0625. Specializes in the area of: textiles/apparels.

CHARLES J. KENNETH ASSOCIATES LTD.
333 No. Broadway
Jericho NY 11753
Contact Paul T. Bianco VP, Mgr. 516/931-3500. FAX: 516/931-3889. Specializes in the areas of: asset; credit; international; investment; lending; trust.

KLING PERSONNEL AGENCY OF WESTCHESTER
599 West Hartsdale Avenue
Suite 202
White Plains NY 10607
Contact Partner. 914/761-3010. Employment agency. Appointment requested. Founded 1959. Specializes in the areas of: Accounting and Finance; Banking; Clerical; Food Industry; Insurance; Manufacturing; Sales and Marketing; Technical and Scientific. Positions commonly filled include: Accountant; Administrative Assistant; Aerospace Engineer; Bank Officer/Manager; Bookkeeper; Buyer; Clerk; Computer Operator; Computer Programmer; Credit Manager; Customer Service Representative; Data Entry Clerk; Draftsperson; EDP Specialist; Electrical Engineer; Financial Analyst; Hotel Manager/Assistant Manager; Insurance Agent/Broker; Legal Secretary; MIS Specialist; Mechanical Engineer; Medical Secretary; Metallurical Engineer; Office Worker; Operations/Production Specialist; Personnel and Labor Relations Specialist; Purchasing Agent; Quality Control Supervisor; Receptionist; Sales Representative; Secretary; Stenographer; Systems Analyst; Technical Writer/Editor; Technician; Typist; Underwriter; Word Processing Specialist. Company pays fee. Number of placements per year: 201-500.

KLING PERSONNEL ASSOCIATES, INC.
180 Broadway, 5th Floor
New York NY 10038
Contact Len Adams, C.P.C., Vice President. 212/964-3640. Employment agency; temporary help agency. Appointment required. Founded 1948. Specialist firm/relationship oriented-offers quality service to candidates seeking careers in Banking/Finance/Insurance. Specializes in the areas of: Banking and Finance; Insurance; Real Estate; Secretarial and Clerical. Positions commonly filled include: Accountant; Actuary; Administrative Assistant; Bank Officer/Manager; Bookkeeper; Claims Representative; Customer Service Representative; Executive Secretary; Financial Analyst; General Manager; Insurance Agent/Broker; International Banker; Legal Secretary; Personnel Director; Receptionist; Secretary; Stenographer; Systems Analyst; Typist; Underwriter; Word Processor. Company pays fee. Number of placements per year: 201-500.

LAROCCO ASSOCIATES, INC.
1133 Avenue of the Americas
New York NY 10036
Contact Claire Cook. 212/921-7670. Specializes in the area of: legal (attorneys; legal administrators; legal secretaries; paralegals).

LLOYD CONSULTANTS
10 Cutter Mill Road, Suite 200
Great Neck NY 11021
Contact Merrill Banks, CPC. 516/466-6670. FAX: 516/466-6028. Specializes in the areas of: computer science (corporate/computer security; consulting; data processing; EDP audit; operations; programming; sales; software engineering; systems; technicians; word processing sales/service); insurance (actuarial; claims; life/health; pension; property/casualty; rating; reinsurance; underwriting); real estate (asset/portfolio management; finance; property management); sales (business products; computers; consumer products; industrial products; management; medical products); temporary services (accounting/bookkeeping; secretaries; word processing).

M & M PERSONNEL, INC.
505 Fifth Avenue, Suite 1800
New York NY 10017
212/986-4959. Employment agency; temporary help agency. No appointment required. Founded 1971. Specializes in the areas of: Secretarial and Clerical; All Office Support. Positions commonly filled include: Administrative Assistant; Bookkeeper; Clerk; Customer Service Representative; Data Entry Clerk; Executive Secretary; Legal Secretary; Medical Secretary; Receptionist; Secretary; Stenographer; Typist; Word Processor. Company pays fee. Number of placements per year: 201-500.

MHR CONSULTANTS, INC.
Civic Center Plaza, P.O. Box 668
Poughkeepsie NY 12601
Contact Joseph F. O'Connor. 914/485-7370. FAX: 914/485-7470. Specializes in the area of: human resources (benefits; compensation; labor relations; management; personnel/industrial relations; recruiting/staffing; training/development).

JOSEPH T. MALONEY AND ASSOCIATES, INC.
61 Broadway, Suite 2215
New York NY 10006
Contact Bonnie Butler, Office Manager. 212/363-9689. Employment agency. Appointment requested. Founded 1971. Specializes in the areas of: Accounting and Finance; Banking; Clerical; Insurance; Legal; Personnel and Human Resources; Sales and Marketing. Positions commonly filled include: Accountant; Administrative Assistant; Attorney; Bank Officer/Manager; Bookkeeper; Brokerage Operator; Claim Representative; Clerk; Computer Operator; Computer Programmer; Credit Manager; Customer Service Representative; Data Entry Clerk; EDP Specialist; Economist; Financial Analyst; Legal Secretary; MIS Specialist; Marketing Specialist; Office Worker; Operations/Production Specialist; Personnel and Labor Relations Specialist; Receptionist; Sales Representative; Secretary; Stenographer; Systems Analyst; Typist; Word Processing Specialist. Company pays fee. Number of placements per year: 501-1000.

MANPOWER TEMPORARY SERVICES OF NEW YORK
1775 Broadway
New York NY 10019
Contact Mitchell Fronstein, President. 212/307-1008. Temporary help service. Appointment requested. Founded 1948. Specializes in the areas of: Banking; Clerical; Fashion; Nonprofit; Printing and Publishing. Positions commonly filled include: Bookkeeper; Clerk; Data Entry Clerk; Dictaphone Typist; Receptionist; Secretary; Statistician; Stenographer; Typist; Word Processing Specialist. Number of placements per year: 1000+.

MITCHELL/MARTIN, INC.
80 Wall St., Ste. 1215
New York NY 10005
Contact Eugene Holtzman. 212/943-1404. FAX: 212/943-0041. Specializes in the areas of: computer science (data processing; programming; software; engineering; systems).

NATEK, NATIONAL TECHNOLOGY CORPORATION
9 Maple Avenue, 2nd Floor
Saratoga Springs NY 12866
Contact Robert J. Bartone. 518/583-0359. FAX: 518/583-0558. Specializes in the area of: computer science (programming).

NETWORK RESOURCES INC.
271 Madison Avenue
New York NY 10016
Contact Nick Mancino. 212/818-9292. FAX: 212/818-1108. Specializes in the areas of: computer science (data processing; operations; technicians) electronics (field service; technicians); telecommunications (data; satellite; voice); temporary services (technical).

NEW YORK - NEW YORK
170 Broadway, Suite 906
New York NY 10038
Contact Marsha Sommer. 212/267-3500. FAX: 212/791-3746. Specializes in the area of: office administration (administrators; clerks; management; receptionists; secretaries; word processing).

NOONE-WALSH ASSOCIATES, INC.
50 Main St.
White Plains NY 10606
914/946-0990. FAX: 914/946-0542. Specializes in the areas of: audit; bookkeeping; budgeting; clerical; financial analysis; public accounting; tax; insurance (actuarial; claims; pension; property/casualty; rating; reinsurance; underwriting).

OFFICE TEMPORARIES, INC.
902 Broadway, 9th Floor
New York NY 10010
Contact Rose Cavagnolo, Vice President. 212/995-2400. Temporary help service. No appointment required. Specializes in the areas of: Accounting and Finance; Advertising; Banking; Broadcasting; Clerical; Communications; Fashion; Film; Finance; Food Industry; Insurance; Nonprofit; Personnel and Human Resources; Printing and Publishing; Public Relations; Retail; Television; Textiles. Positions commonly filled include: Accountant; Administrative Assistant; Assistant Manager; Bookkeeper; Clerk; Computer Operator; Computer Programmer; Customer Service Representative; Data Entry Clerk; Demonstrator; EDP Specialist; Factory Worker; General Laborer; Legal Secretary; Light Industrial Worker; Medical Secretary; Office Worker; Receptionist; Stenographer; Typist; Word Processor. Company pays fee. Number of placements per year: 1000+.

OMNI RECRUITING, INC.
275 Madison Avenue
New York NY 10016
Contact Gerald Kaufman. 212/683-7800. FAX: 212-779-0342. Specializes in the area of: computer science (corporate/computer security; consulting; data processing; EDP audit; operations; programming; sales; software engineering; systems); electronics (engineering; field service; manufacturing; sales/marketing; technicians); security (computer; corporate; institutional).

THE ORIGINAL TEMPO SERVICES, INC.
1900 Hempstead Turnpike
East Meadow NY 11554
Contact Bernard L. Vinson, President. 516/794-6100. Temporary help agency. Appointment required. Founded 1949. The Original Tempo Services Corp. is Long Island's leading temporary personnel service providing office, industrial and home health care personnel. Nonspecialized. Positions commonly filled include: Accountant; Bookkeeper; Clerk; Computer Programmer; Credit Manager; Data Entry Clerk; Draftsperson; Driver; EDP Specialist; Executive Secretary; Factory Worker; Financial Analyst; General Laborer; Legal Secretary; Light Industrial Worker; Marketing Specialist; Medical Secretary; Nurse; Purchasing Agent; Receptionist; Secretary; Stenographer; Systems Analyst; Typist; Word Processor. Company pays fee. Number of placements per year: 1000+.

PC DATA
462 7th Avenue, 4th Floor
New York NY 10018
Contact Vice President. 212/736-5040. Employment agency. Appointment requested. Founded 1971. Specializes in the areas of: MIS/EDP; Management Consulting; Personal Computer Hardware and Software. Positions commonly filled include: Computer Operator; Computer Programmer; MIS Specialist; Management Consultant for MIS; Systems Analyst. Company pays fee.

PEAK SEARCH, INC.
25 W. 31st Street 12 Floor
New York NY 10001
Contact Richard Eichenberg, CPC 212/947-6600. FAX: 212/947-6780. Specializes in the area of: chemical.

PERSONNEL ASSOCIATES, INC.
Courtyard Entrance
731 James Street
Syracuse NY 13203
Contact Peter J. Baskin, CPC. 315/422-0070. FAX: 315/474-7293. Specializes in the area of: insurance (claims; life/health; pension; property/casualty; rating; reinsurance; sales; underwriting).

PERSONNEL POOL, INC.
227 East 45th Street
New York NY 10017
Contact Judy Chudfash, Area Director. 212/983-8800. Temporary help service. No appointment required. Founded 1946. Specializes in the areas of: Finance; Advertising; Banking; Broadcasting; Clerical; Fashion; Insurance; Legal. Positions commonly filled include: Administrative Assistant; Bookkeeper; Clerk; Computer Operator; Customer Service Representative; Data Entry Clerk; Demonstrator; EDP Specialist; Legal Secretary; Legal Librarian; Light Industrial Worker; Medical Secretary; Model; Office Worker; Paralegal; Public Relations Worker; Receptionist; Sales Representative; Secretary; Stenographer; Telex Operator; Typist; Word Processing Specialist. Number of placements per year: 1000+.

PERSONNEL SYSTEMS INC., AGENCY
5 South Ridge Road
Pomona NY 10970
Contact Richard Wexler, Ph.D., CPC. 914/739-0455. FAX: 914/739-1371. Specializes in the areas of: energy (gas; solar; utilities); environmental/hazardous waste.

PERSONNEL UNLIMITED LTD.
170 Broadway, Suite 909
New York NY 10038
Contact Shirley Whelan. 212/962-6310. FAX: 212/962-7733. Specializes in the areas of: audit; bookkeeping; budgeting; clerical; credit; financial analysis; international; lending; public accounting; trainees; trust; human resources (benefits; compensation; management; personnel/industrial relations; recruiting/staffing; training/development); insurance (actuarial; claims; life/health; pension; property/casualty; rating; reinsurance; sales; underwriting); office administration (administrators; clerks; management; receptionists; secretaries; word processing).

PHOENIX EMPLOYMENT AGENCY
25 W. 14th Street, #114
New York NY 10011
Contact Steve Blecher. 212/255-3436. Specializes in the area of: manufacturing/production (factory automation; plant management; quality control; supervisory; technicians).

POSTON PERSONNEL
16 East 79th Street, Suite G-4
New York NY 10021
Contact Jerry Bohne, Licensee/Owner. 212/535-4116 or 212/988-7080. Employment agency. Appointment requested. Nonspecialized. Positions commonly filled include: Administrative Assistant; Advertising Worker; Bookkeeper; Clerk; Commercial Artist; Customer Service Representative; Executive Secretary; Legal Secretary; Marketing Specialist; Medical Secretary; Office Worker; Personnel and Labor Relations Specialist; Public Relations Worker; Receptionist; Sales Representative; Secretary; Stenographer; Technical Writer/Editor; Typist. Company pays fee. Number of placements per year: 51-100.

PRESTIGE PERSONNEL
108-16 72nd Avenue
Forest Hills NY 11375
Contact Solomon Ovadia or Roz Rezmovic, Office Managers. 718/268-6600. Employment Agency. No appointment required. Founded 1978. A complete office service agency for the Queens and Manhattan area. Positions commonly filled include: Bookkeeper; Legal Secretary; Office Personnel; Real Estate Personnel. Number of placements per year: 500+.

PROFESSIONAL PLACEMENT ASSOCIATES
14 Rye Ridge Plaza
Rye Brook NY 10573
Contact Laura J. Schachter. 914/939-1195. FAX: 914/939-1959. Specializes in the area of: medical/health care (dental; doctors; hospitals; medical secretaries; nurses; nursing homes; paraprofessionals).

PROFILE AUTOMATION SERVICES, INC.
662 Franklin Avenue, Suite 451
Garden City NY 11530
Contact Ron Edwards, Vice President. 516/741-6881. Employment agency; temporary help agency. Founded 1979. Specializes in the areas of: Banking and Finance; Computer Hardware and Software; MIS/EDP. Positions commonly filled include: Bookkeeper; Computer Programmer; Data Entry Clerk; EDP Specialist; Management Consultant; Systems Analyst; Technical Writer/Editor; Typist; Word Processor. Individual pays fee. Number of placements per year: 1-50.

QUEENS EMPLOYMENT SERVICE, INC.
29-27 41st Avenue Room 502
Long Island City NY 11101
Contact John E. Thorsen, CPC. 718/784-1010. FAX: 718/784-0402. Specializes in the areas of: food service (institutional; manufacturers; sales); manufacturing/production (factory automation; plant management; quality control; robotics; safety; supervisory; technicians).

THE REMBRANDT PERSONNEL AGENCY, INC.
1422 Avenue J
Brooklyn NY 11230
Contact Shimie Silver, President. 718/258-9202. Employment agency. Appointment required. Placing primarily within the Brooklyn area. Specializes in the placement of office personnel. Positions commonly filled include: Accountant; Administrative Assistant; Advertising Executive; Bookkeeper; Clerk; Commercial Artist; Credit Manager; Customer Service Representative; Data Entry Clerk; Draftsperson; Executive Secretary; General Manager; Insurance Agent/Broker; Legal Secretary; Medical Secretary; Personnel Director; Public Relations Worker; Receptionist; Sales Representative; Secretary;

Stenographer; Typist; Word Processor. Company pays fee. Number of placements per year: 501-1000.

REMER-RIBOLOW & ASSOCIATES
275 Madison Avenue, Suite 1605
New York NY 10016
Contact Adele Ribolow, President. 212/808-0580. Employment agency. Appointment requested. Founded 1955. Specializes in the areas of: Printing and Publishing. Positions commonly filled include: Administrative Assistant; Marketing Specialist; Reporter/Editor; Secretary; Technical Writer/Editor. Company pays fee.

REPUBLIC EMPLOYMENT AGENCY, INC.
181 Broadway, 5th Floor
New York NY 10007
Contact Tony Freddo, President. 212/964-0640. Employment agency. No appointment required. Founded 1963. Specializes in the areas of: Accounting and Finance; Banking; Insurance; Legal; Sales and Marketing. Positions commonly filled include: Accountant; Bank Officer/Manager; Bookkeeper; Broker; Buyer; Credit Manager; Data Entry Clerk; EDP Specialist; Financial Analyst; Legal Secretary; Office Worker; Purchasing Agent; Receptionist; Sales Representative; Secretary; Stenographer; Systems Analyst; Typist; Underwriter; Word Processing Specialist. Company pays fee. Number of placements per year: 201-500.

FRAN ROGERS AGENCY, INC./FRAN ROGERS TEMPS
535 Broadhollow Road, Suite B36
Melville NY 11747
Contact Fran Rogers, President. 516/752-8888. Employment agency; temporary help service. No appointment required. Founded 1975. Specializes in the areas of: Accounting and Finance; Banking; Computer Hardware and Software; Engineering; MIS/EDP; Technical and Scientific. Positions commonly filled include: Accountant; Administrative Assistant; Bookkeeper; EDP Specialist; Electrical Engineer; Financial Analyst; MIS Specialist; Receptionist; Secretary; Systems Analyst; Typist. Company pays fee. Number of placements per year: 201-500.

SALES CAREERS
481 Main Street
New Rochelle NY 10801
Contact John Donahoe, President. 914/632-8800. Employment agency. Founded 1971. Places sales personnel at all levels and specializes in providing career advice to the individual and at no cost to the applicant. Specializes in the areas of: Sales and Marketing. Company pays fee. Number of placements per year: 201-500.

SALES RECRUITERS INTERNATIONAL
371 South Broadway
Tarrytown, NY 10591
Contact Richard J. Harris, CPC. 914/631-0090. Specializes in the areas of: chemical; food service (sales); marketing (consumer products; business products/computers; industrial products; international; market research; product management; sales promotion); packaging; printing (sales); sales (business products; computers; consumer products; industrial products; international; management; services/intangibles).

SHELWOOD ENTERPRISES, INC.
26 Broadway
New York NY 10004
Contact Larry Wittlin, CPC. 212/635-9700. Specializes in the area of: computer science (consulting; data processing; programming; sales).

SIGMA SEARCH, INC.
425 Broadhollow Road, Suite 304
Melville NY 11747
Contact Thea Linker, President. 516/694-7707. Employment agency. Appointment requested. Founded 1983. Specializes in the areas of: Accounting and Finance; Computer Hardware and Software; MIS/EDP; Technical and Scientific. Positions commonly filled include: Accountant; Bookkeeper; Computer Programmer; EDP Specialist; Financial Analyst; MIS Specialist; Systems Analyst. Company pays fee. Number of placements per year: 51-100.

SLOAN PERSONNEL SERVICES
One East 42nd Street
New York NY 10017
Contact Joseph Nocerino. 212/949-7200. FAX: 212/983-0804. Specializes in the areas of: office administration (administrators; clerks; management; receptionists; secretaries; word processing); temporary services (accounting/bookkeeping; secretaries; word processing).

SMITH'S FIFTH AVENUE AGENCY, INC.
17 East 45th Street
New York NY 10017
Contact Arnold Milgaten, President. 212/682-5300. Employment agency. Appointment requested. Founded 1950. Specializes in the areas of: Advertising; Market Research; Sales and Marketing of Consumer Goods. Positions commonly filled include: Advertising Worker; Market Research Professionals; Market Specialist. Company pays fee. Number of placements per year: 201-500.

ALBERTA SMYTH PERSONNEL AGENCY.
305 Madison Ave.
Suite 421
New York NY 10165
Contact E. John Broderick. 212/953-0011. FAX: 212/682-1991. Specializes in the areas of: asset; audit; bookkeeping; budgeting; clerical; credit; credit & collection (commercial; consumer; retail; wholesale); financial analysis; lending; trainees; human services (benefits; compensation; EEO; labor relations; management; personnel/industrial relations; recruiting/staffing; training/development); sales (business products; computers; consumer products; industrial products; international; management; media; medical products; services/intangibles; trainees).

SQUIRES PERSONNEL NETWORK
25 West 45th Street
New York NY 10036
Contact Lee Roberts, President. 212/869-5757. Employment agency. Appointment required. Founded 1986. Specializes in the areas of: Accounting; Advertising; Banking and Finance; Computer Hardware and Software; Insurance; Legal; MIS/EDP; Real Estate; Sales and Marketing; Secretary and Clerical. Positions commonly filled include: Accountant; Actuary; Administrative Assistant; Bookkeeper; Claims Representative; Clerk; Computer Programmer; Credit Manager; Customer Service Representative; Data Entry Clerk; EDP Specialist; Executive Secretary; Legal Secretary, Medical Secretary; Personnel

Director; Public Relations Worker; Purchasing Agent; Receptionist; Sales Representative; Secretary; Stenographer; Systems Analyst; Technical Writer/Editor; Typist; Underwriter; Word Processor. Company pays fee. Number of placements per year: 501-1000.

STAFF BUILDERS INC. BUSINESS SERVICES
122 East 42nd Street, Second Floor
New York NY 10168
Contact Michael Firneno, Executive Vice President, Branch Operations. 212/867-2345. Temporary help service. Appointment requested. Founded 1961. Over 100 offices in the U.S. and Canada. Nonspecialized. Positions commonly filled include: Accountant; Administrative Assistant; Bookkeeper; Clerk; Companion; Computer Operator; Computer Programmer; Customer Service Representative; Data Entry Clerk; Demonstrator; Draftsperson; EDP Specialist; Factory Worker; General Laborer; Health Aide; Legal Secretary; Light Industrial Worker; Medical Secretary; Nurse; Office Worker; Public Relations Worker; Receptionist; Sales Representative; Secretary; Stenographer; Technician; Typist; Word Processing Specialist. Number of placements per year: 1000+.

STAFF BY MANNING, LTD.
38 East 57th Street, 7th Floor
New York NY 10022
Contact Ruth Manning, President. 212/753-8080. Employment agency. Appointment required; unsolicited resumes accepted. Founded 1978. Specializes in career opportunities for top level Executive Secretaries, Administrative Assistants, and Office Managers for top level executives and corporations. Job Evaluations. Contingency. Number of searches conducted per year: 51-100.

SUTTON-LANE PERSONNEL AGENCY, INC.
Westchester Financial Center
50 Main Street
White Plains NY 10606
Contact Dennis Troy, President. 914/682-2191. Founded 1981. Specializes in the area of: Sales, Marketing, Contract Furniture, Interior Design. Common positions filled include: Sales, Marketing, Technical Support Personnel. Company pays fee. Number of placements per year: 101-200.

TEMP FORCE OF EAST MEADOW
1975 Hempstead Turnpike
East Meadow NY 11554
Contact Edward Grant, President. 516/794-9700. Temporary help service. No appointment requested. Founded 1965. Nonspecialized. Positions commonly filled include: Accountant; Bookkeeper; Clerk; Computer Operator; Computer Programmer; Customer Service Representative; Data Entry Clerk; Demonstrator; Driver; Factory Worker; General Laborer; Legal Secretary; Light Industrial Worker; Medical Secretary; Office Worker; Purchasing Agent; Receptionist; Secretary; Statistician; Stenographer; Typist; Word Processing Specialist.

TEMP FORCE OF LONG ISLAND
71A North Franklin Street
Hempstead NY 11550
516/485-5240. Temporary help service. No appointment required. Founded 1965. Branch offices located in: Alabama; Arkansas; California; Colorado; Connecticut; Florida; Illinois; Indiana; Kansas; Maryland; Massachusetts; Michigan; Mississippi; Nevada; New Jersey; New Mexico; New York; Ohio; Oklahoma; Pennsylvania; Tennessee; Utah; Vermont; Virginia. Nonspecialized. Positions commonly filled include: Accountant; Bookkeeper;

Clerk; Computer Operator; Computer Programmer; Customer Service Representative; Data Entry Clerk; Demonstrator; Driver; Factory Worker; General Laborer; Legal Secretary; Light Industrial Worker; Medical Secretary; Office Worker; Purchasing Agent; Receptionist; Secretary; Statistician; Stenographer; Typist; Word Processing Specialist.

TEMP FORCE OF LONG ISLAND
425 Broadhollow Road, Suite 207
Melville NY 11747
516/293-7050. Temporary help service. No appointment required. Founded 1965. Branch offices located in: Alabama; Arkansas; California; Colorado; Connecticut; Florida; Illinois; Indiana; Kansas; Maryland; Massachusetts; Michigan; Mississippi; Nevada; New Jersey; New Mexico; New York; Ohio; Oklahoma; Pennsylvania; Tennessee; Utah; Vermont; Virginia. Nonspecialized. Positions commonly filled include: Accountant; Bookkeeper; Clerk; Computer Operator; Computer Programmer; Customer Service Representative; Data Entry Clerk; Demonstrator; Driver; Factory Worker; General Laborer; Legal Secretary; Light Industrial Worker; Medical Secretary; Office Worker; Purchasing Agent; Receptionist; Secretary; Statistician; Stenographer; Typist; Word Processing Specialist.

TEMP FORCE OF NEW YORK
180 Broadway, Suite 1101
New York NY 10038
Contact Don Carnegie, Manager. 212/267-TEMP. Temporary help service. No appointment required. Founded 1965. Branch offices located in: Alabama; Arkansas; California; Colorado; Conneticut; Florida; Illinois; Indiana; Kansas; Maryland; Massachusetts; Michigan; Mississippi; Nevada; New Jersey; New Mexico; Ohio; Oklahoma; Pennsylvania; Tennessee; Utah; Vermont; Virginia. Nonspecialized. Positions commonly filled include: Accountant; Bookkeeper; Clerk; Computer Operator; Computer Programmer; Customer Service Representative; Data Entry Clerk; Demonstrator; Driver; Factory Worker; General Laborer; Legal Secretary; Light Industrial Worker; Medical Secretary; Office Worker; Purchasing Agent; Receptionist; Secretary; Statistician; Stenographer; Typist; Word Processing Specialist.

TEMPOSITIONS, INC.
420 Lexington Avenue, Room 555
New York NY 10170
Contact Tina Essey Mikkelsen, Director, Personnel. 212/490-7400. Temporary help service. No appointment required. Founded 1962. Offices in New York, California and Florida providing temporary positions in the fields of publishing, advertising, accounting and finance, law, and communications. Multiple divisions include: TemPositions Office Division, filling positions in word processing, secretarial, clerical, telemarketing, administrative assistants, data entry; AcctPositions, specializing in accounting and finance-related personnel; TemPositions Health Care, providing hospitals and group homes with nurses, technicians, therapists, childcare workers, social workers, and nurse's aides. Number of placements per year: 1001+.

PHILLIP THOMAS PERSONNEL, INC.
545 5th Avenue, Suite 608
New York NY 10017
Contact Tina Carberry, President, or Bruce Phillips, Vice President. 212/867-0860. Employment agency; temporary help agency. Founded 1976. We are a full service agency providing quality, college-educated candidates to top-drawer corporations and financial institutions. Specializes in the areas of: Banking and Finance; Fashion; Sales and Marketing; Secretarial and Clerical. Positions commonly filled include: Administrative Assistant; Clerk; Credit Manager; Customer Service Representative; Entry Level Finance

and Investment Banking; Executive Secretary; Financial Analyst; Portfolio and Sales Assistant; Receptionist; Sales Representative; Secretary; Word Processor. Company pays fee. Number of placements per year: 51-100+.

TOWN EAST PERSONNEL AGENCY
200 North Avenue, Suite 8
New Rochelle NY 10801
914/633-8888. Employment agency. Appointment requested. Founded 1974. Nonspecialized. Positions commonly filled include: Accountant; Actuary; Administrative Assistant; Advertising Worker; Architect; Attorney; Automotive Worker; Bank Officer and Manager; Biochemist; Biologist; Bookkeeper; Buyer; Ceramics Engineer; Chemical Engineer; Chemist; Claim Representative; Clerk; Commercial Artist; Computer Operator; Computer Programmer; Construction Worker; Credit Manager; Customer Service Representative; Data Entry Clerk; Dental Assistant; Draftsperson; Driver; EDP Specialist; Factory Worker; Financial Analyst; General Manager; Hotel Manager; Industrial Designer; Industrial Engineer; Insurance Agent/Broker; Legal Secretary; MIS Specialist; Marketing Specialist; Mechanical Engineer; Medical Assistant; Medical Secretary; Metallurgical Engineer; Nurse; Office Worker; Operation/Production Specialist; Pension and Benefits Administrator; Personnel and Labor Relations Specialist; Public Relations Worker; Purchasing Agent; Quality Control Supervisor; Receptionist; Reporter and Editor; Sales Representative; Secretary; Statistician; Stenographer; Systems Analyst; Technical Writer and Editor; Technician; Typist; Underwriter. Company pays fee. Number of placements per year: 100-150.

TRAYNOR CONFIDENTIAL, LTD.
10 Gibbs Street Suite 400
Rochester, NY 14604
Contact Thomas H. Traynor. 716/325-6610. Specializes in the areas of: asset; audit; budgeting; computer science (corporate/computer security; consulting; data processing; EDP audit; operations; programming; software engineering; system); construction (management); credit; credit & collection (commercial; consumer; retail; wholesale); financial analysis; international; investment; lending; public accounting; tax; trainees; trust.

NICHOLAS TRIPOLI ASSOCIATES
251 New Karner Road
Albany NY 12205
Contact Nicholas W. Tripoli. 518/869-8000. Specializes in the areas of: audit; budgeting; financial analysis; international; public accounting; tax.

THE TYLER GROUP
50 East 42nd Street, Suite 2000
New York NY 10017
Contact William P. Conroy, President. 212/972-7200; FAX: 972-7647. Employment agency. Founded 1970. Handling the recent grad to the middle manager with placements in small firms and Fortune 500 companies, introducing the best people to the best companies in New York City, Westchester County, New Jersey, and Long Island. Specializes in the areas of: Accounting; Advertising; Banking and Finance; Insurance; Legal; Manufacturing; MIS/EDP; Publishing; Real Estate; Secretarial and Clerical. Positions commonly filled include: Accountant; Actuary; Administrative Assistant; Bank Officer/Manager; Bookkeeper; Claims Representative; Clerk; Computer Programmer; Credit Manager; Customer Service Representative; Data Entry Clerk; EDP Specialist; Executive Secretary; Financial Analyst; Legal Secretary; Medical Secretary; Personnel Director; Purchasing Agent; Receptionist; Secretary; Statistician; Stenographer; Typist; Underwriter; Word Processor. Company pays fee. Number of placements per year: 400-500.

VINTAGE RESOURCES, INC.
11 E 44th St.
Suite 1608
New York NY 10017
212/867-1001. Employment agency. No appointment required. Founded 1985. Specializes in the areas of: Accounting; Advertising; Legal; Printing and Publishing; Secretarial and Clerical. Positions commonly filled include: Accountant; Administrative Assistant; Bookkeeper; Data Entry Clerk; Executive Secretary; Legal Secretary; Medical Secretary; Receptionist; Secretary; Word Processor; Entry level jobs for college graduates. Company pays fee. Number of placements per year: 201-500.

DON WALDRON AND ASSOC. INC.
450 Seventh Ave., Suite 501
New York NY 10123
Contact Don Waldron. 212/239-9110. Specializes in the areas of: printing (sales); sales (business products; computers; consumer products; industrial products; management; media; medical products; services/intangibles; trainees).

WERBIN ASSOCIATES EXECUTIVE SEARCH, INC.
521 Fifth Avenue, Room 1749
New York NY 10175
Contact Susan Werbin, President. 212/953-0909. Employment agency. Appointment requested. Founded 1978. Specializes in the placement of Data Processing and Operations and Market Research professionals. Specializes in the areas of: Advertising; Banking; Computer Hardware and Software; Insurance; MIS/EDP. Positions commonly filled include: Computer Programmer; EDP Specialist; MIS Specialist; Marketing Specialist; Systems Analyst; Technical Writer/Editor. Company pays fee. Number of placements per year: 50.

WESTCHESTER EMPLOYMENT AGENCY
109 Croton Avenue
Ossining NY 10562
Contact Alan Gordon, Manager. 914/941-8150. Employment agency; temporary help agency. Founded 1961. Specializes in the areas of: Accounting; Advertising; Banking and Finance; Computer Hardware and Software; Construction; Engineering; Food Industry; Health and Medical; Industrial and Interior Design; Insurance; Legal; Manufacturing; MIS/EDP; Nonprofit; Printing and Publishing; Real Estate; Sales and Marketing; Secretarial and Clerical. Positions commonly filled include: Accountant; Actuary; Administrative Assistant; Advertising Executive; Aerospace Engineer; Agricultural Engineer; Architect; Attorney; Bank Officer/Manager; Biochemist/Chemist; Biologist; Biomedical Engineer; Bookkeeper; Ceramics Engineer; Civil Engineer; Claims Representative; Clerk; Commercial Artist; Computer Programmer; Construction Worker; Credit Manager; Customer Service Representative; Data Entry Clerk; Dietician/Nutritionist; Draftsperson; EDP Specialist; Economist; Electrical Engineer; Executive Secretary; Factory Worker; Financial Analyst; General Laborer; General Manager; Hotel Manager; Industrial Designer; Industrial Engineer; Insurance Agent/Broker; Interior Designer; Legal Secretary; Light Industrial Worker; Marketing Specialist; Mechanical Engineer; Medical Secretary; Metallurgical Engineer; Mining Engineer; Nurse; Personnel Director; Petroleum Engineer; Physicist; Public Relations Worker; Purchasing Agent; Receptionist; Reporter; Editor; Sales Representative; Secretary; Statistician; Stenographer; Systems Analyst; Technical Writer/Editor; Technician; Typist; Underwriter; Word Processor. Company pays fee. Number of placements per year: 501-1000.

WINMAR PERSONNEL AGENCY

535 Fifth Avenue Suite 1008
New York NY 10017
Contact Susan Medeloff Winters. 212/687-8977. FAX: 212/687-9853. Specializes in the areas of: human resources (benefits; compensation; EEO; labor relations; management; personnel/industrial relations; recruiting/staffing; training/ development); office administration (administrators; management; secretaries; word processing); temporary services (secretaries; word processing).

WINSTON PERSONNEL INC.

535 Fifth Avenue, Suite 701
New York NY 10017
Contact Dave Silver, VP/Operations. 212/557-5000. Employment agency. No appointment required. Founded 1967. Specializes in Insurance and Health Care personnel recruitment. Specializes in the areas of: Accounting and Finance; Advertising; Architecture; Banking; Clerical; Fashion; Health and Medical; Insurance; Legal; MIS/EDP; Personnel and Human Resources; Printing and Publishing; Sales and Marketing. Positions commonly filled include: Accountant; Actuary; Advertising Worker; Administrative Assistant; Aerospace Engineer; Architect; Attorney; Bank Officer and Manager; Biochemist; Biologist; Biomedical Engineer; Bookkeeper; Buyer; Ceramics Engineer; Chemical Engineer; Chemist; Civil Engineer; Claims Representative; Clerk; Commercial Artist; Computer Operator; Computer Programmer; Credit Manager; Customer Service Representative; Data Entry Clerk; Demonstrator; Dietician; Draftsperson; EDP Specialist; Economist; Electrical Engineer; Financial Analyst; General Manager; Industrial Designer; Industrial Engineer; Insurance Agent/Broker; Legal Secretary; MIS Specialist; Marketing Specialist; Mechanical Engineer; Medical Secretary; Metallurgical Engineer; Mining Engineer; Model; Nurse; Office Worker; Petroleum Engineer; Operations and Production Specialist; Personnel and Labor Relations Specialist; Physicist; Public Relations Worker; Purchasing Agent; Quality Control Supervisor; Receptionist; Reporter and Editor; Sales Representative; Secretary; Statistician; Stenographer; Systems Analyst; Technical Writer and Editor; Technician; Typist; Underwriter; Word Processing Specialist. Company pays fee. Number of placements per year: 1000 +.

WINSTON TEMPORARIES

535 Fifth Avenue
New York NY 10017
Contact Sy Kaye. 212/687-7890. Temporary help service. No appointment required. Founded 1979. Positions commonly filled include: Accountant; Actuary; Advertising Worker; Administrative Assistant; Architect; Attorney; Bank Officer and Manager; Bookkeepers; Buyer; Computer Operator; Computer Programmer; Credit Manager; Customer Service Representative; Data Entry Clerk; Dietician; Demonstrator; Draftsperson; Financial Analyst; General Manager; Legal Secretary; Marketing Specialist; Medical Secretary; Model; Nurse; Office Worker; Personnel and Labor Relations Specialist; Secretary; Statistician; Stenographer; Systems Analyst; Technical Writer and Editor; Typist; Underwriter; Word Processing Specialist. Company pays fee. Number of placements per year: 1001+.

WOODBURY PERSONNEL ASSOC., INC.

375 North Broadway
Jericho NY 11753
Contact Louis Copt, CPC. 516/938-7910. FAX: 516/938-7370. Specializes in the areas of: asset; credit; international; investment; lending; trust; insurance (actuarial; claims; life/health; pension; property/casualty; rating; reinsurance; underwriting); marketing

(consumer products; direct marketing; international; market research; product management); retailing (buying; management; merchandising; operations).

WOODSIDE ON THE MOVE
58-14 Roosvelt Avenue
Woodside NY 11377
Contact Cormac Cullinan, Business Coordinator. 718/476-8449. Employment agency. No appointment required. Founded 1979. As a community based nonprofit organization, Woodside on the Move is dedicated to stimulating the local economy by encouraging local businesses to hire residents. Positions commonly filled include: Administrative Assistant; Bookkeeper; Clerk; Construction Worker; Data Entry Clerk; Driver; Executive Secretary; Factory Worker; General Laborer; General Manager; Light Industrial Worker; Machinist; Plumber; Secretary; Typist; Word Processor. Company pays fee. Number of placements per year: 100-201.

THE WORTH GROUP, INC.
331 Madison Ave., Ste. 704
New York, NY 10017
Contact Al Rosenblum. 212/351-2320. FAX: 212/953-3282. Specializes in the area of: telecommunications (data; voice).

WRIGHT PERSONNEL CONSULTANTS, INC.
525 Route 207
Newburgh NY 12550
Contact James C. Wright, Manager. 914/561-3311. Employment agency; temporary help agency. Appointment required. Founded 1960. Specializes in the areas of: Accounting; Banking and Finance; Computer Hardware and Software; Engineering; Food Industry; Industrial and Interior Design; Insurance; Legal; Manufacturing; MIS/EDP; Sales and Marketing; Secretarial and Clerical; Technical and Scientific. Positions commonly filled include: Accountant; Administrative Assistant; Bank Officer/Manager; Biochemist/Chemist; Biomedical Engineer; Bookkeeper; Claims Representative; Clerk; Computer Programmer; Credit Manager; Customer Service Representative; Data Entry Clerk; Industrial Designer; Draftsperson; EDP Specialist; Executive Secretary; Financial Analyst; General Manager; Legal Secretary; Marketing Specialist; Mechanical Engineer; Metallurgical Engineer; Personnel Director; Purchasing Agent; Receptionist; Sales Representative; Secretary; Stenographer; Systems Analyst; Technician; Typist; Underwriter; Word Processor. Company pays fee. Number of placements per year: 201-500.

EXECUTIVE SEARCH FIRMS OF NEW YORK

ABLE PERSONNEL, INC.
280 Madison Avenue
8th floor
New York NY 10016
Contact Dan Gardner. 212/689-5500. Executive search firm. Appointment required; unsolicited resumes accepted. Founded 1956. Specializes in the areas of: Accounting; Administration; MIS/EDP; Advertising; Affirmative Action; Architecture; Art;

Communications; Construction; General Management; Human Resources; Industrial and Interior Design; Market Research; Marketing; Nonprofit; Operations Management; Printing and Publishing; Procurement; Production; Real Estate; Retailing; Sales and Marketing; Transportation; Women. Contingency. Number of searches conducted per year: 501+.

ALEXADEROSS ASSOCIATES, INC.
280 Madison Avenue
Suite 1104
New York NY 10016
Contact Mr. Ben Lichtenstein, Senior Partner. 212/889-9333. Executive search firm. Appointment requested. Founded 1977. Recruitment firm specializing in Human Resource functions for the Fortune 500 and major Financial Services organizations. Number of searches conducted per year: 50.

ARROW EMPLOYMENT AGENCY MELVILLE, INC.
150 Route 110
Melville NY 11747
Contact Don Becker, President. 516/271-3700. Executive search firm. No appointment required; unsolicited resumes accepted. Founded 1954. Specializes in the areas of: Accounting; Computer Hardware and Software; Engineering; Food Industry; Manufacturing; Personnel and Human Resources; Printing and Publishing; Procurement; Sales and Marketing; Technical and Scientific; Retail. Contingency. Number of searches conducted per year: 201-500.

THE BAILEY AGENCY
14 Church Street
White Plains NY 10601
Contact Frank Deligio, C.P.C., President. 914/946-1383. Executive search firm. Appointment required; unsolicited resumes accepted. Founded 1972. Under present management since 1978. Emphasis on quality placement through extensive recruiter-training and a commitment to high standards in evaluation of candidates and client companies. Member: Bailey System, NAPC, APCNY, BBBT. Specializes in the areas of: Accounting; Administration; Architecture; Banking and Finance; Computer Hardware and Software; Industrial and Interior Design; Insurance; Legal; Office Services. Contingency. Number of searches conducted per year: 201-500.

CAREER GUIDES, INC.
450 7th Avenue
Suite 1200
New York NY 10123
Contact Sy Gellman, C.P.C. 212/697-3358. Executive search firm. Appointment requested; no phone calls; unsolicited resumes accepted. Founded 1954. Specializes in the areas of: Procurement; Sales and Marketing. Contingency. Number of searches conducted per year: 101-200.

CLOSMAN & ASSOCIATES, INC.
Two Penn Plaza, Suite 1500
New York NY 10121
Contact Stan S. Closman, President. 212/244-3100. Executive search firm. Appointment requested; unsolicited resumes accepted. Founded 1968. Specializes in the areas of: Administration and MIS/EDP; Affirmative Action; Banking; Broadcasting; Computer Hardware and Software; Manufacturing; Personnel and Human Resources; Women. Contingency; noncontingency. Number of searches conducted per year: 101-200.

CONTACT
733 3rd Avenue
16th Floor
New York NY 10017
212/223-8111. Executive search firm. Appointment required. Founded 1983. Specializes in the areas of: Accounting; Advertising; Banking and Finance; Computer Hardware and Software; Real Estate; Sales and Marketing. Positions commonly filled include: Actuary; Advertising Executive; Bank Officer/Manager; Computer Programmer; Customer Service Representative; Economist; Financial Analyst; Management Consultant; Marketing Specialist; Personnel Director; Public Relations Worker; Sales Representative; Systems Analyst. Company pays fee. Number of placements per year: 1-50.

CORPORATE CAREERS, INC.
188 East Post Road
White Plains NY 10601
Contact Richard Birnbaum, President. 914/946-2003. Executive search firm. Appointment requested; unsolicited resumes accepted. Founded 1973. Specializes in the areas of: Accounting; Administration, MIS/EDP; Banking; Computer Hardware and Software; Engineering; Finance; Food Industry; General Management; Manufacturing; Personnel and Human Resources; Procurement; Sales and Marketing; Technical and Scientific. Contingency; noncontingency.

CRISPI, WAGNER & CO., INC.
420 Lexington Avenue
Suite 400
New York NY 10170
Contact Nicholas Crispi, President. 212/687-2340. Executive search firm. Appointment required; no phone calls; unsolicited resumes accepted. Founded 1972. We are a firm of investment professionals servicing the investment industry. Specializes in Investment Professionals exclusively. Noncontingency. Number of searches conducted per year: 1-50.

FRANK CUOMO & ASSOCIATES, INC.
111 Brook Street
Scarsdale NY 10583
Contact Frank Cuomo, President. 914/723-8001. Executive search firm. Appointment requested; no phone calls; unsolicited resumes accepted. Founded 1980. Middle management positions in Sales, Marketing, Engineering, Accounting, Manufacturing. Contingency. Number of searches conducted per year: 51-100.

DRUMMOND ASSOCIATES INC.
50 Broadway
New York NY 10004
Contact Chester Fienberg, President. 212/248-1120. Executive search firm. Appointment requested; no unsolicited resumes. Founded 1967. Specializes in the areas of: Banking; Finance. Contingency; noncontingency. Number of searches conducted per year: 26-50.

THE FRY GROUP, INC.
18 East 41st Street
New York NY 10017
Contact John Fry, President. 212/532-8100. Executive search firm. Appointment requested; no phone calls; unsolicited resumes accepted. Founded 1976. Recruits experienced executives for the Communications field. Specializes in the areas of: Advertising; Public Relations. Contingency.

HAWKES-RANDOLPH & ASSOCIATES, INC.
805 Third Avenue, 28th Floor
New York NY 10022
Contact Ted King, President. 212/593-3131. Executive search firm. Appointment required; unsolicited resumes accepted. Founded 1985. Specializes in the areas of: Banking and Finance; Sales and Marketing. Number of searches conducted per year: 101-200.

RUTH HIRSCH AND JIM GRATHWOL ASSOC.
400 Madison Avenue, Suite 1507
New York NY 10017
212/758-4070. Executive search firm. Appointment requested; no phone calls; unsolicited resumes accepted. Founded 1947. Specializes in the areas of: Advertising; Architecture; Art and Design; Construction; Engineering; Real Estate; Quality Control. Contingency.

MANAGEMENT RECRUITERS OF GRAMERCY
Suite 1510, 200 Park Avenue South
New York NY 10003
Contact Steve Schwartz, Manager. 212/505-5530. Executive search firm. Appointment required; no phone calls; unsolicited resumes accepted. Founded 1965. World's largest contingency search firm. Five hundred offices nationwide, doing business under the names "Management Recruiters", "Sales Consultants", "CompuSearch" and "OfficeMates5." Specializes in mid-management/professional positions, $25,000-75,000 per annum. Specializes in the areas of: Accounting; Administration; MIS/EDP; Advertising; Affirmative Action; Architecture; Banking and Finance; Communications; Computer Hardware and Software; Construction; Electrical; Engineering; Food Industry; General Management; Health and Medical; Human Resources; Industrial and Interior Design; Insurance; Legal; Manufacturing; Operations Management; Printing and Publishing; Procurement; Real Estate; Retailing; Sales and Marketing; Technical and Scientific; Textiles; Transportation. Contingency.

MANAGEMENT RECRUITERS OF HUNTINGTON
76 East Main Street
Huntington NY 11743
Contact Sue Goldfarb, Manager. 516/549-6970; FAX: 516/549-2717. Executive search firm. Appointment required; no phone calls; unsolicited resumes accepted. Founded 1965. World's largest contingency search firm. Five hundred offices nationwide, doing business under the names "Management Recruiters", "Sales Consultants", "CompuSearch" and "OfficeMates5." Specializes in mid-management/professional positions, $25,000-75,000 per annum. Specializes in the areas of: Accounting; Administration; MIS/EDP; Advertising; Affirmative Action; Architecture; Banking and Finance; Communications; Computer Hardware and Software; Construction; Electrical; Engineering; Food Industry; General Management; Health and Medical; Human Resources; Industrial and Interior Design; Insurance; Legal; Manufacturing; Printing and Publishing; Procurement; Real Estate; Retailing; Sales and Marketing; Technical and Scientific; Textiles; Transportation. Contingency.

MANAGEMENT RECRUITERS OF MANHATTAN-FIFTH AVENUE
350 Fifth Avenue, Suite 2205
New York NY 10018
Contact Joseph H. Kay, Manager. 212/947-3131. Executive search firm. Appointment required; no phone calls; unsolicited resumes accepted. Founded 1965. World's largest contingency search firm. Five hundred offices nationwide, doing business under the names "Management Recruiters", "Sales Consultants", "CompuSearch" and "OfficeMates5."

Specializes in mid-management/professional positions, $25,000-75,000 per annum. Specializes in the areas of: Accounting; Administration; MIS/EDP; Advertising; Affirmative Action; Architecture; Banking and Finance; Communications; Computer Hardware and Software; Construction; Electrical; Engineering; Food Industry; General Management; Health and Medical; Human Resources; Industrial and Interior Design; Insurance; Legal; Manufacturing; Operations Management; Printing and Publishing; Procurement; Real Estate; Retailing; Sales and Marketing; Technical and Scientific; Textiles; Transportation. Contingency.

MANAGEMENT RECRUITERS OF MANHATTAN/
LEXINGTON AVENUE
Suite 505, 575 Lexington Avenue
New York NY 10022
Contact Jeff Heath, Manager. 212/486-7300; FAX: 212/486-7584. Executive search firm. Appointment required; no phone calls; unsolicited resumes accepted. Founded 1965. World's largest contingency search firm. Five hundred offices nationwide, doing business under the names "Management Recruiters", "Sales Consultants", "CompuSearch" and "OfficeMates5." Specializes in mid-management/professional positions, $25,000-75,000 per annum. Specializes in the areas of: Accounting; Administration; MIS/EDP; Advertising; Affirmative Action; Architecture; Banking and Finance; Communications; Computer Hardware and Software; Construction; Electrical; Engineering; Food Industry; General Management; Health and Medical; Human Resources; Industrial and Interior Design; Insurance; Legal; Manufacturing; Operations Management; Printing and Publishing; Procurement; Real Estate; Retailing; Sales and Marketing; Technical and Scientific; Textiles; Transportation. Contingency.

MANAGEMENT RECRUITERS OF NASSAU COUNTY
77 North Centre Avenue, Suite 211
Rockville Centre NY 11571
Contact Tom Wieder, Manager. 516/536-3111; FAX: 516/536-3138. Executive search firm. Appointment required; no phone calls; unsolicited resumes accepted. Founded 1965. World's largest contingency search firm. Five hundred offices nationwide, doing business under the names "Management Recruiters", "Sales Consultants", "CompuSearch" and "OfficeMates5." Specializes in mid-management/professional positions, $25,000-75,000 per annum. Specializes in the areas of: Accounting; Administration; MIS/EDP; Advertising; Affirmative Action; Architecture; Banking and Finance; Communications; Computer Hardware and Software; Construction; Electrical; Engineering; Food Industry; General Management; Health and Medical; Human Resources; Industrial and Interior Design; Insurance; Legal; Manufacturing; Printing and Publishing; Procurement; Real Estate; Retailing; Sales and Marketing; Technical and Scientific; Textiles; Transportation. Contingency.

MANAGEMENT RECRUITERS OF SUFFOLK COUNTY
100 Crossways Park West
Woodbury NY 11797
Contact Sebastian LiVolsi, Manager. 516/364-9290. Executive search firm. Appointment required; no phone calls; unsolicited resumes accepted. Founded 1965. World's largest contingency search firm. Five hundred offices nationwide, doing business under the names "Management Recruiters", "Sales Consultants", "CompuSearch" and "OfficeMates5." Specializes in mid-management/professional positions, $25,000-75,000 per annum. Specializes in the areas of: Accounting; Administration; MIS/EDP; Advertising; Affirmative Action; Architecture; Banking and Finance; Communications; Computer Hardware and Software; Construction; Electrical; Engineering; Food Industry; General Management; Health and Medical; Human Resources; Industrial and Interior Design;

Insurance; Legal; Manufacturing; Printing and Publishing; Procurement; Real Estate; Retailing; Sales and Marketing; Technical and Scientific; Textiles; Transportation. Contingency.

MANAGEMENT RECRUITERS OF WESTCHESTER COUNTY
570 Taxter Road
Elmsford NY 10523
Contact Bob Neuffer, Manager. 914/592-4370. Executive search firm. Appointment required; no phone calls; unsolicited resumes accepted. Founded 1965. World's largest contingency search firm. Five hundred offices nationwide, doing business under the names "Management Recruiters", "Sales Consultants", "CompuSearch" and "OfficeMates5." Specializes in mid-management/professional positions, $25,000-75,000 per annum. Specializes in the areas of: Accounting; Administration; MIS/EDP; Advertising; Affirmative Action; Architecture; Banking and Finance; Communications; Computer Hardware and Software; Construction; Electrical; Engineering; Food Industry; General Management; Health and Medical; Human Resources; Industrial and Interior Design; Insurance; Legal; Manufacturing; Printing and Publishing; Procurement; Real Estate; Retailing; Sales and Marketing; Technical and Scientific; Textiles; Transportation. Contingency.

MARSHALL-ALAN ASSOC., INC.
25 West 39th Street, Suite 503
New York NY 10018
Contact Alan Massarsky, President. 212/382-2440. Executive search firm. Appointment requested; unsolicited resumes accepted. Founded 1982. Mid-upper management only. Specializes in the areas of: Apparel; Hospitality; Retail. Contingency and retainer. Number of searches conducted per year: 101-200.

JUNE B. MEYER
250 West 57th Street
New York NY 10107
Contact June Meyer, President. 212/333-5900. Executive search firm. Appointment requested; unsolicited resumes accepted. Founded 1978. Services the metal industry. Searches for qualified people in the areas of: Management; Finance; Trading; Purchasing; Selling; Traffic; Administration. Contingency. Number of searches conducted per year: 25.

OFFICEMATES5 OF ROCKLAND
One Bluehill Plaza, Box 1603
Pearl River NY 10965
Contact Tom Malone or Veronica Varian, Co-Managers. 914/735-7015. Executive search firm. Appointment required; no phone calls; unsolicited resumes accepted. Founded 1965. World's largest contingency search firm. Five hundred offices nationwide, doing business under the names "Management Recruiters", "Sales Consultants", "CompuSearch" and "OfficeMates5." Specializes in mid-management/professional positions, $25,000-75,000 per annum. Specializes in the areas of: Accounting; Administration; MIS/EDP; Advertising; Affirmative Action; Architecture; Banking and Finance; Communications; Computer Hardware and Software; Construction; Electrical; Engineering; Food Industry; General Management; Health and Medical; Human Resources; Industrial and Interior Design; Insurance; Legal; Manufacturing; Printing and Publishing; Procurement; Real Estate; Retailing; Sales and Marketing; Technical and Scientific; Textiles; Transportation. Contingency.

PROFESSIONAL MAN ASSOCIATES, INC.
Box 606
Smithtown NY 11787
Contact Alfred J. Lewandowski, President. 516/862-7009. Executive search firm. Appointment requested; unsolicited resumes accepted. Founded 1960. Specializes in the areas of: Computer Hardware and Software; Electronics; Engineering; Technical and Scientific; Technical Management.

SALES CONSULTANTS OF WESTCHESTER-SOUTH
Nine Skyline Drive
Hawthorne NY 10532
Contact Bob Penney, Manager. 914/592-1290. Executive search firm. Appointment required; no phone calls; unsolicited resumes accepted. Founded 1965. World's largest contingency search firm. Five hundred offices nationwide, doing business under the names "Management Recruiters", "Sales Consultants", "CompuSearch" and "OfficeMates5". Specializes in mid-management/professional positions, $25,000-75,000 per annum. Specializes in the areas of: Accounting; Administration; MIS/EDP; Advertising; Affirmative Action; Architecture; Banking and Finance; Communications; Computer Hardware and Software; Construction; Electrical; Engineering; Food Industry; General Management; Health and Medical; Human Resources; Industrial and Interior Design; Insurance; Legal; Manufacturing; Printing and Publishing; Procurement; Real Estate; Retailing; Sales and Marketing; Technical and Scientific; Textiles; Transportation. Contingency.

SALES SEARCH, LTD.
48 Burd Street
Nyack NY 10960
Contact John Ratcliff, C.P.C., President. 914/353-2040. Executive search firm. Appointment required; unsolicited resumes accepted. Founded 1983. Covers all aspects of Sales, Sales Management and Marketing. Specializing in Consumer, Industrial High Tech Communications, EDP, and Technical. Owner has over 20 years of experience. Specializes in the areas of: Communications; Computer Hardware and Software; Electrical; Engineering; General Management; Sales and Marketing; Technical and Scientific. Resume preparation. Contingency.

SAXON MORSE ASSOCIATES
Post Office Box 177
Northside Plaza
Pomona NY 10970-0177
Contact Mr. Stan Case, Executive Vice President. 914/362-1300. Executive search firm. Appointment required; no phone calls; unsolicited resumes accepted. Founded 1965. Retained by Consumer Electronics Manufacturers/Importers and Watch/Clock Manufacturers/Importers to staff domestic and international divisions-Sales/Marketing, Prem./Incent., Accounting/Credit, Licensing, etc. Specializes in the areas of: Computer Hardware and Software; Consumer Electronics; Sales and Marketing. Human Resource Audit. Noncontingency. Number of searches conducted per year: 50+.

SETFORD SHAW ASSOCIATES, LTD
111 Broadway, 10th Floor
New York NY 10006
Contact Edward L. Shaw, President. 212/962-1500. Executive search firm. No appointment required; unsolicited resumes accepted. Founded 1982. Specializes in the areas of: Administration, MIS/EDP; Computer Hardware and Software. Contingency. Number of searches conducted per year: 101-200.

TECHSEARCH SERVICES, INC.
1500 Broadway
Suite 2203
New York NY 10036
Contact David G. Taft, President. 212/302-7010; FAX: 212/575-2618. Executive search firm. No appointment required. Founded 1984. Places high-level individual contributors with technical skills and middle management in Fortune 500 and Financial Services firms. Specializes in the areas of: Banking and Finance; Computer Hardware and Software; MIS/EDP. Positions commonly filled include: Computer Programmer; EDP Specialist; Management Consultant; Marketing Specialist; Systems Analyst. Company pays fee. Number of placements per year: 1-50.

EMPLOYMENT AGENCIES AND TEMPORARY SERVICES OF CONNECTICUT

A & A PERSONNEL SERVICES
11 Asylum St., Ste. 612-613
Hartford CT 06103
Contact Lewis E. Schweitzer. 203/549-5262. FAX: 203/249-9979. Specializes in the areas of: audit; data processing; EDP audit; engineering (aeronautical; chemical; civil; electrical; environmental/hazardous waste; HVAC; industrial; manufacturing; mechanical; nuclear; packaging); financial analysis; operations; public accounting; software engineering; systems; tax; insurance (actuarial; claims; life/health; pension; property/casualty; rating; underwriting). Positions commonly filled include: Accountant; Actuary; Attorney; Aerospace Engineer; Bank Officer/Manager; Bookkeeper; Civil Engineer; Claims Representative; Computer Programmer; Credit Manager; Customer Service Representative; EDP Specialist; Electrical Engineer; Executive Secretary; Financial Analyst; Industrial Designer; Industrial Engineer; Mechanical Engineer; Personnel Director; Purchasing Agent; Sales Representative; Statistician; Systems Analyst; Technician; Underwriter. Company pays fee. Number of placements per year: 51-100.

ALP ASSOCIATES
5 South Science Park
Suite 2031
New Haven CT 06511
Contact Andrew L. Piscitelle, CPC. 203/786-5310. FAX: 203/786-5023. Specializes in the area of: engineering (aeronautical; electrical; environmental/hazardous waste; industrial; manufacturing; mechanical; packaging).

ABRAHAM & LONDON LTD.
P.O. Box 2154
Danbury CT 06813
Contact Stuart R. Laub. 203/798-7537. FAX: 203/798-1784. Specializes in the areas of: marketing (consumer products; business products/computers; direct marketing; industrial products; international; market research; medical products; product management; sales

promotion); sales (business products; computers; consumer products; industrial products; international; management; media; medical products; services/intangibles); telecommunications (data; voice).

ACCOUNTANTS ON CALL
2777 Summer Street
Stamford CT 06905
Contact Marvin H. Sternlicht. 203/327-5100. FAX: 203/327-5567. Specializes in the areas of: audit; bookkeeping; budgeting; clerical; financial analysis; international; public accounting; tax.

AMERICAN INTERNATIONAL, LTD.
25 Sylvan Rd., South
Westport CT 06880
Contact Patricia Putzig/Dorothy Miller. 203/454-1010. FAX: 203/454-9584. Specializes in the areas of: computer science (corporate/computer security; consulting; data processing; EDP audit; operations; programming; sales; software engineering; systems; technicians); marketing (consumer products; business products/computers; direct marketing; industrial products; international; market research; medical products; product management; sales promotion); pharmaceuticals (manufacturing; sales; scientific); sales (business products; computers; consumer products; industrial products; international; management; media; medical products; services/intangibles; trainees); telecommunications (data; satellite; voice).

BAILEY EMPLOYMENT SERVICE OF BRANFORD, INC.
Five South Main Street
Branford CT 06405
Contact Dean Troxell, President. 203/488-2504. Employment agency. Appointment required. Founded 1972. Statewide exposure through ten affiliates. Full service, Engineering, Accounting and Office Services. Specializes in the areas of: Accounting; Computer Hardware and Software; Engineering; Insurance; Legal; Manufacturing, MIS/EDP; Sales and Marketing; Secretarial and Clerical. Positions commonly filled include: Accountant; Administrative Assistant; Aerospace Engineer; Biomedical Engineer; Bookkeeper; Claims Representative; Computer Programmer; Customer Service Representative; Data Entry Clerk; Draftsperson; EDP Specialist; Electrical Engineer; Executive Secretary; Financial Analyst; Industrial Designer; Industrial Engineer; Legal Secretary; Mechanical Engineer; Receptionist; Sales Representative; Secretary; Systems Analyst; Technical Writer/Editor; Technician; Typist; Word Processor. Company pays fee. Number of placements per year: 201-500.

BAILEY EMPLOYMENT SVC.-NORWALK
6 Elm Street
Norwalk CT 06850
Contact Joyce Matusow, CPC. 203/838-2351. Specializes in the area of: office administration (administrators; clerks; management; receptionists; secretaries; word processing).

BATES ASSOCIATES
6527 Main Street
Trumbull CT 06611
Contact Bradford R. Bates. 203/452-9441. FAX: 203/452-9465. Specializes in the areas of: accounting/finance; engineering; environmental/hazardous waste; human resources; manufacturing/production; materials/management; purchasing; security.

BIXBY ASSOCIATES PERSONNEL CONSULTANTS
300 Church Street
Yalesville CT 06492
Contact Kevin Maynes, President. 203/269-1715. Employment agency. Appointment required. Founded 1981. Specializes in the areas of: Accounting and Finance; Banking; Computer Hardware and Software; Construction; Engineering; Insurance; Manufacturing; MIS/EDP; Sales and Marketing; Technical and Scientific. Positions commonly filled include: Accountant; Actuary; Administrative Assistant; Advertising Worker; Aerospace Engineer; Agricultural Engineer; Architect; Attorney; Bank Officer/Manager; Biochemist; Biologist; Biomedical Engineer; Bookkeeper; Buyer; Ceramics Engineer; Chemist; Civil Engineer; Claim Representative; Clerk; Commercial Artist; Computer Operator; Computer Programmer; Construction Worker; Credit Manager; Customer Service Representative; Data Entry Clerk; Dietician; Draftsperson; EDP Specialist; Economist; Electrical Engineer; Financial Analyst; Food Technologist; General Manager; Industrial Designer; Industrial Engineer; Insurance Agent/Broker; Legal Secretary; MIS Specialist; Marketing Specialist; Mechanical Engineer; Medical Secretary; Metallurgical Engineer; Mining Engineer; Office Worker; Operations/Production Specialist; Personnel and Labor Relations Specialist; Petroleum Engineer; Physicist; Public Relations Worker; Purchasing Agent; Quality Control Supervisor; Receptionist; Reporter/Editor; Sales Representative; Secretary; Statistician; Stenographer; Systems Analyst; Technical Writer/Editor; Technician; Typist; Underwriter; Word Processing Specialist. Company pays fee. Number of placements per year: 101-200.

CHARTER PERSONNEL SERVICES
P.O. Box 1070
Danbury CT 06813
Contact Louise V. Fornabaio, President. 203/744-6440. Temporary help service. No appointment required. Founded 1977. Nonspecialized. Positions commonly filled include: Accountant; Biochemist; Biologist; Biomedical Engineer; Bookkeeper; Buyer; Chemical Engineer; Chemist; Civil Engineer; Clerk; Computer Operator; Customer Service Representative; Data Entry Clerk; Draftsperson; EDP Specialist; Electrical Engineer; Industrial Designer; Industrial Engineer; Legal Secretary; Mechanical Engineer; Medical Secretary; Office Worker; Paralegal; Purchasing Agent; Quality Supervisor; Receptionist; Secretary; Statistician; Stenographer; Technical Writer/Editor; Technician; Word Processing Specialist. Company pays fee.

CHENEY ASSOCIATES
3190 Whitney Avenue
Hamden CT 06518
Contact Timothy W. Cheney. 203/281-3736. FAX: 203/281-6881. Specializes in the areas of: consulting; data processing; EDP audit; operations; programming; software engineering; systems.

CHOICE PERSONNEL
733 Summer Street
Suite 406
Stamford CT 06901
Contact Pat Michael/Steve Klein. 203/324-4744. FAX: 203/964-9344. Specializes in the areas of: office administration (administrators; clerks; receptionists; secretaries; word processing); temporary services (accounting/bookkeeping; secretaries; word processing).

CREATIVE OPTIONS
50 Washington St.
South Norwalk CT 06854
Contact Holly Hinds. 203/854-9393. Specializes in the areas of: account management; art; copy; production/traffic; sales promotion; packaging (design); public relations (agency; corporate).

DAWSON PERSONNEL, INC.
100 Constitution Plaza, Suite 400
Hartford CT 06103
Contact Jean Dawson, President. 203/249-7721. Employment agency; temporary help service. Appointment requested. Founded 1977. Specializes in the areas of: Accounting and Finance; Advertising; Banking; Clerical; Computer Hardware and Software; Engineering; Insurance; Legal; Manufacturing; MIS/EDP; Personnel and Human Resources; Printing and Publishing; Sales and Marketing; Technical and Scientific. Positions commonly filled include: Accountant; Actuary; Administrative Assistant; Advertising Worker; Aerospace Engineer; Agricultural Engineer; Architect; Attorney; Bank Officer/Manager; Biochemist; Biologist; Biomedical Engineer; Bookkeeper; Buyer; Ceramics Engineer; Chemist; Civil Engineer; Claim Representative; Clerk; Commercial Artist; Computer Operator; Computer Programmer; Credit Manager; Customer Service Representative; Data Entry Clerk; Demonstrator; Draftsperson; EDP Specialist; Economist; Electrical Engineer; Financial Analyst; Food Technologist; General Manager; Industrial Designer; Industrial Engineer; Insurance Agent/Broker; Legal Secretary; Light Industrial Worker; MIS Specialist; Marketing Specialist; Mechanical Engineer; Medical Secretary; Metallurgical Engineer; Mining Engineer; Office Worker; Operations/Production Specialist; Personnel and Labor Relations Specialist; Petroleum Engineer; Physicist; Printing Specialist; Public Relations Worker; Purchasing Agent; Quality Control Supervisor; Receptionist; Reporter/Editor; Sales Representative; Secretary; Statistician; Stenographer; Systems Analyst; Technical Writer/Editor; Technician; Typist; Underwriter; Word Processing Specialist. Company pays fee. Number of placements per year: 101-200.

DITECH RESOURCES
110 Washington Avenue
North Haven CT 06437
Contact Diane Brecciaroli, CPC. 203/234-9030. FAX: 203/234-6302. Specializes in the area of: engineering (aeronautical; chemical; civil; electrical; manufacturing; mechanical).

DIVERSIFIED EMPLOYMENT SERVICES, INC.
531 Whalley Avenue
New Haven CT 06511
Contact D. William DeRosa Jr., President. 203/397-2500. Employment agency; temporary help agency. Founded 1970. Broad based areas of employment with individuals specialized to each area. Permanent, temporary and contract personnel. Specializes in the areas of: Accounting; Computer Hardware and Software; Engineering; Industrial and Interior Design; Manufacturing; MIS/EDP; Secretarial and Clerical; Technical and Scientific. Positions commonly filled include: Accountant; Administrative Assistant; Biochemist/Chemist; Biomedical Engineer; Bookkeeper; Clerk; Computer Programmer; Credit Manager; Customer Service Representative; Data Entry Clerk; Executive Secretary; EDP Specialist; Electrical Engineer; Industrial Designer; Industrial Engineer; Legal Secretary; Medical Secretary; Metallurgical Engineer; Personnel Director; Purchasing Agent; Receptionist; Secretary; Stenographer; Systems Analyst; Technical Writer/Editor; Technician; Typist. Company pays fee. Number of placements per year: 51-200.

DUNHILL PERSONNEL OF NEW HAVEN
59 Elm Street
Suite 520
New Haven CT 06510
Contact Donald Kaiser, President. 203/562-0511. Employment agency; temporary help service; resume service. Founded 1978. Specializes in the areas of: Accounting and Finance; International Sales and Management; Office Personnel; Sales and Marketing. Positions commonly filled include: Accountant; Data Entry Personnel; Marketing Manager; Sales Representative; Secretary.

EMPLOYMENT OPPORTUNITIES, INC.
213 Main Street
Danbury CT 06810
Contact Geanette Petroski. 203/792-9536. FAX: 203/798-1653. Employment agency; temporary help service. No appointment required. Founded 1977. Specializes in the areas of: chemical; engineering (chemical; electrical; environmental/hazardous waste; HVAC; industrial; manufacturing; mechanical; packaging); materials management (inventory control [raw/in process]; MRP systems; production control/planning; purchasing); pharmaceuticals (manufacturing; scientific); scientific research & development (product development; research & development; sales; technicians). Company pays fee. Number of placements per year: 1001+.

FELLOWS ASSOCIATES, INC.
34 Bloomfield Ave.
Windsor CT 06095
Contact Linda C. Fellows. 203/688-8110. FAX: 203/688-1562. Specializes in the areas of credit; investment; lending; office administration (administrators; clerks; management; receptionists; secretaries).

MICHAEL GARBI ASSOC.
1351 Washington Boulevard
Stamford CT 06902
Contact Georgia Siomkos. 203/967-2629. Specializes in the areas of: audit; budgeting; corporate/computer security; consulting; data processing; EDP audit; financial analysis; international; operations; programming; public accounting; sales; software engineering; systems; tax; technicians; word processing sales/service; human resources (benefits; compensation; EEO; labor relations; management; personnel/industrial relations; recruiting/staffing; training/development); office administration (administrators; clerks; management; receptionists; secretaries; word processing).

THE GOEDERT GROUP
110 N. Washington Ave.
North Haven CT 06473
Contact Patrick J. Goedert, CPC. 203/234-6340. Specializes in the area of: sales (business products; computers; consumer; products; industrial products; international; management medical products; services/intangibles; trainees).

STANLEY HERZ AND COMPANY, INC.
300 Broad St. #502
Stamford CT 06901
Contact Stanley Herz. 203/358-9500. Specializes in the areas of: audit; budgeting; consulting; data processing; EDP audit; financial analysis; international; programming; public accounting; systems; tax.

HIGH-TECH RECRUITERS
30 High Street, Suite 104A
Hartford CT 06103
Contact Clement W. Williams, CPC. 203/527-4262. FAX: 203/724-4796. Specializes in the areas of: corporate/computer security;. data processing; EDP audit; programming; software engineering; systems; technicians; word processing sales/service.

HIPP WATERS ASSOCIATES
209 Bedford Street
Stamford CT 06901
Contact Donald Hutchinson, CPC. 203/246-4477. FAX: 203/247-0371. Specializes in the areas of: audit; bookkeeping; budgeting; clerical; financial analysis; international; public accounting; tax; office administration (administrators; clerks; management; receptionists; secretaries; word processing); sales (business products; computers; consumer products; industrial products; international; management media; medical products; services/intangibles; trainees).

HIPP WATERS ASSOCIATES
209 Bedford Street
Stamford CT 06901
Contact Robert Clemenza, CPC. 203/357-8400. FAX: 203/324-5819. Specializes in the areas of: asset; audit; bookkeeping; budgeting; corporate/computer security; consulting; credit; clerical; data processing; EDP audit; electronics (engineering; field service; manufacturing; sales/marketing; technicians); engineering (aeronautical; chemical; civil; electrical; environmental/hazardous waste; HVAC; industrial; manufacturing; mechanical; nuclear; packaging); entry level (management trainees; support staff); financial analysis; investment; international; lending; operations; programming; public accounting; sales; software engineering; systems; tax; technicians; trainees; trust; insurance (actuarial; claims; life/health; pension; property/casualty; rating; reinsurance; sales; underwriting); sales (business products; computers; consumer products; industrial products; international; management; media; medical products; services/intangibles; trainees)

HIPP WATERS OFFICE PERSONNEL
209 Bedford Street
Stamford CT 06901
Contact Andrea Mattola. 203/866-9900. FAX: 203/857-0849. Specializes in the areas of: office administration (administrators; clerks; management; receptionists; secretaries; word processing); temporary services (accounting/bookkeeping; professional industrial; sales; secretaries; technical; word processing).

HIPP WATERS OFFICE PERSONNEL
209 Bedford Street
Stamford CT 06901
Contact Jane Blocker, CPC. 203/327-1200. FAX: 203/359-4627. Specializes in the areas of: office administration (administrators; clerks; management; receptionists; secretaries; word processing); temporary services (accounting/bookkeeping; professional industrial; sales; secretaries; technical; word processing).

THE HIRE GROUP
P.O. Box 330068
West Hartford, CT 06133-0068
Contact Donald J. Berardo, CPC. 203/233-8266. Specializes in the areas of: asset; credit; international; investment; lending; trainees; trust.

LABOR FORCE OF AMERICA
102 New Haven Avenue
Milford CT 06460
Contact Robert Martin, Vice President Marketing. 203/878-6821. Employment agency; temporary help service. No appointment required. Founded 1975. Nonspecialized. Positions commonly filled include: Accountant; Clerk; Computer Operator; Computer Programmer; Construction Worker; Credit Manager; Customer Service Representative; Data Entry Clerk; Demonstrator; Draftsperson; Driver; EDP Specialist; Electrical Engineer; Factory Worker; General Laborer; Industrial Engineer; Legal Secretary; Marketing Specialist; Mechanical Engineer; Metallurgical Engineer; Office Worker; Purchasing Agent; Quality Control Supervisor; Receptionist; Sales Representative; Secretary; Stenographer; Typist; Word Processing Specialist. Company pays fee. Number of placements per year: 1001+.

LOFT SYSTEMS
4675 Main St. Commerce Park
Bridgeport CT 06606
Contact Lawrence Loft. 203/371-5638. FAX: 203/374-3821. Specializes in the areas of: audit; bookkeeping; budgeting; clerical; financial analysis; international; public accounting; tax; office administration (administrators; clerks; management; receptionists; secretaries; word processing); temporary services (accounting/bookkeeping; professional industrial; sales; secretaries; technical; word processing).

MJF ASSOCIATES
187 N. Main St., P.O. Box 132
Wallingford CT 06492
Contact Matt Furman, CPC. 203/284-9878. FAX: 203/284-9871. Specializes in the area ot: sales (computers; industrial products; international; management; medical products).

MANPOWER, INC. OF WATERBURY/
dba MANPOWER TEMPORARY SERVICES
P.O. Box 2738
Waterbury CT 06723
Contact G. W. Post, General Manager. 203/756-8303. Temporary help agency. Appointment required. Founded 1955. Specializes in the areas of: Accounting; Clerical; Office Automation; Secretarial. Positions commonly filled include: Accountant; Administrative Assistant; Bookkeeper; Clerk; Construction Worker; Customer Service Representative; Data Entry Clerk; Draftsperson; Executive Secretary; General Laborer; Legal Secretary; Light Industrial Worker; Medical Secretary; Receptionist; Sales Representative; Secretary; Stenographer; Technical Writer/Editor; Technician; Typist; Word Processor. Company pays fee. Number of placements per year: 1000+.

A.R. MAZZOTTA PERSONNEL
50 Riverview Center
Middletown CT 06457
Contact Arlene R. Mazzotta. 203/347-1626. Specializes in the areas of: audit; bookkeeping; budgeting; clerical; financial analysis; public accounting; tax; office administration (administrators; clerks; management; receptionists; secretaries; word processing); temporary services (accounting/bookkeeping; secretaries; word processing/sales).

McKNIGHT PERSONNEL SERVICES

60 Guernsey Avenue
Post Office Box 1172
Stamford CT 06904
Contact Richard F. McKnight, President. 203/357-1891. Employment agency. Appointment requested. Founded 1974. Specializes in the areas of: Accounting and Finance; Clerical; Personnel and Human Resources; Sales and Marketing. Positions commonly filled include: Accountant; Administrative Assistant; Bank Officer/Manager; Bookkeeper; Buyer; Clerk; Credit Manager; Customer Service Representative; Data Entry Clerk; EDP Specialist; Financial Analyst; General Manager; Legal Secretary; Light Industrial Worker; Marketing Specialist; Office Worker; Receptionist; Sales Representative; Secretary; Typist; Word Processing Specialist.

MICRO/TEMPS AND EDP/TEMPS OF CONNECTICUT

37 North Avenue
Norwalk CT 06851
203/847-6600. Temporary help service. No appointment required. Founded 1976. Branch offices located in: California; Connecticut; Illinois; Maryland; Massachusetts; Michigan; New York; Ohio; Pennsylvania; Virginia. Specializes in the areas of: Accounting and Finance; Banking; Computer Hardware and Software; Engineering; Insurance; Manufacturing; MIS/EDP; Nonprofit; Personnel and Human Resources; Printing and Publishing; Technical and Scientific. Positions commonly filled include: Computer Operator; Computer Programmer; EDP Specialist; MIS Specialist; Systems Analyst; Technical Writer and Editor. Company pays fee. Number of placements per year: 1001+.

J. MORRISSEY & COMPANY

Landen Building
2 Capital Avenue
Hartford CT 06106
Contact James D. Morrissey, CPA, CPC. 203/246-9373. Specializes in the areas of: audit; bookkeeping; budgeting; clerical; corporate/computer security; consulting; data processing; EDP audit; financial analysis; international; operations; programming; public accounting; sales; software engineering; systems; tax; word processing sales/service; temporary services (accounting/bookkeeping; secretaries; word processing).

NEW ENGLAND PERSONNEL, INC.

900 Main St.
Hartford CT 06103
Contact Kathryn Clark. 203/525-8616. FAX: 203/293-0817. Specializes in the area of: office administration (administrators; clerks; management; receptionists; secretaries; word processing).

PELMARK PERSONNEL INC.

40 Hoyt Street
Stamford CT 06905
Contact Catherine Peluso, CPC. 203/348-0555. FAX: 967-3772. Specializes in the area of: office administration (clerks; receptionists; secretaries; word processing).

PERSONNEL PRIORITIES, INC.

Spencer's Corner/201
Centerbrook CT 06409
Contact Dinny LaFage. 203/767-0517. FAX: 203/767-1152. Specializes in the areas of: office administration (administrators; clerks; management; receptionists; secretaries; word processing); temporary services (accounting/bookkeeping; secretaries; word processing).

QUALITY CONTROL RECRUITERS
P.O. Box 1900
Bristol CT 06010
Contact Charles V. Urban, CPC. 203/582-0003. FAX: 203/585-7395. Specializes in the area of: manufacturing/production (quality control).

RKS RESOURCES
22 5th St.
Stamford CT 06905
Contact Roseanne Shegirian, CPC. 203/359-9290. FAX: 203/359-8743. Specializes in the area of: office administration (administrators; clerks; management; receptionists; secretaries; word processing).

THE REILLY GROUP
1344 Silas Dean Highway
Rocky Hill CT 06067
Contact Chris Reilly, CPC. 203/563-4874. FAX: 203/563-3310. Specializes in the areas of: real estate (asset/portfolio management; finance; property management); sales (industrial products; medical products).

RESEARCH TECHNOLOGIES, INC.
490 Old Toll Road
Madison CT 06443
Contact Michael Haburay, Jr., CPC. 203/421-3088. FAX: 203/421-4542. Specializes in the areas of: electronics (engineering; field service; manufacturing; sales/marketing; technicians); engineering (aeronautical; chemical; electrical; environmental/hazardous waste; HVAC; industrial; manufacturing; mechanical; nuclear; packaging; physics); environmental/hazardous waste; scientific research & development (product development; research & development).

RIORDAN ASSOCIATES
Post Office Box 17232
West Hartford CT 06117
Contact John Riordan, Manager. 203/236-5776. Temporary help service. No appointment required. Founded 1970. Specializes in the areas of: Engineering; Manufacturing. Positions commonly filled include: Draftsperson; Electrical Engineer; Industrial Designer; Industrial Engineer; Mechanical Engineer; Operations and Production Specialist; Quality Control Supervisor; Technical Writer and Editor; Technician. Company pays fee. Number of placements per year: 51-100.

RITA PERSONNEL, INC.
60 Washington Place
Hamden CT 06518
Contact Barbara J. Russota. 203/248-0333. FAX: 203/288-8389. Specializes in the area of: insurance (claims; life/health; property/casualty; rating; sales; underwriting).

N.C. ROGERS ASSOCIATES
100 Prospect Street
Stamford CT 06901
Contact Nancy C. Rogers. 203/359-2500. FAX: 203/969-3787. Specializes in the areas of: office administration (administrators; clerks; management; receptionists; secretaries; word processing); temporary services (accounting/bookkeeping; sales; secretaries; word

processing).

SNELLING AND SNELLING
109 Greenwich Avenue
Greenwich CT 06830
Contact Nancy O. Stitzel, Manager. 203/622-0020. Employment agency. Appointment requested. Founded 1953. Nonspecialized. Positions commonly filled include: Accountant; Administrative Assistant; Advertising Worker; Aerospace Engineer; Architect; Bank Officer/Manager; Bookkeeper; Buyer; Ceramics Engineer; Civil Engineer; Claims Representative; Clerk; Commercial Artist; Computer Operator; Computer Programmer; Credit Manager; Customer Service Representative; Data Entry Clerk; Demonstrator; Draftsperson; EDP Specialist; Economist; Electrical Engineer; Financial Analyst; General Manager; Hotel Manager/Assistant Manager; Industrial Designer; Industrial Engineer; Insurance Agent/Broker; Legal Secretary; MIS Specialist; Marketing Specialist; Medical Secretary; Office Worker; Operations/Production Specialist; Personnel and Labor Relations Specialist; Physicist; Public Relations Worker; Purchasing Agent; Quality Control Supervisor; Receptionist; Reporter/Editor; Sales Representative; Secretary; Statistician; Stenographer; Systems Analyst; Technical Writer/Editor; Technician; Typist; Underwriter; Word Processing Specialist. Company pays fee.

SNELLING AND SNELLING
64 Wall Street
Norwalk CT 06850
Contact Robert Mouat, Manager. 203/853-1281. Employment agency; temporary help service. Appointment requested. Founded 1960. Specializes in the areas of: Mechanical; Technical and Scientific. Positions commonly filled include: Accountant; Actuary; Administrative Assistant; Advertising Worker; Aerospace Engineer; Agricultural Engineer; Bank Officer/Manager; Biochemist; Biologist; Biomedical Engineer; Bookkeeper; Buyer; Ceramics Engineer; Chemist; Civil Engineer; Claim Representative; Clerk; Computer Operator; Computer Programmer; Credit Manager; Customer Service Representative; Data Entry Clerk; Draftsperson; Driver; EDP Specialist; Electrical Engineer; Financial Analyst; Food Technologist; General Manager; Industrial Engineer; Insurance Agent/Broker; Legal Secretary; Light Industrial Worker; MIS Specialist; Marketing Specialist; Mechanical Engineer; Medical Secretary; Metallurgical Engineer; Office Worker; Operations/Production Specialist; Personnel and Labor Relations Specialist; Physicist; Public Relations Worker; Purchasing Agent; Quality Control Supervisor; Receptionist; Sales Representative; Secretary; Statistician; Stenographer; Systems Analyst; Technical Writer/Editor; Technician; Typist; Underwriter; Word Processing Specialist. Company pays fee. Number of placements per year: 201-500.

STAFF BUILDERS, INC. OF NORWALK
1234 Summer Street
Stamford CT 06905
203/853-1411. Temporary help service. Appointment requested. Founded 1961. Branch offices located in: Arizona; California; Connecticut; District of Columbia; Florida; Georgia; Illinois; Indiana; Kansas; Louisiana; Maryland; Massachusetts; Michigan; Minnesota; Missouri; Nevada; New Jersey; New Mexico; New York; Ohio; Oklahoma; Oregon; Pennsylvania; Rhode Island; Tennessee; Texas; Virginia; Washington. Nonspecialized. Positions commonly filled include: Accountant; Administrative Assistant; Bookkeeper; Clerk; Computer Operator and Computer Programmer; Customer Service Representative; Data Entry Clerk; Demonstrator; Draftsperson; Driver; EDP Specialist; Factory Worker; General Laborer; Health Aide and Companion; Legal Secretary; Light Industrial Worker; Medical Secretary; Nurse; Office Worker; Public Relations Worker; Receptionist; Sales

Representative; Secretary; Stenographer; Technician; Typist; Word Processing Specialist. Company pays fee. Number of placements per year: 1001+.

THE STAMFORD GROUP
155 Sycamore Street
Glastonbury CT 06033
Contact William Peoples. 203/657-3868. FAX: 203/657-2713. Specializes in the areas of: electronics (engineering; field service; manufacturing; sales/marketing; technicians); medical/health care (health physics; hospitals; nurses); packaging (design; engineering; manufacturing); scientific research & development (product development; research & development; sales; technicians).

TECH/AID OF CONNECTICUT
21 New Britain Avenue
Rocky Hill CT 06067
203/529-5710. Temporary help service. No appointment required. Founded 1969. Tech/Aid is a division of Technical Aid Corporation and has branch offices located in: Arizona; California; Connecticut; Illinois; Maryland; Massachusetts; New Hampshire; Pennsylvania; Rhode Island; Texas; Virginia. Specializes in the areas of: Architecture; Cable Television; Computer Hardware and Software; Construction; Engineering; Manufacturing; Technical and Scientific. Positions commonly filled include: Aerospace Engineer; Architect; Buyer; Ceramics Engineer; Chemical Engineer; Civil Engineer; Draftsperson; Electrical Engineer; Estimator; Factory Engineer; Industrial Designer; Industrial Engineer; Mechanical Engineer; Metallurgical Engineer; Mining Engineer; Petroleum Engineer; Operations and Production Specialist; Purchasing Agent; Quality Control Supervisor; Technical Writer and Editor; Technician. Company pays fee. Number of placements per year: 1001+.

UNI/SEARCH OF WATERBURY, INC.
195 Grove Street
Waterbury CT 06710
Contact Donald Rulli, General Manager. 203/753-2329; FAX 203/575-1513. Employment agency. Founded 1967. Generalist agency priding itself on professionalism and integrity. Positions commonly filled include: Accountant; Administrative Assistant; Advertising Executive; Aerospace Engineer; Bank Officer/Manager; Biochemist/Chemist; Biomedical Engineer; Bookkeeper; Ceramics Engineer; Civil Engineer; Claims Representative; Clerk; Computer Programmer; Credit Manager; Customer Service Representative; Data Entry Clerk; Draftsperson; EDP Specialist; Electrical Engineer; Executive Secretary; Financial Analyst; General Manager; Industrial Designer; Interior Designer; Legal Secretary; Management Consultant; Marketing Specialist; Mechanical Engineer; Medical Secretary; Metallurgical Engineer; Personnel Director; Purchasing Agent; Receptionist; Sales Representative; Secretary; Statistician; Stenographer; Systems Analyst; Technical Writer/Editor; Technician; Typist; Underwriter; Word Processor. Company pays fee. Number of placements per year: 201-500.

VANNA/ROWE, INC.
11 Mountain Avenue
P.O. Box 514
Bloomfield CT 06002
Contact Margaret Vannah. 203/243-0424. FAX: 203/243-0252. Specializes in the areas of: computer science (programming; software engineering; systems); engineering (electrical).

EXECUTIVE SEARCH FIRMS OF CONNECTICUT

THE CAMBRIDGE GROUP, LTD
830 Post Road East
Westport CT 06880
Contact Joseph B. Ryan, Vice President-Executive Search. 203/226-4243. Executive search firm. Appointment required; no phone calls; unsolicited resumes accepted. The Cambridge Group is one of the largest centralized information services recruitment organizations in the Northeast. Incorporated in 1974, the firm has enjoyed steady growth and now employs more than 20 full-time professionals who serve a diverse clientele. The Cambridge Group is one of the first firms to provide both retainer executive search and non-retainer technology. The Executive Search Division identifies and assists in recruiting key managers and individual contributors. The Cambridge Group matches candidates to demanding requirements for characteristics such as managerial strength, political sensitivity, and communication skills. The Camridge Group provides non-retainer recruitment services in four areas of information technology: General Business Systems, Systems Software and Operations, Telecommunications, and Expert Systems. The positions filled by the firm range from information specialists to senior level executives. The Cambridge Group concentrates solely on information technology recruitment.

DUNHILL OF GREATER STAMFORD, INC.
213 Danbury Road
Wilton CT 06897
Contact Katherine W. Strakosch, C.P.C., President. 203/762-7722. Executive search firm. Appointment required; no phone calls; unsolicited resumes accepted. Founded 1975. Specializes in the areas of: Sales and Marketing, predominantly in the chemical and chemically-related marketplaces. Contingency. Number of searches conducted per year: 1-50.

HARRIS HEERY AND ASSOCIATES, INC.
40 Richards Avenue
Norwalk CT 06854
Contact William Heery, President. 203/857-0808. Executive search firm. Founded 1981. A specialized retainer and outplacement firm concentrating in consumer marketing on a national basis. Specializes in the areas of: Food Industry; HHP, HBA; Sales and Marketing. Positions commonly filled include: Advertising Executive; Marketing Specialist. Number of placements per year: 51-100.

MANAGEMENT RECRUITERS OF FAIRFIELD
140 Sherman Street
Fairfield CT 06430
Contact Rush Oster or Joan Oster, Co-Managers. 203/255-2299. Executive search firm Appointment required; no phone calls; unsolicited resumes accepted. Founded 1965. World's largest contingency search firm. Five hundred offices nationwide, doing business under the names "Management Recruiters", "Sales Consultants", "CompuSearch" and "OfficeMates5." Specializes in mid-management/professional positions, $25,000-75,000 per annum. Specializes in the areas of: Accounting; Administration; MIS/EDP; Advertising; Affirmative Action; Architecture; Banking and Finance; Chemicals and Pharmaceuticals; Communications; Computer Hardware and Software; Construction; Electrical; Engineering; Food Industry; General Management; Health and Medical; Human Resources; Industrial and Interior Design; Insurance; Legal; Manufacturing; Operations

Management; Printing and Publishing; Procurement; Real Estate; Retailing; Sales and Marketing; Technical and Scientific; Textiles; Transportation. Contingency.

MANAGEMENT RECRUITERS OF HAMDEN
105 Sanford Street
Hamden CT 06514
Contact Jackson P. Burke, Manager. 203/248-0770. Executive search firm. Appointment required; no phone calls; unsolicited resumes accepted. Founded 1965. World's largest contingency search firm. Five hundred offices nationwide, doing business under the names "Management Recruiters", "Sales Consultants", "CompuSearch" and "OfficeMates5." Specializes in mid-management/professional positions, $25,000-75,000 per annum. Specializes in the areas of: Accounting; Administration; MIS/EDP; Advertising; Affirmative Action; Architecture; Banking and Finance; Chemicals and Pharmaceuticals; Communications; Computer Hardware and Software; Construction; Electrical; Engineering; Food Industry; General Management; Health and Medical; Human Resources; Industrial and Interior Design; Insurance; Legal; Manufacturing; Operations Management; Printing and Publishing; Procurement; Real Estate; Retailing; Sales and Marketing; Technical and Scientific; Textiles; Transportation. Contingency.

MANAGEMENT RECRUITERS OF WATERBURY
45 Freight Street
Waterbury CT 06702-1880
Contact Jack Bourque, Manager/Owner. 203/755-9228; FAX 203/753-7047. Executive search firm. Appointment required; no phone calls; unsolicited resumes accepted. Founded 1965. World's largest contingency search firm. Five hundred offices nationwide, doing business under the names "Management Recruiters", "Sales Consultants", "CompuSearch" and "OfficeMates5." Specializes in mid-management/professional positions, $25,000-75,000 per annum. Specializes in the areas of: Accounting; Administration; MIS/EDP; Advertising; Affirmative Action; Architecture; Banking and Finance; Chemicals and Pharmaceuticals; Communications; Computer Hardware and Software; Construction; Electrical; Engineering; Food Industry; General Management; Health and Medical; Human Resources; Industrial and Interior Design; Insurance; Legal; Manufacturing; Operations Management; Printing and Publishing; Procurement; Real Estate; Retailing; Sales and Marketing; Technical and Scientific; Textiles; Transportation. Nonspecialized. Contingency. Number of placements per year: 501+.

OFFICEMATES5 OF STAMFORD
15 Bank Street, Suite 204
Stamford CT 06901
Contact Mr. Lynn W. Moore, General Manager, or Barbara G. Moore, Manager. 203/324-2232. Executive search firm. Appointment required; no phone calls; unsolicited resumes accepted. Founded 1965. World's largest contingency search firm. Five hundred offices nationwide, doing business under the names "Management Recruiters", "Sales Consultants", "CompuSearch" and "OfficeMates5." Specializes in mid-management/professional positions, $25,000-75,000 per annum. Specializes in the areas of: Accounting; Administration; MIS/EDP; Advertising; Affirmative Action; Architecture; Banking and Finance; Chemicals and Pharmaceuticals; Communications; Computer Hardware and Software; Construction; Electrical; Engineering; Food Industry; General Management; Health and Medical; Human Resources; Industrial and Interior Design; Insurance; Legal; Manufacturing; Operations Management; Printing and Publishing; Procurement; Real Estate; Retailing; Sales and Marketing; Technical and Scientific; Textiles; Transportation. Contingency.

SALES CONSULTANTS OF NEW HAVEN
265 Bic Drive
Milford CT 06460
Contact Ron Fink, Manager. 203/878-9800. Executive search firm. Appointment required; no phone calls; unsolicited resumes accepted. Founded 1965. World's largest contingency search firm. Five hundred offices nationwide, doing business under the names "Management Recruiters", "Sales Consultants", "CompuSearch" and "OfficeMates5." Specializes in mid-management/professional positions, $25,000-75,000 per annum. Specializes in the areas of: Accounting; Administration; MIS/EDP; Advertising; Affirmative Action; Architecture; Banking and Finance; Chemicals and Pharmaceuticals; Communications; Computer Hardware and Software; Construction; Electrical; Engineering; Food Industry; General Management; Health and Medical; Human Resources; Industrial and Interior Design; Insurance; Legal; Manufacturing; Operations Management; Printing and Publishing; Procurement; Real Estate; Retailing; Sales and Marketing; Technical and Scientific; Textiles; Transportation. Contingency.

SALES CONSULTANTS OF STAMFORD
1055 Washington Boulevard
Stamford CT 06901-2204
Contact J. Robert Wright, General Manager, or Elaine Brachfeld, Manager. 203/978-0033; FAX 203/967-3573. Executive search firm. Appointment required; no phone calls; unsolicited resumes accepted. Founded 1965. World's largest contingency search firm. Five hundred offices nationwide, doing business under the names "Management Recruiters", "Sales Consultants", "CompuSearch" and "OfficeMates5." Specializes in mid-management/professional positions, $25,000-75,000 per annum. Specializes in the areas of: Accounting; Administration; MIS/EDP; Advertising; Affirmative Action; Architecture; Banking and Finance; Chemicals and Pharmaceuticals; Communications; Computer Hardware and Software; Construction; Electrical; Engineering; Food Industry; General Management; Health and Medical; Human Resources; Industrial and Interior Design; Insurance; Legal; Manufacturing; Operations Management; Printing and Publishing; Procurement; Real Estate; Retailing; Sales and Marketing; Technical and Scientific; Textiles; Transportation. Contingency.

RESUME AND CAREER COUNSELING SERVICES OF CONNECTICUT

A & A RESUME SERVICE
11 Asylum Street, Suite 612-613
Hartford CT 06103
Contact Lewis E. Schweitzer. 203/549-5262. A resume and career counseling service.

EMPLOYMENT AGENCIES AND TEMPORARY SERVICES OF NEW JERSEY

AARON PERSONNEL AND AARON ENGINEERING
151 West Passaic Street
Rochelle Park NJ 07662
Contact Charlotte Gold or Dianne Mack, Owners. 201/845-6011. Employment agency. Appointment requested. Founded 1982. Specializes in the areas of: Accounting and Finance; Clerical; Computer Hardware and Software; Engineering; Fashion; Insurance; MIS/EDP; Technical and Scientific. Positions commonly filled include: Accountant; Administrative Assistant; Aerospace Engineer; Biochemist; Biomedical Engineer; Bookkeeper; Buyer; Chemical Engineer; Chemist; Claims Representative; Clerk; Computer Operator; Computer Programmer; Credit Manager; Customer Service Representative; Data Entry Clerk; Driver; EDP Manager; Electrical Engineer; Financial Analyst; Food Technologist; General Engineer; Industrial Engineer; Legal Secretary; MIS Specialist; Mechanical Engineer; Medical Secretary; Office Worker; Operations/Production Specialist; Personnel and Labor Relations Specialist; Physicist; Purchasing Agent; Quality Control Supervisor; Receptionist; Sales Representative; Secretary; Stenographer; Systems Analyst; Technical Writer/Editor; Technician; Typist; Word Processing Specialist. Company pays fee. Number of placements per year: 201-500.

ACCOUNTANTS ON CALL
505 Thornall St.
Edison NJ 08837
Contact Sue-Ellen Hepworth. 908/321-1700. FAX: 908/494-4386. Specializes in the area of: accounting/finance.

ACCOUNTANTS ON CALL
354 Eisenhower Pkwy
Livingston NJ 07039
Contact Rita Silverstein. 201/533-0000. FAX: 201/553-1504. Specializes in the area of: accounting/finance.

ACCOUNTANTS ON CALL
East 80 Route 4, Ste. 430
Paramus NJ 07652
Contact Ellyn Small. 201/843-8882. FAX: 201/843-8572. Specializes in the area of: accounting/finance.

ACCOUNTANTS ON CALL
5 Independence Way
Princeton Corporate Center
Princeton NJ 08540
Contact Sue-Ellen Hepworth. 609/452-7117. FAX: 908/494-4386. Specializes in the area of: accounting/finance.

ACCOUNTANTS ON CALL
Park 80 W. Plaza II
Garden State Pkwy. Interstate 1080
9th Fl.
Saddle Brook, NJ 07662.
Contact Stewart C. Kibes, CPA. 201/843-0006. FAX: 201/843-4936. Specializes in the area of: accounting/finance.

RAYMOND ALEXANDER ASSOCIATES
420 Minnisink Rd.
Totowa NJ 07512
Contact Karen Jezierski. 201/256-1000. FAX: 201/256-5871. Specializes in the area of: accounting/finance.

AMERICAN PLACEMENT SERVICES, INC.
1999 E. Marlton Pike
Cherry Hill NJ 08003
Contact Jay Garfield, CPC. 609/424-6542. FAX: 609/4224-5368. Specializes in the area of: insurance (actuarial; claims; life/health; property/casualty; rating; reinsurance; sales; underwriting).

APPLIED PERSONNEL, INC.
758 Route 18 P.O. Box 545
East Brunswick NJ 08816
Contact Ann Lee Stein. 908/238-2500. FAX: 908/238-9099. Specializes in the areas of: audit; bookkeeping; budgeting; clerical; credit & collection (commercial; wholesale); entry level (management trainees; support staff); office administration (administrators; clerks; management; receptionists; secretaries; word processing); sales (business products; computers; consumer products; industrial products; international; management; media; medical products; services/intangibles; trainees).

ASSURANCE PERSONNEL & HEALTHCARE
151 West Passaic Street
Rochelle Park NJ 07662
201/845-6050. Temporary help service. Appointment requested. Founded 1961. Branch offices located in: Arizona; California; Connecticut; District of Columbia; Florida; Georgia; Illinois; Indiana; Kansas; Louisiana; Maryland; Massachusetts; Michigan; Minnesota; Missouri; Nevada; New Jersey; New Mexico; New York; Ohio; Oklahoma; Oregon; Pennsylvania; Rhode Island; Tennessee; Texas; Virginia; Washington. Nonspecialized. Positions commonly filled include: Accountant; Administrative Assistant; Bookkeeper; Clerk; Companion; Computer Operator; Computer Programmer; Customer Service Representative; Data Entry Clerk; Demonstrator; Draftsperson; Driver; EDP Specialist; Factory Worker; General Laborer; Health Aide; Legal Secretary; Light Industrial Worker; Medical Secretary; Nurse; Office Worker; Public Relations Worker; Receptionist; Sales Representative; Secretary; Stenographer; Technician; Typist; Word Processing Specialist. Company pays fee. Number of placements per year: 1001+.

BERMAN & LARSON ASSOCIATES
140 Route 17 North
Suite 204
Paramus NJ 07652
Contact Robert Larson. 201/262-9200. FAX: 201/262-7060. Specializes in the areas of: computer science (corporate/computer security; consulting; EDP audit; programming; software engineering; systems).

BLAIR PERSONNEL SERVICE
1130 Rt. 46 PO Box 5306
Parsippany NJ 07054
Contact Bruce Campbell. 201/335-6150. Specializes in the areas of: office administration; public relations; temporary services.

BROOKS EXECUTIVE PERSONNEL, INC.
140 Sylvan Ave. P.O. Box 1155
Englewood Cliffs NJ 07632
Contact Bunny Brooks/Marty Kay. 201/585-7200. FAX: 201/585-9897. Specializes in the areas of: audit; biotechnology scientific; budgeting; chemical; computer science (corporate/computer security; consulting; data processing; EDP audit; programming; systems); engineering (aeronautical; chemical; civil; electrical; environmental/hazardous waste; food service (institutional; manufacturers; restaurants; sales; supermarkets); industrial; manufacturing; mechanical; nuclear; physics); financial analysis; international; public accounting; tax; insurance (actuarial; claims; life/health; pension; property/casualty; rating; reinsurance; sales; underwriting); office administration (administrators; clerks; management; receptionists; secretaries; word processing); temporary services (accounting/bookkeeping; professional industrial; sales; secretaries; technical; word processing).

BROOKS EXECUTIVE PERSONNEL, INC.
BP TEMPS, INC.
140 Sylvan Avenue
Englewood Cliffs NJ 07632
Contact Marty Kay, Principal. 201/585-7200. Employment agency; temporary help agency. Appointment required. Founded 1984. Specializes in the areas of: Accounting; Banking and Finance, Computer Hardware and Software; Engineering; Food Industry; Industrial and Interior Design; Insurance; MIS/EDP; Manufacturing; Sales and Marketing; Technical and Scientific; Secretarial and Clerical. Positions commonly filled include: Accountant; Actuary; Administrative Assistant; Aerospace Engineer; Agricultural Engineer; Biochemist/Chemist; Biologist; Biomedical Engineer; Bookkeeper; Ceramics Engineer; Civil Engineer; Claims Representative; Clerk; Computer Programmer; Credit Manager; Customer Service Representative; Data Entry Clerk; EDP Specialist; Economist; Electrical Engineer; Executive Secretary; Factory Worker; Financial Analyst; General Manager; Insurance Agent/Broker; Industrial Engineer; Legal Secretary; Light Industrial Worker; Marketing Specialist; Mechanical Engineer; Medical Secretary; Metallurgical Engineer; Mining Engineer; Personnel Director; Petroleum Engineer; Physicist, Purchasing Agent; Receptionist; Sales Representative; Secretary; Statistician; Stenographer; Systems Analyst; Technician; Typist; Word Processor. Company pays fee. Number of placements per year: 201-500.

CAREER CENTER, INC.
194 Passaic Street
Post Office Box 1036
Hackensack NJ 07601
Contact Barry Franzino, Jr., C.P.C., President. 201/342-1777. Employment agency; temporary help service. Appointment requested. Founded 1969. Specializes in the areas of: Accounting and Finance; Advertising; Banking; Bilingual Communication; Clerical; Computer Hardware and Software; Engineering; Fashion; Insurance; Manufacturing; MIS/EDP; Personnel and Human Resources; Sales and Marketing; Technical and Scientific. Positions commonly filled include: Accountant; Administrative Assistant; Bank Officer/Manager; Bookkeeper; Buyer; Chemical Engineer; Chemist; Civil Engineer; Claim Representative; Clerk; Computer Operator; Computer Programmer; Credit Manager; Customer Service Representative; Data Entry Clerk; Draftsperson; EDP Specialist; Electrical Engineer; Financial Analyst; Industrial Designer; Industrial Engineer; Legal Secretary; MIS Specialist; Marketing Specialist; Mechanical Engineer; Medical Secretary; Metallurgical Engineer; Mining Engineer; Office Worker; Operations/Production Specialist; Personnel and Labor Relations Specialist; Petroleum Engineer; Purchasing Agent; Quality Control Supervisor; Receptionist; Sales Representative; Secretary;

Stenographer; Systems Analyst; Technician; Typist; Underwriter; Word Processing Specialist. Company pays fee. Number of placements per year: 1001+.

CAREERS FIRST, INC.
305 U.S. Route 130
Cinnaminson NJ 08077
Contact Gail Duncan. 609/786-0004. Specializes in the areas of: computer science (corporate/computer security; consulting; data processing; EDP audit; operations; programming; sales; software engineering; systems; technicians; word processing sales/service).

CHINA HUMAN RESOURCES GROUP
20 Nassau St., #401
Princeton NJ 08542
Contact Christine Casati. 609/682-4521. FAX: 609/683-9670. Specializes in the area of: international/overseas placement).

CITIZENS EMPLOYMENT SERVICES, INC.
Six Ames Avenue
Rutherford NJ 07070
Contact Rose Natiello, Manager. 201/460-0026. Employment agency; temporary help service. Appointment requested. Founded 1969. Specializes in the areas of: Banking; Clerical; Computer Hardware and Software; Insurance; Manufacturing; Sales and Marketing. Positions commonly filled include: Accountant; Actuary; Bank Officer/Manager; Bookkeeper; Chemical Engineer; Claims Representative; Computer Operator; Computer Programmer; Credit Manager; Customer Service Representative; Data Entry Clerk; EDP Specialist; Electrical Engineer; Industrial Engineer; Insurance Agent/Broker; Legal Secretary; Light Industrial Worker; Mechanical Engineer; Office Worker; Operations/Production Specialist; Purchasing Agent; Quality Control Supervisor; Receptionist; Sales Representative; Secretary; Stenographer; Systems Analyst; Technician; Typist; Underwriter; Word Processing Specialist. Number of placements per year: 1001+.

DATA HUNTERS, INC.
215A First Street
Hohokus NJ 07423
Contact Bette Rosenfeld & Ray Radleight. 201/447-4880. FAX: 201/447-4956. Specializes in the areas of: computer science (corporate/computer security; consulting; data processing; operations; programming; software engineering; systems).

DUNHILL-MIDDLESEX
100 Menlo Park
11 Edison NJ 08837
Contact Ken Altreuter. 908/549-6100. Specializes in the area of: engineering (HVAC; mechanical; packaging).

FINANCIAL RECRUITMENT GROUP
155 Park Ave., #208
Lyndhurst NJ 07071
Contact Bob Conlin. 201/939-9036. FAX: 201/939-6545. Specializes in the areas of: audit; budgeting; financial analysis; international; public accounting; tax.

GARDEN STATE EMPLOYMENT
35 Beaverson Blvd.
Brick NJ 08723
Contact Joan Lindsay. 908/920-5700. FAX: 908/920-5055. Specializes in the areas of: legal (attorneys); retailing (buying; management; merchandising; operations; sales).

GENERAL PERSONNEL & TECHNICAL SERVICES
1209 East Grand Street
Elizabeth NJ 07201
Contact E. C. Sheridan, President. 908/289-7050. Employment agency; temporary help service. Appointment requested. Founded 1960. Nonspecialized. Positions commonly filled include: Accountant; Administrative Assistant; Bank Officer/Manager; Bookkeeper; Buyer; Chemical Engineer; Chemist; Civil Engineer; Claims Representative; Clerk; Computer Operator; Construction Worker; Credit Manager; Customer Service Representative; Data Entry Clerk; Demonstrator; Draftsperson; Electrical Engineer; Food Technologist; General Manager; Hotel Manager/Assistant Manager; Industrial Engineer; Legal Secretary; Light Industrial Worker; Marketing Specialist; Mechanical Engineer; Office Worker; Operations/Production Specialist; Personnel and Labor Relations Specialist; Purchasing Agent; Quality Control Supervisor; Receptionist; Sales Representative; Secretary; Stenographer; Technician; Typist; Underwriter; Word Processing Specialist. Company pays fee. Number of placements per year: 501-1000.

G.L. GRANT & ASSOC.
96 Park Street
Montclair NJ 07042
Contact Georgia Grant. 201/744-5766. FAX: 201/744-2988. Specializes in the areas of: computer science (EDP audit; programming; software engineering; systems; technicians).

HALLMARK & HALLMARK TEMPS
140 Route 17 North
Paramus NJ 07652
Contact Diane C. Goldman. 201/939-3443. FAX: 201/261-4469. Specializes in the areas of: audit; bookkeeping; budgeting; clerical; financial analysis; international; public accounting; tax; office administration (administrators; clerks; management; receptionists; secretaries; word processing); temporary services (accounting/bookkeeping; secretaries; word processing).

HIGH POWER PERSONNEL
215 W. Union Avenue
Bound Brook NJ 08805
Contact Robert T. Holloway, CPC. 908/560-9331. FAX: 908/560-8295. Specializes in the areas of: biotechnology scientific; temporary services (accounting/bookkeeping; secretaries; technical; word processing).

HIPP WATERS ASSOCIATES
433 Hackensack Avenue
Hackensack NJ 07601
Contact Rosemary Jackson, CPC. 201/488-6666. FAX: 201/488-9592. Specializes in the areas of: audit; bookkeeping; budgeting; clerical; financial analysis; international; public accounting; tax; office administration (administrators; clerks; management; receptionists; secretaries; word processing); sales (business products; computers; consumer products; industrial products; international; management; media; medical products; services/intangibles; trainees); temporary services (accounting/bookkeeping; professional industrial; sales; secretaries; technical; word processing).

H. NEUMAN ASSOCIATES
P.O. Box 6448
Lawrenceville NJ 08648
Contact Helen Neuman, CPC. 609/883-3700. Specializes in the areas of: clerks: receptionists; secretaries; word processing); pharmaceuticals (scientific).

J & J TEMPORARIES
One World Fair Drive, Suite 302
Somerset NJ 08873
908/356-2020. Temporary help service. No appointment required. Founded 1972. Specializes in the areas of: Clerical; Construction. Positions commonly filled include: Bookkeeper; Clerk; Computer Operator; Construction Worker; Data Entry Clerk; Demonstrator; Driver; Factory Worker; General Laborer; Legal Secretary; Light Industrial Worker; Medical Secretary; Office Worker; Receptionist; Secretary; Stenographer; Typist; Word Processing Specialist. Company pays fee. Number of placements per year: 1001+.

KARLYN PERSONNEL, INC./DBA KARLYN ASSOCIATES
210 Sylvan Ave.
Englewood Cliffs NJ 07632
Contact Karen Dickson. 201/871-9800. FAX: 201/894-1186. Specializes in the areas of: apparel/textile; office administration; retailing.

LAKELAND PERSONNEL, INC.
50 North Morris Street P.O. Box 171
Dover NJ 07802
Contact W.E. Gandenberger, CPC. 201/366-7474. FAX: 201/366-6422. Specializes in the areas of: office administration (administrators; clerks; management; receptionists; secretaries; word processing); temporary services (accounting/bookkeeping; professional industrial; sales; secretaries; technical; word processing).

LANCASTER ASSOCIATES
94 Grove Street
Somerville NJ 08876
Contact Ray Lancaster, Jr., CPC. 908/526-5440. Specializes in the areas of: computer science (corporate/computer security; consulting; data processing; EDP audit; operations; programming; software engineering; systems; technicians).

MIS SEARCH
450 Hurman Meadow Blvd., 3rd Fl.
Secaucus NJ 07094
Contact Brad Violette. 201/330-0080. Specializes in the area of: computer science.

MARTIN PERSONNEL ASSOCIATES
100 West Mount Pleasant Ave.
Livingston NJ 07039
Contact Martin Untermeyer, CPC. 201/994-1900. FAX: 201/994-7426. Specializes in the area of: marketing (industrial products; medical products); sales (consumer products; industrial products; management; medical products).

MERLIN INTERNATIONAL
17 South Franklin Turnpike, Box 313
Ramsey NJ 07446
Contact Jim Cinquina. 201/825-7220. FAX: 201/825-1043. Specializes in the areas of: biotechnology scientific; pharmaceuticals (manufacturing; sales; scientific).

MILLIE KIPP ASSOCIATES, INC.
703 Broad St.
Shrewsbury NJ 07702
Contact Millie Kipp, CPC. 908/842-4442. FAX: 908/842-9015. Specializes in the areas of: insurance (claims; property/casualty); office administration (administrators; management; receptionists; secretaries).

ONLINE CAREER SEARCH, INC.
One Greentree Centre Suite 203
Marlton NJ 08053
Contact Robert T. Kelly, CPC. 609/985-0110. FAX: 609/985-9394. Specializes in the areas of: computer science (consulting; data processing; EDP audit; operations; programming; software engineering; systems).

THE PALMER GROUP
1 Eves Dr., Ste. 111
Marlton NJ 08053
Contact Susan Davies. 609/985-1992. Specializes in the areas of: environmental/hazardous waste; sales (business products; consumer products).

PLANT CAREERS
70 Washington Avenue
Dumont NJ 07628
Contact Richard R. Odierna. 201/501-0805. Specializes in the area of: manufacturing/production.

POMERANTZ PERSONNEL
1065 Route 22 West
Bridgewater NJ 08807
Contact Gary Pomerantz, President, or Mary Pomerantz, Executive Vice President. 908/526-8280. Employment agency; temporary help service. Appointment requested. Founded 1974. Specializes in the areas of: Accounting and Finance; Architecture; Banking; Bilingual Communication; Broadcasting; Clerical; Computer Hardware and Software; Construction; Engineering; Food Industry; Insurance; Legal; Manufacturing; MIS/EDP; Minorities; Nonprofit; Personnel and Human Resources; Printing and Publishing; Sales and Marketing; Technical and Scientific; Transportation. Positions commonly filled include: Accountant; Administrative Assistant; Aerospace Engineer; Bank Officer/Manager; Biochemist; Biologist; Biomedical Engineer; Bookkeeper; Buyer; Ceramics Engineer; Chemical Engineer; Chemist; Civil Engineer; Claims Representative; Clerk; Computer Operator; Computer Programmer; Credit Manager; Customer Service Representative; Data Entry Clerk; Demonstrator; Draftsperson; Driver; EDP Specialist; Electrical Engineer; Factory Worker; Financial Analyst; Food Technologist; General Laborer; General Manager; Industrial Designer; Industrial Engineer; Insurance Agent/Broker; Legal Secretary; Light Industrial Worker; MIS Specialist; Marketing Specialist; Mechanical Engineer; Medical Secretary; Metallurgical Engineer; Office Worker; Operations/Production Specialist; Personnel and Labor Relations Specialist; Physicist; Purchasing Agent; Quality Control Supervisor; Receptionist; Sales Representative; Secretary; Stenographer; Systems Analyst; Technical Writer/Editor;

Technician; Typist; Underwriter; Word Processing Specialist. Company pays fee. Number of placements per year: 1001+.

POMERANTZ PERSONNEL
385 West Ferris
East Brunswick NJ 08816
Contact Gary Pomerantz, President, or Mary Pomerantz, Executive Vice President. 908/238-4780. Employment agency; temporary help service. Appointment requested. Founded 1974. Specializes in the areas of: Accounting and Finance; Architecture; Banking; Bilingual Communication; Broadcasting; Clerical; Computer Hardware and Software; Construction; Engineering; Food Industry; Insurance; Legal; Manufacturing; MIS/EDP; Minorities; Nonprofit; Personnel and Human Resources; Printing and Publishing; Sales and Marketing; Technical and Scientific; Transportation. Positions commonly filled include: Accountant; Administrative Assistant; Aerospace Engineer; Bank Officer/Manager; Biochemist; Biologist; Biomedical Engineer; Bookkeeper; Buyer; Ceramics Engineer; Chemical Engineer; Chemist; Civil Engineer; Claims Representative; Clerk; Computer Operator; Computer Programmer; Credit Manager; Customer Service Representative; Data Entry Clerk; Demonstrator; Draftsperson; Driver; EDP Specialist; Electrical Engineer; Factory Worker; Financial Analyst; Food Technologist; General Laborer; General Manager; Industrial Designer; Industrial Engineer; Insurance Agent/Broker; Legal Secretary; Light Industrial Worker; MIS Specialist; Marketing Specialist; Mechanical Engineer; Medical Secretary; Metallurgical Engineer; Office Worker; Operations/Production Specialist; Personnel and Labor Relations Specialist; Physicist; Purchasing Agent; Quality Control Supervisor; Receptionist; Sales Representative; Secretary; Stenographer; Systems Analyst; Technical Writer/Editor; Technician; Typist; Underwriter; Word Processing Specialist. Company pays fee. Number of placements per year: 1001+.

POMERANTZ PERSONNEL
300 Raritan Avenue
Highland Park NJ 08904
Contact Gary Pomerantz, President, or Mary Pomerantz, Executive Vice President. 908/246-7100. Employment agency; temporary help service. Appointment requested. Founded 1974. Specializes in the areas of: Accounting and Finance; Architecture; Banking; Bilingual Communication; Broadcasting; Clerical; Computer Hardware and Software; Construction; Engineering; Food Industry; Insurance; Legal; Manufacturing; MIS/EDP; Minorities; Nonprofit; Personnel and Human Resources; Printing and Publishing; Sales and Marketing; Technical and Scientific; Transportation. Positions commonly filled include: Accountant; Administrative Assistant; Aerospace Engineer; Bank Officer/Manager; Biochemist; Biologist; Biomedical Engineer; Bookkeeper; Buyer; Ceramics Engineer; Chemical Engineer; Chemist; Civil Engineer; Claims Representative; Clerk; Computer Operator; Computer Programmer; Credit Manager; Customer Service Representative; Data Entry Clerk; Demonstrator; Draftsperson; Driver; EDP Specialist; Electrical Engineer; Factory Worker; Financial Analyst; Food Technologist; General Laborer; General Manager; Industrial Designer; Industrial Engineer; Insurance Agent/Broker; Legal Secretary; Light Industrial Worker; MIS Specialist; Marketing Specialist; Mechanical Engineer; Medical Secretary; Metallurgical Engineer; Office Worker; Operations/Production Specialist; Personnel and Labor Relations Specialist; Physicist; Purchasing Agent; Quality Control Supervisor; Receptionist; Sales Representative; Secretary; Stenographer; Systems Analyst; Technical Writer/Editor; Technician; Typist; Underwriter; Word Processing Specialist. Company pays fee. Number of placements per year: 1001+.

PRINCETON EXECUTIVE SEARCH

P.O. Box 7373
Princeton NJ 08543
Contact Andrew B. Barkocy, CPC. 609/896-3260. Specializes in the areas of: asset; audit; bookkeeping; budgeting; clerical; credit; financial analysis; international; investment; lending; public accounting; tax; training; trust; human resources (benefits; compensation; labor relations; management; personnel/industrial relations; recruiting/staffing; training/development).

RPA MANAGEMENT, INC.

P.O. Box 158
Fair Lawn NJ 07410
Contact Rick Pascal. 201/794-7223. FAX: 201/794-8314. Specializes in the areas of: audit; bookkeeping; budgeting; clerical; financial analysis; international; public accounting; tax.

RSVP SERVICES

Suite 614 One Cherry Hill Mall
Cherry Hill, NJ 08002
Contact Howard Levin. 609/667-4488. Computer science (corporate/computer security; programming; software engineering; systems).

READY PERSONNEL READY TEMPS

21 Path Plaza (Concourse Level)
Jersey City NJ 07306
Contact Denise Arthur & Jean Frank. 201/420-1900. FAX: 201/420-4411. Specializes in the areas of: legal (legal administrators; legal secretaries; paralegals); office administration (administrators; clerks; management; receptionists; secretaries; word processing); temporary services (accounting/bookkeeping; secretaries; word processing).

S-H-S INT'L OF CHERRY HILL

929 N Kings Highway
Cherry Hill NJ 08034
Contact Lee Grant, CPC. 609/779-9030. FAX: 609/779-0898. Specializes in the areas of: accounting/finance; computer science; engineering; insurance; office administration; sales.

SANFORD ROSE ASSOCIATES

P.O. Box 156
Colts Neck NJ 07722
Contact John Fodor, Director. 908/946-7465. Employment agency. No appointment required. Headquarters located in Akron, OH. Operates 92 offices throughout the United States. Specializes in the areas of: Engineering; Manufacturing; MIS/EDP. Positions commonly filled include: Electrical Engineer; Industrial Engineer; Mechanical Engineer. Company pays fee. Number of placements per year: 1001+.

SCIENTIFIC SEARCH

Plaza Office Center, Suite 309
Route 73 & Fellowship Road
Mt. Laurel NJ 08054
Contact Robert I. Greenberg. 609/866-0200. FAX: 609/722-5301. Specializes in the areas of: asset; computer science (corporate/computer security; consulting; data processing; EDP audit; operations; programming, software engineering, systems) credit; engineering (aeronautical; chemical; civil; electrical; environmental/hazardous waste; HVAC; industrial; manufacturing; mechanical; nuclear; packaging); investment; lending; trust.

SEARCH CONSULTANTS, INC.
10 Forest Avenue P.O. Box 402
Paramus NJ 07653-0502
Contact Walter Perog, CPC. 201/843-5090. FAX: 201/843-8334. Specializes in the area of: human resources (benefits; compensation; EEO; labor relations; management; personnel/industrial relations; recruiting/staffing; training/development).

SEARCH EDP, INC.
150 River Road, Buld. C Ste. 3
Montville NJ 07045
Contact Joseph Hauser, CPC. 201/335-6600. FAX: 201/335-8053. Specializes in the areas of: computer science (consulting; data processing; EDP audit; operations; programming).

SELECT FINDERS CORP.
1129 Bloomfield Avenue
West Caldwell NJ 07006
Contact Allen MacWright, CPC. 201/575-0370. FAX: 201/575-8332. Specializes in the areas of: asset; credit; investment; lending; trainees; trust; human resources (benefits; compensation; labor relations; management; personnel/industrial relations; recruiting/staffing; training/development); office administration (administrators; clerks; management; receptionists; secretaries; word processing).

SNELLING & SNELLING
450 Springfield Ave.
Summit NJ 07901
Contact Richard O. Leggett, CPC. 908/273-6500. FAX: 908/273-4379. Specializes in the area of: office administration (administrators, clerks; management; receptionists; secretaries; word processing).

STAFF BUILDERS
622 Georges Road
North Brunswick NJ 08902
Contact Barbara Van Alstyne, President. 908/246-1687. Temporary help agency. No appointment required. Founded 1970. Servicing Middlesex, Somerset and Mercer Counties with the best in temporary help and home health agencies. Specializes in the areas of: Advertising; Food Industry; Health and Medical; Secretarial and Clerical. Positions commonly filled include: Accountant; Administrative Assistant; Bookkeeper; Claims Representative; Clerk; Computer Programmer; Construction Worker; Customer Service Representative; Data Entry Clerk; Driver; Executive Secretary; Factory Worker; General Laborer; Light Industrial Worker; Legal Secretary; Marketing Specialist; Model; Nurse; Receptionist; Sales Representative; Secretary; Stenographer; Technician; Typist; Word Processor. Company pays fee. Number of placements per year: 1000+.

SUMMIT GROUP, INC.
51 Gibraltar Drive
Morris Plains NJ 07950
Contact Gary W. Pezzutti, President. 201/898-0700. Employment agency. Appointment requested. Founded 1981. Specializes in the areas of: Accounting and Finance; Engineering; Manufacturing; Materials Management; Personnel and Human Resources; Production Control; Technical and Scientific. Positions commonly filled include: Accountant; Aerospace Engineer; Biomedical Engineer; Buyer; Ceramics Engineer; Chemical Engineer; Chemist; Customer Service Representative; Draftsperson; Electrical Engineer; Financial Analyst; General Manager; Industrial Designer; Industrial Engineer; Inventory Control Manager; Marketing Specialist; Materials Manager; Mechanical

Engineer; Metallurgical Engineer; Operations and Production Specialist; Personnel and Labor Relations Specialist; Production Control Manager; Purchasing Agent; Quality Control Supervisor; Systems Analyst; Technical Writer/Editor. Company pays fee. Number of placements per year: 51-100.

TOPAZ INTERNATIONAL, INC.
383 Northfield Ave.
West Orange NJ 07052
Contact Ronni L. Gaines. 201/669-7300. FAX: 201/669-9811. Specializes in the area of: legal (attorneys; legal administrators; legal secretaries; paralegals).

UNITEMP TEMPORARY PERSONNEL
95 Route 17 South
Paramus NJ 07652
Contact P. Sheehan, Vice President. 201/845-7444. Temporary help service. No appointment required. Founded 1969. Specializes in the areas of: Accounting and Finance; Banking; Clerical; Computer Hardware and Software; Insurance; Legal; Personnel and Human Resources; Printing and Publishing; Sales and Marketing; Women. Positions commonly filled include: Accountant; Advertising Worker; Administrative Assistant; Bookkeeper; Clerk; Computer Operator; Computer Programmer; Customer Service Representative; Data Entry Clerk; Demonstrator; Driver; EDP Specialist; General Laborer; Legal Secretary; Light Industrial Worker; MIS Specialist; Medical Secretary; Office Worker; Quality Control Supervisor; Receptionist; Secretary; Stenographer; Systems Analyst; Typist; Word Processing Specialist. Company pays fee. Number of placements per year: 1000+.

WINTERS & ROSS
442 Main Street
Fort Lee NJ 07024
Employment agency. 201/947-8400. Appointment requested. Founded 1981. Specializes in the areas of: Accounting and Finance; Clerical; Computer Hardware and Software; Fashion; MIS/EDP; Personnel and Human Resources; Technical and Scientific. Positions commonly filled include: Accountant; Administrative Assistant; Bookkeeper; Buyer; Clerk; Computer Operator; Computer Programmer; Credit Manager; Customer Service Representative; Data Entry Clerk; EDP Specialist; Financial Analyst; General Manager; Legal Secretary; Office Worker; Operations/Production Specialist; Personnel and Labor Relations Specialist; Purchasing Agent; Receptionist; Secretary; Stenographer; Typist; Word Processing Specialist. Company pays fee. Number of placements per year: 201-500.

EXECUTIVE SEARCH FIRMS OF NEW JERSEY

EXECUTIVE EXCHANGE CORP.
560 Sylvan Avenue
Englewood Cliffs NJ 07632
Contact Liz Glosser, Owner. 201/871-4646 or 201/223-6655. Executive search firm. Apppointment preferred; unsolicited resumes accepted. Professional recruitment in data processing, retail, and computer-related sales. Our business has grown consistently each year: from 45 placements in 1981 to 170 in 1987; from average starting salary of $18K in 1981 to $32K in 1987; from one to two offices. Revenue has increased an average of 15%

per year. Specializes in the areas of: Computer Hardware and Software; Retailing; Sales and Marketing. Contingency.

GRAHAM ASSOCIATES, INC
111 Madison Avenue, Suite 100
Morristown NJ 07960
Contact W. M. Stephenson, President. 201/455-0805. Executive search firm. Appointment required; no phone calls; unsolicited resumes accepted. Founded 1973. Strong Technical orientation. Conducts searches for: Engineering, Scientific Salesperson; Marketing Executive in Chemicals, Plastics, Pharmaceuticals, Instrumentation, Process Control, and Industrial Electronics. Contingency. Number of searches conducted per year: 51-100.

MANAGEMENT RECRUITERS OF NORTH BRUNSWICK
669 Nassau Street
North Brunswick NJ 08902
Contact Alan D Best, Manager. 908/545-1900. Executive search firm. Appointment required; no phone calls; unsolicited resumes accepted. Founded 1965. World's largest contingency search firm. Five hundred offices nationwide, doing business under the names "Management Recruiters", "Sales Consultants", "CompuSearch" and "OfficeMates5." Specializes in mid-management/professional positions, $25,000-75,000 per annum. Specializes in the areas of: Accounting; Administration; MIS/EDP; Advertising; Affirmative Action; Architecture; Banking and Finance; Communications; Computer Hardware and Software; Construction; Electrical; Engineering; Food Industry; General Management; Health and Medical; Human Resources; Industrial and Interior Design; Insurance; Legal; Manufacturing; Operations Management; Printing and Publishing; Procurement; Real Estate; Retailing; Sales and Marketing; Technical and Scientific; Textiles; Transportation. Contingency.

MANAGEMENT RECRUITERS OF PASSAIC COUNTY-NORTH
750 Hamburg Turnpike
Pompton Lakes NJ 07442
Contact David Zawicki, Manager. 201/831-7778. Executive search firm. Appointment required; no phone calls; unsolicited resumes accepted. Founded 1965. World's largest contingency search firm. Five hundred offices nationwide, doing business under the names "Management Recruiters", "Sales Consultants", "CompuSearch" and "OfficeMates5." Specializes in mid-management/professional positions, $25,000-75,000 per annum. Specializes in the areas of: Accounting; Administration; MIS/EDP; Advertising; Affirmative Action; Architecture; Banking and Finance; Communications; Computer Hardware and Software; Construction; Electrical; Engineering; Food Industry; General Management; Health and Medical; Human Resources; Industrial and Interior Design; Insurance; Legal; Manufacturing; Operations Management; Printing and Publishing; Procurement; Real Estate; Retailing; Sales and Marketing; Technical and Scientific; Textiles; Transportation. Contingency.

MANAGEMENT RECRUITERS OF PASSAIC COUNTY-SOUTH
1373 Broad Street
Clifton NJ 07013
Contact Brian Wittlin, Manager. 201/473-1600. Executive search firm. Appointment required; no phone calls; unsolicited resumes accepted. Founded 1965. World's largest contingency search firm. Five hundred offices nationwide, doing business under the names "Management Recruiters", "Sales Consultants", "CompuSearch" and "OfficeMates5." Specializes in mid-management/professional positions, $25,000-75,000 per annum. Specializes in the areas of: Accounting; Administration; MIS/EDP; Advertising; Affirmative Action; Architecture; Banking and Finance· Communications; Computer

Hardware and Software; Construction; Electrical; Engineering; Food Industry; General Management; Health and Medical; Human Resources; Industrial and Interior Design; Insurance; Legal; Manufacturing; Operations Management; Printing and Publishing; Procurement; Real Estate; Retailing; Sales and Marketing; Technical and Scientific; Textiles; Transportation. Contingency.

MANAGEMENT RECRUITERS OF SPARTA
Suite 201, 191 Woodport Road
Sparta NJ 07871
Contact Lance Incitti, Manager. 201/729-1888; FAX: 201/729-1620. Executive search firm. Appointment required; no phone calls; unsolicited resumes accepted. Founded 1965. World's largest contingency search firm. Five hundred offices nationwide, doing business under the names "Management Recruiters", "Sales Consultants", "CompuSearch" and "OfficeMates5". Specializes in mid-management/professional positions, $25,000-75,000 per annum. Specializes in the areas of: Accounting; Administration; MIS/EDP; Advertising; Affirmative Action; Architecture; Banking and Finance; Communications; Computer Hardware and Software; Construction; Electrical; Engineering; Food Industry; General Management; Health and Medical; Human Resources; Industrial and Interior Design; Insurance; Legal; Manufacturing; Operations Management; Printing and Publishing; Procurement; Real Estate; Retailing; Sales and Marketing; Technical and Scientific; Textiles; Transportation. Contingency.

McCORMICK & ASSOCIATES
3086 Route 27, Suite 5
Kendall Park NJ 08824
Contact Harriet McCormick, President. 908/297-8600. Executive search firm No appointment required. Founded 1981. All staff college graduates; most have advanced degrees. Specializes in the areas of: Advertising; Banking and Finance; Computer Hardware and Software; Engineering; Legal; MIS/EDP; Sales and Marketing; Technical and Scientific. Positions commonly filled include: Accountant; Advertising Executive; Aerospace Engineer; Attorney; Bank Officer/Manager; Biochemist/Chemist; Biologist; Biomedical Engineer; Computer Programmer; EDP Specialist; Electrical Engineer; Financial Analyst; Industrial Engineer; Management Consultant; Mechanical Engineer; Personnel Director; Physicist; Purchasing Agent; Sales Representative; Statistician; Systems Analyst; Technical Writer/Editor. Company pays fee. Number of placements per year: 201-500.

MANAGEMENT RECRUITERS OF STANHOPE
Waterloo Executive Plaza
4 Waterloo Road
Stanhope NJ 07874
Contact Arthur Young, Manager. 201/691-2000. Executive search firm. Appointment required; no phone calls; unsolicited resumes accepted. Founded 1965. World's largest contingency search firm. Five hundred offices nationwide, doing business under the names "Management Recruiters", "Sales Consultants", "CompuSearch" and "OfficeMates5". Specializes in mid-management/professional positions, $25,000-75,000 per annum. Specializes in the areas of: Accounting; Administration, MIS/EDP; Advertising; Affirmative Action; Architecture; Banking and Finance; Communications; Computer Hardware and Software; Construction; Electrical; Engineering; Food Industry; General Management; Health and Medical; Human Resources; Industrial and Interior Design; Insurance; Legal; Manufacturing; Operations Management; Printing and Publishing; Procurement; Real Estate; Retailing; Sales and Marketing; Technical and Scientific; Textiles; Transportation. Contingency.

OFFICEMATES5 OF BRIDGEWATER
1120 Route 22 East
Bridgewater NJ 08807
Contact David Campeas or Barry Smith, Co-Managers. 908/725-2595; FAX: 908/725-0439. Executive search firm. Appointment required; no phone calls; unsolicited resumes accepted. Founded 1965. World's largest contingency search firm. Five hundred offices nationwide, doing business under the names "Management Recruiters", "Sales Consultants", "CompuSearch" and "OfficeMates5." Specializes in mid-management/professional positions, $25,000-75,000 per annum. Specializes in the areas of: Accounting; Administration; MIS/EDP; Advertising; Affirmative Action; Architecture; Banking and Finance; Communications; Computer Hardware and Software; Construction; Electrical; Engineering; Food Industry; General Management; Health and Medical; Human Resources; Industrial and Interior Design; Insurance; Legal; Manufacturing; Operations Management; Printing and Publishing; Procurement; Real Estate; Retailing; Sales and Marketing; Technical and Scientific; Textiles; Transportation. Contingency.

ORION CONSULTING, INC.
115 Route 46
Building B, Suite 13
Mountain Lakes NJ 07046
Contact James Dromsky, President. 201/538-0030. Executive search firm. Appointment required; unsolicited resumes accepted. Founded 1982. Specializes in the areas of: Accounting; Administration; Advertising; Banking and Finance; Chemicals and Pharmaceuticals; Communications; Computer Hardware and Software; Construction; Electrical Engineering; Food Industry; General Management; Health and Medical; Human Resources; Industrial and Interior Design; Insurance; Legal; Manufacturing; Military; Operations Management; Procurement; Sales and Marketing; Technical and Scientific; Transportation. Noncontingency. Outplacement. Job evaluations. Human Resource Audit. General H/R consulting. Number of searches conducted per year: 51-100.

SALES CONSULTANTS OF MORRIS COUNTY
364 Parsippany Road
Parsippany NJ 07054
Contact Ernie Bivona, Manager. 201/887-3838. Executive search firm. Appointment required; no phone calls; unsolicited resumes accepted. Founded 1965. World's largest contingency search firm. Five hundred offices nationwide, doing business under the names "Management Recruiters", "Sales Consultants", "CompuSearch" and "OfficeMates5." Specializes in mid-management/professional positions, $25,000-75,000 per annum. Specializes in the areas of: Accounting; Administration; MIS/EDP; Advertising; Affirmative Action; Architecture; Banking and Finance; Communications; Computer Hardware and Software; Construction; Electrical; Engineering; Food Industry; General Management; Health and Medical; Human Resources; Industrial and Interior Design; Insurance; Legal; Manufacturing; Operations Management; Printing and Publishing; Procurement; Real Estate; Retailing; Sales and Marketing; Technical and Scientific; Textiles; Transportation. Contingency.

SALES CONSULTANTS OF SPARTA
Suite 105, 70 Sparta Avenue
Sparta NJ 07871
Contact Harvey Bass, Manager. 201/729-9771; FAX 201/729-1170. Executive search firm. Appointment required; no phone calls; unsolicited resumes accepted. Founded 1965. World's largest contingency search firm. Five hundred offices nationwide, doing business under the names "Management Recruiters", "Sales Consultants", "CompuSearch" and "OfficeMates5". Specializes in mid-management/professional positions, $25,000-75,000 per

annum. Specializes in the areas of: Accounting; Administration; MIS/EDP; Advertising; Affirmative Action; Architecture; Banking and Finance; Communications; Computer Hardware and Software; Construction; Electrical; Engineering; Food Industry; General Management; Health and Medical; Human Resources; Industrial and Interior Design; Insurance; Legal; Manufacturing; Operations Management; Printing and Publishing; Procurement; Real Estate; Retailing; Sales and Marketing; Technical and Scientific; Textiles; Transportation. Contingency.

SEARCH EAST, INC.
1600 Route 22
Union NJ 07083
Contact Bob Dougherty, Manager. 908/687-8300. Contingency middle management search firm. Appointment required. Founded 1975. Specializes in the areas of: Accounting; Banking and Finance; Computer Hardware and Software; Engineering; Food Industry; Insurance; Manufacturing; MIS/EDP; Technical and Scientific. Positions commonly filled include: Actuary; Aerospace Engineer; Bank Officer/Manager; Biomedical Engineer; Claims Representative; Computer Programmer; EDP Specialist; Electrical Engineer; Industrial Designer; Industrial Engineer; Insurance Agent/Broker; Mechanical Engineer; Technical Writer/Editor. Company pays fee. Number of placements per year: 51-100.

VIP EXECUTIVE PERSONNEL
140 Sylvan Avenue, Suite 9
Englewood Cliffs NJ 07632
Contact Phyllis Scott, President. 908/947-8600. Executive search firm. Appointment required; unsolicited resumes accepted. Full service agency founded in 1977, specializing in the health care industry. Specializes in the areas of: Women's Placement; Accounting; Advertising; Construction; Engineering; General Management; Health and Medical; Libraries; Office Support; Retail Apparel; Retailing; Sales and Marketing; Warehousing. Contingency.

Professional and Trade Associations

Anyone who has conducted a job search has heard the dictum, "It s not what you know, it's who you know." While the validity of this comment has just as often been exaggerated, it does contain more than a grain of truth. Connections can never replace good old hard work as the best method of finding employment, but they can't hurt.

If you don't have an uncle in high places who can set up some interviews for you with a few of his friends, don't worry. Most people don't. The important thing to remember is that in most instances, connections do not materialize out of thin air -- they are created. That means that anyone who works at it can make them.

One of the best ways to meet people in your area of interest is through professional trade associations. Trade associations exist so that professionals in an industry can meet, share information about trends in the field, and arrange new business. Many of them regularly publish newsletters and magazines that will help you stay abreast of the current state of your industry. In addition, many associations hold regular meetings, and these meetings may present you the opportunity not only to learn more about the field you hope to enter, but also to establish connections.

With this in mind, we have included this directory of professional associations. Many of the addresses listed are for headquarters offices only. Inquire about local chapters in your area.

ACCOUNTING

**AMERICAN INSTITUTE OF
CERTIFIED PUBLIC ACCOUNTANTS**
1211 Avenue of the Americas
New York NY 10036
212/575-6200

For more information, contact:

NATIONAL SOCIETY OF PUBLIC ACCOUNTANTS
1010 North Fairfax Street
Alexandria VA 22314
703/549-6400

ADVERTISING, MARKETING, PUBLIC RELATIONS

AMERICAN ASSOCIATION OF ADVERTISING AGENCIES
666 Third Avenue, 13th Floor
New York NY 10017
212/682-2500

BUSINESS-PROFESSIONAL ADVERTISING ASSOCIATION
Metroplex Corporate Center
100 Metroplex Drive
Edison NJ 08817
201/985-4441

PUBLIC RELATIONS SOCIETY OF AMERICA
33 Irving Place
New York NY 10003
212/995-2230

TELEVISION BUREAU OF ADVERTISING
477 Madison Avenue
New York NY 10022
212/486-1111

For more information, contact:

AMERICAN ADVERTISING FEDERATION
1400 K Street NW
Suite 1000
Washington DC 20005

AMERICAN MARKETING ASSOCIATION
250 South Wacker Drive
Suite 200
Chicago IL 60606
312/648-0536

APPAREL AND TEXTILES

AMERICAN APPAREL MANUFACTURERS ASSOCIATION
2500 Wilson Boulevard
Suite 301
Arlington VA 22201
703/524-1864

AMERICAN TEXTILE MANUFACTURERS INSTITUTE
1801 K Street NW
Suite 900
Washington DC 20006
202/862-0500

NORTHERN TEXTILE ASSOCIATION
230 Congress Street
Boston MA 02110
617/542-8220

TEXTILE RESEARCH INSTITUTE
Box 625
Princeton NJ 08542
609/924-3150

ARTS AND ENTERTAINMENT/LEISURE

AMERICAN FEDERATION OF MUSICIANS
1501 Broadway, Suite 600
New York NY 10036
212/869-1330

AMERICAN FEDERATION OF TELEVISION AND RADIO ARTISTS
260 Madison Avenue
New York NY 10016
212/532-0800

THEATRE COMMUNICATIONS GROUP
355 Lexington Avenue
New York NY 10017
212/697-5230

For more information, contact:

AMERICAN ASSOCIATION OF ZOOLOGICAL PARKS & AQUARIUMS
Oglebay Park
Wheeling WV 26003
304/242-2160

NATIONAL ENDOWMENT FOR THE ARTS
1100 Pennsylvania Avenue NW
Washington DC 20506
202/682-5400

BANKING/SAVINGS AND LOAN

INSTITUTE OF FINANCIAL EDUCATION/CHAPTER 18
Empire of America
Federal Savings Association
501 Balmore Avenue
East Meadow NY 11554
516/485-4884

For more information:

AMERICAN BANKERS ASSOCIATION
1120 Connecticut Avenue NW
Washington DC 20036
202/663-5221

BANK ADMINISTRATION INSTITUTE
Plaza 1000, Suite 202
Voorhees NJ 08043
609/424-3233

INDEPENDENT BANKERS ASSOCIATION OF AMERICA
One Thomas Circle NW
Suite 950
Washington DC 20005
202/659-8111

INSTITUTE OF FINANCIAL EDUCATION
111 East Wacker Drive
Chicago IL 60601
312/644-3100

NATIONAL COUNCIL OF SAVINGS INSTITUTIONS
1101 15th Street NW
Suite 400
Washington DC 20005
202/857-3100

BOOK AND MAGAZINE PUBLISHING

AMERICAN BOOKSELLERS ASSOCIATION
137 West 25th Street, 11th Floor
New York NY 10001
212/463-8450

ASSOCIATION OF AMERICAN PUBLISHERS
220 East 23rd Street
New York NY 10010
212/689-8920

MAGAZINE PUBLISHERS ASSOCIATION
575 Lexington Avenue, Suite 540
New York NY 10022
212/752-0055

WRITERS GUILD OF AMERICA EAST, INC.
555 West 57th Street, Suite 1230
New York NY 10019
212/245-6180

For more information:

WRITERS GUILD OF AMERICA WEST, INC.
8955 Beverly Boulevard
Los Angeles CA 90048
213/550-1000

BROADCASTING

INTERNATIONAL RADIO AND TV SOCIETY
420 Lexington Avenue
Suite 531
New York NY 10170
212/867-6650

TELEVISION BUREAU OF ADVERTISING
477 Madison Avenue
New York NY 10022
212/486-1111

WOMEN IN RADIO & TV, INC./NEW YORK
245 5th Avenue, Suite 2103
New York NY 10016
212/481-3038

For more information, contact:

BROADCAST EDUCATION ASSOCIATION
1771 N Street NW
Washington DC 20036
202/424-5355

CABLE TELEVISION ASSOCIATION
1724 Massachusetts Avenue NW
Washington DC 20036
202/775-3550

NATIONAL ASSOCIATION OF BROADCASTERS
1771 N Street NW
Washington DC 20036
202/429-5300

NATIONAL ASSOCIATION OF BUSINESS
AND EDUCATIONAL RADIO
1501 Duke Street
Suite 200
Alexandria VA 22314
703/739-0300

WOMEN IN RADIO AND TV, INC.
1101 Connecticut Avenue NW
Suite 700
Washington DC 20036
202/429-5102

CHARITABLE, NON-PROFIT, HUMANITARIAN

NATIONAL ASSOCIATION OF SOCIAL WORKERS
545 8th Avenue
6th Floor
New York NY 10018
212/947-5000

For more information, contact:

NATIONAL ASSOCIATION OF SOCIAL WORKERS
7981 Eastern Avenue
Silver Spring MD 20910
301/565-0333

NATIONAL ORGANIZATION FOR HUMAN
SERVICE EDUCATION
National College of Education
2840 Sheridan Road
Evanston IL 60201
708/256-5150

CHEMICALS & RELATED: PROCESSING, PRODUCTION, DISPOSAL

AMERICAN INSTITUTE OF CHEMICAL ENGINEERING
345 East 47th Street
New York NY 10017
212/705-7338

AMERICAN INSTITUTE OF CHEMISTS/NEW YORK
c/o Joel Freeman
6 Darcy Lane
Eastchester NY 10709

DRUG, CHEMICAL, AND ALLIED TRADES ASSOCIATION
#2 Two Roosevelt Avenue
3rd Floor
Syosset NY 11791
516/496-3317

For more information, contact:

AMERICAN CHEMICAL SOCIETY
Career Services
1155 16th Street NW
Washington DC 20036
202/872-4600

AMERICAN INSTITUTE OF CHEMISTS
7315 Wisconsin Avenue, Suite 525 E
Bethesda MD 20814
301/652-2447

**ASSOCIATION OF STATE & INTERSTATE
 WATER POLLUTION CONTROL ADMINISTRATORS**
444 North Capital Street NW
Suite #330 N
Washington DC 20001
202/624-7782

WATER POLLUTION CONTROL FEDERATION
601 Wythe Street Avenue NW
Alexandria VA 22314
703/684-2400

COLLEGES AND UNIVERSITIES/EDUCATION

AMERICAN ASSOCIATION OF SCHOOL ADMINISTRATORS
1801 North Moore Street
Arlington VA 22209
703/528-0700

ASSOCIATION OF AMERICAN UNIVERSITIES
One Dupont Circle NW
Suite 730
Washington DC 20036
202/466-5030

COMMUNICATIONS

COMMUNICATIONS WORKERS OF AMERICA/NEW JERSEY
Allan Kaufman, CWA Representative
10 Rutgers Place
Trenton NJ 08618
609/392-2771

COMMUNICATIONS WORKERS OF AMERICA/NEW YORK
Jan D. Pierce - VP
80 Pine Street, 37th Floor
New York NY 10005
212/344-2515

For more information, contact:

COMMUNICATIONS WORKERS OF AMERICA
1925 K Street NW
Washington DC 20006
202/728-2300

UNITED STATES TELEPHONE ASSOCIATION
900 19th Street NW, Suite 800
Washington DC 20006
202/835-3100

COMPUTERS: HARDWARE, SOFTWARE AND SERVICES

ASSOCIATION FOR COMPUTING MACHINERY
11 West 42nd Street, 3rd Floor
New York NY 10036
212/869-7440

For more information, contact:

**ADAPSO/THE COMPUTER SOFTWARE AND SERVICES
 INDUSTRY ASSOCIATION**
1300 North 17th Street, Suite 300
Arlington VA 22209
703/522-5055

ASSOCIATION FOR COMPUTER SCIENCE
P.O. Box 19027
Sacramento CA 95819
916/421-9149

IEEE COMPUTER SOCIETY
1730 Massachusetts Avenue NW
Washington DC 20036-1903

SEMICONDUCTOR INDUSTRY ASSOCIATION
4300 Stevens Clark Boulevard, Suite 271
San Jose CA 95129
408/246-2711

CONSTRUCTION

ASSOCIATION OF BUILDERS & OWNERS OF GREATER NEW YORK
122 East 42nd Street
Suite 1518
New York NY 10168
212/986-2626

For more information, contact:

**BUILDING OFFICIALS AND CODE
ADMINISTRATORS INTERNATIONAL, INC**
4051 West Flossmoor Road
Country Club Hills IL 60478
708/799-2300

CONSTRUCTION INDUSTRY MANUFACTURERS ASSOCIATION
111 East Wisconsin Avenue, Suite 940
Milwaukee WI 53202
414/272-0943

INTERNATIONAL CONFERENCE OF BUILDING OFFICIALS
5360 South Workman Road
Whittier CA 90601
213/699-0541

NATIONAL ASSOCIATION OF HOME BUILDERS
15th & M Streets NW
Washington DC 20005
202/822-0200

ELECTRICAL AND ELECTRONICS

INSTITUTE OF ELECTRICAL AND ELECTRONICS ENGINEERS
345 East 47th Street
New York NY 10017
212/705-7900

INTERNATIONAL BROTHERHOOD
OF ELECTRICAL WORKERS/LOCAL 3
158-11 Harry Van Arsdale, Jr. Avenue
Flushing NY 11365
718/591-4000

For more information:

AMERICAN ELECTROPLATERS AND SURFACE FINISHERS SOCIETY
12644 Research Parkway
Orlando FL 32826
407/281-6441

ELECTROCHEMICAL SOCIETY
10 South Main Street
Pennington NJ 08534-2896
609/737-1902

ELECTRONIC INDUSTRIES ASSOCIATION
2001 Pennsylvania Ave NW
Washington DC 20006
202/457-4900

ELECTRONICS TECHNICIANS ASSOCIATION
602 N. Jackson Street
Greencastle IN 46135
317/653-8262

INTERNATIONAL BROTHERHOOD OF ELECTRICAL WORKERS
1125 15th Street NW
Washington DC 20005
202/833-7000

INTERNATIONAL SOCIETY OF CERTIFIED
ELECTRONICS TECHNICIANS
2708 West Berry
Ft. Worth TX 76109
817/921-9101

NATIONAL ELECTRICAL MANUFACTURERS ASSOCIATION
2101 L Street NW, Suite 300
Washington DC 20037
202/457-8400

NATIONAL ELECTRONICS SALES AND SERVICES ASSOCIATION
2708 West Berry
Ft. Worth TX 76109
817/921-9061

ENGINEERING AND ARCHITECTURE

AMERICAN SOCIETY OF CIVIL ENGINEERS
345 East 47th Street
New York NY 10017
212/705-7496

AMERICAN SOCIETY OF LANDSCAPE ARCHITECTS
Paul A. Pietrotaolo, Chapter Secretary
Port Authority: NY/NJ
73 East One World Trade Center
New York NY 10048
212/466-2130

ILLUMINATING ENGINEERING SOCIETY OF NORTH AMERICA
345 East 47th Street
New York NY 10017
212/705-7926

UNITED ENGINEERING TRUSTEES
345 East 47th Street
New York NY 10017
212/705-7000

For more information, contact:

AMERICAN INSTITUTE OF ARCHITECTS
1735 New York Ave NW
Washington DC 20006
202/626-7300

AMERICAN SOCIETY FOR ENGINEERING EDUCATION
11 Dupont Circle NW
Suite 200
Washington DC 20036
202/293-7080

**AMERICAN SOCIETY OF HEATING, REFRIGERATING
 AND AIR CONDITIONING ENGINEERS**
1791 Tullie Circle NE
Atlanta GA 30329
404/636-8400

AMERICAN SOCIETY OF NAVAL ENGINEERS
1452 Duke Street
Alexandria VA 22314
703/836-6727

AMERICAN SOCIETY OF PLUMBING ENGINEERS
3617 Thousand Oaks Boulevard
Suite #210
Westlake CA 91362
805/495-7120

AMERICAN SOCIETY OF SAFETY ENGINEERS
1800 East Oakton Street
Des Plaines IL 60018
708/692-4121

INSTITUTE OF INDUSTRIAL ENGINEERS
25 Technology Park
Norcross GA 30092
404/449-0460

NATIONAL ACADEMY OF ENGINEERING
2101 Constitution Avenue NW
Washington DC 20418
202/334-3200

NATIONAL SOCIETY OF PROFESSIONAL ENGINEERS
1420 King Street
Alexandria VA 22314
703/684-2800

SOCIETY OF FIRE PROTECTION ENGINEERS
60 Batterymarch Street
Boston MA 02110
617/482-0686

FABRICATED METAL PRODUCTS/PRIMARY METALS

MASTERS ASSOCIATION OF METAL FINISHERS
Claude Blaser
799 Broadway, Room 321
New York NY 10003
212/475-7070

For more information, contact:

AMERICAN CASTE METALS ASSOCIATION
455 State Street
Des Plaines IL 60016
708/299-9156

AMERICAN POWDER METALLURGY INSTITUTE
105 College Road East
Princeton NJ 08540
609/452-7700

ASSOCIATION OF IRON AND STEEL ENGINEERS
Three Gateway Center
Suite 2350
Pittsburgh PA 15222
412/281-6323

NATIONAL ASSOCIATION OF METAL FINISHERS
111 East Wacker Drive, Suite 600
Chicago IL 60601
312/644-6610

FINANCIAL SERVICES/MANAGEMENT CONSULTING

AMERICAN MANAGEMENT ASSOCIATION
Management Information Service
135 West 50th Street
New York NY 10020
212/586-8100

ASSOCIATION OF MANAGEMENT CONSULTING FIRMS
230 Park Avenue, Suite 544
New York NY 10169
212/697-9693

FINANCIAL ANALYSTS FEDERATION
1633 Broadway
Room 1602
New York NY 10019
212/957-2860

FINANCIAL EXECUTIVES INSTITUTE
10 Madison Avenue
P.O. Box 1938
Morristown NJ 07962-1938
201/898-4600

COUNCIL OF CONSULTANT ORGANIZATIONS
230 Park Avenue
Suite 544
New York NY 10169
212/697-8262

NEW YORK CREDIT AND FINANCIAL MANAGEMENT ASSOCIATION
520 8th Avenue
New York NY 10018
212/268-8711

SECURITIES INDUSTRY ASSOCIATION
120 Broadway
New York NY 10271
212/608-1500

For more information, contact:

AMERICAN FINANCIAL SERVICES ASSOCIATION
Fourth Floor, 1101 14th Street NW
Washington DC 20005
202/289-0400

AMERICAN SOCIETY OF APPRAISERS
P.O. Box 17265
Washington DC 20041
202/478-2228

FEDERATION OF TAX ADMINISTRATORS
444 North Capital Street NW
Washington DC 20001
202/624-5890

INSTITUTE OF FINANCIAL EDUCATION
111 East Wacker Drive
Chicago IL 60601
312/644-3100

NATIONAL ASSOCIATION OF CREDIT MANAGEMENT
8815 Centre Park Drive
Suite 200
Columbia MD 21045-2117
301/740-5560

NATIONAL ASSOCIATION OF REAL ESTATE INVESTMENT TRUSTS
1129 20th Street NW
Suite 705
Washington DC 20036
202/785-8717

NATIONAL CORPORATE CASH
 MANAGEMENT ASSOCIATION
52 Church Hill Road
Newtown CT 06470
203/426-3007

FOOD: PROCESSING, PRODUCTION, AND DISTRIBUTION

AMERICAN ASSOCIATION OF CEREAL CHEMISTS/NEW YORK
William Graham, VP
c/o Florasynth
410 East 62nd Street
New York NY 10021
212/371-7700

PESTICIDE ASSOCIATION OF NEW YORK STATE
Dr. David Marsden
4561 Frank Gay Road
Marcellus NY 13108
315/673-1303

For more information, contact:

AMERICAN ASSOCIATION OF CEREAL CHEMISTS
3340 Pilot Knob Road
St. Paul MN 55121
612/454-7250

AMERICAN SOCIETY OF AGRICULTURAL ENGINEERS
2950 Niles Road
St. Joseph MI 49085
616/429-0300

AMERICAN SOCIETY OF BREWING CHEMISTS
3340 Pilot Knob Road
St. Paul MN 55121
612/454-7250

DAIRY AND FOOD INDUSTRIES SUPPLY ASSOCIATION
6245 Executive Boulevard
Rockville MD 20852
301/984-1444

NATIONAL AGRICULTURAL CHEMICALS ASSOCIATION
1155 15th Street NW
Suite 900
Washington DC 20005
202/296-1585

NATIONAL DAIRY COUNCIL
6300 North River Road
Rosemont IL 60018
708/696-1020

UNITED FOOD AND COMMERCIAL
 WORKERS INTERNATIONAL UNION
1775 K Street NW
Washington DC 20006
202/223-3111

GENERAL MERCHANDISE: RETAIL AND WHOLESALE

NATIONAL RETAIL MERCHANTS ASSOCIATION
100 West 31st Street
New York NY 10001
212/244-8780

HEALTH CARE AND PHARMACEUTICALS/HOSPITALS

NATIONAL HEALTH COUNCIL
350 5th Avenue, Suite 1118
New York NY 10018
212/268-8900

NEW YORK DENTAL SOCIETY
30 East 42nd Street, Suite 1606
New York NY 10017
212/986-3937

NEW YORK COUNTY MEDICAL SOCIETY
40 West 57th Street
New York NY 10019
212/399-9040

PHARMACEUTICAL SOCIETY OF THE STATE OF NEW YORK
Pine West Plaza IV
Washington Avenue Extension
Albany NY 12205
518/869-6595

For more information, contact:

AMERICAN ACADEMY OF PHYSICIAN ASSISTANTS
950 North Washington Street
Alexandria VA 22314
703/836-2272

AMERICAN COLLEGE OF HEALTHCARE EXECUTIVES
840 North Lake Shore Drive
Chicago IL 60611
312/943-0544

AMERICAN DENTAL ASSOCIATION
211 East Chicago Avenue
Chicago IL 60611-9985
312/440-2500

AMERICAN HEALTH CARE ASSOCIATION
1201 L Street NW
Washington DC 20005
202/842-4444

AMERICAN MEDICAL ASSOCIATION
535 North Dearborn Street
Chicago IL 60610
312/645-5000

AMERICAN OCCUPATIONAL THERAPY ASSOCIATION
1383 Piccard Drive
Rockville MD 20850
301/948-9626

AMERICAN PHARMACEUTICAL ASSOCIATION
2215 Constitution Avenue NW
Washington DC 20037
202/628-4410

AMERICAN PHYSICAL THERAPY ASSOCIATION
1111 North Fairfax Street
Alexandria VA 22314
703/684-2782

**AMERICAN SOCIETY FOR BIOCHEMISTRY
AND MOLECULAR BIOLOGY**
9650 Rockville Pike
Bethesda MD 20814
301/530-7145

AMERICAN SOCIETY OF HOSPITAL PHARMACISTS
4630 Montgomery Avenue
Bethesda MD 20814
301/657-3000

AMERICAN VETERINARY MEDICAL ASSOCIATION
930 North Meacham Road
Schaumburg IL 60196
708/605-8070

CARDIOVASCULAR CREDENTIALING INTERNATIONAL
P.O. Box 611
Dayton OH 45419
513/294-5225

MEDICAL GROUP MANAGEMENT ASSOCIATION
1355 South Colorado Boulevard
Suite 900
Denver CO 80222
303/753-1111

NATIONAL MEDICAL ASSOCIATION
1012 Tenth Street NW
Washington DC 20001
202/347-1895

HOTEL AND RESTAURANT RELATED

THE AMERICAN HOTEL AND MOTEL ASSOCIATION
295 Lafayette Street, 7th Floor
New York NY 10012
212/941-5858

NEW YORK STATE RESTAURANT ASSOCIATION
505 8th Avenue, 7th Floor
New York NY 10018
212/714-1330

For more information, contact

**COUNCIL ON HOTEL, RESTAURANT
 AND INSTITUTIONAL EDUCATION**
1200 17th Street NW
Washington DC 20036
202/331-5990

**THE EDUCATION FOUNDATION OF
 THE NATIONAL RESTAURANT ASSOCIATION**
150 North Michigan Avenue
Suite 2000
Chicago IL 60601
312/853-2525

INSURANCE

ACTUARIAL SOCIETY OF GREATER NEW YORK
John M. Fenton - Secretary
Tillinghast/Towers Perrin
245 Park Avenue
New York NY 10167

AMERICAN COUNCIL OF LIFE INSURANCE/NEW YORK
1270 Avenue of the Americas
Suite 2411
New York NY 10020-0474

INSURANCE INFORMATION INSTITUTE
110 William Street
New York NY 10038
212/669-9200

For more information, contact:

ALLIANCE OF AMERICAN INSURERS
1501 Woodfield Road
Suite 400 West
Schaumburg IL 60173
708/330-8500

AMERICAN COUNCIL OF LIFE INSURANCE
1001 Pennsylvania Avenue NW
Washington DC 20004-2599
202/624-2000

AMERICAN INSURANCE ASSOCIATION
1130 Connecticut Avenue NW
Suite 1000
Washington DC 20036
202/828-7100

NATIONAL ASSOCIATION OF LIFE UNDERWRITERS
1922 F Street NW
Washington DC 20006
202/331-6000

SOCIETY OF ACTUARIES
475 North Martingale Road
Suite 800
Schaumburg IL 60173-2226
708/706-3500

LEGAL SERVICES

FEDERAL BAR ASSOCIATION/EMPIRE STATE CHAPTER
Molly Strum
GPO Box 2
New York NY 10116

For more information, contact:

AMERICAN BAR ASSOCIATION
750 North Lake Shore Drive
Chicago IL 60611
312/988-5000

FEDERAL BAR ASSOCIATION
1815 H Street NW, Suite 408
Washington DC 20006
202/638-0252

NATIONAL ASSOCIATION FOR LAW PLACEMENT
1666 Connecticut Avenue, Suite 450
Washington DC 20009
202/667-1666

NATIONAL ASSOCIATION OF LEGAL ASSISTANTS
1601 South Main Street, Suite 300
Tulsa OK 74119
918/587-6828

NATIONAL FEDERATION OF PARALEGAL ASSOCIATIONS
Suite 201, 104 Wilmot Road
Deerfield IL 60015
708/940-8800

NATIONAL PARALEGAL ASSOCIATION
P.O. Box 629
Doylestown PA 18901
215/297-8333

MISCELLANEOUS ASSOCIATIONS

AMERICAN FEDERATION OF SMALL BUSINESS
407 South Dearborn Street, Suite 500
Chicago, IL 60605
312/427-0206

NATIONAL COOPERATIVE BUSINESS ASSOCIATION
1401 New York Ave. NW
Suite #1100
Washington DC 20005
202/638-6222

NATIONAL SMALL BUSINESS UNITED
1155 15th Street NW
Suite 710
Washington DC 20005
202/293-8830

MISCELLANEOUS MANUFACTURING

NATIONAL TOOLING AND MACHINING ASSOCIATION/NEW YORK
9 Pine Hill Court
Northport NY 11768
516/261-2877

For more information, contact:

NATIONAL ASSOCIATION OF MANUFACTURERS
1331 Pennsylvania Avenue, NW
Suite 1500
Washington DC 20004
202/637-3000

NATIONAL MACHINE TOOL BUILDERS
7901 Westpark Drive
McLean VA 22102-4269
703/893-2900

NATIONAL SCREW MACHINE PRODUCTS ASSOCIATION
6700 West Snowville Road
Breckville OH 44141
216/526-0300

NATIONAL TOOLING AND MACHINING ASSOCIATION
9300 Livingston Road
Fort Washington MD 20744
301/248-1250

THE TOOLING AND MANUFACTURING ASSOCIATION
1177 South Dee Road
Park Ridge IL 60068
312/693-2347

NEWSPAPER PUBLISHING

THE DOW JONES NEWSPAPER FUND/NEW YORK
World Financial Center
200 Liberty Street
New York NY 10281
212/416-2000

THE NEWSPAPER GUILD
133 West 44th Street
New York NY 10036
212/575-1580

For more information, contact:

AMERICAN NEWSPAPER PUBLISHERS ASSOCIATION
Box 17407
Dulles International Airport
Washington DC 20041
703/648-1000

AMERICAN SOCIETY OF NEWSPAPER EDITORS
P.O. Box 17004
Washington DC 20041
202/648-1144

THE DOW JONES NEWSPAPER FUND
P.O. Box 300
Princeton NJ 08543-0300
609/520-4000

INTERNATIONAL CIRCULATION MANAGERS ASSOCIATION
P.O. Box 17420
Washington DC 20041
703/620-9555

NATIONAL NEWSPAPER ASSOCIATION
1627 K Street NW
Suite 400
Washington DC 20006
202/466-7200

NATIONAL PRESS CLUB
529 14th St. NW
Washington DC 20045
202/662-7500

PAPER PRODUCTS AND PACKAGING/CONTAINERS

AMERICAN PAPER INSTITUTE
260 Madison Avenue
New York NY 10016
212/340-0600

For more information, contact:

TECHNICAL ASSOCIATION OF THE PULP AND PAPER INDUSTRY
P.O. Box 105113
Atlanta GA 30348
404/446-1400

PETROLEUM AND ENERGY RELATED/MINING AND DRILLING

**AMERICAN INSTITUTE OF MINING,
 METALLURGICAL AND PETROLEUM**
345 East 47th Street
New York NY 10017
212/705-7695

For more information, contact:

AMERICAN ASSOCIATION OF PETROLEUM GEOLOGISTS
P.O. Box 979
Tulsa OK 74101
918/584-2555

AMERICAN GAS ASSOCIATION
1515 Wilson Boulevard
Arlington VA 22209
703/841-8400

AMERICAN GEOLOGICAL INSTITUTE
4220 King Street
Alexandria VA 22302
703/379-2480

AMERICAN NUCLEAR SOCIETY
555 North Kensington Avenue
La Grange Park IL 60525
708/352-6611

AMERICAN PETROLEUM INSTITUTE
1220 L Street NW
Washington DC 20005
202/682-8000

**AMERICAN SOCIETY OF TRIBOLOGISTS
AND LUBRICATION ENGINEERS**
840 Busse Highway
Park Ridge IL 60068
708/825-5536

CLEAN ENERGY RESEARCH INSTITUTE
P.O. Box 248294
Coral Gables FL 33124
305/284-4666

GEOLOGICAL SOCIETY OF AMERICA
3300 Penrose Place
P.O. Box 9140
Boulder CO 80301
303/447-2020

SOCIETY OF EXPLORATION GEOPHYSICISTS
P.O. Box 702740
Tulsa OK 74170-2740
918/493-3516

PRINTING

ASSOCIATION OF GRAPHIC ARTS
5 Penn Plaza
New York NY 10001
212/279-2100

NATIONAL ASSOCIATION OF PRINTERS AND LITHOGRAPHERS
780 Pallisade Avenue
Teaneck NJ 07666
201/342-0700

TECHNICAL ASSOCIATION OF THE GRAPHIC ARTS
Box 9887
Rochester NY 14614
716/272-0557

For more information, contact:

BINDING INDUSTRIES OF AMERICA
70 East Lake Street
Chicago IL 60601
312/372-7606

PRINTING INDUSTRIES OF AMERICA
1730 North Lynn Street
Arlington VA 22209
703/841-8100

REAL ESTATE

APARTMENT OWNERS AND MANAGERS ASSOCIATION
65 Cherry Plaza
Watertown CT 06795
203/274-2589

BROOKLYN BOARD OF REALTORS
186 Joralemon Street
Suite 16
Brooklyn NY 11201
718/875-5185

For more information, contact:

BUILDING OWNERS AND MANAGERS ASSOCIATION
1521 Ritchie Highway, P.O. Box 9709
Arnold MD 21012
301/261-2882

INSTITUTE OF REAL ESTATE MANAGEMENT
430 North Michigan Avenue
Chicago IL 60611
312/661-1930

INTERNATIONAL ASSOCIATION OF CORPORATE
 REAL ESTATE EXECUTIVES
440 Columbia Drive, Suite 100
West Palm Beach FL 33409
407/683-8111

INTERNATIONAL REAL ESTATE INSTITUTE
8383 East Evans Road
Scottsdale AZ 85260
602/998-8267

NATIONAL ASSOCIATION OF REAL ESTATE INVESTMENT TRUSTS
1129 20th Street NW
Suite 705
Washington DC 20036
202/785-8717

NATIONAL ASSOCIATION OF REALTORS
430 North Michigan Avenue
Chicago IL 60611
312/329-8200

RUBBER AND PLASTICS

SOCIETY OF PLASTIC ENGINEERS
14 Fairfield Drive
Brookfield Centre CT 06804
203/775-0471

SOCIETY OF PLASTICS INDUSTRY
355 Lexington Avenue
New York NY 10017
212/370-7340

TRANSPORTATION/SHIPPING/AUTOMOTIVE

AMERICAN INSTITUTE OF AERONAUTICS AND ASTRONAUTICS
555 West 57th Street
New York NY 10019
212/247-6500

MOTOR VEHICLE MANUFACTURERS ASSOCIATION/NEW YORK
534 Merrick Foad
Room 2
Lynbrook, L.I.
Long Island NY 11563
516/599-9105

NATIONAL MARINE MANUFACTURERS ASSOCIATION
353 Lexington Avenue
New York NY 10016
212/684-6622

For more information, contact:

AIR LINE EMPLOYEES ASSOCIATION
5600 South Central Ave
Chicago IL 60638
312/767-3333

AIR TRANSPORT ASSOCIATION OF AMERICA
1709 New York Ave NW
Washington DC 20006
202/626-4000

AMERICAN TRUCKING ASSOCIATION
2200 Mill Road
Alexandria VA 22314-4677
703/838-1700

ASSOCIATION OF AMERICAN RAILROADS
50 F Street NW
Washington DC 20001
202/639-2100

AUTOMOTIVE SERVICE ASSOCIATION
1901 Airport Freeway, Suite 100
Bedford TX 76021
817/283-6205

AUTOMOTIVE SERVICE INDUSTRY ASSOCIATION
444 North Michigan Avenue
Chicago IL 60611
312/836-1300

AVIATION MAINTENANCE FOUNDATION
P.O. Box 2826
Redmond WA 98073
206/828-3917

INSTITUTE OF TRANSPORTATION ENGINEERS
Suite 410
525 School Street SW, Suite 410
Washington DC 20024
202/554-8050

MARINE TECHNOLOGY SOCIETY
1825 K Street NW
Suite 218
Washington DC 20006
202/775-5966

MOTOR VEHICLE MANUFACTURERS ASSOCIATION
7430 2nd Avenue
Suite 300
Detroit MI 48202
313/872-4311

NATIONAL AERONAUTIC ASSOCIATION OF USA
1815 North Fort Meyer Drive
Arlington VA 22209
202/265-8720

NATIONAL AUTOMOTIVE DEALERS ASSOCIATION
8400 Westpark Drive
McLean VA 22102
703/821-7000

NATIONAL INSTITUTE FOR AUTOMOTIVE SERVICE EXCELLENCE
13505 Dulles Technology Drive
Herndon VA 22071
703/742-3800

NATIONAL MARINE MANUFACTURERS ASSOCIATION
401 North Michigan Avenue
Suite 1150
Chicago IL 60611
312/836-4747

PROFESSIONAL AVIATION MAINTENANCE ASSOCIATION
500 NW Plaza, Suite 809
St. Ann MO 63074
314/739-2580

SHIPBUILDERS COUNCIL OF AMERICA
1110 Vermont Ave. NW, Suite 1250
Washington DC 20005
202/775-9060

UTILITIES

NEW YORK POWER AUTHORITY
1633 Broadway
New York NY 10019
212/468-6000

AMERICAN WATER WORKS ASSOCIATION
Charles Seal, Section Secretary
c/o U.S. Pipe & Foundry
P.O. Box 307
Tarrytown NY 10591
914/332-0980

For more information, contact:

AMERICAN WATER WORKS ASSOCIATION
6666 West Quincy Avenue
Denver CO 80235
303/794-7711

Index

Alphabetical Index to Tri-State Employers

INDEX TO GREATER NEW YORK EMPLOYMENT
SERVICES

A

Index of Professional Associations

W

AVAILABLE AT YOUR LOCAL BOOKSTORE

Knock 'em Dead With Great Answers to Tough Interview Questions
Will you have the answers when the recruiter asks: Why do you want to work here? What can you do for us that someone else cannot? How much money do you want? Why do you want to change jobs? In *Knock 'em Dead*, Martin Yate gives you not only the best answers to these and scores of more difficult questions, but also the best way to answer--so that you'll be able to field any tough question, and get the job and salary that you deserve. 6x9 inches, 204 pages, paperback, $7.95.

Resumes that Knock 'em Dead
In *Resumes that Knock 'em Dead*, Martin Yate reviews the marks of a great resume: what type of resume is right for each applicant, what always goes in, what always stays out, and why. Every single resume in *Resumes that Knock 'em Dead* was used by a real individual to successfully obtain a job. No other book provides the hard facts for producing an exemplary resume. 8 1/2x11 inches, 216 pages, $7.95.

Cover Letters that Knock 'em Dead
Cover Letters that Knock 'em Dead shows not just how to write a "correct" cover letter, but how to write a cover letter that offers a powerful competitive advantage in today's tough job market. *Cover Letters that Knock 'em Dead* gives the essential information on composing a cover that wins attention, interest and job offers. 8 1/2x11 inches, 184 pages, $7.95.

ALSO OF INTEREST...
The JobBank Series
There are now 18 *JobBank* books, each providing extensive, up-to-date employment information on hundreds of the largest employers in each job market. Recommended as an excellent place to begin your job search by *The New York Times, The Los Angeles Times, The Boston Globe, The Chicago Tribune*, and many other publications, *JobBank* books have been used by hundreds of thousands of people to find jobs.

Books available: *The Atlanta JobBank--The Boston JobBank--The Chicago JobBank--The Dallas-Ft. Worth JobBank--The Denver JobBank--The Detroit JobBank--The Florida JobBank--The Houston JobBank--The Los Angeles JobBank--The Minneapolis JobBank--The New York JobBank--The Ohio JobBank--The Philadelphia JobBank--The Phoenix JobBank--The St. Louis JobBank--The San Franciso JobBank--The Seattle JobBank--The Washington DC JobBank*. Each book is 6x9 inches, over 250 pages, paperback, $12.95.

If you cannot find a book at your local bookstore, you may order it directly from the publisher. Please send payment including $3.75 for shipping and handling (for the entire order) to : Bob Adams, Inc., 260 Center Street, Holbrook, MA 02343. Credit card holders may call 1-800-USA-JOBS (in Massachusetts, 617-767-8100). Please first check at your local bookstore